T5-BPY-682

LAY PARTICIPATION IN CRIMINAL TRIALS

The Case of Croatia

Sanja Kutnjak Ivković

Austin & Winfield, Publishers
Lanham • New York • Oxford

176558

Copyright © 1999 by
Sanja Kutnjak Ivkovich

Austin & Winfield, Publishers
4720 Boston Way
Lanham, Maryland 20706

12 Hid's Copse Rd.
Cumnor Hill, Oxford OX2 9JJ

All rights reserved
Printed in the United States of America
British Library Cataloging in Publication Information Available

Library of Congress Cataloging-in-Publication Data

Kutnjak Ivkovich, Sanja.
Lay participation in criminal trials : the case of Croatia / Sanja Kutnjak Ivkovich
p.   cm.
q.   Includes bibliographical references and index.
1. Criminal justice, Administration of—Croatia. 2. Jury—Croatia. 3. Lay judges. 4.
Judicial process. I. Title.
KKZ5292.4.K88   1999   345.4972—dc21   99—20600 CIP

ISBN 1-57292-130-7 (cloth: alk. ppr.)

Editorial Inquires:
Austin & Winfield, Publishers
4720 Boston Way
Lanham, Md. 20706
(301) 459-3366
Website: www..univpress.com
To Order: (800)462-6420

The paper used in this publication meets the minimum
requirements of American National Standard for Information
Sciences—Permanence of Paper for Printed Library Materials,
ANSI Z39.48—1984

For my mom and my husband

Contents

176558

Acknowledgments

The writing of this book was a challenging and a most pleasurable task. I was privileged to enjoy the help and support of many people and institutions during various stages of this project. It gives me extreme pleasure to extend my most sincere gratitude to all of them. At the same time, my greatest fear is that I will not manage to give everyone due credit.

The nucleus of this book is my dissertation in Criminology. Although it has undergone a thorough revision and considerable expansion in several directions, the fact remains that my dissertation committee at the University of Delaware contributed to the book with their fine scholarship and support. Valerie P. Hans, my dissertation advisor, Allan L. McCutcheon, Frank R. Scarpitti, and James J. Magee were an inspiring committee; they not only provided valuable feedback at various stages of my graduate studies, but also made an important prediction — that this research will be published as a book. I am happy to say that they were correct. I am particularly appreciative of the role Valerie P. Hans has played in my academic career.

I was fortunate to have received dedicated help and support from a broad network of family and friends. My husband, Zoran Ivković, was the first and the most vigorous reader of each draft. I am grateful for his commitment and contribution and I thank him for his love and patience. My mother, Nevenka Kutnjak, demonstrated virtually unlimited patience while carrying out some of the clerical aspects of the data collection and literature search. My father-in-law, Božidar Ivković, and my uncle, Danko Cobović, were instrumental in certain phases of data collection. Valentin Puževski was a source of tremendous encouragement and support.

The support and assistance of Judge Vladimir Gredelj, the President of the Regional Court of Bjelovar and the President of the Association of Croatian Judges, has been most generous. He assisted me with the data collection in every possible way and was the single most important contributor from the Bjelovar Region. However, his contribution extended far beyond data collection. His ability, enthusiasm, and energy continue to be an inspiration. Morena Šporčić-Beti, a judge at the District Court of Zagreb and an old friend (that is, a friend for many years), was particularly helpful in communicating with the respondents from the District Court of Zagreb. Davor Baranić, a court clerk at the District Court of Zagreb, provided his assistance with collecting the data from lay judges. His efficiency and cooperation are much appreciated. I would also like to thank Jadranka Božičević, Darko Pavičić, and Petar Perušić for their kind assistance in collecting the data. I extend my deepest gratitude to Prof. Stanislav Pomorski from the Rutgers University Law School, who generously provided me with a detailed description of a study on lay participation carried out in Poland in the 1970s.

Tara Zend edited this book with professionalism and commitment. I am very grateful for her friendly support and availability at the most awkward timers. Eilika Wöhl-Ban helped me clarify many dilemmas related to research studies published in German and German legal codes. My father-in-law, Božidar Ivković, assisted with translations from German.

I take this opportunity to thank the then Minister of Justice Ivica Crnić, Branko Košutić, Josip Kardum, The President of the Supreme Court Milan Vuković, then Justice of the Supreme Court Vesna Milošević, and then Justice of the Supreme Court Vladimir Primorac for their interest in and support of my research. I express my gratitude to the presidents of courts and state attorneys for facilitating the data collection at their courts/offices. Also, Vladimir Meznarić, then President of the Association of Attorneys of Zagreb, provided invaluable assistance by supplying a list of attorneys practicing criminal law. Special thanks are due to the presidents of the courts where questionnaires were distributed to lay judges: Rajko Bagić, then President of the District

Court of Zagreb; Vladimir Gredelj, then President of the District Court of Križevci; Vojko Madirazza, then President of the Regional Court of Zagreb; and Ivan Ernjak, then President of the Regional Court of Bjelovar. I would also like to thank all of the participants in this study, for without their individual effort of filling in the questionnaires this study would not have been possible.

Finally, a number of colleagues and friends have read the manuscript or some of its individual chapters and have provided invaluable comments. I am profoundly thankful to Katie Bartakovic (Brock University, Canada), Charles Donahue (Harvard Law School, USA), Valerie P. Hans (University of Delaware, USA), Franjo Hirjan, (Office of the National State Attorney, Croatia) Josip Kregar (University of Zagreb Law School, Croatia), Mattias Kumm (Harvard Law School, USA/Germany), Maximo Langer (Harvard Law School, USA/Argentina), Dubravko Ljubić (Constitutional Court, Croatia), Stefan Machura (University of Bochum, Germany), Otwin Marenin (Washington State University, USA), Peter Murray (Harvard Law School, USA), Lana Petö-Kujundžić (Regional Court of Zagreb, Croatia), Stephan Thaman (Saint Louis University School of Law, USA), Margaret Vandiver (University of Memphis, USA), Neil Vidmar (Duke Law School, USA), Josip Vrandečić (Yale University, USA), and Mateja Vraničar (Ministry of Finance, Slovenia).

Preface

Legal decision-making has involved lay participants since antiquity. Like a thread that weaves through the fabric of history, ordinary citizens have been a part of many decision-making bodies through various times and across different societies. The thread sometimes became thinner and almost invisible; at other times it grew stronger and more prominent.

In this book I examine forms of lay participation across the world today and across time. I follow the development of mixed tribunals, decision-making bodies composed of professional judges and lay judges who decide cases jointly. I focus on lay participation in two countries: Germany, a western democracy and a cradle of mixed tribunals, and Croatia, a country in transition.

Croatian mixed tribunals are the central theme of the book. Specifically, I focus on the interaction among tribunal members during trial and deliberation. In addition to developing a theoretical framework that models the interaction, the book presents results of an extensive empirical study of mixed tribunals I recently conducted in Croatia. I examine mixed tribunals at the point in time when the system of mixed tribunals demonstrates its endurance by continuing to exist in the societies which abolished the communist regime and are undertaking a transition toward democracy.

I devote the first part of Chapter 1 to a detailed description of various forms of lay participation in decision-making across the world. The jury is examined as an integral and historical part of the legal systems of common-law countries (e.g., the United States, the United Kingdom), as well as a recently introduced part of the legal systems of the countries in transition (Russia) and western countries with a very long tradition of featuring no lay participation

(Spain). Also discussed are magistrates in the United Kingdom and justices of the peace in the United States, as well as people's courts, a form of decision-making characteristic of socialist countries (e.g., Cuba, former Yugoslavia, former USSR). The chapter proceeds with an examination of mixed tribunals, a form of lay participation in which professional judges and lay judges make legal decisions jointly. Mixed tribunals are utilized in many countries whose legal systems are based on Roman or civil law. Finally, the discussion focuses on countries that utilize no lay participation in legal decision-making (e.g., Japan, Saudi Arabia). In the second part of Chapter 1 I perform a detailed analysis of the reasons for the introduction of lay participation into the decision-making in criminal cases, as well as an analysis of the criticisms of lay participation.

Chapters 2 and 3 trace the development of lay participation in Germany and Croatia. Germany, one of the western democracies, has a long and rich history of lay participation, while Croatia, a country in transition, did not have lay participation in criminal cases until the mid-1940s (except for a few brief encounters with the jury system in the 19th century). Contemporary legal systems in Germany and Croatia are described from the perspective of the selection process of lay judges, the types of cases lay judges participate in, the types of courts they serve at, and the rights and responsibilities they have. Emphasis is placed on the rights and duties of lay judges as active members of the courtroom workgroup, as fact-finders, and as decision-makers in criminal trials. Particularly interesting are the changes in the *Croatian Criminal Procedure* (1998) that affected mixed tribunals several years after the country steered away from the communist regime.

Very few of the cases decided in common-law countries are tried by the jury. Yet, there is a very extensive body of literature on the jury. On the other hand, while a substantial portion of the cases in civil-law countries is tried by mixed tribunals, there are very few studies on mixed tribunals. In Chapter 4 I review previous studies on mixed tribunals, the majority of which were conducted in the 1960s/1970s. The focus of the chapter is on the empirical studies of mixed tribunals which examined positive and negative features of lay participation, the impact of lay judges' contribution toward the task of mixed tribunals, the frequency and importance of lay judges' participation, and lay judges' ability to understand evidence and apply the law.

Chapter 5 provides a theoretical framework for the interaction among professional judges and lay judges in the tribunal. Elements of status characteristics theory, a theory used in psychological literature to model interaction in small task-oriented informal groups, have been modified and adopted to explain the interaction in the mixed tribunal, a small formal group.

Chapter 6 commences the empirical part of the book. I provide a brief summary of basic facts about Croatia, its judicial system, and the courtroom workgroup. I also describe the methodology used in the study — the questionnaire and its distribution — and continue with a description of the respondents (professional judges, lay judges, state attorneys, and attorneys).

How do trials by mixed tribunals look like? Who has the dominant role in the tribunal during trial? In Chapter 7 I provide a legal framework for trials by mixed tribunals and examine the respondents' perceptions about the activity of mixed tribunals during trial. I focus on the frequency and importance of questions lay judges asked of the defendant, witnesses, and expert witnesses. A detailed analysis is performed in order to determine the impact of lay judges' demographic characteristics (e.g., gender, age, occupational prestige, education) on the perceived frequency and importance of lay judges' participation during trial. Furthermore, I study the importance and the reported frequency of their reading the case file.

Chapter 8 examines what happens after the parties provide closing arguments at the end of the trial and mixed tribunals are left to deliberate and decide the case. What happens behind closed doors? Who talks and who listens? The only persons present in the deliberation room — members of the tribunals themselves — were asked to provide their views. Professional judges and lay judges answered questions concerning the beginning of deliberation, frequency and importance of lay judges' comments, frequency and topics of disagreements, and ways of resolving disagreements. The analysis also includes an examination and a comparison of the opinion furnished by professional judges, state attorneys, and attorneys about lay judges' abilities to understand evidence, evaluate it critically, and to understand and apply the law. These evaluations are compared to the lay judges' evaluations of their own abilities.

In Chapter 9 I examine the respondents' general opinion about mixed tribunals. The respondents compared trials by mixed tribunals to trials by professional judge alone, by a professional tribunal, and by jury. This chapter also examines the respondents' answers about the future of mixed tribunals and possible improvements to the system of mixed tribunals.

In the concluding chapter of the book, I examine the results of this study as they relate to the "big picture." I argue, based on status characteristics theory and the results of this study, that problems experienced by lay judges in mixed tribunals are very likely to surface in the work of any decision-making group composed of professional and lay members, regardless of whether their task is reaching a verdict in a criminal case, a decision about the suspension of a medical license, or a decision in a disciplinary procedure against a student. I discuss possible improvements to the system of mixed tribunals. This discussion extends far beyond the borders of the Croatian legal system and can be applied to improve the quality of proceedings and decision-making process by mixed tribunals or indeed any tribunal composed of professional and lay members.

Chapter 1

Forms and Features of Lay Participation

Lay participation in legal decision-making has been present since antiquity. It has long been considered to be a cornerstone of the democratic administration of justice. In fact, legislators in most countries did not leave the responsibility of deciding the guilt and determining the punishment in criminal cases solely to professional judges.

Lay participants are persons who have neither advanced education in legal issues nor systematic training in legal decision-making. They are selected and empowered to decide legal cases jointly either with fellow lay participants or with professional judges. Professional judges, on the other hand, are law school graduates who have passed the bar exam and have been appointed or elected as judges. They represent the government and the state and may wear robes, wigs, or other symbols of their position.

1.1 Forms of Lay Participation

In some countries professional judges are assigned the responsibility of conducting trials in serious criminal cases and deciding legal issues, while lay participants have the responsibility of deciding the facts and the guilt of the defendant (the jury system, utilized in, e.g., the United Kingdom, the United States, Canada). Other countries assign all of these functions to a tribunal composed of both professional judges and lay participants (the system of mixed tribunals, utilized in, e.g., Austria, Croatia, Finland, Germany, Hungary, Poland, and Sweden). However, even in the countries with very extensive systems of lay participation, there is a tendency to treat less serious cases differently in order to reduce the expenses associated with trials. This can be achieved by assigning only the least serious cases to be tried by lay persons (the system of justices of the peace in the United States or magistrates in the United Kingdom), by reducing the size of the decision-making group (smaller mixed tribunals for less serious offenses), or by replacing the decision-making group with only one individual, a professional judge (the latter two solutions are characteristic of legal systems that utilize mixed tribunals, such as Croatia and Germany).

1.1.1   The Jury

Kalven and Zeisel described the Anglo-American jury as a "remarkable political institution" (1966, p. 3):

> ... it recruits a group of twelve laymen, chosen at random from the widest population; it convenes them for the purpose of the particular trial; it entrusts them with great official powers of decision; it permits them to carry on deliberations in secret and to report out their final judgment without giving reasons for it; and, after their momentary service to the state has been completed, it orders them to disband and return to private life.

The jury has a long tradition in common-law countries (e.g., the United States and the United Kingdom). According to Kalven and Zeisel (1966, p. 13), in the mid-1960s, over 80% of all jury trials in criminal cases worldwide took place in the United States.[1]

Although trial by jury is a typical feature of the United Kingdom, Australia (Hale, 1973), and New Zealand (Burns, 1973), it is not as widespread in the other Commonwealth countries. For example, while the jury became a

---

[1]Trial by jury is a constitutional right of the defendants in criminal cases in the United States (Amendment VI of the *Constitution of the United States*, 1791).

part of the criminal justice system in 1845 in the former British colony Hong Kong (Duff *et al.*, 1990, 1992), there is no trial by jury in India, the most populous Commonwealth country (Kawaley, 1989). Similarly, it seems that in African countries, if introduced at all, trials by jury are limited primarily to capital offenses (Jearey, 1961a, 1961b; Kawaley, 1989). On the other hand, the jury is often found in the Commonwealth countries of the Caribbean; it is even a constitutional right in some, for example, the Bahamas and Bermuda (Kawaley, 1989).

Outside the common-law countries, trials by jury are not very frequent. They are utilized, for example, in Austria (trials by jury are reserved for the most serious cases, whereas the less serious cases are left to the jurisdiction of mixed tribunals). Japan, a country in which there is formidable respect toward professional judges and, as a consequence, no lay participation, utilized the jury earlier in this century (Dean, 1995).

While the utilization of the jury system in civil cases may be questioned in the United States (Litan, 1993) and the United Kingdom,[2] its utilization in criminal cases has recently been increasing in some other countries. For example, Russia (Thaman, 1995) and Spain (Thaman, 1998), both non-common-law countries, recently reintroduced the jury system into their respective criminal justice systems (1993 and 1995, respectively);[3] there has been a recent debate on its introduction in Japan (Lempert, 1992).

Even in the countries that provide the defendant with the right to a jury trial, for example, the United States, very few criminal cases are actually tried by jury; rather, the majority of the cases do not go to trial at all because

---

[2]As Dean (1995, p. 381) argued, a gradual erosion of jury trials started in 1976 with the recommendations of the James Committee (*Interdepartmental Committee on the Distribution of Criminal Business between the Crown Court and the Magistrates' Court*). This decline continued with the findings and recommendations by the Roskill Committee in 1986 (Dean, 1995, p. 381).

[3]Interestingly, while the new Spanish jury has been introduced in all 50 provinces of Spain, the new Russian jury has been introduced in only 9 out of 89 regions of Russia (Thaman, 1998, p. 404).

they are resolved through plea bargaining.[4] As Kalven and Zeisel (1966, p. 14) wrote, "[a] fundamental fact about the jury trials is that it is the mode of final disposition for only a small fraction of all criminal prosecutions." In 1997 in the United States, as many as 92% of the total number of federal criminal cases that were not dismissed were resolved through plea bargaining; a very small percentage (7%) of all the federal cases tried in U.S. District Courts were tried by jury (*1997 Sourcebook of Criminal Justice Statistics*, 1998, p. 419). Similarly, the percentage of felonies tried by jury at state courts in the United States in 1994 was only 6%; the overwhelming majority of the cases in state courts (89%) were resolved through plea bargaining (*1997 Sourcebook of Criminal Justice Statistics*, 1998, p. 422). Juries are not more frequent in civil cases in the United States either. For example, less than 1% of all civil cases terminated in state courts in 1988 and 2% of all civil cases terminated in federal courts in 1991 were jury trials (Galanter, 1993, p. 63). A study by Wilhjelm (in Anderson, 1990, p. 846) showed a decline in the use of juries in Denmark from 2% of criminal trials in the 1950s to 0.4% in 1980.

There are two types of juries in the United States — the grand jury and the petit jury. The grand jury, composed of between 6 to 23 persons, depending on the state (*State Court Organization 1993*, 1995, p. 280-282), decides about the indictments. The petit jury or the trial jury, composed of either 12 persons in the federal system or between 6 and 12 persons in the state systems (*State Court Organization 1993*, 1995, p. 274-279), decides the guilt of the defendant in felony cases (*State Court Organization 1993*, 1995). A six-member jury was found to be constitutional in *Williams v. Florida* (1970); four states use

---

[4]This is in sharp contrast with jury trials in Russia, where the guilty plea by the defendant does not mean that the defendant has waived the right to trial by jury. Rather, the guilty plea is just another incriminating piece of evidence that will eventually be evaluated by the jury (Thaman, 1995, p. 103). However, in cases in which the defendant fully admits his guilt, the professional judge who presides over the jury trial has the option, provided that both parties give their consent, of limiting the trial to the disputed pieces of the evidence only, or, if there are no such pieces, of going directly into the sentencing stage. Interestingly, none of professional judges in the period of the first two years of jury trials in modern Russia (1993-1995) exercised that option (Thaman, 1995, p. 104).

six- (Connecticut and Florida) or eight-member juries (Arizona and Utah) for non-capital felonies, and a number of other states use six- to eight-member juries for misdemeanor cases. The U.S. Supreme Court limited the minimal jury size to six; as was argued in *Ballew v. Georgia* (1978, p. 239), "the purpose and functioning of the jury in a criminal trial is seriously impaired, and to a constitutional degree, by a reduction in size to below six members." Although the U.S. Supreme Court in *Apodaca v. Oregon* (1972) decided that jury decisions need not be unanimous, the great majority of the states still require a unanimous decision in felony cases (Louisiana and Oregon being exceptions); even for civil trials, there are only several states that require only a majority decision (*State Court Organization 1993*, 1995, p. 274-279). Six-member juries must reach a unanimous decision (*Burch v. Louisiana*, 1979).

Trials in the common-law countries are adversarial proceedings in which the parties perform active roles. This is especially true of the prosecutor, who has the burden of proving beyond a reasonable doubt that the defendant committed the crime. In trials by the petit jury, the professional judge usually conducts the trial and gives legal instructions to the jury.[5] The jury makes an independent determination of the factual issues in the case; jurors decide the guilt or liability of the defendant.[6] In most criminal cases they do not determine the sanction; this issue is left to the professional judge and is typically resolved in subsequent proceedings. The exception to this rule involves the death sentence; juries frequently decide the death penalty cases as well. In such cases, jurors need to be "death qualified jurors." In other words, persons who *a priori* oppose the death penalty are systematically excluded from jury duty in capital cases (*Witherspoon v. Illinois*, 1968). In some countries or

---

[5]The newly introduced Spanish jury has a more active role — it may ask questions, examine documents, and take notes (Thaman, 1998, p. 304-306).

[6]The Continental version of the jury (which has recently been reintroduced into the Spanish criminal justice system) reaches a special verdict — the professional judge provides jurors with a list of factual questions and the jurors need to answer whether they found these facts to be proven or not (Thaman, 1998, p. 321).

states, for example, Texas, juries decide not only the guilt, but also determine the penalty. Civil juries typically determine damage awards.

In common-law countries, jurors are not required nor do they provide explanations or reasons for their verdicts. If they acquit the defendant (for whatever reason), the parties are not allowed to appeal their decision. In that sense, the jury's verdict is final. The jury in Spain, on the other hand, does need to provide reasons for its decision (Thaman, 1998, p. 364), so that "a reasonable appellate decision can be facilitated;" the verdict should be written and the reasons for it should be enumerated (Thaman, 1998, p. 322). Even the jury acquittal can be reversed, as was the case in one of the first jury trials in Spain; in the Otegi murder case, "the reversal was met with satisfaction, not only by the families of the victims [two police officers were killed], but also by supporters of trial by jury" (Thaman, 1998, p. 410).

Although the typical "division of labor" between the jury and the trial judge is that the jury determines the facts in the case while the professional judge decides the legal issues, juries may implicitly affect the application of the law as well. If the jury does not perceive that the mandatory sanction (or the sanction jurors believe to be likely) is fair, although it decides neither the legal issues in the case nor the sanction, the jury can effectively halt the application of that sanction by returning the "not guilty" verdict. In other words, juries do not need to explain the reasons for their verdicts and thus do not need to follow the law; they can bend the law by acquitting the defendant regardless of the strength of the evidence against him ("nullification;"[7] *Cargill v. State*, 1986) if they believe that following the letter of the law would result in an unjust verdict.[8]

---

[7]Green (1985) studied early examples of jury nullification — medieval cases in which jurors found elements of self-defense in killings although the technical elements of self-defense according to the law were not fulfilled.

[8]The Spanish jury is prohibited from engaging in jury nullification (Thaman, 1998, p. 376).

1.1.2 Magistrates and Justices of the Peace

The second form of lay participation, magistrates and justices of the peace, is used mostly in countries whose legal systems are based on common law. For example, stipendiary magistrates and lay magistrates are a part of the criminal justice system in the United Kingdom, while justices of the peace and magistrates (both of whom can be either professional lawyers or lay persons) are a part of the criminal justice system in the United States.

The 27,000 magistrates in England and Wales sentenced over 90% of offenders in England and Wales in the 1980s (Parker *et al.*, 1989, p. 1). Justices of the peace, an essential element of the U.S. criminal justice system, sit in courts of limited jurisdiction and decide primarily minor traffic and criminal law violations, as well as small civil claims (*State Court Organization 1993*, 1995, p. 69-76; Silberman, 1979, p. 27-29).

Interestingly, while the function of a magistrate may be performed by either lay persons (lay magistrates) or lawyers — barristers or solicitors of at least seven years' standing (stipendiary magistrates), the overwhelming majority of magistrates in the United Kingdom are in fact lay magistrates. Indeed, in a study of magistrates in four cities from four different parts of the United Kingdom, out of over 500 magistrates serving at the respective courts, only one (0.2%) was a stipendiary magistrate (Parker *et al.*, 1989). This result should not be surprising because justice administration by lay persons is a prominent feature of the British legal system. Furthermore, some earlier studies also indicated that most magistrates in the United Kingdom were lay magistrates; for example, there were as many as 23,000 lay magistrates and only 50 stipendiary magistrates in the United Kingdom in 1977 (Diamond, 1990). At the same time, there were 20,280 state judicial posts in the United States, out of which 13,217 were filled by justices of the peace who were not lawyers (Silberman *et al.*, 1979).

An interesting question, raised by Provine (1981), is why lawyers in the United States tolerate lay judges. According to Provine (1981, p. 29), such tolerance is possible because lawyers have little contact with lay judges (parties are typically not represented by a lawyer since the sanctions are light and there is no realistic possibility of incarceration) and, moreover, the court system would incur a heavy financial burden if lay judges were to be replaced by lawyers.

The emergence of lay judges in the United States was brought on by the lack of trained lawyers and the persistent dislike of the (English) legal profession (Silberman, 1979, p. 335). The former problem persisted well into the 1970s; Kress and Stanley found that, "lawyers are simply unavailable for the positions of town and village justices in sixty-six percent of the towns and villages in New York State" (in Silberman, 1979, p. 10).

Lay magistrates and stipendiary magistrates in the United Kingdom have essentially the same rights and duties and may preside over the same types of cases. They differ, however, in terms of education, frequency of service, reward for their service, and the degree of their independence.

Stipendiary magistrates are persons trained in law (barristers or solicitors of at least seven years' standing), while lay magistrates, as their name suggests, do not have a background in law. Lay magistrates in the United Kingdom have been required to take mandatory basic training since 1966 (Reichert, 1973; Baldwin, 1974; Baldwin, 1975).[9] Similarly, magistrates or justices of the peace in the United States may be required to take mandatory training in the rudimentary principles of law. For example, such requirements are made of magistrates in West Virginia and Georgia and of justices of the peace in Texas (Silberman, 1979, p. 319-325; *State Court Organization 1993*, 1995, p. 77, 90).

Lay magistrates' training includes legal education in substantive and procedural issues, as well as practice in observing the courtroom behavior of their more experienced colleagues (Baldwin, 1974, 1975). Although, "the training programs are not intended to make lawyers out of lay magistrates" (Reichert,

---

[9]However, research studies (Baldwin, 1975) reported that this training varied greatly in depth and variety of courses offered.

1973, p. 138), this additional set of seminars on legal issues further removes lay magistrates from their "lay" element. They do not become lawyers as a consequence of their training, but they do grow more accustomed to and aware of the expectations and pressures for the uniformity of the system. Parker *et al.* (1989, p. 171) found in their study of four British courts that at each of the courts the novice magistrates were socialized and obtained their *rite de passage* to become real magistrates through watching and sitting with more experienced colleagues. Parker *et al.* (1989, p. 171) further wrote:

> Magistrates are lay people, predominantly middle-aged, middle class and highly 'respectable'. They are, in the main, intelligent and sensible people who, in their own domestic, professional or business lives, would insist on applying rules like consistency, accountability and financial management. Yet, as magistrates, they collectively become something else. They put on the mask and play in role and become highly selective in which parts of their life-experienced 'selves' they employ when acting as magistrates. Their socialization, their training and the absorption of the magistrates' ideology defines where and how the selection is made.

Diamond (1990) concluded that lay magistrates tended to be more lenient than stipendiary magistrates in part because of the difference in formal legal education; however, she primarily attributed lay magistrates' greater leniency to the fact that they held part-time positions (Diamond, 1990, p. 209). On the other hand, Provine (1986, p. 100) found that non-lawyer judges in New York were more severe than lawyer judges and that non-lawyers judges were more favorably disposed toward the police and the prosecution. Nevertheless, Provine's overall conclusion (1986, p. 114) was that:

> Observation and interviews yielded no support for the argument that lay judges are more likely than lawyers to be biased in favor of local residents, racially prejudiced, or oversensitive to defendants who do not show proper deference.

Lay magistrates are less concerned with the official goals of sentencing than stipendiary magistrates are. They are also more likely to focus on each defendant they try. Bond and Lemon (1981) studied two groups of lay magistrates:

one group had only one year of experience at the bench without any legal training, while the other group attended the obligatory training in law. They concluded that one year of experience at the bench influenced lay magistrates to become more deterrence-oriented with a stronger emphasis on punishment, while the obligatory training in law attenuated these tendencies.

Lay magistrates in the United Kingdom are employed part-time and can sit in 26 half-day sessions in the court per year; stipendiary magistrates, on the other hand, are employed full-time. Therefore, stipendiary magistrates earn their salary by performing their duty, while lay magistrates are volunteers who receive only recompense for their expenses and a modest travel allowance. It is important to keep in mind that, as Reichert (1973, p. 139) emphasized:

> Even if the English were not satisfied with their magistrates' courts, it would be almost impossible to eliminate them in the near future. First, the number of solicitors and barristers in England required to replace the magistrates with professional judges or stipendiaries would seriously cripple the legal profession; second, the cost of paying professional full-time magistrates would place an additional strain on an economy that is already heavily burdened with fiscal problems.

Finally, stipendiary and lay magistrates do not possess the same degree of independence; while stipendiary magistrates preside over cases alone, lay magistrates must sit in panels of two or three lay judges (Diamond, 1990).

1.1.3   Lay Courts

Unlike magistrates and justices of the peace, who try cases in regular state courts and follow the procedural rules prescribed by the state, lay courts are typically not a part of the regular state court system and "the rules of the game" are not precisely specified in advance. Lay courts or various forms of popular justice could be found in the (former) socialist states (Ramundo, 1965; Butler, 1972; Smith, 1974; Reichel, 1994), Western democracies (Fisher, 1975; Merry and Milner, 1993), as well as in some African countries (Smith, 1968; Ross, 1973; Salman, 1983; Makamure, 1985; Grant and Schwikkard, 1991).

While the state systems in socialist countries introduced lay courts in pursuit of the official ideology of the subsequent transformation of society and the replacement of laws by socialist morality, as was the case in the former Soviet Union (Smith, 1974, p. 239), lay courts in African countries typically developed as a consequence of the inadequacies of formal courts and/or ideological role they played, as was the case in South Africa (Grant and Schwikkard, 1991, p. 305). The exceptions to the latter rule occurred in the instances in which colonial legal systems were changed in the direction of a socialist regime, as was the case in Zimbabwe (Makamure, 1985), and lay courts served to implement the socialist concept of popular justice. Consequently, the systems of lay courts in socialist countries were relatively uniform, while lay courts in African countries differed greatly in their organization, nature, and scope.

Interestingly, Felstiner and Drew (1978, p. 27) argued that lay courts in industrialized societies had been primarily a socialist phenomenon, while American forms of lay courts had been based on African, non-industrial models. On the other hand, Merry and Milner (1993, p. 9) argued that, "[m]any of the U.S. experiments in community mediation traced their ancestry to Soviet, Cuban, and Chinese examples." However, the emphasis of American lay courts is quite different and is marked with an American flare — "helping individuals achieve full personhood" (Merry and Milner, 1993, p. 9). Merry (1993, p. 37) further elaborated on the differences in perspectives:

> In countries with Anglo-American legal systems, popular justice is described as the opposite to an adversarial, rights-based, act-oriented legal system. In societies with socialist law, popular justice is presented as the expression of popular consciousness and authority, opposed to the control of the central elite. Many Third World countries equipped with colonial Anglo-American legal systems are developing customary-law forms of popular justice to reclaim a law suppressed during the colonial era. Procedures are conciliatory rather than adversarial, the characteristics of the Anglo-American legal system.

The first appearance of lay courts in countries with Marxist ideology was recorded in the Soviet Union in December 1917 (only two months after the October Revolution). The early lay courts, called comrades' courts, were initially formed in some units in the Petrograd military district and were subsequently extended via Trotsky's 1918 Decree to the entire Red Army "as a means of strengthening military discipline" (Ramundo, 1965, p. 703; Butler, 1972, p. 202). Soon thereafter, Lenin's 1919 Decree mandated that disciplinary comrades' courts be formed in the local sections of trade unions (Ramundo, 1965, p. 704).

These first lay courts were introduced with the purpose of improving the workers' discipline and productivity. Other petty violations were soon added to the list. The 1921 Decree extended the jurisdiction of comrades' courts to also include "immoral acts of individual members of the collective: hooliganism, obscene behavior, rudeness on the job, petty abuses, petty thefts, etc." (Ramundo, 1965, p. 704). Therefore, jurisdiction was effectively expanded from the narrow spectrum of violations of labor discipline to the more general jurisdiction over personal misconduct. Once the jurisdiction of Soviet lay courts had been extended, comrades' courts mushroomed in factories and neighborhoods. In fact, Ramundo (1965, p. 705) stated that there were more than 45,000 comrades' courts in the Soviet Union in 1938.

Comrades' courts — non-professional, three member tribunals popularly elected to rule on minor disputes (Smith, 1974, p. 240) — had a dual purpose: they were considered to be a developer of "the new Soviet man" and were also considered to be a controller of society's unruly and immoral elements (Ramundo, 1965, p. 1). Communism was perceived as a form of public self-government and it was believed that, in order to attain it, the people living in socialism (which was viewed as the preparatory stage of social development), should be educated "to the point that the collective sense of right or wrong becomes so ingrained that social pressure replaces law as the social control mechanism" (Smith, 1974, p. 239). It was believed that social classes would eventually be eliminated, that the law would be replaced by communist morality, and that the need for the state and state mechanisms (including courts) would ultimately disappear. Consequently, the state and the law would "wither away." One of Lenin's policies, that of maximum participation of the masses in public administration and the building of communism, was aimed at educating the people and preparing them for this step; it thus found a thorough application in comrades' courts.

Due to the role they played in the development of communist morality ("state compulsion to enforce acceptable standards is to be gradually replaced by a sense of community morality"), these lay courts were officially not considered to be a part of the state judicial apparatus (Ramundo, 1965, p. 698, 701; Smith, 1974, p. 250), although, as some authors argued, the line between regular courts and comrades' courts was not very clear in the areas of supervision and procedure (Butler, 1972, p. 206). The procedure was not particularly legalistic; comrades' courts were not restricted by any set of formal rules of procedure. Moreover, as Savitskii and Keizerov pointed out, if and when comrades' courts did use formal procedural rules, they were criticized for distorting their "popular justice" character by creating "an artificial barrier between the comrades' courts and the collective which elected it" (in Ramundo, 1965, p. 713).

The change in legislation during World War II (the shift of jurisdiction from comrades' courts to regular criminal courts) and other reasons (e.g., the lack of uniform legislation) led toward the virtual disappearance of comrades' courts at the time (Ramundo, 1965, p. 705; Butler, 1972, p. 202; Smith, 1974, p. 242). Comrades' courts were reintroduced once again in the 1950s as "an extension of control into the areas which in most societies are regulated by moral norms and not regulated by regular courts" (Ramundo, 1965, p. 726). In 1963 there were 197,000 comrades' courts in the Soviet Union (Ramundo, 1965, p. 708). Consequently, approximately half a million people served as lay judges in comrades' courts.[10] Comrades' courts began to appear in various forms in other countries of Eastern Europe with varying degrees of success.

---

[10]See also Friedgut (1979, p. 247).

Poland introduced comrades' courts in 1946 and reintroduced them in 1955, the former German Democratic Republic and Romania introduced them in 1953, followed by Hungary in 1956 and the former Czechoslovakia in 1959 (Butler, 1972, p. 207). However, comerades' courts in these countries did not have a long and happy life (Butler, 1972).

Although the former Yugoslavia did not adopt comrades' courts, it did develop a different form of lay courts — "reconciliation boards" — and put it to use predominantly in rural areas. A study on lay courts in the former Yugoslavia found that Yugoslav lay courts heard about 20,000 civil cases and 5,000 criminal cases annually in one of the Yugoslav republics (Felstiner and Drew, 1978, p. 27). Cases placed under the jurisdiction of lay courts were mostly simple civil cases and minor criminal cases. Criminal cases decided by lay courts were typically the least serious ones (e.g., slander, insult), that is, the ones that were not initiated *ex officio*, but by the initiative of the victim.

Reconciliation boards had a very specific place in the system of justice administration in the former Yugoslavia. The victim needed to initiate the case and bring charges at the regular court. Judges at regular courts tried to redirect the parties to the reconciliation boards in order to decrease their own caseload. However, there is another, more important but hidden reason for the existence of reconciliation boards: decision made by a criminal court would disappoint at least one party and, as a consequence of the trial, the relationship that typically existed between the parties before the dispute had developed would likely be broken. The idea behind reconciliation boards was to try to preserve that relationship through the use of negotiating techniques, which would make both parties feel like winners and would reaffirm their relationship.

Therefore, it is not surprising that the rules of civil and criminal procedure were generally not observed in the reconciliation board proceedings. Rather, the hearings had the form of narrative accounts of the disputes; the parties talked to each other and to the court in a way that liberated them from following strict norms and legal jargon. In addition, the parties were typically not represented by lawyers. All of these characteristics created the impression that reconciliation boards were not typical courts in which uneducated parties could not follow complex legal rules. The proceedings were not held in the courthouse, but rather in a local community office.

Once the parties stated their respective viewpoints, a general discussion usually followed, upon the conclusion of which the board tried to resolve the dispute. Felstiner and Drew (1978, p. 27) reported that formal reconciliation occurred in 60-80% of the cases. The "verdict" given by the board was written in the form of a contract between the parties.

The structure of this process and the features of the decision-making mechanism implied that it was particularly important who the judges were. Judges — members of reconciliation boards — were lay persons of social and political influence, persons whose credibility guaranteed that their "wise" decisions would be accepted as such. This was particularly true and important in the rural areas, which is where reconciliation boards were used most frequently.[11]

China does not utilize lay courts; rather, it provides for another way of lay persons' decision-making in informal groups called mediation committees. Mediation committees can be described as (Reichel, 1994, p. 254):

> ... small groups ... of 10 to 20 people to which everyone in China, except small children, belongs. The units are organized at places of work, neighborhoods, schools, and the like, so each person is likely to belong to several such groups (especially one at work and one in the neighborhood). The resulting peer pressure from these constant companions provides the glue holding together an informal sanctioning process.

In the 1980s there were more than 800,000 mediation committees, each of which consisted of five to eleven members, and a total of six million mediators elected by popular vote for two-year terms (Leng and Chiu, 1985, p. 68). Clark (1989, p. 61) reported that there was a unit of mediation committee for almost every 1,700 citizens (with approximately 700,000 mediation committees across the country).

---

[11]See Felstiner and Drew (1978, p. 28) for a thorough discussion of this and other reasons for the greater usage of reconciliation boards in rural areas.

Each member of Chinese society belongs to several such units, but observers (Troyer, 1989, p. 27) argue that the work unit organization is a more powerful association than the neighborhood unit. These units have an extensive power over their members, and, for example, "once a person is assigned to a work unit, it is difficult to change jobs" (Troyer, 1989, p. 27) because the unit may be reluctant to approve the change. In that sense, the membership is not voluntary.

The idea of mediation committees, which are not a part of the official state apparatus but are unofficially considered to be the lowest level of the criminal justice system (Reichel, 1994, p. 254), is related to both the views and philosophy of the socialist morale and a long-lasting dislike for the legal profession. The dislike of lawyers dates back at least to Imperial China, when one could be sentenced to a three-year sentence for helping the parties in a case prepare legal documents (McCabe, 1989, p. 121). McCabe (1989, p. 117) provided an example of the way these attitudes are expressed in the emperor's response to the criticism of the courts in the 17th century:

> The good citizens, who may have difficulties among themselves, will settle them like brothers, by referring them to the arbitration of some old man or the mayor of the commune. As for those who are troublesome, obstinate, and quarrelsome, let them be ruined in the law courts — that is the justice that is due to them.

Similar attitudes have persisted over time, culminating with the extensive prosecution of lawyers in the late 1950s, resulting in only 2,000 lawyers in the 1970s and 12,000 lawyers in the 1980s in a country of one billion (McCabe, 1989, p. 121). Mao encouraged popular participation, while condemning the bureaucracy and the development of technocracy (technical experts), including the courts (McCabe, 1989, p. 118). After his death in 1976, the People's Republic of China started a legal development program, which included the development of the first comprehensive code of substantive law and procedural law (MaCabe, 1989, p. 118). Clark (1989, p. 63) connected this increased activity with the orientation of mediation committees:

With the extensive development of the formal legal system in the thrust toward the rule of law, people's justice at the local level is increasingly becoming a legal education and prevention force in the country. This is not to say that local units do not handle important conflict matters; but ... the drive to bring legal education to the grass roots throughout the entire country, coupled with the expansion of trained personnel at the lowest levels of the official bureaucracy, has allowed the focus of this remaining mass organization to concentrate on early intervention and education about potentially problematic behavior.

Mediation committees serve as a filter, a transmission board, and the enforcer of the norms, values, and rules that the government deems appropriate and broadcasts through the media. Mediation boards are in charge of enforcing such norms and, therefore, controlling the behavior of their members, ranging from "misbehavior and outright deviance to questions of health care and family planning" (Reichel, 1994, p. 255). Clark (1989, p. 63) described the jurisdiction of these committees:

Actual cases range from domestic quarrels, to neighborhood disturbances, to economic squabbles over the sale of goods, to juveniles' neglecting school or work, to minor theft. Technically, these committees do not handle criminal cases, but it seems evident that some of their cases could have been handled under the criminal or public security code.

These committees handled up to 90% of civil cases in China; in 1981 they handled 2.8 times as many civil and minor criminal cases as basic people's courts did (Leng and Chiu, 1985, p. 68). The methods used are highly non-legalistic and non-formalistic and include discussions and persuasion (McCabe, 1989, p. 64).

1.1.4 Mixed Tribunals

Historically, Germany is a "country of origin" of contemporary mixed tribunals. Mixed tribunals are typically utilized in countries of Central, Eastern, and Northern Europe (i.e., in general, in the countries whose legal systems are based on civil law).

Mixed tribunals span across different ideologies; they have been a part of the court system in the current and former socialist countries, for example, China (McCabe, 1989), Poland (Kubicki and Zawadzki, 1970), Hungary (Kulcsár, 1972, 1982), the former Czechoslovakia (Krystufek, 1976), the former German Democratic Republic (Buchholz, 1986), and the former Yugoslavia (Kamhi and Čalija, 1974; Ljubanović, 1983, 1989), as well as in Western democracies, for example, Germany (Görlitz, 1970; Casper and Zeisel, 1972; Klausa, 1972; Gerken, 1988), Austria (Frassine et al., 1979), Denmark (Anderson, 1990), Finland, and Sweden (Klami and Hämäläinen, 1992).

Mixed tribunals are a unique form of lay participation in legal decision-making because professional judges and lay judges (also referred to as lay assessors) hear the case together and need to determine and decide both factual and legal issues in the case. The size of mixed tribunals varies from the most common one, a three-member tribunal composed of one professional judge and two lay judges (and has been utilized in, e.g., China, Croatia, Germany, Poland), to a nine-member tribunal, which was composed of three professional judges and six lay judges (and had been utilized in Germany until its abolishment in 1974).

Unlike the systems that utilize jury trials, in which the defendants can select between a bench trial and a jury trial and the guilty plea eliminates the trial,[12] the systems that utilize mixed tribunals do not allow the defendants to choose the decision-maker in criminal cases; if the law mandates that a mixed tribunal has the jurisdiction, the case will indeed be tried by a mixed tribunal. Such statutory provisions and the fact that plea bargaining plays a very limited role in civil-law systems together imply that the percentage

---

[12]The new Spanish jury is an exception to this rule; since the right to a jury trial is not provided as either a constitutional right or a procedural right of the defendant, the defendant may not waive it (Thaman, 1998, p. 258).

of cases tried by lay participants is larger in the countries that utilize mixed tribunals than in the countries that utilize the jury.

Casper and Zeisel reported that, although the majority of criminal cases (388,619 or 83%) tried in West German courtrooms in 1969 were tried by a professional judge alone, the number of trials by mixed tribunals in the same year was fairly large — mixed tribunals conducted approximately 80,000 trials of adult offenders (Casper and Zeisel, 1972, p. 143). On the other hand, fewer offenses were placed under the jurisdiction of a professional judge in Sweden. Nelson reported that there were 12,000 trials by a professional judge alone and 63,000 trials by mixed tribunals at Swedish district courts in 1984, that is, as many as 84% of trials were conducted by mixed tribunals (Nelson, 1987, p. 136). Similarly, Klami and Hämäläinen (1992, p. 35) reported that the overwhelming majority of criminal cases (89%) tried in Swedish courtrooms in 1985 were tried by mixed tribunals.

The number of lay judges required to sit in trials by mixed tribunals is by no means minor. Kubicki and Zawadzki (1970, p. 97) reported that approximately 50,000 lay judges were elected in Poland, a country of 32.6 million inhabitants according to the 1970 Census (*1979/80 Statistical Yearbook*, 1981, p. 73), for a single term of office. These numbers suggest that approximately 153 lay judges per 100,000 inhabitants served at the time. Rácz (1972, p. 412) reported that approximately 17,000-18,000 lay judges were selected triennially in Hungary, a country of 10 million inhabitants according to the 1970 Census (*1979/80 Statistical Yearbook*, 1981, p. 73). It follows that there were 170 lay judges per 100,000 inhabitants in Hungary at the time. Richert (1983, p. 8) reported that 27,000 lay judges served in criminal courts in West Germany in 1976. According to the 1970 Census, there were 60.7 million inhabitants living in West Germany (*1979/80 Statistical Yearbook*, 1981, p. 73). The rate of lay judges per 100,000 inhabitants was somewhat smaller than the rates in other countries (mostly in Eastern Europe) — 45 lay judges per 100,000. Buchholz (1986, p. 218) reported that approximately 40,000 lay judges were elected in the 1980s for criminal and civil courts and 10,000 lay judges were elected for labor courts in the former German Democratic Republic, a country of 17 million inhabitants (*1979/80 Statistical Yearbook*, 1981, p. 73). The rate in East Germany (234 lay judges per 100,000 inhabitants) at the time was higher than the rate in West Germany. As of January 1, 1997, there were 60,947 lay judges (including juvenile lay judges) in (reunited) Germany (*Bundesministerium der Justiz*, 1997, p. 7-12), which is approximately 75 lay judges per 100,000 inhabitants.[13]

In the former Yugoslavia, a country with a population of 23.4 million in 1987 (*Statistical Calendar of Yugoslavia*, 1989, p. 33), there were 54,149 lay judges in regular courts in 1987 (*Statistical Calendar of Yugoslavia*, 1989, p. 151). In other words, approximately 231 lay judges per 100,000 inhabitants served at the time. Similarly, Ljubanović (1983, 1989) reported that there were 2,207 selected lay judges and 863,292 inhabitants in the part of former Yugoslavia where he conducted his study of mixed tribunals, which yielded an average of 256 lay judges per 100,000 inhabitants.

Mixed tribunals are heterogeneous groups that consist of lay judges and professional judges who try cases jointly; the judges sit together during trial, hear and examine evidence, and deliberate. Thus, professional judges and lay judges decide both factual and legal issues in the case jointly. Professional judges in mixed tribunals have an opportunity to "correct" the views of lay judges and to explain the law; at the same time, lay judges have the opportunity to "correct" the professional judges' views by bringing the fresh approach of an average citizen.

The size of the tribunal may vary in accordance with the seriousness of the case; although the general rule is that the number of lay judges at the trial level exceeds the number of professional judges in the tribunal and, consequently, lay judges can outvote professional judges, this is not always the case. For example, German *Grosse Strafkammer* decides felony cases and is composed of three professional judges and two lay judges (Wolfe, 1996, p. 324). Swedish

---

[13]The population of Germany in 1999 is estimated at approximately 81.76 million (*Germany: Facts and Figures*, 1997).

mixed tribunals also vary in size (Klami and Hämäläinen, 1992, p. 34), from the smallest ones — the four-member tribunal (one professional judge and three lay judges) — to the largest ones — the eight-member tribunal (two professional judges and six lay judges).

The Croatian *Criminal Procedure Law* (1998) distinguishes between mixed tribunals of three different sizes. The size and the composition of the tribunal change depending on the seriousness of the offense. Offenses for which the prescribed sanction is between three and fifteen years of imprisonment are tried by a "small tribunal," which is composed of one professional judge and two lay judges (Articles 18 and 20, *Criminal Procedure Law*, 1998). Offenses for which the prescribed sanction is fifteen years of imprisonment are tried by a "large tribunal," which is composed of two professional judges and three lay judges (Article 20, *Criminal Procedure Law*, 1998). Finally, offenses for which the prescribed sanction exceeds fifteen years of imprisonment (the so-called "long-term imprisonment" — twenty to forty years of imprisonment) are tried by an even larger tribunal, which is composed of three professional judges and four lay judges (Article 20, *Criminal Procedure Law*, 1998). The latter is a recent addition which, unlike the more seasoned "small tribunals" and "large tribunals," was not present in the previous criminal procedure laws of Croatia.

In some types of cases the eligibility of lay judges may be predicated upon special qualifications. For example, lay judges in juvenile cases need to have professional experience with education of juveniles (e.g., being a teacher or a social worker). German law requires that juvenile lay judges need to be trained and experienced in juvenile education (Article 35, *Juvenile Court Code*, 1974).

Soon after the mixed tribunals were introduced into Yugoslav courtrooms in 1945, the *Criminal Procedure Law* of 1948 (Article 314) required the candidates for lay judges who were to try juvenile cases (i.e., participate in the work of the so-called "juvenile mixed tribunals") to be experienced in the education of juveniles. In the parlance of jury terminology, these lay judges were "blue-ribbon" lay judges — experts in the specific area which is highly relevant to the decisions in the case and in which the professional judge was not trained in.[14]

Croatia features a typical continental European system of mixed tribunals. As mentioned earlier, professional judges and lay judges hear cases and reach decisions about both facts and legal issues in the case jointly. The respective positions of the tribunal members are normatively specified. In general terms, lay judges and professional judges are equals during trial and deliberation; their votes have the same weight. Thus, two lay judges can outvote a professional judge in small tribunals, and, similarly, three lay judges can outvote two professional judges in large tribunals. On the other hand, although lay judges (elected persons without legal education or systematic training in legal decision-making) and professional judges have the same decision-making power, only professional judges (professional lawyers appointed as professional judges) may preside over the work of the tribunals; that is, not all members are charged with the same responsibilities. For example, the presiding judge conducts the trial, interrogates the defendant(s), witnesses, and expert witnesses, and lets the other members of the tribunal speak (Article 297, *Criminal Procedure Law*, 1998). The presiding judge, upon completing his/her own examination, has the duty to allow other members of the tribunal to ask questions directly of the defendant, witnesses, and expert witnesses.

The tribunal in civil-law systems has a more active role than the professional judge in common-law systems; the tribunal has the responsibility of both deciding which evidence to examine and examining that evidence. There are numerous differences between the jury and mixed tribunals because the underlying legal systems are very distinct. For illustrative purposes, I will use examples of Croatia (a civil-law country) and the United States (a common-law country).

---

[14]The next *Criminal Procedure Law* (1953, Article 415) expanded these requirements even further by requiring that lay judges who were to try juvenile cases had to be either professors, teachers, educators, or other persons who had experience in the education and upbringing of juveniles.

There is a tendency in both types of systems to avoid bias in lay participants, but the ways of achieving this goal differ. Jurors are selected for a particular trial. During the selection process, called *voir dire*, the professional judge and the attorneys have the right to ask questions of potential jurors in order to detect bias. Once attorneys detect bias in prospective jurors, they may ask for challenges for cause. If the judge grants the challenge, the indicated prospective jurors will be excluded. Attorneys also may ask, usually without giving any reasons (peremptory challenges), that certain potential jurors be excluded, up to a predetermined maximum number of such jurors. It is important to note that attorneys do not tend to select jurors who are not biased; rather, they tend to select jurors who would, in their mind, better suit the purpose of their clients. In other words, if attorneys do detect bias, they would not challenge potential jurors as long as the direction of the bias serves their clients.

No similar mechanism exists in the context of trials by mixed tribunals. Lay judges are not selected for each case; rather, they are elected once for a period of several years during which they sit in a number of cases. Although a process similar to *voir dire* does not exist, lay judges can be challenged once elected. For each trial, lay judges can be excused for the same reasons for which professional judges can be excused. These include, for example, intense friendship or hostility with the parties or attorneys in the case, or kinship with the parties or attorneys in the case.

The second important difference between the jury and mixed tribunals relates to the delineation of "who decides what." As mentioned earlier, in the context of jury trials, juries usually decide only the guilt, while professional judges determine the sentence. On the other hand, lay judges in mixed tribunals not only decide the guilt (like jurors do), but also determine the sanction. Furthermore, lay judges decide the guilt and determine the sentence *jointly* with professional judges.

The third difference is centered around the question of whether the decision has to be explained. Juries do not have an obligation to explain, or give reasons for, their verdict.[15] The jury foreperson conveys the decision reached by the jury by answering simple questions, for example, whether or not the jury found the defendant guilty of particular count(s) of the indictment, or whether or not the factual questions in the case have been proven. As discussed earlier, since the jury does not give an explanation for its decisions, it has the power to decide on any grounds, regardless of whether or not its reasons are legally acceptable. On the other hand, lay judges in mixed tribunals are in a completely different position: the mixed tribunal they sit in has to state the reasons for its decision in the form of a written verdict. Furthermore, the parties can appeal the verdict if, for example, those reasons were not clearly stated in the verdict or the reasoning given in the verdict contradicts the law.

Finally, the important difference is the finality of the decision. If the jury finds the defendant guilty, the professional judge passes the sentence and the decision may be appealed. If, on the other hand, the jury acquits the defendant (finds the defendant not to be guilty), such a decision is final, that is, there is no possibility of appeal. By contrast, regardless of whether the mixed tribunal finds the defendant guilty or innocent, appeal is possible. The parties can appeal the verdict not only if the verdict contradicts the law, but also if the written verdict violates the rules of logic or the factual issues have not been determined correctly. The appellate decision may be either in the hands of a professional tribunal (composed of professional judges only, as is the case in Croatia) or in the hands of a mixed tribunal (composed of both professional judges and lay judges, as is the case in Sweden). The justification for the use of professional tribunals at the appellate level is that the decision at the appellate stage is a complex legal decision which is not easily accessible to the persons not trained in law.

Mixed tribunals in African countries operated on quite a different principle, one based on the Indian legislation: not only did professional judges and lay

---

[15]An interesting counterexample is the new Spanish jury which needs to provide the reasons for its decision (Thaman, 1998, p. 364). Based on the legal requirement that "reasons shall be given for all criminal judgments," the legislator decided to apply this rule even to the new jury trials.

judges perform different roles, but they also had very different decision-making powers. In fact, lay judges did not participate in legal decision-making with professional judges; rather, they were considered to be "experts" or "advisors" on the subject of local laws and customs and were expected to provide their individual opinion. In that sense, lay judges were truly lay *assessors* who had expertise on local laws and could assist professional judges in colonial, British-based courts in dealing with the cases which required some familiarity and adaptation to local customs. Their opinion, however, did not bind the professional judge (Gray, 1958; Jearey, 1961b, p. 88).

Although the professional judge in the former British African Territories was not bound by the lay judges' opinion and the final decision in the case rested with the professional judge (Jearey, 1961b, p. 85), the Court of Appeal for Eastern Africa held that it was desirable that lay judges provide reasons for their opinion (Jearey, 1961b, p. 88). Richings (1976, p. 114) wrote that lay judges in the South African courtrooms had been employed only in an advisory capacity until 1935 and that since then "they have been full members of the court on the questions of fact." Ross (1973) pointed out that if the professional judge disagreed with the *unanimous* opinion of lay judges in the East-African countries of Tanzania, Kenya, and Uganda, the professional judge had to record the reasons for disagreement in writing. Gray (1958, p. 6) stated that, based on *R. v. Mwita* (1948), professional judges were not required, but were recommended, to explain in their opinion the reasons for disagreement with the lay judges' opinion.

Lay assessors in South Africa who participated in death-penalty cases did not resemble a typical profile of lay judges; the statutory requirement was that lay judges should have *legal* experience or other skill relevant to the trial and it seems that the overwhelming majority of lay judges in South-African courtrooms who actually decided on factual issues in death-penalty trials were lawyers (van Zyl Smit and Isakow, 1985, p. 221). Unlike European lay judges, who decided both factual issues and legal issues in the case, South-African lay judges participated only in deciding factual issues, but not in legal issues or sentence (van Zyl Smit and Isakow, 1985, p. 225-226). In 1991, lay participation was introduced at lower courts as well; moreover, lay participants at lower courts need not be legally trained.

Interestingly, some African countries in the past concurrently utilized both jury trials and trials by mixed tribunals. The choice of the decision-maker depended on a number of factors, such as the defendant's choice (Siera Leone; Jearey, 1960, p. 136), seriousness of the crime (Nigeria; Jearey, 1960, p. 144), the defendant's origin (Kenya; Jearey, 1961a, p. 43), inability to summon a sufficient number of jurors (Southern Rhodesia; Jearey, 1961a, p. 44).

1.1.5   Absence of Lay Participation

Some countries, such as Japan (Lempert, 1992; Dean, 1995), South Korea (Chang and Janeksela, 1996), Saudi Arabia (Solaim, 1971; Moore, 1987; Reichel, 1994; Moore, 1996), Bahrain (Moore, 1996),[16] and the Netherlands (Griffiths, 1997), do not feature any lay participation in their respective criminal justice systems (although some of them may have done so in the past). For example, the *Courts Law* (1984) of Israel stipulates that only lawyers may be legal decision-makers. In fact, the *Courts Law* (1984) requires judges to

---

[16]Islamic law (*Shari'a*) is one of the major legal systems distinct from both the civil-law systems and the common-law tradition. Unlike the aforementioned two legal traditions, it is believed that Islamic law is not created by men for men; it does not contain a codified set of legal rules. Rather, it is based on the Islamic religion. There are two primary sources (*Qur'an* — a set of principles believed to have been revealed by God through Muhammad — and *Sunna* — a set of decisions of the Prophet respecting circumstances not addressed in *Qur'an*) and two secondary sources (*Ijma* — a consensus of jurist decisions made in the absence of a ruling by either God or Muhammad — and *Qiyas* — a method of analysis or reasoning by analogy; Moore, 1996, p. 390). Consequently, professional judges (*kadi*) who serve at the *kadi* courts in, for example, Saudi Arabia are different from their counterparts in the common-law systems or civil-law systems; they begin their advanced education by attending a five-year preparatory religious school, upon the completion of which they enroll in one of the four *Shari'a* law schools (law schools in Saudi Arabia do not have university status; Reichel, 1994, p. 217). *Kadi* are employed by the state and serve as full-time judges. Furthermore, upon their selection by the Ministry of Justice, they are required to complete a three-year course of judicial training at the Higher Judicial Institute (Reichel, 1994, p. 217).

be law-school graduates and to have several years of experience after the bar exam either in legal practice or in another law-related activity (e.g., being a law-school professor).

Some countries continue to limit lay participation in other decision-making groups. For example, the Netherlands recently further reduced lay participation by abolishing it in social insurance tribunals and limiting it to only non-court proceedings and tribunals, such as medical disciplinary tribunals (Griffiths, 1997, p. 153). Griffiths (1997, p. 156, 158) interpreted this reluctance to rely on lay participation as follows:

> The special expertise that the Dutch attribute to judges — and the ignorance, emotionalism and lack of wise judgment they attribute to the average person — is generally regarded by them as a fatal objection to the jury ... It is my conclusion that the lack of expertise with regard to the finding of facts that the Dutch attribute to juries is not so much a well-founded description of the jury system as it is a typical expression of a particular political culture ... In general, Dutch political culture is characterized by a deep respect for professionals, based on their academic training and the specialized knowledge and competence they are supposed to possess. In other cultures respect is earned in other ways (age, wealth, power, etc.). Such a fundamental cultural difference has profound consequences for the way public institutions which require broad societal support are organized.

Japan, a prominent example of a country that presently features no lay participation in criminal trials, employed the jury in criminal cases earlier in this century, had since abolished it altogether, and has recently debated its reintroduction in civil cases (Lempert, 1992; Dean, 1995). The jury was introduced in Japan by the *Jury Law* of 1923 (which did not come into effect until 1928). As an integral part of the process of the opening up of Japan to the West, the jury was given initial consideration in the late 19th century (Dean, 1995, p. 383). In the 1880s Japanese legislators adopted the French inquisitorial system by passing both the *Penal Code* and the *Code of Criminal Instruction* (i.e., the *Criminal Procedure Code*). Although some voices were raised in favor of introducing the jury system as well, this did not happen. The new *Code of Criminal Procedure* of 1922 added elements of German criminal procedure (Dean, 1995, p. 384-385). At that point, consideration was given to both the jury and mixed tribunals, but the Japanese government decided to introduce the jury. According to Dean (1995, p. 386), this decision

> ... was not due to an overwhelming distrust of professional judges, or that they exhibited signs of being in need of restraint; instead there was a desire to see people participate in the administration of justice and the jury was seen as part of the process of democratisation.

Rather than deciding on the defendant's guilt, jurors provided a special verdict — they answered a series of factual questions asked by the professional judge. Their answers did not bind the professional judge, who had the right to order a retrial if he found the decision to be "improper" (Lempert, 1992, p. 37; Dean, 1995, p. 387). The decline of the jury began only two years after its introduction; over the 15-year period of its existence, there were fewer than 500 jury trials (Dean, 1995, p. 388). In 1942 the percentage of eligible cases in which jury trials were waived reached a staggering 98%, resulting in only two jury trials in 1942 (Dean, 1995, p. 388). Not surprisingly, the jury was abolished in 1943.

A number of reasons contributed toward this demise (Urabe, 1976, p. 486; Lempert, 1992, p. 38; Dean, 1995, p. 388). First, there was already a mixture of criminal procedure based on legislation in two different countries, France and Germany; the jury, which is more suitable for the adversarial procedure (characteristic of the common-law countries) may have added too much to that mixture. Second, there were severe limitations on appeals in jury trials. Third, trials by jury were expensive. Fourth, answers provided by the jury did not bind the professional judge. Finally, people in Japan have a greater tendency to trust professional judges (or public officials in general) than people who live in Western democracies do. In fact, Dean argued that, as a consequence of the immense respect toward authority (created and maintained via strict hi-

176558

erarchical structures and rules in Japanese society), the Japanese "trusted the findings of professional judges more than they valued the opinion of laymen" (Dean, 1995, p. 388).

After the end of World War II the common-law tradition had a significant influence on Japanese laws. Nevertheless, the American attempts to reintroduce the jury were met with considerable Japanese resistance and were unsuccessful (Dean, 1995, p. 389). About three decades later, a series of scandals that brought to light the inadequacies of the existing inquisitorial procedure by pointing out several gross miscarriages of justice lead toward imminent questions about the independence of the judiciary. Recently, calls for judicial reform and the reintroduction of the jury surfaced (Dean, 1995, p. 395). The most important argument for the introduction of the jury system, its democratic character, was recognized by the Japanese Supreme Court in 1990 (Dean, 1995, p. 401).

Argentina is an example of a country whose legal system is based primarily on the civil-law tradition. Modeled after the U.S. *Constitution*, the Argentinean *Constitution* of 1853 provides for trial by jury.[17] However, unlike the U.S. *Constitution*, which provides an explicit right to a jury trial for the defendants (Amendment VII, 1791), the Argentinean *Constitution* does not guarantee this right to the defendants explicitly. Rather, the Argentinean *Constitution* determines that, "... the Congress will promote ... the establishment of trial by jury" (Article 24), that powers of the Congress include the power "... to establish the civil, commercial, [and] penal codes ... and especially to establish ... general laws for the whole nation ... necessary for the establishment of the jury trial ..." (Article 75.12), and that, "[a]ll the regular criminal trials ... will be tried by juries, after this institution has been established in the Republic ..." (Article 118). This right has not been established either by the Argentinean *Criminal Procedure Code* (1991) or the Argentinean *Criminal Judiciary Act* (1991). The Argentinean *Criminal Judi-*

---

[17]Argentina modified its *Constitution* in 1994, but the changes did not affect the rules pertaining to the jury system.

ciary Act (1991) specifies in Article 12 that a professional tribunal composed of three professional judges will try for crimes specified in Article 25 of the *Criminal Procedure Code* (1991) for which the punishment is three years of imprisonment or more. On the other hand, Article 26 of the *Criminal Procedure Code* (1991) determines that, upon the completion of an investigation, a professional judge alone will try for crimes for which the punishment is up to three years of imprisonment. An exception to this rule is provided in Articles 13 and 17 of the Argentinean *Criminal Judiciary Act* (1991), which stipulate that, regardless of the seriousness of crime and punishment prescribed, the decision-making body for a number of white-collar crimes and economic crimes will be composed of three professional judges.

Interestingly, the executive branch of the Argentinean government proposed the so-called Maier/Binder criminal procedure project to the House of Representatives in 1987, but the laws did not pass. Article 30 of the *Project Concerning the Organization of Criminal Justice and the Office of the Attorney General* (1988) proposed an introduction of mixed tribunals composed of two permanent judges, one lawyer (who is not regularly employed by the state), and two lay persons for felony trials. The same article proposed that mixed tribunals in charge of misdemeanors be composed of one permanent judge, one lawyer, and one lay judge. Appellate decisions were to be made by professional judges only.

Argentina is a federation composed of 23 provinces, each of which has the power to determine its own court organization and criminal procedure. One of the provinces, Cordoba, provides for lay participation in criminal trials for serious crimes. In particular, Article 369 of the *Code of Criminal Procedure of the Province of Cordoba* (1992) explicitly states that,

> ... if the maximum penalty for the crime included in the indictment is 15 years of imprisonment or more, the court [composed of three professional judges; Article 34 *ter.* 3, *Code of Criminal Procedure Law of the Province of Cordoba*, 1992], upon the request by the prosecutor, the private prosecutor, or the defendant, will add two lay persons.

1.2 Positive Functions of Lay Participation

Lay participation in legal decision-making plays a remarkable variety of roles; it is intended to fulfill several positive functions. The most frequently emphasized positive function of lay participation is its **political function**, that is, its tendency to provide for independent and democratic legal decision-making. For example, the *New South Wales Law Reform Commission* (Kawaley, 1989, p. 533-534) examined the jury system and concluded:

> We consider that the jury as an institution is such a crucial and fundamental symbol and component of democracy that it should not be surrendered until, first, it is clearly shown that it operates so incompetently as to deny other democratic rights, and second, that no amount of procedural tinkering can overcome this incompetence.

The democratization of the criminal justice system was recently advocated as the main reason for the introduction of the jury in post-Franco Spain (Thaman, 1998, p. 250). Interestingly, the jury was not legislated as a constitutional or procedural right of the defendant (as is the case in, e.g., the United States — Amendment VI of the *Constitution of the United States*, 1791); rather, the jury was viewed as a "right-duty" (Thaman, 1998, p. 257) of the citizens to participate in the criminal justice system.

At the heart of the political function of lay participation is the notion of being judged by one's peers as opposed to being judged by professional judges. The U.S. Supreme Court even defined the jury through this "peer" issue; the jury is "a body of men composed of the peers or equals of the person whose rights it is selected or summoned to determine" (*Strauder v. West Virginia*, 1879, p. 308). Heath (1993, p. 138) elaborated:

> Trial by one's peers is a belief rooted deep in our heritage and there remains to this day a healthy scepticism to any system that has to be administered by professionals or any law that can only be interpreted by experts. For this reason, [the British] Parliament has limited the number of stipendiary magistrates to one hundred.

A legal process in which lay persons participate is perceived as more democratic than the one handled by the professional elite alone. The political function of lay participation is connected with the very essence of the democratic process:

> ... with the centralization of the administration of justice, e.g., when royal judicial process gained hegemony, lay participation gained political significance (either in the representation of local interest, or as a factor of influence of the 'unprivileged classes' or as the opponent to royal power) which today has crystallized into the principle of the democratic control of the courts (Kulcsár, 1982, p. 34).

Professional judges are perceived as a professional elite and a part of the state legal machinery, which limits their credibility and independence in the eyes of the population. On the other hand, lay participants are supposed to be independent from the state. According to Kulcsár (1982, p. 34), lay participants are not bound by the organizational restrictions in the same way professional judges are, and are thus freed from the state's direct influence.

Lay participants typically do not participate in the decision-making process on a regular basis. Lay magistrates in the United Kingdom are employed part-time and can sit in 26 half-day sessions in the court per year, while stipendiary magistrates are employed full-time (Diamod, 1990). Lay judges who sit in mixed tribunals are selected for a period of several years (typically four or five) and are occasionally summoned to the court to serve on a particular day. Klami *et al.* (1990, p. 93) reported that Swedish lay judges typically serve less than ten days per year. Similarly, Buchholz (1989, p. 218) reported that lay judges in the former German Democratic Republic served for two weeks each year. Although research studies indicate that a certain percentage of selected lay judges (15-30%, depending on the court) does not perform their duty when summoned (Ljubanović, 1983, p. 179), lay judges are considerably more numerous than professional judges[18] and are thus summoned to perform their duty rarely.[19]

Jurors serve even less frequently. In the United States, names are randomly selected from the master list of eligible jurors for *venire* — the list of potential jurors who are eligible for a given period of service (two to four weeks). The *voir dire* process serves to reduce the jury panel of 30 (for a twelve-member jury) to the 14 persons (12 jurors and 2 alternatives) selected for jury duty in a particular case. In other words, jurors are not selected to (occasionally) serve for a period of several years; rather, they were selected to serve in a particular case. Jurors in newly introduced Russian juries serve only once a year for a period of no longer than ten days or until the end of the trial (Thaman, 1995, p. 83).

Lay participants do not earn their salary from this duty, which is another factor that makes them more independent than professional judges are. Lay magistrates in the United Kingdom, for example, are volunteers; they receive compensation only for the expenses associated with their lost salary and a modest travel allowance if they live more than three miles from the court (Diamond, 1990, p. 197). Similarly, lay judges in Croatia receive symbolic amounts of money that cover their travel expenses and an equivalent of between three and five dollars per hour, depending on the type of court at which they serve (*Regulations Concerning Compensation and Awards for Lay Judges*, 1996). In addition, their employers pay them a full salary for the days they are absent from work in order to serve at the court. West German lay judges received 4 DM per hour in 1975 for their service, in addition to the reimbursement for potentially lost income, which was paid at a rate of additional 10 DM per hour (Richert, 1977, p. 500). In the United States, employers in a

---

[18]According to the *1991 Statistical Yearbook* (1991), in 1990 there were 8,928 lay judges and only 800 professional judges at district courts in Croatia.

[19]However, Ljubanović (1983) pointed out that there were exceptions to this rule; it appears that courts frequently tended to summon a smaller number of lay judges who, for reasons of convenience, were more accessible or reliable (e.g., retirees or housewives). These practices raise the question of representativeness of lay judges who actually perform their duty.

few states have the obligation to pay for jurors for the days they are absent from work in order to perform jury duty (*State Court Organization 1993*, 1995, p. 265-268); jurors in some states also receive their daily fees, ranging from four or five dollars (e.g., Illinois, Connecticut) to $30 (Hawaii) or $40 (South Dakota, federal courts).

It is quite interesting to compare these relatively modest daily remuneration rates to the ones paid to lay participants in Spain and Russia. Russian jurors are paid the higher of the following two amounts: either their current salary or one-half of the *pro-rata* salary of a professional judge (Thaman, 1995, p. 83). Thaman (1995, p. 83) reported that jurors were paid 3,500 rubles (slightly less than three dollars at the time) a day for their three days of service, while one juror was paid 13,000 rubles per day because she proved that this was her salary. Thaman (1995, p. 83) explains the reasons for this relatively high rate:

> Reformers hope that this high pay will encourage citizens to appear for jury duty and participate in the administration of justice. This encouragement is particularly necessary because the penalty for a juror's non-appearance is merely a minor fine; the judge has no power to issue a bench warrant or to jail a recalcitrant prospective juror [footnotes omitted].

The jurors in Spain receive even larger sums of money for their services. The *Law on Trial by Jury* (1995) in Section 7(1) stipulates that jurors be remunerated at a rate equivalent to the *per diem* salary of a criminal law judge. The Spanish Ministry of Justice issued a memorandum setting this daily remuneration at 1,270 pesetas per hour or 10,160 pesetas per day (approximately $81.00 per day), in addition to transportation and other expenses (Thaman, 1998, p. 265).

The fact that lay participants receive either no compensation or only symbolic compensation for their work is used to substantiate the claim of their independence from the state. However, absence of compensation may have a negative interpretation as well:

> The trouble is that lay magistrates are not paid — not that they ever should be — and many people equate payment with ability,

unpaid work with amateurism and amateurism with incompetence. What these people fail to see, and what many court clerks, and others even higher in the system, all of whom are in favour of the lay magistracy, fail to see is that although sitting on the bench may be only a part-time unpaid activity, that does not mean that those thus engaged are fools. Many lay magistrates hold extremely important jobs; some have jobs beside which being a Crown Court Judge looks like a hobby (Block, 1996, p. 887).

In the spirit of the jurors who, despite being deprived of food and drink for two days, refused to convict William Penn and William Mead of unlawful assembly (Moore, 1973, p. 83-86), the presence of lay participants is also perceived as a **safeguard against potential tyranny** by the government or government officials. The Justices of the U.S. Supreme Court in *Singer v. United States* (1965, p. 31) wrote that, "the [jury trial] clause was clearly intended to protect the accused from oppression by the Government." In a later decision, *Duncan v. Louisiana* (1968, p. 155), Justice White emphasized that the right to jury trial was guaranteed to criminal defendants in federal and state courts as a safeguard:

A right to jury trial is granted to criminal defendants in order to prevent oppression by the Government. Those who wrote our constitutions knew from history and experience that it was necessary to protect against unfounded criminal charges brought to eliminate enemies and against judges too responsive to the voice of higher authority. The framers of the constitutions strove to create an independent judiciary but insisted upon further protection against arbitrary action. Providing an accused with the right to be tried by a jury of his peers gave him an inestimable safeguard against the corrupt or overzealous prosecutor and against the compliant, biased, or eccentric judge.

It is quite interesting to hear the same arguments echoed in a different part of the world. In the early 1990s the jury was reintroduced in Russia; the system of mixed tribunals was retained and the choice between the two decision-making bodies was left to the defendants (Thaman, 1995, p. 85-86). Yakolev (1988) commented on the draft of the legislation:

Ideally, the court is an open contest between two equal sides
— the defence and the prosecution. The judge must preserve objectivity and make his decisions based on all the evidence. The
judge represents the interests of the state. But does he always
understand these interests correctly? What are we to do with his
objectivity if the case concerns a conflict between a citizen and the
state (represented by this or that organ)? The state can influence
its employees. Whereas the law, rather than someone's interests,
must reign supreme in the court ... We should set up a court of
people's representatives ... Such a measure would be in keeping
with the democratic transformations now going on in our country.
The jury's role in the history of justice is great.

The introduction of the jury in Croatia in 1850, almost 150 years ago, raised
the same sentiments. Šulek (1952, p. 138), a Croatian journalist, emphasized
in 1850 the lay participants' independence as one of the several positive functions of the then newly introduced jury system:

Every citizen wants to have a judge whom one can trust, but a
regular [professional] judge who follows the letter of the law rarely
enjoys such a level of trust. In order to resolve this problem, the
jury, in which honest, able, and unbiased people sit, to whom neither the prosecutor nor the defendant can object, was accepted.
The court composed in this way, of course, is a great benefaction,
and the jury is considered to be the most precious treasure of any
constitutional state. It is impossible to imagine the freedom of
press without the jury.

Interestingly, the same idea — the idea of democracy — is often cited as
an important reason for the introduction of lay participation in both capitalist and (former) communist countries. The role of lay participation in former
communist countries was similar to the role lay participation plays in capitalist countries; however, the underlying ideology was different. According to
Marxist ideology, the ultimate stage of the development of human society is
communism. As the society progresses toward communism, the whole machinery of the state and the state itself will collapse. Behavior would no longer

be controlled by the law and courts; rather, it would be controlled by the approval of the society (David and Brierley, 1968, p. 184). Lay participation in socialism was perceived as a step toward future non-judicial forms of decision-making. Ramundo (1965, p. 693) summarized the role of lay participation:

> Theorists anticipate that this participation will increase as public self-government develops further in the transition from the state of the entire people to the final victory of communism. Once communism is achieved, state and law will have withered away, but the need for regulation and control will remain an inherent feature 'of society at so high a level of its development.' The necessary regulation and control will be supplied by a system of 'self-government' through public or social organizations (rather than a formal state apparatus). [footnotes omitted]

Kulcsár (1982, p. 37) argued that the institutionalization of lay participation in Hungary was a political act because "it meant the implementation of an organized form accepted in all European socialist countries and as such it was a step in building the institutions of the socialist state and socialist state organization."

Similar ideas motivated the introduction of mixed tribunals in the former Yugoslavia. One of the first legal documents of the then future socialist Yugoslavia, *Regulations Concerning the Court Organization* of December 22, 1943, elaborated on the reasons for nurturing lay participation (Jovanović, 1958, p. 41-42):

> Judiciary, as a part of that authority, should respond to the wishes, needs, and opinion of the people in terms of its composition and methods of resolving disputes. Consequently, it [the judiciary] should be democratized, that is, it should result from the people who have to participate directly in the administration of justice. Administration of justice as obligatory passing of the law has to be in the hands of the people, and the leading idea in the administration of justice should be the one expressed in the principles of national-liberation movement. As a guarantee of it, a judicial body imminently has to be composed of the members of the people.

Since the introduction of mixed tribunals in the former Yugoslavia in 1944, a number of legal scholars have written about the political role of mixed tribunals (Čulinović, 1954; Bayer, 1955; Kovačević, 1973). Krapac (1977, p. 14) wrote about the role lay judges played in the criminal justice system:

> Participation of lay judges in legal decision-making is perceived to be the most basic factor of the democratization of the judiciary, to correspond to the basic assumptions of socialist self-management system, and to contribute toward the socialization of the judicial function.

Some authors (e.g., Kovačević, 1973) emphasized that, by performing their duty, lay judges developed and consolidated the notion that the power of the state belonged to the working class. Similarly, Krystufek (1976, p. 302) stated that one of the reasons why mixed tribunals were introduced in the former Czechoslovakia was that the legislator wanted to "bring the judiciary closer to the people."

Lay judges in mixed tribunals also serve as **deterrent safeguards**: by being present in the tribunal, lay judges deter professional judges from reaching arbitrary decisions and from being corrupt or biased. The mere presence of lay judges forces professional judges to state their opinion and to make their reasoning explicit. Borucka-Arctowa (1976, p. 289) considered this to be the **"latent function"** of lay participation. According to Kulcsár (1982, p. 40), the role of the lay judge as a social controller changed as the conditions in the society changed; when the system of mixed tribunals was introduced in socialist Hungary, the emphasis was primarily on political control, whereas "under present-day conditions within advanced socialist society ... the significance of this control is far greater in reconciling the contradiction between the professional who acts out of routine and the lay judge who better senses the specific circumstances."

Although in a different sense, jurors can serve in the deterrent or controlling capacity as well; despite the fact that very few of the cases are actually resolved through jury trials (most are resolved through plea bargaining), the "threat" of jury trial is present in most of the cases and the negotiations between the parties are heavily influenced, among other things, by the estimates of the jury decision in the case. The estimated jury decision guides the behavior of and the decisions reached by the case participants;[20] therefore, the jury affects the "bargaining in the shadow of the law."[21] Wrote Kalven and Zeisel (1966, p. 31-32):

> ... we saw at every stage of this informal process of pre-trial dispositions that decisions are in part informed by expectations of what the jury will do. Thus, the jury is not controlling merely the immediate case before it, but the host of cases not before it which are destined to be disposed of by the pre-trial process. The jury thus controls not only the formal resolution of controversies in the criminal case, but also the informal resolution of cases that never reach the trial stage. In a sense the jury, like the visible cap of an iceberg, exposes but a fraction of its true volume [footnotes omitted].

Lay participation is a form of **citizen participation** in government and the state. In one of the earliest discussions on the subject, Plato wrote (1970, p. 32):

> As for charges of crimes against the state, the first need is to let the man in the street play his part in judging them. A wrong done to the state is a wrong done to all its citizens, who could be justifiably annoyed if they were excluded from deciding such cases.

The U.S. Supreme Court explicitly stated in *Powers v. Ohio* (1991, p. 407) that, "with the exception of voting, for most citizens the honor and privilege of jury duty is their most significant opportunity to participate in the democratic

---

[20]A new branch of consulting — jury consulting — has recently developed in the United States. Jury consulting firms employ various methods, ranging from community surveys, interviews with mock jurors, and discussions of issues in the case with shadow jurors (Galanter, 1993, p. 78). An estimated 300 businesses provided jury consulting services in 1989 (Galanter, 1993, p. 78).

[21]The term "in the shadow of the law" was used by Mnookin and Kornhauser in their paper titled "Bargaining in the Shadow of the Law: The Case of Divorce" (1979).

process." Similarly, the *Constitution of the Republic of Croatia* (1990, Article 44), contains a guarantee that "every citizen of the Republic shall have the right, under equal conditions, to take part in the conduct of public affairs, and have access to public services."

As mentioned earlier, in the former communist countries participation in the government through mixed tribunals was at the same time perceived to be one of the stages in the process of building the communist society in which the political power would be in the hands of the working class. For example, Lapaine (1986, p. 605) wrote about lay participation in the former Yugoslavia:

> Socialist society ... provides a guarantee to the citizens, albeit to a limited extent, as one of their basic rights, to collectively achieve and develop the political, economic, social, and cultural life of the community. The participation of lay judges in the judicature is a specific form of realization of this right. It is regarded that the development and the existence of socialist democracy is impossible without providing the people with opportunities to directly state the law and to thereby develop their own sense of political and social responsibility toward the tasks of the community (i.e., by doing so, toward themselves).

Kulcsár (1982, p. 38) noted that lay participation in legal decision-making in Hungary was just one aspect of the "participation of the lay element in political decisions of society-wide scope."

Researchers (e.g., Tyler, 1990; Thibaut and Walker, 1975) have suggested that people relate issues of loyalty to authority and those of obedience to legal rules of *procedure* by which authorities render legal decisions and not to the actual *outcomes* of these procedures. Tyler (1990, p. 172) reported that the respondents' sense of procedural justice, based on their actual experience, had a serious impact on their views about the legitimacy of authority:

> If people have an experience not characterized by fair procedures, their later compliance with the law will be based less strongly on the legitimacy of legal authorities ... Only if people can trust authorities, rules, and institutions can they believe that

their own long-term interests are served by loyalty toward the organization.

The willingness of the decision-makers to hear the parties in the case and to consider their arguments increases the parties' perceptions of procedural fairness. Tyler (1990, p. 176) argued that, "people feel that their membership and status in the group are confirmed when their views are heard and considered, irrespective of the decisions made by the third party." By their very nature, lay participants have a greater tendency to listen to the arguments presented in the form of a narrative story and in a non-legalistic way (which would also be more appealing to other lay participants in the trial — defendants and witnesses) than professional judges do. Furthermore, the above findings about procedural justice suggest that people have greater confidence in a system in which they perceive that they and their peers have had some input.

An additional function of lay participation, then, lies in the fact that people seem to attribute greater **legitimacy** to legal decisions reached by their peers than to legal decisions reached by professional judges (who are employed by the state); lay participation has "the beneficial effect of reinforcing the confidence of the population in the legal system" (Gomard, 1976, p. 421). Similarly, Justice Hale (1973, p. 102) from the Supreme Court of Western Australia wrote that the jury

> ... enhances respect for and trust in the operation of the criminal courts: a jury is a microcosm of the community, their verdict is a verdict of the community and if they err the error is an error by the people representing the man-in-the-street.

The legitimacy function has been pointed out in former communist regimes too. For example, Roca, a member of the Central Committee of the Communist Party of Cuba (in Berman, 1969, p. 1318), reported that one of the rationales for the introduction of lay judges into the Cuban system was to encourage voluntary compliance with the severe rationing that was in effect in Cuba at the time. Greater compliance would presumably occur as a result of the greater legitimacy of the decisions reached by the members of the community themselves, rather than by professional judges. Popular courts were thus introduced for the purpose of encouraging "acceptance of the laws of a new society by making the courts, which enforce these new laws, not institutions of coercion, but familiar, popularly accepted institutions" (in Berman, 1969, p. 1318). Roca further wrote (in Berman, 1969, p. 1318):

> The fact that the Popular Tribunals are organized and function in the neighborhood, so that neighbors and acquaintances of those being judged can attend the trials and can make these trials truly public, and that the judges sitting in these trials come from the same community in which they live and work, reinforces the idea that the justice they administer is that of the working people, the expression of the power of the working people in the socialist state.

Similarly, legitimacy was advocated as one of the advantages of comrades' courts in the former Soviet Union; "[during the period of intensive building of a communist society] ... the toiling masses participate more widely in state administration, strengthening of legality and safeguarding the public order" (Kaznin, 1963, p. 4).

The results of opinion polls demonstrated that citizens prefer lay decision-makers over decision-makers who are representatives of formal authority. The respondents in the MacCoun and Tyler's study (1988) showed an overwhelming support for the jury system; 97% of respondents viewed the jury system as "somewhat" or "very" important as a national institution. Similarly, eight out of ten respondents evaluated the right to a jury trial as "extremely important," and the remaining respondents rated this right as "important" (McCloskey and Brill, 1983). Furthermore, approximately three out of four respondents in the MacCoun and Tyler study (1988) considered the jury to be a fairer decision-maker than the professional judge (MacCoun and Tyler, 1988, p. 338). Finally, respondents regarded the jury as not only fairer, but also more accurate, less biased, and more representative of minorities than the professional judge (MacCoun and Tyler, 1988, p. 338).

In a Gallup Poll (Doob, 1979a) Canadian respondents were asked about their attitudes toward the criminal jury. The majority of respondents (54%) said that the jury and the professional judge were equally likely to arrive at a just and fair verdict (Doob, 1979a, p. 11). But, the respondents who said that one of the two types of decision-makers was more likely to arrive at a just and fair verdict were four times more likely to select juries than to select professional judges (37% and 9%, respectively, Doob, 1979a, p. 11).

This preference for juries over professional judges is emphasized even more strongly in cases involving serious crimes. MacCoun and Tyler's study (1988, p. 340) suggested that the public overwhelmingly favored jury trials in the cases that featured more serious crimes (murder), whereas it was much less likely to favor jury trials for less serious crimes (shoplifting). Similarly, Doob (1979a, p. 13) reported that the more serious the crime, the more likely the Canadian respondents were to feel that the accused should have the option of a trial by jury.

Unlike their American and Canadian counterparts, three out of ten respondents in Hong Kong did not know what the jury was (Duff *et al.*, 1992, p. 111). Those who were more likely to say that they had not heard about the jury were typically less educated and not fluent in English. The Hong Kong respondents were asked a question that was very similar to the question asked of their Canadian counterparts: to provide their opinion on who would be more likely to arrive at a fair and just verdict. The findings were surprisingly similar to the results of the Canadian Gallup Poll (Doob, 1979a); respondents most frequently said that the jury and the professional judge were equally likely to arrive at a just and fair verdict (48%; Duff *et al.*, 1992, p. 113). The respondents who perceived that one type of decision-maker is more likely to arrive at a just and fair verdict were three times more likely to select juries than to select professional judges (40% and 13%, respectively, Duff *et al.*, 1992, p. 113). The overwhelming majority of respondents (84%) reported that the jury should be kept after the 1997 return of Hong Kong to China (Duff *et al.*, 1992, p. 113).

The recent reintroduction of the jury in Spain was not received with such undivided affection. While the Council of Judges stated that, "the first experiences have generally been positive and that citizens have demonstrated the same common sense, or lack of it, as judges have" (Thaman, 1998, p. 412), the percentage of Spaniards who supported the jury was virtually identical to the percentage of Spaniards who opposed it (43% *v.* 42%; Thaman, 1998, p. 412). Thaman (1998, p. 412) concluded that:

> The fact that it [the jury] lacks solid support among the population, among judges and lawyers, and among law professors means that reforms along the lines of those taken in Germany, France, Italy, and Portugal, converting the classic jury into a 'mixed court,' are certainly possible.

Smaus (1985) surveyed the population of the former West Germany about their general attitudes on the judicial system. One of the questions inquired about the comparison of the quality of the decisions reached by professional judges to the quality of the decisions reached by mixed tribunals. The majority of respondents (65%; Smaus, 1985, p. 171) supported the statement that courts will make better decisions if the decisions are made not only by professional judges but also by members of the public, the respondents' positive opinion about professional judges notwithstanding.[22]

A lack of legitimacy of official courts and the overall criminal justice system in South Africa, which was perceived by the majority of its black citizens, led toward the development of informal people's courts that operated outside of formal legal structures. Colonial law was perceived as a source of oppression and "a source of harassment, humiliation, and degradation" (van Niekerk, 1972, p. 53). The apartheid legislation and its enforcement by the South African police greatly contributed to the dissatisfaction with the imposed sys-

---

[22]The majority of respondents (79%) supported the statement that very few professional judges may be reproached as biased, unjust, or prejudiced (Smaus, 1985, p. 168). Similarly, a high percentage of respondents (74%) agreed with the statement that the majority of professional judges today may serve as examples of honesty. Finally, nine out of ten respondents (87%) perceived professional judges to be just (Smaus, 1985, p. 168).

tem (Grant and Schwikkard, 1991, p. 307). Court proceedings conducted in the official languages not spoken by the black majority and the almost impossible access to legal representation further contributed toward the dislike of the system (Grant and Schwikkard, 1991, p. 307-308). It is by no means surprising that alternative access to justice developed; peoples' courts started to develop in response to the first attempts of the British colonizers to impose a foreign legal system on the people of South Africa (Burman, 1989, p. 152). The perceptions and goals of these alternative courts were in sharp contrast with the perceptions and goals of the official regime. Sachs (1984, p. 99) provided a description of popular justice that, according to Allison (1989), summarized the goals of people's courts:

> ... justice that is popular in form, in that its language was open and accessible; popular in its functioning, in that its proceedings were based essentially on active community participation; and popular in its substance, in that judges drawn directly from the people were to give judgment in the interest of the people.

It seems that being judged by one's peers was perceived to provide and, whenever implemented properly, truly provided for a greater legitimacy of legal decisions across the world. It is, therefore, quite interesting to compare such a positive climate that favored lay participation to the one which led toward the withering of the jury system in Japan. Hirano (in Urabe, 1976) provided the following comment:

> It is undeniable that one of the reasons for the unpopularity of jury trial was the people's preference for trial by 'those people above' rather than by 'their fellows.' Judges, with a sense of their special responsibility to adjudicate cases 'in the name of the Emperor,' tried hard to keep their moral standards as high as those of priests ... People trusted judges partly because they believed that judges with such a mental attitude would act impartially, and partly because of their general respect for public officials serving the Emperor.

Participation in legal decision-making also **educates** lay participants about the ways the legal system actually operates and, as a result, changes their views about the system. Over a century ago, Alexis de Tocqueville (1966, p. 253) wrote that education was the primary function of the jury system; the jury was "one of the most effective means of popular education at society's disposal." Furthermore, "[t]he jury is both the most effective way of establishing the people's rule and the most efficient way of teaching them how to rule" (de Tocqueville, 1966, p. 254). A century later, and in a different part of the world, Rácz (1972, p. 412) wrote about the educational function of a different form of lay participation — mixed tribunals:

> The circumstance that the co-operation of the working people in the work of the judiciary educated them to participate in governmental work, helps to give publicity to the work of the courts and thus it implies great *potentialities for a propaganda of law, for the extension of the knowledge of law or legal erudition of the citizens,* has generally been recognized also as an invaluable merit of the institution of people's assessors [emphasis added].

Research studies on actual jurors show that jury service educated the jurors and enhanced their respect for the criminal justice system (Hans and Vidmar, 1986). Furthermore, the results of a Gallup Poll show that the respondents who had some direct experience or indirect knowledge about jury service were more likely to say that the jury would reach a just and fair verdict (Doob, 1979a).

A study by Pabst *et al.* (1976, p. 164) suggested that the majority of the citizens who failed to wriggle out of jury duty looked back on it as a positive experience and viewed their jury duty as a valuable opportunity, rather than an onerous burden.[23] Similarly, three out of four jurors in the study by Richert (1977, p. 498) evaluated jury duty as "important" and "a worthwhile experience." The majority of jurors (68%) in a study by Consolini (1992, p. 123)

---

[23]However, it is important to keep in mind that approximately one-half of the potential jurors summoned were successful in avoiding jury duty (Richert, 1977, p. 497). Therefore, Pabst *et al.* (1976) may have disproportionately excluded from their sample persons opposed to the jury in the United States.

reported that they had learned something positive or factual while performing their duty.

The overwhelming majority of the surveyed jurors (90%; Pabst *et al.*, 1976, p. 164; Richert, 1977, p. 498-499) looked "favorably" or "more favorably" on jury duty than they did before they had served. Furthermore, Cecil *et al.* (1987, p. 23) found that 85% of the jurors who served in long trials and 93% of those who served in short trials reported that whey would be willing to serve again. However, those who spent a longer time waiting for their duty to commence once they arrived at the court had more negative attitudes about their jury duty than those who waited for a shorter period of time (Pabst *et al.*, 1976, p. 168).

The experience of jury service seems to have a favorable impact on the satisfaction with the criminal justice system as a whole. Allen (1977) found that jurors evaluated justice and equity of the overall legal system more favorably upon the completion of their jury service. Similarly, Consolini (1992, p. 155) reported that jurors who had performed their duty perceived the system to work well and courts to be fair. It is quite interesting to compare these positive evaluations of the criminal justice system with the evaluations provided by the general population. Diamond (1993, p. 286) wrote that citizens who served as jurors seem to have a more positive opinion about the criminal justice system and the courts than the citizens who came in contact with the criminal justice system in other ways (as defendants, witnesses, etc.). Indeed, the overall confidence in the American criminal justice system is low[24] and it is quite possible that the "support for courts is eroded by experience with or knowledge about them" (Sarat, 1977, p. 439). However, jury service seems to be an exception to this rule.

---

[24]Only about 20% of the citizens surveyed in the 1990s had either "a great deal" or "quite a lot" of confidence in the criminal justice system (*1997 Sourcebook*, 1998, p. 105), one-third had "a great deal" or "quite a lot" confidence in local courts (*1997 Sourcebook*, 1998, p. 112), and about one-half had "a great deal" or "quite a lot" confidence in the U.S. Supreme Court (*1997 Sourcebook*, 1998, p. 105).

The overwhelming majority of the surveyed Hong Kong jurors (Duff *et al.*, 1992) reported that they had achieved something by serving as jurors. Some of them mentioned that they had experienced a real trial for the first time, learned about the process and the Hong Kong idea of justice, and sharpened their analytical skills (Duff *et al.*, 1992, p. 104). Some jurors turned out to be sarcastic about their achievements; a juror stated that his achievement as a juror was "to appreciate the waste of precious time and sacrifice of clarity and accuracy when a trial should have been conducted in Cantonese and not English" (Duff *et al.*, 1992, p. 104).[25]

Trials and informal proceedings in socialist countries served the purpose of not only punishing the persons who violated the norms of socialist morale and laws, but also of conveying socialist morality and legality to the public. McCabe (1989, p. 117) argued that the main purpose of the socialist law, especially the criminal law, is to educate. Felkenes (1989, p. 141) wrote about the criminal law in China:

> ... criminal laws and procedures and various kinds of corrective labor laws have a vital role to play. These three branches of Chinese law — especially the first two; criminal laws and criminal procedures — are constantly emphasized in the Chinese Communist Party and governmental media as a primary vehicle for promoting socialist legality; thus they have served as a fundamental cause for the building of the communist system in China.

The contemporary view on the educational role of the law in China has roots in the ancient codes of ethics. Wrote Clark (1989, p. 61):

> Punishing the offenders may diminish their particular unacceptable behavior, but the general population will still only know what is bad — not what is good. Educating the offenders, possible offenders, and the general public in the moral principles of *li* will assure that they also know the correct way to behave. Everyone must therefore be made aware of high morals in a system of human rule.

---

[25] Jury trials in Hong Kong were held in English with translation of witnesses' statements from Cantonese to English.

Education was also mentioned as one of the roles that comrades' courts in the former Soviet Union were supposed to achieve (Article 1, *Statute on Comrades' Courts*, 1961):

> The chief duty of the comrades' courts is to prevent violations of the law and misdemeanors detrimental to society, *to educate people* by persuasion and public influence, and to create an intolerant attitude towards any antisocial acts [emphasis added].

However, the reality of comrades' courts was quite different; the original idea of gradual increase in the involvement of citizens in the work of the government had been twisted into overt control over the lives of citizens in the aspect that Western societies routinely place outside of the state's reach and within the reach of moral or religious norms. In fact, Ramundo (1965, p. 726) wrote that, "education is sought through a rigid form of control which attempts to impose sanctions for attitudes and approaches, in addition to overt acts, which violate the moral code of the builder of communism."

The same philosophy has been applied to lay judges in mixed tribunals in (former) socialist countries. Lay judges can also fulfill the educational role because, "[t]hanks to his direct participation in the administration of justice, a lay assessor [in Poland] can have a considerable share in the preventive and pedagogical activity of the court and in propagating the legal culture among the people" (Kubicki and Zawadzki, 1970, p. 101).

Professional judges may be isolated from, or even unfamiliar with, the values of a particular community. Lay participation has the potential of **introducing community values** into the decision-making process. This notion is rooted in the laws and organization of the states in medieval Europe: the jury passed on local news (and local customs and norms) to the royal judges, who occasionally visited their villages (Sawer, 1965, p. 78).

Allott (1957, p. 250) argued that lay judges in African countries performed two functions — the role of assessors and the role of advisors:

> First, assessors may assess or weigh the evidence and whether an accused is guilty or not, in the light of their special knowledge

of African habits, customs, modes of thought, and language; they are peculiarly qualified to judge the probability of the story told by a witness, and may detect in his demeanour what may escape the presiding judge. In this role the assessor's task is similar to that of a juror's ... Secondly, the assessor's duty is to advise the judge or magistrates on the matters of which they have special knowledge, and to give their view, in the abstract, of what the custom or law is in the circumstances postulated.

Ayyangar wrote in *King Emperor v. Tirumal Reddi* (1901, p. 543) about lay judges as experts in the field of local norms and customs:[26]

> ... in my opinion, assessors are analogous to expert witnesses and in principle the opinion of an assessor is substantially on the same footing as the opinion evidence of expert witness. A brief retrospect of Indian legislation in regard to trial of criminal cases with the aid of assessors would clearly show that such is the correct view and it is also in conformity with the institution of assessors in England, in civil cases, especially in admiralty, ecclesiastical, patent and similar cases.

Lay judges in mixed tribunals have a direct opportunity to introduce community values and, if necessary, to contradict the professional judge. This provides a forum for different social groups to state and defend their voices and for evidence to be evaluated by persons with different knowledge and experience. Similar arguments, albeit raised in a context of socialist morality, were pointed out by Buchholz (1986, p. 216) in connection with the role lay judges performed in the former German Democratic Republic:

> The participation of lay assessors is the most obvious form of citizen participation in the criminal procedure in the GDR. Due to their direct connection with working people, the lay assessors are supposed to introduce the workers' experience, views, and way of thinking and feeling, into jurisdiction. Thus, they contribute to ensuring popular and democratic jurisdiction. This makes the lay

---

[26]The Criminal Procedure Codes in East Africa were based on the Indian *Code of Criminal Procedure* and it was customary to cite cases from India.

assessors an important and direct link between working people and the courts, between material production and the other spheres of social life and the administration of justice.

In India and some African countries, laymen — members of mixed tribunals — inform about and interpret the local practices (Reichert, 1979, p. 352). Similarly, Klami and Hämäläinen (1992, p. 16) argued that lay participation in rural district courts in Finland has been traditionally defended with the saying that, "the mostly well-being peasants sitting as layman assessors possess a 'local knowledge' about agriculture and their neighbours."

The familiarity with local conditions and community values was emphasized as an advantage of lay courts (comrades' courts) over regular courts in socialist regimes too. Comrades' courts were organized within smaller segments of society than regular courts were, and were intended to provide the advantage of being truly judged by one's peers (e.g., fellow factory workers from the same plant, neighbors from the same neighborhood). However, a completely different topic for discussion is whether these peers were actually independent and free to make their own judgment, that is, whether they were unjaded by the official party line. A new direction and changes for comrades' courts were discussed in 1964 (*A New Stage in the Activity of the Comrades' Courts*, 1964, p. 3):

> [T]he comrades' court as a rule, knows better than a people's court the specific situation, conditions of life and the inter-relations of the disputing parties, especially their character and similar facts which have a significant bearing upon the correct resolution of the controversy.

The introduction of community values is very important for the jury system too. Because deliberations are secret and the jurors do not need to explain reasons for their verdicts, jurors can bend the law in order to achieve justice in a particular case. Standards of negligence or self-defense in one community may be different from the corresponding legal standards or norms in another community. Therefore, by applying the standards of a particular community in which the case is tried, jurors can achieve justice that may be different from the one achievable without the opportunity to bend the law.

However, having a group of citizens participate in decision-making will not result in bringing just one, singular voice to the decision-making group. In fact, one of the advantages of group lay participation is that it brings the opportunity for many different voices to be heard during deliberation (assuming, of course, that the membership is not limited to a small selected subset of the population and that members of various groups in the society indeed participate in the process). The U.S. Supreme Court wrote in *Taylor v. Louisiana* (1975, p. 524):

> The purpose of a jury is to guard against the exercise of arbitrary power — to make available the common-sense judgment of the community as a hedge against the overzealous or mistaken prosecutor and in preference to the professional or perhaps overconditioned or biased response of a judge. This prophylactic vehicle is not provided if the jury pool is made up of only special segments of the populace or if large, distinctive groups are excluded from the pool. Community participation in the administration of the criminal law, moreover, is not only consistent with our democratic heritage but is also critical to public confidence in the fairness of the criminal justice system. Restricting jury service to only special groups or excluding identifiable segments playing major roles in the community cannot be squared with the constitutional concept of jury trial.

Therefore, the issue of impartiality and the issue of representativeness of the jury are related; the U.S. Supreme Court argued about a fair cross-section venire requirement, imposed by the Sixth Amendment and further explained in *Taylor v. Louisiana* (1975, p. 528); "no jury was impartial unless it was drawn from sources representative of all segments of the community." In other words, as Abramson (1994, p. 122) argued,

> ... impartiality was accomplished by turning the traditional search for disinterested jurors on its head: we should realistically admit that jury deliberation is but the interplay of group biases.

Paradoxical as it sounds, the *Taylor* court was committed to the notion that the most impartial jury was the jury that most accurately reflected the mix of popular prejudices.

Another interesting situation in which the contribution by lay participants may be crucial is the situation in which a new state emerged and its laws have not been developed or codified. In the cases in which there are serious gaps in the laws, the contribution of lay judges, who may provide a common-law resolution to the problem or are at least as qualified to make decisions following moral norms as professional judges are, is extremely valuable. Such was the case at the end of World War II and immediately thereafter on the territory of the former Yugoslavia. Čulinović (1954, p. 53) described this role as follows:

> ... [in the period] of absence of the new written Yugoslav statutory law, lay participants closed the gaps in the legal system with their familiarity with the common law by facilitating the resolution of legal cases in accordance with the customs and within the boundaries set by the general principles of constitutionality and legality.

In common-law countries, jurors have an opportunity to **soften the rigidity of the legal rules**. Unlike professional judges, who have to follow the law, jurors may either nullify the law or put more weight on the mitigating circumstances if doing so better suits their sense of justice. In that regard,

> Juries reflect the good sense and judgment as well as the conscience of the community; they are a protection against the rigidity of the law because whereas a judge must always stick to the letter of the law a jury can often soften its application to meet the broad justice of the case (Chief Justice of the New Zealand Rotorua Supreme Court, cited in Burns, 1973, p. 109).

In civil-law countries that utilize mixed tribunals, such a softening may take place during deliberation. Lay judges have an opportunity to state an opinion that promotes their sense of justice and, if necessary, to outvote the professional judge by voting for the verdict they feel is just, as long as they remain within the boundaries of the law. Furthermore, in order to explain legal rules to lay participants (either jurors or lay judges in mixed tribunals), professional judges are put in a position to "translate" the rules written in legalistic, professional jargon into laymen's terms. Consequently, lay participation may also serve the function of demystifying the law.

Lay participants also contribute by **focusing closely on a particular case**. Since most lay participants perform their duty only several days per year, each case they decide is new and unique for them. Professional judges, on the other hand, conduct trials for similar cases every day, and, after some time, they may become exposed to the tendency to start deciding cases routinely;

> ... anybody who does nothing but crime day after day, year after year, is not as good a court as a lot of men and women from different walks of life, all pooling their joint experiences [as lay magistrates], and in effect representing the public [Lord Gardiner, former Lord Chancellor of the United Kingdom, cited in Reichert, 1973, p. 139].

Anderson (1990, p. 859) also argued in that direction:

> Perhaps the contribution of the laity in the individual cases lies not in supplementing the qualifications of professional judges, but rather in what lay judges and jurors do *not* have. They are not jaded. As one lay person who has served at all three posts (Municipal and High Court lay judge and High Court juror [in Denmark]) points out, 'The professional judges, who day in and day out work with crime, can hardly avoid being influenced by their work.' [footnote omitted]

Similarly, Joaquín Sánchez-Covisa, the Chief Prosecutor of the Madrid Province, commented about the newly introduced jury trials in Spain (Thaman, 1998, p. 411), "[j]ustice is full of dust. The jury has been like opening the windows to let in fresh air from the streets. A magnificent experience."

In comparison with all other forms of lay participation, lay judges in mixed tribunals have the unique opportunity to focus the attention of the whole tribunal on each and every case. Kubicki and Zawadzki (1970, p. 100) wrote the following about the positive role that lay judges play in the system of justice administration:

> The institution of the lay assessor [lay judge] is one of the means for preventing this danger [danger of professional deformation and routine]. The active role of a lay assessor is that he should represent in court the views and evaluations prevailing currently in the broader public opinion. On their basis he should carry out his individual evaluation of the evidence, the degree of the social danger of the misdeed, and define his attitude towards the problem of the penalty. This is the essence of the function of the social judge. This mission results in the confrontation of the 'fresh' look which the layman takes at the case on trial with the look of the professional judge who is in danger of 'standardization' and staleness caused by the vocational habit.

This "fresh" look of lay participants leads toward another feature of lay participation — lay participation **promotes justice and equity** (Klami and Hämäläinen, 1992) because the lay participants' interpretation of laws may be less formal and strict and more likely to be oriented toward the search for "just" verdicts in legal cases in which a legal decision that would be based solely on the strict interpretation of legal rules would not fulfill the lay participants' sense of justice.

Unlike professional judges, who frequently make legal decisions alone, lay participants typically sit as a group (mixed tribunals, jury, lay courts, magistrates) and have the opportunity to provide different perspectives and discuss factual and legal issues in the case from various viewpoints. Therefore, lay participation in decision-making, especially in the case of the jury or a larger mixed tribunal, provides for another advantage — **group decision-making**. In fact, the U.S. Supreme Court in *Williams v. Florida* (1970, p. 100) used the concept of group decision-making to explain why juries should not be composed of fewer than six members:

> ... the essential feature of a jury obviously lies in the interposition between the accused and his accuser of the common-sense

judgment of a group of laymen, and in the community participation and shared responsibility which results from that group's determination of guilt or innocence. The performance of this role is not a function of the particular number of the body which makes up the jury. To be sure, the number should probably be large enough to promote group deliberation, free from outside attempts at intimidation, and to provide a fair possibility for obtaining a representative cross section of the community.

Several years later, the Supreme Court expanded on the advantages of group decision-making in *Ballew v. Georgia* (1978, p. 232-234):

> Generally, a positive correlation exists between group size and the quality of both group performance and group productivity ... The smaller the group, the less likely are members to make critical contributions necessary for the solution of a given problem. Because most juries are not permitted to take notes, ... memory is important for accurate jury deliberations. As juries decrease in size, then, they are less likely to have members who remember each of the important pieces of evidence or argument. Furthermore, the smaller the group, the less likely it is to overcome the biases of its members to obtain an accurate result. When individual and group decisionmaking were compared, it was seen that groups performed better because prejudices of individuals were frequently counterbalanced, and objectivity resulted. Groups also exhibited increased motivation and self-criticism. All these advantages, except, perhaps, self-motivation, tend to diminish as the size of the group diminishes. Because juries frequently face complex problems laden with value choices, the benefits are important and should be retained. In particular, the counterbalancing of various biases is critical to the accurate application of the common sense of the community to the facts of any given case [footnotes ommitted].

Competence of the jury is based both on its size and its composition (Ellsworth, 1989); the jury is composed of at least six members with different backgrounds, selected in such a manner as to represent different opinions in the community. If the jury is composed in a way that is really representative of different opinions in the community, then the jury, as a heterogeneous group, should provide a greater variety of information and opinion, both of which will be questioned and discussed more thoroughly. This leads toward decisions that are higher in quality than those reached by virtually homogeneous groups of individuals. As Ellsworth (1989, p. 205) pointed out that, "[r]epresentativeness is important not only for ensuring 'the essential nature of the jury as a tribunal embodying a broad democratic ideal,' but because it affects the jury's competence directly."

Similarly, Lord Hailsham, the former Lord Chancellor of the United Kingdom, stated the following (Reichert, 1973, p. 139):

> I would regard the abolition of the lay magistrate as a sheer disaster ... What they lose in professionalism they gain in local knowledge. What they lose in speed they gain in the added humanity of having three quite differently constituted human beings putting their heads together.

Yet another function of lay participation is that lay persons are perceived as **mediators between the formalism of the higher courts and the citizens.** Magistrates and justices of the peace are prime examples of courts in which the legal procedure is more "humanized" and thus more accessible to the average citizen. Interestingly, if appeal to the lay participants' decision is allowed, as is the case, for example, for mixed tribunals or the jury (only when the jury convicts), the majority of countries today utilize professional judges as either the only decision-makers or the predominant decision-makers in appeals.

This section would be incomplete if it did not point out that the mere existence of lay participation on the books does not guarantee an independent and democratic process; the law may never be actually implemented or it may be implemented without the lay participants' real independence from the state. There are several prominent historical examples in which courts with lay participants were anything but independent and democratic, for example, the Revolutionary Tribunal in Paris (1793-1795) and the German *Volksgerichtshof* during the Third Reich (Reichert, 1979, p. 350).

Lay participation in Germany was effectively abolished in 1939. The only remaining form of lay participation was the *Volksgerichtshof* (established in 1934). However, the *Volksgerichtshof* did not truly provide for democratic and independent lay participation; the selection of three lay persons who decided cases jointly with two professional judges was overseen by Hitler himself (Wagner, 1974; Schorn, 1959, p. 102).

The right to jury trial in Hong Kong was perceived as "a safeguard against oppression and a bastion of liberty" (Ip, cited in Duff, 1990, p. 367). The importance of the right to jury trial was further confirmed by the Chinese recognition and a guarantee of the preservation of this right in the subsequent return of Hong Kong to the People's Republic of China in 1997 (Article 86, *The Basic Law of the Hong Kong Special Administrative Region of the People's Republic of China*, 1990).

However, the right to jury trial had a different meaning for an average citizen of Hong Kong. To begin with, the High Court, a court that had jurisdiction over very serious crimes, was the only forum at which the right to jury trial could be exercised (Duff, 1990, p. 368). The jury trial was, therefore, rather rare; out of all the criminal cases heard in Hong Kong in 1988 (1,824 at the District Courts; 147,045 charge cases at the Magistrates' Courts; and 311,792 summons issues at the Magistrates' Courts; Duff, 1990, p. 371) only 296 — less than 0.2% of all the cases (excluding summons cases) — were heard at the High Court. In terms of the number of defendants, 39,265 offenders were prosecuted in 1988 for relatively serious crimes (e.g., burglaries, assault) and it seems obvious that very few of those defendants could have been tried in the 296 cases held at the High Court.

Duff (1990, p. 372) examined whether, despite the apparent scarcity of jury trials, the jury may have played an important role in the decisions reached by the High Court. Duff compared the outcomes of the cases (serious crimes) tried at district courts by professional judge alone to the outcomes of the cases tried at the High Court by professional judge and the jury. His results suggested that the differences in acquittal rates were minimal, as were the rates of discharge of cases (Duff, 1990, p. 372-373); Duff (1990, p. 375) further wrote:

> [o]n looking at the respective rates in the two courts, it is apparent that, with regard to the small number of extremely serious criminal cases which come before them, a judge sitting with a jury produces roughly the same results as a judge sitting alone.

The jury in Hong Kong is a colonial product. Shortly after the establishment of a British colony in Hong Kong in 1843, the jury was introduced by the *Ordinance for the Regulation of Jurors and Juries*. The language of the court proceedings was English (and major criminal trials were conducted in English), which made the majority of Hong Kong residents, who spoke only Cantonese, ineligible for jury service (Duff *et al.*, 1992, p. 1). Indeed, out of approximately four million people in the age group eligible for jury service, only 143,798 people were put on the List of Common Jurors in 1987. Consequently, the list of people eligible and available for jury service is not even remotely representative of the Hong Kong society; "[jurors] are likely to be well educated, middle class, professional or business persons" (Duff *et al.*, 1992, p. 57). Furthermore, people of European, Australasian, and North-American origin, who constituted between 2-3% of the Hong Kong society, filled one-third of the list of potential jurors (Duff *et al.*, 1990, p. 888). Therefore, "the Hong Kong jury is not in the least representative of the Hong Kong community, nor has there been any attempt to make it so" (Duff *et al.*, 1990, p. 881). The selection process itself limits the representativeness of the jury even further; with five peremptory challenges for the defense (although not a large number of peremptory challenges overall), and due to a rather small jury size (seven), the defense attorney has an opportunity to select the jury carefully (Duff *et al.*, 1992, p. 61-68). Duff (1990, p. 379) concluded:

> Therefore, in Hong Kong, the significance of the jury lies primarily in what it is perceived to do, or perceived to be capable of doing, rather than in what it actually does in practice. The jury is seen as a guarantee of impartial and democratic decision making,

free from government or bureaucratic pressures, and in this way
it helps to maintain public confidence in the system of criminal
justice. In other words, the jury is a symbol and it is what it represents, rather than what it does, that is crucial to the considerable
support it attracts.

The Singapore jury system (abolished in 1969 because of its inefficiency)
had very similar features. The requirement that the jurors should understand
English excluded a large percentage of the overall population. Consequently,
Cheang (1973, p. 122) concluded, "[n]obody was ever tried by his peers in this
country. Trial by jury was trial by the English educated."

In South Africa, although lay participation in regular state courts was on
the books, the criminal justice system (under the apartheid) was far from
being democratic. It was argued earlier that lay courts that developed in
South Africa flourished as an alternative method of achieving justice and as
opposition to the oppressive regime. Also described earlier were South African
mixed tribunals that participated in death-penalty cases only; they were far
from achieving any roles in legitimizing the system or serving as means of
citizen participation in the government. A typical lay assessor serving in those
mixed tribunals was anything but a representative member of the community:
"[h]e has a legal background and is in retirement or semi-retirement. It can
also be added that he is white and male" [footnotes omitted] (van Zyl Smit and
Isakov, 1985, p. 222). Professional judges interviewed in the study reported
that they "had considered the appointment of 'non-whites' but that legally
qualified assessors from these groups were not available" (van Zyl Smit and
Isakov, 1985, p. 222). Similarly, Richings (1976, p. 112) wrote that lay judges
were rarely non-white and that the few non-white lawyers tried only non-white
defendants. Only white men were eligible for jury service and it is by no means
surprising that, as Richings (1976, p. 109) argued, "the number of jury trials
was declining rapidly, partly due to their unpopularity with accused persons
— the majority of whom were non-white ..."[27]

---

[27]The juries were abolished in South Africa in 1969 (Strauss, 1973, p. 138; Richings, 1976, p. 109).

The system of lay participation in Kenya (described by Jearey, 1961a) did not promote democracy and equity among the citizens. While Europeans were to be tried by the jury of their peers, other persons were to be tried by the professional judge with the help of lay assessors. As Jearey (1961a, p. 42) pointed out:

> This differentiation (*to use a neutral word*) between Europeans and others is not confined to the provisions regarding mode of trial. It is also to be found in the sections conferring on magistrates jurisdiction, powers of punishment and powers of committal for trial, all of which are drastically reduced where the accused is a European. A precedent for this is, however, to be found in the Indian Codes [emphasis added, footnote omitted].

Still different was the jury system in Southern Rhodesia, originally established at the end of the 19th century and the beginning of the 20th century. Although there were no provisions (on the books) that explicitly discriminated on the basis of skin color, other eligibility requirements ensured that the jury pool consisted predominantly of Europeans (Jearey, 1961a, p. 43-44). In addition, if five qualified jurors were not able to attend the trial, the professional judge had the option of trying the case alone or trying it with the assistance of up to four lay assessors who could be either Europeans or Africans (Jearey, 1961a, p. 44).

Another deviation from the idea of lay participation can be attributed to comrades' courts, a prime example of lay courts in socialist countries. While comrades' courts were supposed to play an important role in the transformation of society from socialism toward communism by providing everyday citizens with opportunities to learn and develop the norms of socialist morals, the reality was quite different; comrades' courts turned out to be a means of achieving and maintaining a firm grip on the lives of ordinary citizens. Instead of trying to achieve an impossible task of having the police monitor each and every group (no matter how small), the legislator turned to comrades' courts and empowered their participants not only to deal with (minor) violations of the laws, but also to enforce adherence to moral norms and to closely monitor for their violation. In the words of Ramundo (1965, p. 727),

> [T]he Soviet need for elaborate societal controls has converted this dream of Marxism-Leninism into a convenient, ideological cover for a form of 'popular control' whose aim is to intervene in every aspect of the existence of the individuals subject to its authority.

1.3　Criticisms of Lay Participation

Despite its many positive features, lay participation is not free from criticisms. Critics of lay participation often point out the lay participants' lack of legal knowledge — the most obvious difference between professional judges and lay participants. Lay persons are also accused of not being able to understand and evaluate evidence. Finally, lay participants are perceived by critics as being biased and prejudiced. A case against the jury was clearly stated by Judge Maude (in Cheang, 1973, p. 131):

> The jury system is most inefficient, slow and costly. The intricate lengthy cases have to be decided by juries who are inexperienced and without any sort of instruction until the last minute, by the judge's summing-up; they are not accustomed to retain the spoken word in their memories, and are not often found to be taking notes; they may often be reluctant, for irrelevant reasons, to accept police evidence; they may be fearful of convicting because of a kind-hearted dislike of being in any way responsible for a fellow human being going to jail; they may well be fearful of their own ability to do the job properly and they may be actuated largely by prejudices of which they are blissfully and totally unaware.

The position that some lawyers express about the introduction of lay persons into the legal decision-making process is vividly portrayed in a historical anecdote from the 19th century involving Thomas McKean, who was at that time the Governor of Pennsylvania. A radical delegation visited the governor and requested expansion of the powers of the justices of the peace (lay persons). The governor responded by taking out his watch and by asking the chairperson of the delegation to repair it. When the chairperson said that he was not a watch repairman, the governor drew an analogy with the law (in Provine, 1986, p. 14):

> The law, gentlemen, is a science of great difficulty and endless complication; it requires a lifetime to understand it. I have bestowed a quarter of a century upon it; yet you who can't mend this little watch, become lawyers all at once, and presume to instruct me in my duty.

Similarly, Dow (1981, p. 196) claimed that, just as surgery patients expect the "surgeon to be a qualified doctor," defendants also expect the decision-maker to be a judge and that to be a real judge requires "no less than a law degree, a license to practice, and trial experience."

A frequent criticism of lay participation in legal decision-making is that lay persons **do not know the law**. Judge Frank (1963, p. 116), one of the prominent critics of the jury system, stated his disapproval of the jury very vividly:

> To comprehend the meaning of many a legal rules requires special training. It is inconceivable that a body of twelve ordinary men ... could merely from listening to the instructions by the judge, gain the knowledge necessary to grasp the true import of the judge's words. For these words have often acquired their meaning as the result of hundreds of years of professional disputation in courts. The jurors usually are as unlikely to get the meaning of those words as if they were spoken in Chinese, Sanskrit, or Choctaw.

In summary, the advocates of professional decision-making would argue that lawyers, unlike lay persons, possess a wide spectrum of relevant knowledge and skills. They know how to read the criminal codes, how to interpret the law and draw legal analogies, what article of the code is relevant and how to apply it; in common-law countries, lawyers also know what precedents are important. Furthermore, lawyers know which facts are important in each case, which evidence may be used to prove the facts, and how to evaluate evidence. Lawyers also know the range of criminal sanctions in criminal cases, the purpose of these sanctions, and how to choose among the listed sanctions in each particular case. Moreover, lawyers are familiar with the procedural rules, the rights of the parties in the case, and the ways parties may exercise those rights.

Lawyers, in comparison with lay participants, know how to "think like lawyers." As Mudd (1983) argued, there are two components of "thinking like lawyers," both of which are important for legal decision-making. First, there is *critical thinking*; it involves clarity, precision, and quality of thinking and is not "different in kind from thinking like a physicist or philosopher" (Mudd, 1983, p. 706).[28] Theoretically, then, educated lay participants would not have any problems fulfilling this requirement. However, lay persons selected to become lay judges or jurors need to constitute a representative sample of the community and the educational level of an average citizen is lower than that of an average lawyer. Typically, the education of an average citizen in the industrialized nations is approximately "graduated from high school" or less,[29] while an average lawyer has at least "graduated from college," and, depending on the educational system, may have additional years of professional schooling. Therefore, in reality there is a gap between the educational level of lay participants and educational level of professional lawyers, and, since education is considered to be an important factor in developing critical thinking skills, lay persons are on average somewhat less equipped with critical thinking skills than lawyers are.

What differentiates professional judges from educated lay judges is the second component, *the ability to use and practice these skills to solve real legal problems*. As described, lawyers learn how to define a legal problem, select facts important for the definition and resolution of the problem, and draw

---

[28]Further details are provided in Chapter 5.

[29]Only 3.6% of the Croatian population 15 years of age or older in 1981 had graduated from college (*1991 Statistical Yearbook*, 1991); 18.4% of the population age 18 and over in the United States in 1990 had graduated from college (*Statistical Abstract of the United States*, 1993).

conclusions through the selection of relevant hypotheses. Following the logic of this argument, experience and practice in solving legal problems are seen as an advantage.

Opponents of lay participation often argue that, because lay participants do not know the law, lay participants tend to decide cases in terms of their values and personal opinion, including their biases and prejudices, rather than in terms of the law. This criticism needs to be addressed for each form of lay participation separately. The first question is "Which law?" Furthermore, how important is the familiarity with the state law? In the case of lay courts, the decision-makers typically rely on their sense of justice and fairness, that is, on customary or common-law, rather than on state law. Therefore, their knowledge of state law is unimportant. Lay magistrates, on the other hand, need to apply state law. To that end, they receive seminars on legal issues. While these seminars do not convert lay magistrates into lawyers, they do provide them with a basis. Jurors typically only need to decide the factual issues in the case and are thus not in a position to decide on the legal issues. It is questionable to what degree the two are separable; moreover, even if the jurors need to decide only on the factual issues in the case, the professional judge provides them with relevant legal instructions prior to deliberation. The immediate question is, then, to what degree do jurors understand these instructions? Mixed tribunals in European countries need to make both factual and legal decisions in the case. However, lay judges make those decisions jointly with a professional judge (a lawyer by education and training) who may help them in their understanding of legal issues. Finally, lay members of African mixed tribunals most often do not actually make decisions; they merely provide advice to professional judges. Their advice is focused on their own local norms and customs, rather than on official rules.

Most of the existing studies that examine lay participants' ability to understand the law and legal issues focused on the jury.[30] As mentioned earlier,

---

[30]See Chapter 4 for an overview of the results of existing studies on mixed tribunals, only some of which addressed the issue of lay judges' ability to understand the law.

jurors, who usually decide only factual issues, receive legal instructions before deliberation. There are two separate issues related to jurors' inability to understand the law provided in the jury instructions: is the law really so complex that it is practically impossible to summarize the most important aspects in a few minutes and/or is the way legal instructions are delivered inappropriate for lay persons? Judge Frank clearly opted for complexity (in Hans and Vidmar, 1986, p. 120):

> [O]ften the judge must state ... [the legal] rules to the jury with such niceties that many lawyers do not comprehend them, and it is impossible that the jury can. Judge Bok notes that 'juries have the disadvantage ... of being treated like children while the testimony is going on, but then being doused with a kettleful of law during the charge that would make a third-year law student blanch.'

The results of research studies generally show that jurors' understanding of legal instructions is very low. A study by Hastie *et al.* (1983, p. 80-81) suggested that the memory of individual jurors about the facts and the law in the case is moderate; on the memory tests individual jurors achieved an average of about 60% accuracy of factual information and less than 30% accuracy of judicial instructions. Advocates of the jury system would argue that, even if some of the jurors are not able to completely understand legal complexities, the ensuing deliberation of twelve people will rectify that shortcoming. Indeed, a study by Hastie *et al.* (1983, p. 80-81) supported this argument. The jury's collective memory turned out to be impressive: the jury achieved an average of 90% accuracy of factual information and 80% accuracy of judicial instructions.

However, the authors (Hastie *et al.*, 1983, p. 231) concluded that jurors experienced more problems with judicial instructions than with evidence and argued that the *nucleus* of the difficulties jurors experienced with the instructions did not lie in the understanding of legal concepts (e.g., "beyond reasonable doubt"), but in the inability to keep in order all the verdict categories and all of their constituent elements. Therefore, Hastie *et al.* (1983, p. 231) concluded that, "improvements are needed in the manner in which the trial judge communicates the law to the jury."

The issue of understandability of legal instructions was examined by both social scientists and legal scholars (Charrow and Charrow, 1979; Elwork *et al.*, 1977; Elwork *et al.*, 1982; Elwork and Sales, 1985; Luginbuhl, 1992; Severance and Loftus, 1982). Their efforts showed that the understandability of these instructions can be improved significantly without sacrificing their legal accuracy. For example, Elwork *et al.* (1977) compared the level of understanding of the respondents who received regular legal instructions on negligence issues, those who received modified instructions, and those who did not receive any instructions. The respondents who did not receive any instructions and the respondents who received regular instructions performed equally poorly, while the respondents who received modified legal instructions performed significantly better. Diamond (1993, p. 95) reported that several states in the United States (e.g., Pennsylvania, Alaska, Arizona, and Florida) systematically modified judicial instructions in response to the mounting concerns about their understandability.[31]

Although jurors would have a better chance of understanding revised legal instructions, it does not necessarily mean that they would follow them. First, jurors need not follow the law; rather, there is a possibility for them to bend the law. Second, jurors may have difficulties following the instructions. An example of instructions which induce difficulty are limiting instructions in the United States and Canada about the proper use of the defendant's prior criminal record. Specifically, when the defendant takes the stand and his or her prior criminal record is revealed, the instructions state that prior criminal record may not be used to determine guilt; it may only be used to determine the credibility of the defendant. In a mock jury experiment, Hans and Doob (1976) showed that respondents had difficulty following these limiting instructions. Juries composed of the respondents who did not learn about the prior criminal

---

[31]For example, The California Supreme Court changed instructions on proximate cause used in negligence cases as a consequence of the study by Charrow and Charrow (1979).

record all returned not guilty verdicts; only 60% of the juries who knew about the prior criminal record did so.

Critics of lay participation in the criminal justice system also argue that lay persons **are not able to understand and evaluate evidence.** Hundreds of journal articles have been published on the question of jury competence and bias.[32] Probably the most frequently cited study on the jury was conducted in the 1950s by Kalven and Zeisel (1966). The research team asked professional judges who had conducted jury trials to reach a hypothetical verdict themselves and to compare that verdict with the real verdict decided by the jury. Most of the time (in approximately four out of five cases), the jury's real and the professional judge's hypothetical verdicts were the same (Kalven and Zeisel, 1966, p. 58). However, this still does not mean that the jurors understood evidence, so Kalven and Zeisel (1966) compared the frequency of disagreement in cases with simple evidence to that which prevailed in cases with complex evidence. The hypothesis was that if disagreement was due to the jurors' difficulty in understanding of evidence, then disagreement should be greater in the cases with complex evidence than in the cases with simple evidence. Since the data show that the jury disagreed with professional judges as frequently in the cases with simple evidence as they did in the cases with complex evidence, Kalven and Zeisel concluded that disagreement could not be attributed to misunderstanding of evidence.

The general impression about the jury's ability to understand and evaluate evidence is positive. This can be probably attributed to the jury's composition of twelve persons (see, e.g., Hastie *et al.*, 1983). The results of Ellsworth's study (1989, p. 217) suggested that "twelve heads are better than one" — as a result of group deliberation by the jury, errors of fact were generally corrected. Individual jurors tended to focus on a piece of evidence that favored their initial verdict preference. According to Ellsworth (1989), this tendency should not be considered as a weakness, but as a benefit of the deliberation

---

[32]See Chapter 4 for a review of research studies on mixed tribunals, some of which address the issue of evidence understanding.

process, since this provides jurors with an opportunity to compare several different interpretations of the event and supporting evidence. A similar set of arguments can be applied to other forms of lay participation as well, because lay participants rarely make legal decisions as individuals — their decisions are group decisions.

Although juries are generally considered to be competent to understand and evaluate evidence, some of the studies point to specific problems juries and jurors might encounter, for example, problems in understanding and evaluation of statistical evidence (Thompson, 1989) and expert evidence (Gross, 1991; Vidmar and Schuller, 1989; Goodman, Greene, and Loftus, 1985; Penrod and Cutler, 1989), as well as problems in eyewitness identification evidence (Loftus, 1974; Loftus, 1996).

In addition to being incompetent, lay participants are usually attacked for **being biased and prejudiced**, and, consequently, for **being more lenient** than professional judges. A critic of jury trials, Judge Frank summarized this argument as follows (in Hans and Vidmar, 1986, p. 131):

> [P]rejudice has been called the thirteenth juror and it has been said that 'Mr. Prejudice' and 'Miss Sympathy' are the names of witnesses whose testimony is never recorded but must nevertheless be reckoned with in trials by jury.

As Hans and Vidmar (1986, p. 133) pointed out, "Miss Sympathy" has two faces: positive feelings about the defendant and negative feelings about the victim. The potential bias and prejudice by lay participants was mostly examined in jury studies (e.g., Kalven and Zeisel, 1966; Ugwuebgu, 1979; Field, 1979), while it received attention in relatively few studies on mixed tribunals (e.g., Casper and Zeisel, 1972).

It was estimated that "Miss Sympathy" and "Mr. Prejudice" appeared in less than 10% of the jury cases. In particular, "Miss Sympathy" was present in 4% of the cases, while the presence of "Mr. Prejudice" was recorded in only 3% of the cases studied by Kalven and Zeisel (1966). Sympathy was extended to young defendants, elderly defendants, female defendants, exceptionally attractive male defendants, or defendants with severe disabilities.

In the same study, Kalven and Zeisel (1966) reported that the jury was more severe than the professional judge in 3% of the cases. Baldwin and McConville (1979a, 1979b) estimated that "Mr. Prejudice" appears in 5-10% of the cases tried in England. It must be noted that Kalven and Zeisel (1966) looked for prejudice only in the cases in which the jury *disagreed* with the professional judge. It is quite possible that *both* the jurors and the professional judge in some cases were biased in the same direction, but such instances were not counted toward the reported 3% of the cases. In most of the 22% of criminal cases in which they disagreed with the professional judge, the jury was more lenient toward the defendant than the professional judge was.

Based on the answers given by professional judges, Kalven and Zeisel (1966) concluded that racial prejudice was present among jurors in some of the cases involving interracial sex. One of the judges observed (Kalven and Zeisel, 1966, p. 398):

> It is my opinion that the jury probably did not take time to consider the evidence but merely based its decision on the fact that a colored defendant was on trial for white slavery involving colored and white prostitutes.

Jury simulation studies in the United States show similar effects of race in sex crimes (Ugwuebgu, 1979; Field, 1979), although this effect was more pronounced in the cases in which the evidence was close than in the cases in which the evidence clearly pointed towards determining either guilt or innocence (Hans and Vidmar, 1986, p. 138). Ugwuebgu (1979) found that the race of the juror, defendant, and victim were all important for the decision: white jurors were more likely to find a black defendant guilty of raping a white victim than in any other racial combination; similarly, black jurors were more likely to find a white defendant guilty of raping a black victim. In a simulated rape case, Field (1979) found that the race of the defendant *and* the victim were important for the decision; black defendants who raped white women were given a more severe sentence than white defendants who raped white women.

Some studies reported the occasional influence of other factors, such as the victim's sexual behavior, the defendant's unattractiveness, immorality, and behavior at trial (Kalven and Zeisel, 1966). Kalven and Zeisel (1966) reported that such influences took place when the case was not clear for acquittal, that is, when the case was close to the borderline of reasonable doubt. The authors concluded (Kalven and Zeisel, 1966, p. 385):

> Although it is ... clear that the jury is often alienated by the unattractiveness of the defendant, we find no cases in which the jury convicts a man, so to speak, for the crime of being unattractive. In the cases examined it is apparent that there is always a considerable link, in the eyes of the jury, between the unattractiveness of the defendant and his credibility.

The issue of leniency in sentencing has been examined in a number of studies that focused on magistrates or justices of the peace. Diamond and Stalans (1989) examined the myth of judicial leniency in sentencing by comparing the sentences given in four cases by professional judges and lay persons (who were neither magistrates nor justices of the piece) in Illinois. In the cases involving burglary and assault, professional judges gave more severe sentences, while the sentences given by lay persons and professional judges in the remaining two cases of drug dealing and purse snatching were of approximately equal severity.

In a subsequent study, Diamond (1990) used simulated cases, courtroom observations, and archival data to compare the work of lay magistrates and stipendiary magistrates in London. The results suggested that sentences given by stipendiary magistrates were more severe than those given by lay magistrates were. Diamond concluded (1990, p. 209) that the greater severity of stipendiary magistrates was partially associated with the difference in formal legal education, while the primary source of lay magistrates' greater leniency appeared to be the fact that theirs was a part-time position. Stipendiary magistrates seemed to be more concerned with general crime control, while lay magistrates were much less concerned with the official goals of sentencing and were instead focused on each particular defendant (Diamond, 1990). A study by Bond and Lemon (1981) would support the position that, as a result of experience, stipendiary magistrates were more concerned with crime control and, therefore, more severe in their sentences. A more recent study by Parker *et al.* (1989, p. 172) concluded that the magistrates "apply the criteria and accepted wisdom they inherit with great vigour and dedication. However, ... the overall impact is highly punitive."

Provine (1986) compared lawyer and nonlawyer judges in New York. The results of her study contradicted those reported by Diamond (1990): according to Provine (1986, p. 100), nonlawyer judges were decidedly more likely to sentence more severely.[33] At the same time, nonlawyer judges were more favorably disposed toward the police and the prosecutors. Moreover, nonlawyer judges considered a smaller number of factors when reaching decisions than lawyer judges did, and, while deciding the punishment, they attributed less importance to the offense itself (Provine, 1986, p. 110). However, Provine's general conclusion was that differences between nonlawyer and lawyer judges were unimportant. Common characteristics included equally effective communication of procedural rights by both types of judges, as well as similarities in imposing bail, handling small claims, and exercising discretion.

Provine also examined the impact of potential bias and prejudice. She concluded that nonlawyer judges were not more biased or prejudiced than lawyer judges were (Provine, 1986, p. 114), and that nonlawyer judges were less critical toward attorneys (prosecutors and defense attorneys) than lawyer judges were (Provine, 1986, p. 101). Finally, Kapardis and Farrington (1981) examined the influence of age, race, gender, and social status of the defendant on the magistrates' decisions. Their conclusion was that lay persons were

---

[33]Approximately 88% of nonlawyer judges claimed to be more severe in sentencing than their lawyer counterparts, whereas only 60% of lawyer judges claimed to be more severe in sentencing than their nonlawyer counterparts.

influenced by gender and social status of the defendants, but not by age and race.

Lay participants are also perceived to be **less efficient** than lawyers, meaning that lay participants require more time than professionals to arrive at legal decisions in cases of comparable difficulty or complexity. Of course, it is almost impossible to compare the efficiency of lay participants and professional judges because they rarely, if ever, decide similar issues in similar cases. This is particularly true of mixed tribunals because they make the decision jointly, while it seems to be pointless to compare the efficiency of the jury and the professional judge because they reach decisions on different issues.

On the other hand, a comparison of the efficiency of lay magistrates and stipendiary (professional) magistrates may be useful. Provine (1986, p. 138) compared professional and lay justices of the peace in New York. Although there were significant differences in the caseload (lawyers decided on average 1,500 cases per year; lay justices decided on average 350 cases per year), it appears that lay justices were less efficient than lawyers: the median number of cases considered per hour was 0.7 for lay justices and 3.5 for lawyers.

One of the disadvantages of lay participation is the potential of **higher costs** associated with trials that involve lay participants. Of course, assessing whether involving lay participants increases costs of the administration of justice is very difficult. The appropriate answer to this question depends primarily on the form of lay participation and on the legal framework of a particular country.[34]

Trials in which lay participants hear cases, provide advice, and/or make decisions *in the same courtroom* with professional judges (i.e., trials by mixed tribunals, trials by jury) will clearly generate expenses that exceed those that would have been incurred if only the professional judge handled the cases (i.e., bench trials). Compared to the expenses of a bench trial, a jury trial introduces additional costs associated with the maintenance of the jury pool, additional

---

[34]See Murray (1998) for an attempt to provide a direct comparison of the relative efficiency, fairness, and costs of civil trials in common-law countries and civil-law countries.

stages of the trial (e.g., *voir dire*, jury instructions, deliberation), and/or a prolonged trial. There are also costs of covering the expenses of jurors' lost salary, their travel expenses, and their daily fee. In addition, other participants in the trial (e.g., the professional judge, attorneys) need to spend more time preparing for the trial and participating in it. Ultimately, the assessment of exactly how much costlier jury trials are depends on the specifics of the legal proceedings in a particular country and, of course, on the remuneration of jurors, transportation costs, and other expenses. An illustrative example of large differences in rates of remuneration, even across countries with comparable standards of living, is the aforementioned difference between the United States and Spain. While compensation in the United States varies and can reach up to $40 (state courts in South Dakota and federal courts), an average American juror receives only $5 per day (*State Court Organization 1993*, 1995, p. 265-268). An average juror in Spain, on the other hand, receives an impressive $81 per day (Thaman, 1998, p. 265).

Comparable calculations for trials by mixed tribunals are somewhat simpler. To begin with, there are costs associated with the selection process of lay judges. Unlike jury trials, trials by mixed tribunals typically are not longer than trials by professional judge alone (exclusive of deliberation); there are no additional stages of the trial to be included if the case is to be decided by a professional judge alone or by a mixed tribunal.[35] The only additional part of trial involves deliberation and voting. Next, there are costs of covering the expenses of the lay judges' lost salary, their travel expenses, and their daily fee, as well as additional costs because the professional judge will spend more

---

[35]For example, the procedure in Croatia may be expedited in the cases tried by professional judge alone (the so-called summary procedure); the usage of this summary procedure was introduced primarily because of the relatively low seriousness of the crime (fine or imprisonment of up to three years), rather than because such trials were to be conducted by professional judge alone (and not by mixed tribunal). Summary procedure is regulated by specific articles of the *Criminal Procedure Law* (Articles 430-445, *Criminal Procedure Law*, 1993; Articles 430-446, *Criminal Procedure Law*, 1998). Article 430 stipulates that issues not regulated in those articles will be resolved according to other rules specified in the *Criminal Procedure Law*.

time on deliberation with lay members than he/she would have required to reach the decision by himself/herself. There are circumstances under which a trial by mixed tribunal may generate even higher costs; these include situations in which a trial has been postponed because the professional judge could not find the appropriate number of lay judges to be present during the trial (e.g., although summoned on time, lay judges did not respond to the court's mail) or when the preceding part of the trial needed to be repeated because the composition of the tribunal had changed in the meantime.

A different set of considerations may apply to the forms of lay participation in which lay participants make legal decisions *instead* of professional judges (i.e., lay courts, magistrates, justices of the peace). The accounting of costs should include costs associated with the selection or appointment of lay judges and costs of their obligatory training. Although the fact that lay participants typically make decisions in a group may suggest high costs, it is often true that the salary provided to a single professional judge may easily exceed the combined costs of remuneration to all lay participants. It is estimated that, "a typical stipendiary disposes of work at three to five times the rate of a typical lay bench" (O'Connor, 1993, p. 453). It may appear that justice by lay magistrates is less expensive than justice by professional magistrates, since lay magistrates are volunteers and professional magistrates are employed by the state. However, the difference could be much smaller, or even completely eliminated, when the salary for a professional court clerk, who performs a great amount of legal work for lay magistrates, is entered into the calculations.[36] Moreover, replacing many (inefficient) lay judges (magistrates, justices of the peace) by fewer (efficient) professional judges would still lead to high costs (Provine, 1981, p. 29). Finally, as Parker *et al.* (1989, p. 172) argued:

> ... the overall impact is highly punitive. Be it giving a fine
> where it will not easily be paid and so lead to prison for default,
> or using community service because 'disciplined' employment is in

---

[36]Unlike lay magistrates, stipendiary magistrates do not have professional court clerks who are barristers or solicitors. Rather, stipendiary magistrates have only clerical assistants (O'Connor, 1993, p. 453).

short supply or slipping requirements on to probation orders because they're a 'good thing', the collective result is to push towards
the prison. Be it committing to Crown Court for sentence or using custody unsparingly, the pressure builds. While magistrates'
justice is arguably cheap to administer, the end result is expensive.

In summary, the overall costs of trials by lay participants are probably
higher than the overall costs of bench trials. However, while weighing such
comparisons, one should keep in mind advantages of trials by lay participants
that go beyond simple cost/benefit analyses. It is quite challenging to place a
monetary value on the functions which trials by lay participants may achieve.
All the benefits of trials by lay participants (i.e., providing for a democratic
process, a potential safeguard against biased judges and overzealous prosecutors, an opportunity for the citizens to participate in the government, an
option to be judged by one's peers) lie at the very root of democratic society
and, as such, have obviously outweighed the criticisms of lay participation in
most of the countries in the world today.

Chapter 2

History of Lay Participation in Germany

This chapter provides a brief overview of the history of lay participation in Germany, a cradle of mixed tribunals. Germany is a country with a long and successful tradition of the actual use of mixed tribunals in its courtrooms, as well as an extensive interest (both theoretical and empirical) in mixed tribunals. The next chapter contains a detailed overview of the historical development of lay participation in Croatia, the country in which I conducted the empirical part of this study.

Examining the development of lay participation in the two countries is particularly instructive because Germany and Croatia are each characteristic of a different historical emergence of contemporary lay participation. While Croatia did not utilize lay participation in legal decision-making until the mid-1940s (except for a few brief encounters with the jury system in the 19th century), participation of lay person in legal decision-making has had a long and rich history in Germany —some form of lay participation was present during most periods of German legal history. Moreover, lay participation in the two countries was founded on very different ideological platforms. In Germany, contemporary lay participation in mixed tribunals, as well as relatively brief recent periods that also featured the jury, were fostered within the confines of a capitalist society which, at least over the past five decades, has been oriented

toward Western-style parliamentary democracy. On the other hand, Croatia
has been a part of socialist Yugoslavia and has begun the process of transition
toward democracy only recently.

2.1   Early History

During the early periods in German history, the assembly of free men was
the governing agency (Dawson, 1960, p. 35). Consequently, any matter of
general interest could have been brought to the assembly (*Thing*). Cases were
initially brought in front of and decided by all the able-bodied male members
of the tribe/community who were free and law-worthy members of the tribe
(*Urteiler*). Cases were decided either at the assemblies held on a regular basis
(e.g., twice a year) or at special assemblies that met solely for the purpose of
resolving a specific case. The laws or legal rules were known to all the men
participating in the assembly; these rules were an inseparable part of their
common group experience (Dawson, 1960, p. 35). Wrote Jolliffe (1961, p.
7-8):

> Our oldest law [English law], *like that of Germans and Celts*,
> is one in which the appropriate maxim is on every man's lips as
> soon as the facts of any case have been determined. From this it
> follows that the court is a meeting of common men, neighbors, a
> folk-moot. Freed from questionings about law, since it has the ac-
> knowledged rules of folkright to apply, it expends its full force upon
> establishing the efficiency and integrity of its means of arriving at
> right judgment [emphasis added].

Trial was conducted by the head of the assembly, called the *Graf, Vogt,
Schultheis,* or *Richter,* who was usually the prince, a priest, or a "law-speaker"
(a person who had wisdom in legal matters; Dawson, 1960, p. 37). Richert
(1983, p. 49) argued that the role performed by the head of the assembly
was similar to the role once performed by the Roman *praetor* — it consisted of
presiding over the proceedings (Richert, 1983, p. 49) and proposing the verdict
(Dawson, 1960, p. 37). However, the head of the assembly did not take part

in the decision-making process; the decision was reached by the assembly. All freemen had the right to attend and take part in the judgment (Forsyth, 1875, p. 36). The consent of the whole assembly was required and the members of the assembly were responsible for the judgment.

The spreading of Christianity and the emergence of increasingly powerful kings in the period from the 5th century to the 9th century contributed to considerable advancements in the structure and organization of decision-making entities. During this period, the *Thing* was refined and the state judiciary system emerged through the king's courts (Benz, 1982).

While in the earlier period the whole *Thing*, headed by the *Richter*, made the decision in a case, the operation of the *Thing* had been streamlined at the beginning of the second period. The head of the assembly would ask only a smaller subset of the assembly to state what the common law of the particular geographic area determined in the case. The members of this smaller group were the community's most respectable freemen, who were called the *Rachimburger* (Benz, 1982). Simply put, there was a trade-off between the tendency to allow for a sufficient number of the *Rachimburger* to hear the case and the tendency to secure efficiency by avoiding large crowds in the proceedings. The usual number of the *Rachimburger* in the group was seven. The *Rachimburger* would suggest, based on the customs and norms, the decision to the rest of the assembly (*Umstand*). If the assembly accepted the proposal, the head of the assembly would issue the ruling.

Interestingly, although there was no possibility of appeal or legal redress, a special mechanism existed for situations in which some of the members of the assembly or the defendant himself was not satisfied with the decision. The way of objecting to the verdict was to accuse the *Rachimburger* of maliciously withholding the content of the law. The conflict between the defendant and the assembly members, or among the assembly members themselves, was resolved by duel or oath (Benz, 1982).

The changes to the *Thing* did not initially alter its original spirit; the entire assembly was still the decision-maker in the case. Over time, however,

the *Thing* that met rarely but regularly (three times a year; Dawson, 1960, p.
38), and did not require a special invitation (summons) to attend, ended up
deciding only the more serious criminal cases. It was called the regular *Thing*
(*Echte Thing*).

The custom of electing the president of the *Thing* by the people was gradually abandoned in favor of granting the appointment by the king (Dawson,
1960, p. 37). For reasons of efficiency, the head of the assembly, who was now
the king's clerk (*Graf*), was empowered to summon only a sufficient number of
the *Rachimburger* to render their opinion on legal issues in less serious cases.
Instead of inviting a large crowd, the president typically summoned only seven
Rachimburger. Such meetings were scheduled irregularly; they met twice per
week or when necessary. This variety of the *Thing* was called the ordered
Thing (*Gebotene Thing*).

The judgment of the *Rachimburger* had the strength of a legal decision in
less important matters, provided that the *Graf* concurred (Dawson, 1960, p.
38). Bestowing decision-making powers in less important matters to a group
of seven instead of having the whole assembly decide each and every case both
preserved group decision-making and attained reasonable efficiency.

Popular courts were subjected to Charlemagne's reforms in the 8th century, *circa* 769-780 (Benz, 1982; Estey, 1951, p. 119). One of the motives
for the reforms was to relieve ordinary free men, whose economic status had
declined substantially, of the burden of court attendance (Dawson, 1960, p.
38); it seems that even infrequent participation presented a heavy burden
for the *Rachimburger*, so they started avoiding their duty by either paying
bribes to or tacitly tolerating fines imposed by the *Grafen* (Richert, 1983,
p. 49; Estey, 1951, p. 119). Charlemagne's reform also sought to limit the
power of the *Grafen* by controlling the level of influence they had over the
court proceedings, especially over the selection of the *Rachimburger* and the
frequency of convening court sessions (Estey, 1951, p. 119). By jointly ad-
dressing the reluctance of the *Rachimburger* to participate and the immense

powers of the *Grafen*, the reform was also aimed at increasing the standard of decision-making and conformity to the law (Dawson, 1960, p. 38).

The reform replaced the *Rachimburger* with lay judges called the *Schöffen* in German or *scabini* in Latin (Richert, 1983, p. 49). The *Schöffen* were selected once; their appointment was for their lifetime and their successors could inherit this right. Although these judges were not formally trained in law — they were mostly respectable local land owners (Dawson, 1960, p. 39; Estey, 1951, p. 123) — they became permanent judges because of the respect they enjoyed in the community and their knowledge of the laws of that community. Furthermore, because of the steady nature of their function, these permanent lay judges were considered to be professional judges. They sat in traditional groups of seven, but also in groups of twelve or fifteen (Dawson, 1960, p. 94). By the late 1400s these groups included fourteen *Schöffen*, leading citizens and merchants, who met three times per week (Dawson, 1960, p. 180). In addition to considerable respect, lay judges were also provided with a tangible incentive to serve — they participated in the distribution of the fines.

In the aftermath of the Northmen descent, Europe was weakened and divided. As a consequence, starting from the 9th century, each of its parts pursued a separate road in building a new court system. In Germany, the same system of lay participation utilized in most of Europe before the Northmen conquest was still in use until the 13th century.

The period from the 9th to the 14th centuries is generally characterized by decentralized court systems; the 13th and the 14th century in Germany were marked by a conflict among church courts, feudal lordships, and privileged cities over determining who would maintain and possibly increase judicial powers. Preservation of the idea of lay participation and utilization of at least some forms of group decision-making were nevertheless a constant factor during this period.[1] The *Schöffen* represented a middle-ground between the total

---

[1]See Benz (1982, p. 21-24) for several examples of legal codes from various parts of Germany, drafted in the 13th and the 14th centuries, that each rely on lay participation in judicial decision-making.

conquest of the judicial function by the state and by the citizen body. It was difficult to establish a common court structure and apply the same legal rules because the rules, maintained through oral tradition, varied greatly from one village to another. While France solved this problem by organizing *ad hoc* juries to testify to the law in each case, Germany retained the *Schöffen* — permanent groups of wise men who knew the laws of a particular community. The procedure was oral; the parties had an active role in order to convince a passive tribunal.[2] The *Schöffen* and other officers of the court were allowed to testify about the facts they had learned in their official capacity (Dawson, 1960, p. 98).

Eventually, the tribunal no longer merely suggested the decision to the assembly; rather, it made the legal decision itself (Dawson, 1960, p. 99). The *Schöffen* courts started to keep records of their decisions in the 14th century.[3] Their decisions included a mixture of adjudication in a particular case and rule-making. Through their work, the *Schöffen* courts helped maintain and preserve rules of their own communities. The *Schöffen* were regarded as "practical men with eyes directed to the concrete instance" (Dawson, 1968, p. 170).

---

[2]See Dawson (1960, p. 99-101), Richter (1983, p. 50), or Benz (1982, p. 29) for an example of a more aggressive form of *Schöffen* courts, the so-called *Vemgerichte*. The *Vemgerichte* were local courts in the 14th century Westfalia. The members of the decision-making body were the free count (*Freigraf*) and the free *Schöffen* (*Freischöffen*); they were "free" because they had jurisdiction over free men, not because they were independent from the crown. The *Freischöffen* swore an oath of secrecy and thus joined the secret society. In addition to their participation in the regular *Thing*, the *Freischöffen* had to investigate and report offenses, to bring up charges, to help in coercing the witnesses and the defendants to attend secret trials (*iudicium secretum* or *Stillgerichte*), and to help execute those who were found guilty in secret trials. Thus, law-finders became inquisitors. The immense power the *Stillgerichte* enjoyed soon wreaked terror and induced fear among the residents of Westfalia. Interestingly, despite protestations of neighboring regions, the *Stillgerichte* exercised their right, bestowed upon them by the crown, to operate outside Westfalia if they deemed it necessary (such trials would require the presence of only three *Freischöffen*). Secret trials were abandoned by the end of the 14th century; the *Stillgerichte* fell victim to their own power. The Emperor, no longer satisfied with their role and performance, revoked their privileges and gave support to the pressure that had been mounting against them. Thus, the *Stillgerichte* were virtually eliminated.

[3]For a detailed treatment and examples of these decisions see Dawson (1968, p. 158-170) and Wigmore (1936, p. 855-856).

As a consequence of the revival of Roman law, the first law schools and universities were founded. The law taught in law schools was not German common law; rather, it was "the law," that is, Roman law. The development of the legal profession supplied additional scores of potential judges who were at the same time trained lawyers — "learned doctors" of Roman and canon law. Trained lawyers and their novel approach to the law were not accepted eagerly:

> Lawyers were seen as foes of the traditional order, eager destroyers of familiar routines, 'modernizers' undermining a culture deeply attached to accustomed ways. Lawyers were outsiders to the social body, unsympathetic to its often irrational folkways, ignorant and contemptuous of its working. Their technical know-how and command of law idiom gave them a powerful instrument for innovation. Lay judges and jurors had to be reminded 'to stick to the old customs and pay no heed to the doctors' [footnotes omitted] (Strauss, 1986, p. 24).

The procedure shifted from being completely oral to being either oral or written (depending on the parties), to being completely written and canonist in nature (Dawson, 1960, p. 105):

> But by 1505 the transition was accomplished. Canonist methods of pleading and proof became standard procedure thereafter; pleadings consisted of an exchange of papers, proof was by means of written interrogatories administered by the court or its delegates, with the answers of witnesses recorded in writing.

That change required additional skills of lay judges, many of whom were illiterate (Richert, 1983, p. 51). The gap between the uneducated *Schöffen* and the educated lawyers grew. It became impossible to cope with the case, to follow the procedure, and to understand the vocabulary used by the parties in the case without any training in Roman and canon law. The situation became even worse with the growth of strong appellate courts (composed overwhelmingly of persons trained in law), which controlled the work of trial courts and

primarily used Roman law. Appellate courts exerted pressure on trial courts
to Romanize their procedures, doctrine, and *personnel* (Dawson, 1960, p. 109;
Benz, 1982, p. 32).

The noblemen complained bitterly about the court procedures ran by the
learned doctors and their rapidly growing power. For example, the Bavarian
Ritterschaft complained to the Bavarian Duke around 1500 (Strauss, 1986, p.
26):

> The benches of the higher courts are no longer occupied as they
> used to be in the old days, but have now come into the hands of
> the learned. And hardly a locally born man [*landmann*] is found on
> the court who knows where the book is kept by which judgment
> should be given, which the foreigners [*auslender*] know nothing
> about and hold in contempt; and out of this contempt new laws
> are made, unheard of in the days of our forefathers and mortal to
> our common rights and customs.

The Duke, however, supported the learned doctors and the role they played
in enhancing the quality of the court system:

> A great number of doctors sit on our high courts because they
> have superior knowledge of the law. And because their legal un-
> derstanding is greater than that of laymen, their judgments are
> more correct and in better agreement with the law. Thus our peo-
> ple are not harmed by faulty verdicts which, when appealed to the
> Imperial Chamber Court, would be rejected there (Strauss, 1986,
> p. 26).

This exchange illustrates the clash between the two irreconcilable tendencies. The tension lasted for decades; eventually, the *Schöffen* fell victim to the
gradual departure from common German law in favor of Roman law. Indeed,
although the *Schöffen* were quite capable of applying the common law of their
particular community, that is, of "finding the law," they could not keep up
with the vigorous "making of the law," which was based on the knowledge of
the law obtainable only in law schools:

The ultimate fate of the *Schöffen* courts is connected with the fate of the substantive law they applied. The *Schöffen* and most of the law they 'found' were submerged in the reception of Roman law. The process began in the fifteenth century; by the end of the sixteenth the *Schöffen* had either been displaced or completely transformed, that is, Romanized (Dawson, 1960, p. 102).

Indeed, the replacement of lay judges by learned doctors of law continued. By the mid-16th century, learned doctors occupied a significant proportion of seats in legal decision-making bodies. Strauss (1986, p. 80-82) provides examples of numerical representation of learned doctors in various German provinces; for example, "... of the thirty-eight assessors sitting on the high court of Hessen in Marburg ... twelve were doctors, one a magister, and another a licentiate."

The promulgation of Roman law was an efficient method of transforming the medieval, fragmented world into a world of uniform, modernized, and powerful states. The inherent qualities of the system of Roman law (originality, clarity, strong conceptualization, cumulative nature) enabled it to stand out as the ideal means of providing the uniformity of legal principles and procedures across German lands (and other parts of Europe). In addition, *Corpus Iuris Civilis* was an imperial law and was thus perceived as a promoter of authority and, consequently, an instrument of new power (Strauss, 1986, p. 59-70).

The way to attain the desired uniformity was to engage in a series of reformations, which "... were revisions of older law codes with more or less massive infusions of Roman elements in both substance and procedure" (Strauss, 1986, p. 60). Codification of criminal law started to establish the power of the state and introduced methods of investigation characteristic of strong governments (Strauss, 1986, p. 124).

Criminal law was standardized throughout the German territory in 1532 by the *Constitutio Criminalis Carolina* (henceforth the *Carolina*), one of the most studied legal documents in history.[4] On the surface, the old common

---

[4]Langbein (1974, p. 141) wrote that, "[t]he importance of the Carolina has made it the subject of a vast body of scholarship [footnotes omitted] which has no counterpart,

law was not discarded completely; one of the clauses of the statute, *clausula salvatoria*, stated that the old common laws were still applicable, as long as they were in accordance with the idea and the content of the new law.

The *Carolina* surfaced in the period in which the process of replacing uneducated judges by those trained in Roman law had already begun. However, as Langbein (1974, p. 175) argued, although *Carolina* was a crucial step in the transition toward a professional judiciary, lay courts were not replaced by professional courts because:

> [i]mperial legislation abolishing the customary courts and substituting professional ones by fiat would have been unthinkable. Elsewhere in Europe more potent central authorities would be unable to effect drastic legislative change in court structure for several centuries.

Although the *Carolina* did not replace lay judges with professional judges explicitly, it is very clear that Charles V introduced the *Carolina* in order to react to the problems that surfaced in connection with lay decision-making. In particular, Charles V explained in the Preamble of the *Carolina* (1532) that "several learned, thoroughly experienced persons" had been commanded to produce a written summary of "how and in what manner judicial proceedings in criminal cases ought best to be conducted according to law and equity." The need for a uniform codex was stated unequivocally (Preamble, *Carolina*, 1532):

> ... most criminal courts are staffed with persons who have not studied, had experience with, or exercised our Imperial law. And that therefore in many places proceedings are often contrary to law and reason, and either the innocent are punished and killed or the guilty reprieved, dismissed and set free through irregular, deceitful, and protracted proceedings with great disadvantage to criminal complainants and to the common weal.

The *Carolina* (Article 104, 1532) regulated that only "a good, legally knowledgeable judge" could conduct trials. However, Charles V was aware that

---

Continental or English, in historical writing about the criminal process."

a complete reorganization of the court system was impossible and that he could not staff all the criminal courts with lawyers (Langbein, 1974, p. 175). Therefore, judges sat together with (permanent) lay judges on the same tribunal. These lay judges were considered to be decision-makers; "because such *Schöffen* in this case act not as witnesses but as cojudges, they shall not therefore be excluded from the court or from the judgment" (Article 91, *Carolina*, 1532). In the cases involving the death penalty, the *Carolina* required that a total of seven lay judges be present; less serious cases required only four lay judges (Dawson, 1960, p. 109-110).[5]

The *Carolina* not only established the dominance of Roman law over the old German common law, but also contained several aspects important for the development of mixed tribunals. For the first time, descriptions of criminal offenses were given as a part of the legal code (Articles 104-180, *Carolina*, 1532). In addition, decision-makers did not make their decision on the basis of the evidence heard, but rather on the basis of the transcripts read (Article 81, *Carolina*, 153). Thus, the process became written, replacing the old oral process.

There was a "dress rehearsal" for the public trial day (*Rechttag*). The decision was made on that occasion (i.e., before the public trial day itself; Langbein, 1974, p. 187) and was based on the case file (Article 81, *Carolina*, 1532):

> Before the Rechttag all that has been gone into shall be read out before the judge and judgment-givers; [all the prior proceedings which the court scribe has transcribed shall be] brought before the judge and judgment-givers. On that basis judge and judgment-givers can discuss among themselves and decide what judgment they wish to speak.

---

[5]Lay judges were present during criminal inquisitions as well, especially when torture was used (Dawson, 1960, p. 110; Benz, 1982).

Although panel members had already decided (and had written down their decision) during the "dress rehearsal," they formally reached the decision on the *Rechttag* as specified in Article 92 (*Carolina*, 1532):

> After both sides have made their submissions, and after everything else has been brought up, and after these matters are finally decided, then the judge, Schöffen, and judgment-givers shall take up with diligent consideration and deliberation everything which was submitted to and done before the court, and shall thence (upon their best understanding of this our criminal courts ordinance and according to the circumstances of each individual case) have formulated in writing the most appropriate and even-handed judgment.

The *Carolina* is an excellent example of a code that keeps the old forms (public shaming and lay courts) *de iure* alive, while *de facto* empowering the new forms (secretive process and professional decision-makers). The formal preservation of old traditions enabled a subtle implementation of a dramatic change. The traces of past times were present; the judge was required to ask lay judges about the law and, upon their discussion, to prepare and announce the final judgment in the case (Article 94, *Carolina*, 1532). However, as Langbein (1974, p. 192) argued, this was just a ritual and the judge had a complete control over the process:

> The whole of the Vorverfahren [the new preliminary process] has been conducted by the judge. He has administered the Indizienlehre's 'probable cause' determination, he has supervised the examination under torture (in the presence of two passive Schöffen-witnesses), he has arranged the verification of the confession, he has handled the taking of witness proofs. Only then, when he has secured confession or full proof, does the judge summon the Schöffen for the pre-Rechttag session of Article 81 at which judge and Schöffen take up the case on the basis of the written record which has been compiled under the direction of the judge. This is already the dress rehearsal, where the judgment is being settled for the Rechttag ... The Vorverfahren has become the functional Hauptverfahren. And the layman is being displaced by the professional.

The emphasis on the written case file (*Akte*), a feature of a typical inquisitorial procedure, was just one element that made lay participation in decision-making difficult. Another element was the focus on legal rules. In addition to serving as a primer on criminal law and procedure, *Carolina* provided a prominent role for the judge at the expense of lay judges ("it sought simultaneously to oust the laymen — to restrict the genuinely deliberative role of the unwieldly court of numerous laymen while enhancing the authority of the judge in their midst;" Langbein, 1974, p. 200).

Furthermore, the *Carolina* developed yet another mechanism for the reception of Roman law in lay courts: the advice-seeking duty. If the court could not resolve the case by applying the *Carolina*, the judges had an "obligation to seek advice from the nearest universities (*hohen schulen*), cities, free cities, or others legally knowledgeable ..." (Article 219, *Carolina*, 1532).

The *Schöffengerichte* — **mixed tribunals** — were born. Consequences of the *Carolina* were long-lasting. In general terms, the use of the *Schöffen* as lay participants in mixed tribunals lasted for another two to three centuries (Dawson, 1960, p. 110), but the practical aspects of trials by mixed tribunals were less than glamorous. To begin with, lawyers, who were literate and trained in the law, probably tended to ignore the lay judges, who did not know the Roman law to be applied in each case. Furthermore, Article 219 of the *Carolina* advised trial courts that they should send the more complex cases to upper courts or law schools in order to obtain their legal opinion. This act was perceived as advisory at the time; it later became obligatory for lower courts. The upper echelons of the hierarchy made the decisions and the lower courts had no choice but to pass the decisions reached by upper courts or law schools.

2.2 Recent Developments

The preceding section focused on the early phases of the history of lay participation in Germany. The reception of Roman law and the consequent changes that occurred in the court system of Germany had a very strong negative impact on lay participation. In particular, the written (rather than oral) format of trial, in addition to the reliance on Roman law (rather than the traditional German common law) expedited and strengthened the need for trained decision-makers. In the aftermath of the *Constitutio Criminalis Carolina* (1532), the period from the 16th to the 18th century was generally marked by the decline of lay participation and its virtual disappearance from German courtrooms; "yet if lay judges were not exterminated, they were brought to a state of subordination" (Dawson, 1960, p. 111).

The Ordinance of 1555 reformed the imperial courts. It did not directly eliminate lay judges; instead, one of the provisions was that the judges be persons with "enough understanding to supervise and direct judicial proceedings" (Smend, 1911, p. 251). Gradually, legal training did become a prerequisite for a president of the panel at imperial courts (Smend, 1911, p. 260). Richert (1983, p. 52) argued that these positions were sought after because being a judge had become a full-time life-long career. Historians noted that similar changes occurred at other courts, including the imperial *Reichshofrat*, where legal education became a requirement in 1654 (Smend, 1911, p. 304).

Despite the general trend, lay participation in the form of mixed tribunals survived the change in some jurisdictions. The size of mixed tribunals (those that survived) typically increased from the usual seven to twelve or more members (Richert, 1983, p. 52); the Ordinance of 1562 in Swabia required twelve members, as was the case in Emmendingen (near Freiburg), the court in Hauenstein required 24, and the court in Freiburg required as many as 30 members (Forsyth, 1875, p. 315-316). Tradition was followed and lay members (*Urteiler*) served as judges, while court proceedings were chaired by an elected official or civil servant.

However, mixed tribunals gradually disappeared from German courtrooms by the mid-19th century. For example, lay judges served in their traditional role until 1715 in Mark-Kleve (Richert, 1983, p. 52-53), until 1786 in Constance, until 1803 in Überlingen (Forsyth, 1875, p. 315-316), until 1813 in

Hamburg (Forsyth, 1875, p. 38), and until 1866 in Schleswig-Holstein (Forsyth, 1875, p. 34-35).

The next pivotal event in the history of German lay participation was the introduction of the jury. The conquering French revolutionary armies, which occupied the left bank of the Rhine at the end of the 18th century, brought with them a special form of the jury in which a professional judge conducted the trial and asked jurors for a special verdict — their opinion on a series of narrowly defined questions of fact (Richert, 1983, p. 53). Although the Prussian administration that overtook the occupied areas upon the fall of Napoleon was generally against the institutions established by the Napoleonic regime, the jury was not abolished. In fact, a commission appointed in 1816 recommended that the jury be retained because of its popularity (Gneist, 1967, p. 135). The hope was that the effects of the absolutist regime could be cushioned at least partially by the opportunity of lay participation (Forsyth, 1875, p. 325-326):

> The hatred felt throughout Germany at the French name was at this period intense, and the people were anxious to obliterate all traces of the military inundation which has swept over them, and to restore the old landmarks of German nationality. Prussia, therefore, looked with no favor upon a tribunal which was the offspring of French domination, but the inhabitants of the Rhineland clung to it with the affection of men who knew by experience the benefits it conferred. The government now adopted a wise course. They appointed a commission of five persons ... who were thoroughly to investigate the practical working of the system, and ascertain by personal inquiry what were the views and wishes of the inhabitants ... After a long and deliberate inquiry, the Commissioners made their report in 1819, and they were unanimous in favor of the continuance of the jury trial.

Several periods in the 19th century (1818, 1819, the 1830s, 1842-44) witnessed parliamentary debates on the jury (Richert, 1983, p. 54). The debates were instigated by the Liberal party, which emphasized the political function of the jury and promoted it as a means of resistance to the absolutist regimes that ruled German lands at the time.

Such a strong political wave was reflected in the constitutional draft prepared by the National Assembly in 1848. The jury court (*Schwurgericht*), structured along the lines of the French model, was proposed for all offenses by the press (Article 142), all serious crimes, and political offenses (Article 179). This opened up possibilities for German states to introduce the jury. The process started the same year and lasted until the early 1850s (Richert, 1983, p. 54). Interestingly, although Bavaria, Prussia, Württemburg, Hanover, Nassau, Oberhessen, Stackenburg, Brunswick, and Oldenburg introduced the jury relatively rapidly, some other German states, such as Saxe-Altenburg, Mecklenburg, Lippe, Hamburg, Lübeck, and Bremen resisted the trend (Richert, 1983, p. 54).

Despite such a dramatic movement for the introduction of the jury, the interest in the jury was soon lost and the voices advocating the reintroduction of mixed tribunals became stronger. The political development that marked the era between 1853 and 1858, and was in no small way responsible for the ultimate fate of the jury, was a successful search for the common political ground by the advocates of the authoritarian state and the advocates of the liberal state.

Richert (1983, p. 55) argued that the ultimate decision to abolish the jury was related to the shortcomings of the jury system in general. Forsyth (1875, p. 328), on the other hand, attributed the jury's apparent lack of success and longevity to the inherent foreignness of the jury:

> Eagerly as trial by jury was demanded in Germany, and gladly as the concession has been received, experience has already proved that institutions, like trees, when transplanted do not flourish with the same vigor as when growing in their native soil.

The movement for the reintroduction of mixed tribunals started with the Hanover legislative reform in 1852 and continued for the next twenty years. At the beginning, mixed tribunals did not replace juries; rather they were assigned to hear less serious cases. Mixed tribunals and the jury co-existed in a number of German states before the unification of the German court system in 1879, which was initiated by the passing of the *Court Organization Act* of 1877 (Richert, 1983, p. 55-57).

Mixed tribunals were reintroduced under the old name (*Schöffengerichte*), but they differed in terms of their role and organization from the former institute of mixed tribunals. The crucial issue was that the separation of functions between the professional judge (*Richter*) and lay members (*Schöffen*) was no longer valid; the professional judge became a member of the tribunal and participated in the decision with lay members. Furthermore, the jurisdiction of lay members was extended; now, professional and lay members were in charge of deciding both the facts and the legal issues in the case. This form of mixed tribunals is identical in all important aspects to the contemporary mixed tribunals in Germany, as well as in a number of other European countries.

The political unification of German states was accompanied by the efforts to establish a unified German legal system. The 1873 court organization proposal included two types of mixed tribunals (small tribunals, composed of one professional and two lay judges and put in charge of less serious cases, and large tribunals, composed of three professional and six lay judges and put in charge of more serious cases), but no jury. The arguments raised at the time were that the new, unified Germany did not need a French institution and that mixed tribunals, the traditional German form of lay participation, had been successfully used to regain public acceptance of justice administration in lower courts in the aftermath of absolutist regimes (Richert, 1983, p. 57-58).

As a consequence of strong support for the jury in the southern German states, the final draft of the *Court Organization Act* of 1877 included both mixed tribunals and the jury. Out of five separate German courts in the first instance, two had lay participants. The *Schöffengerichte*, which met at the lowest courts in the hierarchy (*Amtsgerichte*), were composed of one professional and two lay judges; they had jurisdiction over the cases for which the prescribed penalties were imprisonment for up to three months or a fine of up to five hundred German marks. The *Schwurgerichte*, which met at county courts (*Landgerichte*), were composed of three professional judges and twelve jurors; they were in charge of the cases for which the prescribed punishment exceeded five years of imprisonment and of capital cases.

Although the jury once again became a part of the German court system, the debate about its usefulness and the prejudice of the jury continued. Interestingly, this was not a general debate about the disadvantages of trials by lay persons, but a debate that was limited to the shortcomings of the jury. In fact, the proposals for the elimination of the jury included, for example, the proposition forwarded by a Prussian Ministry of Justice Commission to replace it by either mixed tribunals or a professional judge (Herrmann, 1957, p. 106). Despite numerous proposals for the replacement of the jury system (Richert, 1983, p. 59), the court system established in 1879 persevered until the end of World War I.

Professional judges at that time were professional lawyers. Krüger (1914, p. 134) described the requirements:

> The leading officers of the German courts are professional judges. Their training is the same for the whole Empire. After graduation from a secondary school they have to study at least three years in jurisprudence [courses omitted] and economics. After they have passed rigid examinations of a general and theoretical character, they are admitted to the judicial career as Referendars. They are prepared in the different courts and may after three years of service be admitted to a second more practical examination. After the passage of this examination they have fulfilled the scientific qualification for the juristic career, receive the title 'Assessor,' and are appointed judges if a vacancy occurs.

As Krüger (1914, p. 135) emphasized, the only lay persons who had judicial powers in criminal trials at that time were lay judges in mixed tribunals (*Schöffengerichte*). On the other hand, jurors serving in the *Schwurgericht* courts decided only the guilt, while three professional judges were "required to preside at the trial, to formulate the questions and to mete out the penalty in accordance with the sentence of the jurors" (Exner, 1933, p. 253).

Jury service was considered to be an honor (Section 81, *Court Organization Act*, 1877), and jurors were not paid for their time. Interestingly, Howard (1904, p. 654) emphasized that the list of persons eligible for jury service had a dual purpose; it also served as a list of eligible persons for the service as lay judges in mixed tribunals. The same person could not have been summoned in the same year to serve both as a juror and as a lay judge (Howard, 1904, p. 655); once potential lay judges for that year were selected, the remainder of the list was used to identify potential jurors.

Lay participants were reimbursed only for the travel expenses they encountered in the course of performing their role. In fact, persons who could prove that they could not bear the expenses related to their jury service were exempt from jury service. Persons stripped of their civic rights as a consequence of a judicial decision or persons whose right to dispose of their property had been limited due to a judicial decision could not serve as jurors (Section 32, *Court Organization Act*, 1877). Furthermore, persons who could not perform their service because of their disposition (young age, dependent position, or personal characteristics) or persons occupying other positions in the government were exempt from jury service (Section 33 and Section 34, *Court Organization Act*, 1877). Finally, the law recognized a separate category of persons who did not need to serve, such as physicians, members of the legislature, persons who already served as jurors, or persons over the age of 65 (Section 35, *Court Organization Act*, 1877).

The majority of professional judges who served at the beginning of the Weimar Republic were inherited from the earlier regime and remained relatively conservative despite a general liberalization of the political system. Two sets of reforms were considered in order to improve the situation: the abolition of a life-long appointment of professional judges in favor of a limited-term appointment, and the widening of the jurisdiction of lay participants (Richert, 1983, p. 60). Perhaps surprisingly, the subsequent reform of 1924 ("The Emminger Reform") and the previous requests and proposals had very little in common.

While the jury was abolished completely (and replaced by large mixed tribunals composed of three professional and six lay judges), the name of the court (*Schwurgericht*) and the term used for jurors (*Geschworene*) were both kept in the statute. Exner (1933, p. 253) summarized the most frequent criticisms of the jury system:

> This form of court has been very often criticized, not only on account of its size and cost and not only because the judges were not able to give the reasons for their sentence, since they had not taken part in the deliberation of the jurors; but the most important argument against the former jury was the following: the jurors, without any legal adviser, had to decide upon a sentence and in doing this they often made the most serious mistakes.

This was the end of the jury in German courtrooms, except for a brief reintroduction in Bavaria immediately after World War II (1948-1950).

On the other hand, while the proposals advocated an expansion of the jurisdiction of mixed tribunals, the reform of 1924 achieved mostly the opposite effect. The jurisdiction of a professional judge alone was expanded at the expense of mixed tribunals; a professional judge alone took over from mixed tribunals the jurisdiction of some of the cases for which the maximum penalty was up to ten years of imprisonment. The ratio of the cases tried by a professional judge alone and a small mixed tribunal changed rapidly; while 97% of the cases before the reform were tried by a small mixed tribunal, over 85% of the cases in the years immediately following the reform (1924 and 1925) were tried by a professional judge alone (Richert, 1983, p. 61). Finally, the reform expanded the jurisdiction of mixed tribunals in another direction — mixed tribunals became a part of the appellate system. Small tribunals reviewed appeals in the cases decided in the first instance by a professional judge alone, while large tribunals reviewed appeals in the cases decided in the first instance by small mixed tribunals. Interestingly, while the majority of tribunal members in small appellate tribunals were lay judges (one professional judge and two lay judges), the majority of members of large appellate tribunals were professional judges (three professional judges and two lay judges).

While Nazi Germany emphasized the importance of the participation of the "Volk" in the administration of justice, partially to maintain the German tradition of lay participation, in reality the average person had almost no opportunity to participate. In 1934 the selection system was changed in order to ensure that lay participants would be the supporters of the Nazi regime. The long history of lay participation in Germany effectively came to its end in 1939, when lay participation in criminal courts was (supposedly temporarily) abolished. The only court in which lay participants remained involved in the administration of justice was the *Volksgerichtshof*, which was created in 1934 to hear treason cases, but any resemblance with full-fledged lay participation was due to chance: Hitler himself was involved in the selection of the three lay persons who sat with two professional judges (Wagner, 1974; Schorn, 1959, p. 102).

The post-World War II Germany once again turned to mixed tribunals and made them an important part of the court system. The court system in Germany today is regulated by the *Court Organization Act* of May 9, 1975. The court system consists of ordinary courts, in charge of criminal and civil cases, and specialized courts, including labor courts, social courts, financial courts, and administrative courts. The courts at the lowest level — trial courts — are state courts, while the highest court is always a federal court. The federal court at the highest level of the hierarchy of ordinary courts is the *Bundesgerichtshof*.

Since the focus of this book is on lay participation in regular or ordinary courts, I will focus the presentation on the description of the selection process and rights and duties of lay judges in ordinary German courts. Lay judges generally do not participate in civil trials.[6] By contrast, lay judges are full-

---

[6]There are two exceptions to this rule: lay judges participate in trials in commercial cases at the *Landgerichte* and in trials in agricultural disputes at the *Amtsgerichte*, the

fledged participants in criminal trials. The least serious cases (those with
the penalty of up to two years of imprisonment) are tried by a professional
judge alone (*Einzelrichter* or *Strafrichter*) at the *Amtsgerichte* (Article 25,
Court Organization Act, 1975), while somewhat more serious cases (those with
the penalty of up to four years of imprisonment) are tried by a small mixed
tribunal (*Schöffengericht*), composed of one professional judge and two lay
judges (Article 29, *Court Organization Act*, 1975). Based on the prosecutor's
motion and the complexity of the case, the presiding professional judge may
decide to expand the tribunal and include an additional professional judge
(Casper and Zeisel, 1972, p. 142). Such complex cases, then, are tried by the
expanded small mixed tribunal (*Erweitertes Schöffengericht*). The legislature
prescribed a general rule that is applicable to all mixed tribunals: the presiding
judge of the tribunal can only be a professional judge (Article 28, *German
Judicial Code*, 1972).

It seems that a relatively small percentage of less complex cases in the late
1960s and the 1970s were tried by mixed tribunals; the bulk of these cases
at the *Amtsgerichte* were tried by a professional judge alone. Official court
statistics do not report the percentage of cases decided by mixed tribunals.
However, some estimates are available. For example, there were 972,336 cases
tried at the *Amtsgerichte* in 1974 (Richert, 1983, p. 67); that number includes
both the cases tried by a professional judge alone and by mixed tribunals.
On the other hand, Casper and Zeisel (1972, p. 143) reported that there were
70,466 trials by mixed tribunals at the *Schöffengerichte* in 1969. Prefaced with
an obvious *caveat* that the two numbers do not pertain to the same year, a
rough estimate, obtained by dividing the latter with the former, would suggest
that it is very likely that at most up to 10% of these cases were tried by mixed
tribunals.

Serious criminal cases (exceeding four years of imprisonment), certain cases
of political and economic crimes, and crimes listed in Article 76 of the *Court
Organization Act* (1975) are tried at the *Landgerichte* by large mixed tribunals

---

Oberlandesgerichte, and the *Bundesgerichtshof*.

— the *Grosse Strafkammern.* These large mixed tribunals consist of three professional judges and two lay participants (Article 74, *Court Organization Act*, 1975). Compared to the original organization from 1924 (two professional judges and six lay judges), the size of the tribunal has been reduced in 1975. The *Act* refers to lay participants as lay judges (*Schöffen*) rather than as jurors (*Geschworene*). According to Richert (1983, p. 67), in 1974 there were 9,941 cases tried by these large mixed tribunals at county courts (*Landgerichte*). In the reality of the everyday German legal system, trials by large tribunals represent a small percentage of all criminal cases — about 1%.

Finally, a separate court in the hierarchy deals with the cases involving treason - the *Oberlandesgericht.* The tribunal is composed of five professional judges. These cases are very rare in the overall German court statistics; for example, there were only 30 such cases tried in 1974 (Richert, 1983, p. 67).

The German *Court Organization Act* of 1975 provides room for lay judges even at the appellate level. Decisions by a professional judge alone may be appealed to small mixed tribunals (*Kleine Strafkammern*), composed of one professional judge and two lay judges (Article 76, *Court Organization Act*, 1975). Decisions by small mixed tribunals at the *Amtsgerichte* may be appealed to large mixed tribunals, composed of three professional judges and two lay judges (*Grosse Strafkammern*), at the *Landgerichte*. Finally, decisions by the *Grosse Strafkammern* may be appealed to the *Oberlandesgericht*, where appeals are decided by professional tribunals.

The German court system recognizes separate courts for juvenile offenders. These courts were introduced into the German court system in 1923. The least serious cases are decided by a professional judge alone (*Jugendrichter*), while more serious cases are decided by the *Jugendschöffengerichte*, which meet at the *Amtsgerichte* and are composed of one professional judge and two lay judges, or by the *Jugendstrafkammern*, which meet at the *Landgerichte* and are also composed of one professional judge and two lay judges.

The federal system establishes the basic principles of the selection process, while the individual states have the option of providing additional requirements and regulations. The latter are valid if individual states remain within the federal boundaries. The consequences of violating these rules are serious; specifically, there will be grounds for legal redress if the process used for the selection of lay judges was in conflict with the statutory provisions, if the court was not composed in accordance with the legal rules, or if a lay judge who was excluded from the case participated in the trial (Article 338, *Criminal Procedure Law*, 1987).

Selection of lay judges rests on the basic principle that lay judges be representative of the community with respect to their gender, age, occupation, and social status (Articles 36 and 42, *Court Organization Act*, 1975). Gender plays an especially important role for juvenile courts; the rules require that, if reasonably possible, one of the lay judges should be a woman, and the other one a man. A violation of this rule does not have serious consequences; it cannot be used as the grounds for appeal or revision (Schorn, 1959, p. 85).

Eligibility requirements for lay judges are relatively simple: German citizenship, the right to hold public office, and the absence of court-determined punishment of more than six months of imprisonment (Article 32, *Court Organization Act*, 1975). Lay judges are persons with no legal training and without extensive experience in the criminal justice system; in particular, the *Act* excludes persons who have obtained experience as actors in the criminal justice system (e.g., professional judges, state attorneys, attorneys, notaries public) or persons who spent at least eight years working in the criminal justice system (Article 34, *Court Organization Act*, 1975).

Interestingly, to be classified as "suited," citizens need to meet both the minimum and the maximum age requirement (25 and 70 years of age, respectively). Furthermore, those who did not live in the community for over a year, or are mentally or physically infirm, will be classified as "unsuited." In addition, there is a group of citizens who "should not" be called to perform their lay judges' function; this group includes the federal president, members of either state or federal governments, judges, prosecutors, lawyers (persons in legal occupation should not serve; Article 34, *Court Organization Act*, 1975), governmental employees in general, and lay judges who have already served eight years as lay judges (Article 34, *Court Organization Act*, 1975).

Richert (1983, p. 100) analyzed the criteria used to assess the ability of lay judges and concluded that those criteria lead to a population of potential lay judges that is not representative of the German population; "these requirements prevent more than two out of every three Germans from serving as lay judges." Indeed, according to Richert's calculations (1983, p. 101), only 31.5% of the total (West) German population was eligible to serve as lay judges. At the same time, as many as 67.8% of that same population was eligible to vote (Richert, 1983, p. 102).

As a consequence of the special needs of juveniles, the requirements for the lay judges at juvenile courts are more extensive. Juvenile lay judges need to be "pedagogically capable and experienced in juvenile education" (Article 35, *Juvenile Court Code*, 1974). However, these qualifications can be interpreted in different ways to include, for example, only persons who have official training and education in dealing with juveniles or, for example, all the persons who have children.

Although lay judges who serve at juvenile courts should have special skills related to the education of juveniles, a study conducted by Gerken (1988) revealed that only one-third of the sampled lay judges from Hamburg actually had some professional experience with children or education in pedagogy. Furthermore, despite the expectations by the legislature, and in accordance with the finding that the majority of the sampled lay judges did not have the required professional expertise, lay judges did not perceive the projection of their expected expertise to be a part of their role as lay judges in juvenile cases (Gerken, 1988).

The election process for lay judges starts with the determination, made by the president of the county court (*Landgericht*), of the number of lay judges necessary for the trials at both the adult courts and the juvenile courts. The names of potential lay judges are placed on the list of nominees (*Vorschlagslist*) by accepting nominations from the community government, by soliciting suggestions from various agencies and organizations, or by randomly drawing names from the voter registration lists (Wolfe, 1996, p. 327). Once the list of nominees is composed, it is displayed publicly for a week to allow for challenges. Generally, the nomination lists are supposed to contain at least twice the number of lay judges needed. Interestingly, Wolf reported that the number of names on these lists is sometimes in precise correspondence to the number of lay judges to be selected for the court (Wolf, 1987, p. 234). Upon the expiration of the period of public challenge, lists are forwarded to the court. Lay judges who are selected from the list for a particular court are assigned to participate in criminal cases in a random fashion (Wolf, 1987, p. 236).

If severe violations of the selection process occur, persons who were selected despite the letter of the law should not become lay judges and, consequently, should not have the powers of a judge (Wolf, 1987, p. 234). If persons who should not participate in the trial as lay judges nevertheless participated, the verdict is not automatically null. However, it can be nullified as a result of an appeal by the parties.

Richert (1983) examined demographic characteristics of lay judges in 1976 and compared them with the demographic characteristics of the population. Compared to the general adult population, men were overrepresented — three out of four lay judges were men. Women were represented with higher percentages in mixed tribunals in East Germany at the time; between 1953 and 1974, the proportion of female lay judges increased from 35% to 48% (Richert, 1983, p. 84). Similarly, middle-age citizens were overrepresented in West Germany; approximately two-thirds of lay judges and one-third of citizens were in the age group 41-60. Finally, certain occupational groups were overrepresented (civil servants, self-employed individuals), while other occupational groups were underrepresented (retired persons, housewives, blue-collar workers). Not surprisingly, the percentage of blue-collar workers who served as lay judges in East Germany was higher (Richert, 1983, p. 84).

Article 1 of the *German Judicial Code* (1972) states that the power to administer justice is in the hands of professional judges (*Berufsrichter*) and lay judges (*Schöffen*). The fundamental principle of independence of the judiciary, including lay judges, was stated in Article 97 of the *Constitution of the Federal Republic of Germany* (1994). However, the principle of independence of the judiciary does not mean that the judges, both professional and lay, are free to decide cases irrespective of the law; in fact, they have to follow the law (and may not bend it).

In terms of their power, the *Court Organization Act* of 1975 states in Article 30 that lay judges exercise the judicial office "in full extent," unless there is an exception regulated by the law. The interpretation of the meaning of "full extent" is a topic of debate among legal scholars (Klausa, 1972; Kühne, 1985; Wassermann, 1982). In order to preserve the principle of neutrality of decision-makers, the law stipulates that lay judges may be exempt from the case for the same reasons that apply to professional judges (Wolf, 1987, p. 237).

Lay judges have certain duties, such as attending the trial sessions they have been called to participate in and protecting the secrecy of deliberations in which they have participated. They take an oath before they start performing their duty for the first time. Furthermore, if they violate the law, lay judges may be punished and/or dismissed from duty (Wolf, 1987, p. 237).

This determination of the actual extent of the role(s) played by professional judges and lay judges is of crucial importance in German courtrooms because of the nature of German criminal procedure, which provides the judges with an active role. Lay judges have the same legal status during trial as professional judges do and their votes have the same power (Article 30, *Court Organization Act*, 1975). In order to avoid the pressure of conforming with the vote(s) cast by the professional judge(s), the law requires that the voting be conducted in a particular order — lay judges vote first (Article 197, *Court Organization Act*, 1975). Furthermore, the law does not require unanimous decisions, but rather a majority vote (Article 196, *Court Organization Act*, 1975).

Lay judges' role is limited to trial (preliminary investigation is conducted by a professional judge alone). As a consequence of the inquisitorial nature of the process, the role of the presiding judges is an active, truth-seeking role. Primary responsibility for the truth-seeking function rests either with the presiding judge or the judge appointed to lead the case (Article 194, *Court Organization Act*, 1975). The presiding judge has the responsibility of directing the trial and deliberation.

However, the lay judges' role is somewhat more limited than the role performed by professional judges even during trial. For example, the right to ask questions of participants is not the same — the lay judges' right to ask questions is less pronounced. Their turn comes only after the other professional judges in the tribunal have asked questions; moreover, lay judges are placed at the very end of the list of other trial participants who are allowed to ask questions, that is, after the prosecutor, the defendant, and his/her attorney (Article 240, *Criminal Procedure Code*, 1987). In addition, only the presiding judge (who must be a professional judge) may label questions as unsuitable or irrelevant and thus disallow them (Article 241, *Criminal Procedure Code*, 1987). The final decision as to whether the question should be allowed is resolved by the tribunal (Article 242, *Criminal Procedure Code*, 1987).

The presiding professional judge has access to the entire court file, which includes investigation reports, police reports, charging documents, and arrest warrants (Schreiber, 1974, p. 941, 949). The most important part of the documentary materials is undoubtedly the indictment (*Anklageschrift*). Its inaccessibility to lay judges has been the centerpiece of controversy. Presiding professional judges prepare for the trial (and make procedural decisions on whom to call to appear at the trial) by reading the case file and thus necessarily have to have access to the entire file. Not allowing complete access to lay judges is usually viewed as a corollary to the principles of German criminal procedure: decisions should be made based on the evidence brought before the trial court (Article 261, *Criminal Procedure Code*, 1987); evidence should be presented orally (principle of orality), and not read from case files (Article 250, *Criminal Procedure Code*, 1987). In other words, the evidence deemed important for the case should be presented during the trial; the principle of directness of evidence (Article 250, *Criminal Procedure Code*, 1987) states that a person whose perception is pertinent to the proof of a fact should examine the fact during the trial itself. While there is no legal rule in any of the statutes that would prohibit lay judges from gaining access to this documentary material, the Federal Court of Justice repeatedly established this principle in the course of hearing and deciding on appeals from criminal courts (the proceedings in administrative, labor, and financial courts do not have such provisions). Furthermore, prior to 1982 the state ministries of justice established a rule (Rule Number 126) that prevented lay judges from having access to the *Anklageschrift* (Wolfe, 1996, p. 333).

However, the importance of those rulings is quite different in Germany than it would be in the United States; since Germany is a Roman-law country, lower courts are not bound by the decisions of higher courts (the *stare decisis* principle does not have any effect).

There is an interesting quirk in the regulations that govern accessibility of pre-trial documents, one that speaks volumes about the differential degree of confidence in tribunal members' integrity and ability. Namely, if other professional judge(s) sit in the tribunal (in addition to the presiding professional judge), all professional judges have the same access to the documentary materials. The right of non-presiding professional judges to have such access has been confirmed by the courts; it has been motivated by the assertion that no legal rule prohibits it, and that granting such access to all professional judges would enable them to function effectively. While the same arguments could be applied in support of equal access by lay judges, the law and legal practice do not seem to be heading in that direction.

2.2.1 Broader Perspective

The development of lay participation in Germany over the past several decades was not an isolated phenomenon; soon after the end of World War I, the use of mixed tribunals once again started to spread across Europe (e.g., Italy and the Swiss Cantons reintroduced mixed tribunals in the 1920s and 1930s). Debates over the form of lay participation continued with unabated passion.

For example, the Third International Congress for Criminal Law in Italy in 1933 posed as one of the questions for debate whether to accept the jury or mixed tribunals as the favorite form of lay participation in the criminal process. The participants clearly expressed their varied preferences,[7] and the text of the resolution stated that the selection of one form of lay participation over the others depended on the traditions within each nation. For mixed tribunals, the resolution suggested that the number of lay members should be twice the number of professional judges, and that the selected lay members should be able to fulfill the necessary moral and intellectual requirements and should be selected in such a manner as to represent all social classes (Bayer, 1940, p. 39).

The former Soviet Union adopted mixed tribunals in 1918. The second *Decree on Courts* of 1918 determined that civil cases would be decided by a tribunal composed of three permanent judges and four lay judges, while criminal cases would be decided by one permanent judge and twelve lay judges (Rácz, 1972, p. 400). The 1936 *Constitution of the Soviet Union* established the constitutional principle of lay participation (in the form of lay assessors) in the judicial system.

After World War II, a number of countries that adopted a socialist regime under the influence of the Soviet Union (including the former Yugoslavia) introduced mixed tribunals into their respective legal systems (Rácz, 1972). Mixed tribunals further survived the fall of communism in the late 1980s and early 1990s and are an integral part of the criminal processes of most countries in transition toward democracy. The next chapter explores the historical development of lay participation in Croatia.

---

[7]Six speakers supported mixed tribunals, four supported the jury, and three argued for professionals as the only decision-makers (Bayer, 1940, p. 39).

Chapter 3

History of Lay Participation in Croatia

This chapter is devoted to the history of lay participation in Croatia. Croatia was for a long time associated with or was a part of the Austro-Hungarian Union. After World War I Croatia became a part of the Yugoslav Union and was a part of socialist Yugoslavia from the end of World War II to 1991. Croatia has since been an independent country.

Unlike Germany, Croatia did not have lay participation in legal decision-making until the mid-1940s (except for a few brief encounters with the jury system in the 19th century). While fact-finding lay participation did exist in the form of medieval juries, modern legal decision-making was not entrusted to lay persons until the end of World War II. The ideological platform for the introduction of mixed tribunals into Croatian courtrooms was the communist ideology, which had been implemented by the Communist party in the days of socialist Yugoslavia. The Communist party held a firm grip on political life in the former Yugoslavia until the late 1980s. In the early 1990s, Croatia gained its independence and is currently regarded as a country in transition toward democracy. Perhaps surprisingly, the general sweep of the relics of the communist past bypassed mixed tribunals. In fact, the extent of the changes to the system of mixed tribunals is minimal in comparison with the vast overall changes that took place in Croatia over the past decade.

Mixed tribunals evolved in a series of socio-political and legal developments as the contemporary form of lay participation in legal decision-making in Croatia. These developments were numerous and frequent, each time reflecting the underlying changes of Croatian society, as well as the political system governing Croatia. Therefore, a rigorous description of the resulting legal changes, coupled with the highlights of the changing social reality, is an important stepping-stone toward the appreciation of contemporary mixed tribunals. Special attention is paid to the technicalities of the legal codes since the 1950s. There were many changes in that period; the legal culture changed frequently, as witnessed by five constitutions in Yugoslavia (1945, 1946, 1954, 1963, and 1974), interspersed with numerous amendments and, most recently, the *Constitution of the Republic of Croatia* (1990). Consequently, the organization of the courts and the court practices changed frequently as well. Mixed tribunals survived all of these changes, albeit with refinements that were gradually built into legislation. However, the general trend was a narrowing of the jurisdiction of mixed tribunals in both civil and criminal cases.

3.1   Lay Participation before 1944

Croatian tribes arrived in Southern Europe in the 7th century. Similar to German tribes, all adult male members of Croatian tribes formed assemblies; these assemblies were in charge of reaching important decisions on crucial issues, including legal decisions concerning the offenders and their crimes (Čulinović, 1946).

Despite frequent wars with its neighbors and internal power struggles, Croatia maintained its presence on European maps for several centuries. Finally, the Croatian noblemen signed a contract (*Pacta Conventa*) with the Hungarian King Koloman in 1102. The Croatian Kingdom *de facto* lost its independence, although Croatia *de iure* remained a separate country which was only loosely linked in a union with Hungary and had its own *Ban* (viceroy), parliament, tax system, currency, and military (Macan, 1992, p. 49).

Medieval Croatia did not correspond in its territory to the modern, 20th century Croatia; while certain parts of Croatia were either under Venetian rule or were independent (i.e., the Republic of Dubrovnik), other parts were in the union with Hungary. In 1527, Ferdinand, the Austrian Emperor, became the Croatian and Hungarian King as well.

Some forms of lay participation, such as the (fact-finding) jury, had existed in medieval Croatia. Indeed, lay judges are called *suci porotnici* in Croatian; the literal translation into English would be "judges-jurors;" the root of the second word is "rota" (oath) — medieval lay judges swore an oath at the beginning of their mandate or trial, that is, prior to their participation in the work of a typical medieval fact-finding jury. This root led some legal scholars to believe that the first form of lay participation, the origin of mixed tribunals and the jury, dates from the 12th century (Ogorelica, 1899, p. 39; Čulinović, 1946, p. 72), while others (Bayer, 1940; Krapac, 1987) argued that these (fact-finding) juries were not forms of lay participation in legal *decision-making*.

Several medieval statutes (e.g., *Vinodol Statute* of 1288, *Dubrovnik Statute* of 1332, *Poljice Statute* of 1440) introduced the fact-finding jury. Just like lay participants in much of Europe at the time, jurors (*rotnici* or *porotnici* in Croatian) were initially invited to swear an oath. It is important to note that the function of such a fact-finding jury was not to act as a decision-maker and reach a legal decision based on the knowledge jurors acquired during trial; rather, the jurors were used as evidence about the credibility of the defendant and were required to provide their personal knowledge about the case.

The statutes specified the number of jurors that the party in the case needed to call when charged with a particular offense in order to prove that his/her statement was true. If the defendant could not find a sufficient number of jurors to swear, the defendant could swear himself/herself as many times as necessary to obtain the required number of oaths. Article 56 of the *Vinodol Statute* (1288) provides an example for rape, "[i]f there be no jurors, or there be not as many, that women hath to swear instead of those whom are missing."

The number of required oaths was, for example, 50 for murder (Article 68, *Vinodol Statute*, 1288), 25 for robbery and 12 for theft (Article 9, *Vinodol Statute*, 1288), 3 for false testimony (Article 52, *Vinodol Statute*, 1288), 1 for insult (Article 28, *Vinodol Statute*, 1288). Other statutes, for example, the *Dubrovnik Statute* of 1332 (*Dubrovački statut*) and the *Poljice Statute* of 1440 (*Poljički statut*), also recognized and attached an important role to the jurors in the fact-finding jury.

Barada (1952) and Dabinović (1940) maintained that medieval lay judges also acted as decision-makers, not only as members of the (fact-finding) jury. Barada (1952) argued that lay judges (*rotnici*) were decision-makers; he provided an example from the *Vinodol Statute* (Article 73: "and serfs must be called before the royal court, in front of the lay judges.") Similarly, Dabinović (1940, p. 134) argued that, in addition to participating as members of the fact-finding jury, lay persons also participated as decision-makers in legal cases, both during the period of Croatian King Petar Krešimir (1058-1075) and in the Vinodol Republic.

Feudal courts, which were in charge of crimes committed by serfs, did not develop any procedural rules until the 18th century; even after that period, there was no guarantee that feudal courts would follow the rules (Čulinović, 1946, p. 75). Noblemen were tried by the king's courts, while common citizens were tried by city courts. Peasants or common citizens were not eligible to become judges at any of the courts, while the role of lay assessors was performed by noblemen. For example, a court in charge of serious crimes, the *Ban's* Court (*Sedes Judiciaria* or *Županijski sudbeni stol*) was composed of state officials and an unspecified number of honorary assessors of noble status appointed by the *Ban* (Article 28, *Act of 1723*; Čulinović, 1946, p. 53). Similarly, the National Judicial Bench (*Zemaljski sudbeni stol*), one of the four courts at the top of the hierarchy in the Hungarian Monarchy, was composed of at least five professional judges and about six assessors appointed by the king from the noble class. The Judicial Bench (*Sudbeni stol*) was in charge of trials to noblemen and was at the same time the appellate court for the other courts deciding criminal cases in the first instance. It was composed of seven noblemen (Article 13, *Act of 1478*, Čulinović, 1946, p. 52). The court reform of 1723 affected this court by expanding it to 23 members, including four king's assessors, two *Ban's* assessors, and four surplus assessors appointed by the king.

The court system of Croatia was reorganized in 1850; feudal courts were abolished and regular courts were introduced instead. The Ministry of Justice developed a uniform court system by establishing 57 district courts (*kotarski sudovi*), 7 national courts (*zemaljski sudovi*), and the Higher *Ban's* Court (*viši banski sud*). According to the *Code* of 1850, the highest court of Croatia was the Cassation Court in Vienna (Čulinović, 1946, p. 89). A decade later the highest court of Croatia became the newly established Bench of Seven (*Stol sedmorice*).

The Austrian *Criminal Procedure Law* of 1850 replaced the inquisitorial procedure, which was in use since medieval times (Čulinović, 1946, p. 80-81), with a procedure that was based on the accusatory principles — separation of the prosecution function from the judicial function, the principle of material truth, and the principle of free evaluation of evidence. Lay participation was introduced for the offenses committed by the press. Since Croatia was a part of the Habsburg Monarchy at the time, it is not surprising that the first form of lay participation in modern decision-making introduced in Croatia dates back to 1850, the year in which the jury was introduced in Austria and Croatia for the offenses committed by the press (Čulinović, 1946, p. 88). Josip Jelačić, the *Ban* of Croatia at the time, introduced jury trials for offenses by the press by passing the *Interim Law* of 1849 (Bayer, 1955, p. 148).

Despite its limited jurisdiction, the introduction of the jury was welcomed by the Croatians. The prospect of the first trial by jury in Zagreb was announced in the press by journalist Bogoslav Šulek in 1850. The first paragraph in his column vividly portrayed the social climate (Šulek, 1952, p. 136):

> On Monday, we, the citizens of Zagreb, shall participate in the administration of the most noble civil law, brought to us by the

new age; we shall witness an event yet unseen in Zagreb, in which
a free citizen shall try a free citizen — we shall have the *jury.*

Bayer (1955, p. 148) argued that the *Interim Law* of 1849 was written so
superficially and inadequately that the first trial, held on February 6, 1850,
turned into a major scandal and the substantive issues in the case were never
decided.

Be that as it may, the new absolutist regime in Vienna abolished jury
trials for offenses by the press in 1852, that is, only two years later, and instead introduced a professional tribunal composed of six professional judges
(Čulinović, 1946, p. 88). This legal change, of course, affected Croatia. The
new *Criminal Procedure Law* of 1853, authored by Hye-Glunek, was considered to be a step back toward the inquisitorial system (Bayer, 1940, p. 40).
After the collapse of absolutism in Austria, Julius Glaser, then Minister of
Justice and a Professor of Law, developed a new, more democratic and more
advanced *Code of Criminal Procedure* in 1873 (the so-called "Glaser Law").
It established the institution of the state prosecutor and the initiation of the
prosecutions *ex officio*, the principle of material truth, the principle of free
evaluation of evidence, the principle of public trial, and the principle of oral
trial. In addition, the *Code* placed the jury in charge of trials for the most
serious criminal cases.

At that time, Croatian legislators were limited in their actions by the Austrian and Hungarian crown. The laws in Croatia were drafted by the Croatian
Parliament and submitted to Franz Joseph I, the Austrian and Hungarian
Emperor, for his approval. However, despite a high level of control and supervision, Croatian laws were not literal copies of the Austrian or Hungarian
laws. Indeed, the 1870s were marked by *Ban* Ivan Mažuranić, who promulgated numerous legislative and judicial reforms and modernized the Croatian
state.

Although the Croatian Parliament modeled the new *Criminal Procedure
Law* of 1875 after the *Glaser Law*, the jury system was not introduced. Rather,
the Croatian *Code of Criminal Procedure for Offenses by the Press* of 1875

empowered the jury to try only for a very limited subset of crimes — offenses by the press. A month later, the Parliament passed the *Code Concerning the Compilation of Lists of Jurors* of 1875, which regulated the jury organization and jurisdiction of the jury. It described in detail eligibility requirements for jury service, how the selection process operated, and what issues were under the jurisdiction of the jury.

The October 13, 1874 discussion in the Croatian Parliament (the *Sabor*) focused on the jury and the types of cases the jury should decide. The debate, focusing on the positive and negative features of lay participation (the political function in particular), examined the need for the introduction of the jury at the time when the inquisitorial theory of evidence was abolished, and when lay assessors were introduced as decision-makers next to professional judges in local courts for the civil cases of small value (Sirotković and Margetić, 1990, p. 156). Danilo Stanković, one of the Members of the Parliament, reminded the Parliament why the jury enjoyed such a support ("the most beautiful flower of the criminal justice system") as the decision-maker in the cases involving offenses by the press (*Eighty-Fifth Parliament Session*, 1874, p. 1537):

> No one sensible cannot thus be opposed to this institution [the jury], nor is the government opposed to it, because it introduced the jury in the law on offenses by the press. It did so because the jury in press offenses is a *corollarium* of free press. This is the principle, one upon which the *Code Concerning the Use of Press* is based, and which the Sabor [Croatian Parliament] accepted. Since the press is considered to be an expression of public opinion, it is quite acceptable that it be tried by another factor of public opinion, that is, the jury. Our daily experience teaches us that the press comes into conflict with many, naturally, with the government as well, so that the government is frequently a party in the cases brought against the press. Indeed, when one immerses oneself into such cases, one has to be convinced that these are matters that by their very nature do not belong under the jurisdiction of the courts [the professional judges] but can be tried justly only by the jury.

Danilo Stanković further argued that the jury should not be introduced for political offenses, because (*Eighty-Fifth Parliament Session*, 1874, p. 1538):

> ... the jury is useful only when it is an institution of law, and not a political one ... In the heat of political battle the voice of justice fades away; and, at least my subjective opinion is that in those upsetting moments professional judges are more objective than the jurors. That is to be expected. Professional judges are outside of the battle of political parties, whereas jurors are not. Such jurors would try like Eol's harp. Such a jury is very dangerous, because history teaches us that whenever the jury tried political offenses, the state suffered too. It is quite different when the jury is an institution of law, when [it] tries a swindler, a thief, or a murderer. It is then considered as a judge who follows the law, justice, and fairness. But if it tries only for political offenses, I think and I am concerned, that it is there just to make the politics and not to try the case.

Another Member of the Parliament, Napoleon Špun-Strižić, a lawyer and a judge, argued that it really did not matter whether they introduced the jury for political offenses in addition to offenses by the press for a very simple reason: there were very few such offenses in Croatia (*Eighty-Fifth Parliament Session*, 1874, p. 1539). However, if the jury were introduced, the question remained whether it would be able to guarantee legal protection:

> Badly mistaken are those who think that the jury will save freedom. Despite the good intentions of Montesquieu and others who defended the jury, history teaches us that during the [French] Republic the jury sentenced to death everyone who did not support the Republicans. In fact, a famous gentleman from that era, Carnot, explicitly stated: 'It is not asked whether one is guilty, but whether one is a member of the minority or the majority.' When Napoleon became the French Emperor, he retained the jury. But he established new requirements for carrying out the jury duty, so that this institution became a lever of imperialism. What was the consequence? If the defendant was a republican, he was undoubtedly sentenced, while an imperialist remained safe from it [the jury]

... From this historical analysis please draw your own conclusions about the political value of the jury, as your reason commands.

By contrast, Josip Turelli (*Eighty-Fifth Parliament Session*, 1874, p. 1539) argued that the jury should be introduced for political offenses:

> I think that the jury is the pride of the constitution of every state because it is nothing but the division of power between the crown and the public. If that is the case, I cannot comprehend why this institution should be excluded exactly where these questions are the most delicate, where it is necessary to exclude the almighty influence of the state — on the issues that concern the state on the one hand and the public on the other hand.

Eventually, the jury was introduced to decide offenses by the press in 1875. Čulinović (1954, p. 43) argued that the jury in Croatia "was born out of fear from tyranny of the government and the belief that the introduction of the jury would drastically change the judicial system of Croatia." Offenses by the press were decided by the Royal Judicial Bench (*Kraljevski sudbeni stol*) in Zagreb (Article 3, *Code of Criminal Procedure for Offenses by the Press*, 1875). The composition of the court depended on the seriousness of the offense; for the offenses with the maximum penalty of up to five years in prison the Bench was composed of the court (*sudište* — the presiding judge, three additional professional judges, and a secretary) and twelve members of the jury (Article 15, *Code of Criminal Procedure for Offenses by the Press*, 1875), while more serious cases were tried by the Bench that consisted of the court (the presiding judge, *five* additional professional judges, and a secretary) and twelve members of the jury (Article 15, *Code of Criminal Procedure for Offenses by the Press*, 1875). The facts and guilt were decided by a twelve-member jury, while the sanction was determined by the court. The Royal Judicial Bench in Zagreb had regular meetings scheduled every three months (Article 16, *Code of Criminal Procedure for Offenses by the Press*, 1875) and could schedule additional meetings at other times. Jurors were not appointed but elected from the juror registry.

The rules regulated in detail *the eligibility requirements for jury duty*. It is instructive to perform a detailed exploration of these requirements and compare them with the requirements for lay judges today. In addition to a general rule which specified eligibility for jury service, there were a number of more detailed rules that established who was exempt or excluded from jury service. Only male citizens between 30 and 60 who could read and write, had lived in the district for at least one year, and paid taxes in the amount of at least 20 forints were eligible (Article 2, *Code Concerning the Compilation of Lists of Jurors*, 1875). Regardless of the amount of taxes they paid, the following persons were also eligible: persons who obtained doctoral honors in any field, persons who graduated with honors from a professional school or any higher technical university, persons who were regular members of the Yugoslav Academy of Sciences and Arts, attorneys, notaries, and professors. This catalog of acceptable persons was very consistent with the values of Croatian society (as well as most European societies) at the time: potential jurors were to be distinguished men, either by their wealth, their education, or by their professional standing.

In addition, there were persons who were exempt from jury service and persons who were excluded. Those *excluded* from jury service were either persons who were physically or psychologically unable to perform the service, who had limited civil rights, who were under investigation, or who had been convicted for certain offenses. Some men were *exempt* from jury service because of the conflicts between their profession and jury service (teachers, religious leaders, professional judges, soldiers, postal workers, state officials). Finally, there was a category of persons who were *pardoned* from jury service (members of the Parliament during Parliament sessions, employees in Royal Service, public teachers, doctors of medicine, and jurors who were active the previous year).

The *Code* mandated that jury service was not a paid service. In fact, even the expenses the jurors had incurred, such as lost salary, were not reimbursed. However, as Bayer (1940, p. 43) argued, jurors could not have encountered high travel and lodging expenses because only the residents of a city in which the court was located were potentially eligible for jury duty at that court.

The law also regulated the *selection process* of potential jurors; that process bore some similarities with the jury selection in the United States today. The names of all eligible persons (who were not relieved from the service) were placed on the initial juror list. The information about each person included the person's name, age, class or occupation, and address (Article 6, *Code Concerning the Compilation of Lists of Jurors*, 1875). The public had one week to examine the registry and to complain either that some eligible persons were not included on the list or that the list contained the names of persons who were not eligible for service. Furthermore, a person who was on the list could write a statement containing the reasons why his name should be removed from the list (Article 7, *Code Concerning the Compilation of Lists of Jurors*, 1875).

The City Council sought to select from the initial juror list such persons who could be particularly successful in performing their jury duty because of their common sense, honesty, and "honorable reasoning" (Article 9, *Code Concerning the Compilation of Lists of Jurors*, 1875). The law required that there be one juror on the list for every 50 persons living in a given community (Article 10, *Code Concerning the Compilation of Lists of Jurors*, 1875). Based on these selection criteria, a new list, the so-called annual jury registry, was compiled, printed, and distributed to the courts.

For each session, the court compiled the official registry (*službeni imenik*) from the annual jury registry by picking 36 regular and 9 substitute jurors for each session. The first 9 names were substitute jurors, while the remaining 36 were regular jurors. The process itself was supposed to be recorded in the form of a written document (Article 12, *Code Concerning the Compilation of Lists of Jurors*, 1875).

The presiding judge invited the 45 jurors to attend the court session. Before each trial, the *voir dire* process would be conducted and 12 jurors would be selected to decide the facts in the case. The regular 36 jurors were called first;

if an insufficient number of regular jurors were present (i.e., less than 36), the court would add the necessary number of substitute jurors (Article 19, *Code of Criminal Procedure for Offenses by the Press*, 1875). Jurors who were called for service and failed to appear at the court (without offering a valid excuse) were assessed a fine of 50 forints (Article 20, *Code of Criminal Procedure for Offenses by the Press*, 1875).

In the *voir dire* process the parties, the victim, and the jurors themselves would examine whether exclusionary reasons existed. From the perspective of common-law countries, this is a rather unusual part of the *voir dire* process because the list of reasons why potential jurors should be excluded resembled very closely the reasons for the exclusion of professional judges. These reasons were listed in the statute and the *voir dire* process did not include general questioning about the juror's interests and biases toward the defendant, the case, or the general topic of the session (e.g., attitudes toward the police).

Exclusionary reasons included a relationship of the juror with the defendant or the victim, a potential material gain or damage to the juror that would result from either acquittal or the sentence, the fact that the juror participated as a party or a witness in a pending criminal case, the fact that the juror participated either as a defense attorney or attorney for the plaintiff in the previous or a pending case, and the fact that the juror participated earlier in the same capacity in the same criminal case (Article 21, *Code of Criminal Procedure for Offenses by the Press*, 1875).

The number of jurors retained after this screening process had been completed needed to be at least 30. Next, the presiding judge drew the jurors' names in random order and the parties could exercise their peremptory challenges (Article 22, *Code of Criminal Procedure for Offenses by the Press*, 1875). The number of challenges was the same for both parties but, if the number of jurors was odd, the defendant was afforded an additional opportunity. The process terminated either when there were twelve jurors who had not been eliminated or when the number of names left in the bowl and the number of jurors who had not been eliminated at that point added to twelve. The twelve selected jury candidates then became the jury in the case. In addition, one or two potential jurors were kept together with the jury. They would become jurors if the regular jurors were not able to perform their function (Article 25, *Code of Criminal Procedure for Offenses by the Press*, 1875). The jurors then took a very lengthy oath specified by the *Code* (Article 29, *Code of Criminal Procedure for Offenses by the Press*, 1875).

The *Code* (1875) described the procedure in detail. It also specified the rules that governed the formulation of the questions the jury had to answer. The jury was supposed to determine the factual issues in the case: whether the facts that showed that the constituent elements of the offense were established, whether the defendant committed the crime, and whether the crime was conducted intentionally or negligently. In addition, jurors determined the existence of the circumstances that would limit the responsibility of the defendant, as well as other mitigating and aggravating circumstances. Ogorelica (1899, p. 804) and Bayer (1940, p. 45) argued that the questions and issues the jurors had to decide included legal issues as well; not only were the jurors supposed to decide the defendant's guilt (factual issues), but they also had to determine whether the constituent elements of the crime were present (legal issues).

The jurors were left in the deliberation room and their first task was to select the foreman (*prvnik*) by a majority vote (Article 40, *Code of Criminal Procedure for Offenses by the Press*, 1875). The *Code* contained detailed instructions to the jurors on their decision-making and on the (lack of) rules that limit the ways they can evaluate evidence (Article 40, *Code of Criminal Procedure for Offenses by the Press*, 1875). If the jurors had some questions, they were allowed to contact the presiding judge, who was to provide the answers (Article 41, *Code of Criminal Procedure for Offenses by the Press*, 1875) but was not allowed to be present during deliberation and voting.

The voting was oral and individual, with the foreman voting last (Article 42, *Code of Criminal Procedure for Offenses by the Press*, 1875). For the majority of the questions a simple majority vote was sufficient, while two-thirds of jurors needed to agree on the issues of guilt and aggravating circumstances (Article 43, *Code of Criminal Procedure for Offenses by the Press*, 1875). While an acquittal by the jury could not be changed by professional judges (Article 48, *Code of Criminal Procedure for Offenses by the Press*, 1875), a guilty decision could be reversed by the appellate court and the case could be returned for a new trial by a new presiding judge and a new jury if the professional judges at the appellate court expressed an unanimous opinion that the jurors made an error while deciding the principal issues in the case (Article 46, *Code of Criminal Procedure for Offenses by the Press*, 1875).

Positive views about the jury were also expressed in Dalmatia (*Dalmacija*), now a Mediterranean region of The Republic of Croatia, which had been under the direct administrative control of the Austrian regime at the time. Austrian laws regulating criminal procedure and criminal law were applied to Dalmatia directly. Consequently, under Austrian law, the jurisdiction of the jury was more extensive in Dalmatia than in (continental) Croatia.[1] In particular, in addition to being in charge of trials for offenses by the press, the jury in Dalmatia was also in charge of trials for other serious crimes as specified by the law. The editors of *Narodni list* (*Il Nazionale*), the political gazette of the People's Party (*Narodna Stranka*), the leading political party in Dalmatia at the time, praised the jury with utmost enthusiasm (*Narodni list*, 1874, p. 1):

> Last Wednesday the jury met for the first time in the District Court of Zadar ... The jury is not a novelty to our people, because, following the old tradition, the people knew and know how to settle their disputes and to reconcile their brotherly blood through '*good people*'; good people are nothing but today's jurors.
>
> These good people, instead of mediating between people in their village or neighborhood as they had done until today, are henceforth called in as jurors to the imperial and royal court to voice their verdict solemnly and publicly and to perform a good deed as

---

[1]See Bayer (1940, p. 48-50) for a detailed description of the differences between the criminal laws and criminal procedure codes applicable in Dalmatia and those applicable in (continental) Croatia.

conscientiously and fairly as they did in their own village on the basis of friendly agreement.

Our people should rejoice in this development, because it not only achieves the public good, but also extends praise and honor.

The editors further made a direct connection between the medieval juries and the modern jury of the 19th century (*Narodni list*, 1874, p. 1):

By embracing the jury, that grand and enlightened Europe finally adopted one of the oldest and universal customs of the Slavic people! What is innately attached to the Slavic heart from ancient times, she [Europe] today presents to the world as the important acquisition of the freedom and progress of the 19th century! We Slavs are truly unenlightened and undeveloped!

The editors praised the jury that decided a murder case for its wisdom and high quality of decision-making. That praise undoubtedly contained political overtones, as is clear from the following passage (*Narodni list*, 1874, p. 1):

What is even dearer to the people's heart is the fact that the jurors who demonstrated so far, especially in Italy, that they were not up to the task, attested with their first verdict in Zadar to the high level of wisdom and sense of justice harbored by our people. We admired the agility and the natural ability of some of our good people during the interrogation of the witnesses and the defendant in the murder trial held at this court last Wednesday. The best lawyers, who followed and studied the trial with the greatest dedication, upon hearing the verdict said that even the most skilled jurors in England could be proud of this decision. But even this will not convince our people's oppressors that we are fit to be free [independent], that we don't need the guardianship by either the Hungarians or the Germans [Austrians], that the people ... can prove themselves with a pen and in the battlefield, in the courtroom and wherever, [and] that the people have virtues which their oppressors may only envy.

Despite enthusiasm and positive words in favor of the jury in offenses by the press, and a very detailed regulation of both the criminal procedure and the selection system, the jury did not have a long future in Croatia. In fact, the Ministry of Justice composed a letter and submitted it to the Parliamentary Judiciary. In the letter, they proposed the suspension of the jury for a period of three years. The suspension was approved by a majority vote in the Parliament in 1884 (*Mjesečnik*, 1884, p. 699). The Ministry claimed that the jury did not fulfill the expectations (*Mjesečnik*, 1884, p. 697):

> Whenever the state, upon the introduction of the jury, prosecuted someone for offenses by the press in a jury trial, the indictment was very unsuccessful, unless the decision was requested from the jury in the most obvious cases, in which the violation of the law was not in doubt and the offender was known. Such a repeated failure in recent times prompted the government to completely abstain from prosecution of offenses by the press and to try instead to prevent the distribution of the newspapers that contain punishable writings by using other legitimate means, such as first forfeiting the newspapers and then obtaining the permission to forfeit the newspapers from the regular criminal court. The consequences of such a pause in the administration of justice on the part of our press are well-known; most ruthless attacks were launched against the government and its institutions, the Sabor, certain unpopular persons, existing laws and orders, immoral acts were approved, and, not infrequently, brute force was instigated. The government has the duty to establish the rule of law, and, to that end, in its opinion, no recourse is left but to transfer the jurisdiction over offenses by the press to regular courts; according to experience and to the present state of distress and fear, it is not reasonable to expect that the jurors will be able to keep their objectivity and independence, which are prerequisites for a just verdict.

It seems that the jury performed exactly as it should have — as the protector of the citizens (journalists) against the government. It is not surprising that the Ministry of Justice, a state institution, supported another state institution — the public prosecutor's office. What might seem surprising is the fact that the Parliamentary Judiciary Committee, which was supposed to represent the interests of the public, eagerly supported this proposition (*Mjesečnik*, 1884, p. 698):

While discussing the basis for the Code, the Judiciary Committee was led on the one hand by the reasons the high government stated in its letter, and on the other hand by the abuse of the press, which in our homeland fueled inflamed and unrestrained political passion with such intensity that any cool-headed patriot has to be afraid that the freedom of press will fall victim to such harsh terrorism.

This suggests that there had been more complex and serious reasons behind the abolition of the jury, an institution that was so enthusiastically endorsed and regulated in such detail less than a decade before. Indeed, in order to obtain a thorough understanding of the reasons that lead toward the abolition of the jury system in Croatia, it is necessary to examine the political situation in Croatia between the 1850s and 1884.

The period from 1848 until the end of the 19th century was characterized by intermittent periods of liberalism and strong voices for Croatia's independence from the Monarchy, which were intertwined with periods of absolutism and dominance by the Monarchy. The revolution in Hungary and Italy placed the Emperor of the Austrian Monarchy in a vulnerable position and made him amenable to compromise with other constituent parts of the Monarchy (Sirotković and Margetić, 1990, p. 141). A new *Ban*, Colonel Josip Jelačić, was appointed in Croatia in 1848. One of his first acts was to establish a new election order and to allow for the first session of the new post-feudal Croatian Parliament. The Parliament abolished feudalism and decided to change the relationship with both Hungary and Austria. The contract with Hungary was declared void and future relationships were deemed dependent upon the recognition of the Croatian state by Hungary (Sirotković and Margetić, 1990, p. 141). The Parliament requested from Austria that the relations be established on the federal principle with Croatia having a new government responsible to the Croatian Parliament. The new government was eventually established and it had control over the interior affairs, the military, finance, administration of justice, and education.

Unfortunately, the end of the revolution in Hungary and the consequent political change in Austria in 1849 resulted in the abolition of the new Croatian government in 1850 (Sirotković and Margetić, 1990, p. 142). The Austrian Emperor Franz Joseph I endorsed absolutism in 1851. "Bach's Absolutism," named after Bach, the Minister of the Interior who enforced it, created a more dependent position of the countries within the Monarchy. Consequently, during the entire period of absolutism (1851-1860), Croatia was completely dominated by the central government in Austria and the new Croatian government lost its powers. The Croatian *Ban* was directly responsible to the Austrian government and the country was controlled by government employees from Austria. Wrote Sirotković and Margetić (1990, p. 143):

> The wave of Germanization of offices and schools overflowed Croatia. Suppression of the freedom of press, prosecution of liberal writers, the system of total police control, supported by the armed forces of the newly formed gendarmerie, illegal arrests, and economic harassment of the opposition — all of these were tested methods of the absolutist regime in the fight against liberal elements. The whole state apparatus was used with the purpose of achieving the basic political goal of absolutism — the strengthening of German hegemony in the strictly centralized Austrian Monarchy.

The awakening of nationalism across the countries in the Monarchy, problems with the budget, economic crisis, disasters in the military area and in the domain of foreign politics, were among the factors which contributed toward the Emperor's decision to dismiss Bach in 1860. In 1860 the October Diploma reinstated the old constitutional system in all the countries of the Monarchy (Sirotković and Margetić, 1990, p. 143). However, only a few months later, in February 1861, the Emperor made another decision which strengthened the centralist government — he established the Imperial Tribunal. Some of the members of the Tribunal were supposed to be representatives of the parliaments of the constituent countries of the Monarchy, but the Hungarian Parliament and the Croatian Parliament refused to send their representatives. In the aftermath of unsuccessful attempts to attain control over the situation, the Emperor was left with no other option but to dismiss the Croatian Parliament in 1861 and to sign an agreement with Hungary in 1867 (*Austro-Hungarian Compromise*, 1867). This *Compromise* changed the legal status of Hungary; Hungary was recognized as a separate part of the Monarchy with a separate government and parliament. Furthermore, the *Compromise* had a profound effect on the organization of the entire Monarchy; the Monarchy was now divided into two parts: the Austrian part and the Hungarian part (Macan, 1992, p. 306).

The still unsettled relationship between Croatia and Hungary was resolved by the *Compromise* of 1868. This *Compromise* had *de iure* recognized Croatia as an independent country with its own government and parliament, but *de facto* put Hungary in a position of dominance over Croatia. Certain functions, such as the administration of justice, internal affairs, education, and religion remained in the jurisdiction of the Croatian institutions, while other functions, such as tax collection and finances, were placed in the joint jurisdiction of Croatian and Hungarian institutions (Sirotković and Margetić, 1990, p. 149). Such an arrangement left Croatia in a position wherein 55% of the taxes collected in Croatia were sent to Hungary; this triggered unrest and dissatisfaction with the current status of the country (Sirotković and Margetić, 1990, p. 149). Furthermore, the *Compromise* had *de facto* stipulated that the *Ban* of Croatia could only be a person loyal to the Hungarian government. The *Ban* was no longer responsible to the Croatian Parliament. Not surprisingly, a wave of unrest and opposition toward Hungary grew rapidly. At the same time, the government further aggravated the situation by prosecuting the press and persons who raised their voices in opposition to the *Compromise* (Macan, 1992, p. 309). In fact, Eugen Kvaternik, a leader of the Party of Rights, one of the political parties in Croatia, organized a short-lived rebellion and declared Croatia an independent country in 1871.

Ivan Mažuranić served as the Croatian *Ban* from 1873 to 1880. During his term in office, he conducted a number of reforms that modernized Croatia and engaged in active legislative activity together with the Croatian Parliament. He left his mark on political life even while he was still a chancellor of the Croatian Court Office — in 1862 he persuaded the Austrian Emperor to allow him to establish the Bench of Seven (*Stol Sedmorice*) as the highest court in Croatia and to thus remove Croatia from the jurisdiction of the highest courts in either Hungary or Austria (Beuc, 1989, p. 77; Sirotković and Margetić, 1990, p. 155). During his regency he carried out a comprehensive judicial reform by separating the judicial and executive branches of government (*Law Concerning Judicial Authority*, 1874), by establishing the independence of the judiciary, and by determining the jurisdiction of each of the courts in the hierarchy (Beuc, 1989, p. 77). In addition, he reorganized the executive branch and substituted a large number of districts (*kotar*) for a smaller number of regions (*podžupanija*) in order to reduce the costs associated with the bureaucracy (Beuc, 1989, p. 77). He also established a number of national ministries, including the ministries of health, education, culture (Sirotković and Margetić, 1990, p. 170), agriculture, and the Office of Statistics (Beuc, 1989, p. 77). He sponsored the law that established elementary schools and prescribed obligatory elementary school education, as well as the law that established the first modern Croatian university (Beuc, 1989, p. 77; Sirotković and Margetić, 1990, p. 170). He also introduced the law which established the concept of accountability of the *Ban* and other high-ranking Croatian government officials for violations of legal rules (Beuc, 1989, p. 77; Sirotković and Margetić, 1990, p. 169).

Furthermore, he promulgated the *Criminal Procedure Code* of 1875. This law established the principle of free evaluation of evidence, the principle of material truth, the principle of oral trial, and the principle of directness of trial (Sirotković and Margetić, 1990, p. 168). More than one-half of a century later, it served as a basis for the *Criminal Procedure Law* of 1929. Mažuranić also sponsored three laws dealing with the press: the *Code of Criminal Procedure for Offenses by the Press* of 1875, which introduced the jury into the Croatian criminal process (albeit for a limited number of offenses), the *Code Concerning the Compilation of Lists of Jurors*, and the *Code Concerning the Use of the Press* (Sirotković and Margetić, 1990, p. 168).

Next was the period of Khuen-Hĕderváry. *Ban* Károly Khuen-Hĕderváry, a powerful Hungarian statesman who served as the Croatian *Ban* for twenty years (1883-1903), was a zealous enforcer of the Hungarian influence in all aspects of life in Croatia. His main objective was a thorough Hungarization of Croatia, which ranged from a rigorously enforced ban on the use of the Croatian language in all schools, public offices, public places, and cultural events to a vigorous attempt to limit and crush Croatian nationalist sentiment in political life. A constant state of unrest was typical of this period. The opposition toward the *Ban* and the Hungarian Monarchy grew increasingly stronger despite very successful efforts by the *Ban* to control the country. The unrest culminated with the burning of the Hungarian flag during the Emperor's visit to Croatia in 1895. Finally, the conflict between the Austrian and Hungarian parts of the Monarchy (which was spurred by Hungary's quest for independence from the Monarchy), in addition to unrest in Croatia, led toward the end of Hĕderváry's rule. Not surprisingly, Khuen's period was deemed a difficult one:

> Khuen's absolutistic regime remained a bad remembrance. He arrived to calm Croatia down by force and to make Croatia a Hungarian province. Characteristics of his regency were prosecutions and prisons, dismissal from service, despotism at elections, suppression of the freedom of speech and press, economic exploitation, and violation of the clauses of the Croatian-Hungarian Compromise (Macan, 1992, p. 321).

In light of the historical events that took place at the time, it is by no means surprising that Khuen's rule had a detrimental impact on the Croatian legal system. The Hungary-dominated Croatian Ministry of Justice proposed the abolition of the jury in 1884 (only a year later Khuen became the *Ban*) and the pro-Hungarian dominance in the Croatian Parliament insured that such a proposal be accepted by the majority in the Parliament. Jury trials for offenses by the press were "temporarily postponed" precisely because the jury *did* perform its political function — it provided the voice of people and protected the defendants against oppression by the regime. The jury system, introduced in 1875 for offenses by the press, was "temporarily postponed for three years" in 1884 and was never reintroduced. It was finally abolished by the infamous *Vidovdan Constitution* of 1921.

Although the jury system in Croatia did not last very long, it enjoyed popular support. At the same time, the ruling regimes tried to abolish it and to establish professional judges as the only decision-makers. This was just as true of the Austrian and Hungarian regimes before 1918 as it was true of the Kingdom of Serbs, Croats, and Slovenians (1918-1929) and the Kingdom of Yugoslavia (1929-1941). Indeed, while Nikola Ogorelica, a highly respected Croatian lawyer and scholar, designed a draft of the *Jury Law*, at the same time the *Vidovdan Constitution* (1921), which applied to the Kingdom of Serbs, Croats, and Slovenians, eliminated the jury as a decision-maker for offenses by the press from Croatian courtrooms.

Article 13 of the *Vidovdan Constitution* (1921) stated that all offenses by the press were to be tried by regular courts. Since the law did not abolish the jury system directly, this rule was interpreted by the legal experts as an indirect abolition of the jury system (Bayer, 1940, p. 42). The matter was laid to rest by the *Judicial Criminal Procedure Law* (1929), which reaffirmed that professional judges were the only decision-makers. The same was true of the *Regular Courts Law* (1929) — professional judges were the only decision-makers in regular courts (Article 7).

Such a development was by no means surprising because the rulers of Croatia were once again moving toward centralization. This time, Croatia was a part of the Kingdom of Yugoslavia and the King in Belgrade consistently increased the centralization of his power from the introduction of the 1921 *Vidovdan Constitution* to the putsch in 1929. The constant tension among political parties in the Yugoslav Parliament in Belgrade culminated with the assassination of several Parliament Members from Croatia in 1928. One of the fallen victims was Stjepan Radić, the leader of the Croatian Peasants' Party, which was the strongest political party in Croatia at the time. The political character of the assassination was completely transparent. In the months preceding the tragedy, the Croatian Peasants' Party entered into a coalition with the Independent Democratic Party, led by S. Pribičević. The joint platform was the fight against Serbian hegemony and continued centralization of power. In the aftermath of the assassination, the King seized the moment and took the power over completely on the night of January 5, 1929:

> The King abolished the Constitution and nullified earlier institutions of limited parliamentarism: he dismissed the National Assembly and political parties, imposed the censorship of the press, and strengthened the rules of the *Law Concerning the Protection of the State*. With the slogan that 'nothing cannot and should not come between the King and the people,' the King inaugurated the open absolutist regime, known in our Constitutional history as King Aleksandar's Dictatorship of January the 6th (Sirotković and Margetić, 1990, p. 251).

The desire to sustain the absolutist regime prompted the King to entrust legal decision-making only to professional judges, who were (compelled to be) loyal to the regime, rather than to allow members of the public, especially in those areas of the country which were unhappy with the political solution, to make decisions in legal cases. Since the power was concentrated in his hands (and not in the hands of the Parliament), the King had the opportunity to do so.

The attitudes toward the jury varied considerably across Yugoslavia; at the First Congress of Lawyers of the Kingdom of the Serbs, Croats, and Slovenians, held in 1925, the first topic on the schedule was the issue of whether lay participation should be allowed in the criminal process (Bayer, 1940, p. 160). By that time, Professor Nikola Ogorelica from Croatia had completed the draft of the *Jury Law*. The whole project was motivated by the notion that

> ... it is impossible to deny the fact that the jury is regarded as an important historical achievement that increased the reputa-

tion of the system of justice administration among the people and awakened the trust of the people in its independence and impartiality, because its decisions corresponded to the legal conscience of the people (Bayer, 1940, p. 161).

Ogorelica also emphasized the democratic character of the jury which allows members of various social classes to participate in the administration of justice (Bayer, 1940, p. 161). Professor Dolenc from Slovenia pointed out that an overwhelming 90% of the voters at the poll voted for the introduction of the jury into the Yugoslav judicial system (Čulinović, 1954, p. 47).

Although quite a number of professors of law who participated in the work of the Congress supported the idea of lay participation in the criminal process, the Congress concluded in its *Memorandum* that, "the majority, especially from the geographic areas with no jury, raised their voices against the participation of lay persons in the system of administration of justice" (in Bayer, 1940, p. 161). One of the strongest voices in the opposition of lay participation was that of Professor Božidar Marković from Belgrade.

The first post-World War I *Criminal Procedure Law* was drafted in 1921 by two professors. While one, Prof. Nikola Ogorelica from Zagreb, was a strong supporter of the jury, the other, Prof. Božidar Marković from Belgrade, was its strong opponent. The *Criminal Procedure Law* did not become law until after the King took power during the putsch orchestrated in January of 1929, at which point the law had undergone certain changes. Marković wrote (in Bayer, 1940, p. 166) that the *Criminal Procedure Law* did not change in any *substantive* way (compared to the draft of 1921), suggesting either that the jury was not established by the draft or, if the jury existed in the draft, the deletion of the jury from the *Criminal Procedure Law* did not represent a substantive change (*sic!*). Regardless, as Bayer (1940, p. 167) emphasized, "the Criminal Procedure Law of 1929 was one of the first Acts by the Dictatorship of January the Sixth, and it is quite understandable that it embraced the principle of complete exclusion of lay persons from criminal trials."

County courts (*kotarski sudovi*) had jurisdiction over less serious criminal offenses and regional courts (*okružni sudovi*) had jurisdiction over more serious criminal offenses in the first instance (trial); regional courts (*okružni sudovi*) and courts of cassation (*kasacioni sudovi*) were in charge of the second instance (appeal). A professional judge alone was the decision-maker in cases tried at county courts (Article 7, *Regular Courts Law*, 1929), while a tribunal composed of five professional judges was in charge of appeals (Article 34, *Regular Courts Law*, 1929). Regional courts decided cases via professional tribunals composed of three members, and the most serious criminal cases were decided by five-member professional tribunals (Sirotković and Margetić, 1990, p. 248).

Interestingly, although the general and predominant tendency of the regime was to remove lay persons from legal decision-making, one form of lay participation was actually introduced by the same *Regular Courts Law* (1929) — that of "honorable judges." Honorable judges were merchants or "persons familiar with the mining and maritime issues." However, this form of lay participation was not introduced because it provided the possibility for the citizens to participate in the government and express their voice; rather, this was a form of lay participation used in a relatively small number of cases dealing with commercial disputes and it insured that the professional judges' expert opinion on the law could be supplemented with the expert opinion on the issues of commerce. In this sense, it is difficult to talk about honorable judges as lay judges because, although they did not have a thorough and comprehensive formal legal education, they were called primarily because they were experts in certain other fields (although the law required of them to have not only substantive knowledge in their area of expertise, but also to be familiar with the legal regulations pertinent to their area of expertise).

The law prescribed that, for a very small subset cases tried by commerce courts, tribunals were composed of two professional judges and one honorable judge (Article 30, *Regular Courts Law*, 1929). Therefore, the law made it impossible for honorable judges to outvote the professionals. The position

of honorable judges — experts in certain fields — during trial and deliberation was equal to that of professional judges (Article 77, Item 2, *Regular
Courts Law*, 1929). Honorable judges were appointed by the Minister of Justice (Čulinović, 1946, p. 122). This service was not paid, but was nevertheless
obligatory.

The 1933 *Decree Concerning Honorable Judges* further specified eligibility
requirements and rights and duties of honorable judges, their mandate, and the
ways their service could be terminated. Honorable judges had to be citizens
of the Kingdom of Yugoslavia who were at least 30 years of age, who were
independent, who, by the pursuit of their occupation, had become familiar
with commerce, the shipping industry, or the mining industry and with the
pertinent laws and customs, who were not bankrupt, who had not lost their
civil rights or the right to perform public service as a result of a sentence
in a criminal case (and were not under investigation for such a case), who
lived in the same city where the court met, and who were not related to the
professional judges at the courts at which they were to be appointed (Article 6,
Decree Concerning Honorable Judges, 1933). The *Decree* further specified that
if some of these conditions were no longer fulfilled after the honorable judge
was appointed, the service would be terminated (Article 16, *Decree Concerning
Honorable Judges*, 1933).

3.2   Lay Participation after 1944

Hitler asked the Yugoslav government in March of 1941 to join the *Axis Pact*
signed by Germany, Italy, and Japan. The Yugoslav government reluctantly
accepted and signed the *Pact*. Massive protests throughout the country en-
sued overnight, and a putsch in Belgrade overturned the government. German
aggression started a few days later, on April 6, 1941, with a surprise attack on
Belgrade and several other cities. The country experienced a rapid military
collapse in only 12 days. The Yugoslav Kingdom was occupied and was imme-

diately dissolved into several entities. Some were placed under direct control of either Germany or Italy, while quisling governments were established in others. The court system of the Kingdom of Yugoslavia was retained for the most part and new types of courts were added to the system (Čulinović, 1946, p. 129).

Before the formation of socialist Yugoslavia in 1945, lay participation in Yugoslavia was more the exception than the rule. Socialist regimes created under the auspices of the USSR after World War II followed the example of the USSR and, in the spirit of Marxist ideology regarding the decomposition of the state and the transfer of the state's functions to the people, tended to see lay participation as one of the ways this decomposition of the state was to be carried out. Socialist Yugoslavia was no exception to the rule; lay participants — lay judges in mixed tribunals — were a part of the criminal process from the very beginning.

In the midst of the war, small regions of the country were controlled by the partisan forces led by the Communist Party and Josip Broz Tito. Unlike the quisling regimes that had established the court system, which consisted of both regular and specialized courts, the troops led by the Communist Party did not have an established official territory and, at the same time, were not in a position to organize and establish a regular court system on the (temporarily) liberated territories. Consequently, from the collapse of the Kingdom of Yugoslavia in April 1941 to the fall of 1944, trials on liberated territories were conducted by members of the community under the supervision of a respectable citizen. These trials were not conducted by mixed tribunals but by "popular courts" (Čulinović, 1954). Nevertheless, the Communist Party performed a crucial role in the establishment of mixed tribunals in Yugoslavia.

On the territory of Croatia, the organizational principles of the new judicial system were established by the *Regulations Concerning Court Organization* of December 22, 1943. The *Regulations* (1943) elaborated on the reasons for the particular way of establishing the new court system (Jovanović, 1958, p. 41-42):

... the people [are] the source and drain of authority, and only the people are sovereign; above them there is no and cannot be any other authority. Judiciary, as a part of that authority, should respond to the wishes, needs, and opinion of the people in terms of its composition and methods of resolving disputes. Consequently, it [the judiciary] should be democratized, that is, it should result from the people who have to participate in the administration of justice directly. The administration of justice as an obligatory passing of law has to be in the hands of the people, and the leading idea in the administration of justice should be the one expressed in the principles of the national-liberation movement. As a guarantee of it, a judicial body imminently has to be composed of the members of the people ... During the national-liberation movement the people abolished the old authority, including the old system of the administration of justice, and developed its own people's judiciary that reflects the people's principles and corresponds to the people's wishes and needs.

Mixed tribunals were introduced in Croatia in 1944, that is, at the time when the war was still in progress but large portions of the territory were liberated. The pertinent regulation, the *Regulations Concerning Court Organization*, was issued by the National Anti-Fascist Council of People's Liberation of Croatia (*Zemaljsko antifašističko vijeće narodnog oslobodjenja Hrvatske*). Professional judges and other lawyers throughout the liberated territories discussed whether some form of lay participation should be introduced (Čulinović, 1954, p. 49). Those who argued for lay participation pointed out that the introduction of lay judges (called "temporary judges" at the time) would increase the democratic character of the new criminal justice system. At the Congress held later that same year, the advocates of lay participation also emphasized that the jury would contribute toward further development of the socialist character of society. It was argued that a lay judge or a juror should not be limited, and, in the case of mixed tribunals, lay judges and professional judges should be equals during trial and deliberation (Čulinović, 1954, p. 50). Opponents argued that the selection process of professional judges (called "permanent judges" at the time), wherein judges were to be selected from the people and by the people and were thus expected to be closely connected to the voters, reflected the democratic character of the government in formation. Such an arrangement would eliminate the need to introduce lay judges, a step that, according to Čulinović (1954, p. 50), was regarded by some as politically unnecessary and legally wrong.

The tribunals consisted of three members: one presiding permanent judge and two temporary judges (Article 7, *Regulations Concerning Court Organization*, 1944). The war was a likely cause of a shortage of trained lawyers who could perform the function of professional judges on liberated territories. There was no possibility to train new lawyers at the law schools. Most of the lawyers already trained were perceived to be loyal to the old regime, and the lawyers trained in the old Yugoslavia loyal to the new regime were primarily sent to serve at the newly established military courts. Regular courts were advised to have one lawyer, serving as a law clerk, who would provide technical assistance with the cases. There was another reason that made the need for persons trained in law less pressing and the adequacy of lay persons appropriate at that point; the old laws were not utilized any longer and the new laws were not drafted yet; consequently, as Jovanović (1958, p. 47) argued, these mixed tribunals did not have legal rules to apply and they made legal decisions based on general principles of justice. However, in the period of several months immediately before and after the liberation, the situation changed rapidly because quite a large number of legal rules were drafted and passed.

The legislature did not require presiding judges to be lawyers but rather to consider their judicial service as a full-time occupation. Permanent judges were in charge of the organization and everyday functioning of courts; they also invited temporary judges to attend court sessions and to thereby perform their service.

Temporary judges could be either female or male citizens of age who were "viceless." They were elected by the people (or by the representatives of the people) and were called "assessors" (*prisjednici*). The differences between permanent and temporary judges were twofold; they included the frequency of service and the types of activities performed while at service. As their name suggests, temporary judges were invited to perform their service occasionally. They were present only during trials and deliberations, both in criminal cases and in civil cases, during which their rights equaled those of permanent judges. Permanent judges also performed preparatory tasks for trials (such as scheduling trials and inviting all the parties to attend).

The partisans, a national-liberation anti-fascist force lead by the Communist Party, started the final liberation of the Yugoslav territory in the fall of 1944. Finally, World War II ended in Yugoslavia on May 15, 1945. The partisans and the Communist Party emerged victorious. The new country, Democratic Federative Yugoslavia (*Demokratska Federativna Jugoslavija*) had its federal government established in March of 1945 and, by the end of May of 1945, all the constituent parts had their own governments. According to the international treaty signed in 1944 between the old Yugoslav royal government and the representatives of the partisans, the organization of the state was to be resolved by the post-war elections.

In September of 1945, immediately after the conclusion of World War II, the new *Law Concerning the Organization of the People's Courts* introduced mixed tribunals composed of three members, among whom the distinction was based not on their education but on the *frequency of their service*. Therefore, the principle of collective decision-making was established as a rule.

There were two types of participants in the tribunals: permanent judges (called "judges") and temporary judges (called "assessors" — "*prisuditelji*"). While permanent judges performed their function full-time, temporary judges perform theirs rather infrequently — up to 15 days per year (Article 15, *Law Concerning the Organization of the People's Courts*, 1945). Interestingly, there was no debate in the Federal Parliament about the proposed and accepted solution dealing with lay judges (Jovanović, 1958, p. 53); the new law was determined to be in accordance with the earlier view of lay participation, established during the national-liberation movement.

Legal education as the basis for the differentiation between lay judges and professional judges, though not of immediate importance for regular courts at the time, played a role in the domain of military courts. As early as 1945, the *Law Concerning the Organization and Jurisdiction of Military Courts in the Yugoslav Army* stated that the judges at military courts were supposed to be ranked military officers who were professional lawyers, while assessors could be other members of the military (Article 24, *Law Concerning the Organization and Jurisdiction of Military Courts in the Yugoslav Army*, 1945).

Legal requirements detailed in the *Law Concerning the Organization of People's Courts* were less strict; whenever possible, educated candidates for the position of permanent judges would be preferred (Article 17), thus establishing general education, not legal education *per se*, as one of the criteria relevant for the selection of professional judges. However, each regular court was supposed to have a law clerk, a trained lawyer, whose task was to help the judges with their cases (Article 54, *Law Concerning the Organization of People's Courts*, 1945). As mentioned earlier, the discussion in the Federal Parliament related to the new law on the organization of courts led to the conclusion that permanent judges should not be required to be lawyers. The speaker for the majority, Miloš Minić, emphasized that if such a requirement were to be reinstated, the old apparatus and the old judges with all the scars from the old regime would return (in Jovanović, 1958, p. 55).

It could also be argued that the legislature assumed that there was an insufficient number of trained lawyers loyal to the new regime who could take the positions of professional judges, and imposing only general education as a requirement for potential permanent judges was an attempt to deal with such a shortage. The data (Table 3.1) on the professional judges at people's courts[2] in Croatia in August 1946 refute this argument: only about 14% of permanent (professional) judges were not lawyers. Although the law specified that educated candidates would be more desirable for the position of perma-

---

[2]In the spirit of Marxist ideology, the term "people's courts" was used for regular courts to emphasize that the courts belonged to the people.

nent judges, the data from Table 3.1 show that this guideline was not followed entirely: whereas clerks, who possessed higher levels of education than farmers or workers, accounted for only 15% of all permanent judges who did not have an education in law, farmers and workers accounted for as many as 72%. It seems apparent that such demographics were driven at least partially by the ideological platform of communism and the supposedly leading role of farmers and workers in the process of political and social transformation.

There were three additional changes regulated by the *Law Concerning the Organization of the People's Courts* (1945). All mixed tribunals at regular courts were supposed to be composed of three members — one judge and two assessors. For the first time, lay members were theoretically in a position to outvote the professional judge, since lay judges constituted the majority in mixed tribunals. The length of mandate for lay judges and professional judges was equalized: 3 years at lower courts and 5 years at upper courts (Articles 24, 32, 39, and 49, *Law Concerning the Organization of the People's Courts*, 1945). Finally, the jurisdiction of mixed tribunals was limited to the first instance (trial), in which lay judges and professional judges had equal rights, while appellate decisions were made by professional tribunals only. Interestingly, mixed tribunals were introduced even for trials in the first instance at the supreme courts of the republics and provinces, and at the Supreme Court of the Federation (Article 37, *Law Concerning the Organization of the People's Courts* (1945).

This was a period of rapid development of the court system and laws were drafted and updated constantly. The law that was passed only one year later, in 1946, introduced two new developments: it further specified the differences between professional judges and lay judges (Article 16, *Law Concerning the Organization of the People's Courts*, 1946) and addressed the fact that professional judges were the only decision-makers at the appellate level, as stated in Article 119 of the *Constitution* (1946). The *Law Concerning the Organization of the People's Courts* (1946) determined that legal decisions in the first instance (trial) were to be made by mixed tribunals, unless there were conflicting

Table 3.1: Professional judges at people's courts in Croatia in August 1946.[a]

Permanent judges

A: Status

Lawyers	275
	(86%)
Non-lawyers	46
	(14%)
	Total: 324
	(100%)

B: Occupation of non-lawyers

Farmers	17
	(37%)
Workers	16
	(35%)
Clerks	7
	(16%)
Craftsmen	2
	(4%)
Other occupations	4
	(8%)
	Total: 46
	(100%)

[a]Source: Čulinović, 1946, p. 194.

rules in other statutes. This opened up the possibility that a separate statute could determine a special subset of court cases for which the decision-maker would be a professional judge alone rather than a mixed tribunal. The new *Criminal Procedure Law* of 1948 did not utilize this opportunity for any subset of criminal cases.

The *Constitution* (Article 119, 1946) established that courts try cases in tribunals composed of professional judges and lay judges. Professional judges were persons who performed their role as their occupation, while lay judges were persons who retained their original occupation and were invited to perform their service as lay judges only infrequently. However, they were still considered to be equals during trial and deliberation (Article 16, *Law Concerning the Organization of the People's Courts*, 1946). The new *Law Concerning the Organization of the People's Courts* (1946) did not require professional judges to be lawyers. In fact, professional judges and lay judges could be any citizens if their civil rights were not withheld (Article 20). However, the *Law* (1946) instructed the committees which appointed lay judges and professional judges to select such persons who will be able to fulfill the assigned functions in the criminal justice system. In particular, the requirement was that professional judges should have an adequate level of education (Article 20, *Law Concerning the Organization of the People's Courts*, 1946). The observed expert knowledge of a particular lay judge would be utilized extensively; the *Law* (Article 38) instructed professional judges to frequently call on lay judges who have specialized expert knowledge in relevant field.

The new *Law* of 1946 also provided detailed instructions on the responsibility of lay judges and professional judges, including criminal, civil, and disciplinary responsibility/liability, and the process of relieving lay judges from their duty. While the 1945 *Law* specified that only professional judges could decide the appeals, the 1946 *Law* stated that, if a three-member professional tribunal could not be composed at a particular regional court, two lay judges would decide the appeal together with one professional judge. In this instance, the *Law* not only involved lay judges in appellate decisions, but it also gave lay judges the power to outvote the professional judge at the appellate level. This decision was yet another consequence of the war and the unavailability of a sufficient number of persons trained in law.

The Communist Party won the first elections for both houses of the Federal Parliament in 1945; approximately 90% of the electorate voted for the People's Front (*Narodni front*). At its first session in 1945 the new Parliament abolished the monarchy, stripped the King of his rights, and declared the new country to be a federative republic.

The basic principles of the new socialist regime were specified for the first time in the aforementioned *Constitution* of 1946. The *Constitution* (Article 6, 1946) declared that all power springs from the people and belongs to the people. The people exercise it through their representatives in the institutions of the government (Article 6, *Constitution*, 1946). All these institutions are just representatives — not holders — of power. Courts, as a part of state apparatus, are subordinate to the people's representative body (Čulinović, 1946, p. 174). Jovanović (1958, p. 89) described the reasons for the introduction of lay participation in the criminal justice system:

> The new court did not develop as a guarantee and the right of an individual to be tried by his peers or equals, nor did it develop as a guarantee of the citizens against the tyranny of a professional judge. For such a new court no one fought with a gun or a pen. The requirements of the political revolution were for the working people to take over all the power in the country, including the court authority as the constituent element of the united people's authority.

The political system of 1946 was established as the centralized system of state government (Sirotković and Margetić, 1990, p. 378). This is by no means surprising because this was the period of an intensive building of the state, legal system, and society in general. Regional units still did not gain power and the federal government was dominant. Furthermore, the economy was characterized as a socialist state-controlled economy. One of the characteristics of such an economy is the development of an extensive bureaucratic apparatus. In addition, private property was nationalized. All these changes were justified as being necessary at the first stage on the long road toward achieving a communist society; immediately after the working class takes over from the capitalist class, there is a need for a strong dictatorship of the proletariat that preserves the power of the working class. A part of that dictatorship involves an intensive search for the opposition and appropriate methods of dealing with it.

Legalistic procedures were not routinely employed for all the individuals accused of committing crimes. Treatment of individuals accused of political crimes is particularly illustrative of the way justice was distributed in the period of dictatorship of the proletariat. After the end of World War II, and in keeping with the Marxist doctrine of dictatorship of the proletariat, the Communist Party tended to consolidate and further to strengthen its power. In the process, it tended to eliminate its political enemies, especially those who fought against it during the war. Lampe (1996, p. 224) provided an account of such use of judicial proceedings in Croatia:

> Judicial proceedings also played a significant, officially trumpeted role in the Communist consolidation of power in Croatia. By June 1945, trials began with the well deserved conviction of leading figures from the Jasenovac death camp and those Ustaša leaders who had not escaped to Germany or Italy. The trials quickly grew to include a significant number of Catholic priests, some of whom were guilty of forced conversions and war crimes.

The judiciary played a role in the removal of political opponents from social life and the political scene. Lampe (1996, p. 234) describes these processes in the subsequent period (1946-1947):

> ... Communist control of the judicial system made political opposition riskier than it had ever been in the first Yugoslavia [pre-World War II Yugoslavia] ... the UDBa [State Security Administration] exercised unrestricted powers to arrest, imprison, and even execute political opponents without public charges or trials

... Rough estimates vary, but the numbers of people the UDBa executed in 1946-1947 probably run to five figures and those held in concentration camps at least to six ... Convictions from the new network of people's courts, judges, and public prosecutors (the latter specifically created to root out political opposition) added to the camp population. The system worked without regard to due process or defendant's rights, in the fashion of military courts which continued to operate after the war. When Agrarian Party leader Dragoljub Jovanović complained that the new Communist prosecutors had become 'the all-powerful organs of the judiciary,' he only hasted his own arrest and nine-year sentence in April 1947. His judge doubtless met the 'fundamental moral qualifications,' which the party's chief prosecutor at the Mihailović trial, Miloš Minić, explained as 'infinite loyalty' regardless of prior legal training.

The open confrontation with Stalin in 1948 and the refusal by the majority of Yugoslav leaders to allow Yugoslavia to become one of the satellites of the former Soviet Union almost resulted in another war. Furthermore, the prosecution of political opponents grew even more rampant after the dispute with the Soviet Union. Lampe (1996, p. 248) wrote about the prosecution of supporters of the Stalin regime:

> In the eyes of the KPJ [Communist Party of Yugoslavia] leadership, arrests and 'hard time' were needed to send an effective message to the party's large membership. The 16,000 members whose arrest was later acknowledged (the actual number was probably higher) did indeed do hard time ... Less than one-fifth even received a trial, civilian or military. Most were simply seized under the 'administrative procedures' to which all party members could be subjected ... The party's reputation did not suffer until the details of Goli otok [one of the camps] were made public during the 1980s. Yet by 1953, Aleksandar Ranković admitted that nearly half of the 36,000 formal arrests for all major crimes in 1950 had been unjustified.

The resulting economic isolation from the countries of the socialist bloc oriented Yugoslavia toward the West and toward the development of its own brand of socialism called "self-management" (*samoupravljanje*). The state no longer controlled the entire economy; according to the *Fundamental Law Concerning Management of State Companies by the Workers' Council* (1950), workers now had the power to run organizations through workers' councils (*radnički savjeti*). That is, lay participation, at least on paper, was quite extensive — employees had the opportunity to control the work of the professionals and to actually run the company.

The theory of self-managed socialism reached its peak in the 1970s. This is, for example, how Trajković (1984, p. 9) described self-management in his book about the judicial system:

> The essential feature of self-management democracy is that the freedom, rights and duties of man and citizen, as determined under the Constitution, are an inseparable part and source of socialist self-management democratic relations, in which man is freed from any exploitation and arbitrariness and, with his labour, can create conditions for his own overall development and free expression, ensuring the safety of his own person and respect for human dignity.

Theoretical arguments that were developed had far-reaching consequences; during the entire period of the former Yugoslavia, lay participants were a part of the system and their role was always described as very important for the overall process of socialization and further development of society. Important aspects of this theory which related to the issue of lay participation were very similar to those developed in other socialist countries.[3] In general, the socialist period was viewed merely as a preparatory stage for the society of the future — communist society. It was further argued that, as a society advances from a socialist state organization (especially from its first stage of dictatorship of the proletariat) toward a communist society, factories and organizations would be successfully transferred into the hands of the working class; formal boundaries, such as the state mechanism and the official rules, would at that time become

---

[3]See Chapter 1 for a discussion of theoretical underpinnings of lay courts in socialist countries.

obsolete. Workers would have internalized the norms and would have learned how to run society. This societal takeover (*podruštvljavanje*) included also the process in which laws were to become social norms and lay judges were to replace professional judges. Indeed, lay participation played an important role in this process of socialization and self-management (Kovačević, 1973). Bajić-Petrović (1985a, p. 43) described the role of lay participation in this socialization process:

> In the process of relinquishing the strict forms and frames of judicial decision-making, in assigning important authority to self-management courts, in the separation of subjects of decision-making into more diverse, elastic forms, in the socialization of court functions, and in insuring sincere self-management of the social functions, we think that the existence of the decision-making in which lay judges participate becomes the question of principle. This institution [mixed tribunals] has a political color, but also has an important social role: [the achievement of] justice for the people and toward the people. Public opinion is a participant and a subject in the creation and control of the court decision.

Similarly, Čulinović (1954) described positive features of trials by mixed tribunals that have been noted in everyday judicial practice over a ten-year period since the tribunals have been introduced: in accordance with the political theory of socialism, lay participation was perceived to increase the democratic character of the Yugoslav judicial system by involving workers in legal decision-making and by providing them with an opportunity to participate in the government directly; furthermore, the presence of lay participants decreased the formalism of professional judges. One of the more interesting positive features Čulinović (1954) pointed out was that lay participants played a crucial role at the time when legal norms were not fully developed; in such a legal environment, it was very useful to have someone who was familiar with the local traditions and customs be a member of the tribunal.

By the mid-1950s, there were numerous criticisms of lay participation. The first congress of lawyers in the socialist Yugoslavia examined the issue of lay participation and its implementation, which was perceived to be one of the weak spots of the new legal system (Jovanović, 1958, p. 100). One of the most serious problems associated with lay participation was the disorderly response of lay judges to the court summons to perform their duty. A number of professional judges spoke at the congress about this problem and its consequences — trial delays, lack of interest, negative attitudes by professional judges. Jovanović (1958) talked about the lack of legal knowledge, about the discrepancy between the type of work regularly performed by lay judges at their places of employment (physical work) and that required of them in the courtroom (intellectual work), about their inability to be thinkers independent of professional judges. A paper published by Vladimir Bayer, Professor of Law, in the *Zbornik Pravnog fakulteta u Zagrebu* (Collected Papers of the University of Zagreb Law School), begins with the statement that, "the frequent question seems to be a question of whether lay participation in our country today is justified" (1955, p. 142). One of the leading daily newspapers in the country, *Politika*, in the same year published a letter written by M. Brajković, one of the lay judges from Croatia, in which he claimed that lay judges were "more like observers than like equal members of tribunals" (in Jovanović, 1958, p. 106).

By 1953 the effects of World War II were diminishing, basic laws had been drafted, and the large changes in the style of company management were occurring. The new *Constitutional Law* of 1953 was drafted in order to incorporate those changes. Lay participation in legal decision-making was considered to be one of the forms of direct participation of citizens in the government and, consequently, a constituent element of the new system of self-management (Ljubanović, 1989, p. 28). In the spirit of this wave of lay participation in self-management in the economy, it is not surprising that the new law that regulated the court organization provided more details about lay judges and their selection. The 1954 *Courts Law* established a general rule that legal decisions were to be made by mixed tribunals, unless specified otherwise by separate laws (Article 13). The 1954 *Courts Law* opened the possibility for some other specific legal codes (civil or criminal procedure laws, for example) to determine the delineation between the offenses to be tried by professional judges and those to be tried by mixed tribunals. As a result, the 1954 *Judicial Criminal Procedure Law* placed twenty-two offenses, those punishable by either fine or imprisonment of up to two years, under the jurisdiction of a professional judge alone (Articles 18 and 20, *Judicial Criminal Procedure Law*, 1954). Čulinović (1954, p. 53) argued that this was done with the purpose of increasing the efficiency while simplifying the process at the same time. The *Commentary Concerning the Criminal Procedure Law* (1953) also contains other arguments for the introduction of a professional judge alone instead of mixed tribunals for the least severe criminal cases. These arguments included the reduction in cost, an opportunity for a better selection process because of a lowered demand for lay judges, and an opportunity for lay judges to focus on more serious criminal cases. Vasiljević *et al.* (1975, p. 23) argued that this decision would lead toward a drastic decrease in lay participation.

The 1954 *Courts Law* limited jurisdiction of mixed tribunals in one aspect, but extended it in another. Depending on the type of case and the possible sanction, "large tribunals," which were to be composed of two professional judges and three lay judges, were introduced in parallel with the existing "small tribunals," which were composed of one professional judge and two lay judges. These tribunals were in charge of trials for the offenses punishable by either the death penalty or imprisonment of up to 20 years. Although mixed tribunals were in charge of a certain number of offenses, they were not included as decision-makers for appellate decisions. In other words, final decisions were made by professional judges.

The law featured specific rules on a number of issues related to mixed tribunals: requirements for professional judges and lay judges, the election process of lay judges, their rights and duties, and the changes in the jurisdiction of mixed tribunals.

Eligibility requirements for professional judges and lay judges featured a clear distinction on the basis of education. One of the requirements for the position of a professional judge was legal education, in particular graduation from law school (Article 46, *Courts Law*, 1954). Moreover, depending on the type of court, professional judges needed to pass the bar exam, or both pass the bar exam and obtain experience in working on legal issues. On the other hand, lay judges had to be citizens of Yugoslavia, 27 years of age or older, who had not been convicted for offenses which limit moral adequacy for this service, and who were able to perform this duty in general (Article 47, *Courts Law*, 1954). The law did not specify nor did it provide guidance in any way on how a person can prove that he/she is able to perform this function or, on the other hand, what the factors that would make someone unable to be a lay judge at face value should be.

The law also described the election process, lay judges' rights and duties, and conditions for dismissal from service. It followed the idea of providing the people with the possibility of selecting their own representatives for the court by giving the people's representatives the right to make a choice. That is, potential lay judges for local courts were proposed and elected by the people's committees (*narodni odbor*), a committee of local residents (Article 51, *Courts Law*, 1954).

Interestingly, the law specified general rights and duties of professional judges and lay judges in the same articles, rather than listing their roles and their rights and duties separately. Professional judges and lay judges could not be held liable for their vote or opinion (Article 56, *Courts Law*, 1954); however, if they committed a crime, either in the course of their duty (e.g., by accepting bribes) or off-duty (e.g., by committing murder), they were liable in criminal court and, if applicable, in civil court (Articles 66 and 67, *Courts Law*, 1954). Neither professional judges nor lay judges could be prosecuted for crimes they committed in the course of their duty without the approval of the disciplinary board (Article 57, *Courts Law*, 1954). No such stipulations existed for crimes committed off-duty. In the performance of their duty, professional judges and lay judges were bound only by the law and their conscience (Article 53, *Courts Law*, 1954). They also had the responsibility of thoroughly examining the evidence in the cases they were assigned to decide (Article 60, *Courts Law*, 1954). Finally, they could be excused from a particular case (Article 61, *Courts Law*, 1954).

On the other hand, professional judges and lay judges differed with respect to their selection process, qualifications, occupations, mandate (a two-year term for lay judges *v.* an unlimited term for professional judges; Article 53, *Courts Law*, 1954), payment for their service (or the absence thereof), and, to a degree, rights and duties in the criminal process. Nevertheless, once the trial began, professional judges and lay judges were equals (Article 11, *Courts Law*, 1954). Although the *Criminal Procedure Law* of 1948 did not state explicitly that only professional judges could be presiding judges, it was clear from the rules describing the role the presiding judge had to perform that this role could only be performed by a professional judge. However, the principle of collective decision-making was important and lay judges were determined to be equals to the presiding professional judge. Lay judges were mentioned explicitly in some of the rules that provided them with the right to ask questions of defendants, witnesses, and expert witnesses directly (Articles 222, 228, and 232, *Criminal Procedure Law*, 1948).

A lay judge's service could be terminated at his/her own request, when it was determined that the lay judge could not perform his/her role because of the general or moral inability to do so, or when it was determined that the lay judge performed his/her role disorderly (Article 79, *Courts Law*, 1954).

The *Criminal Procedure Law* (Article 314, 1948) required potential lay judges for juvenile mixed tribunals to be experienced in the education of juveniles. This was the first time the lay judges for juvenile mixed tribunals were supposed to be different in some aspect from the lay judges for trials of adult offenders; in jury terminology, lay judges for mixed tribunals were "blue-ribbon" lay judges — experts in the specific non-legal area important for the decision in the case. The next *Criminal Procedure Law* (1953, Article 415) expanded this requirement even further by requiring that lay judges be selected from the ranks of professors, teachers, educators, and other people who had experience in the education and upbringing of children. The changes in 1954 did not concern only the regulation of regular courts, but also the changes in commerce courts and military courts. The tribunals introduced for trials of commerce cases were different from mixed tribunals for regular courts because they required potential lay judges to possess a professional level of knowledge and/or experience in commerce (Article 28, *Commerce Courts Law*, 1954). This represented the introduction of lay judges who were specialists in certain areas into the judicial system of socialist Yugoslavia. These tribunals bore similarities with the tribunals for commerce offenses from the period of the Kingdom of Yugoslavia — requirements set in front of lay judges who served in commerce resembled those specified for "honorary judges."

Mixed tribunals at military courts were a part of the legal system of socialist Yugoslavia since its very beginning. They tried all offenses committed by military personnel and some offenses, related to breaches of national security, committed by civilians. The new *Military Courts Law* of 1954 retained mixed tribunals as an integral part of military courts. Lay judges eligible for service in such tribunals had to be military persons of rank over 27 years of age (Article 25, *Military Courts Law*, 1954). Unlike lay judges at other courts, and like professional judges at military courts, lay judges at military courts were appointed by the top commander of the military forces, Josip Broz Tito (Article 23, *Military Courts Law*, 1954).

Over the next decade, certain problems in the work of mixed tribunals were detected. As Kamhi and Čalija (1974, p. 17) noted,

> In that short period of 18 years, between 1945 and 1963, our jury system [system of mixed tribunals] has undoubtedly shown certain qualities, as well as many weaknesses that are characteristic of the jury [mixed tribunals] in general and are the reason why lay participation in trials is attacked with such intensity. Moreover, in addition to these general weaknesses, certain weaknesses have surfaced that are specific for our jury [mixed tribunals] and are undoubtedly rooted in the structure of the system of mixed tri-

bunals, which our country took over so uncritically from the Soviet Union.

The problems Kamhi and Čalija (1974) referred to were observed by professional judges and were a result of their interaction with lay judges. As described by Kamhi and Čalija (1974, p. 17-19), professional judges had a lengthy list of grievances. They complained that lay judges did not respond to the court's mail and that they repeatedly had to rely on the same lay judges, which made the concept of representation of the people next to impossible to implement. Lay judges often did not appear for the next court session in the same case, and professional judges routinely had to rely on substitute lay judges. Furthermore, lay judges were frequently unfamiliar with the subject of trial and deliberation and, because of a large caseload, professional judges typically did not have time to introduce the topic to the lay judges. Consequently, lay judges assumed a passive role in the proceedings. In addition, lay judges had serious problems in applying the law because they did not have legal education and tended to rely on professional judges.

Kamhi and Čalija (1972, p. 19) argued that the legislature was aware of these problems when the new *Constitution* was passed in 1963. Although the *Constitution* retained the system of mixed tribunals, the statement that all the cases were to be decided by mixed tribunals unless specifically determined by a separate law (as it appeared in the *Courts Law* of 1954), was considerably mellowed. Article 137 of the 1963 *Constitution* states that, "[p]rofessional judges and lay judges participate in legal proceedings. Federal statutes may prescribe that only professional judges participate in certain courts and in certain cases."

While the *Constitution* of 1946 contained an explicit statement that professional judges and lay judges were equals during trial and deliberation, no such rule appeared in the text of the *Constitution* of 1963. By not regulating the institution of mixed tribunals in general, the *Constitution* provided an opportunity for separate laws dealing with different subject matters to provide solutions that would seem most suitable.

Following the new *Constitution*, the court system was reorganized, but the changes in subsequent laws, including changes in the *Criminal Procedure Law* (1967), the *Civil Procedure Law* (1965), the *Basic Law on the Courts of General Jurisdiction* (1965), the *Commerce Courts Law* (1965), and the *Military Courts Law* (1965) provided very limited changes in the existing system of mixed tribunals. Aside from expanding the jurisdiction of mixed tribunals by a small degree (by allowing lay judges to be members of appellate tribunals only in the rare instances in which these tribunals conducted trials), changes were minimal. In the cases in which the mixed tribunal decides an appeal, the tribunal is composed of two professional judges and three lay judges (Article 5, *Law Concerning Amendments and Supplements to the Criminal Procedure Law*, 1965).

Two changes relevant for mixed tribunals took place in 1965. The age limit of 27 was reduced to 18 by the *Basic Law on the Courts of General Jurisdiction* (1965). In addition, this law further specified that additional requirements for lay judges (e.g., their educational level and/or occupation) could be imposed in other statutes; the law specifically mentioned that lay judges who sit in juvenile cases should be occupationally related to juveniles (Article 41, *Basic Law on the Courts of General Jurisdiction*, 1965). Indeed, Article 430 of the *Criminal Procedure Law* of 1967 stated that lay judges for juvenile cases should be elected from the ranks of professors, teachers, educators, and other persons experienced in dealing with juveniles.

The new (Croatian, not Federal) *Courts Law* of 1967 elaborated on the process of election of lay judges. This process was very similar to the election process regulated by the *Regular Courts Law* of 1977 (with subsequent changes in 1986, 1988, 1990, and 1991). Since the latter was on the books at the time the empirical part of this study was conducted, its relevant details will be discussed shortly.

Decentralization became the key word in the politics of the 1970s and had a prominent role in the new *Constitution* of 1974. The new *Constitution*, which declared the basic constitutional right of citizens to participate in trials as members of mixed tribunals (Article 229, *Constitution*, 1974), provided a greater degree of autonomy to the constituent parts of Yugoslavia — six socialist republics and two socialist autonomous provinces. The majority of the state functions were in the jurisdiction of the republics and their local parliaments, while the prespecified functions remained in the hands of the federal parliament. The *Constitution* of 1974 (Article 221) specified that the judicial function was to be performed by regular courts; the organization of regular courts and administration of justice were no longer a federal issue (Article 220, *Constitution*, 1974). Consequently, the 1974 *Constitution* contained only several articles dealing with the very few courts that were still under federal jurisdiction: the Federal Court (Articles 369-371) and military courts (Articles 281 and 221).

The situation was somewhat complicated by the fact that criminal procedure, which regulated the issue of whether the case was in the jurisdiction of a professional judge alone or a mixed tribunal, remained under the regulatory power of the Federal Parliament (*Savezna skupština*). To complicate matters even further, while the criminal procedure statute was supposed to provide the delineation between cases tried by a professional judge alone, a small tribunal, and a large tribunal on the basis of the severity of punishment, the range of punishment prescribed for a particular offense was to be determined primarily by individual criminal law code of *each republic*.

Consequently, the aforementioned *Regular Courts Law* of 1977 was a Croatian law, drafted by the Croatian Parliament. Similarly to all the other republics (with the exception of Slovenia), the organization of the court system remained almost identical to the prior organization established by the federal *Basic Law on the Courts of General Jurisdiction* of 1965. District courts had jurisdiction over trials in less serious criminal cases; regional courts had jurisdiction over trials in more serious criminal cases, as well as appellate jurisdiction over the cases tried at district courts. The supreme court of a republic had appellate jurisdiction in the cases tried by regional courts in that republic.

Although the *Regular Courts Law* was originally drafted in 1977, certain sections of the law were subsequently changed (1986, 1988, 1990, and 1991).[4] This law specified the requirements for being a lay judge, the election and dismissal process, and the lay judges' rights and duties. Any citizen of age (18 years) who was "able and worthy" to perform the lay judges' duty, as witnessed by that person's "personal and working characteristics," could be a lay judge.

The *Regular Courts Law* of 1988 also regulated the *election process* of lay judges. The election process was initiated by the president of a particular court (Article 103, *Regular Courts Law*, 1988), who suggested to the parliament of that district/region the number of lay judges to be elected. The parliament would then conduct the election. During the process, professional judges from the respective court would give their opinion about the candidates. The parliament's final selection of the candidates is then distributed to the potential lay judges and to the court.

The law further specified mechanisms of *dismissal* of lay judges from duty. The reasons for dismissal were threefold: reasons related to the election process (e.g., eligibility requirements for lay judges were not satisfied at the time election took place), reasons related to the inability to perform jury duty (e.g., a lay judge requested to be dismissed from duty, a lay judge has not performed the duty at all or performed it irregularly without having offered acceptable reasons for absenteeism, or a lay judge was sentenced to imprisonment of six months or more), and reasons related to the misuse of the position (e.g., a lay judge violates legal rules, damages the reputation of the court).

Although the law prescribed that lay judges be dismissed from duty if they exhibited absenteeism, this rarely happened in practice. Problems related to

---

[4]Some of the changes introduce different wordings of certain rules, replace, or delete the whole articles. Other changes, such as the change in 1988, provided the whole text of the law with all the previous changes incorporated. The most recent restated version of the *Regular Courts Law* is that of 1988. For expository convenience, I will refer to the *Regular Courts Law* of 1977 and its subsequent changes as the *Regular Courts Law* (1988). That is, I will not explicitly enumerate all the subsequent changes and will cite the most recent restated version.

the reluctance of lay judges to participate had been noticed for some time; for example, Čulinović (1954) and Jovanović (1958) wrote about these problems in the 1950s. A few studies conducted in the 1980s (Ljubanović, 1984; Bajić-Petrović,[5] 1985a, 1985b) examined how this rule was implemented. They generally found that, although a number of lay judges indeed did not respond to the court's mail and did not participate in trials at all or participated only infrequently, the process of dismissing them from duty had never been initiated.

What are the consequences of the practice of not dismissing lay judges who do not respond to the courts' mail? The *Criminal Procedure Law* (1993, Article 354)[6] required that the same tribunal try the case (i.e., that the same professional judges and lay judges be present at all sessions in the case). In general, if the members of the tribunal were not the same (in particular, if the presiding professional judge was not the same or the adjournment had lasted over one month), the trial had to start again (Article 295, *Criminal Procedure Law*, 1993). In all other cases, provided that the adjournment was less than 30 days and the same professional judge was present, there was a possibility that the court would not hear the testimonies again; rather, the testimonies given in front of the preceding tribunal would be read if the parties in the case agreed to it. Therefore, one immediate consequence was that either the court session was postponed, and the duration of the process increased, or that the principle of oral presentation of evidence in front of the decision-makers would have been violated by reading the transcripts of the earlier testimonies.

---

[5]This study was conducted in Vojvodina, an autonomous province and a part of the Socialist Republic of Serbia within the former Yugoslav Federation at the time.

[6]The federal *Criminal Procedure Law* of 1977 had been periodically changed (1977, 1985, 1987, 1989, 1990) and had subsequently been adopted as the Croatian *Criminal Procedure Law* in 1991. It was further changed in 1993 and in 1996, and one of the changes in 1993 included a printing of the restated version. Therefore, I will refer to it as the *Criminal Procedure Law* of 1993 — not only was it the most recent restated version at the time the study was conducted, but it was in all important aspects that pertain to this book very similar to the original *Criminal Procedure Law* of 1977.

In order to avoid postponing the court sessions because the assigned lay judges did not respond to the court's mail, courts relied only on the lay judges who *did* respond. Courts prepared lists of reliable lay judges and formed a pool of "reserve" lay judges. According to Bajić-Petrović (1985a, 1985b), one of the long-term consequences was selective reelection of only those lay judges who responded to the courts' mail. As Ljubanović (1984) pointed out, this solution contradicted the idea of involving as many citizens in the criminal justice system as possible.

In addition, Bajić-Petrović (1985a, 1985b) stated that this problem influenced the atmosphere in the courtroom by making the presiding professional judge less favorably disposed and less sensitive toward the lay judges' opinion. In other words, the irresponsible behavior of (some) lay judges may have had serious consequences on the interaction between the professional judge and the lay judges who responded to the court's mail and were willing to participate in the process.

Violating the rules that regulate the presence of tribunal members in the courtrooms by, for example, proceeding with the trial even when one of the tribunal members was not present, would create a basis for appeal. That is, this particular violation had a very serious consequence — it constituted an absolute violation of the *Criminal Procedure Law* (Article 354, *Criminal Procedure Law*, 1993) and was one of the reasons why the appellate court had to disallow the verdict and return the case to be tried again (Article 375, *Criminal Procedure Law*, 1993).

The lay judges who responded to the court's mail and participated in the process were compensated only for the expenses they incurred, such as lost salary, and were given a modest remuneration (Article 106, *Regular Courts Law*, 1988). For example, according to the most recent *Regulations Concerning Compensation and Awards of Lay Judges* (1996), in addition to their travel expenses and lost salary, lay judges are entitled to receive an award for their work. This award is calculated on a *pro-rata* basis and is dependent upon the type of court: at district courts the rate is 20 kunas or $3 per hour, while it is somewhat higher at regional courts (25 kunas or $4 per hour) and at commercial courts (30 kunas or $5 per hour).

In general terms, the functions of both professional judges and lay judges are public and, therefore, subject to legal rules (Article 14, *Regular Courts Law*, 1988). The letter of the law was worded so that all rules about the rights and duties of professional judges applied to lay judges as well, unless stated otherwise (Article 107, *Regular Courts Law*, 1988). Both categories of judges had the duty of protecting the legal system and the laws and upholding the reputation of the court. They had immunity from being prosecuted for a vote and/or statement given during trial and/or deliberation (Article 15, *Regular Courts Law*, 1988).

Lay judges and professional judges were once again deemed to be equals during trial and deliberation (Article 13, *Regular Courts Law*, 1988); their votes had the same power. Professional judges had additional rights and responsibilities as the presiding members of the tribunals, such as maintaining order in the courtroom or allowing the parties to speak. These additional rights and duties of professional judges in the criminal process, as regulated by the *Criminal Procedure Law* (1993), will be discussed in detail in subsequent chapters.

The *Regular Courts Law* (Article 13, 1988) left the resolution on whether a certain type of case would be tried by a mixed tribunal or a professional judge alone to specific codes of procedure. The *Criminal Procedure Law* (1993) regulated that, depending on the type and maximum seriousness of the sanction to be imposed (as specified in the laws dealing with the area of substantive criminal law), the decision-maker in the criminal trial may have been either a mixed tribunal or a professional judge alone. When the maximum sanction for the offense was a fine or imprisonment for less than one year, a professional judge alone had the jurisdiction over the case (Article 21, *Criminal Procedure Law*, 1993). When the maximum sanction was harsher, the case was to be tried by a mixed tribunal. Unlike the situation in the United States, where defendants may choose to waive their right to a jury trial, the defendant could not choose between the trial by a professional judge alone and the trial by a mixed tribunal.

The size and the composition of the tribunal changed depending on the seriousness of the offense. "Small tribunals," composed of one professional judge and two lay judges, had jurisdiction over offenses for which the maximum sanction was between one and fifteen years of imprisonment (Article 21, *Criminal Procedure Law*, 1993). Offenses for which the maximum sanction exceeded fifteen years of imprisonment were tried by a "large tribunal," composed of two professional judges and three lay judges (Article 21, *Criminal Procedure Law*, 1993).

Criminal cases that reached instances above the first instance (appeal, extraordinary legal redress) were decided by professional tribunals only (Article 21, *Criminal Procedure Law*, 1993). There was one exception to this rule: when the appellate court conducted the trial session in order to reexamine the evidence, the tribunal was composed of two professional judges and three lay judges (Article 23, *Criminal Procedure Law*, 1993). Similar to mixed tribunals, the size of professional tribunals in the second instance depended on the seriousness of the offense: when the maximum sanction was less than fifteen years, the tribunal was composed of three professional judges, while for offenses for which the maximum sanction exceeded fifteen years of imprisonment, the tribunals consisted of five professional judges (Article 23, *Criminal Procedure Law*, 1993). Finally, all the criminal cases that reached the third instance (extraordinary legal redress) were decided by professional tribunals composed of five professional judges (Article 23, *Criminal Procedure Law*, 1993).

Although Croatia has been exposed to tremendous social, political, and legislative changes since 1977, that is, the year when both the *Regular Courts Law* and the *Criminal Procedure Law* were passed into law, the changes that occurred until 1993 did not result in any major changes in the way criminal proceedings were conducted nor in the way the work of mixed tribunals was regulated. The only noteworthy (yet temporary) changes were motivated by the war in Croatia — the jurisdiction of mixed tribunals was temporarily reduced at the trial level and, at the same time, temporarily expanded at the appellate level in 1991; jurisdiction reverted to the previous scope in 1996. Substantial changes to the organization of the court system and criminal law and procedure were codified in 1994 and 1998, respectively.

Not unlike the countries of the former socialist block in Europe, in its efforts to initiate a process of transition toward democracy, the Croatian Parliament introduced amendments to the Croatian *Constitution* in early 1990. These amendments allowed for the existence of political parties other than the ruling Communist Party, and have thereby abolished the Communist Party's four-decade monopoly over political life in Croatia. The first multi-party elections for the Croatian Parliament and local governments were held in the spring of 1990 and the first session of the newly elected multi-party Croatian Parliament was held on May 30, 1990.

Soon thereafter, the Presidentship of Croatia embarked upon carrying out numerous changes, some of which inevitably affected the judicial system. It was proclaimed that all the political and ideological characteristics of the old regime had to be erased. In June of 1990 the Croatian Parliament decided that all the characteristics of socialist/communist ideology should be removed from the *Constitution* and the laws. Consequently, in July 1990 Croatia added new amendments to the *Constitution*, which introduced changes in the organization of the state and government. However, Kregar *et al.* (1991) argued that these changes were symbolic; it was clear that social transformation would not be achieved on the basis of reconstruction of the old *Constitution*, and that a new *Constitution* was necessary.

The new Croatian *Constitution* was enacted by the Croatian Parliament in December 1990. Croatia was established as a parliamentary multi-party repub-lic. The basic principles of the new *Constitution* included political democracy, the rule of law, and the principle of market economy. Unlike the governmental organization in the socialist/communist regime, in which the same body was in charge of both the legislative and the executive authority (Kregar *et al.*, 1991), the new Croatian *Constitution* is based on the principle of the division of authority into legislative, executive, and judicial branches.[7] The Parliament also made a move toward subsequent transformation of public property into private property.

The new *Constitution* (1990) did not provide a detailed regulation of lay participation, but it did establish the basic principle. Although the political system in Croatia started to change dramatically, the form of lay participation to be utilized in Croatia remained lay participation in mixed tribunals. Democratization was emphasized as the reason for keeping the mixed tribunals; Article 118 of the *Constitution* (1990) states that, "justice shall be administered by judges and lay assessors in conformity with the law." The actual organization of the court system was left to be regulated by a separate law (*Courts Law*), while the process of drawing lines between the jurisdiction of a professional judge alone, small tribunals, large tribunals, and professional tribunals was left for the laws dealing with substantive issues (*Criminal Procedure Law*). The *Constitution* further regulated that, "judges and lay assessors who take part in the administration of justice shall not be called to account for an opinion given in the process of judicial decision-making" (Article 119, *Constitution*, 1990).

At the same time, the political situation in the former Yugoslavia was deteriorating. In an effort to find a peaceful solution, presidents of the six Yugoslav republics proposed that the governments of each republic organize a referendum and that citizens determine the future of the Yugoslav Federation (Perić, 1995, p. 91). On May 23, 1991 the President of the Republic of Croatia declared that the citizens have decided that the Republic of Croatia should become an independent state. About a month later, on June 25, 1991, Croatia unilaterally declared its independence from Yugoslavia. Within days, the war in Croatia began.

---

[7]Kregar *et al.* (1991, p. 150) argued that, "the separation of power (although emphasized in the Constitution as one of its fundamental principles) has not been consistently carried out because of a shift in favour of the executive power and the institution of the President of the Republic, which should primarily be ascribed to the specific conditions under which the Constitution was enacted."

The temporary limitation of the jurisdiction of mixed tribunals was ordered by the *Presidential Decree* of 1991 (1991b, Article 3): instead of deciding cases for which the maximum potential sanction to be imposed was over one year, mixed tribunals were to decide only the cases for which the maximum potential sanction to be imposed was over five years, leaving other cases to be decided by a professional judge alone. This change was made in order to increase the efficiency of courts and to ensure that cases be decided in conditions of war (during which it may not always have been possible to have lay judges present in the courtrooms).

Another decree (Article 9, *Presidential Decree*, 1991a) extended the jurisdiction of mixed tribunals to appellate decisions on procedural issues during trials (in instances in which a three-member professional tribunal could not be assembled). Clearly, in anticipation of war, changes were made to accommodate legal decision-making even in circumstances in which it may not have been feasible to have three qualified professional judges decide the appeals.

Furthermore, military courts were established. However, lay participation was not a part of military courts; all decisions were made by professional judges, either by a professional judge alone or by a professional tribunal. For the offenses for which the sanction to be imposed was up to five years of imprisonment, a professional judge was the decision-maker in the first instance (Article 4, *Presidential Decree*, 1991b), while the more serious offenses were decided by professional tribunals of three.

Both decrees were abolished in 1996 (*Presidential Decree*, 1996), that is, once it became clear that the war was over and that the process of peaceful reintegration of the remaining Croatian territory was underway. The country went through extensive changes in territorial organization; it has been reorganized into a system of twenty regions. The court system in Croatia was changed at the beginning of 1994 (*Courts Law*, 1994). The courts in the Republic of Croatia are: district courts, regional courts, military courts,[8] com-

---

[8]Military courts have been abolished by the *Presidential Decree* of 1996.

merce courts, the High Commerce Court of Croatia, the Administrative Court
of Croatia, and the Supreme Court of Croatia (Article 13, *Courts Law*, 1994).

Several changes that were introduced by the *Courts Law* of 1994 affected
mixed tribunals. They relate to the issues of qualifications and election of lay
judges. According to the *Courts Law* of 1994, every Croatian citizen who is
18 years of age and is worthy of carrying out the lay judge's duty may be
elected as a lay judge (Article 68, *Courts Law*, 1994). Lay judges at district,
commerce, and regional courts are now elected by regional parliaments, based
on the suggestions made by districts or city councils, the union, the employers'
associations, and the chambers of commerce (Article 70, *Courts Law*, 1994).
Lay judges at all other courts are elected by the House of Representatives of
the Croatian Parliament, based on the suggestions made by the Minister of
Justice (Article 70, *Courts Law*, 1994). In a manner similar to that from the
Regular Courts Law (1988), the respective court has an opportunity to evaluate
potential lay judges before the final decision is made, albeit this evaluation is
now to be performed only by the president of the court (and no longer by
all the professional judges serving at the court). The lay judges' mandate
remained the same (i.e., four years), with the possibility of reelection (Article
69, *Courts Law*, 1994).

In addition, this law now provides for the wording of the oath to be taken
by lay judges (Article 71, *Courts Law*, 1994) and specifies who will administer
the solemn act of taking the oath. Finally, this law regulates the situations in
which criminal proceedings or the procedure of dismissal from lay judge's duty
has been initiated against a lay judge (Article 72, *Courts Law*, 1994). In such
situations, the president of the court will not ask the lay judge to perform lay
judge's duty until these proceedings are resolved.

The new *Criminal Procedure Law* (1998) establishes that the cases that
are tried at district courts and for which the maximum penalty is either fine
or imprisonment for up to three years are to be tried by a professional judge
alone (Article 18, *Criminal Procedure Law*, 1998). For the offenses that are
tried at district courts and for which the maximum punishment is between

three and ten years of imprisonment, the decision is made by a mixed tribunal composed of one professional judge and two lay judges (Article 18, *Criminal Procedure Law*, 1998). Similarly, for the offenses that are tried at regional courts and for which the maximum punishment is between ten and fifteen years of imprisonment, the decision is made by a mixed tribunal composed of one professional judge and two lay judges (Article 20, *Criminal Procedure Law*, 1998). Decisions in the cases with a maximum punishment of fifteen years of imprisonment are made by mixed tribunals composed of two professional judges and three lay judges (Article 20, *Criminal Procedure Law*, 1998).

The new *Criminal Code* of 1998 introduced a new penalty for particularly serious felonies — long-term imprisonment of 20-40 years (the previous maximum penalty was 20 years of imprisonment). Naturally, the *Criminal Procedure Law* of 1998 contains rules dealing with the offenses punishable with long-term imprisonment. In particular, such offenses are to be tried by mixed tribunals composed of three professional judges and four lay judges (Article 20, *Criminal Procedure Law*, 1998).

Decisions on appeal, unless they require a trial session, are decided by professional tribunals (Articles 20 and 22, *Criminal Procedure Law*, 1998). The size of the professional tribunal varies from three professional judges for the least serious offenses to seven professional judges for the most serious offenses. If the case on appeal requires a trial session (hearing), the tribunal is composed of professional judges and lay judges. The number and composition of the tribunal depend on the seriousness of punishment and vary from a five-member tribunal for the least serious cases at regional courts (two professional judges and three lay judges; Article 20, *Criminal Procedure Law*, 1998) to a seven-member tribunal for the most serious cases at the Supreme Court (three professional judges and four lay judges; Article 22, *Criminal Procedure Law*, 1998). All the cases that reach the third instance (extraordinary legal redress) are decided by professional tribunals. The size of the professional tribunal at the Supreme Court varies from three for the least serious cases to seven for the most serious cases (Article 22, *Criminal Procedure Law*, 1998). The other rules dealing with the work of mixed tribunals remained very similar to the rules provided in the *Criminal Procedure Law* of 1993.

Juvenile criminal procedure was previously a part of the *Criminal Procedure Law*; in 1998 a separate criminal procedure was established for juvenile offenders (*Juvenile Courts Law*, 1998). District courts, regional courts, and the Supreme Court now have separate divisions for juveniles (ages 14 through 18). It is noteworthy that none of the cases involving juveniles are tried by a professional judge alone; mixed tribunals are in charge of all juvenile cases. Unlike the mixed tribunals for adult offenders, the size of which depends on the seriousness of the offense, mixed tribunals for juveniles are *always* composed of one professional judge and two lay judges (Article 57, *Juvenile Courts Law*, 1998), unless the trial is conducted by an appellate tribunal, in which case the tribunal consists of two professional judges and three lay judges (Article 57, *Juvenile Courts Law*, 1998).

The *Juvenile Courts Law* (1998) also regulates trials of younger adult offenders (ages 18 through 21), as well as trials for crimes in which the victims were children (these crimes are listed in Article 117). Younger adult offenders indicted for crimes for which the punishment is up to fifteen years of imprisonment are tried by mixed tribunals composed of one professional judge and two lay judges. If the punishment exceeds fifteen years of imprisonment or if the crimes victimized children, the tribunals are composed of two professional judges and three lay judges (Articles 115, 125, *Juvenile Courts Law*, 1998).

Similar to the earlier statutes, the new *Juvenile Courts Law* (1998) requires that lay judges selected to decide juvenile cases must have special qualifications and skills. They are elected from the ranks of professors, teachers, and other persons who have experience with the education of juveniles (Article 40, *Juvenile Courts Law*, 1998). Furthermore, the *Law* requires lay members in each mixed tribunal to be of different gender (Article 57).

Chapter 4

Previous Research on Mixed Tribunals

In common-law countries, the overwhelming majority of the defendants plead guilty and proceed directly into the sentencing stage of the process. Consequently, very few trials are held and, even then, defendants have the option of selecting between a bench trial and a jury trial. Overall, juries actually decide very few of the cases. For example, the overwhelming majority of all felony state trials in the United States in 1994, about 89%, were plea bargained and the remaining 11% were divided between bench trials and jury trials; jury trials accounted for only 6% of all felony state trials (*1997 Sourcebook*, 1998, p. 422).

Unlike their counterparts in common-law systems, defendants in civil-law systems do not have the option of pleading guilty and proceeding directly to sentencing; rather, each case will be tried. Furthermore, defendants in civil-law systems do not have the right or the option of selecting between a bench trial and a trial by mixed tribunals. In fact, decision-makers for various types of cases are prescribed by statutes and are usually determined according to the severity of the offense to be tried and/or by certain characteristics of the offender (age, military status). Therefore, if the prosecutor proceeds with the indictment, each case will be tried and a large percentage of these cases will be tried by mixed tribunals. For example, Kubicki and Zawadzki

(1970, p. 321) reported that at the time their study was conducted mixed tribunals decided "almost half the total number of cases considered in penal proceedings." Recently, I was able to gain access to two registries from Croatian courts, both of which confirm this expectation. Specifically, the registry of criminal cases tried at the District Court of Bjelovar showed that in 1997 three-quarters of criminal cases were tried by mixed tribunals and only one-quarter by a professional judge alone, and the registry of criminal cases at the Regional Court of Bjelovar showed that in 1997 the overwhelming majority of cases were tried by large tribunals (90%), while the remaining 10% were tried by small tribunals.

A very clear paradox surfaces: while very few of the cases tried in common-law countries are tried by jury, there is a very extensive body of literature on the jury; on the other hand, while a substantial portion of the cases in civil-law countries is tried by mixed tribunals, there are very few studies on tribunals. This is all the more remarkable in light of the fact that mixed tribunals have been used extensively over a long period of time in a number of European countries.

Several studies that examined the process of selection of lay judges and its impact on the representativeness of lay judges (Ljubanović, 1984; Bajić-Petrović, 1985a, 1985b; Richert, 1983; Gerken, 1988) were discussed in the context of historical developments and contemporary systems of mixed tribunals in Chapters 2 and 3. This chapter focuses on the empirical studies of mixed tribunals that examined the impact of lay judges' contribution toward the decision, the frequency and importance of lay judges' participation, and positive and negative features of lay participation (Table 4.1). The common feature of these studies is that they are mostly of an empirical nature, with virtually no attempt to establish a theoretical framework for the study of mixed tribunals, other than simply focusing on positive and negative features of lay participation. Another common feature of most of the studies is that they were conducted in the late 1960s or early 1970s.

In terms of the methodology available for the study of mixed tribunals, there are common limitations across countries. Deliberations by mixed tribunals are secret and the records from these deliberations are both inaccessible and uninformative because they rarely contain any information other than the actual votes and dissents. Nevertheless, their examination is prohibited to all, with the exception of the appellate court when it decides the appeal. Having an inside helper (i.e., being a participant-observer as a professional judge, as was the case for Lucas [in Kalven and Zeisel, 1966], or having the approval for court apprentices to observe deliberations, as was the case in the Polish study [Kubicki and Zawadzki, 1970]) may eliminate successfully at least some of the institutional barriers. In the absence of such conveniences, researchers are typically limited to interviewing or surveying professional judges and lay judges (and possibly other participants in trials by mixed tribunals) about their experiences during trial and deliberation.

4.1 Literature Review

The attempts to study and evaluate the significance and contribution by lay judges started well before the 1960s; Casper and Zeisel (1972, p. 139) reported that in 1908 Mittermaier and Liepmann published the results of a series of studies considered to be "the most serious evaluation of *Shöffengerichte* and *Schwurgerichte* yet."

There was another noteworthy pre-1960s study. Lucas (1944; in Kalven and Zeisel, 1966, p. 519) examined disagreements between three professional judges, one being himself, and three lay judges in 123 appellate criminal cases tried at a Danish appellate court. Since he wanted to study the contribution made by lay judges, he recorded the votes on guilt and sentence for each judge. His results suggested that the decision was unanimous in the great majority of the cases (85%), whereas in the remaining 15% of the cases at least one lay judge disagreed with the majority and voted for an acquittal or a lesser charge. He concluded that when lay judges disagreed, they favored the defendants more than they favored the prosecution. The general conclusion offered by Lucas (in Kalven and Zeisel, 1966, p. 519) was that, "lay judges have made no significant contribution to his court." However, two methodological problems need to be considered before one can accept this conclusion. First, is only counting the votes really a valid measure of lay judges' contribution to the work of the tribunal and the final decision in the case? Second, can the researcher who was at the same time a member of the tribunals be objective?

Krystufek (1976, p. 301) participated in the study of mixed tribunals conducted in the former Czechoslovakia in 1963. The study was sponsored by the Czechoslovakian Academy of Sciences and was described as "the first sociological project in the field of law in Czechoslovakia after 1948." Despite the importance of the project, Krystufek reported that the research was suspended while he was studying abroad, and that another scholar withdrew from the project, so the study was never finished. He concluded that, "the author unfortunately has no access to original materials and this belated report can therefore be based only on his memory" (Krystufek, 1976, p. 306). Since the study was never completed, only the preliminary findings were available.

Questionnaires were sent to representative samples (of unknown size) composed of lay judges and professional judges, attorneys, public prosecutors, and litigants in Prague. The survey was preceded by informal interviews with lay judges and other participants, and followed by formal interviews with litigants.

The results revealed that presiding professional judges had full discretion over the selection of lay judges for each case, so, as Krystufek (1976) pointed out, they could select those lay judges whom they approved of or whom they preferred. Professional judges had a very concrete mechanism with which they could force lay judges to comply with their opinion: they evaluated lay judges and therefore controlled their reelection. The paradox of the system was that if lay judges participated wholeheartedly, they would most likely not be reelected. In other words, if lay judges tried to participate fully by bringing community values and achieving the "latent" function, they would

Table 4.1: Summary of reviewed research studies on mixed tribunals.

Authors (Year of Publication)	Country	Sample	Method	Focus
Casper & Zeisel (1972)	West Germany	570 trials/deliberations	PJs report on their own and LJs' behavior in all trials held over a period of 3 months	LJ's participation in trial; LJs' contribution in deliberation; initial disagreement & resolution; reasons for disagreement; Mr. Prejudice and Ms. Sympathy
Frassine et al. (1979)	Austria	550 trials/deliberations	PJs report on their own and LJs' behavior in all trials held over a period of 3 months	LJ's participation in trial; LJs' contribution in deliberation; initial disagreement & resolution; reasons for disagreement; Mr. Prejudice and Ms. Sympathy
Gerken (1988)	West Germany	20 LJs interviewed, 25 LJs surveyed	interviews, survey	selection process (juvenile LJs); LJs' activity in trial & deliberation; disagreement on guilt/sanction
Görlitz (1970)	West Germany	70 PJs	survey	general opinion about LJs' contribution to the decision; disagreement in trial & deliberation
Kamhi & Čalija (1974)	the former Yugoslavia	100 PJs, 196 LJs (district & regional courts)	survey; interviews (individual and focus groups)	selection process; LJs' interest in participation; LJs' impact on the verdict; importance of LJs' participation; disagreement; PJs' treatment of LJs; general opinion; Mr. Prejudice and Mrs. Sympathy; improvements to the system

Table 4.1: continued

Authors (Year of Publication)	Country	Sample	Method	Focus
Klami & Hämäläinen (1992)	Sweden Finland	36 Swedish PJs, 80 Swedish LJs, 46 Finnish PJs, 190 Finnish LJs	survey, experiment (3 hypothetical cases)	positive & negative features; LJs' understanding of evidence & law; standard of proof for PJs and LJs
Klausa (1972)	West Germany	124 PJs (39 for criminal cases), 191 LJs (56 for criminal cases)	interviews, survey	positive & negative features; LJs' understanding of evidence & law; selection process; LJs' impact on the decision; disagreement & resolution; improvements to the system
Krystufek (1976)	the former Czechoslovakia	LJs, PJs, state attorneys, attorneys from Prague	interviews, survey	selection process; LJs' impact on the decision; positive & negative features; general opinion
Kubicki & Zawadzki (1970) Pomorski (1975) Borucka-Arctowa (1976)	Poland	257 criminal cases, 127 community meetings; 292 LJs & 50 PJs interviewed; 2,565 LJs, 100 PJs, 200 prosecutors, & 100 attorneys surveyed	observations (trials, community meetings); interviews (292 LJs & 50 PJs); surveys (LJs, PJs, prosecutors, attorneys)	frequency & importance of LJs' participation in trial & deliberation; LJs' role; severity of sentencing; disagreement & resolution; general opinion; Mr. Prejudice & Ms. Sympathy

Table 4.1: continued

Authors (Year of Publication)	Country	Sample	Method	Focus
Kulcsár (1972, 1982)	Hungary	1,223 LJs (450 from Budapest, 773 from other areas), 126 PJs; 2,857 trials/deliberations	surveys (LJs, PJs); PJs report on their own and LJs' behavior in all trials held over a period of 3 months	LJs' information-gathering activity; LJs' questions & comments (frequency & importance); LJs' disagreement; PJs' reaction to LJs' disagreement; freq. of wrong verdicts if no LJs
Lucas (1944)	Denmark	123 appellate cases (all criminal cases other than major felonies tried before a jury)	participant observation (the author was one of the 3 PJs participating with 3 LJs)	frequency of disagreement on guilt & sentence
Ljubanović (1983, 1989)	the former Yugoslavia	16 presidents of district and regional courts, 101 LJs, 30 PJs, 4 prosecutors, 4 attorneys	surveys	selection process; summons; LJs' activity in trial & deliberation; disagreement & resolution; general opinion; criticisms of lay participation; positive & negative features; improvements to the system;

challenge professional judges, which would inevitably lead toward disagreement and would ultimately present a serious risk of not being reelected.

Although lay judges had access to court records and thus had opportunities to familiarize themselves with the cases before trials, they rarely exercised this right (Krystufek, 1976). Based on a set of informal interviews, Krystufek (1976) concluded that lay judges in criminal cases generally formed and expressed their opinion, which was typically not the case in civil trials. He found two reasons why lay judges did not express their opinion in civil cases: lay judges were either not present during all the hearings or the issues were legally or technically complex, which discouraged lay judges from active participation. Interestingly, if lay judges in the tribunal possessed specialized non-legal technical knowledge about the case, they usually expressed their opinion, and the tribunal tended to rely on their expertise.

Krystufek (1976) reported that lay judges in criminal cases generally formed and expressed their opinion. However, he was not able to be more precise in telling us about the frequency of lay judges' participation, the extent of their participation during the whole trial/deliberation, the impact of demographic variables on the frequency and type of lay judges' activity, frequency of disagreement, and the ways of resolving these disagreements.

It is clear that the results of the study were the product of the times in which the project was carried out. For example, although the research team promised anonymity to the respondents, the attorneys participating in the study provided the responses that conformed to the political expectations of the socialist state, which "proclaimed the lay judges as an indisputably positive feature of the socialist judiciary," while their informal responses tended to be quite different (Krystufek, 1976, p. 304).

Approximately at the same time (mid- to late-1960s) a number of projects on mixed tribunals was conducted in other countries in continental Europe — Poland, Austria, Germany, the former Yugoslavia, and Hungary. The most comprehensive project of all was conducted in Poland under the auspices of the Institute of Legal Sciences of the Polish Academy of Sciences (Kubicki and Zawadzki, 1970, p. 98).

The research team in Poland (Kubicki and Zawadzki, 1970; Pomorski, 1975; Borucka-Arctowa, 1976) combined several methods of data collection. Researchers observed 127 community meetings in which candidates for lay judges were nominated (Kubicki and Zawadzki, 1970, p. 101), court apprentices observed 257 actual criminal cases between 1964 and 1967 (Pomorski, 1975, p. 204), researchers interviewed 177 inexperienced lay judges, 115 experienced lay judges, and 50 professional judges (Kubicki and Zawadzki, 1970, p. 102), and researchers surveyed 2,565 lay judges, approximately 200 prosecutors, 100 professional judges, and 100 attorneys (Kubicki and Zawadzki, 1970, p. 102). Furthermore, in order to achieve objectivity, professional judges and lay judges participating in the observed trials were not told about the study.

This study provided a unique opportunity to contrast two views, one obtained by comparing the opinion about the perceived impact on the outcome of the process and the other obtained through observations by court apprentices of actual trials and deliberations. Although the majority of lay judges were convinced that they exerted considerable influence on the outcome of the case (almost 90%), the majority of lawyers (51% of professional judges, 73% of prosecutors, and 85% of attorneys) stated that lay judges played no role in the proceedings and the outcome of the case (Kubicki and Zawadzki, 1970, p. 103).

The observations of deliberations revealed quite an interesting pattern; they suggested that deliberations may be classified into four broad types, ranging from deliberations in which there was absolute dominance by the professional judge to deliberations in which real discussion developed (Type I to Type IV; Kubicki and Zawadzki, 1970, p. 105). Although the underlying assumption was that deliberations by mixed tribunals would include *discussions* by members of the tribunals, the observations suggested that in approximately one-half of the observed deliberations professional judges dominated over the work of the tribunal completely and either imposed their opinion or stubbornly maintained it despite attempts by lay judges to influence them (Kubicki and Zawadzki, 1970, p. 105). Consequently, in the majority of the cases (60%), the professional judge was dominant during deliberation, while in the remaining 40% of the cases (Type IV deliberation) lay judges expressed their personal views and evaluations concerning the case (Kubicki and Zawadzki, 1970, p. 106). It is important to note that this was only an *explicit* influence; Pomorski (1975) and Borucka-Arctowa (1976) argued that there was also an *implicit* influence of lay judges — their presence in the tribunal itself — through which lay judges realized their "latent" function (Borucka-Arctowa, 1976).

The results pointed out that lay judges typically did not prepare for the trial by reading the case file (only 9% of lay judges reported that they read the case file). Approximately one-third of professional judges tried to acquaint lay judges with the case before the beginning of the trial, mostly by focusing on the degree of social harm, value of the evidence, and the defendant's guilt (Kubicki and Zawadzki, 1970, p. 104). Lay judges received information about the legal issues in the case (i.e., legal classification of the behavior) from the professional judge before the trial in less than 20% of trials (Kubicki and Zawadzki, 1970, p. 104).

Furthermore, the majority of lay judges did not participate actively during trial (66% of lay judges did not ask questions at all and only 5% asked questions systematically; Kubicki and Zawadzki, 1970, p. 104). However, professional judges did not display much eagerness to stimulate lay judges into performing their role more actively either; only one-quarter of professional judges asked lay judges whether they had any questions during trial (Kubicki and Zawadzki, 1970, p. 104).

A part of the process of determining the significance of the lay judges' contribution included an examination of the frequency of disagreement and its resolution. In the Polish study, lay judges and professional judges were virtually unanimous on the issue of guilt; they disagreed in only 4% of the cases (Kubicki and Zawadzki, 1970, p. 106), which may be a reflection of the fact that, according to Kubicki and Zawadzki (1970, p. 106), the defendant's guilt was usually obvious, especially because of the relatively frequent confessions by the defendant. On the other hand, lay judges tended to disagree with professional judges more often on sentencing issues; this occurred in 54% of the cases (Kubicki and Zawadzki, 1970, p. 106). Most disagreements between professional judges and lay judges were resolved during discussions in deliberation (40% of cases with disagreement) or by a compromise under the dominance of a professional judge (44% of cases with disagreement), while in the remaining cases with disagreement either professional judges or lay judges were outvoted or wrote *votum separatum* (Kubicki and Zawadzki, 1970, p. 107). In other words, it seems that an attempt to measure the frequency of lay judges' disagreement through the frequency with which they outvoted professional judges would likely result in a very small percentage of disagreements in the tribunal, most of which would be resolved through a compromise of one form or another.

When there were disagreements, lay judges were usually the more lenient ones; in 75% of the cases with disagreement, they influenced verdicts in favor of the defendant. The reason for such a relatively high percentage of cases in which lay judges disagreed on sentencing issues, according to Pomorski (1975), stemmed from the fact that lay judges seemed to be guided more by the personal circumstances of the defendant and his/her subjective faults than by the nature of the offense itself or by the official criminal policy. Thus, "Miss Sympathy" (Hans and Vidmar, 1986) seemed to be occasionally present in the Polish courtrooms and, according to Pomorski (1975), more so for older lay judges, highly educated lay judges, and female lay judges. It is interesting that the lay judges' vote was anything but uniform; while 60% of lay judges stated that they were frequently, or at least sometimes, inclined to pronounce a more severe sentence than professional judges were, a similar percentage (72%) stated that they were frequently, or at least sometimes, inclined to pronounce a more lenient sentence than professional judges were (Kubicki and Zawadzki, 1970, p. 108).

In order to investigate this issue further, researchers asked professional judges and lay judges to evaluate the same hypothetical case (Kubicki and Zawadzki, 1970, p. 108). Of course, asking respondents to provide individual verdicts in hypothetical cases has two serious shortcomings: first, hypothetical and real situations may not lead toward the same resolution, and second, group deliberation is missing. The results showed a discrepancy between professional judges and lay judges; forty-four percent of lay judges selected a sentence that was similar to the sentence selected by 74% of professional judges (Kubicki and Zawadzki, 1970, p. 108). Interestingly, professional judges were much more uniform in the range of sentences they picked; "the sentences pronounced by the lay assessors, though they tend generally to be more lenient, do not differ essentially in their structure, but are much more differentiated and show a tendency to be extreme in both directions" (Kubicki and Zawadzki, 1970, p. 108).

Finally, the results of the survey showed that, despite of rather infrequent direct impact lay judges had on the work of the tribunal, the majority of lay judges, professional judges, state attorneys, and attorneys agreed that mixed tribunals should be kept in the system (Kubicki and Zawadzki, 1970, p. 110). The fact that lay judges were substantially more likely to have a positive view about the system was by no means surprising; while 90% of lay judges supported the idea of keeping mixed tribunals, that idea was supported by only 70% of professional judges, 67% of attorneys, and 65% of state attorneys (Kubicki and Zawadzki, 1970, p. 110).

Approximately at the same time, in the late 1960s, Casper and Zeisel (1972) studied mixed tribunals in West Germany. Casper and Zeisel asked only professional judges to report on the interaction in the tribunal and the lay judges' impact on the final decision in the case. Researchers asked professional judges at courts of various levels and composition to write reports on trials by mixed tribunals in which they had participated. They reported on every trial they had participated in within a three-month period, with but one exception: they were asked to report on only every third trial by the most frequent mixed tribunals (*Schöffengerichte*), which are composed of one professional and two lay judges. The overall number of trials reported about was 570 (Casper and Zeisel, 1972, p. 570).

Lay judges were not perceived to be very active during trial; the majority did not ask any questions (Caper and Zeisel, 1972, p. 150). However, this summary masks an important difference: while in the majority of the cases tried at the *Schöffengericht* or the *Grosse Strafkammer* (54% and 60%, respectively) professional judges reported that lay judges did not ask questions at all, in the majority of cases (67%) tried at the *Schwurgericht*, the majority of professional judges said not only that lay judges asked questions, but that their questions were questions of merit ("good questions"). This is an important finding, especially in light of the fact that cases tried at the *Schwurgericht* were estimated to be more difficult, that evidence was more complex (Tables 14 and 15, Casper and Zeisel, 1972, p. 149), and that trials lasted longer (Casper and Zeisel, 1972, p. 150). Furthermore, although confessions were almost as frequent in the cases tried at other courts as they were in the cases tried by the *Schwurgericht* (Table 9, Casper and Zeisel, 1972, p. 146), deliberations either with or without full confession were longer at the *Schwurgericht* (Casper and Zeisel, 1972, p. 151). Two factors seem to have contributed to this finding. First, cases tried by the *Schwurgericht* were the most serious, resulting in or aiming at the victim's death. Second, the composition and size of the tribunal that tried cases at the *Schwurgericht* was very different from the other tribunals; the tribunal was composed of nine members (three professional judges and six lay judges), whereas the other two tribunals had up to five members (*Schöffengericht*: one professional judge and two lay judges; *Grosse Strafkammer*: three professional judges and two lay judges). Overall, it seems that group interaction and its dynamics were different in the *Schwurgericht* than in other courts.

Casper and Zeisel (1972) examined the issue of initial disagreement and the way it was resolved. They reported that, according to professional judges, disagreements were more frequent on sentencing issues than on the question of guilt (Casper and Zeisel, 1972, p. 153).[1] When cases with full confessions were excluded from the analysis, the pattern of disagreements on guilt was clear: as the number of judges in the tribunal increased, disagreements became more likely (Casper and Zeisel, 1972, p. 152), being the most frequent at the *Schwurgericht*. Overall, professional judges reported that the cases tried at the *Schwurgericht* had a substantially higher percentage of initial disagreements between professional judges and lay judges on both guilt and sentencing issues than the cases tried at either the *Schöffengericht* or the *Grosse Strafkammer* (Tables 22 and 24, Casper and Zeisel, 1972, p. 153-154). The researchers (Casper and Zeisel, 1972, p. 153) also reported that lay judges disagreed more frequently with professional judges when professional judges disagreed between or among themselves.

The study further explored the intensity of disagreement. Casper and Zeisel focused on two tribunals that each had two lay judges — the *Schöffengericht* and the *Grosse Strafkammer*. They reported that about one-half of the cases in which there was an initial disagreement between professional judges and lay judges featured the initial disagreement of only one lay judge (Casper and Zeisel, 1972, p. 154), whereas the other half featured an even stronger disagreement — that of both lay judges. Interesting patterns emerged: when only one lay judge disagreed on the issue of guilt, the lay judge was more likely to favor the defendant than to favor the prosecution, whereas in the cases in which both lay judges disagreed, lay judges were equally likely to favor the defendant as they were to favor the prosecution (Table 26, Casper and Zeisel, 1972, p. 154).

Casper and Zeisel (1972) found that in 19 out of 34 *Schöffengericht* and *Grosse Strafkammer* cases (misdemeanors, felonies, less serious crimes, minor political offenses) in which there was initial disagreement on guilt, "professional judges said that the evaluation of evidence was a task of some difficulty" (Casper and Zeisel, 1972, p. 155). Lay judges were twelve times more likely to

---

[1]This finding is consistent with the results reported in the Polish study (Kubicki and Zawadzki, 1970).

disagree on the issue of guilt if the evidence in the case was complex and the conclusion was not simple than if the evidence in the case was clear and the conclusion was simple (Casper and Zeisel, 1972, p. 164), which clearly suggests that complexity of evidence was related to frequency of disagreement. As for the direction of disagreement, in the 19 cases in which professional and lay judges disagreed on the question of guilt, lay judges were more lenient in 11 cases and more severe in 8 cases (Casper and Zeisel, 1972, p. 157).

The authors also tried to study the factors which might influence lay judges to disagree in a particular case. In minor cases prior criminal record was not important, whereas in more serious cases lay judges relied on prior criminal record to prove that the defendant was dangerous (Casper and Zeisel, 1972). According to professional judges, lay judges were sometimes guided by such factors as the personality of the defendants, unattractiveness, nationality, defendants' lifestyle, morality, and prejudices towards professional drivers in traffic accidents. In quite a number of cases, more than a single factor seemed to matter. For example, in a case of attempted robbery, lay judges found three factors to be important: the defendant's pleasant personality, the store owner's bad reputation, and the fact that the defendant was a foreigner[2] (Casper and Zeisel, 1972, p. 159).

Similar issues surfaced when lay judges disagreed with professional judges on sentencing and took into account such extrinsic factors as defendants' illness, nationality, poor financial situation, deprivation in childhood, hard times, age, different standards of negligence for professional drivers and medical doctors. In a case in which the defendant, a doctor, drove under the influence of alcohol, hit another car, and caused damage below 1,000 DM, the lay judge who favored more severe punishment argued that, "when a doctor commits an offense like this, his guilt must be viewed as being greater than that of an ordinary citizen" (Casper and Zeisel, 1972, p. 170).

---

[2]One of the lay judges stated that he had a "weakness for all foreignness" because he, being Jewish, had lived abroad during the war.

Finally, it is interesting to examine how disagreements were resolved. Out of all disagreements regarding guilt (6.5% of all cases), lay judges affected the verdict in 21% of such cases; furthermore, in disagreements on sentence, lay judges affected 22% of the decisions (Casper and Zeisel, 1972, p. 187-188). However, it is crucial to understand that this impact on the verdict was measured exclusively as the impact on the cases with initial disagreement in which the lay judge won, whereas other studies tell us that the lay judges' initial disagreements ended in a compromise much more frequently than in the lay judge's *votum separatum*. This study, however, suggests that lay judges were more likely to surrender than to compromise (Tables 38 and 39, Casper and Zeisel, 1972, p. 187, 188). This leads to the earlier conclusion: when all the cases were examined, including those with a full confession, lay judges affected the verdict in 1.4% of the cases (Casper and Zeisel, 1972, p. 189). The authors (Casper and Zeisel, 1972, p. 189) concluded that:

> The traceable overall effect of the lay judges on the verdicts of the German criminal courts is indeed small. Whether it is politically negligible as well is difficult to say. The answer depends upon the goals one seeks to accomplish through lay participation.

Casper and Zeisel's study (1972) on mixed tribunals in Germany reported results on the issue of lay judges' contribution which were in sharp contrast to those presented in the Polish study (Pomorski, 1975). When all cases were examined, including those with full confessions, lay judges in Casper and Zeisel's study affected the verdict in a mere 1.4% of all cases (1972, p. 189), whereas the Polish lay judges were found to impact the verdict in as many as 40% of all cases (Kubicki and Zawadzki, 1970, p. 106). How can such huge differences between the two be explained?

First, the methodology may account for much of the reported discrepancies: Casper and Zeisel, using the same method Kalven and Zeisel used in *The American Jury* (1966), relied on the professional judges' impression of the deliberation process. Serious doubts about the accuracy of results may be raised if only one party in the interaction is asked to evaluate both its own behavior and the behavior of the other party. The authors themselves were well-aware of this problem (Casper and Zeisel, 1972, p. 189):

> We had no opportunity to hear from the lay judges in the trials and it is possible that they have a different view of what goes on or is prevented from going on in the deliberation room.

Second, while researchers in Poland considered cases in which professional judges were not absolutely dominant, resulting in 40% of the cases in which lay judges had some explicit influence, Casper and Zeisel (1972) assumed that lay judges influenced cases only when they initially disagreed with professional judges, including in the calculations even the cases with full confessions (where disagreement over the issue of guilt was not very realistic). Casper and Zeisel's assumption of the lack of lay judges' influence in the absence of disagreement with professional judges thus disregarded the lay judges' latent function.

Frassine *et al.* (1979) conducted a study on mixed tribunals in Austria in 1967. The methodology was very similar to the one employed by Casper and Zeisel (1972) in the German study.[3] Nineteen professional judges, members of mixed tribunals composed of two professional judges and two lay judges, were asked to observe and record their deliberations in criminal cases. The cases included in the study involved 550 defendants (Frassine *et al.*, 1979, p. 89).

The study focused on the perceived frequency of initial disagreements between professional judges and lay judges on the issues of guilt and sentence, the reasons for such disagreements, and the ways of resolving them. According to professional judges, lay judges disagreed with them on the issues of guilt very infrequently (in less than 10% of the cases with no confessions and in less than 5% of all the cases) and, when they did disagree, their opinion favored the defendant much more frequently than it favored the prosecution (Frassine *et al.*, 1979, p. 91). Similar to the results reported by Casper and Zeisel (1972), lay judges were perceived to be more likely to disagree when the evidence was not clear than when the evidence was clear (Frassine *et al.*, 1979, p. 104).

---

[3]This is by no means surprising because one of the co-authors of Frassine *et al.* (1979) was Hans Zeisel.

Out of all the initial disagreements, most (60%) were resolved because lay judges have changed their opinion; thirty-two percent featured a direct impact of lay judges either because professional judges changed their opinion or because lay judges persisted with a *votum separatum* (Frassine *et al.*, 1979, p. 92). Overall, in 3% of the cases without confession (1.5% of all the cases) lay judges had a direct impact on the decision on guilt in the case.

Professional judges in Austria, just like their counterparts in Germany, were more likely to say that lay judges disagreed more frequently with them on the issue of sentence. However, disagreement was still not very frequent; professional judges said that lay judges initially disagreed with them in 27% of the cases (Frassine *et al.*, 1979, p. 105), and an initial disagreement on sentence was more likely when there was an initial disagreement on guilt (Table 17, Frassine *et al.*, 1979, p. 118).

Unlike disagreements on guilt, the lay judges' disagreements on sentencing were distributed in a more equitable fashion; when an initial disagreement on sentencing surfaced, according to professional judges, lay judges were as likely to argue for a more lenient sanction as they were to push for a harsher sanction. The only cases in which lay judges made some direct impact on the sentence were the cases in which both lay judges disagreed with professional judges and argued for a more lenient punishment (Frassine *et al.*, 1979, p. 106), because professional judges persuaded lay judges to change their opinion in the majority of cases with initial disagreement on sentence (66%). The final impact lay judges had on the sanction was not very strong; lay judges were perceived to make some impact in only 3% of all the cases, mostly by making the decision more lenient (Frassine *et al.*, 1979, p. 106).

According to professional judges, the most dominant reasons for more lenient/harsher sanctions expressed by lay judges were the characteristics of the defendant and, to a lesser degree, characteristics of the offense itself (Frassine *et al.*, 1979, p. 116). Overall, in the majority of the cases, the lay judges' initial sentencing decision was identical to the final sentence (because disagreement on sentence was not very frequent); this was especially the case for less serious sanctions (Frassine *et al.*, 1979, p. 119).

Approximately at the same time, another researcher in Germany was studying mixed tribunals, but his methodology and aim were different. By interviewing professional judges and lay judges who participated in criminal cases, Klausa (1972) wanted to obtain their general opinion about mixed tribunals, as well as their opinion about the selection process. As a part of a larger study which examined the impact and perceived contributions by lay judges in mixed tribunals in various branches of law (e.g., criminal law, administrative law, financial law, labor law), Klausa interviewed 124 professional judges and 191 lay judges. I will provide a brief summary of his findings as they pertain to the area of criminal law. In particular, I will focus on the subset of 39 professional judges and 56 lay judges who decided criminal cases.

Surprisingly, there was a great level of agreement between professional judges and lay judges about the importance of lay participation; two out of three professional judges and almost all lay judges perceived lay participation in a favorable light (either as a "great advantage" or as an "advantage;" Klausa, 1972, p. 54), and very few of the professional judges (13%) and none of the lay judges reported that lay participation should be abolished.

When asked to specify reasons for their opinion, professional judges were somewhat more skeptical of lay participation than lay judges were. Professional judges and lay judges resorted to typical positive features of lay participation: legitimacy of decisions, democracy, and latent function. Professional judges and lay judges who tried juvenile cases perceived these functions in even more positive terms than their counterparts who engaged in trials of adult offenders (Klausa, 1972, p. 69). For example, none of the professional judges who tried juvenile cases voted for the abolition of lay participation. In addition to the common themes expressed by the respondents from adult courts, the respondents from juvenile courts also added the educational experience and pedagogy as important functions performed by lay judges (Klausa, 1972, p. 70).

In terms of criticisms of lay participation, professional judges emphasized the lack of ability to understand the law, subjectivity, emotionalism, and a problematic selection process, as well as the expense, outvoting of professional judges, and lost time. Lay judges were more uniform in their critique; they emphasized problems with their selection process, emotionalism, and the lack of knowledge about the law (Klausa, 1972, p. 69).

The study also incorporated questions about lay judges' abilities to understand the law and evaluate evidence. At the outset, the majority of professional judges evaluated the intellectual level of lay judges as "average" (Klausa, 1972, p. 71). It was, therefore, not surprising that the overwhelming majority of professional judges (85%; Klausa, 1972, p. 73) perceived that lay judges understand evidence, but only the minority (42%) perceived that lay judges understand legal issues. By contrast, the majority of lay judges perceived the material presented to be "interesting and understandable" (Klausa, 1972, p. 75).

Professional judges (74% of the professional judges for adult offenders and 50% of the professional judges for juveniles) perceived that lay judges made a difference in terms of the final outcome of the case (Klausa, 1972, p. 76). Deliberations were not perceived as being consistently and systematically dominated by professional judges. In fact, the majority of lay judges perceived that professional judges collaborated with them gladly (Klausa, 1972, p. 76). Klausa (1972, p. 213) further concluded that lay judges participated more frequently when professional judges accepted them as partners.

The majority of professional judges reported that they had been outvoted by lay judges during their career, and an even greater percentage of lay judges (whose "careers" as lay judges are much shorter than those of professional judges) said that they had experienced the same (Klausa, 1972, p. 77). Interestingly, a number of professional judges sent a very clear message about the importance of lay judges' participation; they emphasized that experienced professional judges cannot be outvoted, that is, that there were methods to be used to persuade lay judges. Klausa (1972, p. 79) argued that lay judges probably had some impact, but the observed discrepancy in the perceived frequency of outvoting was a result of the fact that formal outvoting of lay judges probably happened rarely because, although there were initial disagreements (especially on sanctions), initial disagreements were most often resolved in a compromise and thus did not result in outvoting. The overall impression, however, was that the impact of lay judges may not be all that important (Klausa, 1972, p. 79):

> The presiding judge can generally neutralize the impact of lay judges. That is particularly true for the three professional judges in the criminal tribunal. If they withhold the necessary information from lay judges, lay judges may not make a decision. In addition to information, lay judges need encouragement. This has been confirmed by many interviewed professional judges in all branches of law, who lean toward the professional tribunal. Some also added that many of their colleagues perceive that [encouragement] as a burden, and that lay judges seemed to them like juveniles.

Lay judges had generally positive attitudes about their service; the majority said that they would agree to be reelected (Klausa, 1972, p. 76) and that their opinion about lay judges' role improved over time (Klausa, 1972, p. 74). Lay judges and professional judges both had ideas for further improvement of the system of mixed tribunals. While professional judges emphasized a better selection process, better education of lay judges, the introduction of "blue-ribbon lay judges," and the dismissal of lay judges not eager to participate, lay judges, in addition to these same factors, also placed emphasis on gaining access to the case file.

Another study conducted in Germany in the 1960s, much like Casper and Zeisel's study (1972), also relied on answers provided only by professional judges. Görlitz (1970) distributed questionnaires to 70 professional judges at administrative courts. Although six out of ten professional judges showed a positive general opinion about lay judges, only the minority of professional judges (39%) said that lay judges performed their duties and slightly fewer than one-half of professional judges (43%) said that lay judges contributed nothing or almost nothing to the decision-making process (Görlitz, 1970, p. 194-195). Not surprisingly, professional judges who said that their general opinion about lay judges was negative were also more likely to say that lay judges contributed very little or virtually nothing at all (Görlitz, 1970, p. 195). Conversely, professional judges who evaluated lay judges in a positive light were more likely to say that lay judges performed their expected role. Görlitz (1970, p. 197) summarized the results in the following way: "It is clear that, despite the widespread positive general opinion about lay participation, the overwhelming majority of professional judges did not accept this institution in the form determined by the official ideology of the organization."

According to the majority of professional judges (90%), disagreements with lay judges occurred very infrequently or never (Görlitz, 1970, p. 228). Furthermore, professional judges who said that lay judges did not contribute toward the decisions were also more likely to say that lay judges did not disagree with them. Finally, Görlitz (1970, p. 306) concluded:

> The research conducted in the administrative jurisdiction of Hessen clearly manifested that lay judges are outsiders in organizational terms who practically do not participate in the process of decision-making. That way, the purpose of lay participation, which is social control of judicial power, was not fulfilled ... The tendency to perceive lay judges as a political counterbalance or institutionalized public would negate the results of research and would entail the hiding of reality.

Kamhi and Čalija (1974) conducted a study on mixed tribunals in 1969 in the Republic of Bosnia and Herzegovina (which was at the time a part of the former socialist Yugoslavia). The authors distributed questionnaires to 100 professional judges and 196 lay judges from district and regional courts across the Republic. Since the majority (84%) of all professional judges suggested that lay judges showed more interest in criminal cases than in civil cases, it would have been interesting to compare the answers about lay judges' activity given by professional judges who decided civil cases with the answers given by professional judges who decided criminal cases. Unfortunately, the authors did not conduct such an analysis; similarly, the answers provided by the respondents who decided cases at district courts were not separated from those provided by their counterparts from regional courts. The reasons for the lay judges' greater interest in criminal cases, according to the respondents, were the nature of criminal law (which is less complex than civil law), the presence of logic (which is more emphasized in criminal cases), and the perception that social relationships regulated by criminal law are familiar to the average citizen.

The first part of the study by Kamhi and Čalija (1974) focused on the interest of lay judges to participate in legal decision-making. The majority of professional judges (71%; Kamhi and Čalija, 1974, p. 42) stated that lay judges were not motivated to participate because they had to leave work, lay judges' role was perceived as a burden, lay judges' role was imposed upon lay judges by the Communist party, and the majority of retired persons (who were over-represented relative to other age groups) regarded their lay judges' duty as a method of disposing of abundant amounts of free time (Kamhi and Čalija, 1974, p. 43-44). Professional judges emphasized that the length of service was negatively related to the interest in participating; more experienced lay judges were more likely to display a lower level of interest.

The overwhelming majority of lay judges reported that they did not perceive their duty as a burden, but rather as an honorary duty which they were glad to perform (Kamhi and Čalija, 1974, p. 51). Lay judges who evaluated their duty as a burden offered several reasons for their opinion; some of these reasons resembled those expressed by professional judges (absence from work), while others were unique to their perspective (participation in the trials in which they were not familiar with the topic of the trial, a lack of respect by the presiding professional judge; Kamhi and Čalija, 1974, p. 51-52). Although the majority of professional judges emphasized distinctly that lay judges felt more comfortable deciding criminal cases and even provided reasons for their opinion, less than one-half of lay judges agreed with them (Kamhi and Čalija,

1974, p. 52); one-third of lay judges said that they felt more comfortable making legal decisions in civil cases, 46% said the same about criminal cases, while 22% said that the type of case did not make any difference.

The substantial majority of lay judges (95%) reported that they responded to the court's mail and a surprisingly high percentage of the same lay judges (38%) said that they had been summoned over the phone or by courier to come to the court immediately to replace lay judges who had not responded to the court's mail (Kamhi and Čalija, 1974, p. 55). A rather predictable finding was that three out of four professional judges reported that the participation of lay judges had a significant impact on the speed with which trials proceeded. According to the majority of respondents, this finding was primarily driven by the difficulties in obtaining a required number of lay judges every morning so that the court could operate without delays and continuances; it was not a consequence of the extent of the impact lay judges had on trials and/or deliberations (Kamhi and Čalija, 1974, p. 56).

A part of the survey included questions about the perceived frequency and importance of lay judges' activity. According to professional judges, the majority of lay judges did not touch upon the issues of merit and mostly discussed peripheral and less important issues; 16% of professional judges reported that lay judges discussed the issues of merit and an additional 16% reported that lay judges partially discussed the issues of merit (Kamhi and Čalija, 1974, p. 60). The main reasons why few lay judges discussed the issues of merit in the case were perceived to be their lack of legal knowledge, low educational level in general, lack of interest in participating in general, and the inability to summon lay judges well in advance and provide them with an opportunity to familiarize themselves with the case (Kamhi and Čalija, 1974, p. 60).

Kamhi and Čalija (1974) also examined the contribution lay judges made to the tribunal. They did not measure the initial disagreement nor how disagreement was resolved; rather, they asked whether the verdicts were reached as unanimous or majority verdicts. Seventy-five percent of professional judges and lay judges agreed that the verdicts were unanimous. Consequently, the researchers concluded that lay judges contributed actively in 25% of all the cases (Kamhi and Čalija, 1974, p. 65), mostly on sentencing issues in criminal cases. Lay judges argued that the discrepancy on sentencing issues did not occur as a result of their lack of legal knowledge about criminal sanctions, but rather out of the impressions that their sense of fairness may not have overlapped completely with the outcome of the case if the criminal code were followed (Kamhi and Čalija, 1974, p. 76).

Lay judges had a more positive outlook on their ability to participate in trials than professional judges did; four out of five lay judges said that, despite their lack of legal knowledge, they could be equal partners to professional judges (Kamhi and Čalija, 1974, p. 69). Lay judges further argued that the obstacles that disallowed or diminished active participation did not stem from their lack of legal knowledge; rather, they were primarily centered around the lack of information about and insufficient preparation for trials.

Furthermore, the majority of lay judges perceived that professional judges had a very professional attitude toward them and required of them to state their opinion frequently. If true, these results would contradict the usual criticism that lay judges are not very active during trial or deliberation.

In the cases with disagreement, the majority of professional judges (58%; Kamhi and Čalija, 1974, p. 67, 78) reported that they had never been in a position in which they had to accept the lay judges' opinion on how the case was to be ultimately resolved. On the other hand, as many as 54% of lay judges reported that they encountered such events, although *very rarely*. Interestingly, the majority of professional judges (54%; Kamhi and Čalija, 1974, p. 66) reported that they had experienced being outvoted by lay judges at least once during their career (although, admittedly, such instances were very rare).

The professional judges' overall opinion about lay judges and their participation was not very positive. In fact, 40% of the professional judges reported that lay judges had no impact on the verdict (i.e., their participation neither improved nor decreased the quality of the decision), while 23% reported that the decisions would have been more correct had lay judges not participated in the decision-making (Kamhi and Čalija, 1974, p. 85). Kamhi and Čalija (1974, p. 59) provided the following description of their findings:

> Lay judges are not only equals to professional judges according to the law, but they also constitute the majority in each tribunal. However, because of professional superiority of professional judges, in practice lay judges, despite the formal equality with professional judges and their numerical advantages, end up occupying the inferior position. In such conditions, they, according to the opinion of many, leave the trial and decision-making to professional judges — experts. And, to make attitudes even more negative, since the tribunal includes only one professional judge, in practice collective decision-making becomes individual decision-making.

That the overwhelming majority of professional judges advocated changes in the then existing system of mixed tribunals was by no means surprising (Kamhi and Čalija, 1974, p. 91). Professional judges were more likely to recommend that lay judges and the system of mixed tribunals be retained in criminal cases than to make such a recommendation for civil cases; furthermore, most respondents (78%) believed that the scope of mixed tribunals should be limited to trials in the first instance (Kamhi and Čalija, 1974, p. 93). Lay judges had a more positive opinion about the system of mixed tribunals in general and they wanted to retain lay judges in both civil and criminal cases; ninety percent of lay judges perceived that lay judges were very useful in the legal decision-making process (Kamhi and Čalija, 1974, p. 94), primarily because of the reasons of legitimacy, democracy, and deterrence of professional judges' misconduct.

In regard to improving the system, both professional judges and lay judges agreed that lay judges did not receive as much assistance from professional judges as they needed. Both groups believed that lay judges would have been more active had the professional judge provided more assistance (Kamhi and Čalija, 1974, p. 107). The respondents also proposed the introduction of short seminars for lay judges, the purpose of which would have been to familiarize lay judges with their rights and responsibilities as lay judges.

Another study in which lay judges were not perceived as very active during trial and deliberation was conducted in Hungary by Kulcsár (1972). As a result of the author's negative findings, the Hungarian Ministry of Justice curtailed the use of lay judges, limiting their presence only to serious criminal cases and family and divorce cases.

Kulcsár (1972, 1982) included over 1,000 lay judges (450 lay judges from Budapest and 773 lay judges from other areas of Hungary) and over 100 professional judges into his study. The majority of the lay judges were quite experienced because they had been elected at least three years before they participated in the study. There was a clear discrepancy between the occupational profile of the surveyed lay judges and that of the general population. Furthermore, even among the surveyed lay judges, there was a core group that had been called to perform their duty more frequently than other lay judges (Kulcsár, 1982, p. 69); forty-three percent of professional judges reported that they customarily made proposals to call in certain lay judges (Kulcsár, 1982, p. 71). However, Kulcsár (1982, p. 66) was well-aware of the potential problems this may have created; he emphasized that this may have had a negative impact on lay judges because they may have been strongly influenced by the organization and the expectations that the organization imposed upon them and, consequently, less likely to bring the fresh, unjaded input of citizens unburdened by the court system and its expectations.

A comparison of lay judges' and professional judges' opinion on a variety of sentencing issues, as well as on a variety of general issues (including family, social, and moral issues) showed that lay judges were more conservative (Kulcsár, 1982, p. 76-78). Although professional judges said very rarely that they would have *ever* reached a wrong judgment if it were not for lay judges (14%), the majority of lay judges perceived that professional judges welcomed their participation (Kulcsár, 1982, p. 95). It is very revealing to contrast this perception of being generally welcome to participate in the work of the tribunal with the next finding.

Kulcsár (1982, p. 95) reported a very interesting result: while approximately one-half of lay judges had an opinion that was in disagreement with the professional judge's opinion, the majority of them (55% in Budapest and 72% in other regions) did not express their disagreement. It is quite possible that lay judges did not *openly* express their disagreement with professional judges because they felt that professional judges either would not consider their opinion or would accept it only rarely (52% of lay judges in Budapest and 68% in other areas reported that professional judges either never or rarely accepted their opinion; Kulcsár, 1982, p. 96). Rather, lay judges tried to find a way to incorporate their opinion and to shape the direction in which the discussion was going without actually creating a confrontational atmosphere in the tribunal. Indeed, the results showed that the perceived acceptance of their opinion by a professional judge and the willingness to express that opinion were related. While the lay judges who said that they rarely expressed their differing opinion were more likely to say that their opinion was rarely accepted by professional judges, the lay judges who said that they expressed their differing opinion more often were more likely to say that professional judges repeatedly accepted their opinion (Kulcsár, 1982, p. 97). Therefore, the results of this study challenge the validity of the results reported in the studies in which the researchers asked *only* professional judges to report on lay judges' disagreement; such studies took into consideration only the opinion about *explicit* disagreements as perceived by professional judges, while there still may have been plenty of room for lay judges to try to persuade professional judges indirectly, that is, without stating their differing opinion explicitly.

One of the crucial elements for a successful decision is the process of information gathering. Professional judges typically enjoy an advantage because they have access to the case file. The results of the Hungarian study also showed that lay judges rarely read the case file (Kulcsár, 1982, p. 101). Kulcsár (1982, p. 102) recorded that reading the case file or collecting preliminary information about the case in general before the trial started was related to the frequency of asking questions of merit during trial and making comments of merit during deliberation.[4]

Lay judges were not perceived as very active either during trial or during deliberation. The overwhelming majority (70% in Budapest and 82% in other areas) did not report asking any questions during trial (Kulcsár, 1982, p. 103), but lay judges were perceived to be somewhat more active while trying certain types of criminal cases, such as violent crimes and "crimes against the family, youth, and sexual morals" (40% of lay judges asked questions of merit in those cases, as opposed to lower percentages in criminal trials in general — 22% for Budapest and 14% for other areas; Kulcsár, 1982, p. 104). The majority of lay judges were not perceived as making substantial contributions to the subject discussed during deliberation either; Kulcsár (1982, p. 105) reported that the majority of lay judges (51% in Budapest and 67% in other areas) did not make *any* comments of merit during deliberation. Those who made comments of merit usually focused on sentencing issues (Kulcsár, 1982, p. 113). In fact, Kulcsár (1982, p. 109) wrote that, "the ratio of opposing votes by the people's assessors is so low that it can hardly be expressed in percentages."

One of the more recent studies is the study by Gerken (1988). It was conducted on a relatively small sample of respondents; Gerken interviewed 20 lay judges and distributed questionnaires to an additional 25 lay judges (1988, p. 105). The results of her study pertaining to the election process and qualifications of juvenile lay judges were presented in Chapter 2. Here, I will focus on Gerken's results concerning the interaction in the tribunal and lay judges' contribution toward the work of the tribunal.

Lay judges expressed their concerns regarding the possibility of their effective participation during trial, partially because of their perceived inability to

---

[4]Thirty-three percent of lay judges who obtained preliminary information (by reading the case file or by asking questions of the professional judge) asked questions of merit, as opposed to 12% of those who did not obtain preliminary information about the case. Similarly, 49% of those who obtained preliminary information made comments of merit, as opposed to 18% of those who did not obtain preliminary information about the case.

formulate questions in the "proper" way and partially because they perceived that professional judges saw them as a burden on the road toward a more efficient trial (Gerken, 1988, p. 110). Furthermore, not having access to the case file turned out to be perceived as a real obstacle for successful participation (Gerken, 1988, p. 111). Overall, lay judges felt that they were being suppressed into a subordinate role (Gerken, 1988, p. 121).

Deliberation was perceived as a more relaxed forum where lay judges could state their opinion (unless they were pressured by time). Another factor that had an impact on the lay judges' willingness to participate actively was the smooth way in which professional judges presented their arguments. The most prominent and active role lay judges performed reportedly took place during the part of deliberation that focused on sanctions or educational measures (since the defendants were juveniles). However, appreciating the purposes of educational measures (as opposed to sanctions for adults) and the spectrum of these educational measures were also a problem (Gerken, 1988, p. 111). Typical problems pinpointed by lay judges included the lack of ability to determine the relative severity of the case and the moral dilemma they encountered in the process of sentencing someone to a prison term.

It is particularly interesting that lay judges who tried juvenile cases were supposed to be professionals in juvenile education, persons who were more likely to understand and be able to lead the discussion in terms of purposes of educational measures, yet, according to Gerken (1988), lay judges did not fulfill these requirements. Not surprisingly, such lay judges were not very helpful in drawing the line and distinguishing between the purposes of punishments for adult and juvenile offenders.

In a study conducted in Croatia, then a part of the former Yugoslavia, Ljubanović (1983, 1989) distributed short questionnaires to 16 presidents of district and regional courts, 101 lay judges, 30 professional judges, 4 state attorneys, and 4 defense attorneys. Lay judges were surveyed at 16 courts, at which the exact numbers of lay judges elected to serve varied from 47 lay judges at the smallest court to 340 lay judges at the largest court, with an average of 138 lay judges per court (Ljubanović, 1983, p. 143). It is possible that there was selection bias. Ljubanović (1989, p. 63) stated that, "for example, 340 lay judges were elected for the District Court of Osijek, out of whom we surveyed 5, who participated, on average, in 69 trials per year. Similarly, 139 lay judges were elected for the District Court of Vukovar, and 7 surveyed lay judges participated on average in 60 trials annually." Furthermore, the results suggested that the surveyed lay judges were quite an experienced group; on average, these lay judges participated in trials 24 times over the course of the preceding year (Ljubanović, 1983, p. 186). Specifically, two-thirds of the surveyed lay judges participated in trials more than 10 times over the course of the preceding year, and some had participated as many as 85 or even 100 times (Ljubanović, 1983, p. 186). In addition to telling us something about the practice employed by the courts involved in the study, these summary statistics also tell us plenty about the bias in the sample.

Ljubanović (1983, 1989) focused on several issues, starting with the election process and the actual summons of lay judges to the court. He reported that lay judges were elected in a timely fashion, although the selection process typically included some deviations from the letter of the law. For example, although the opinion about potential lay judges should be given by all the professional judges from a particular court, Ljubanović found that only the presidents of courts provided their opinion about the candidates;[5] the majority of professional judges reported that they did not have *any* impact on the selection of potential lay judges. Although one of the requirements for the lay judges was the ability to perform the lay judge's duty, Ljubanović's study (1983, 1989) suggested that the courts and other bodies involved in the election process neither knew how to evaluate this ability nor developed mechanisms for its evaluation. Furthermore, although the law required that lay judges who refuse to perform their duty by not replying to the court summons should be dismissed from their duty, the results obtained by Ljubanović (1983, 1989) suggested that this was not the case; instead of dismissing those lay judges,

---

[5]This practice was recently build into law. See Chapter 3 for details.

court presidents opted not to summon them again and instead repeatedly called the "reliable" lay judges.

The majority of court presidents and lay judges agreed that most lay judges were interested in performing their functions (Ljubanović, 1983, p. 193-194). In terms of their actual participation in trials, the majority of professional judges said that lay judges obtained at least some level of preparation for trials, although this preparation frequently amounted only to oral summation by the professional judge immediately before the trial started. An unusually high percentage (44%) of (quite experienced) lay judges reported that they familiarized themselves with case files before trials started. They were also perceived to be rather active during trial; according to the opinion expressed by approximately one-half of professional judges, lay judges were perceived to follow trials carefully and the majority actually asked questions during trials (Ljubanović, 1983, p. 210). Although the overwhelming majority of lay judges also reported that they followed trials carefully, only one-quarter of them said that they had asked questions of defendants, witnesses, and expert witnesses (Ljubanović, 1983, p. 213).

Lay judges turned out to be even more active during deliberation; two-thirds of lay judges said that they participated actively during deliberation and voting (Ljubanović, 1983, p. 247) and approximately one-half of lay judges reported that they stated their opinion openly and did not merely accept the opinion expressed by professional judges (Ljubanović, 1983, p. 221). Despite such a powerful statement about their own frequency of contribution, lay judges claimed that decisions were made unanimously because disagreeing opinions were harmonized. The statements by professional judges tell us more about the way these disagreeing opinions became harmonized. Although approximately one-half of professional judges stated that they had cases during their careers in which the disagreement persisted until after the voting, they predominantly said that in such cases lay judges held the minority vote (Ljubanović, 1983, p. 218). A number of professional judges said that they actually accepted the lay judge's opinion in very few such cases; according to professional judges, in the great majority of such cases the lay judge was the one who changed his/her opinion and accepted the professional judge's opinion. Consistent with the findings of earlier studies (e.g., Casper and Zeisel, 1972), it seems that most of the (initial) disagreements in the tribunals were resolved in a simple way — lay judges changed their opinion.

Lay judges said that professional judges helped them perform their function either by explaining the relevant legal rules, by familiarizing them with the case, or by summarizing the evidence (Ljubanović, 1983, p. 226). Indeed, professional judges were quite aware that they might have helped the lay judges by familiarizing them with the case before the trial started.

Not surprisingly, the overwhelming majority of lay judges and a substantial number of professional judges said that lay judges were quite resistant to outside influences (Ljubanović, 1983, p. 228-229). A surprisingly large percentage of professional judges (77%), especially in view of the corresponding percentages reported by other studies (e.g., Kamhi and Čalija, 1974), reported that they found lay participation to be useful (Ljubanović, 1983, p. 242). Professional judges who explained their opinion stated that lay judges had extensive experience, that they knew local customs and norms, and that some of the lay judges had specific expert knowledge or skills useful for certain cases (Ljubanović, 1983, p. 242). It is quite interesting to contrast this general positive opinion about the usefulness of lay judges in the decision-making process with the professional judges' answers to the question about the frequency of decisions in which the decision would have been wrong if no lay judges were present. In particular, only one out of 30 professional judges (3%) and 7 out of 101 lay judges (7%) said that they had such a case (Ljubanović, 1983, p. 245).

Professional judges typically complained about the lay judges who refused to perform their duty, which resulted in the aforementioned solution wherein the same group of lay judges was constantly being called to the court (Ljubanović, 1983, p. 251). Consequently, the ideas for the improvement of the system were partially focused on the election process — selection of lay judges who were not too occupied with their careers and who showed genuine interest in participation. Interestingly, the majority of professional judges in the study (80%) argued that the current system of mixed tribunals should not be changed and, at the same time, that the jurisdiction of mixed tribunals should not be extended to appellate decisions (Ljubanović, 1983, p. 254).

A part of the potential contribution made by lay judges (one of the positive features of trials with lay participants) includes their educational role. The majority of lay judges did not discuss their duty as lay judges with the citizens and they perceived that the citizens were not interested in hearing about their experience (Ljubanović, 1983, p. 230, 232).

The most recent study on mixed tribunals was conducted in Finland and Sweden. Klami and Hämäläinen (1992) distributed detailed questionnaires to 36 Swedish professional judges, 80 Swedish lay judges, 46 Finnish professional judges, and 190 Finnish lay judges. The purpose of the study was dual: to obtain general opinions about positive and negative features of lay participation and to obtain comparable estimates of appropriate decision in three hypothetical scenarios.

Respondents were asked to pick the three strongest reasons for the introduction of lay participants into the legal decision-making process by agreeing or disagreeing (on a five-point scale) with the statements summarizing positive features of lay participation. There was a striking (although not entirely unexpected) difference; while lay judges perceived that they provided an important contribution to the tribunal by fulfilling various positive functions of lay participation, professional judges painted a much gloomier picture about the realization of these positive features. In particular, lay judges were more likely to argue that there were important reasons for lay participation.[6] Lay judges primarily perceived that the reasons for the introduction of lay participants included participation of different social groups, group decision-making,

---

[6]For 10 out of 12 statements the scores for lay judges were higher than the scores for professional judges, sometimes even as many as 2 points on a five-point scale (Klami and Hämäläinen, 1992, p. 55).

knowledge of local norms and customs, confidence in the decisions, and general arguments of democracy. Professional judges, on the other hand, did not perceive any of these reasons to be as important as lay judges did. In fact, both Finnish and Swedish professional judges perceived the "latent function" to be the most important contribution/function — "when lay judges are participating in adjudication, the professional judge must make his reasoning understandable to them" (Klami and Hämäläinen, 1992, p. 55). The authors further wrote (Klami and Hämäläinen, 1992, p. 56):

> Lawyers do not think that lay judges are any significant factor when protection of minorities is concerned: neither do they think that lay judges fulfil any particularly democratic function ... Swedish lay judges do not really think that they are a factor counterbalancing professional severity ... Neither do they think that laymen have any particular abilities when sanctions are chosen ... Finnish judges do not really think that lay judges — as they are now appointed — are promoting democracy or the confidence of people in the judiciary.

Discrepancies were not as large for the set of questions dealing with negative features of trials by mixed tribunals. A set of nine statements was presented to the respondents, who had either to agree or disagree with the statements involving typical criticisms of lay participation ("Mr. Prejudice," "Mrs. Sympathy," leniency), as well as with the statements describing their interaction in the tribunal (a professional judge persuades lay judges whenever he wants to; a professional judge does not bother to explain the legal background of a case). Interestingly, none of the nine statements was strongly supported either by lay judges or by professional judges. Professional judges tended to agree with the statements claiming that lay judges were emotional and that professional judges persuaded lay judges if they wanted to. Lay judges, on the other hand, did not perceive themselves to be so easily influenced by professional judges. Klami and Hämäläinen were actually surprised to learn that professional judges did not support the statement that they could easily persuade lay judges more strongly, especially in the light of the low percentage of "lay verdicts;" their explanation was that the respondents probably understood that question as meaning that professional judges have to persuade *all* disagreeing lay judges, while it was sufficient to persuade *only one* lay judge to have the majority vote (Klami and Hämäläinen, 1992, p. 58).

In the second part of the study the respondents were asked to evaluate three hypothetical scenarios. The authors concluded that the results did not show any substantial disagreement between professional judges and lay judges in terms of the punishment (Klami and Hämäläinen, 1992, p. 90). Finally, the respondents were asked for their personal opinion about the minimum and maximum punishment for eleven crimes, ranging from espionage and incest to fencing and drunk driving. Although individual differences emerged, the aggregate picture was that both professional judges and lay judges from Finland and Sweden were relatively content with the range of punishment provided by the law (Klami and Hämäläinen, 1992, p. 93).

4.2   Summary

Previous studies consistently reported about the low frequency of lay judges' participation and the small impact their participation had on the final product, the verdict. As may be expected, lay judges tended to be more active during deliberation than during trial. They were more likely to voice their opinion (to the point of disagreeing with the professional judge) when the discussion focused on the sentencing issues than when the discussion targeted the defendant's guilt. The extent of measured contribution differs from study to study, which is not surprising in view of the different methodologies and measures employed.

Although professional judges generally have a more critical opinion about mixed tribunals than lay judges do, both professional judges and lay judges find reasons for the retention of mixed tribunals in the criminal justice system. Despite some differences among the opinions expressed by professional judges in various studies, the common pattern was that professional judges primarily emphasized the political function as the most important feature of trials by mixed tribunals. At the same time, lay judges typically perceived that they made contributions to the legal decision-making process itself.

The reviewed research on mixed tribunals yielded a number of interesting and important findings; at the same time, there are at least three concerns that should be raised. They pertain to the age of most of the studies, the choice of methodology, and (the lack of) theoretical underpinnings.

The overwhelming majority of the studies on mixed tribunals were conducted about three decades ago. At the time when most of the studies were carried out, the former Czechoslovakia, Poland, Hungary, and the former Yugoslavia were communist countries, which implies that the underlying ideology of lay participation was quite different from that embraced in the West. After the collapse of the iron curtain, these countries started the process of transition toward democracy and the question remains to what degree this change of the underlying political philosophy affected mixed tribunals (which, apparently, survived the early transition period and are still a part of the system of justice administration in the countries in transition). Even the studies on German mixed tribunals have aged; they target the former West Germany, and were conducted before the reunification of Germany.

The reviewed studies often focused on a very small number of respondents (e.g., 20 respondents) and/or relied on only one source (e.g., professional judges) to describe the interaction in the tribunal. The choice of methodology is clearly an extremely important issue because it may have had quite an impact on the results these studies reported, especially those about the contribution of lay judges to trial and deliberation. Asking only professional judges to observe and report on their own behavior and on the behavior of lay judges may have yielded results that are different from those that would be obtained had researchers been allowed to observe both trials and deliberations or if all participants in the decision-making process (professional judges *and* lay judges) were surveyed.

Finally, the focus of these studies was on the empirical examination of the interaction in the tribunal and the contribution by lay judges, while theoretical arguments aimed at explaining that interaction were not raised. The only reported discussion that did not involve strictly empirical analysis revolved around positive and negative features of lay participation (i.e., arguments *pro* and *contra* lay participation).

In the present study, which analyzes Croatian mixed tribunals in the 1990s, I address all three concerns. First, the data were collected in 1993, and are thus very recent. At the time the data were collected, Croatia was in the early stages of transition toward democracy. Communism fell, the former Yugoslavia disintegrated, and Croatia was subjected to aggression (Croatia was still partially occupied by the Serb paramilitary forces at the time). On the legislative side, many laws have been drafted and passed, and many relics of the communist past have been eradicated. Mixed tribunals resisted such a clean-up because their positive features transcended the underlying political systems. Second, the data were collected from both professional judges and lay judges, as well as from state attorneys and attorneys (who, although not members of the tribunal and thus absent during deliberation, were regular "observers" of their work during trial). Moreover, data were collected at different levels of the court/office hierarchy, from district courts/offices to the Supreme Court in two different regions in Croatia. Third, I establish a theoretical foundation that explains the interaction in mixed tribunals (Chapter 5).

Chapter 5

Theoretical Issues

The review of earlier studies on mixed tribunals in the previous chapter indicates that most of the researchers have placed a strong emphasis on a variety of empirical results and observations, but have rarely focused on developing a theoretical framework for the study of mixed tribunals. If some theoretical issues were discussed, the authors primarily focused on positive and negative features of lay participation. This chapter provides a theoretical framework for the interaction in mixed tribunals by utilizing status characteristics theory (Berger *et al.*, 1977, 1980, 1986), a psychological theory that aims at explaining interaction in small groups. A brief overview of the relevant literature will lead naturally toward status characteristics theory and its application to mixed tribunals.

5.1   Mixed Tribunals and Social Psychology

According to the basic propositions of social psychology, mixed tribunals are *small groups* (Fisher, 1974, p. 7) — they fulfill the condition of enabling face-to-face interactions among all group members (Balkwell, 1994). In terms of their purpose and function, mixed tribunals are task-oriented, formal, and heterogeneous groups; each of these attributes merits due attention.

5.1.1   Mixed Tribunals as Task-Oriented Groups

According to Gergen (1974), to qualify as a task-oriented group, the group needs to be centered on a specific task. Mixed tribunals indeed qualify; their task is that of legal decision-making, that is, deciding the defendant's guilt and, if appropriate, determining the sentence. Interestingly, legal decision-making in criminal cases has not been studied in detail from the standpoint of the psychology of decision-making (Lloyd-Bostock, 1989).

The process of decision-making is usually presented as a continuum with an *automatic* response on one end and a *non-automatic* response on the other end (Lloyd-Bostock, 1989). At the automatic end of the continuum, the decisions are reached by classifying a new situation according to a previously developed classification; the response is skill-based. Green (in Kerr *et al.*, 1982, p. 13) found in an archival analysis of legal decisions that, when a case was legally similar to the preceding case, there was a direct relationship between the severity of the sentences imposed in those two cases — the first decision sets a precedent for the second one. This is by no means a surprising result. In fact, we develop and promulgate legal rules advocating that the punishment should be proportionate to the crime. Furthermore, we expect judges to be consistent in their decisions. Therefore, it is quite understandable that professional judges with considerable experience routinely tend to rely on their reasoning and decisions in previous cases. Similarly, results of research studies show that extensive prior experience in jury service set the standards for those jurors regarding the decisions reached in new cases (Kerr *et al.*, 1982).

At the other, non-automatic end, a classification is not developed and each new situation requires an assessment and a weighing of alternatives and solutions based on more general knowledge. In other words, each case is treated like a new situation. Typical jurors are likely to participate in perhaps only one case in their lives and are thus likely to employ such an approach.

Sentencing is considered to be placed in the middle of this continuum (Lloyd-Bostock, 1989). However, depending on the experience and skill of a particular decision-maker, this task can be shifted toward either end of the continuum: less experienced professional judges are more likely to make decisions in a less automatic way; conversely, more experienced professional judges are more likely to make decisions in a more automatic way. For example, in a study by the Centre for Criminological Research at Oxford, most of the 25 interviewed judges described the sentencing process as "an intuitive process, using such terms as 'instinct,' 'hunch,' and 'feeling'" (in Lloyd-Bostock, 1989, p. 63).

However, "automatic" does not necessarily mean "simple," nor does it necessarily have negative connotations. A skilled professional is likely to decide not only more efficiently, but also more consistently. A good example may be a skilled medical doctor, who makes decisions more quickly and more efficiently than a student of medicine. Similarly, professional judges are more likely to recognize facts important in the case and to apply a sentence which is consistent with the other cases that have occurred during their careers than lay judges are. Nevertheless, fine details of the case may be lost and minimized if such an approach is used in the process; lay judges, on the other hand, would be more likely to focus on such details. Assuming that these are the ways in which a typical professional judge and a typical lay judge approach a case (and further assuming that they can understand each other and work together), their union might be quite beneficial.

Another set of considerations is related to the question of exactly to what extent the knowledge of the law plays a role in legal decision-making in criminal cases in a typical Continental law system. The goal legal decision-makers need to fulfill is to reach a legal decision in accordance with the law. While deciding and applying the law, decision-makers may be faced with various types of problems. They may have a case in which the legal rules are clear, a case in which the existing norms are conflicting, or a case in which there are no legal rules that apply. How, then, do decision-makers resolve legal cases in each of these situations? A useful tool for this discussion is Peczenik's theory of legal reasoning (in Klami and Hämäläinen, 1992, p. 19). Peczenik identified four levels of legal reasoning:

1. *Sources of law* — If there is a clear statutory rule or a precedent that applies, the decision-makers follow the law. Legal decisions in Croatia and in most of the countries that utilize mixed tribunals are supposed to be rule-bound.[1] Since the decision-making at this level is accomplished by applying pure legal knowledge, professional judges have every advantage in comparison with lay judges; they know the legal rules and the sources of legal doctrine. An overwhelming majority of the cases in the first instance, that is, the cases of interest in the context of mixed tribunals,[2] are decided at this level of legal reasoning.

2. *Conceptual stipulations* — If there is no clear statutory rule or a precedent that applies, legal reasoning will focus on the legal terms employed in the case. At this level professional judges will still have a considerable advantage over lay judges because professional judges possesses a systematic appreciation of the legal order, not only the knowledge of the set of changing rules. Professional judges will conceptualize the legal terms at hand in a broad context and as an integral part of the entire body of legal concepts.

3. *Legal principles* — In the absence of legal rules and well-established meanings of legal terms, legal principles become a foundation for the legal decision. Professional judges still have an advantage over lay judges because they can "think like lawyers;" since the decision is rule-bound, professional judges will try to develop arguments that will keep the legal decision as close as possible to the spirit of the law or particular legal norms. However, that advantage is considerably less pronounced than it

---

[1]Lay judges in mixed tribunals, contrary to jurors, do not have the right to bend the law.

[2]Croatian mixed tribunals decide only cases in the first instance. Cases decided in the second or third instance are decided by professional tribunals (unless a hearing is required). See Chapter 3.

was at the first two levels. Here, lay judges are more likely to be active and to challenge the professional judge by questioning the application of a particular legal principle. In other words, reasoning at this level can benefit from general problem-solving skills and ability to think critically (traits that can be possessed by lay judges as well) to a higher extent than was possible at the previous two levels.

4. *Moral Considerations* — When the legal decision requires a choice between legal principles, moral considerations become important. In other words, if there are several legal principles and the legal decision could not satisfy all the legal principles simultaneously, the decision-maker needs to select among the conflicting legal principles and their respective goals. The way the latter is typically accomplished is by applying moral norms. It is only at this, the highest level of legal reasoning, that lay judges are not at a disadvantage compared to professional judges. The crucial issue is no longer that of legal knowledge, but that of a morally just decision. However, as was emphasized by Klami and Hämäläinen (1992, p. 21), "such cases are in these days of ever expanding legislation extremely rare in the courts of first instance."

In summary, the professional judge dominates over lay judges at the first two levels and, to some extent, at the third level of the above typology of legal reasoning, since the legal reasoning employed in the decision-making process at these levels is primarily a question of in-depth legal knowledge. Therefore, knowing the law and knowing "how to think like a lawyer" is important for the majority of the cases resolved in the first instance.

Mudd (1983) argued that "thinking like a lawyer" entails two important components. First, there is the *critical thinking* that involves clarity, precision, and quality of thinking and is not "different in kind from thinking like a physicist or philosopher" (Mudd, 1983, p. 706). Second, there is *the ability to use and practice these skills to solve real legal problems* (Mudd, 1983).

In theory, lay judges have the right to read the case file even before the trial starts and to thus familiarize themselves with the legal rules to be applied in the case. Furthermore, the professional judge is in the deliberation room together with the lay judges and can explain the law in a way that would make the content of the legal norms more understandable to them. If the professional judge explains the law, are some of the lay judges better able to understand the law than others? The discussion, therefore, leads itself naturally to the first component of "thinking like a lawyer" (Mudd, 1983) — critical thinking. Dressel and Mayhew (1954, p. 179-180) identified five critical thinking skills:

1. the ability to define a problem;

2. the ability to select pertinent information for the solution of the problem;

3. the ability to recognize stated and unstated assumptions;

4. the ability to formulate and select relevant and promising hypotheses; and

5. the ability to draw conclusions validly and to judge the validity of inferences.

It follows that educated lay participants can fulfill the critical thinking requirement. Moreover, educated lay judges will be better able to define legal problems and provide relevant hypotheses than lay judges with lower levels of education. Therefore, when legal rules are the key issue for the resolution of the case (the first two types of legal reasoning), which, according to Klami and Hämäläinen (1992), occurs in the overwhelming majority of the cases, lay judges with higher levels of education will have an advantage over lay judges with lower levels of education.

What differentiates professional judges from educated lay judges is the second component, *the ability to use and practice these skills to solve real legal problems.* Only lawyers receive legal education and systematic training in

defining a legal problem, selecting factors that are important for the definition and resolution of the problem, forming relevant hypotheses, and drawing
appropriate conclusions. Furthermore, only lawyers have the opportunity to
practice legal decision-making regularly and to thereby amass considerable
experience.

On the other hand, it is important to note that the roles played by professional judges and lay judges do not overlap completely and that lay judges
may actually be more familiar with the social rules that prevail in a particular city or area than professional judges. As discussed in Chapter 1, positive
functions of lay participation are realized precisely through the introduction
of community norms and values into the criminal justice system (within the
legal limits). The question is, then, to what degree will these social norms play
a significant role in the decision-making process, especially because lay judges
and professional judges are not empowered to bend the law and substitute
legal for social or moral norms.

In fact, the majority of lay judges in the Polish study (72%) thought that
lay judges served a function in counteracting the tendency of statutory law to
ignore the realities of life (Borucka-Arctowa, 1976). Borucka-Arctowa (1976)
argued that the "social" role performed by lay judges and the "professional"
role performed by professional judges may be perceived as mutually complementary.

The majority of professional judges, on the other hand, may have a different
view about the lay judges' role and their capacity to make legal decisions; it
would not be surprising if professional judges believed that judicial decision-
making requires "no less than a law degree, a license to practice, and trial
experience" (Dow, 1981, p. 196). That is, professional judges would emphasize
the "professional" role over the "social" role, both for themselves and for lay
judges.

Sentiments or community values might lead jurors to change the rules
somewhat or to decide even contrary to the legal rules. The same will not work
for mixed tribunals; mixed tribunals have to decide following the legal rules and

subsequently to explain the reasons for their decision in the form of a written verdict (written by the presiding professional judge) which may be reviewed on appeal by a tribunal composed of professional judges. Furthermore, the appeal may be initiated by either party, regardless of whether the decision was an acquittal or a conviction. A serious violation of the rules, either procedural or substantive, provides grounds for appeal and annulment of the verdict and the return of the case for trial *de novo*.

In the large majority of cases, as was argued by Klami and Hämäläinen (1992), legal questions require simple application of legal rules. In the cases involving the third and the fourth level of legal reasoning, there is more room for social values and moral values in general to be incorporated into the decision-making process and into the final decision in the case.

5.1.2   Mixed Tribunals as Formal Groups

Mixed tribunals are formal groups because the positions of the tribunal members are normatively specified in advance, before the tribunal members actually enter the courtroom and meet in order to decide a legal case: professional lawyers, appointed as professional judges, are the presiding judges in the tribunal, whereas persons without education in law and training in legal decision-making, elected as lay judges, serve as tribunal members.

In order to demonstrate that Croatian mixed tribunals are indeed formal groups, I provide a brief review of the system of mixed tribunals in Croatia as it was at the time this study was conducted (i.e., in mid-1993).[3]

The *Croatian Criminal Procedure Law* of 1993 and the *Presidential Decrees* of 1991 distinguished between mixed tribunals of two sizes — "small tribunals" and "large tribunals." The size and the composition of the tribunal depended on the seriousness of the offense. Offenses for which possible sanctions ranged between 5 and 15 years of imprisonment were tried by a "small tribunal," which was composed of one professional judge and two lay judges (Article

---

[3]A more detailed description of the past systems and the contemporary system of mixed tribunals in Croatia was furnished in Chapter 3.

9, *Presidential Decree*, 1991a). Offenses for which the prescribed sanction exceeded 15 years of imprisonment were tried by a "large tribunal," which was composed of two professional judges and three lay judges (Article 21, *Criminal Procedure Law*, 1993).

In general terms, lay judges and professional judges are equals during trial and deliberation (Article 13, *Regular Courts Law*, 1988) and their votes have the same weight. Thus, two lay judges can outvote a professional judge in a small tribunal and, similarly, three lay judges can outvote two professional judges in a large tribunal. Although lay judges and professional judges were intended to be equals, only professional judges may preside over the work of a mixed tribunal. That is, responsibilities assigned to the tribunal members are clearly not identical.

Indeed, there are several important differences between the professional judges' and lay judges' responsibilities. The presiding judge conducts the trial, interrogates the defendant, witnesses, and expert witnesses, and lets the other members of the tribunal and parties in the case speak (Article 292, *Criminal Procedure Law*, 1993). After the presiding judge has completed his/her examination, he/she has the duty to allow other members of the tribunal to ask the defendant, witnesses, and expert witnesses questions directly.

After the defendants, witnesses, and expert witnesses are examined and the examination of other evidence in the case is completed, the prosecutor, the victim, the defense attorney, and the defendant give their closing statements (Article 339, *Criminal Procedure Law*, 1993). Once the closing statements are provided, and if the tribunal does not conclude at that point that it is necessary to examine additional evidence, the presiding professional judge will declare that the trial has concluded and the tribunal will prepare for deliberation (Article 344, *Criminal Procedure Law*, 1993).

Decisions are made after oral discussion and voting (Article 116, *Criminal Procedure Law*, 1993). The vote of each member carries the same weight, regardless of whether the member is a lay judge or a professional judge. The presiding judge votes last, after all the other members of the tribunal have

already cast their votes (Article 116, *Criminal Procedure Law*, 1993). The presiding professional judge directs deliberation and voting, and has the responsibility of ensuring that the tribunal engages in a discussion of all the issues "fully and universally" (Article 116, *Criminal Procedure Law*, 1993). The *Criminal Procedure Law* (1993) does not regulate the order in which the discussion during deliberation should proceed.

However, since these roles are only partially predetermined by this legal structure and the order of deliberation is not predetermined at all, it is quite possible that the professional judge is just the first among the equals once the case reaches the deliberation room. In other words, although the law provides a more active role for professional judges during trial, if there were no other factors that would give a higher status to professional judges, one would not be surprised if the interaction between professional judges and lay judges in the deliberation room assumed more egalitarian tones.

5.1.3   Mixed Tribunals as Heterogeneous Groups

Finally, mixed tribunals are inherently *heterogeneous groups*, since tribunal members differ with respect to at least one characteristic (Gergen, 1974). Characteristics of special interest here, as well as throughout this book, are legal education and experience in legal decision-making. In addition, mixed tribunals are heterogeneous with respect to various demographic variables (e.g., age, gender, education, occupation).

The influence of homogeneity and heterogeneity on productivity and effectiveness of small groups other than mixed tribunals has been studied, but the research findings are somewhat contradictory. The results of Hoffman and Maier's study (1961) and Gillespie and Mileti's study (1981) strongly support the idea of superiority of heterogeneous groups over homogeneous groups in terms of the quality of group decisions. When many alternative solutions need to be examined to solve a problem, heterogeneity tends to increase the problem-solving ability of the group and may thus help the group find the correct solution (Gergen, 1974).

Hoffman and Maier (1961) grouped students into homogeneous and heterogeneous groups on the basis of the results of their personality-test scores and asked them to resolve diverse types of problems. The results suggested that heterogeneous groups were more successful in terms of the quality of their decisions. The authors emphasized two major reasons for such success: in heterogeneous groups there is a greater diversity of information available for solving problems and there is a greater tendency for individual members to question the others' assumptions and opinions than in homogeneous groups (Hoffman and Maier, 1961).

In addition, research studies show that heterogeneity increases the group's potential problem-solving activity (Collins and Guetzkow, 1964), since heterogeneous groups offer more numerous and more varied alternatives, fewer random errors, fewer constant biases, and a better criticism of suggested solutions. Heterogeneous group composition seems to be more helpful in cognitive aspects of task performance and less helpful in the area of personal relations (Collins and Guetzkow, 1964). Furthermore, the results of Collins and Guetzkow's study (1964) also suggest that group heterogeneity is more beneficial when the task is difficult and when the distinguishing characteristics are important for the task.

Gender may serve as an illustrative example of the effect of group heterogeneity on group performance. Research studies showed that women and men behave differently in both homogeneous and heterogeneous groups (e.g., Aries, 1976; Henley, 1977; Piliavian and Martin, 1978; Skvoretz, 1981; Martin, 1985; Taps and Martin, 1990). Hoffman and Maier (1961) suggested that both women and men emphasize their different perspectives or styles of social interaction more strongly in heterogeneous groups than in homogeneous groups. Men benefit in heterogeneous groups because the presence of women gives them more opportunities to participate than they would have in homogeneous, male-only groups and because interaction tends to be less dominance-oriented (Taps and Martin, 1990). Women, on the other hand, benefit in heterogeneous groups because the presence of men adds legitimacy to their task-oriented goals and pursuits (Taps and Martin, 1990).

A study by Piliavian and Martin (1978) partially contradicts this hypothesis. Piliavian and Martin (1978) examined the effect of sex-role stereotype on the style of social interaction for both homogeneous and heterogeneous groups. They hypothesized that both women and men would exhibit more sex-role stereotyping in mixed-sex groups than in single-sex groups.[4] The results of their study suggest that the initial differences in the style of social interaction change as the group composition changes, but in a direction that contradicted their hypothesis. In homogeneous groups, female participants exhibited mostly socio-emotional contributions, while in heterogeneous groups their contributions were more task-oriented and less socio-emotional. Male students performed task-oriented contributions in both homogeneous and heterogeneous groups.

Group heterogeneity may have a negative influence on the quality of group decisions as well. Negative influence may be caused by a variety of differences among group members, such as status differences, differences in attitudes toward the group's goal, or personality differences (Gergen, 1974). Exline and Ziller (1959) studied the effects of group members' diverse status positions on decision-making. Their results showed that the groups with more diverse status levels experienced more conflict and made incorrect decisions more frequently than the groups with less diverse status levels (Exline and Ziller, 1959). According to Paicheler (1979), the mere presence of women and men in the same group may have negative effects on the quality of the decision.

One of the negative effects of group heterogeneity is that some group members systematically tend to get fewer opportunities to participate. Taps and Martin (1990) argued that heterogeneous groups have disadvantages for members with lower status; women's chances of participating and demonstrating

---

[4]A typical stereotype of female contribution to a group task is "socio-emotional" contribution, while a typical stereotype of male contribution to a group task is "task" contribution (Piliavian and Martin, 1978).

competence are lower in gender-skewed groups (i.e., one woman in a predominantly male group) than in all-female groups. They found that the type of contribution a woman makes in a group depends on the composition of the group. In a predominantly male group, the most influential and well-liked impact made by the woman is when she gives external attributional accounts; in a predominantly female group, maximum impact is achieved when a woman gives internal attributional accounts. In gender-balanced groups, a woman is comparably influential and well-liked when she gives either internal or external accounts (Taps and Martin, 1990). Furthermore, it seems that it matters not only that there is minority participation, but also what the relative size of the minority group is. Results of some research studies suggested that the lower the proportional representation of women in heterogeneous groups, the more poorly women fare, particularly with regard to influence on other group members (Izraeli, 1985; Taps and Martin, 1990).

5.2 Status Characteristics Theory and Mixed Tribunals

Status characteristics theory, developed by Berger *et al.* (1977, 1980, 1986), explains the interaction among the members of small task-oriented groups. The theory states that individuals who interact in task-oriented groups typically acquire expectations about the potential task-related contributions of members of their group (Berger *et al.*, 1977, Berger *et al.*, 1980; Berger *et al.*, 1986, Balkwell, 1994). These expectations are crucial for the interaction in the group because they influence their observable power and prestige behaviors in the group. The bases for these expectations are *status characteristics*.

Status characteristics can be viewed as attributes possessed by members of a group whose culturally specified meaning makes such characteristics potentially relevant to the performance of the group's task (Balkwell, 1994, p. 124). Each status characteristic has a *state* that is evaluated more positively than other states. For example, a number of studies examined this theory by studying the influence of status characteristics, such as gender (Carli, 1991; Ridgeway, 1982; Berger *et al.*, 1980; Meeker and Weitzel-O'Neil, 1977) or race (Terrell *et al.*, 1977), on the perceived competence to perform a certain task. In the case of gender, a typical modern western society appreciates males more highly than it appreciates females; "whatever is thought of as manly is more highly valued than what is thought of as womanly" (Harding, 1986, p. 18). Studies reported that both sexes evaluated males more favorably than females (Lockheed and Hall, 1976); a paper or a lecture was evaluated less positively if it was attributed to a female (Goldberg, 1968, Mischel, 1974). As a matter of terminology, for some status characteristics, such as education or income, it is more natural to speak of *levels* rather than *states*.

Status characteristics can be either specific or diffuse (Carli, 1991; Balkwell, 1994). *Specific status characteristics* are *directly* related to the group task. *Diffuse status characteristics* are at best *indirectly* related to the group task; they are more general in nature (i.e., they are believed to have wide-ranging connotations for performance). Diffuse status characteristics include, for example, education, gender, age, and race.

5.2.1   Specific Status Characteristics and Mixed Tribunals

Professional judges in mixed tribunals are persons with a legal background; they are law school graduates who have completed their apprenticeship, have passed the bar exam, and have a certain number of years of experience working on legal issues after passing their bar exam. In other words, professional judges are persons with legal knowledge and systematic training and experience in resolving legal issues — they are experts in law. Lay judges, on the other hand, are persons who are neither educated in law nor trained and experienced in resolving legal issues. Professional judges and lay judges in mixed tribunals thus differ with respect to two specific status characteristics (i.e., characteristics directly relevant to the task at hand — legal decision-making): **legal education and experience in legal decision-making acquired through systematic**

training and regular practice. Because they possess high states on both specific status characteristics, professional judges are very likely to have a higher status in the tribunal than lay judges do.

Lay judges can also possess certain experience in legal decision-making. Clearly, those lay judges who have served for a long period of time have been involved in more trials by mixed tribunals than novice lay judges. However, their experience is gathered *ad hoc* and only sporadically; it lacks systematic training and is not a regular activity. Such a delineation is very subtle because there is a potential to regard any kind of prior experience in trials by mixed tribunals as a characteristic that is very important for the task. Indeed, in the context of the jury, *any* prior experience with jury service affords those who possess it a higher status on the jury. In mixed tribunals, however, its importance is overshadowed by the distinction between professional judges and lay judges with respect to *systematic* training in and *regular* practice of legal decision-making. Lay judges' experience is not comparable to that possessed by professional judges and having higher levels of it will not serve to bridge the status gap between lay judges and professional judges. Thus, lay judges' experience, although potentially important for the group task, truly belongs to the ranks of diffuse status characteristics; it is likely, nevertheless, to be among the most important diffuse status characteristics.

5.2.2 General Hypotheses of Status Characteristics Theory

Status characteristics theory may be summarized by four general hypotheses about the operation of status processes in task-oriented groups (Balkwell, 1994). The first hypothesis, the *salience hypothesis*, suggests that if a status characteristic important for the task discriminates among the group members, then this status characteristic will become operative or activated (Balkwell, 1994). This hypothesis undoubtedly plays a role in mixed tribunals, since the difference between professional judges and lay judges is derived for the most part from specific status characteristics.

The second hypothesis, the *burden of proof hypothesis*, asserts that any salient status characteristic will come to link its possessor to the possible outcomes of the group's task (Balkwell, 1994). Therefore, any activated status characteristic will contribute to the structuring of social interaction, unless it is stated clearly that this status characteristic is *not* related to task competence. Legal education and systematic training and experience in legal decision-making will certainly influence social interaction — it will be structured so as to reflect different states of the two status characteristics possessed by professional judges and lay judges, respectively.

The third hypothesis, the *aggregation hypothesis*, describes how group members combine all status information on multiple characteristics to form aggregated performance expectations for themselves and for others (Balkwell, 1994). It is also implicitly assumed that group members will (tacitly) agree, at least to some extent, on what characteristics are more important than others, how status information is combined, and on what the performance expectations of each group member are. Specific legal knowledge and systematic training and experience in legal decision-making, possessed by professional judges but not by lay judges, will tend to be considerably more important characteristics for the formation of aggregated performance expectations than diffuse status characteristics (e.g., age or gender of professional judges and lay judges).

The fourth hypothesis, the *translation hypothesis*, asserts that a member's production of performance outcomes is a function of aggregated performances held for the member relative to the performances held by other group members (Balkwell, 1994). In the long run, the group members with higher aggregated performance expectations will also exhibit more intense activity in the group. For mixed tribunals, this hypothesis implies that professional judges, members who are more qualified to decide legal cases, are also likely to be more active over time. This prediction is further reinforced by the normative specification (provided by the law), which establishes professional judges as leaders in charge of legal proceedings and affords them more opportunities to speak.

5.2.3 Processing Salient Status Information

According to status characteristic theory, information about specific and diffuse status characteristics determines the expectation hierarchy in a group. The theory further implies that diffuse status characteristics will be more important in interactions among strangers who possess little or no information about the members' relative competence or ability at the group task (Carli, 1991). In the context of mixed tribunals, the expectation is that diffuse status characteristics will have little impact on the opinion of lay judges about the professional judge's competence to make legal decisions, since specific status characteristics are available: although professional judges and lay judges may be strangers, lay judges, by simply knowing that a particular member of the tribunal is a professional judge, will evaluate that member as knowledgeable and skillful in deciding legal issues. In other words, although professional judges and lay judges may be strangers, they will still have enough information about the specific status characteristics to form expectations, simply based on the fact that they know that some of them are *professional* judges and some of them are *lay* judges.

If lay judges have had prior experience in deciding cases with the same professional judge, they will also base their evaluation on the opinion they have formed about the previous performance of that professional judge. This opinion, based on actual practical experience, will either reinforce the overall positive opinion about the ability of one of the members of the judicial profession to contribute toward the task or weaken it.

The only direct information a professional judge may have about a lay judge's competence is his/her previous experience with the same lay judge. If the professional judge does not have such information, a general evaluation about lay judges' competence in legal decision-making (likely along the lines of a stereotype) would probably be used. In other words, by knowing that the tribunal member is a lay member, the professional judge may reach a general conclusion about the lay judge's competence on the basis of the opinion about the competence of the whole group to contribute toward a successful completion of the task. However, as is true with all professions, many members of the legal profession probably think that only educated and trained members of a profession are qualified to make professional decisions; therefore, they limit in their mind the capacity of lay persons to make quality legal decisions.

Performance expectations of group members may develop based not only on status positions external to the group (status characteristics), but also on *status cues*. Status cues are defined as indicators, markers, or identifiers of the different social status people possess (Berger *et al.*, 1986, p. 1). These are the aspects of a person's appearance (e.g., an expensive suit), behavior (e.g., extensive vocabulary), or surrounding possession (e.g., diploma on the wall) which can be used to draw conclusions about status. Status cues activate a status-organizing process and are affected by the operation of that process (Berger *et al.*, 1986, p. 3).

Status cues can be either *task cues* or *categorical cues* (Berger *et al.*, 1986). Task cues give information about performances taking place during the interaction itself (e.g., voice level, physical position within the group, gestures, speech rate), while categorical cues give information about "who these people are" or the larger social groups these people belong to (e.g., having a beard and wearing a conservative business suit and a tie are categorical cues to the gender state "male").

When the level of information about status characteristics is limited, the expectations are based solely on cues or the information revealed during group interaction (Rashotte and Smith-Lovin, 1997, p. 237). In the context of mixed tribunals, plenty of information about specific status characteristics is available in advance, before the trial begins. Professional judges know before lay judges enter into the courtroom that lay judges do not have legal education and that they are not trained to make legal decisions (i.e., that they have low status based on both specific status characteristics). Similarly, lay judges know in advance that they will join a *professional* judge (i.e., a person with both legal education and, most likely, substantial experience in trials by mixed tribunals).

Since plenty of information about the members' states of specific status characteristics is available at the outset (and status hierarchies may develop based in part on that information), cues will be less important *if* they point in the same direction; there is a general prediction of a decreasing marginal return on influence for status and task cues pointing in the same direction (Balkwell and Berger, 1996). This reduced effect has been called the *attenuation principle* (Berger *et al.*, 1977). On the other hand, if status characteristics and task cues are not congruent, task cues may serve to alter the initial status hierarchies. Generic examples are the results of empirical studies (e.g., Ridgeway, 1981, 1982) which show that the behavior during interaction can enhance the influence of (initially low-status) women in mixed sex groups. In fact, the gradual changes in the original expectations of the perceived competence of women in the work force from the 1950s until the present can be explained by the interaction and the impact of conflicting task cues that suggested competence in contrast to the expectations associated with gender (their diffuse status characteristic).

Therefore, if the message about performance sent by task cues is similar to the status established on the basis of status characteristics, the original status hierarchy will be reinforced and the impact of these task cues will be minimal and decreasing at the margin. On the other hand, if a professional judge sends cues which suggest that he/she is not very experienced (i.e., there is a conflict between specific status characteristics and task cues), the lay judges' expectations about his/her ability to perform the task will decrease. Thus, the original status hierarchy may be altered if either professional judges or lay judges send cues inconsistent with the status hierarchy that initially had been established on the basis of specific status characteristics.

5.2.4 Combining Specific and Diffuse Status Characteristics

Each professional judge and each lay judge is a person with at least two specific and a number of diffuse status characteristics. How do the lay judges' or professional judges' status (based on their legal education and experience in legal decision-making — specific status characteristics) combine with their race, gender, education, or nationality (diffuse status characteristics)?

The aggregation hypothesis (Balkwell, 1994) implies that the performance expectation and power of each group member will include information about all status characteristics, regardless of whether they are specific or diffuse, but different weights will be attached to them. The expectation is that specific status characteristics, that is, characteristics directly relevant to the task, will be more important (weigh more heavily) for the aggregate expectation than diffuse status characteristics (which are related to the task only indirectly). In the context of mixed tribunals, legal education and experience in legal decision-making will have a stronger impact (and weigh more heavily) on the overall expectation about the professional judges' or lay judges' ability to decide legal cases than, for example, their gender — after all, the former is directly related to the task while the latter is not.

Therefore, the primary and dominant bases of professional judges' high status and lay judges' low status are specific status characteristics, whereas diffuse status characteristics are expected to play a very marginal role, if any. For example, although it seems plausible that a relatively inexperienced, young, female professional judge will have a lower status than an experienced, older, male professional judge, the relative strength of specific status characteristics still suggests that the status of either of these two professional judges would be higher than the status of, for example, an older physician serving as a lay judge.[5]

---

[5]The focus here is not on discussing occupational prestige (lawyers *v.* medical doctors). Rather, the discussion focuses on their respective status in the tribunal (based on their specific and diffuse status characteristics and the way they relate to their task — legal decision-making).

5.2.5   Diffuse Status Characteristics and Mixed Tribunals

The common trait of all diffuse status characteristics is that they are secondary to specific status characteristics; they are related to the group task only indirectly. However, not all the diffuse status characteristics are equally (un)important for the group task. Indeed, lay judges' experience and education are likely to have a stronger impact than, for example, occupation, gender, or age. If specific and diffuse status characteristics were viewed as the two opposite endpoints of a continuum, then lay judges' experience and education would be considerably closer to specific status characteristics than virtually any other diffuse characteristic. On the other hand, if specific and diffuse status characteristics are viewed as a rigid dichotomy, lay judges' experience and education are less likely to fit comfortably into such a framework than almost any other characteristic. Lay judges' experience and education are discussed in detail; occupation and gender will also receive due attention.

Experience

Although lay judges do not have formal training in legal decision-making, participation in several trials and deliberations may provide them with some experience, which may also impact their opinion about their own abilities and thus possibly change the frequency of their participation. Lay judges' experience may thus reinforce or weaken the opinions or expectations (of themselves and others) professional judges and lay judges have formed already.

Although the primary differences among members of mixed tribunals will be based on their education in law and training in legal decision-making, it is quite possible that the length of the mandate served by lay judges (or the actual experience) may have an impact on their interaction in the tribunal and their status. In other words, large differences between professional judges and lay judges will persist, but it is also likely that lay judges' experience will serve to differentiate among the lay judges' status. Not surprisingly, results of research studies show that lay judges do not have a clear view of what is expected of them and what their rights in the process are (Borucka-Arctowa, 1976, p. 289). Lay judges undoubtedly benefit from trial experience — more experienced lay judges will be more knowledgeable about the criminal process, about some basic concepts of substantive law, and their expectations of their own role in the process will be more refined.

In every social interaction we try to modify our behavior and respond to the signals sent by the audience. In the context of mixed tribunals, professional judges and other lay judges are the audience for a lay judge. Lay judges at the beginning of their mandate (below 1 year) are still in the process of learning social rules in a new social setting and are thus probably not sure what their role is; they will probably participate less frequently than lay judges who are already familiar with those rules (lay judges with a mandate over 1 year). On the other hand, lay judges with a mandate of over 3 years have already sat in numerous trials and, if professional judges routinely failed to encourage them to participate actively, they may have reacted by reducing the frequency of their participation. For example, Arzt (1982, p. 154) reported that the longer lay judges participate in mixed tribunals, the less likely they will be to attempt to influence the outcome.

In terms of the type of experience, it is possible that the type of court at which judges serve (professional and lay alike) will impact their quantity and quality of participation. Since there is no reasonable basis to expect that the abilities and the quality of lay judges elected to serve at district courts would in any respect be distinguishable from the abilities and the quality of lay judges elected to serve at regional courts, some other factors obviously need to be recognized as important for the potential differences in opinion about lay judges' abilities and the frequency of their participation in the work of mixed tribunals at the two different types of courts.

First, the seriousness of crimes tried for at district courts and regional courts is not the same; the law determined that the crimes to be tried at regional courts are punishable by harsher penalties than the crimes tried for at district courts. Therefore, greater seriousness of cases may encourage both professional judges and lay judges at regional courts to behave at least somewhat differently from their counterparts at district courts; lay judges may be more active and professional judges may be more willing to discuss the case with other tribunal members.

Second, the composition of the tribunal generally changes as the court level increases. Professional judges at district courts try cases only in small tribunals, whereas professional judges at regional courts try cases in both small and large tribunals. Small mixed tribunals, composed of one professional judge and two lay judges, are in charge of trials for crimes with the maximum penalty of up to 15 years of imprisonment (Article 23, Item 1, *Criminal Procedure Law*, 1993). Large mixed tribunals, composed of two professional judges and three lay judges, are in charge of trials for crimes with the maximum penalty of 15 or more years of imprisonment (Article 23, Item 1, *Criminal Procedure Law*, 1993). It is quite possible that presiding professional judges in large tribunals provide more opportunities for all members to participate and engage in discussion by simply providing more "floor time" for another professional judge (their colleague and associate at work of equal rank) sitting as a member of the same tribunal. Consequently, the professional judges' experience with mixed tribunals at districts court may be quite different from that of professional judges at regional courts. If indeed there are such differences, it is possible that they would also affect the opinion held by lay judges and state attorneys. That same influence would not be likely to affect attorneys as well, because they represent clients at both court levels and are thus not subject to differential exposure to the same extent that the other two categories of lawyers are.

Third, the size of the tribunal itself may make a difference; it is clearly easier to ignore two additional tribunal members (in a small tribunal) than to ignore four additional members (in a large tribunal).

Furthermore, status characteristics theory may serve as a useful framework to differentiate between the opinions held by lawyers (i.e., professional judges) who participate in trials by mixed tribunals and reach legal decisions *jointly* with lay judges and those held by lawyers who just observe trials by mixed tribunals (i.e., state attorneys and attorneys). Indeed, although all lawyers (professional judges, state attorneys, and attorneys) are law-school graduates who have in addition undergone rigorous training in legal decision-making (either as court apprentices or as apprentices serving at state attorneys' offices or attorneys' offices), their opinions about lay judges themselves and about lay judges' expected contributions toward the achievement of the group task may be somewhat different.

An interesting issue is to what extent lawyers rely on stereotypes about lay judges. Professional judges certainly have ample opportunities to form their opinion of lay judges at least in part on the basis of actual interaction with them. On the other hand, it is quite possible that, as a result of the lack of actual and (more or less) accurate information based on actual interaction with lay judges, state attorneys and attorneys may be more vulnerable toward accepting stereotypes about lay judges.

Of course, not all groups of lawyers necessarily share the same stereotypes about lay judges. Despite the fact that professional judges, state attorneys, and attorneys all attended the same law schools, their *socialization* into the legal profession may have been different; after all, within the legal culture there are particular legal subcultures. By learning the norms, both formal and informal, of the subculture a lawyer belongs to by virtue of the lawyer's role in the criminal justice system, the lawyer would also accept the stereotypes that exist in and are shared by the members of the specific legal subculture to which the lawyer belongs. It seems equally clear that different types of experience, specific to each legal subculture, can yield different stereotypes.

Education

Education, another potentially "more than diffuse" diffuse status characteristic, will be more highly correlated with the ability to understand the evidence in the case and to apply the law than any other diffuse status characteristic.

If, as is most often the case, legal rules are the key issue for the resolution of the case, that is, if the first two levels in Peczenik's typology of legal reasoning are employed (in Klami and Hämäläinen, 1992, p. 19), then lay judges with higher levels of education will have an advantage over lay judges with lower levels of education. Although lay judges with higher levels of education will not know the law and the intricacies of the legal procedure, if relevant legal rules are explained to them, they will likely have fewer problems in developing logically correct arguments and conclusions than lay judges with lower levels of education. Thus, if and when the professional judge explains the law, the performance expectation of the lay judges with higher levels of education will be higher, *ceteris paribus*, from that of the lay judges with lower levels of education.

If there are no clear legal rules that can be applied to the case, that is, if the third or the fourth level in Peczenik's typology is employed, legal principles and moral considerations guide the decision-making process. Lay judges with higher levels of education will have an advantage over lay judges with lower level of education in such cases as well, albeit for a different reason — they will likely possess better critical thinking skills, which will enable them to better analyze the problem, develop competing hypotheses, and draw logical conclusions.

Understandability of evidence is not the only factor that has a major impact on the assessment of the role of a particular piece of evidence in the network of other evidence in the case; the question of the standard of proof may also play a significant role. Sharper critical thinking skills are again a potentially valuable asset. As suggested by the results of the study on jurors conducted by Costantini and King (1980-81), because of their education and exposure to different ideas and viewpoints, lay judges with higher levels of education will be less likely to have prejudices. Furthermore, more highly developed critical thinking skills are likely to make their possessors less susceptible to impressions created by the demeanor and language projected by the lawyers and other more educated parties in the case.

Occupational Prestige

Members of the legal profession, lawyers in general and professional judges in particular, have high status in virtually every society; they are highly respected and rewarded.[6] As Rueschemeyer (1987) pointed out, the legal profession derives this power from its highly specialized knowledge.

The legal profession is one of the most highly ranked occupations. For example, according to Treiman's (1977) international occupational prestige scale (which has been validated in a number of countries), lawyers in general, and professional judges in particular, are ranked extremely highly. On the scale from 6 (narcotics peddlers) to 90 (chiefs of states), the prestige score for professional judges is as high as 78 (Treiman, 1977). The same prestige score is attributed to scientists, physicians/medical doctors, and university professors. Professional judges are outranked only by the most distinguished members of society: medical researchers (79), chief physicians in hospitals (80), provincial governors (82), high church officials (83), university presidents (86), ambassadors (87), and chiefs of states (90).

Although having a high-status occupation will not help lay judges gain the status that could rival the status possessed by professional judges, it may be beneficial in bridging the status gap. Individuals who have power and privilege are highly valued; therefore, occupations that are powerful and privileged are highly regarded (Treiman, 1977). Lay judges whose occupations belong to the

---

[6]Members of many professions tend to formalize and maintain the boundaries of their profession by limiting the number of new members through classification exams or bar exams (with a purpose of maintaining the high market position of the current members) and thus derive a relatively high income. Building such boundaries and thereby controlling the supply of legal professionals is all the more important in countries in which wealth and status of the legal profession are relatively high (Abel, 1985). However, even in the countries with an economically powerful bar, not all of the members of the legal profession are equally powerful; there is an informal differentiation within the profession based on the clientele and expertise, as described in a study of Chicago lawyers (Heinz and Laumann, 1982). Similarly, not all of the members of the legal profession in a country earn equally high salaries; according to Abel (1985), income depends on a number of factors, including the country specifics of the labor market, specialization, geographic differences, age, and employment sector (private v. public).

more prestigious group(s) are expected to be more accustomed to problem-solving group conversations in which their word is respected and valued. Lay judges whose occupations are more prestigious are likely to participate more frequently (but not as frequently as professional judges) than lay judges whose occupations are less prestigious because they expect that their questions and comments would be more appreciated and valued by the professional judge, a person whose occupation is at the high end on the occupational prestige scale. In other words, occupation may lead toward differentiation of performance expectations among lay judges and may provide some lay judges with more opportunities to participate than others; it may also result in more positive evaluations of their participation.

Gender

In the context of the study of interaction and group performance of mixed tribunals, gender is a diffuse status characteristic. It is possible that female professional judges might be evaluated as somewhat less able to perform than male professional judges, but both would still have a much higher status than that possessed by lay judges.

The impact of differences between the states or levels of diffuse characteristics possessed by professional judges and lay judges in mixed tribunals has not been systematically examined in previous research studies. However, there are a number of studies that examined such differences *separately* for professional judges and for lay participants.

The percentage of women in the legal profession in Croatia has been rising steadily. Approximately one-half of professional judges at district courts in Croatia in the 1990s were women.[7] Aggregate percentages do not tell the whole story, however; while percentages may be approaching an even split between women and men, female professional judges on average still have lower status. Indeed, the percentage of women among professional judges decreases with

---

[7]See Chapter 6 for details on the demographics of professional judges, lay judges, state attorneys, and attorneys in Croatia.

the increase of the court level (from district courts, regional courts, to the Supreme Court); while slightly over 50% of all professional judges at district courts were female, that percentage decreases to 40% at regional courts, and to only 25% at the Supreme Court (*1997 Statistical Yearbook*, 1997, p. 473). These percentages incorporate the recent drastic increase of the percentages of women among professional judges, especially among the professional judges at regional courts (from 20% in the early 1980s, 30% in the late 1980s, to 40% in the 1990s; *1991 Statistical Yearbook*, 1991, p. 356; *1993 Statistical Yearbook*, 1993, p. 446; *1997 Statistical Yearbook*, 1997, p. 473).

Similar trends have been taking place among attorneys — female lawyers are mostly located at the bottom of the bar; while in the 1990s 30% of attorneys were women, the percentage of attorneys' apprentices (lawyers who are preparing for their bar exam and are employed by attorneys at a junior level) is as high as 60%; the percentage of women among attorneys increased from only 10% in the 1980s to 30% in the 1990s (*1991 Statistical Yearbook*, 1991, p. 374; *1992 Statistical Yearbook*, 1993, p. 460; *1997 Statistical Yearbook*, 1997, p. 475).

Given a chronic lack of published research on the topic of gender in the legal profession in Croatia, I will appeal to the results of a few American research studies to suggest that it is likely that the increase of the percentage of women among Croatian lawyers has not changed the legal profession. Rather, women who joined the profession have likely adopted (willingly or not) the traditional male-dominated legal culture.

Martin (1990, p. 208) argued that the impact of gender on the work of professional judges may be noticed on a number of issues: decisional output (especially in cases involving sexual discrimination), conduct of courtroom business (especially in regard to biased behavior by other members of the courtroom workgroup), influence of sex-role attitudes held by male colleagues (especially at appellate courts), and administrative behavior in hiring female law clerks. However, other research studies generally found that such differences were of minor importance and impact. Specifically, research studies suggested that either female judges did not "speak in a different voice" (Gruhl *et al.*, 1981) or deviated from the norms established by the workgroup even when confronted with an issue of great concern to women, such as sexual assault (Spohn, 1995), or that some female judges sometimes did speak in a different voice, but this was limited to a narrow category of cases (Gottschall, 1983; Walker and Barrow, 1985; Gryski *et al.*, 1986; McCormick and Job, 1993).

An explanation for such surprisingly small differences may be that female judges, or female lawyers in general, are assimilated into the legal culture, which is predominantly male; students in law schools are trained to "think like lawyers," which in a male-dominated culture means to "think like males." Indeed, Menkel-Meadow (1989, p. 313) noted that "own research efforts and other evidence ... seem to indicate that women in law are being assimilated into the traditional culture of the profession rather than bringing the innovations often urged by feminist lawyers."

In the context of mixed tribunals, although gender may occasionally have a limited impact on some aspects of the professional judges' work, none of those differences are likely to have a noticeable impact on the professional judges' status, both in relation to other professional judges and in relation to lay judges.

Faced with the absence of studies on the impact of gender on lay members of mixed tribunals, I draw upon the their closest substitute, that is, on the results of jury studies that focused on the issue of gender. In jury deliberations, gender is an important factor from the moment jurors enter the jury room and decide where to sit; the jury usually selected the foreperson from the jurors seated at either end of the table (Strodtbeck and Hook, 1961), and men were more likely to take a seat at the end of the table than women (Hawkins in Marder, 1987). Furthermore, the frequency (quantity) of participation was perceived to be a more important predictor for the leadership position than the quality of participation (Sorrentino and Boutillier, 1975; Smith and Malandro, 1985); jurors who participated more frequently during deliberations were likely to be more influential and to be perceived as leaders (Regula and Julian,

1973). When the figures were adjusted for the difference in proportion of men and women on the jury, it was observed that male jurors offered 40% more comments than female jurors (Hastie *et al.*, 1983). Even when the foreperson was excluded from the calculation, male jurors still had a higher participation rate during deliberation than female jurors (Marder, 1987). Strodtbeck *et al.* (1957) and Hastie *et al.* (1983) also found that men were more likely to be selected as foremen.

In the context of trials by mixed tribunals, the issue of leadership is clearly not resolved among lay members of the tribunal; that position is reserved for the professional judge by means of a rigorous normative specification. One of the consequences of normative specification is that gender is completely irrelevant for the issue of leadership of the tribunal. At best, gender may serve as a tool of differentiation among lay members in the tribunal; that effect, however, is likely to be minimal.

Place of Residence

Place of residence is a sociological concept which incorporates numerous factors, most of which are interconnected and very difficult to isolate. Populations of a big city and a small town may differ in terms of educational levels, occupational prestige, marital status, number of children, impersonality in relationships, individualism, conflicting norms and values, rate of social change, level of political tolerance, and level of informal social control.

Under a plausible assumption that there is a certain difference in status between professional judges and lay judges (based on specific status characteristics — legal education and systematic training and experience in deciding legal cases), an interesting question is whether the size of the gap in status between the two groups is in any way dependent upon the size of the place of residence?

Because place of residence is a complex set of factors, some of these factors may tend to reduce the status gap, while others may pull in the opposite direction. It is, therefore, very difficult to provide exact estimates of how the aggregation of these factors would influence the difference in status between professional judges and lay judges.

Lay judges' educational level, one of the aforementioned diffuse status characteristics, may have a positive impact on the status of lay judges. The average educational level of city population typically exceeds that of people living in small towns.[8] Furthermore, a higher percentage of big-city inhabitants hold occupations that can be classified as prestigious according to Treiman's international occupational scale (Treiman, 1977). Having a more prestigious occupation, such as that of a physician or a university professor, may increase the lay judge's status and power in the tribunal. Based on higher educational levels and more prestigious occupations, the status gap between professional judges and lay judges would likely be smaller in the big city.

Lay judges in small towns are more likely to know the professional judge personally or to know someone who knows the professional judge. This factor in itself may change the status of lay judges in the tribunal by making the atmosphere less formal and more conducive for asking questions and participating in discussions. Furthermore, residents of small towns may appreciate and enjoy the sense of community more than those who live in a big city. This sense of belonging to the community may stimulate small-town residents to be enthusiastic and motivated to participate in trials by mixed tribunals more actively than their counterparts from a big city.

The direction of the aggregate effect of all the factors that characterize place of residence on the status gap is uncertain. In addition to the above considerations, another possibility is that the factors may cancel each other, resulting in a negligible overall impact. Finally, it is also possible that different factors will play dominant roles at different stages of the legal proceedings (i.e., the trial stage and the deliberation stage).

---

[8]The study was conducted in two regions of Croatia. Educational differences between the small-town population (the Bjelovar Region) and the big-city population (the Zagreb Region) were considerable; while more than 48% of the active population in small towns did not finish elementary school, the same was true of only about 18% of the big-city population. See Chapter 6 for details.

5.2.6   Differing Perspectives

Status characteristics theory is mostly concerned with the status of the person about whom the judgment is made (lay judge, professional judge), while the position of the person making the judgment is not considered to be as important. But, as results from the field of political sociology suggest (Smith, 1981), the position of the person making the judgment may be important as well. Smith (1981) emphasized a sense of position from which members of the dominant group view their relations with members of racial out-groups.

If this line of reasoning is applied to mixed tribunals, it can be argued that a professional judge's judgment about lay judges' ability would differ from that passed by a lay judge. In general, the opinion about one's own ability (or about the ability of the members within the same status group) would be higher than the opinion given by members from a different status group; this principle may well be applicable in the context of mixed tribunals.

Similarly, opinions about lay judges' ability and potential contribution toward the group task may differ among various groups of lawyers. Simply put, while professional judges have an opportunity to participate in legal decision-making jointly with lay judges, state attorneys and attorneys do not have such an opportunity (they are just "observers" of trials by mixed tribunals) and are thus more likely to rely on stereotypes about lay judges' ability to make high-quality legal decisions.

5.2.7   Consequences of Status Differences

A number of researchers have studied how performance expectations can be inferred from status cues. The results of their studies support status characteristics theory: individuals of higher status are more likely to interrupt and are more successful in interrupting when they interact with lower status individuals than when they interact with higher status individuals (O'Barr, 1982; Roger and Nesshoever, 1987; Rogers and Jones, 1975, p. 92). Other studies showed that high status individuals are more likely to speak first during interactions (Lamb, 1981; Ridgeway *et al.*, 1985), speak quickly (Sorrentino and Boutillier, 1975), speak loudly (Packwood, 1974), and have a relaxed body posture (Tuzlak and Moore, 1984). Quantity and quality of verbal contributions to a group interaction affect the opinion group members have about the speaker's competence, influence, and leadership ability (Sorrentino and Boutillier, 1975; Carli, 1991).

Professional judges, who have a higher status in the tribunal on the basis of their legal knowledge and training and experience in legal decision-making, are supposed to be *more competent*, to be *evaluated as more competent*, and to *actually perform better* and *more frequently* in achieving the resolution of the group task — making a legal decision — than lay judges are. However, professional judges' and lay judges' roles may not be identical, both from the perspective of normative specification and from the perspective of the respective functions they perform. Indeed, lay judges may be better qualified or prepared to discuss social norms and community values than professional judges are. Consequently, although professional judges are very likely to be better able to sort out legal issues in the case, lay judges may be more familiar with the social values of a particular community.

The theory implies that high status members will be *given more opportunities to make contributions* to the group, and that their *contributions are more likely to receive favorable reactions* from others (Berger *et al.*, 1980). As Balkwell (1994) pointed out, groups tend to allocate more or less "floor time" among their members in direct relation to how useful a particular contribution is expected to be, which is in turn inferred from the members' status.

Therefore, professional judges are *expected to participate more frequently* during trial and deliberation than lay judges. When a tribunal member participates, his/her comment will be regarded more highly if he/she is a professional judge.[9] The theory also implies that the high status members, such as professional judges in mixed tribunals, will be *selected as leaders more often*

---

[9]Of course, this conclusion would be highly predictable for any informal small group that consists of members with different status and levels of specific status characteristics.

(Carli, 1991). On the other hand, mixed tribunals, as emphasized earlier, are *formal* groups, and a part of their interaction is normatively specified. It is known in advance that the presiding professional judge will be in charge of questioning the witnesses and that other members of the tribunal may ask questions only after he/she has completed the questioning. By imposing such a legal rule, the *Criminal Procedure Law* (1993; 1998) provided some formal boundaries for the interaction in the tribunal during trial. The interaction patterns, status, and positions determined during trial may well be translated into the deliberation room and have a significant impact on the interaction in the tribunal behind closed doors as well.

Even when high and low status individuals behave in a similar way, higher status individuals are evaluated more positively (Humphrey, 1985). Interestingly, Meeker and Weitzel-O'Neill (1977) theorized that low status members were not only perceived as less competent, but were also perceived as lacking legitimacy if they contributed more than was expected for an individual of their status. In other words, high status members are expected to further enhance their status, while an attempt made by low status members to increase their status is considered as illegitimate. The only circumstances in which low status members are allowed to contribute more legitimately are when they are explicitly put in that position by a leader or when they show a desire to help the group resolve the task instead of achieving their own goals (Carli, 1991).

In addition, according to status characteristics theory, high status members are supposed to be *more influential* than low status members (Carli, 1991). When this argument is applied to mixed tribunals, it may be assumed that professional judges will be more influential than lay judges. Berger *et al.* (1977) specifically state that high status members will be expected to wield more influence when disagreements occur, so that disagreements will be resolved in their favor. The theory argues that the strength of the argument is not of primary importance; rather, the most important factor is the power of the source. In other words, rather than primarily believing the strength of the argument itself, the members will also think about the source of the comment.

It is quite possible that, for example, over time this repeated activity by professional judges and lay judges may reinforce the higher status of professional judges and, at the same time, further weaken the lower status of lay judges.

Chapter 6

Data Collection

I begin this chapter with a brief summary of basic facts about Croatia, its judicial system, the criminal process in Croatia, and the courtroom workgroup involved in trials by mixed tribunals. Next, I discuss the methodology used in this study — detailed questionnaires. Finally, I describe how and where questionnaires were collected from the respondents (professional judges, lay judges, state attorneys, and attorneys), as well as the respondents' demographic characteristics. This chapter sets the stage for a detailed analysis of the empirical results in Chapters 7, 8, and 9.

6.1   Croatia and Its Judicial System

6.1.1   Basic Facts about Croatia

The Republic of Croatia (*Republika Hrvatska*) is both a Central-European and a Mediterranean country with a territory of 21,829 square miles (56,610 square kilometers) and a population of 4.7 million (*1997 Croatian Almanac*, 1998). Eight out of ten citizens declared themselves as ethnic Croats and 78% are Roman Catholics (*1997 Croatian Almanac*, 1998). Croatia currently has two national and eight regional daily newspapers, 108 licensed radio stations, and ten TV stations (*1997 Croatian Almanac*, 1998).

Croats have been living in Southeastern Europe for more than thirteen centuries. History has witnessed an independent Croatian Kingdom and a union with Hungary and Austria. The Mediterranean parts of Croatia were periodically ruled by Italy. Following the collapse of the Austro-Hungarian Monarchy in 1918, Croatia became a part of the Kingdom of Serbs, Croats, and Slovenians (subsequently renamed the Kingdom of Yugoslavia). After World War II, Croatia became a socialist republic within the newly formed communist-dominated Yugoslav federation. In the midst of the recent war in Croatia, the Republic of Croatia was recognized as an independent and sovereign country by 1992.

Croatia is currently in transition toward a democratic society and market economy. Croatia features a small open economy, that is, its economy is characterized by a small internal market, a high share of trade in gross domestic product, a small share in world trade, and little influence on world prices (*1997 Croatian Almanac*, 1998). The economy and infrastructure of Croatia were among the most advanced in Eastern Europe when communism collapsed in the late 1980s. However, the events in the early 1990s, culminating in the war in Croatia (and soon thereafter in Bosnia and Herzegovina) and Croatia's subsequent independence from Yugoslavia, changed the economic landscape. The countries of the former Yugoslav federation virtually disappeared from the list of Croatia's major trading partners (with the exception of a moderate presence of Slovenia and Bosnia and Herzegovina).

Furthermore, the war brought considerable destruction to Croatia's infrastructure, triggered a major refugee crisis and loss of life and property, virtually annihilated the tourism industry in Croatia for several years, and created high unemployment (17% in December 1994; *The World Factbook*, 1995). Interestingly, although the per capita gross domestic product in Croatia decreased sharply from $5,106 in 1990 to $2,079 in 1992, after which it increased to $3,786 in 1995 (*1997 Croatian Almanac*, 1998), tight monetary policy was successful in controlling inflation and keeping it at relatively low levels (3% in 1994; *The World Factbook*, 1995).

The Croatian state is a multiparty parliamentary democracy. Although there were 40 officially registered political parties in Croatia by the end of 1993

(*Croatia: Facts and Figures*, 1997), the Croatian Democratic Union controls the vast majority of the seats. Despite the recent war, the political situation in the country remained relatively stable since the first multiparty elections in 1990.

6.1.2 Croatian Judicial System

There is a clear separation of the legislative, executive, and judicial functions of the government. The legislative function is performed by the Parliament (consisting of 100-160 members of the House of Representatives and 63 members of the House of Counties), the executive function is performed by the President and the Government, and the judicial function is performed by over 1,000 judges at the courts of various levels. The Supreme Court is the highest of the three regular judicial tiers, followed by regional courts (*okružni sudovi*; since 1994 *županijski sudovi*), and then by district courts (*općinski sudovi*). Criminal trials are held at district courts and at regional courts (Articles 16 and 17, *Courts Law*, 1994), while appeals are decided at regional courts and at the Supreme Court (Articles 17 and 22, *Courts Law*, 1994). At the time when this study was conducted, the courts of general jurisdiction were the Supreme Court, 14 regional courts, 6 military courts,[1] and 99 district courts.

Jurisdiction of district courts extends in the first instance over criminal cases for which the punishment prescribed in the *Criminal Procedure Law* does not exceed 10 years of imprisonment, civil cases, inheritance cases, and labor disputes (Article 16, *Courts Law*, 1994). These courts also execute verdicts and perform a number of other administrative functions, such as those of a land-registry office.

Regional courts also try criminal cases in the first instance, but only for the offenses for which the prescribed punishment exceeds 10 years of imprisonment. In addition, they have a special section that conducts investigations in criminal cases. If the state attorney or other prosecutor (private or subsidiary) decides

---

[1]Military courts have since been abolished by the *Presidential Decree* of 1996.

to prosecute, these cases will be subsequently tried at either district courts or regional courts. Regional courts also have an appellate jurisdiction over the criminal cases and civil cases tried by district courts (Article 17, *Courts Law*, 1994).

The constitutional principle of lay participation in the judicial process is stated in Article 118 of the *Constitution of the Republic of Croatia* (1990): "Lay judges participate in trials, in accordance with the law." The composition of mixed tribunals in the period from 1990 to 1998 was reviewed in Chapter 3. In short, at the time when the study was conducted,[2] offenses punishable by a fine or by imprisonment of up to 5 years were tried by a professional judge alone; offenses punishable by 5 or more years of imprisonment were tried by a mixed tribunal. The mixed tribunal consisted of one professional judge and two lay judges (*small tribunal*) for offenses punishable with imprisonment between 5 and 15 years, or by two professional judges and three lay judges (*large tribunal*) for offenses punishable by prison terms exceeding 15 years of imprisonment. Small tribunals met at both district courts and regional courts, while large tribunals met only at regional courts.

6.1.3   Croatian Criminal Procedure

Croatian criminal procedure, as regulated by the *Criminal Procedure Law* (1993),[3] is typical of the criminal procedures utilized in civil-law countries. Following the usual dichotomy of the type of criminal procedure ("inquisitorial" procedure utilized by civil-law countries and "accusatory" procedure utilized by common-law countries; Schlesinger *et al.*, 1988), Croatia's criminal procedure could be classified as inquisitorial. However, the term "inquisitorial" may be misleading because it equates modern criminal procedures in

---

[2]The study was conducted in 1993. At the time, the jurisdiction of mixed tribunals was limited by the *Presidential Decree* of 1991; it was subsequently reinstated to its original pre-war jurisdiction by the *Presidential Decree* of 1996.

[3]As discussed in Chapter 3, I will provide a description of the criminal procedure rules that were valid at the time when the data for this study were collected (i.e., in 1993).

civil-law countries and the medieval inquisitorial procedure. Indeed, Langbein remarked (1977, p. 1):

> Ango-American culture has long been beset with a pervasive myth about the conduct of criminal justice in European states. Continental criminal procedure is thought to be unjust and oppressive. It is called 'inquisitorial,' a term that has lost its neutral meaning and is now largely an epithet harkening back to the witchcraft trials and heresy persecutions of distant centuries. Among English-speaking peoples the belief is widespread (and quite mistaken) that in Continental procedure the accused is presumed guilty until he proves himself innocent ... The crux of the difference between common law and Continental procedure can be simply stated. It is the contrast between adversarial and nonadversarial fact-finding and law-applying ... In Continental systems the court that decides the case also has the active role in investigating the facts and formulating the issues in dispute. The court inquires, from which comes the word 'inquisitorial.' Comparativists have mostly given up the effort to rehabilitate that word, and in current usage we speak of the 'nonadversarial' or 'investigatory' character of Continental procedure.

Croatian authors (e.g., Bayer, 1988) approached the problem of the inadequacies of the term "inquisitorial" as it applies to Croatian criminal procedure by arguing that Croatian criminal procedure, as well as contemporary criminal procedures utilized in other civil-law countries across the globe today, are actually examples of a *mixed* criminal procedure, which includes elements of the medieval inquisitorial procedure and of the English accusatory procedure. Specifically, the foundation of modern criminal codes in civil-law countries is the French *Code d'instruction criminelle* of 1808, which was a synthesis of the elements of inquisitorial criminal process utilized in France before the Revolution of 1789 and the elements of accusatory criminal process (built upon the English model) introduced in 1791.

Although inquisitorial elements dominate the preliminary, investigation stage of the Croatian criminal process (the initiation of criminal process *ex officio*, the secrecy, the limitation on the defendant's rights, the right to question the defendant), accusatory elements are present as well (separation of the prosecutorial role, which is performed by the state attorney, and the investigative role, which is performed by the investigative judge). Trial is dominated by accusatory elements (the decision is made on the basis of the evidence presented during the trial, not on the basis of the dossier; the prosecutor and the defendant participate in the trial by making statements and by proposing the evidence to be examined and the witnesses and expert witnesses to be heard; the trial is oral and public; the principle of direct evaluation of evidence is applied), although inquisitorial elements are present as well (the active role of the court; the right of the court, the prosecutor, and the defense attorney to question the defendant).[4]

The Croatian *Criminal Procedure Law* (1993) distinguishes among three forms of criminal process: the regular criminal process, the summary criminal process, and the juvenile criminal process. The basic assumption is that the norms of the regular criminal process apply unless the *Criminal Procedure Law* (1993) determines otherwise. The juvenile criminal process applies to offenders ages 14 through 18 and provides for special provisions because of the offender's young age (Articles 452-492, *Criminal Procedure Law*, 1993). Summary criminal process, which somewhat streamlines the procedure, is used when the prescribed sanction is either a fine or up to three years of imprisonment (Articles 430-446, *Criminal Procedure Law*, 1993). The regular criminal process, reviewed in detail below, applies in trials of adult offenders for crimes for which the prescribed sanction exceeds three years of imprisonment.

The Croatian criminal process has several distinct phases: investigation, indictment and control of indictment, trial, appeal, and execution of the decision (Bayer, 1988, p. 109). The criminal process officially starts when an investigative professional judge produces a written decision declaring that the

---

[4]See Bayer (1988, p. 19-23) for details.

investigation is to commence.[5] The offender can appeal this decision to a professional tribunal.[6]

However, the initial decision by the investigative judge to open the investigation may be made only when there is reasonable suspicion that the offender has committed the crime (Article 157, *Criminal Procedure Law*, 1993) and only upon the prosecutor's request (Article 158, *Criminal Procedure Law*, 1993). The prosecutor has to follow the form determined by the law (Article 158, *Criminal Procedure Law*, 1993) and to describe the basis for reasonable suspicion. The latter clearly suggests that the prosecutor will have conducted a pre-investigation in order to learn that there is reasonable suspicion.

The prosecutor will typically base his/her suspicion on the criminal report (a written report or an oral report to the prosecutor stating that the crime has been committed, who the offender is, and the evidence that provides the basis for the suspicion; Bayer, 1988, p. 115). If the report is not complete, the prosecutor will contact the police in order to collect the missing pieces and to thus obtain sufficient information to make a decision on whether or not there is an adequate basis for the request to open an investigation. Therefore, although the criminal process formally starts with the investigation, there is a phase that precedes this investigation (during which the prosecutor and the police play a very active role). In fact, the police may interview citizens (although not as offenders, witnesses, and expert witnesses) and the citizens have the right to refuse to cooperate (Article 151, *Criminal Procedure Law*, 1993).

Once the investigative judge receives a request for an investigation from the prosecutor, the investigative judge will examine the case file compiled by the police and the prosecutor, and interview the offender (who has the right to

---

[5]The *Criminal Procedure Law* (1993, Article 160) determines that in the cases in which the prosecutor perceives that there is sufficient evidence for the indictment there is no need for the prosecutor to request that an investigation be open.

[6]If the offender appeals, the investigation will not begin until the professional tribunal issues its ruling. At that time, the investigation will begin only if the tribunal upheld the original investigative judge's decision.

have an attorney present) in order to decide whether there are sufficient legal grounds for the opening of the investigation (Article 159, *Criminal Procedure Law*, 1993). If the investigative judge determines that there are insufficient legal grounds for the opening of the investigation, the investigative judge will nevertheless forward the case to the professional tribunal, which will then issue the final ruling regarding the opening of the investigation (Article 159, *Criminal Procedure Law*, 1993). If, on the other hand, the investigative judge determines that there are sufficient legal grounds for the opening of the investigation, the investigative judge will produce a written decision. This decision may be appealed to the professional tribunal by both the prosecutor and the offender (Article 159, *Criminal Procedure Law*, 1993).

The purpose of investigation is to collect evidence that will aid both the prosecutor's decision on whether to bring the indictment and the investigative judge's decision on whether to end the investigative process once the investigation has been completed (Article 157, *Criminal Procedure Law*, 1993).

Unlike the medieval inquisitorial procedure, the modern mixed procedure recognizes the separation of powers between the prosecutor (who brings the indictment) and the investigative judge (who is an independent arbiter). The role of the investigative judge is an active one; the investigative judge decides which evidence will be examined and which witnesses will be examined. The prosecutor and the defendant have extensive rights during the investigation, including the right to propose the evidence and witnesses to be examined, the right to be present during these proceedings, and the right to examine the whole case file.

When the investigative judge decides that the investigation is completed, the investigative judge sends the case file to the prosecutor (Article 174, *Criminal Procedure Law*, 1993). The prosecutor has no discretionary power in regard to bringing the indictment; following the principle of legality, if there are reasonable grounds to believe that the offense has been committed by the offender, the prosecutor must bring charges against the defendant. Following the format prescribed by the law (Article 262, *Criminal Procedure Law*, 1993), the prosecutor drafts the indictment and sends it to the trial court.

Unlike the medieval inquisitorial procedure, the modern Croatian criminal procedure provides the defendant with the right to submit a written objection to the indictment to a professional tribunal (Article 267, *Criminal Procedure Law*, 1993). Furthermore, in certain cases the presiding judge of the mixed tribunal assigned to try the case may also exercise the right to question the indictment and submit an objection to a professional tribunal (Article 277, *Criminal Procedure Law*, 1993). This accusatory element in the criminal procedures of the civil-law countries is typically overlooked. As Schlesinger *et al.* (1988, p. 477) emphasized:

> Under the traditional civil-law practice, the dossier now goes to a three-judge panel — on a higher level of the judicial hierarchy. Only if this panel, having studied the dossier and having given defense counsel an opportunity to submit arguments and to suggest the taking of additional evidence, determines that there exists what we [the American tradition] would call 'reasonable cause,' will the accused have to stand trial. (It should be noted here how misleading it can be to call the continental procedure 'inquisitorial' and to contrast it with our allegedly 'adversary' process. Under continental procedure, the accused has a two-fold opportunity to be heard — first in the course of the preliminary investigation, and again when the three-judge panel examines the dossier — *before* any decision is made whether he has to stand trial. This should be compared with the completely nonadversary grand jury proceeding by which in the overwhelming majority of American jurisdictions a prosecutor can obtain an indictment.)

After the indictment has been declared valid (as determined in Article 278, *Criminal Procedure Law*, 1993), the professional judge who is assigned to try the case will determine the date for the beginning of the trial and summon the defendant, witnesses, and expert witnesses (Articles 279-286, *Criminal Procedure Law*, 1993). The professional judge has control over the trial (Article 292, *Criminal Procedure Law*, 1993) and has the responsibility of providing for a thorough examination of the case. If the case is tried by a mixed tribunal, the role of the presiding professional judge during trial is more active than the roles of other members of the tribunal (either professional judges or lay judges). The trial is oral and public.[7]

I will provide a more detailed overview of the trial and deliberation/voting stages of the criminal process in the subsequent chapters. A short account of these stages is as follows. After the proper composition of the tribunal, the presence of the summoned individuals, and identity of the defendant have been determined and the defendant has been informed that he/she may propose the evidence to be examined, make statements, and ask questions of co-defendants, witnesses, and expert witnesses, the trial officially begins with the reading of the indictment by the prosecutor (Article 315, *Criminal Procedure Law*, 1993). Next, the presiding professional judge checks whether the defendant has understood the indictment and the defendant (who does not take the oath) is provided with an opportunity to provide his/her defense in a coherent statement (Article 316, *Criminal Procedure Law*, 1993).

Although the defendant has the right to remain silent (Article 316, *Criminal Procedure Law*, 1993), in the majority of the cases the defendant does not exercise this right; rather, the defendant usually provides a statement in which he/she either confesses or provides his/her own account of the events. The confession by the defendant (either before trial or during trial) does not end the trial stage — the defendant does not have the right to plead guilty and waive the right to trial; even the most complete confession does not absolve the tribunal (or, if applicable, the professional judge alone) of the responsibility to examine other evidence and question witnesses and expert witness (Article 323, *Criminal Procedure Law*, 1993). The statement by the defendant is followed by the questioning by the presiding judge, other members of the tribunal (if applicable), the prosecutor, the victim(s), the defense counsel, the

---

[7]The public may be excluded, as determined by Articles 287-290, *Criminal Procedure Law* (1993).

co-defendants, and the expert witnesses (Articles 317-318, *Criminal Procedure Law*, 1993).

Upon receiving the suggestions made by the prosecutor and the defendant, the mixed tribunal (or, if applicable, the professional judge alone) determines the evidence to be examined and the witnesses and expert witnesses to be heard. The next stage of trial consists of the examination of evidence and the questioning of witnesses and expert witnesses (Article 322, *Criminal Procedure Law*, 1993). At the completion of the trial stage, the prosecutor, the defense attorney, and the defendant give closing statements and the mixed tribunal (or, if applicable, the professional judge alone) declares that the trial is over (Articles 339-344, *Criminal Procedure Law*, 1993). Everybody, except for the tribunal members and the court typist, then leaves the courtroom and the tribunal is ready to commence the next stage — deliberation and voting.

In general terms, if the case is tried by a mixed tribunal, professional judges and lay judges need to reach a joint (majority) decision on the guilt and, if appropriate, the sentence. The votes of lay judges have the same weight as the votes of their professional counterparts, and, since lay judges outnumber professional judges in the tribunal, they may outvote professional judges.

The decision, based only on the facts determined during the trial, is proclaimed publicly (Articles 345-347, *Criminal Procedure Law*, 1993), that is, the parties and the public are invited back into the courtroom, where the decision is stated and the reasons for the verdict are explained (Article 352, *Criminal Procedure Law*, 1993). Soon thereafter, the presiding professional judge (or, if applicable, the professional judge alone) writes the verdict and sends copies to the parties in the case (Articles 356-358, *Criminal Procedure Law*, 1993). The verdict may be appealed by the prosecutor and/or by the defendant on both the law and the facts (Articles 359-391, *Criminal Procedure Law*, 1993).[8] In certain cases, the *Criminal Procedure Law* (1993) allows for extraordinary

---

[8]Interestingly, the appeal may request that new evidence be heard by the appellate tribunal, and, if the appellate tribunal agrees with the request, the appellate tribunal examines the new evidence in a trial session.

legal redress (Articles 400-429, *Criminal Procedure Law*, 1993). If the appeal and extraordinary legal redress have been unsuccessfully exhausted or waived altogether, the verdict will be executed.

6.1.4   Courtroom Workgroup

The members of the courtroom workgroup who routinely participate in trials by mixed tribunals are professional judges, lay judges, state attorneys, and attorneys.[9] Professional judges and lay judges are members of mixed tribunals; state attorneys and attorneys often argue cases in front of mixed tribunals and are thus in a position to observe the work of mixed tribunals during the trial stage. I now provide an account of eligibility requirements, the selection process, and available statistics for each of the four groups. These accounts will set the stage for the description of the respective populations to which the respondents belong (furnished later in this chapter) and for the analyses and discussions of the results of this study (furnished in subsequent chapters).

At the time when the study was conducted, the law required that **professional judges** be law school graduates who have passed the bar exam and who fulfill general employment requirements and other legal requirements (Article 75, *Regular Courts Law*, 1988). By setting the bar exam requirement, the legislature implicitly mandated that a professional judge had to have at least two years of experience as a court apprentice,[10] as an apprentice at the state attorney's office, or as an apprentice with an attorney, or at least four years of

---

[9]I frequently refer to defense attorneys simply as "attorneys" in order to avoid confusion; although defense attorneys defend their clients most of the time, they can also prosecute on behalf of their clients in some cases.

[10]Court apprentices are law school graduates who serve at the courts either as volunteers or as paid employees. The nature of their service is similar to that of law clerks in the United States. Court apprentices undergo periodic rotations and thus spend a few months at each of the court's divisions. In each rotation they clerk for a judge with a different specialty (e.g., pre-trial investigation, criminal trials, civil trials, juvenile trials, appeals). At the conclusion of their two-year period of service, court apprentices take the bar exam. The court at which the apprentices served will offer associate level positions to a few of those who pass the exam; others continue their careers at another court, at one of the state attorney's offices, in private practice, or as in-house attorneys.

experience on other law-related jobs, as these are the necessary requirements for the bar exam. Article 49 of the new *Courts Law* (1994) retained the same basic requirements: a law degree and the bar exam. The newly added requirement for appointment to the bench is a minimum of two years of law-related work experience after the bar exam (Article 50, *Courts Law*, 1994). Prior to 1994, this requirement was nevertheless implicit because the established practice was (and still is) to precede the appointment to the bench with an appointment at the associate level.

Interestingly, while there was no prohibition for professional judges to be members of the Communist Party during the communist regime, the post-communist period features an explicit and strict prohibition: professional judges neither may be members nor may participate in the activities of *any* political party (Article 60, *Courts Law*, 1994).

While a person who fulfills these requirements may be appointed to the bench at one of district courts, more extensive experience is required for an appointment to the bench at a regional court: at least six years of experience as a professional judge, state attorney, attorney, or public notary, at least eight years of experience as an associate at a regional court or at the Supreme Court, or at least ten years of experience at other law-related tasks (Article 51, *Courts Law*, 1994).

For candidates previously employed as professional judges, one of the factors considered in the appointment process is previous performance at a bench. The factors taken into account include (1) quality of legal decisions and adherence to deadlines, (2) diligence, (3) ability to express himself/herself orally and in writing, (4) ability to communicate with parties in the cases in a respectful manner, (5) relationships with other judges and court employees and off-duty behavior, (6) ability to perform administrative tasks, and (7) distinguishing characteristics, including published scholarly and professional papers (Article 52, *Courts Law*, 1994). Another important element in the appointment decision at higher courts is an evaluation of the candidate's previous work, which is given by the presiding judge or the judicial council.

The Ministry of Justice determines and maintains the desired number of professional judges at each court and announces a vacant judicial position when necessary. The Ministry administers technical aspects of the selection process and sends a list of candidates who fulfill the requirements for the position to the State Judicial Council (Articles 16-18, *State Judicial Council Law*, 1993). The State Judicial Council, formed in 1993, makes the final selection from the list (Article 12, *State Judicial Council Law*, 1993).

The number of district court judges gradually increased from 680 in 1981 to its peak in 1989 (823 judges), and then started gradually to decrease to approximately 600-650 in the 1990s (the numbers range from 745 in 1991 to 549 in 1995). There are fewer judges at regional courts (280-300 in the 1980s and 200-250 in the 1990s); the numbers decreased from 276 in 1991 to 212 in 1995. In addition, each year there were between 160-205 court apprentices in the 1980s and between 100-160 court apprentices in the 1990s (Table 6.1).

On average, from being a minority (38-39% in 1981-82), women gradually constituted one-half (48% in 1988-90) or even the majority (55% in 1993-1995) of professional judges at district courts (Table 6.1). The percentage of female professional judges at regional courts increased gradually from 20% in the early 1980s, to 30% in the late 1980s, and to 40% in 1996.

Lay judges are persons who do not have a legal education and who earn their living from other full-time occupations or are retired.[11] Lay judges spend only a few days per year performing their lay judges' role and receive "compensation for the expenses, including lost salary, in addition to the reward" (Article 73, *Courts Law*, 1994). The terms and conditions for the expenses and rewards are determined by the Ministry of Justice (Article 73, *Courts Law*, 1994).

Generally, the number of lay judges vastly exceeds the number of professional judges; there have been on average 5,000-6,000 lay judges at district

---

[11]The eligibility requirements for lay judges and their selection process, both those that applied when the study was conducted and the contemporary ones, were described in Chapter 3.

Table 6.1: Number and gender composition of professional judges by year.[a]

Year	Supreme Court (1)		Regional Courts (14)		District Courts (99)		Apprentices	
	All	Women	All	Women	All	Women	All	Women
1981	32	4 (12.5%)	280	51 (18.2%)	680	261 (38.4%)	178	NA
1982	29	5 (17.2%)	279	57 (20.4%)	696	270 (38.8%)	182	NA
1983	28	3 (10.7%)	277	64 (23.1%)	719	289 (40.2%)	167	NA
1984	27	3 (11.1%)	291	70 (24.1%)	723	317 (43.8%)	198	NA
1985	31	6 (19.4%)	290	79 (27.2%)	747	336 (45.0%)	193	NA
1986	34	7 (20.6%)	293	85 (29.0%)	785	358 (45.6%)	205	NA
1987	31	7 (22.6%)	297	88 (29.6%)	792	375 (47.3%)	205	NA
1988	37	10 (27.0%)	294	88 (29.9%)	812	389 (47.9%)	190	NA
1989	39	9 (23.1%)	303	92 (30.4%)	823	394 (47.9%)	182	NA
1990	39	9 (23.1%)	297	91 (30.6%)	800	385 (48.1%)	116	NA
1991	32	8 (25.0%)	276	88 (31.9%)	745	355 (47.7%)	92	NA
1992	29	7 (24.1%)	263	87 (33.1%)	669	334 (49.9%)	127	NA
1993	27	7 (25.9%)	260	90 (34.6%)	704	384 (54.5%)	96	NA
1994	27	7 (25.9%)	244	82 (33.6%)	647	358 (55.3%)	139	NA
1995	25	10 (40.0%)	212	69 (32.5%)	549	302 (55.0%)	152	NA
1996	25	10 (40.0%)	246	98 (39.8%)	659	404 (61.3%)	160	NA

---

[a]Sources: *1991 Statistical Yearbook* (1991), p. 356, *1993 Statistical Yearbook* (1993), p. 446, *1997 Statistical Yearbook* (1997), p. 473.

courts in the 1990s (the numbers range from 7,828 in 1991 to 4,981 in 1996) and 1,300 lay judges at regional courts in the 1990s (the numbers range from 1,520 in 1991 to 1,188 in 1996). The numbers were larger in the 1980s; there were approximately 9,500 lay judges at district courts and 2,000 lay judges at regional courts (Table 6.2). The percentage of female lay judges is substantially smaller than the percentage of female professional judges; on average, only 16% - 20% of lay judges at district courts and 17% - 22% of lay judges at regional courts have been women (Table 6.2).

The presiding judge summons lay judges to come to the court on a particular day and perform their duty (Article 45, *Judicial Proceedings Act*, 1988). Each court keeps a registry of lay judges. In addition to contact information and other basic information about the lay judges (name, address, telephone number, date of birth, marital status, nationality, education, occupation, gender), this registry includes records of the lay judges' performance of their duty (the date of the scheduled trial, record of attendance, absenteeism and related reasons [if applicable], other data about participation in the trial, and the signature of the presiding judge of the mixed tribunal).

At the time when this study was conducted, the law required that **state attorneys** be law school graduates who have passed the bar exam and who fulfill general employment requirements and other legal requirements (Article 30, *Public Prosecutor Law*, 1977). The new law of 1995 (*State Attorneys Law*, 1995) retained most of these requirements; in addition, it specified more precisely the level of experience required for each position. In particular, persons to be selected to serve as state attorneys at district offices need to have no experience other than that required for the bar exam (two years of experience as a court apprentice, an apprentice with a state attorney, or an apprentice with an attorney) or, if they did not serve as apprentices at state attorneys' offices, attorneys' offices, or at courts, they need to have an additional two years of experience working on legal tasks after the bar exam (Article 37, *State Attorneys Law*, 1995). State attorneys at regional offices need to have more experience; upon passing the bar exam, they need to have at least three years of experi-

Table 6.2: Number and gender composition of lay judges by year.[a]

Year	Supreme Court (1) All	Women	Regional Courts (14) All	Women	District Courts (99) All	Women
1981	29	7 (24.0%)	1,296	358 (18.6%)	9,382	1,530 (16.3%)
1982	29	7 (24.0%)	1,861	343 (18.4%)	9,372	1,514 (16.2%)
1983	29	7 (24.0%)	1,914	345 (18.0%)	9,380	1,668 (17.8%)
1984	15	2 (13.3%)	1,938	350 (18.1%)	9,642	1,667 (17.3%)
1985	15	2 (13.3%)	1,990	347 (17.4%)	9,706	1,738 (17.9%)
1986	15	2 (13.3%)	1,972	329 (16.7%)	9,878	1,777 (18.0%)
1987	15	2 (13.3%)	1,959	325 (16.6%)	9,786	1,832 (18.7%)
1988	15	2 (13.3%)	1,810	329 (18.2%)	9,453	1,847 (19.5%)
1989	15	2 (13.3%)	1,594	294 (18.4%)	9,486	1,882 (19.8%)
1990	15	2 (13.3%)	1,586	296 (18.7%)	8,928	1,727 (19.3%)
1991	15	2 (13.3%)	1,520	287 (18.9%)	7,828	1,641 (21.0%)
1992	NA	NA	1,292	251 (19.4%)	6,634	1,250 (18.8%)
1993	NA	NA	1,285	250 (19.5%)	6,607	1,277 (19.3%)
1994	NA	NA	1,266	244 (19.3%)	6,302	1,211 (19.2%)
1995	NA	NA	1,208	268 (22.2%)	5,434	1,047 (19.3%)
1996	NA	NA	1,188	251 (21.1%)	4,981	964 (19.4%)

[a]Sources: *1991 Statistical Yearbook* (1991), p. 356, *1993 Statistical Yearbook* (1993), p. 446, *1997 Statistical Yearbook* (1997), p. 473.

ence as state attorneys, attorneys, or judges, or at least six years of experience as misdemeanor judges, notaries public, or as associates with the state attorneys, or at least ten years of experience in working on other law-related tasks (Article 37, *State Attorneys Law*, 1995). In other words, the requirements for district state attorneys and regional state attorneys are very similar to the requirements for district professional judges and regional professional judges, respectively (Article 37, *State Attorneys Law*, 1995). The requirements for state attorneys at the national office include even more extensive experience (Article 37, *State Attorneys Law*, 1995).

Interestingly, while state attorneys were prohibited to be members of the Communist Party (Article 33, *Public Prosecutor Law* 1989), the prohibition of political party membership was lifted at the very beginning of the period of transition toward democracy (Article 7, *Changes and Additions to the State Attorneys Law of 1989*, 1990). In 1993, the name of the institution was changed from the Public Prosecutor to the State Attorney.

The Minister of Justice determines the number of assistants to state attorneys at each office on the basis of recommendations furnished by the State Attorneys of the Republic of Croatia (Article 34, *State Attorneys Law*, 1995). State attorneys and their assistants are appointed by the State Judicial Council (Article 35, *State Attorneys Law*, 1995; Article 12, *State Judicial Council Law*, 1993). State attorneys are appointed for a period of eight years with a possibility of reappointment, while their assistants are hired as permanent employees (Article 35, *State Attorneys Law*, 1995). State attorneys have the duty to prosecute criminal offenders and to protect the constitutionality and the rule of law (Article 2, *State Attorneys Law*, 1995).

The state attorneys' system consists of the Office of the National State Attorney, 14 Offices of the Regional State Attorney, and about 60 Offices (62 Offices before 1996 and 57 Offices after 1996) of the District State Attorney. The *1997 Statistical Yearbook* (1997) indicates that there were approximately 330-380 state attorneys and their assistants each year in the 1980s and approximately 300 state attorneys and their assistants each year in the period

Table 6.3: Number of state attorneys & assistant state attorneys by year.[a]

Year	National Office (1)	Regional Offices (14)	District Offices (62)	Apprentices
1981	18	108	205	58
1982	18	108	208	60
1983	16	110	213	53
1984	16	113	218	56
1985	16	112	222	67
1986	16	115	222	62
1987	15	118	234	73
1988	17	121	238	58
1989	16	121	235	50
1990	16	118	231	37
1991	17	117	210	41
1992	17	104	195	43
1993	17	101	210	32
1994	15	96	195	38
1995	15	96	202	41
1996	14	97	174	46

[a]Sources: *1991 Statistical Yearbook* (1991), p. 358, *1993 Statistical Yearbook* (1993), p. 448, *1997 Statistical Yearbook* (1997), p. 474.

1992-1996 (Table 6.3), out of whom very few (15-18) were employed at the National Office, 100-120 were employed at regional offices, and about 200 were employed at district offices (200-240 in the 1980s and 170-200 in the 1990s). In addition, each year there were approximately 60 apprentices in the 1980s and approximately 40 apprentices in the 1990s.

Attorneys are lawyers who are allowed to provide legal counseling and represent clients in the legal processes (Article 3, *Attorneys Law*, 1994). The *Attorneys Law* (1994) lists the requirements for registration as an attorney. These requirements are very similar to the requirements required by the *Attorneys Law* (1972). They include, among others, a law degree, the bar exam, at least three years of experience as an apprentice with a state attorney, attorney, or as a court apprentice, or at least five years of experience at other

Table 6.4: Number and gender composition of attorneys by year.[a]

Year	Attorneys		Apprentices	
	All	Women	All	Women
1981	777	57 (7.3%)	109	43 (39.4%)
1982	811	59 (7.3%)	161	63 (39.1%)
1983	748	62 (8.3%)	175	66 (37.7%)
1984	785	72 (9.2%)	202	68 (33.7%)
1985	806	76 (9.4%)	207	56 (27.1%)
1986	821	83 (10.1%)	215	68 (31.6%)
1987	847	85 (10.0%)	217	77 (35.5%)
1988	881	99 (11.2%)	242	84 (34.7%)
1989	954	127 (13.3%)	261	100 (38.3%)
1990	1,085	172 (15.9%)	338	144 (42.6%)
1991	1,221	232 (19.0%)	380	171 (45.0%)
1992	1,310	281 (21.5%)	418	202 (48.3%)
1993	1,513	356 (23.5%)	436	233 (53.4%)
1994	1,782	458 (25.7%)	483	263 (54.5%)
1995	1,939	535 (27.6%)	509	299 (58.7%)
1996	2,036	583 (28.6%)	522	293 (56.1%)

[a]Sources: *1991 Statistical Yearbook* (1991), p. 374, *1992 Statistical Yearbook* (1993), p. 460, *1997 Statistical Yearbook* (1997), p. 475.

law-related tasks (Article 31, *Attorneys Law*, 1972; Article 48, *Attorneys Law*, 1994). One will not be registered as an attorney if one is employed or is a subject of a pending criminal investigation or a trial for an offense prosecuted *ex officio* (Article 31, *Attorneys Law*, 1972; Article 48, *Attorneys Law*, 1994).[12]

There is a special provision for law professors; they can be registered as attorneys even without the required experience if they have passed the bar exam (Article 50, *Attorneys Law*, 1994).[13] The *Attorneys Law* of 1972 did not even require law professors to pass the bar exam before they were allowed to practice law as attorneys (Article 33, *Attorneys Law*, 1972).

A license can be denied to a candidate who has been sentenced for a crime committed against the state, for misuse of official position, for a crime involving illegal economic gain, or any other crime committed because of "immoral motives" (Article 49, *Attorneys Law*, 1994; similarly, Article 32, *Attorneys Law*, 1972). Such a person cannot be registered as an attorney for at least ten years from the moment the punishment has been served, the sentence has been pardoned, or the statute of limitations has expired (Article 49, *Attorneys Law*, 1994; similarly, Article 32, *Attorneys Law*, 1972).

The number of attorneys gradually increased from the 1980s to the early 1990s (from approximately 800 to 1,310 in 1992), and then even more rapidly from 1992 to 1996 (from 1,310 to 2,036; Table 6.4). Less than one-third of attorneys are women (Table 6.4), but the percentage of women has increased dramatically from less than 10% in the early 1980s to almost 30% in the mid-1990s. The number of apprentices increased from 150 in the early 1980s, to 200-250 in the late 1980s, to 500 in the 1990s (Table 6.4). Female apprentices constituted approximately 40% of the apprentices in the 1980s, while that percentage increased to 55-60% in the 1990s (Table 6.4).

---

[12]The great majority of offenses listed in the *Criminal Code* are prosecuted *ex officio* by the state attorney. Other offenses, typically less serious ones, can be prosecuted by the victim.

[13]One of the requirements for the bar exam is two years of experience as a court apprentice, an apprentice with a state attorney or an attorney, or four years of experience at other law-related tasks.

6.2 Data and Methodology

6.2.1 Courts and Offices Included in the Study

The data were collected primarily in two regions of Croatia — the Zagreb Region and the Bjelovar Region. The hierarchical structure of the courts in which the data were collected is shown in Figure 6.1. In addition, because the number of professional judges at the first instance in the respective criminal divisions of the Regional Courts in Zagreb and in Bjelovar was small, I also surveyed professional judges from the Regional Courts in Osijek, Rijeka, Zadar, and Varaždin. The hierarchical organization of the state attorneys' offices in which the data were collected is shown in Figure 6.2.

The Zagreb Region and the Bjelovar Region differ in terms of *demographic and socio-economic characteristics*, as well as in terms of the organization of their respective courts. Zagreb is the political, administrative, business, cultural, and educational center of the country. The city population was 953,607 in 1991 (*1992 Statistical Yearbook*, 1993, p. 464). Bjelovar, the 17th largest city in Croatia (66,039 inhabitants in 1991; *1992 Statistical Yearbook*, 1993, p. 464), is the center of a region dominated by agriculture, food industry, and building materials industry.

The data in Table 6.5 show the educational levels of the active population between the ages 15 and 60 in each city in which data were collected. "Active population," according to the Croatian Central Bureau of Statistics, consists of individuals capable of work, ages 15 to 60, who are either working and have registered at the public employment office, are out of work and have registered at the public employment office, are serving their military service, or are in prison.[14] The general pattern is: as the size of the city decreases, the percentage of active population in lower educational levels increases. In towns with population below 60,000, over one-half of the population did not

---

[14]The definition of active population excludes housewives. According to the terminology used by the Croatian Central Bureau of Statistics, adding the population of housewives to active population yields the "working contingent."

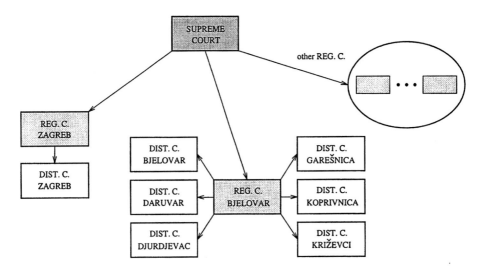

Figure 6.1: Courts of general jurisdiction at which the data for this study were collected.

finish elementary school, whereas this can be said about only 18% of Zagreb's population. Thirteen percent of Zagreb's inhabitants had graduated from college, whereas only 3% or fewer of the inhabitants in smaller towns have college degrees.

The Zagreb Region and the Bjelovar Region differ not only in terms of their demographic and socio-economic characteristics, but also in terms of the *organization of their respective courts*. The Regional Court of Zagreb, as a court of second instance (appellate court), has jurisdiction over the District Court of Zagreb (as well as other district courts in the Zagreb Region); the District Court of Zagreb is the largest district court in the country with 24 professional judges in the Criminal Division alone (in June 1993). The jurisdiction of the Regional Court of Bjelovar in the second instance extends over a number of smaller district courts, each of which has several professional judges who decided criminal cases as a part of their caseload. These district courts are located in smaller cities, including Daruvar, Djurdjevac, Garešnica, Koprivnica, Križevci, and Vrbovec.

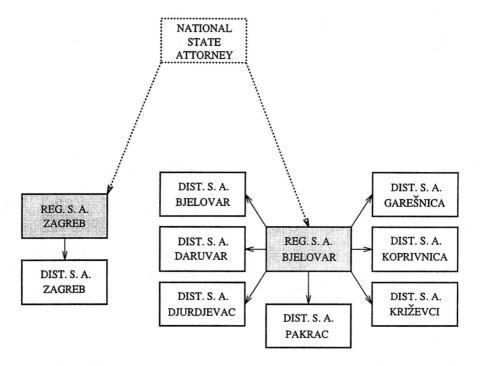

Figure 6.2: Hierarchical organization of the state attorneys' offices at which the data for this study were collected (data were not collected at the National State Attorney's Office, denoted here with dashed lines).

Table 6.5: Education of active population in the cities in which the data were collected.[a]

city	active population size	less than elementary school	elementary school	high school	some college	college	unknown
Bjelovar	30,558	47.77%	17.29%	28.68%	2.70%	3.32%	0.24%
Daruvar	15,232	52.99%	12.23%	29.55%	2.79%	2.34%	0.10%
Djurdjevac	22,184	62.82%	18.51%	16.02%	1.55%	1.04%	0.06%
Garešnica	10,135	59.35%	18.43%	19.03%	1.86%	1.21%	0.12%
Koprivnica	30,716	51.00%	18.24%	25.63%	2.21%	2.80%	0.12%
Križevci	20,346	60.77%	16.01%	19.00%	2.32%	1.78%	0.12%
Zagreb	399,333	17.96%	15.97%	48.11%	5.00%	12.52%	0.44%

[a]Source: *1981 Census of Population, Households, and Residences; Active Population and Employed Workers,* 1986.

Table 6.5: Continued.[a]

city	active population size	less than elementary school	elementary school	high school	some college	college	unknown
Osijek	65,871	25.40%	15.30%	47.20%	5.00%	6.90%	0.26%
Rijeka	231,027	22.83%	17.58%	47.41%	6.19%	5.61%	0.38%
Varaždin	45,236	36.23%	16.80%	38.39%	4.10%	4.36%	0.12%
Zadar	41,546	23.80%	16.78%	46.34%	5.52%	7.23%	0.33%

[a]This part of Table 4.2. lists the cities that are neither in the Zagreb Region nor in the Bjelovar Region.

6.2.2 Selecting the Method

During the design stage, I considered various methods of data collection with the intent to select the most appropriate methodology that would at the same time be feasible. Unfortunately, there are inherent legal limitations and some otherwise desirable methods had to be discarded.

Observation of trials and deliberations with the appropriate mechanism of recording relevant information during trial and deliberation would have been very informative. Not only would observation provide an opportunity to directly measure frequency, importance (relevance), and content of lay judges' and professional judges' questions and comments, but they would also provide first-hand insight into the dynamics of interaction between professional judges and lay judges. Yet, as appealing as observation sounds, it was (and still is) illegal to observe and/or record deliberations by mixed tribunals (Article 118, *Criminal Procedure Law*, 1993; Article 142, *Criminal Procedure Law*, 1998).

The only persons present in the courtrooms during deliberations, in addition to the members of the tribunals themselves and the court typist, are court apprentices. The law does not allow court apprentices to be present during deliberation (Article 118, *Criminal Procedure Law*, 1993; Article 142, *Criminal Procedure Law*, 1998), yet, their presence is tolerated by both parties in the case and the mixed tribunal because it is viewed as a part of the training and valuable learning experience provided to court apprentices. Trying to involve court apprentices in the study by asking them to observe deliberations and record relevant information was the only feasible way to carry out observations; the law does not make any provisions for the presence of researchers, and the courts were not willing to allow my presence (or the presence of other researchers) in the courtrooms. I began by obtaining the permission from the President of the District Court in Zagreb to involve court apprentices. They were given permission to observe deliberations and record the relevant information, pending the approval of each professional judge. After a very short period of time, that is, a few days and but a few observed trials, problems began to mount. In particular, professional judges, although they initially agreed to this method of data collection in their courtrooms, expressed a concern that state attorneys and/or attorneys might take advantage of the situation and claim a violation of criminal procedure by arguing that court apprentices were not only present during deliberations (which by itself was something they might have been prepared to tolerate), but were also recording potentially sensitive information about those deliberations. A modified strategy of recording relevant information from memory *after* the deliberation fell victim to the same kinds of arguments. Consequently, the courtroom doors were closed both *de iure* and *de facto* for social science observation during deliberations.

Another potential method of data collection was the analysis of archival data. Unfortunately, the use of archival data is both illegal and of limited use. First, the *Criminal Procedure Law* (1993, Article 89; 1998, Article 81) requires the tribunal to record only the course of deliberation and voting and to place its final decision in a sealed envelope to be kept with the case file in the court archives. Thus, members of mixed tribunals did not record their deliberations in detail; in practice, tribunals recorded little more than their final decision. That is, very little information relevant to this study could have been uncovered even it were legal to examine these records. Second, such an examination would have been illegal because only the members of the tribunal that decides the appeal or legal redress are allowed to open the sealed envelope (Article 89, *Criminal Procedure Law*, 1993).

It would have been beneficial to interview professional judges and lay judges and to thus obtain both perspectives. Unfortunately, professional judges either declined to be interviewed altogether, or replied by only briefly and informally stating their (most often negative) opinion about mixed tribunals. At that point I decided not to pursue in-depth interviews. At best, I could have interviewed a certain (small) number of lay judges. However, this would have created the same kind of asymmetry that was seen in some of the earlier studies (e.g., Casper and Zeisel, 1972), wherein only one group of participants in trials by mixed tribunals (e.g., professional judges) was involved in the study.

A natural step at this point was to use questionnaires[15] to determine the respondents' *perceptions* of the frequency, content, and importance of lay participation, as well as their perceptions about the system of mixed tribunals in general. To compensate for the infeasibility of interviews, I included several open-ended questions and, in particular, invited the respondents to write down at the end of the questionnaire any additional comments they might have.

6.2.3 Questionnaires

Each respondent in the study filled out an appropriate questionnaire (in Croatian). Among the most extensive questionnaires were those distributed to professional judges at district courts; their questionnaire contained 59 items covering several topics about mixed tribunals. I will describe the main features of that questionnaire and will then use it as a reference point for a description of the questionnaires filled out by other categories of respondents.

Professional Judges from District Courts

The first section in the questionnaire explored *how professional judges evaluated the behavior of lay judges during trial*. Items inquired about the frequency and importance of the questions asked by lay judges ("According to your experience, how frequently do lay judges ask questions during trial?"; "How would you evaluate the importance of the questions asked by lay judges during trial?"). Professional judges were asked to identify the gender, age, and educational categories of typical lay judges who were more likely to ask questions during trial. A question also inquired about the frequency with which lay judges read the case file prior to trial.

The second section in the questionnaire dealt with *professional judges' perception of lay judges' evaluation of evidence*. The questions asked here were related to lay judges' ability to understand and evaluate evidence ("Do you

---

[15]One might argue that mock trials and deliberations could have been considered. I decided against mock trials because I was interested in what goes on in actual trials rather than in simulated ones.

feel that lay judges are generally able to understand evidence?"; "Generally speaking, lay judges evaluate evidence: ..."). Next, professional judges were asked about possible reasons why lay judges may have encountered difficulties in understanding of evidence. Two questions required a comparison between lay judges' understanding of simple and complex evidence and some related issues.

The third section in the questionnaire focused on *deliberation*. The first few questions in this part covered the summation by professional judges, its frequency, purpose, and a possible influence on lay judges' activity during deliberation. Professional judges were then asked to estimate the frequency and list the topics of lay judges' questions and comments during deliberation. Professional judges were further asked to rank the types of comments according to the frequency with which they were mentioned ("During deliberation, the majority of YOUR comments are focused on the following issues..."; "During deliberation, the majority of comments made by LAY JUDGES are focused on the following issues..."). Finally, professional judges were also asked to assess the importance of lay judges' comments and to identify major problems with those comments.

The fourth section examined *disagreement during deliberation*. A question about the frequency of disagreement was asked first ("According to your experience, how frequently do lay judge(s) disagree with you during deliberation?"). Next, professional judges were asked to identify the topic of disagreement and to assess whether the summation at the beginning of deliberation had influenced the frequency of disagreement. Two separate questions were asked about leniency, one dealing with leniency in disagreement and another dealing with leniency in general. Finally, a question inquired how frequently lay judges had outvoted the professional judge ("How frequently have you been outvoted by lay judges?").

The fifth section dealt with *general opinions about mixed tribunals* ("What is your view of the system of mixed tribunals in general?"). In addition, the questionnaire inquired about the professional judges' view at the beginning of their mandate at the criminal division. The respondents were invited to rank various positive/negative characteristics of mixed tribunals by importance ("Which of the following do you see as positive features of trials by mixed tribunals, as compared to trials by a professional judge alone?"; "Which of the following do you see as serious problems with trials by mixed tribunals, as compared to trials by a professional judge alone?"). Two additional questions examined the selection of lay judges and the impact of such selection on the quality of trials by mixed tribunals. The respondents were further invited to rank the suggested improvements to the system of mixed tribunals by their importance. Professional judges were also asked whether any changes in the system of mixed tribunals were desirable. Furthermore, the respondents were asked to state their preference for decision-makers and were offered three comparisons (mixed tribunal *v.* a professional judge alone, mixed tribunal *v.* the jury, and mixed tribunal *v.* professional tribunal).

Finally, a number of questions inquired about the professional judges' *demographic characteristics* (age, gender, marital status, number of children). Questions were also asked about their graduation year, the length of their mandate as professional judges at the criminal division, the length of their mandate as professional judges in general, the number of cases they had tried, the number of criminal cases tried last month, and the number of criminal cases tried last month in a mixed tribunal. The questionnaire asked about the opinion held by law professors and lawyers with whom professional judges usually communicate ("Do you happen to remember what the opinion of your professors of criminal procedure and civil procedure at the Law School was about mixed tribunals?"; "What is the opinion about mixed tribunals most frequently expressed in the circle of lawyers with whom you usually communicate?").

Most questions in the questionnaire asked the respondents to select the most appropriate answer from the list of offered answers. Questions about frequency offered the answers "never," "sometimes," "frequently," "very frequently," and "always." Other questions included, in addition to the option of circling one of the answers provided in the questionnaire, the opportunity for respondents to write down what they thought the appropriate answer was. Several questions asked professional judges to rank the offered answers or options according to the importance they attached to them. Finally, the last question was entirely open-ended; it invited respondents to write comments about any aspect of mixed tribunals which, in their opinion, had not been addressed adequately in the questionnaire.

Professional Judges from Regional Courts

The questionnaire distributed to professional judges at regional courts (who sit in both small tribunals and large tribunals) was very similar to that distributed to professional judges at district courts. It was expanded by only one question which focused on obtaining information about the pattern of disagreement in large tribunals (a question inapplicable to the framework of district courts) — professional judges were asked to compare cases in which two professional judges agree with the cases in which two professional judges disagree and to report the frequency of their disagreement with lay judges.

Supreme Court Justices

Professional judges from the Criminal Division of the Supreme Court filled out a shortened questionnaire. A number of questions asked of other professional judges were omitted (e.g., questions about the behavior of lay judges during trial and deliberation) because the Justices do not conduct trials in mixed tribunals. Professional judges from this group were asked about mixed tribunals in general, about their perceptions of lay judges' ability to evaluate evidence, and about their own demographic characteristics. There were only two additional questions. One asked the Justices to compare professional judges and lay judges with respect to their leniency. The second question was: "Have you ever tried criminal cases in a mixed tribunal as a professional judge?"

State Attorneys and Attorneys

State attorneys and attorneys were presented with similar questionnaires. Both categories of respondents observe the behavior of professional judges and lay judges during trial (but not during deliberation). Consequently, they were asked almost all of the questions about the behavior of lay judges during trial that were asked of professional judges in the first section of the professional judges' questionnaire. All the questions from the third and fourth sections of the professional judges' questionnaire about deliberation and disagreements during deliberation were excluded since state attorneys and attorneys cannot be present during deliberation. Questions about lay judges' ability to evaluate evidence and all the general questions about mixed tribunals were identical to those asked of professional judges. Questions from the last part of the questionnaire (demographic characteristics) were adapted to state attorneys and attorneys (e.g., "How many years have you been a state attorney?"). Two additional questions pertaining to leniency and experience in trials in mixed tribunals were identical to those asked of professional judges from the Supreme Court.

Lay Judges from District Courts

Questionnaires distributed to lay judges were similar to those distributed to professional judges. However, the wording in some of the questions needed to be changed to accommodate different perspectives. For example, professional judges were asked: "How often do you ask lay judges whether they have some questions during trial?" The wording was changed for the corresponding question in the lay judges' questionnaire: "When the defendant, a witness, or an expert witness is cross-examined, how often does the professional judge ask you whether you have any questions for that person?" In most instances, changes were very simple: "How often do lay judges read the case file?" *v.* "How often do you read the case file?"

In the first part of the questionnaire, lay judges were asked how frequently they had asked questions or read the case file in the last 10 trials, and how frequently professional judges asked them whether they had any questions in the last 10 trials. Questions about lay judges' evaluation of evidence, deliberation, and disagreement during deliberation were very similar to the respective questions asked of professional judges. Questions about the selection of lay judges (from the part of the questionnaire that dealt with general opinions about mixed tribunals) were left out. Lay judges were asked how long their mandate had been, whether they sat only in criminal cases, whether they sat in civil cases as well, and what had motivated them to become lay judges. They were invited to provide the level of satisfaction related to their experience as lay judges. Finally, they were asked about their age, gender, marital status, number of children, educational level, and occupation.

An issue that I had to resolve specifically for lay judges was how to code occupations. Besides the impractical approach of making a new occupational classification, the choices included the Hodge-Siegel-Rossi classification used by the General Social Survey (Davis and Smith, 1990), an international classification produced by Treiman (1977), and an occupational classification specifically designed for Yugoslavia by Hammel (1970).

Although Hammel's classification seemed inviting at the outset, I discarded it for a number of reasons. First, Hammel's study was outdated — too many social and political changes have occurred since the mid-1960s to render Hammel's scale applicable to the present time. Second, Hammel's sample was confined to blue- and white-collar workers in a machine factory (50 respondents) and in a construction firm (50 respondents). None of the respondents were college-educated. In short, Hammel's sample was small and was not representative of the population of Yugoslavia at the time (nor would it be representative of the population of Croatia today).[16]

---

[16]Another interesting fact is that Hammel's classification is based not on the *occupational prestige* but on the *occupational desirability*. Occupations were ranked on a five-point scale in terms of their desirability, "if you had all opportunities in your life to become whatever you wanted" (in Treiman, 1977, p. 41). This exposes the scale to another dimension of mea-

Given the choice of the two remaining scales, I chose Treiman's occupational scale (1977) for two reasons. First, although studies that compare the occupational prestige scale for the United States and appropriate scales in some other industrialized countries show a very high correlation (.91), no data that would compare the social structure and prestige of occupations in the United States and Croatia are available, particularly not those that would correspond to the present social structure in Croatia. In that sense, it is hard to determine the applicability of the Hodge-Siegel-Rossi scale to the present study. Second, and perhaps more important, Treiman's occupational scale has been validated in a number of countries around the world and has thus been shown to be fairly robust to a variety of social and political contexts. However, it appears that the results should be robust to the choice of the occupational scale because there is a high correlation between Treiman's international occupational scale and the Hodge-Siegel-Rossi scale.

My final remark on the subject of occupational scales is at the same time a *caveat*. While studies generally show that the prestige hierarchy appears to be virtually unchanged over time, "less stability might be expected in societies undergoing rapid social change, especially change that affects the class structure, such as the communist revolutions of Eastern Europe" (Treiman, 1977, p. 74). An analogous remark may be in order for the recent changes (in the opposite direction) that took place throughout the former Eastern Europe. In order to ensure that the analyses presented in subsequent chapters would not be affected by possible changes in the occupational prestige scale, I will dichotomize the scale of occupational prestige into "high" and "low" and will

---

surement error; current situation on the job market could intervene by (temporarily) altering the desirability of a certain occupation. Another fact, pointed out by Treiman (1977, p.44), is that non-prestige ratings are substantially less highly correlated with the worldwide average (international scale) than prestige ratings are. This observation, although not in itself crucial for the present study, renders Hammel's methodology undesirable for cross-cultural applications. In other words, using Hammel's scale in this study would have complicated future attempts to use potential replications of this study in a number of countries for cross-cultural comparison because job markets are not integrated and are differentially exposed to risks of time-varying demand for certain professions on the respective job markets, all of which can bias measurement of occupational desirability.

thus make the application of Treiman's scale considerably less sensitive to the fluctuations of rankings of occupational prestige in countries in transition.

Lay Judges from Regional Courts

Questionnaires for lay judges from regional courts had one question added to those asked of lay judges from district courts; it was a question about disagreement among lay judges and/or between lay judges and professional judges when professional judges disagreed between themselves. The intent of this additional question was to obtain information about the pattern of disagreement in large tribunals.

6.2.4   Respondents

Over a period of several months, from spring of 1993 to late summer of 1993, data were collected from four categories of respondents: professional judges, lay judges, state attorneys,[17] and attorneys. In this section I provide a description of how the data were collected at each particular court/office and describe each group of respondents in terms of their respective demographic characteristics and professional experience.

Professional Judges

Professional judges who participated in the study tried and decided criminal cases in the first instance at district courts and regional courts. I contacted the professional judges at district courts in Zagreb (the Zagreb Region), Bjelovar, Daruvar, Djurdjevac, Garešnica, Koprivnica, Križevci, Vrbovec, and Varaždin (the Bjelovar Region). Similarly, I contacted the professional judges who decided criminal cases in the first instance (trial) at regional courts in Bjelovar, Osijek, Rijeka, Varaždin, Zadar, and Zagreb. Finally, I also successfully solicited participation in the study from the professional judges from the Criminal Division of the Supreme Court.

---

[17]Henceforth, I refer to both state attorneys and their assistants as "state attorneys."

First, permission to distribute questionnaires was obtained from the president of each court that participated in the study. The questionnaires were then distributed to all professional judges who decided criminal cases in the first instance at district courts and regional courts and to all professional judges who decided criminal cases at the appellate level at the Supreme Court. A cover letter, attached to each questionnaire, described the topic and the purpose of the study, informed respondents that their participation in the study was voluntary, and stated that their responses would be confidential.

The response rate at the District Court of Zagreb was 92%; 22 out of 24 professional judges working in the criminal division participated in the study. Since the first contact with the judges had been established in January 1993, six professional judges were temporarily relocated to the Military Court. They were contacted as well (5 out of 6 professional judges participated). The overall response rate for all professional judges in this group was 90% (27 out of 30 professional judges).

Demographic characteristics of the professional judges from the District Court of Zagreb who participated in the study were as follows: 59% were female and 78% were married. Eighty-two percent had been judges 5 years or more; about 55% had been judges over 10 years. The majority (78%) had been judges at the criminal division for at least 5 years; about 41% of the judges had been at the criminal division for over 10 years.

The response rate at district courts in the Bjelovar Region was 100% (all 29 professional judges responded: 3 from Bjelovar, 2 from Daruvar, 4 from Djurdjevac, 4 from Garešnica, 4 from Koprivnica, 3 from Križevci, 3 from Varaždin, and 6 from Vrbovec).

Demographic characteristics of professional judges from district courts in the Bjelovar Region who decide criminal cases were as follows: 59% were female and 48% were married. The majority had been judges at least 5 years (86%) and nearly one-half (48%) had been judges for more than 10 years. The majority had been judges at the criminal division for at least 5 years (63%) and 30% had been judges at the criminal division for more than 10 years.

The response rate at the regional court level was 92%. A total of 24 professional judges responded: 2 from Bjelovar, 3 from Osijek, 7 from Rijeka, 4 from Varaždin, 2 from Zadar, and 6 from Zagreb. Fifty percent of the surveyed professional judges from regional courts were female and 71% were married. The majority had been judges at least 5 years (92%) and 67% had been judges for more than 10 years. The majority had been judges at the criminal division for at least 5 years (86%) and one-half had been judges at the criminal division for over 10 years.

The response rate at the Criminal Division of the Supreme Court was 77% (10 out of 13 Justices participated). The majority of respondents from the Criminal Division of the Supreme Court were male (60%) and married (60%). Almost all of them had been judges for at least 10 years (90%), and 40% had been judges for over 25 years. Ninety percent had tried criminal cases. Seventy percent had been judges at the Supreme Court between 1 and 5 years.

Lay Judges

One of the problems related to the survey of lay judges was that they do not have a regular courtroom where they can be contacted. The courtroom in which they will sit is not known until just a few moments before the trial. A court official acts as a dispatcher for lay judges by maintaining the registry of lay judges and sending correspondence to them. Lay judges report to the dispatcher as soon as they arrive to the court to collect their trial schedule for the day. With the permission of the presidents of the District Court of Zagreb, the District Court of Križevci, the Regional Court of Zagreb, and the Regional Court of Bjelovar, the dispatcher at each of the courts invited lay judges to participate in the study and presented them with copies of the questionnaire and the cover letter.

There is a master list of lay judges at each of the courts, but many lay judges do not appear at the court when summoned. According to the dispatchers, they are only technically lay judges and probably do not have experience as lay judges. Therefore, data collection efforts were focused on those lay judges who regularly responded to the court's mail and actually sat in mixed tribunals.[18]

One hundred thirty-nine lay judges regularly responded to the Court's mail at the District Court of Zagreb, out of whom 122 (i.e., 88%) decided to participate in the study. About one-half of them were female (49%) and 67% were married. As for education, 16% of the respondents had less than a high school degree, almost one-half of the respondents had graduated from high school (46%), and the remaining lay judges either had an associate's degree (22%) or a college degree (17%). The majority of lay judges said that criminal cases constituted approximately one-half of all the cases that they had decided, and 25% of lay judges said that criminal cases constituted more than one-half of all the cases they had decided. Sixty-three percent of respondents reported that they had been lay judges for more than one year.

Eighty lay judges responded regularly to the Court's mail at the District Court of Križevci. Fifty-three of them filled out the questionnaire, resulting in a response rate of 66%. Ninety-one percent of the respondents were male and 88% were married. As for education, 51% of the respondents had less than a high school degree, 25% graduated from high school, and the remaining lay judges either had an associate's degree (9%) or a college degree (15%). The majority of lay judges said that criminal cases constituted approximately one-half or more of all the cases they had decided (68%). All respondents had been lay judges for more than one year; approximately 68% had been lay judges for over three years.

Lay judges at the Regional Court of Bjelovar were also included in the study. Seventy-seven lay judges responded to the court's mail. In comparison with district courts, there is usually a smaller number of cases tried at regional

---

[18]It is certainly possible, even likely, that their opinion about mixed tribunals may be quite different from the opinion held the by the lay judges who do not respond to the court's mail. Since the primary purpose of this research was to study the interaction and activity in the tribunal (rather than to study general opinion about mixed tribunals), it was natural to exclude the lay judges who did not respond to the court's mail and did not have actual experience in trials by mixed tribunals.

courts. In addition, once lay judges arrive to the court, trials at regional courts generally take a longer time than trials at district courts. These two factors have resulted in a smaller number of lay judges present at the courts; therefore, a smaller number of lay judges from regional courts participated in the study. At the Regional Court of Bjelovar, all 33 lay judges assigned to mixed tribunals over a period of several months (41% of all lay judges who responded to the court's mail) filled out the questionnaire.

Approximately one-quarter of the respondents were female and 79% were married. Thirty-three percent of the respondents had less than a high school degree, 40% graduated from high school, and the remaining lay judges either had an associate's degree (12%) or a college degree (15%). The great majority of lay judges said that criminal cases constituted at least one-half of all the cases they had decided and 91% said that criminal cases were dominant. When asked about the duration of their mandate as lay judges, 94% of the respondents reported that they had been lay judges for more than three years; around 75% had been lay judges for over four years.

Approximately 250 lay judges were on the official list of lay judges at the Regional Court of Zagreb. As was the case with the Regional Court of Bjelovar, a smaller number of cases and longer trials led to a smaller number of lay judges. Only 24 of the summoned lay judges came to the court during the data collection period, out of whom 21 (88%) filled out the questionnaire.

Fourteen percent of the respondents were female and 81% were married. Only 5% of the respondents had less than a high school degree; more than one-half of all respondents had graduated from high school (57%), and the remaining lay judges either had an associate's degree (33%) or a college degree (5%). All the respondents said that criminal cases constituted more than one-half of all the cases that they had decided and 85% of the respondents said that criminal cases constituted most of the cases they had decided. Ninety-five percent of the respondents reported that they had been lay judges for more than three years; about 43% had been lay judges for more than four years.

State Attorneys

State attorneys were contacted at district and regional state attorneys' offices in the Zagreb Region and the Bjelovar Region. The response rate at the District State Attorney's Office in Zagreb was 67% (20 out of 30). The majority of the respondents had been assistant district attorneys for less than three years (65%); one-quarter of the respondents were assistant district attorneys for less than a year. The great majority had not tried criminal cases as professional judges (80%). Sixty percent of the respondents were female and 55% were married.

State attorneys in Bjelovar, Daruvar/Pakrac,[19] Djurdjevac, Garešnica, Koprivnica, and Križevci were invited to participate in the study. Questionnaires were also distributed to state attorneys and assistant state attorneys at the offices in Čazma, Virovitica, and Vrbovec, which do not come under the jurisdiction of the Regional State Attorney's Office in Bjelovar (and are not shown in Figure 6.2), but are adjacent to the Bjelovar Region.

The response rate was 100% (all 20 district state attorneys/assistant district state attorneys responded). The majority of the respondents had been district state attorneys/assistant district state attorneys 5 or more years (85%) and 60% for over 10 years. The great majority had not tried criminal cases as professional judges (84%). Forty-five percent of the respondents were female and 80% were married.

The response rate at the Regional State Attorney's Office in Zagreb was 65% (13 out of 20). When asked how long they had been a district and/or regional state attorney/assistant attorney, the majority of the respondents responded "over 10 years" (85%). The majority had not tried criminal cases as professional judges (83%). Sixty-two percent were female and 58% were married.

All five regional state attorneys and assistant regional state attorneys in Bjelovar also participated in the study. All of the respondents had been re-

---

[19]Due to the war in Croatia in the early 1990s, in 1993 the Pakrac Office of the District Attorney was located in Daruvar.

gional attorneys/regional assistant attorneys for 5 or more years, and 80% for over 10 years. Eighty percent had not tried criminal cases as professional judges. Sixty percent of the respondents were female; all the respondents were married.

Attorneys

Finally, attorneys in Zagreb, Bjelovar, and Križevci were contacted and invited to participate in the study. A list of all the attorneys who practice law in Zagreb was obtained from the Executive Secretary of the Association of Attorneys of Zagreb. At my request, the president of the Association highlighted the 169 attorneys from the list who either practiced criminal law exclusively or practiced in law firms in which at least 30% of the activity was in criminal law. He also wrote a letter to the members of the Association in which he indicated his support for the study and invited members to participate in it. Out of the 169 highlighted attorneys, 140 leased mailboxes in the mailroom located in the basement of the building in which the District Court of Zagreb, the District Attorney's Office, and the Regional Attorney's Office are located. Copies of the questionnaire with the cover letter and a copy of the letter from the president of the Association were placed into their mailboxes. On each letter, there was a note asking the attorneys to place the completed questionnaires into a clearly marked box in the mailroom. Questionnaires, together with self-addressed and stamped envelopes, were mailed to the 29 remaining attorneys who did not have their mailboxes in the basement of the Court building. After a period of two weeks, attorneys were contacted and asked whether they had received the questionnaire; they were invited to fill out their copy of the questionnaire and return it. In the process, more questionnaires were distributed. After three additional weeks, attorneys were contacted again and still more questionnaires were distributed.

Out of 169 attorneys from the list, 8 reported (over the phone or on the questionnaire booklet cover) that they did not practice criminal law. The researcher was not able to contact 42 attorneys because they had closed their offices (they either disconnected their phone number or removed the firm name from the building) since the directory of attorneys maintained by the Association of Attorneys of Zagreb was last updated. All of the remaining 119 attorneys from the list were contacted and 76 filled out the questionnaire (64% response rate).

The majority of respondents had been attorneys for at least 5 years (65%); about 49% had been attorneys for over 10 years. Eighty-three percent of the respondents had not tried criminal cases as professional judges. Eighteen percent were female and 75% were married.

Attorneys in Križevci and Bjelovar were contacted as well. The procedure used for data collection was similar to the procedure used for attorneys in Zagreb. All 9 attorneys in Križevci responded, as did 17 out of 19 attorneys in Bjelovar. The resulting response rate was 93% (26 out of 28). The majority of the respondents had been attorneys for at least 5 years (54%); about 39% had been attorneys over 10 years. Sixty-nine percent of the respondents had not tried criminal cases as professional judges. Twenty-three percent were female and 73% were married.

6.2.5 More on Experience

Empirical analyses reported in this book are based on the respondents' perceptions and opinions about mixed tribunals. It was thus essential to have experienced respondents, so that expressed judgments and opinions could have been based on solid personal observation. Actual experiences and perceptions about these experiences are certainly not the same. Actual experience influences the participants' opinion and behavior. For example, one year of trial experience influenced the opinion magistrates had about the purposes of sanctioning (Bond and Lemon, 1981); the decisions reached by professional judges became more automatic (Lloyd-Bostock, 1989).

In light of the likely influence of the respondents' experience, the immediate question is how experienced the respondents (professional judges, lay judges, state attorneys, and attorneys) were in performing their respective functions in the criminal justice system in general and in participating in trials by mixed tribunals in particular. At the outset, I establish reasonable thresholds for differentiation between experienced and inexperienced respondents. For professional judges, state attorneys, and attorneys (i.e., for lawyers), I assert that a respondent was experienced if he/she had had at least 5 years of experience in performing his/her respective function in the criminal justice system.

The nature of the service performed by lay judges is quite different. They participate in trials by mixed tribunals infrequently and different thresholds of experience need to be devised. As mentioned in Chapter 3, the lay judges' mandate was four years. After four years lay judges could have been elected again (Article 103, *Regular Courts Law*, 1988), either reelected back to the same court or elected to another court. I thus group lay judges according to their experience as follows: novice lay judges (up to one year of service), experienced lay judges (one to three years of service), and very experienced lay judges (three or more years of service).

Professional Judges

It may be quite possible that professional judges were experienced as professional judges in general, but have had very limited experience with mixed tribunals. Therefore, in order to gain an in-depth look at their experience, I examined both the professional judges' length of service as professional judges and the extent of their experience in trials by mixed tribunals.

The great majority of professional judges from district courts and regional courts (86%) had been professional judges for at least 5 years, that is, they were experienced professional judges (Table 6.6). This percentage varies slightly, with the lower limit at 82% for professional judges from the District Court of Zagreb, and the upper limit at 90% for professional judges from regional courts and from the Supreme Court.[20] In fact, the majority of the judges from

---

[20]The questions asked of professional judges at the Supreme Court were identical to those asked of other professional judges. However, the answers offered to the Supreme Court

district courts (52%), regional courts (62%), and the Supreme Court (90%) had been professional judges for over 10 years. Generally, and in accordance with the standard career paths of professional judges, the higher the court, the longer the experience. On the other hand, there were no statistically significant differences (χ^2=0.23, $d.f.$=1, $Phi = .064, p > .05$, n.s.) in the length of service between professional judges from district courts in the two regions, that is, the Zagreb Region and the Bjelovar Region.

The number of years at the bench is not in itself a sufficient measure of the professional judges' experience in trials by mixed tribunals. Professional judges could have been deciding mostly cases other than the criminal ones; they could have been working in the areas of civil law, family law, labor law, and so on. To clarify the nature of the professional judges' experience, two additional questions were asked of them.

The first question inquired how long they had been judges at the criminal division. In general, the majority of professional judges (78%) were experienced in conducting criminal trials because they had been judges at a criminal division for at least five years (78% at the District Court of Zagreb, 70% at the district courts in the Bjelovar Region, and 86% at regional courts; Table 6.6). Only regional courts and the Supreme court had over one-half of the professional judges who participated in the study with more than 10 years of experience at the criminal division. Again, the differences between the experience at the criminal division between professional judges from district courts in the Zagreb Region and in the Bjelovar Region were not statistically significant (χ^2=0.39, $d.f.$=1, $Phi = -.085, p > .05$, n.s.).

---

judges were different. Possible answers to the question inquiring about experience as a judge were: "less than 10 years," "10-15 years," "15-20 years," "20-25 years," and "over 25 years." Possible answers to the question inquiring about experience as a judge at the Criminal Division of the Supreme Court were: "less than 1 year," "1-5 years," "5-10 years," "10-15 years," and "over 15 years." Not surprisingly, virtually all the Supreme Court judges had had at least 10 years of experience as judges. At the same time, 78% of the Supreme Court judges had been at the Criminal Division of the Supreme Court between one and five years.

Table 6.6: Duration of being a judge[a]/being a judge at the Criminal Division.[b]

| | Being a judge | | | | Being a judge at the Criminal Division | | | |
	Prof. j. Dist. C. ZG	Prof. j. Dist. C. BJ	Prof. j. Reg. C.	Prof. j. All D & R	Prof. j. Dist. C. ZG	Prof. j. Dist. C. BJ	Prof. j. Reg. C.	Prof. j. All D & R
less than 1 yr	3.7%	0.0%	4.8%	2.6%	3.7%	14.8%	4.8%	7.8%
1-3 yrs	3.7%	0.0%	4.8%	2.6%	3.7%	7.4%	4.8%	5.2%
3-5 yrs	11.1%	13.8%	0.0%	9.1%	14.8%	7.4%	4.8%	9.1%
5-10 yrs	25.9%	37.9%	28.6%	31.2%	37.0%	40.7%	33.3%	37.7%
more than 10 yrs	55.6%	48.3%	61.9%	54.5%	40.7%	29.6%	52.4%	40.2%
N	27	29	24	80	27	29	24	80

[a]Question: "How many years have you been a judge?"
[b]Question: "How many years have you been a judge at the Criminal Division?"

Professional judges who served at the criminal division did not necessarily spend their time by only conducting trials by mixed tribunals; they could have decided mostly criminal cases tried by a professional judge alone (less serious cases); or, they could have been conducting mostly criminal investigations. Depending on the court level, they may also have acted as investigators or decided appeals. Thus, an additional question inquired about the number of trials by mixed tribunals in which the professional judges had participated in order to determine the professional judges' experience in trials by mixed tribunals.

I regard 200 trials in mixed tribunals to be a reasonable threshold that delineates between the professional judges who were experienced in trials in mixed tribunals and the professional judges who were not. The majority of respondents (75%) were experienced; they had tried over 200 cases in mixed tribunals (Table 6.7). This percentage ranges from 70% for professional judges from district courts in the Bjelovar Region and professional judges from regional courts to 85% for professional judges from the District Court of Zagreb.

An interesting question is whether different measures of experience employed in this section lead to similar assessments of the professional judges' experience. Indeed, how long would a typical professional judge need to serve as a judge to decide 200 cases in mixed tribunals? Professional judges were asked how many trials in mixed tribunals they had decided "last month," that is, during the period of one month prior to their participation in this study. For example, the average for professional judges from the District Court of Zagreb was 4.31 cases per judge per month. Questionnaires were distributed to them in May and June of 1993; thus, for each professional judge from the District Court of Zagreb, the term "last month" indicated a one-month period during April, May, and early June of 1993. These months are typical in terms of caseload, whereas early January, late June, July, August, and late December are very light because of the holidays and vacations. As a plausible heuristic, it is thus appropriate to assume that one year of service as a professional judge accounts for about 9-10 months worth of a typical caseload.

Table 6.7: Number of cases tried in mixed tribunals with a verdict.[a]

	Prof. j. Dist. C. ZG	Prof. j. Dist. C. BJ	Prof. j. Reg. C.	Prof. j. All D & R
0	0.0%	0.0%	0.0%	0.0%
1-9	3.7%	0.0%	12.5%	2.5%
10-50	7.4%	6.9%	12.5%	8.8%
51-100	0.0%	3.4%	4.2%	2.5%
101-200	3.7%	20.7%	8.3%	11.3%
more than 200	85.2%	69.0%	70.8%	75.0%
N	27	29	24	80

[a]Question: "In how many cases in your career in which you tried in a mixed tribunal have you reached a verdict?"

This enables a rough but informative calculation: 200 trials in mixed tribunals typically required between 4.6 and 5.2 years of service as a professional judge.

Thus, the thresholds for the two measures of experience, that is, five years of service as a professional judge and 200 cases tried in mixed tribunals, should identify similar percentages of experienced professional judges. Indeed, according to both measures of experience, the great majority of surveyed professional judges had been experienced professional judges who have had experience in trials in mixed tribunals. This is a comforting finding; it establishes that the professional judges who participated in the study have had sufficient opportunities to observe (and, in fact, participate in) trials by mixed tribunals.

Lay Judges

The lay judges' experience in criminal trials by mixed tribunals was evaluated by examining the length of their service as lay judges, the types of cases they predominantly decided (criminal/civil), and the number of criminal cases they decided "last month," that is, during the period of one month prior to their participation in this study.

The majority of the lay judges who participated in the study were very experienced; fifty-four percent had been lay judges over 3 years (Table 6.8). Lay judges from regional courts served as lay judges for a significantly longer period of time than lay judges from district courts (χ^2=75.39, $d.f.$=2, Phi = .584, $p < .001$). Indeed, 95% of the surveyed lay judges from the Regional Court of Zagreb and 91% of the surveyed lay judges from the Regional Court of Bjelovar had served for over 3 years. By contrast, only 30% of the surveyed lay judges from the District Court of Zagreb and 68% of the surveyed lay judges from the District Court of Križevci had served for over 3 years. Furthermore, three out of four lay judges from the Regional Court of Bjelovar had been lay judges for over 4 years, compared to one out of five lay judges from the District Court of Zagreb, one out of four lay judges from the District Court of Bjelovar, and one out of two lay judges from the Regional Court of Zagreb. That is, lay judges from the Regional Court of Bjelovar were much more experienced than their counterparts from the other courts that participated in the study; typical lay judges from the Regional Court of Bjelovar were probably in (at least) their second mandate as lay judges.

The types of cases decided by lay judges from regional and district courts differed significantly (χ^2=118.16, $d.f.$=3, Phi = .721, $p < .001$); the majority of lay judges from regional courts decided mostly criminal cases (66% of all lay judges from regional courts), whereas the majority of lay judges from district courts decided both criminal cases and civil cases (96% of all lay judges from district courts). This difference is by no means surprising; it is due to the jurisdiction of these courts. District courts conduct trials in both criminal

Table 6.8: Mandate of lay judges.[a]

	Lay j. Dist. C. ZG	Lay j. Dist. C. KŽ	Lay j. Reg. C. ZG	Lay j. Reg. C. BJ	Lay j. Dist. C. All	Lay j. Reg. C. All	Lay j. All R & D
less than 6 months	0.9%	0.0%	0.0%	0.0%	0.6%	0.0%	0.5%
6 months - 1 yr	26.1%	0.0%	0.0%	0.0%	17.9%	0.0%	13.6%
1 - 2 yrs	28.7%	11.3%	0.0%	0.0%	23.2%	0.0%	17.6%
2 - 3 yrs	14.8%	20.8%	4.8%	6.3%	16.7%	5.7%	14.0%
3 - 4 yrs	9.6%	32.1%	52.4%	15.6%	16.7%	30.2%	19.9%
more than 4 yrs	20.0%	35.8%	42.9%	75.0%	25.0%	62.3%	33.9%
N	122	53	21	33	175	54	229

[a]Question: "How many years have you been a lay judge at this court?"

cases and civil cases, while regional courts conduct trials only in criminal cases (Table 6.9).

Interestingly, the two groups of lay judges from regional courts reported different levels of involvement in criminal cases. Lay judges from the Regional Court of Bjelovar were less likely to say that they predominantly decided criminal cases than lay judges from the Regional Court of Zagreb. This result is related to the fact that typical lay judges from the Regional Court of Bjelovar had been lay judges for a longer period of time than their counterparts from the Regional Court of Zagreb. Three out of four lay judges from the Regional Court of Bjelovar said that they had been lay judges for over four years — they were serving at least in their second mandate. If this were their second mandate at the Regional Court, they would still have had no opportunity to participate in the decision-making in civil cases (mixed tribunals do not try civil cases at regional courts; appellate decisions in civil cases are made by three-member professional tribunals). It follows that they had probably served at district courts in their earlier mandate(s) and had thus gained experience in civil cases as members of mixed tribunals at district courts.

Lay judges were also asked about the ratio of criminal cases in all the cases they had decided (Table 6.10). Lay judges from district courts had a different experience in terms of the types of cases they decided than lay judges from regional courts: the majority of lay judges from district courts said that criminal cases constituted one-half or less than one-half of the cases they had decided (71% overall; 76% at the District Court of Zagreb and 60% at the District Court of Križevci), whereas the great majority of lay judges at regional courts (94% overall; 100% at the Regional Court of Zagreb and 91% at the Regional Court of Bjelovar) said that criminal cases constituted more than one-half of the cases they had decided (χ^2=74.25, $d.f.$=3, Phi = .577, $p < .001$).

Lay judges' experience in criminal trials by mixed tribunals was also determined on the basis of the number of criminal cases (in which lay judges sat in a tribunal) that had reached a verdict during the "last month," that

Table 6.9: Types of cases tried by lay judges.[a]

	Lay j. Dist. C. ZG	Lay j. Dist. C. KŽ	Lay j. Reg. C. ZG	Lay j. Reg. C. BJ	Lay j. Dist. C. All	Lay j. Reg. C. All	Lay j. All R & D
only criminal	1.7%	7.7%	85.7%	54.5%	3.5%	66.7%	18.5%
only civil	0.0%	0.0%	0.0 %	0.0%	0.0%	0.0%	0.0%
both	98.3%	92.3%	14.3%	45.5%	96.5%	33.3%	81.5%
N	122	53	21	33	175	54	229

[a]Question: "Do you sit in criminal or civil cases, or both?"

Table 6.10: Proportion of criminal cases in the cases tried by lay judges.[a]

	Lay j. Dist. C. ZG	Lay j. Dist. C. KŽ	Lay j. Reg. C. ZG	Lay j. Reg. C. BJ	Lay j. Dist. C. All	Lay j. Reg. C. All	Lay j. All R. & D
almost all	10.0%	8.0%	85.0%	66.7%	9.4%	73.6%	24.7%
more than 1/2	14.2%	32.0%	15.0%	24.2%	19.4%	20.8%	19.7%
one-half	43.3%	28.0%	0.0%	6.1%	38.8%	3.8%	30.5%
less than 1/2	26.7%	14.0%	0.0%	0.0%	22.9%	0.0%	17.5%
only a few	5.8%	18.0%	0.0%	3.0%	9.4%	1.9%	7.6%
N	122	53	21	33	175	54	229

[a]Question: "How many of the cases that you sit in are criminal cases?"

is, during the month that preceded their participation in the study. On average, lay judges from the Regional Court of Zagreb decided fewer cases in the month preceding their participation in the study (2.10) than lay judges from the District Court of Zagreb (4.28).

As an aside, a comparison between the numbers of cases decided "last month" by professional judges and by lay judges at the same court was interesting. At the District Court of Zagreb, the number of cases decided in mixed tribunals "last month" was virtually identical for professional judges and lay judges (4.31 v. 4.28), whereas professional judges from the Regional Court of Zagreb sat in far more criminal cases tried by a mixed tribunal "last month" than their lay counterparts (4.67 v. 2.10). Differences across courts are likely due to the differences in their internal organization, availability of professional judges and/or lay judges, the expected case throughput, and so on.

In summary, the majority of lay judges who participated in this study were very experienced in trials by mixed tribunals. This is true in both regions and at both court levels: although lay judges from regional courts had decided fewer criminal cases "last month" than lay judges from district courts, they have also served as lay judges for a substantially longer period of time.

State Attorneys and Attorneys

The overwhelming majority of district state attorneys in the Bjelovar Region and regional state attorneys had been serving at their respective positions for 5 years or more (85% and 94%, respectively; Table 6.11), while percentages of district attorneys in Zagreb, attorneys in Zagreb, and attorneys in the Bjelovar Region who had been district attorneys or attorneys for 5 years or more are considerably smaller (29%, 65%, and 55%, respectively).[21] However, it is important to emphasize that, although there are differences in the percentages of the respondents from each group who had served/practiced for 5 years or

---

[21]The differences in the length of service/practice among the six groups of respondents under present consideration were statistically significant (χ^2=20.24, d.f.=5, Phi = .360, p < .001).

more, the majority of respondents in all but one group were experienced, that is, they had been state attorneys/attorneys for 5 years or more. The only group of respondents in this study in which the majority of respondents had less than five years of experience were the district state attorneys from Zagreb. The majority of respondents from this group had less than 3 years of experience (65%).

The respective roles state attorneys and attorneys play in trials by mixed tribunals are each different from the role played by professional judges; while professional judges participate in the work of the mixed tribunal both during trial and during deliberation and are active (and often dominant) decision-makers, state attorneys and attorneys each present their case during trial, take no part in deliberation, and do not participate in decision-making. Relative to the members of mixed tribunals, state attorneys and attorneys merely *observe* the work of the mixed tribunal and the interaction among its members and are exposed only to a part of its activities. Thus, I assert that the number of trials by mixed tribunals in which state attorneys and attorneys need to participate in order to be regarded as experienced in trials by mixed tribunals is set at only 150, that is, three-quarters of the threshold set for professional judges.

To assess the experience of state attorneys and attorneys according to that criterion, state attorneys and attorneys were asked to report the number of trials by mixed tribunals that resulted in verdicts in which they had participated (represented the State or a client) during the one-month period prior to their participation in the study ("last month").

On average, regional state attorneys participated in more such cases "last month" (6.79) than other categories of attorneys. District state attorneys and attorneys in the same geographic area on average participated in approximately the same number of such cases "last month" (2.72 *v.* 2.70 in the Zagreb Region; 3.65 *v.* 3.31 in the Bjelovar Region). Using the smallest of these averages (2.70) and assuming, as was done for professional judges, that one year of service/practice accounts for 9-10 months of a full caseload (the data were

Table 6.11: Duration of being a state attorney/attorney.[a]

	Dist. State a. ZG	Dist. State a. BJ	Reg. State a.	Att. ZG	Att. BJ	State a. R & D	Att. All
less than 1 yr	29.5%	5.0%	5.6%	5.3%	7.7%	13.6%	5.9%
1-3 yrs	36.2%	5.0%	0.0%	18.6%	23.1%	14.2%	19.8%
3-5 yrs	5.9%	5.0%	0.0%	10.7%	15.4%	3.7%	11.9%
5-10 yrs	11.8%	25.0%	11.1%	16.1%	16.0%	15.4%	15.8%
more than 10 yrs	17.6%	60.0%	83.3%	49.3%	38.5%	52.5%	46.5%
N	20	20	18	76	26	58	102

[a]Question: "How many years have you been a state attorney/attorney?"

collected during the "high season" of court activity in 1993), a simple computation reveals that participating in 150 trials by mixed tribunals would have required at most between 5.5 and 6.2 years of service/practice.

Thus, in light of the average length of service reported by most groups of state attorneys and attorneys (with the exception of district state attorneys from Zagreb), the majority of state attorneys and attorneys were experienced both in terms of the length of their service and the estimated number of trials by mixed tribunals in which they had participated.

Chapter 7

Mixed Tribunals during Trial

This chapter focuses on trial, the first opportunity for lay judges to participate in the criminal process. Upon a brief review of the legal details of trials by mixed tribunals according to the *Criminal Procedure Law* of 1993, this chapter examines several important issues related to trial: perceptions about the frequency with which professional judges provided opportunities for lay judges to participate (measured as perceptions about the frequency with which professional judges invited lay judges to ask questions), perceptions of the frequency of lay judges' participation during trial (measured as perceptions about the frequency with which lay judges asked questions), and perceptions about the importance of lay judges' participation (measured as perceptions about the importance of lay judges' questions). Influences of lay judges' demographic characteristics (e.g., gender, age, education, occupational prestige, length of mandate) and other factors (e.g., whether lay judges read the case file, the complexity of evidence in the case) are examined as well. At the conclusion of the chapter, empirical findings about trial are placed into the theoretical framework developed in Chapter 5.

7.1   Legal Framework of Trial

According to Article 298 of the *Criminal Procedure Law* (1993), the professional judge who presides over the work of the mixed tribunal opens the session, announces the case to be tried, and determines whether the tribunal has been composed in accordance with the law and whether all the persons who were invited are present. If all the invited persons (or at the very least the parties) are present,[1] the professional judge invites the defendant to take the stand with the purpose of checking the identity of the defendant and asking the defendant to provide the court with his/her demographic data (Article 312, *Criminal Procedure Law*, 1993). The professional judge then asks the witnesses and expert witnesses to leave the courtroom and to wait outside until they are called to testify. Next, the professional judge provides the private prosecutor (the victim) with the opportunity to assert the indemnity claim (Article 313, *Criminal Procedure Law*, 1993).

The professional judge instructs the defendant about his/her rights during the trial (e.g., the right to ask questions of the co-defendants, witnesses, and expert witnesses), upon which the trial officially starts with the act of reading the charges to the defendant (Articles 314-315, *Criminal Procedure Law*, 1993). The next step in the trial is the questioning of the defendant.

The general order of trial is determined by the *Criminal Procedure Law* (1993), but it may be changed if the circumstances (specified in the statute) so require (Article 293, *Criminal Procedure Law*, 1993). The defendant is asked whether he/she understands the charges; if the defendant answers in the negative, the professional judge has the responsibility to explain the charges to the defendant in a way that will be understandable to him/her (Article 316, *Criminal Procedure Law*, 1993). The defendant is then given the opportunity to present his/her defense.

Unlike the defendants in the common-law systems, the defendants in the civil-law systems have to give a statement. However, they have the right to remain silent or to refuse to answer a particular question. Specifically, Article 218 of the *Criminal Procedure Law* (1993), which determines the rules

---

[1]Legal consequences of missing the court day were regulated by Articles 299-303 of the *Criminal Procedure Law*, 1993.

of questioning the defendant by the investigative judge during investigation, is also applicable to the examination of the defendant during trial.

The trial proceeds with the examination of witnesses and expert witnesses in the case and the presentation of other evidence (Article 322, *Criminal Procedure Law*, 1993). The tribunal determines the evidence to be presented and witnesses and expert witnesses to be questioned. Subsequently, the tribunal asks questions of the witnesses and expert witnesses. The presiding professional judge determines the order in which the evidence is to be presented (Article 322, *Criminal Procedure Law*, 1993). After the examination of the evidence is completed, the parties (the public prosecutor, the private prosecutor, the defense attorney, and the defendant) give their respective closing arguments and the tribunal determines that the trial is over (Articles 339-344, *Criminal Procedure Law*, 1993). The parties then leave the courtroom and the tribunal is ready to start the deliberation (Article 344, *Criminal Procedure Law*, 1993), a topic of the next chapter.

Professional judges and lay judges have equal voting powers in the decision-making process (Article 13, *Regular Courts Law*, 1988). However, the presiding judge is always a professional judge. Although this requirement was not specified *per se*, it clearly follows from the additional responsibilities assigned to the presiding judge of the tribunal that the presiding judge has to be a person who is highly knowledgeable of the legal proceedings. According to the *Regular Courts Law* (1988), the presiding judge examines the correctness and soundness of the charging document (Articles 263, 268), assigns a defense attorney to an indigent defendant (Article 71), conducts preparatory actions for the trial (Article 279), decides motions for new evidence to be examined (Article 282), asks for additional lay judges to be assigned in case of a long trial (Article 283), decides about the postponement of the trial (Article 286), determines that the trial has started and announces the case to be tried (Article 300), determines whether the tribunal has been composed according to law (Article 291), oversees the order in the courtroom (Articles 294, 295,343), and manages the trial (Articles 292, 318, 327); the presiding judge also carries out the examination of the defendants, witnesses, expert witnesses, and other evidence in the case, provides the parties with the opportunity to state their closing arguments (Article 339), announces that the trial is over and the deliberation begins (Article 344), dictates and signs the trial transcript (Article 309), announces the verdict and briefly explains the reasons for it (Article 352), instructs the parties about appeal (Article 354), and signs the written verdict (Article 356).

One of the key roles the presiding judge performs during trial is the examination of the defendant(s), witnesses, and expert witnesses;[2] the presiding judge also lets the other members of the tribunal speak (Article 292, *Criminal Procedure Law*, 1993). Although lay judges have the right to ask questions of the defendants, witnesses, and expert witnesses directly and without the approval of the presiding professional judge, having a presiding professional judge who is intimately familiar with procedural rules, who conducts the trial, and who asks questions before lay judges are given an opportunity to do so, may place lay judges in an uncomfortable position. The presiding professional judge may provide opportunities for lay judges (and, if applicable, another professional judge) to participate in the trial by inviting them to ask questions of the defendant(s), witnesses, and expert witnesses. However, the presiding professional judge has no procedural duty to *invite* other members of the tribunal to ask questions. While discussing Article 318 of the *Criminal Procedure Law* (1993)[3] Jemrić (1987, p. 371) stated:

> The president of a tribunal is not responsible for asking the members of the tribunal, nor other participants in the trial listed in subsection 1 of this Article, whether they have any questions for the defendant.

On the other hand, the presiding professional judge has the duty to *allow* other members of the tribunal to ask the defendant(s), witnesses, and expert

---

[2]The examination of the defendant(s), witnesses, and expert witnesses is regulated by Articles 318 and 327 of the *Criminal Procedure Law* (1993).

[3]The wording of this Article was identical to the wording of Article 318 contained in the *Criminal Procedure Law* (1977).

witnesses questions directly, *after* the presiding professional judge had completed his/her own examination. In a manner that reflects these procedural rules, the examination conducted by the presiding professional judge is called the *fundamental* examination, and the examination conducted by lay judges, the second professional judge (if applicable), and all other parties listed in Article 318 of the *Criminal Procedure Law* (1993), that is, the prosecutor, the defense attorney, the victim, the legal guardian, the legal representative, co-defendant(s), and expert witnesses, is called the *supplementary* examination. Members of the tribunal are not allowed to ask any questions *before* the presiding professional judge has completed his/her examination. However, the rule does provide the presiding professional judge with the opportunity to allow other members of the tribunals to ask questions if they indicate that they have questions before the professional judge is done with his/her examination.

In practice, professional judges occasionally ask lay judges whether they have any questions, probably to give them opportunities to participate actively. However, since the frequency of providing such opportunities for lay judges is not regulated by the law and is thus dependent upon the presiding professional judge and his/her style and preference, the frequency of inviting questions from lay judges can differ tremendously across presiding professional judges. For example, the results of the Polish study (Kubicki and Zawadzki, 1970), the only study of mixed tribunals in which actual trials were observed, suggested that professional judges asked lay judges whether they had any questions in 23% of the observed 257 criminal cases.

7.2 Initiation of Supplementary Examination

One of the items in the questionnaire inquired how frequently professional judges asked lay judges whether they had any questions.[4] When the answers

---

[4]Possible answers were "always," "very frequently," "frequently," "sometimes," and "never." For the purpose of statistical comparison among various groups of respondents, the answers were recoded as follows: "never" and "sometimes" as "rarely"; "always" to "frequently" as "often."

by all twelve different groups of professional judges, lay judges, state attorneys, and attorneys were compared (Table 7.1), it was very clear that members of different groups selected significantly different answers (χ^2=53.62, $d.f.$=11, Phi=.339, $p < .001$).[5]

The analysis is first focused on the frequency with which **professional judges** reported inviting lay judges to ask questions. Seventy percent of professional judges from the District Court of Zagreb and 52% of professional judges from district courts in the Bjelovar Region reported that they infrequently ("sometimes" or "never") invited lay judges to ask questions (χ^2=2.04, $d.f.$=1, Phi= -.191, $p > .05$, n.s.).[6] When the responses by professional judges from district courts were compared to the responses by professional judges from regional courts, it turned out that the majority of professional judges from district courts (61%) reported that they invited lay judges to ask questions only infrequently ("sometimes" or "never"), while the majority of professional judges from regional courts (75%) reported doing so frequently (χ^2=8.57, $d.f.$=1, Phi= -.327, $p < .01$).

The answers given by **lay judges** about the frequency with which professional judges invited them to ask questions were in agreement with those given

---

[5]The usual technique for determining which pairs of groups were significantly different is to apply some of the methods of multiple comparisons, such as the Marascuillo method (Glass and Hopkins, 1984, p. 391-392). In this particular case, using such a test of significance (e.g., chi-square) seemed inadequate because its power depends heavily on the sample size. Since most of the pairs that needed to be compared feature small sample sizes (approximately 20 respondents), the differences that are considered to be substantively important do not turn out to be statistically significant. For example, when the responses by professional judges from the District Court of Zagreb are compared to the responses by professional judges from regional courts, it becomes apparent that, while the majority of professional judges from the District Court of Zagreb (56%) reported that they *sometimes* asked lay judges for questions, the majority of professional judges from regional courts (62.5%) said that they *always* asked for questions. These differences, as substantively important as they obviously are, were not found to be statistically significant by the Marascuillo method (χ^2=9.55, $d.f.$=11, $p > .05$, n.s.).

[6]Although the difference was not statistically significant (primarily due to the relationship between the power of the test and small sample sizes), I consider the difference of 19% to be substantively important. The Phi-value suggests that there is a relationship between region and the reported frequency of inviting questions.

Table 7.1: Frequency of inviting questions from lay judges.[a]

	Prof. j. Dist. C. ZG	Prof. j. Dist. C. BJ	Prof. j. Reg. C.	Dist. State a. ZG	Dist. State a. BJ	Reg. State a.	Att. ZG	Att. BJ
never	14.8%	0.0%	4.2%	30.0%	15.0%	0.0%	5.3%	15.4%
sometimes	55.6%	51.7%	20.8%	50.0%	45.0%	11.1%	46.1%	42.3%
frequently	3.7%	6.9%	4.2%	10.0%	20.0%	5.6%	10.5%	3.8%
very frequently	3.7%	13.8%	8.3%	5.0%	5.0%	38.9%	19.7%	15.4%
always	22.2%	27.6%	62.5%	5.0%	15.0%	44.4%	18.4%	23.1%
N	27	29	24	20	20	18	76	26

[a]Question wording differed for professional judges, state attorneys/attorneys, and lay judges: **professional judges:** "How often do you ask lay judges whether they have questions during trial?"; **state attorneys/attorneys:** "How often do professional judges ask of lay judges if they have some questions during trial?"; **lay judges:** "When a defendant, a witness, or an expert witness is cross-examined, does the professional judge usually ask you if you have any questions for that person?"

Table 7.1: Continued.

	Lay j. Dist. C. ZG	Lay j. Dist. C. KŽ	Lay j. Reg. C. ZG	Lay j. Reg. C. BJ	Prof j. All R & D	State a. All R & D	Att. ZG & BJ	Lay j. All R & D
never	8.3%	3.8%	0.0%	3.0%	6.3%	15.5%	7.9%	5.8%
sometimes	54.2%	37.7%	23.8%	21.2%	43.7%	36.2%	45.1%	42.7%
frequently	22.5%	20.8%	0.0%	24.2%	5.0%	12.1%	8.8%	20.3%
very frequently	10.8%	13.2%	14.3%	9.1%	8.7%	15.5%	18.6%	11.4%
always	4.2%	24.5%	61.9%	42.2%	36.3%	20.7%	19.6%	19.8%
N	122	53	21	33	80	58	102	229

by professional judges: professional judges from regional courts seemed to invite questions from lay judges more frequently than professional judges from district courts. While the majority of lay judges from regional courts (76%) reported that professional judges invited them to ask questions frequently, the majority of lay judges from district courts (56%) reported that professional judges invited them to ask questions only very infrequently ("sometimes" or "never"; χ^2=16.87, $d.f.$=1, Phi= -.273, $p < .001$). In addition, the answers given by lay judges revealed some regional differences: professional judges from the Zagreb Region were perceived to be somewhat more likely to invite lay judges to ask questions than professional judges from the Bjelovar Region (43% $v.$ 65%; χ^2=10.21, $d.f.$=1, Phi= -.212, $p < .01$).

The "observers" of trials, **state attorneys** and **attorneys**, were also asked to report about the frequency with which professional judges invited lay judges to ask questions. Region did not seem to be an important factor for the opinion of attorneys (χ^2=0.32, $d.f.$=1, Phi=.056, $p > .05$, n.s.), while it turned out to be somewhat more influential for state attorneys (χ^2=1.90, $d.f.$=1, Phi= -.218, $p > .05$, n.s.);[7] although the majority of district state attorneys from both regions reported that professional judges invited lay judges to ask questions infrequently, the percentages were more compelling in the Zagreb Region (80%) than in the Bjelovar Region (60%).

Another interesting topic is the impact of the type of court on attorneys' and state attorneys' perceptions about the frequency with which presiding professional judges invited lay judges to ask questions. The majority of district state attorneys (70%) reported that professional judges invited lay judges to ask questions infrequently, whereas the majority of regional state attorneys (89%) reported that professional judges invited lay judges to ask questions very frequently (χ^2=17.24, $d.f.$=1, Phi= -.545, $p < .001$).[8]

---

[7]As is often the case in these analyses, small sample sizes impact the power of the chi-square test, resulting in non-significant results. The Phi-value, the power of which is not as affected by sample size, suggests that region is related to the perceived frequency of professional judges' invitations.

[8]As mentioned earlier, such an inquiry is not appropriate for attorneys; attorneys, unlike

Perceptions by professional judges, lay judges, and state attorneys clearly suggested that professional judges from district courts invited lay judges to ask questions less frequently than professional judges from regional courts did. Indeed, while six out of ten respondents from district courts reported that professional judges invited lay judges to ask questions infrequently, eight out of ten respondents from regional courts reported that professional judges invited lay judges to ask questions either always or very frequently (χ^2=36.88, $d.f.$=1, Phi=.319, p < .001). This result holds uniformly for each of the three groups of respondents. Sixty-one percent of *professional judges* from district courts reported that they invited lay judges to ask questions infrequently, while 75% of professional judges from regional courts said that they invited lay judges to ask questions either always or very frequently. Similarly, 70% of *state attorneys* from district offices reported that professional judges invited lay judges to ask questions infrequently, while 89% of state attorneys from regional offices reported that professional judges invited lay judges to ask questions frequently. Finally, 56% of *lay judges* from district courts reported that professional judges invited lay judges to ask questions infrequently, while 76% of lay judges from regional courts reported that professional judges invited lay judges to ask questions either always or very frequently.

Several factors may have contributed to the latter finding. First, seriousness of criminal cases plays an important role. Professional judges who preside over trials at regional courts try more serious cases (e.g., rape, murder) than their counterparts at district courts. Consequently, they are likely to initiate more thorough examination of the defendant(s), witnesses, and expert witnesses by appealing to the different perspectives provided by the heterogeneity of the tribunal. Second, ignoring lay judges in a large tribunal is much more difficult than doing so in a small tribunal. Third, another key reason for this seems not only to be the increased number of lay judges in the tribunal but also the presence of another professional judge. That is, the presiding

---

state attorneys, did not practice exclusively at one type of court; they represented clients in cases tried at both district *and* regional courts.

professional judge is likely to seek an opportunity to invite a colleague, another professional judge and an associate at work of equal rank, to clarify the remaining unclear issues; the wording of the question such as: "Do **you** have any questions?," though potentially targeting primarily the other professional judge, would provide *both* another professional judge and the three lay judges in the tribunal with more opportunities to ask questions.

The *Criminal Procedure Law* (1993) did not explicitly require professional judges to ask lay judges whether they have any questions. Therefore, it would be interesting to see whether lay judges were familiar with what the law stated on this specific point. To that end, lay judges were asked: "Do you happen to know whether the gesture of asking whether you have any questions is a part of the prescribed criminal procedure or is it left to the discretion of a particular professional judge?" Possible answers were: "this is regulated by the Criminal Procedure Law," "this is left to the professional judge to resolve," "this depends on the case," and "I am not sure."

Surprisingly, on average only 14% of lay judges from each court circled the answer that would be "correct" ("left to the professional judge to resolve"); the percentage ranged from 10% for lay judges from the District Court of Križevci, to 16% of lay judges from the District Court of Zagreb. These small differences were not statistically significant ($\chi^2=1.20$, $d.f.=3$, $Phi=.074$, $p > .05$, n.s.). Also non-significant were differences between the groups of respondents from the two regions ($\chi^2=0.60$, $d.f.=1$, $Phi= -.052$, $p > .05$, n.s) and differences between the two types of courts ($\chi^2=0.08$, $d.f.=1$, $Phi=.019$, $p > .05$, n.s.).

The answer that was selected most frequently by three out of four categories of lay judges was that this issue is "regulated by the Criminal Procedure Law." The range is from 35% for lay judges from the Regional Court of Zagreb to 50% for lay judges from the Regional Court of Bjelovar. Respondents from the District Court of Zagreb most frequently said that "this depends on the case" (39%). In summary, lay judges were not familiar with the fact that the frequency with which presiding professional judges invited lay judges to ask questions depended on the discretion of a particular professional judge.

7.3   Lay Judges' Questions

A crucial question is what the expectation of lay judges' activity should be, that is, what reference point should be used. Is it realistic to expect that lay judges should ask questions after each testimony? While that would serve to promote very active lay participation, it would also imply that trials would be unduly long and that presiding professional judges would often fail to fulfill their mission. Is it, then, more reasonable to expect that lay judges would ask questions only occasionally, perhaps not even at each trial?

Criminal Procedure Law (1993) distinguishes between the fundamental and supplementary examinations of the defendant(s), witnesses, and expert witnesses. The former, chronologically the first one, is obligatory and is conducted by the presiding professional judge. The latter is somewhat arbitrary because its realization depends on the will of the other members of the tribunal. In light of the normatively specified roles and order of examinations, it is not reasonable to expect that lay judges would ask as many questions as presiding professional judges. Thus, any comparison of the frequency of lay judges' questions with the frequency of presiding professional judges' questions would be neither fair nor meaningful.

In general, the court has the responsibility of truthfully and completely determining all the facts (both exculpatory and inculpatory ones) important for decision-making in accordance with the law (Article 15, *Criminal Procedure Law*, 1993). In particular, the presiding professional judge has the responsibility (based on Article 292 of the *Criminal Procedure Law*, 1993) to conduct a versatile discussion of the case, to search for the truth, and to eliminate the elements that are stalling the process. Since the presiding professional judge is charged with such a strictly defined statutory duty, it follows that each professional judge would tend to ask all questions that he/she considers to be relevant.

The results of the Polish study on mixed tribunals suggest that lay judges thought that their presence improved the conformity of court verdicts to public opinion (Borucka-Arctowa, 1976, p. 289). This "latent function" of lay judges (Borucka-Arctowa, 1976, p. 289), the function that makes the very presence of lay judges an instrument of social control over the work of professional judges, seemed to put certain pressure on professional judges to fulfill their statutory duty more fully and carefully than they would have had lay judges not been present. Analogous arguments can be made in the context of this study; if professional judges indeed fulfilled their duty, as the legislator had expected, and as had clearly been intended by the letter of the law, little room would have been left for lay judges' questions. The expectation is thus that lay judges asked questions only very infrequently.

On the other hand, lay judges contribute to the case by bringing knowledge of the values in a particular community and by focusing on a particular defendant and his/her circumstances. It is quite possible that the function they perform is similar to the function performed by jurors — to "apply a measure of fairness and equity to a case that a judge, preoccupied with the fine points of the law, will ignore" (Hans and Vidmar, 1986, p. 116). In fact, 72% of lay judges in the Polish study felt that lay judges served a function in counteracting the tendency of statutory law to ignore the realities of life, facing "social" and "professional" functions in the tribunal (Borucka-Arctowa, 1976, p. 289). Borucka-Arctowa further reported that lay judges in the Polish study perceived the different roles played by themselves and by professional judges as "mutually complementary."

Interestingly, in a study by Kamhi and Čalija (1974), both lay judges and professional judges emphasized that lay judges played a more important and more active role in criminal trials than in civil trials. The respondents in their study believed that general life experience (i.e., knowledge about the state of affairs in the community and awareness of typical relationships that are likely to be resolved by resorting to criminal acts) — an element brought by lay judges — was of greater importance in criminal matters than in civil matters.

Following the logic that lay judges perform a function that is only partially similar to that of professional judges, the factors which professional judges and lay judges take into consideration when evaluating each testimony overlap only partially. Accordingly, the expectation is that lay judges would ask questions more frequently than the viewpoint that lay judges merely seek opportunities for a "correction" would seem to suggest. About 30% of lay judges in the Polish study (Borucka-Arctowa, 1976) asked questions during trial, having therefore actively intervened in the course of trial. As Borucka-Arctowa explained (1976, p. 290),

> A lay judge will intervene actively only when the professional judge does not take due account of circumstances which the lay judge feels are essential to the case, or when the questions the lay judge poses may help to elucidate the case.

The question that arises naturally is whether the mixed tribunal of three or five members is large enough to offer a positive climate for the exchange of different opinions. The results of jury studies on the issue of size of the jury and quality of decision-making were summarized in *Ballew v. Georgia* (1978). The issue was whether juries of fewer than six members were unconstitutional because they deprived the accused of a meaningful trial by jury. The U.S. Supreme Court wrote that, "a positive correlation exists between group size and the quality of both group performance and group productivity" and that, "the chance for hung juries would decline accordingly" in smaller juries (*Ballew v. Georgia*, 1978, p. 232, 236). The Court held that six was the minimum jury size to ensure high quality of decision-making.

However, it would be inappropriate to conclude on the basis of jury studies that mixed tribunals of fewer than six members do not provide quality atmosphere for decision-making: the composition of mixed tribunals is different from that of juries, the legal systems are different, and mixed tribunals have their own safeguards against the bias of lay judges (e.g., participation of a professional judge in each tribunal, the legal requirement to furnish a detailed written opinion as an integral part of the verdict).

According to the results by Casper and Zeisel (1972), the size of the tribunal may be important for the frequency with which lay judges ask questions of defendant(s), witnesses, and expert witnesses. Specifically, Casper and Zeisel (1972) reported that German lay judges did not ask questions during trial in more than one-half of the cases tried by smaller tribunals (one professional member and two lay members or three professional members and two lay members), whereas they asked questions in 96% of the cases tried by larger tribunals (three professional members and six lay members). Casper and Zeisel (1972) attributed that finding to the increasing levels of complexity of evidence. Interestingly, the official commentary to the draft of the German statute which had abolished nine-member tribunals in 1974 stated that the objective of such a change was to "facilitate the cooperation of lay and professional judges, for which goal the smaller panel is more fit" (Langbein, 1981, p. 213).

The potential impact of the size of the tribunal on the frequency with which lay judges ask questions during trial is likely tied with the frequency with which professional judges invited lay judges to ask questions. As discussed earlier, professional judges from regional courts (i.e., for the most part, professional judges in large tribunals) invited lay judges to ask questions far more frequently than professional judges from district courts (i.e., professional judges in small tribunals). It would, therefore, not be surprising to learn that lay judges in large tribunals indeed asked questions more frequently than their counterparts in small tribunals.

7.3.1 Lay Judges' Awareness of their Right to Ask Questions

Were lawyers, who participate in criminal trials on a regular basis, convinced that lay judges were aware of their right to ask questions of the defendant(s), witnesses, and expert witnesses during trial? Professional judges, state attorneys, and attorneys were asked: "Do you think that lay judges in general are aware that they may ask questions during trial?"[9]

---

[9]The offered answers were: "Yes," "No," and "I am not sure." In the analyses below, the answers were divided into two groups — "Yes" and "Other."

The majority in almost all categories of respondents answered in the affirmative. The data indicate, however, that the respondents were not unanimous
in their opinion: only 30% of district state attorneys in Zagreb thought that
lay judges were aware of the possibility, whereas the majority in all other
groups of respondents reported that, in their opinion, lay judges were aware
that they may ask questions during trial (the majority percentage ranged from
65% for district state attorneys in the Bjelovar Region, 70% for attorneys, 75%
for professional judges from district courts, 78% for regional state attorneys,
to 83% for professional judges from regional courts).

A comparison of responses from all groups yielded statistically significant
differences (χ^2=18.47, $d.f.$=5, Phi=.278, p < .01). Because the responses
given by district attorneys from Zagreb were considerably different from those
given by any other group of respondents, it is possible that the statistical significance was driven by their presence. Indeed, when the answers by district
state attorneys from Zagreb were excluded from analysis, multiple comparisons between groups revealed that there were no statistically significant differences among the responses provided by the remaining groups of respondents
(χ^2=1.99, $d.f.$=4, Phi=.096, p > .05, n.s.).

The answers given by district state attorneys from Zagreb were significantly different from the answers given by *any* other group of respondents,
with the exception of district state attorneys from the Bjelovar Region.[10] Finally, chi-square analysis was also performed to compare the answers provided
by district state attorneys from Zagreb with the pooled answers given by all
other respondents. The results suggested a very clear pattern: while less than
30% of district state attorneys from Zagreb said that lay judges were aware

---

[10]The lack of statistical significance was not primarily due to the similarity among the
responses by the two groups of district attorneys; rather, it was due to the lack of power
of the test, which was in turn due to small sample sizes (20 respondents in each group).
When the opinion of district state attorneys from Zagreb was compared to the opinion
held by each of the remaining groups of respondents, significant differences were observed
as follows: with professional judges from district courts (χ^2=13.73, $d.f.$=5, p < .05); with
professional judges from regional courts (χ^2=14.61, $d.f.$=5, p < .05); with regional state
attorneys (χ^2=11.52, $d.f.$=5, p < .05); and with attorneys (χ^2=12.70, $d.f.$=5, p < .05).

of their right to ask questions, 73% of all the other respondents said the same $(\chi^2=15.61, d.f.=1, Phi=-.257, p < .001)$.

The reason for such a markedly different opinion by district state attorneys from Zagreb may lie in the extent of their experience. The majority of respondents from that group selected the answer "I am not sure" (55%), rather than "No." In sharp contrast, the percentage of those who selected the answer "I am not sure" was well below 30% for all the other groups of respondents. It is noteworthy that district state attorneys from Zagreb were the least experienced among all the groups of respondents who were lawyers — 70% of district attorneys from Zagreb had been state attorneys for less than five years.[11] It may well be that their experience in trials by mixed tribunals was insufficient to determine with certainty that lay judges were aware whether they could ask questions.

In general, the majority of professional judges, state attorneys, and attorneys agreed in their view that lay judges were aware that they could ask questions during trial. The next question, then, is how frequently did lay judges exercise this possibility?

7.3.2 Frequency of Lay Judges' Questions

Lay judges and other categories of respondents were asked about the frequency with which lay judges asked questions during trial. Questions were worded somewhat differently in order to focus on different types of experiences; the question asked of lay judges targeted their own activity, while the question asked of professional judges, state attorneys, and attorneys relied on their perceptions about lay judges' activity. Consequently, the results for lay judges will be presented separately from the results for other categories of respondents.

Lay judges were asked to report how frequently in the last 10 trials they had asked questions during trial, exclusive of deliberation.[12] All four groups of

---

[11]See Chapter 6 for details on the experience of various groups of respondents.

[12]There were six possible answers, ranging from "in all 10 trials" to "in none of the trials."

lay judges most frequently said that they had asked questions *in only a few* of the last ten trials (Table 7.2); the percentages ranged from 38% of lay judges from the Regional Court of Bjelovar, slightly more than 50% of lay judges from district courts (51% of lay judges from the District Court of Križevci and 53% of lay judges from the District Court of Zagreb), to 65% of lay judges from the Regional Court of Zagreb. In fact, when the two answers from the lower end of the scale were merged ("never" and "in only a few cases" into "infrequently"), the results showed that the majority of respondents in all four groups reported asking questions infrequently; the percentage varied from 52% of lay judges at the Regional Court of Bjelovar, to more than 60% of lay judges at district courts, to 76% of lay judges at the Regional Court of Zagreb.

Lay judges from the District Court of Zagreb and the Regional Court of Zagreb were more likely to say that they asked questions infrequently[13] (80% for both groups) than lay judges from the respective courts in the Bjelovar Region (66% for the District Court of Križevci and 69% for the Regional Court of Bjelovar; χ^2=4.79, $d.f.$=1, Phi= -.147, $p < .05$).[14] A similar comparison by the type of court did not reveal any significant differences (χ^2=0.09, $d.f.$=1, Phi= -.020, $p > .05$, n.s.). It is also interesting to point out that, on average, one out of ten lay judges in each of the four groups said that he/she did not ask questions in *any* of the last 10 trials.

When the results of this study are compared to the results of the study by Kubicki and Zawadzki (1970), it seems that the majority of lay judges in the Croatian sample reported asking questions more frequently than was recorded for lay judges in the Polish study. Specifically, apprentices in the Polish courts reported that the majority of lay judges did not ask questions at all (66%), 28% asked questions sporadically, and 5.4% asked questions systematically (Kubicki

---

[13]For the purpose of this analysis, those who reported asking questions "in less than one-half of the cases," "in only a few cases," or "never" were deemed to have asked questions "infrequently;" those who reported asking questions "in all 10" through "in one-half" were deemed to have asked questions "frequently."

[14]Responses from lay judges from different courts in the same region were grouped together.

Table 7.2: Lay judges' self-reported frequency of asking questions.[a]

	Lay j. Dist. C. ZG	Lay j. Dist. C. KŽ	Lay j. Reg. C. ZG	Lay j. Reg. C. BJ	Lay j. Dist. C. All	Lay j. Reg. C. All	Lay j. All R & D
all 10	1.7%	7.5%	5.0%	0.0%	3.4%	1.9%	3.0%
more than 1/2	12.2%	11.3%	5.0%	18.8%	11.9%	13.4%	12.2%
one-half	6.1%	15.1%	10.0%	12.5%	8.8%	11.5%	9.4%
less than 1/2	15.7%	5.7%	5.0%	15.6%	12.7%	11.5%	12.4%
a few	52.2%	50.9%	65.0%	37.5%	51.8%	48.2%	51.0%
never	12.2%	9.4%	10.0%	15.6%	11.4%	13.4%	11.9%
N	122	53	21	33	175	54	229

[a]Question: "How frequently have you asked questions in the last 10 trials (exclusive of deliberations)?"

and Zawadzki, 1970, p. 104). Of course, caution needs to be exercised while interpreting this comparison because the Croatian figures are based on the respondents' perceptions on their own activity, while the Polish figures were recorded by observers (court apprentices).

Did lay judges underestimate or overestimate the frequency of their participation? As a part of their everyday practice, professional judges, state attorneys, and defense attorneys are present during trials regularly and are able to observe the behavior of lay judges on a continual basis. The following question was asked of professional judges, state attorneys, and attorneys: "According to your experience, how frequently do lay judges ask questions during trial?"[15] The majority of respondents within each group said that lay judges *sometimes* asked questions (Table 7.3); the overwhelming majority of lawyers (75% overall; 76% of attorneys from the Bjelovar Region, 80% of attorneys from the Zagreb Region, 83% of professional judges from regional courts, 89% of professional judges from the District Court of Zagreb, 90% of professional judges from the Bjelovar Region and district state attorneys from the Bjelovar Region, 100% of regional state attorneys, and only 55% of the least experienced group of lawyers — district attorneys from Zagreb) reported that lay judges only *sometimes* asked questions.[16]

Because lay judges and lawyers were asked questions that were focused on different types of experience — own behavior in the last 10 trials (lay judges) and general experience with mixed tribunals, that is, behavior of others (lawyers) — it is not appropriate to formally compare the answers to the two questions using tests of significance. Still, they can be examined and contrasted

---

[15]The answers ranged from "never" to "always" on a five-point scale.

[16]As a result of the fact that the respondents almost exclusively selected two out of five possible answers — "never" and "sometimes," it was not possible to conduct a chi-square analysis even when the answers were grouped as follows: "always" through "frequently" v. "sometimes" through "never." The only feasible approach was to contrast "never" responses v. all other responses. In that case, no significant differences were detected among the percentages of the respondents within each group who selected "never" ($\chi^2=3.40$, $d.f.=2$, $Phi=.120$, $p > .05$, n.s.).

Table 7.3: Frequency with which lay judges asked questions as perceived by others.[a]

	Prof. j. Dist. C. ZG	Prof. j. Dist. C. BJ	Prof. j. Reg. C.	Dist. State a. ZG	Dist. State a. BJ	Reg. State a.	Att. ZG	Att. BJ
always	0.0%	0.0%	0.0%	0.0%	0.0%	0.0%	1.3%	4.0%
very frequently	0.0%	0.0%	4.2%	0.0%	0.0%	0.0%	0.0%	0.0%
frequently	0.0%	0.0%	8.3%	0.0%	0.0%	0.0%	1.3%	0.0%
sometimes	88.9%	89.7%	83.3%	55.0%	90.0%	100.0%	80.3%	76.0%
never	11.1%	10.3%	4.2%	45.0%	10.0%	0.0%	17.1%	20.0%
N	27	29	24	20	20	18	76	26

[a] According to your experience, how frequently do lay judges ask questions during trial?"

Table 7.3: Continued.

	Prof j. All R & D	State a. All R & D	Att. ZG & BJ
always	0.0%	0.0%	2.0%
very frequently	1.3%	0.0%	0.0%
frequently	2.5%	0.0%	1.0%
sometimes	87.5%	81.0%	79.2%
never	8.7%	19.0%	17.8%
N	80	58	102

in broad terms.[17] Within each group of respondents (lay judges themselves, professional judges, state attorneys, and attorneys), the majority reported that lay judges only *sometimes* asked questions during trial. There were some interesting differences as well: lay judges on average seemed to report that lay judges asked questions more frequently than other categories of respondents had assessed; the percentage of those who answered "always" through "frequently" within each group of respondents was higher for lay judges than for any group of lawyers. Within the same category of respondents, be they lay judges or some other category of respondents, the answers provided by respondents from the Bjelovar Region appeared to be slightly more positive than the answers provided by respondents from the Zagreb Region.

7.3.3 Demographic Characteristics

The broad conclusion of the previous analysis was that lay judges asked questions infrequently. However, these were estimates for lay judges as a group, and it is entirely plausible that some lay judges may have been more active than others. The purpose of the analyses that follow is to determine the demographic characteristics possessed by lay judges who were more likely to report asking questions during trial.

A problem that needs to be kept in mind when discussing the influence of demographic characteristics on the frequency of asking questions is the issue of adequate representation of all segments of society in the pool of lay judges. While the idea of lay participation is to obtain full participation in the legal decision-making process from all segments of society, this is not an easy task to accomplish. When a certain age group, for example, is overrepresented in the pool of lay judges, it is more difficult for respondents to judge whether the higher level of activity they report for older lay judges is due to the truly

---

[17]To express all the answers using a similar measure, answers by lay judges were recoded as follows: "in all 10 trials" as "always," "in more than one-half of trials" as "very frequently," "in one-half of trials" as "frequently," "in less than one-half of trials" and "in a few trials" as "sometimes," and, finally, "never" as "never."

higher level of activity of older lay judges, to the fact that older people are more likely to be lay judges, or to both of these factors.

This section is devoted to the importance of several demographic variables for the frequency with which lay judges asked questions during trial.[18] Demographic characteristics selected for the analysis are gender, age, education, occupational prestige, and mandate.

Studies on juries suggest that the variation in the amount of group participation during deliberation is related to the characteristics of the individuals themselves: men, more educated jurors, and those with higher-status occupations are more likely to speak (Hans and Vidmar, 1986, p. 108). The available studies on mixed tribunals did not address this issue.

The propositions of status characteristics theory, described in Chapter 5, are used as a theoretical basis for the explanation of the interaction among the members of mixed tribunals. It is predicted that members who possess high states of specific characteristics, that is, members who have legal education and systematic training and experience in legal decision-making, will have a higher status in the tribunal and, consequently, will have more opportunities to participate; furthermore, once they participate, their contributions will be evaluated as more important. Lay judges, although not endowed with extensive experience in legal decision-making that can parallel the experience possessed by professional judges, may differ amongst themselves with respect to the length of service or the type of experience (i.e., serving at regional courts *v.* serving at district courts). Diffuse status characteristics are expected to have limited impact, if any, on the participation in the work of the tribunal. Still, not all diffuse status characteristics are the same; some may be more important in terms of legal decision-making (e.g., education or occupational prestige) than others (e.g., gender). The following sections develop hypotheses for several diffuse characteristics and present corresponding empirical results.

---

[18]In order to use chi-square tests, answers "in all 10 trials" through "in about one-half of all the trials" were merged ("frequent"), as were the answers "in less than one-half of the trials" through "in none of the trials" ("infrequent").

Gender

The analysis of the possible influence of gender on the frequency of participation calls for an examination of the issue of adequate representation. Women were traditionally excluded from public service in the past. They did not serve as lay participants until the introduction of mixed tribunals in the Soviet Union in 1917 (Silberman, 1979, p. 365). Following the general principle of equality between women and men, socialist countries introduced more women as lay participants than capitalist countries. The proportion of female lay judges in the Soviet Union in 1975 was 53%, in the Land of Brandenburg in East Germany in 1974 it was 48% (Silberman, 1979, p. 365), while at the same time the proportion of female lay judges in West Germany in 1975 was only 23%.

The proportion of female lay judges in Croatia in 1992 varied between 13% and 21%, depending on the type of court (Table 6.2 in Chapter 6). Among the lay judges who participated in the study, the percentage of female respondents was below or about 25% at three out of four courts (9% at the District Court of Križevci, 14% at the Regional Court of Zagreb, and 25% at the Regional Court of Bjelovar). This fact may have influenced the answers (provided by lawyers) to the questions targeted at the impact of lay judges' demographic characteristics on lay judges' activity during trial; it is difficult to analyze the possibly low frequency of questions asked by female lay judges when there are very few female lay judges to begin with. The situation may have been somewhat different at the District Court of Zagreb, where the percentage of female lay judges out of the 122 lay judges who participated in the study was considerably higher (49%).

In light of a complete absence of treatment of this issue in any of the existing studies on mixed tribunals, in developing the hypotheses I will appeal to the results of jury studies. Jury studies show that, perhaps not surprisingly, all jurors do not participate equally during deliberations; men tend to speak more than women (Hans and Vidmar, 1986, p. 108). The jury, however, typically does not feature members who possess high levels of specific status characteristics, which gives prominence to diffuse status characteristics. In mixed tribunals, specific status characteristics are expected to be more important than the diffuse ones. Therefore, differences in participation between groups of lay judges, who differ only in terms of their diffuse status characteristics are expected to be minimal, if any. The potential impact of different states/levels of diffuse status characteristics on lay judges' activity needs to be assessed via arguments specific to a particular status characteristic. To date, most societies tend to appreciate males more highly than they appreciate females. Consequently, it is expected that, if there are some differences in lay judges' activity with respect to their gender at all, male lay judges will contribute more frequently and will have more opportunities to participate than female lay judges.

The analysis starts with an examination of the possible influence of lay judges' gender and the self-reported frequency of asking questions during trial. When answers to this question by lay judges from all the four courts were pooled, the chi-square test showed no significant differences in the self-reported frequency of questions between female and male lay judges ($\chi^2=0.33$, $d.f.=1$, $Phi=-.039$, $p > .05$, n.s.).

Lawyers were also asked about their perceptions and possible differences in the frequency of participation between female and male lay judges.[19] Interestingly, while the majority of professional judges (60%) stated that gender had no bearing on the frequency with which lay judges asked questions, an identical percentage of state attorneys thought that the opposite was true. Attorneys were divided: approximately one-half said that gender was an important factor and the other half said that gender was not important.

Did the respondents who said that gender had a bearing on the frequency with which lay judges asked questions consider female or male lay judges to be more likely to ask questions? Less than 20% of those who reported that gen-

---

[19]The question was worded as follows: "Would you agree with the following statement: 'Female lay judges are more likely to ask questions during trial than male lay judges'?" The offered answers were: "strongly agree," "agree," "no bearing," "disagree," and "strongly disagree."

der was important within each of the three categories of respondents thought that women were more likely to ask questions; the great majority (94% of the professional judges who reported some influence of gender and 38% of professional judges overall; 81% of the attorneys who reported some influence of gender and 41% of attorneys overall; 85% of the state attorneys who reported some influence of gender and 51% of state attorneys overall) considered that male lay judges were more likely to ask questions than female lay judges.

A separate analysis was performed for the District Court of Zagreb as the court with both by far the largest number of lay judges among the courts included in the study and an approximately equal percentage of female and male lay judges. Although the majority of both female and male lay judges reported that they asked questions during trial (72% and 88%, respectively), female lay judges were somewhat less likely to say so than male lay judges (χ^2= 4.41, $d.f.$=1, Phi= -.197, $p < .05$).

Interestingly, the perceptions of lawyers (professional judges, state attorneys) who practiced law at the District Court of Zagreb judges lead to a different conclusion. The majority of professional judges and state attorneys who practiced law at the District Court of Zagreb (63% and 55%, respectively) replied that gender had no bearing on the frequency of lay judge's participation. However, there were significant differences among the answers with respect to their choice of who would be more active; although the majority of respondents who said that gender would be important reported that male lay judges would be more active than female lay judges, the percentage was higher for professional judges than for state attorneys (100% of the professional judges who reported that gender was important and 37% of professional judges overall; 56% of the state attorneys who reported that gender was important and 25% of state attorneys overall; χ^2= 6.04, $d.f.$=2, Phi=.359, $p < .05$).

Age

Age is an important factor for determining eligibility requirements for participation in the criminal justice system. The *Regular Courts Law* (1988, Article

102) imposed the minimum age required for lay judges — 18 years of age ("full age"). As Silberman emphasized, despite the broadening of the minimum and maximum age requirement for lay participants in criminal justice systems, most lay participants are still middle-aged persons (Silberman, 1979, p. 367). According to Silberman (1979, p. 368), the predominance of middle-aged persons among lay participants was reported in Canada, Great Britain, Austria, West Germany, France, Hungary, Poland, Czechoslovakia, Denmark, Sweden, and the United States. Not surprisingly, the majority of lay judges who participated in this study were also middle-aged: fifty-seven percent were in the age group 51-65 years of age and an additional 22% were in the age group 36-50 years of age.

The issue of adequate representation, raised above for gender, can be raised for age as well. Is the higher frequency of questions asked by middle-aged lay judges a result of their numerical predominance, of their higher activity itself, or of both of these factors? Is this a result of their socialization in different times, different degree of self-esteem, or different degree of sense of responsibility for their lay participation?

The results show that some age groups of lay judges reported asking questions during trial less frequently than others;[20] the youngest group of lay judges (35 and below) reported more frequently that they rarely asked questions than the three older groups of lay judges did ($\chi^2= 4.34$, $d.f.=2$, $Phi=.141$, $p > .05$, n.s.).[21]

The majority of professional judges, state attorneys, and attorneys reported that there was a relationship between age and the frequency of questions asked.[22] Although the majority within each group of lawyers said that

---

[20]The lay judges' answers to the question about the frequency of questions in the last 10 trials were grouped according to the same age categorization as in the observers' question.

[21]Although chi-square analysis did not yield statistically significant differences, I consider the differences of above 20% to be substantively important. In particular, the lay judges from the youngest group were 21% more likely than the lay judges in the second youngest group, 28% more likely than the lay judges in the second oldest group, and 33% more likely than the lay judges in the oldest group to say that they asked questions infrequently.

[22]The question asked of professional judges, state attorneys, and attorneys was: "Lay

age was an important factor, there were statistically significant differences among the three groups (χ^2= 18.26, *d.f.*=2, *Phi*=.276, p < .001). The largest difference was found between attorneys (85%) and professional judges (57%); it was also statistically significant (χ^2=18.10, *d.f.*=1, *Phi*= -.316, p < .001).

To which age group did an average lay judge who asked more questions belong? Professional judges, state attorneys, and attorneys all opted for a lay judge who was neither young (i.e., 35 and below) nor old (i.e., 66 and above). In fact, less than 10% of the respondents within each group who said that age was important selected the youngest group (35 and below) or the oldest group (66 and above) as the most active one; the two competing age groups were 36-50 and 51-65. The majority of professional judges and attorneys who thought that age was an important factor (53% and 61%, respectively) asserted that lay judges from the age group 51-65 were most active in asking questions during trial, while state attorneys equally favored the two competing age groups (approximately 40% chose each competing age group).

A separate analysis of the answers provided by respondents from the District Court of Zagreb showed that the youngest group of lay judges reported asking questions during trial less frequently than the other three groups of lay judges (χ^2= 3.84, *d.f.*=3, *Phi*=.185, p > .05, n.s.).[23] Interestingly, the majority of professional judges and state attorneys who practiced law at the same court (59% and 70%, respectively) reported that age and frequency of lay judges' questions were related.

Education

The *Regular Courts Law* (1988) did not impose a minimum educational requirement as a limit for selection of lay judges; lay judges could have even

---

judges who belong to the following age group are most likely to ask questions during trial: (a) 35 and below; (b) 36-50; (c) 51-65; (d) 66 and above; (e) no difference."

[23]Although the differences were not statistically significant, I consider the differences of at least 20% to be substantively important. The youngest group of lay judges was 19% more likely than the second youngest group, 24% more likely than the second oldest group, and 27% more likely than the oldest group of lay judges to report rarely asking questions during trial.

Table 7.4: Education of lay judges from the District Court of Zagreb and education of the active population of Zagreb.

	active population ZG[a]	lay judges Dist. C. ZG
below elementary school	17.96%	0.0%
elementary school	15.97%	15.8%
high school	48.11%	45.8%
some college	5.0%	21.7%
college	12.52%	16.7%
unknown	0.4%	-
N	399,333	120

[a]Source: *1981 Census of Population, Households, and Residences; Active Population and Employed Workers*, 1986.

been persons who could not read and/or write as long as they were worthy of being lay judges and could have performed that role with dignity.

Assuming the selection process tended to maintain adequate representation of different educational levels, the expectation is that educational levels of lay judges corresponded closely to those of the city/district population in general. A comparison of the educational levels of the active population in Zagreb and the surveyed lay judges from the District Court of Zagreb (122 lay judges or 88% of the pool of lay judges who responded to the Court's mail and actually performed their duty as lay judges; Table 7.4) reveals some similarities: the most dominant level in both the active population and the sample was "graduated from high school." On average, the surveyed lay judges tended to be more educated than the overall active population.[24]

---

[24]Similar comparisons for the other three groups of lay judges were not performed because

Jury studies show that the more educated jurors tend to speak more during deliberations (Hans and Vidmar, 1986, p. 108). In the domain of mixed tribunals, education is a rather interesting variable. In the parlance of status characteristics theory, although not a specific status characteristic, education may be quite important. Through their education, the more educated lay judges have adopted more abstract ways of thinking and problem solving, have interacted with a wider variety of people and have thus become more sensitive to different ideas and positions; furthermore, the more educated lay judges, even if not involved actively, would have at least been present during classroom discussions. Therefore, the expectation is that, if any differences with respect to education are present at all, lay judges with higher educational levels will ask more questions than their less educated counterparts.

The answers given by lay judges indicated that educational level did not influence their activity in asking questions during trial ($\chi^2 = 1.88$, $d.f.=1$, $Phi = -.093$, $p > .05$, n.s.). Interestingly, the majority of professional judges, state attorneys, and attorneys had the opposite view:[25] fifty to seventy percent of professional judges, state attorneys, and attorneys said that education was related to the frequency with which lay judges asked questions during trial (51%, 59%, and 71%, respectively). Among the respondents who emphasized the importance of education, the majority within each category (59% of the professional judges who reported education as important and 30% of professional judges overall; 76% of the state attorneys who reported education as important and 45% of state attorneys overall; and 61% of the attorneys who reported education as important and 43% of attorneys overall) said that lay judges who graduated from high school were the most likely to participate actively by asking questions during trial. A separate analysis was conducted for the respondents who took part in trials at the District Court of Zagreb. The

---

of small sample sizes.

[25] The question asked of professional judges, state attorneys, and attorneys was: "In your opinion, lay judges who most frequently ask questions during trial have the following level of education: (a) below high school; (b) graduated from high school; (c) graduated from college; (d) no difference."

analysis led to the same conclusion: while there were no differences among the self-reported frequency of questions by lay judges' education (χ^2= 1.52, *d.f.*=1, *Phi*= -.116, *p* > .05, n.s.), the majority of professional judges and state attorneys who practiced law at the District Court of Zagreb (52% and 61%, respectively) reported that education was related to the frequency with which lay judges asked questions during trial. Among those professional judges and state attorneys who considered education to be important, the majority (50% of the professional judges who considered education as important and 26% of professional judges overall; 55% of the state attorneys who considered education to be important and 33% of state attorneys overall) perceived that lay judges who had graduated from high school were the most active group of lay judges.

Occupational Prestige

The expectation is that lay judges whose occupations were more prestigious would have asked questions more frequently because, unlike their counterparts with less prestigious occupations, they would have felt that their questions and comments had been appreciated and valued more highly by professional judges, persons whose occupation is itself on the higher level of the occupational prestige scale. Reported occupations were classified on the basis of prestige of each occupation using Treiman's international occupational scale (Treiman, 1977).[26]

In accordance with theoretical developments from Chapter 5, when all the lay judges who participated in the study were pooled, their self-reported frequencies of asking questions during trial did not differ significantly by occupational prestige (χ^2=1.61, *d.f.*=1, *Phi*=.092, *p* > .05, n.s.). Among the four groups of lay judges, only lay judges from the District Court of Zagreb

---

[26]Occupations were coded on the basis of Treiman's international occupational scale (Treiman, 1977) as those with lower prestige, which included occupations coded with numerical values from 10 to 45, and those with higher prestige, which included occupations coded with numerical values from 46 to 78. See Chapter 6 for a description of Treiman's occupational scale.

displayed differences that were (marginally) statistically significant ($\chi^2=3.92$, $d.f.=1$, $Phi=.198$, $p < .05$); while the majority in both groups reported asking questions infrequently, lay judges having more prestigious occupations tended to be less likely to say that they asked questions infrequently than lay judges having less prestigious occupations (73% $v.$ 89%, respectively).

Mandate

Croatian lay judges were unlikely to know their rights and duties as lay judges at the beginning of their mandate, because they typically received no training or education on that topic: by their very nature, they did not possess a law-school education; by the virtue of the environment in which they performed their duty as lay judges, they were not given an opportunity to take part in a separate training for lay judges. The results of the Polish study point in the same direction; "A fair number of lay judges just beginning their activities, have not real views about their rights" (Borucka-Arctowa, 1976, p. 289).

As mentioned earlier, lay judges' mandate is four years, after which they can be reelected to the same court or elected to serve at another court. It is certainly tempting to predict that novice lay judges would ask fewer questions than more experienced lay judges. Such a prediction, though not entirely untrue, would not encompass the impact of routine on the work of lay judges, and would thus be somewhat flawed.

In every social interaction we try to modify our own behavior and respond to the signals sent by the audience. In terms of mixed tribunals, professional judges and other lay judges are the audience for lay judges. Lay judges at the beginning of their mandate (below one year) were still in the process of learning social rules in a new setting and were thus probably not sure what their role was, so they asked questions less frequently than lay judges who knew these rules (lay judges who served for more than one year). On the other hand, lay judges with a mandate of over three years had sat in relatively many trials and perhaps had seen that professional judges did not value their questions highly (the next topic in this chapter), or, even more encompassing, had realized that their input had influenced the outcome rarely, if ever. An element of routine could also have developed, whereby lay judges slowly, as their mandate approached three years, started to reduce the frequency of asking questions during trial. As a consequence, the level of activity of very experienced lay judges (mandate over three years) could easily have been reduced over time. Indeed, Arzt (1982, p. 154) reported that the longer a lay judge participates in mixed tribunals, the less likely the lay judge will be to attempt to influence the outcome.

The expectation is thus that lay judges have been the most active in the period during which they were no longer novice lay judges, but were not yet very experienced (and perhaps not as disillusioned). In other words, it is expected that the frequency with which lay judges asked questions during trial will have reached its peak "in the middle" of their mandate.

The influence of mandate on the frequency of asking questions is examined using two measures. The first is a comparison of self-reported frequency of asking questions during trial by lay judges' mandate. It is based on two questions asked of each lay judge — one querying for the frequency of asking questions during trial and the other querying for the lay judge's mandate.[27] The second is a comparison of the self-reported frequency of asking questions at the beginning of the mandate and later in the mandate. It is based on a single question asked of each lay judge who was in at least the second year of his/her mandate. The question called for a comparison between the frequency of asking questions during trial at the beginning of the lay judge's mandate and the frequency of asking questions during trial later in the lay judge's mandate.[28]

---

[27]The question was worded as follows: "How many years have you been a lay judge at this court?" The offered answers were: "less than 6 months," "6 months to 1 year," "1 to 2 years," "2 to 3 years," "3 to 4 years," and "over 4 years."

[28]The wording of the question was: "Please answer the following question only if you are NOT in the first year of being a lay judge: During your first year as a lay judge, you asked questions during trial..." The offered answers ranged on a five-point scale from "much more frequently than you do now" to "much less frequently than you do now," with "equally frequently" in the middle of the scale.

Interestingly, and contrary to the above hypothesis, when the answers by all lay judges in the study were pooled, the differences among lay judges with different mandates were not statistically significant. Several ways of grouping lay judges according to their mandate were explored; the most powerful grouping, although not powerful enough to be statistically significant, was to merge novice lay judges (below one year) and very experienced lay judges (above three years) and to then compare their answers with the answers given by lay judges in the middle (one to three years) of their mandate (χ^2=1.16, $d.f.$=1, Phi=.074, p > .05, n.s.).

On the other hand, the self-reported frequency with which lay judges from the District Court of Zagreb asked questions during trial contradicted this conclusion and instead supported the above hypothesis; lay judges who had either less than one year of experience or more than three years of experience (treated as one group for statistical purposes) were less likely to say that they asked questions during trial than lay judges in the middle (one to three years) of their mandate (χ^2=7.14, $d.f.$=1, Phi=.257, p < .05). Although the majority of lay judges within each of the groups formed on the basis of their mandate reported that they asked questions during trial infrequently, lay judges who were in the middle of their mandate (1 to 3 years) were significantly less likely to say that they asked questions during trial infrequently than either novice lay judges (below 1 year) or very experienced lay judges (above 3 years). The corresponding percentages were 69% for lay judges in the middle of their mandate *v.* 88% for lay judges with less than 1 year of experience and 91% for lay judges with more than 3 years of experience.

Most of the lay judges who participated in this study were elected in 1990 or earlier; the lay judges who were elected since 1990 were selected from analogous pools of candidates and according to the same laws as their more experienced colleagues. There is thus no reason to believe that either the characteristics of these three groups of lay judges or their election process differed substantially. Therefore, the factors that influenced lay judges of differing mandates to report asking questions during trial more or less frequently need to be looked for elsewhere. For example, the behavior and attitudes of professional judges probably had a large impact. The general finding, supported by some results in this chapter and in the next two chapters, is that professional judges as a group (and especially professional judges from district courts) did not perceive lay judges to participate actively nor did they evaluate their contributions as very important. Furthermore, the general opinion professional judges had about mixed tribunals was negative. It is quite likely that lay judges detected, either directly or indirectly, such an attitude and, not surprisingly, adjusted their own behavior accordingly.

The second question asked lay judges with at least one year of experience as lay judges to compare their frequency of asking questions during trial at the beginning of their mandate to that which prevailed later in their mandate. The majority of lay judges at each of the four courts shared the same opinion — they said that they did not ask questions with the same frequency as they had done earlier in their mandate (χ^2=1.30, $d.f.$=3, Phi=.082, $p > .05$, n.s.). The percentage of lay judges who reported that their frequency of asking questions during trial had changed since the beginning of their mandate as lay judges was the highest for lay judges from the Regional Court of Zagreb (70%), the lowest for lay judges from the Regional Court of Bjelovar (55%), and intermediate for lay judges from district courts (58%).

The most frequently reported direction of change of frequency of asking questions during trial was a *decrease*; the range of reported percentages is between 60-65% for the lay judges from regional courts who reported a change in the frequency with which they asked questions during trial (which amounts to between 33-45% of all the surveyed lay judges from regional courts) and between 52-56% for the lay judges from district courts who reported a change in the frequency with which they asked questions during trial (which amounts to between 30-33% of all the surveyed lay judges from district courts). Neither region nor the type of court produced significant differences.

The majority of professional judges agreed with the opinion of the majority of lay judges themselves: the frequency with which a lay judge asks questions during trial changes as the lay judge's mandate moves from its beginning onward. Specifically, the majority of the professional judges from regional courts who supported this opinion agreed with lay judges by saying that lay judges' activity decreased later in their mandate (67% of the professional judges from regional courts who perceived that a mandate influenced the frequency of lay judges' questions during trial, i.e., 42% of all surveyed professional judges from regional courts). Contrary to that, the majority of professional judges from district courts said that lay judges' activity increased later in their mandate (the percentages are 63% and 65% of the professional judges from district courts who perceived that mandate impacted the frequency of lay judges' questions during trial, respectively, which constituted 37% and 45% of all surveyed professional judges from the two courts, respectively).

7.4 Frequency of Reading the Case File

Although one of the principles of Croatian criminal procedure is that the legal decision may be based only on the evidence selected by the tribunal and presented orally during trial, the presiding professional judge clearly finds it very helpful to consult with the case file generated during the earlier stages of the process (in particular the investigation by the investigative professional judge and the indictment by the prosecutor) in order to determine which evidence needs to be examined and which witnesses have to be heard (as well as to subsequently reach the appropriate legal decision). Under certain conditions, the *Criminal Procedure Law* (1993, Article 317) allowed earlier statements by the witnesses and the defendant to be read. If the defendant changed his/her statement (as compared to the earlier statement given to the investigative judge), the law required the professional judge to draw the defendant's attention to such a discrepancy and to ask the defendant to provide reasons for it (Article 317, *Criminal Procedure Law*, 1993).

Reading the case file and being familiar with its content is of crucial importance for an understanding of the case. Reading the case file presents an opportunity for lay judges to become familiar with the case even before the trial starts. It is expected that the lay judges who read the case file will ask questions during trial more frequently, since they have become more familiar with the case and are thus already actively involved in the process; in addition, the lay judges who read the case file are probably more interested in the trial than the lay judges who do not read the case file, and, as a result of their interest and the information they gathered from the case file, they will ask more questions than other lay judges.

Lay judges in Kulcsár's study (1972) were not given sufficient time to study the case file in advance; they emphasized the difficulty of participating fully and actively when they did not have the opportunity to read the case file. Borucka-Arctowa (1976) reported the same problems in the Polish study.

The question about the frequency with which lay judges read the case files was asked of both lay judges and professional judges.[29] Lay judges from all the four courts said that they, on average, only *sometimes* read the case file (Table 7.5). While approximately nine out of ten lay judges from regional courts reported reading the file at least occasionally, only seven out of ten lay judges from district courts reported the same (χ^2=9.15, *d.f.*=1, *Phi*= -.202, $p < .01$). In other words, lay judges from district courts were significantly more likely to say that they *never* read the case file than lay judges from regional courts.

Professional judges were asked a similar question, but the question asked of professional judges targeted their general experience.[30] The overall finding is that lay judges read the case file rarely, if ever (Table 7.6); more than 90% of professional judges and more than 70% of lay judges reported that lay judges rarely ("sometimes" or "never") read the case file. There were some minor

---

[29]The question for lay judges was worded as follows: "How often do you read the case file?" The offered answers ranged from "always" to "never." For the purpose of the analyses reported below, the lay judges' responses to the question about the frequency of reading the case file were grouped: "always" through "sometimes" as "at least occasionally," and "never" as simply "never."

[30]The question was worded as follows: "According to your experience, how frequently do lay judges read the case file?"

Table 7.5: Lay judges' self-reported frequency of reading the case file.[a]

	Lay j. Dist. C. ZG	Lay j. Dist. C. KŽ	Lay j. Reg. C. ZG	Lay j. Reg. C. BJ	Lay j. Dist. C. All	Lay j. Reg. C. All	Lay j. All R & D
always	1.7%	11.5%	5.0%	0.0%	4.7%	1.9%	4.0%
very frequently	4.2%	3.8%	5.0%	6.1%	4.1%	5.7%	4.5%
frequently	15.1%	11.5%	5.0%	18.2%	14.0%	13.1%	13.8%
sometimes	48.7%	51.9%	75.0%	69.7%	49.5%	71.8%	54.8%
never	30.3%	21.2%	10.0%	6.1%	27.5%	7.6%	22.8%
N	122	53	21	33	175	54	229

[a]Question: "How often do you read the case file?"

discrepancies, however; while the majority of professional judges from district courts in the Bjelovar Region (62%) and professional judges from regional courts (63%) said that lay judges *sometimes* read the case file, the majority of professional judges from the District Court of Zagreb (67%) reported that lay judges *never* read the case file $(\chi^2=9.76, d.f.=2, Phi=.349, p < .01)$. Nevertheless, at least 30% of professional judges within each of these three groups reported that lay judges did not read the case file at all.

The influence of region on the frequency of reading the case files was analyzed by first pooling professional judges from district courts with lay judges from both district and regional courts in each region and then comparing the results by region. The results suggested that respondents from the Zagreb Region reported less frequently that lay judges read the case file only rarely than respondents from the Bjelovar Region did $(\chi^2=4.35, d.f.=1, Phi= -.134, p < .05)$.

An analysis of the frequency with which lay judges asked questions during trial indicated that lay judges' education did not influence the frequency with which they asked questions. Other categories of respondents (professional judges, state attorneys, and attorneys) disagreed and said that education was important, that is, that more educated lay judges asked questions more frequently. Although the conclusion was that education of lay judges did not influence the self-reported frequency of asking questions directly, it seems that there may be an indirect influence: it is quite likely that lay judges with higher educational levels were more likely to read the case file, and those who read the case file were more likely to ask questions.

The results indeed revealed some differences: lay judges with higher levels of education were more likely to say that they read the case files than lay judges with lower levels of education[31] $(\chi^2=5.17, d.f.=1, Phi= -.175, p < .05)$; one-

---

[31]Lay judges were divided into two groups on the basis of their self-reported education — "lower" (high school diploma or less) and "higher" (at least some college). As before, the answers about the frequency of reading the case file were grouped into "at least occasionally" ("always" to "sometimes") and "never" (simply "never").

Table 7.6: Frequency of reading the case file as perceived by professional judges.[a]

	Prof. j. Dist. C. ZG	Prof. j. Dist. C. BJ	Prof. j. Reg. C.	Prof. j. All D & R
always	0.0%	3.4%	0.0%	1.2%
very frequently	0.0%	3.4%	4.2%	2.5%
frequently	0.0%	0.0%	4.2%	1.3%
sometimes	33.3%	62.1%	62.5%	52.5%
never	66.7%	31.0%	29.1%	42.5%
N	27	29	24	80

[a]Question: "How often do lay judges read the case file?"

third of lay judges with lower levels of education and one-sixth of lay judges with higher levels of education reported *never* reading the case file.[32]

Was reading the case file important for the frequency of questions asked during trial? The answers by all lay judges were pooled and suitably recoded for the purpose of this analysis.[33] The results show that lay judges who reported reading the case file at least occasionally were significantly more likely to say that they often asked questions during trial than lay judges who reported not reading the case file (χ^2=7.69, *d.f.*=1, *Phi*= -.188, $p < .05$).

7.5   Evidence Complexity and Frequency of Asking Questions

Lay participants' ability to understand and evaluate evidence was discussed earlier in the book, including the results of studies on the jury and mixed tribunals on this topic. A frequently raised argument was that lay participants have more problems in understanding the important issues in the case when issues in the case become more complex. Are the complexity of evidence and the frequency of participation in the work of the tribunal related?

When respondents were asked if the frequency of asking questions depends on the complexity of evidence in the case,[34] the expectation was that they would say that lay judges usually asked more questions in the cases with complex evidence than in the cases with simple evidence. A rationale in support

---

[32]A *caveat* is in order: it is quite possible that reading the case file may have different connotations for different lay judges — while one lay judge may have understood it as reading the file from cover to cover, another lay judge may have interpreted it as merely browsing through the file. However, the results indicate discrepancies that are very large and are thus unlikely to be due solely (nor indeed primarily) to such differing interpretations.

[33]The self-reported frequency with which lay judges asked questions during trial was recoded into "often" ("always" to "frequently") and "rarely" ("sometimes" to "never"). The self-reported frequency of reading the case file was recoded into "at least occasionally" ("always" to "sometimes") and "never" (simply as "never").

[34]Lay judges were asked: "When the evidence in the case is complex, difficult to understand, are you: 'less likely to ask questions' or 'more likely to ask questions'?" Respondents also had the option of saying that the complexity of evidence did not have a bearing on the frequency with which lay judges asked questions.

of such an expectation would be the desire of lay judges to clarify the evidence. On the other hand, it is also quite possible to argue that (at least some) lay judges may have asked fewer questions in the cases that feature complex evidence in order to avoid embarrassment.

The majority of lay judges said that the complexity of evidence influenced the frequency with which they asked questions; more than 70% within each group of lay judges thought that the complexity of evidence was important (χ^2=5.81, $d.f.$=3, Phi=.162, p > .05, n.s.). However, lay judges were not unanimous in telling in what direction the complexity of evidence influenced the frequency of their questions (Table 7.7): the percentage of lay judges who said that they asked more questions and the percentage of lay judges who said that they asked fewer questions in the cases with complex evidence at both district courts was similar (approximately 50% of the lay judges who reported that there was a relationship between the complexity of evidence and the frequency of questions, which amounts to 35-40% of the overall number of lay judges surveyed at district courts). The most frequent opinions expressed by lay judges from the two regional courts were contradictory; the majority of lay judges from the Regional Court of Zagreb said that the frequency with which they asked questions decreased (67% of the lay judges who reported a relationship between the complexity of evidence and the frequency of asking questions, which accounts for 50% of the overall number of lay judges surveyed at the Regional Court of Zagreb), while the majority of lay judges from the Regional Court of Bjelovar said that their frequency of asking questions increased (63% of the lay judges who reported a relationship between the complexity of evidence and the frequency of asking questions, which accounts for 52% of the overall number of lay judges surveyed at the Regional Court of Bjelovar).

Interesting hypotheses may be developed about the interaction of the lay judges' education, the complexity of evidence in the case, and the frequency with which lay judges asked questions during the trial. For example, it could be argued that, in the cases in which the evidence is complex, lay judges with lower educational levels would ask questions relatively more frequently

Table 7.7: Evidence complexity and self-reported frequency of asking questions by lay judges.[a]

	Lay j. Dist. C. ZG	Lay j. Dist. C. KŽ	Lay j. Reg. C. ZG	Lay j. Reg. C. BJ	Lay j. Dist. C. All	Lay j. Reg. C. All	Lay j. All R & D
less likely to ask questions	39.0%	43.1%	50.0%	30.3%	40.2%	38.0%	39.7%
no influence	28.0%	11.8%	25.0%	18.2%	23.1%	20.8%	22.6%
more likely to ask questions	33.1%	45.1%	25.0%	51.5%	36.7%	41.2%	37.8%
N	122	53	21	33	175	54	229

[a]Question: "When the evidence in the case is complex (difficult to understand), you are:"

than lay judges with higher educational levels because the former would have more problems in following complex evidence (as a result of their less frequent exposure to and experience with abstract problem solving). On the other hand, it could be argued that the more educated lay judges would ask more questions in the cases with complex evidence because lay judges with lower educational levels might have more problems in following the testimony, as a consequence of which they might decide to base their judgment about the credibility of the witness on personal factors (rather than to try to understand complex arguments); therefore, they would not be interested in asking questions at all.

It turned out that lay judges' education had no bearing on the matter; the percentage of lay judges who reported that they asked questions more/less frequently as a result of the complexity of evidence in the case was not related to their education (χ^2=1.12, $d.f.$=1, Phi=.081, $p > .05$, n.s.).[35]

A similar question was asked of professional judges, state attorneys, and attorneys (Table 7.8). The majority within each of these groups of respondents (more than 66% of professional judges; seventy-five percent of state attorneys and attorneys) indeed agreed with lay judges in saying that the complexity of evidence was related to the frequency with which lay judges asked questions (χ^2=2.18, $d.f.$=4, Phi=.096, $p > .05$, n.s.).[36] The lawyers' answers suggest the direction of this relationship; the overwhelming majority of professional judges, state attorneys, and attorneys who emphasized the issue of evidence complexity (more than 90% of those who reported a relationship between the complexity of evidence and the frequency of lay judges' questions in all three groups of lawyers, which constitutes 60-70% percent of all surveyed respondents in each group) said that lay judges asked questions *less frequently* in the cases with complex evidence than in the cases with simple evidence.

---

[35]The reported value of the chi-square test is calculated based only on the answers "less likely" and "more likely" (to ask questions during the trial). The differences remained non-significant when the "no bearing" answer was included in the analysis.

[36]All "observers" were grouped into three groups: professional judges, state attorneys, and attorneys.

Table 7.8: Evidence complexity and frequency of questions by lay judges during trial as perceived by others.[a]

	Prof. j. Dist. C. ZG	Prof. j. Dist. C. BJ	Prof. j. Reg. C.	Dist. State a. ZG	Dist. State a. BJ	Reg. State a.	Att. ZG	Att. BJ
less likely to ask questions	48.1%	65.5%	66.7%	55.6%	80.0%	72.2%	68.0%	72.0%
no influence	48.1%	24.1%	29.2%	44.4%	15.0%	16.7%	26.7%	20.0%
more likely to ask questions	3.7%	10.3%	4.2%	44.4%	15.0%	16.7%	26.7%	20.0%
N	27	29	24	20	20	18	76	26

[a]Question: "When the evidence in the case is complex (difficult to understand), lay judges are:"

Table 7.8: Continued.

	Prof j. All R & D	State a. All R & D	Att. ZG & BJ
less likely to ask questions	60.0%	69.2%	69.0%
no influence	33.7%	25.7%	25.0%
more likely to ask questions	6.2%	5.2%	6.0%
N	80	58	102

The majority of lay judges and "observers" agreed that the complexity of evidence influenced the frequency with which lay judges asked questions (χ^2=3.93, $d.f.$=3, Phi=.093, $p >$ .05, n.s.).[37] Since most of the disagreements revolved around the direction of the change, the next step was to include all three original answers in the analysis. The differences among the answers furnished by various groups of respondents were statistically significant (χ^2=73.26, $d.f.$=6, Phi=.400, $p <$ .001). There was a sharp difference between the answers provided by lawyers and those provided by lay judges; while 60-70% of all professional judges, state attorneys, and attorneys (which is, at the same time, more than 90% of the lawyers who perceived that there was an impact of evidence complexity on the frequency of lay judges' questions) suggested that lay judges asked questions less frequently in the cases with complex evidence than in the cases with simple evidence, only 40% of all lay judges (which is, at the same time, 51% of the lay judges who acknowledged the impact of case complexity) agreed.

Since the majority of respondents, including lay judges themselves, said that lay judges asked questions only infrequently, it may be that lay judges did not feel comfortable to increase/change their frequency of asking questions of the defendants, witnesses, expert witnesses, and professional judges when complex evidence was introduced into the case. Therefore, a question was asked about the change in the frequency of asking for explanations in response to complex evidence.[38]

The majority (more than 60%) in each of the four groups of respondents (i.e., professional judges, lay judges, state attorneys, and attorneys) argued that the complexity of evidence was related to the perceived frequency of

---

[37]The answers were dichotomized into "no bearing" and "some bearing." The latter included both "less likely" and "more likely." Respondents were grouped into four groups according to their roles in the criminal justice system: professional judges, lay judges, state attorneys, and attorneys.

[38]The question was worded as follows: "When the evidence in the case is complex, how often do lay judges ask for explanations during the trial, compared to the cases with simple evidence?" The offered answers were "more frequently," "less frequently," and "equally frequently," as well as the answer that lay judges in general "do not ask for any explanations."

explanation inquiries (χ^2=46.62, d.f.=6, Phi=.364, $p < .001$). Interestingly, the results suggested that members of tribunals (professional judges and lay judges) had an opinion different from the opinion held by the observers of trials (state attorneys and attorneys). While 65% of the professional judges and lay judges who reported the impact (which constituted 39% and 49% of the overall respective populations surveyed in this study) said that lay judges asked for explanations *more frequently* in the cases with complex evidence than in the cases with simple evidence, the overwhelming majority of state attorneys and attorneys (76% and 89% of those who reported the impact, respectively, which constituted 54% and 58% of overall respective populations) reported that lay judges asked for explanations *less frequently* in the cases with complex evidence than in the cases with simple evidence.

The differences between the responses given by non-members (state attorneys and attorneys) and members of mixed tribunals (professional judges and lay judges) may be a result of different interpretations of the question. Non-members are present during trial, but they cannot be present during deliberation and voting; members of mixed tribunals, on the other hand, are present during the whole process. It may be the case that, while answering this question, non-members focused on trial only, whereas the members of mixed tribunals focused on the whole process, deliberation included.

7.6 Importance of Lay Judges' Questions

In general, status characteristics theory predicts that the participation by low-status members is typically perceived less positively. It is expected that the questions asked by lay judges would be seen as less important than the questions asked by professional judges. If lay judges were asked to assess the importance of their own questions, they would probably value lay judges' questions more highly than other groups of respondents would. After all, since lay judges asked questions only infrequently, once they did, they undoubtedly perceived those questions as very important. Moreover, it would not be reasonable to expect lay judges to characterize their own statements as insignificant. There-fore, lay judges were not asked to evaluate the importance of their own ques-tions. On the other hand, professional judges, state attorneys, and attorneys were asked to evaluate the importance of questions asked by lay judges during trial.[39]

The expectation was that few professional judges would classify lay judges' questions as very important. After all, if considerable importance were at-tached to lay judges' comments, this could be interpreted negatively for pro-fessional judges — they did not cover all the important issues during their fundamental examination. The latter argument assumes, of course, that there is a shared understanding among various groups of respondents as to what encompasses important issues. Moreover, attaching minimal importance to lay judges' questions can also be a consequence of the fact that professional judges generally held more negative opinions about mixed tribunals in general and lay judges in particular.

The results are striking: only 5% of all 240 professional judges, state attor-neys, and attorneys thought that lay judges' questions during trial were impor-tant (Table 7.9); the overwhelming majority of lawyers within each groups said that these questions were either only somewhat important or not important at all.[40] The chi-square comparison of these answers suggested that there were significant differences in the way these respondents evaluated the importance of lay judges' questions ($\chi^2=15.42$, $d.f.=7$, $Phi=.258$, $p < .01$).

It seemed quite possible that both the type of court and region influenced their answers. For example, while only 25% of professional judges from re-gional courts described lay judges' questions as "not important at all," 41% of professional judges from district courts in the Bjelovar Region reported the

---

[39]Professional judges, state attorneys, and attorneys were asked: "How would you evaluate the importance of questions asked by lay judges during trial?" The offered answers were: "very important," "important," "somewhat important," and "not important."

[40]Because of the small frequencies with which respondents picked the first two offered answers, it was not possible to use the chi-square test to compare the differences among the groups of respondents. Comparison was only possible when answers were dichotomized ("not important" as one category and all the other answers as another).

Table 7.9: Importance of lay judges' questions as perceived by others.[a]

	Prof. j. Dist. C. ZG	Prof. j. Dist. C. BJ	Prof. j. Reg. C.	Dist. State a. ZG	Dist. State a. BJ	Reg. State a.	Att. ZG	Att. BJ
very important	0.0%	0.0%	0.0%	0.0%	0.0%	0.0%	0.0%	0.0%
important	0.0%	10.3%	12.5%	5.9%	10.0%	0.0%	1.4%	7.7%
somewhat important	46.2%	48.3%	62.5%	23.5%	55.0%	64.7%	41.1%	53.8%
not important	53.8%	41.4%	25.0%	70.6%	35.0%	35.3%	57.5%	38.5%
N	27	29	24	20	20	18	76	26

[a]Question: "How would you evaluate the importance of questions asked by lay judges during trial?"

Table 7.9: Continued.

	Prof j. All R & D	State a. All R & D	Att. ZG & BJ
very important	0.0%	0.0%	0.0%
important	7.6%	5.6%	3.1%
somewhat important	51.9%	48.1%	44.4%
not important	40.5%	46.3%	52.5%
N	80	58	102

same, as did the majority of professional judges (54%) from the District Court of Zagreb. When the analysis was performed with the purpose of comparing the answers provided by professional judges from district courts with the answers provided by professional judges from regional courts, larger (though not statistically significant) differences were observed: while one-quarter of professional judges from regional courts described lay judges' comments as not important, such was the case with approximately one-half of professional judges from district courts (χ^2=3.44, d.f.=1, Phi= -.209, p > .05, n.s.).[41] In other words, the type of court seems to be related to the perceptions about the importance of the questions raised by lay judges.

Similarly, while only one-third of state attorneys from regional offices and district offices in the Bjelovar Region evaluated lay judges' questions as not important, more than two-thirds of state attorneys from district offices in the Zagreb Region said the same (χ^2=5.89, d.f.=1, Phi= -.330, p < .05). Due to the fact that the answers by district state attorneys from the Bjelovar Region and the answers by regional state attorneys were very similar (in both groups 35% reported that questions were not important), when the answers were compared by the type of office (district v. regional), differences did not exceed 20% despite the fact that the answers provided by district state attorneys from the Zagreb Region were very different (71% reported that questions were not important; χ^2=1.21, d.f.=1, Phi= -.150, p > .05, n.s.).

A preliminary examination of the results indicated that regional differences seemed to be important. Consequently, further analysis was performed with

---

[41] Although the difference exceeded 20% (25% v. 47%), the chi-square test did not indicate statistical significance due to small sample sizes (55 in one group and 24 in another group). The Phi-value, on the other hand, exceeds .200, suggesting the potential existence of a relationship. Despite the lack of statistical significance, I consider these answers to be substantively different. Particularly illustrative of this point is a comparison of these results (not determined to be significantly different by value of the chi-square test) with the results of the analysis of the same issue by region (presented in detail at the conclusion of this section). The difference in percentages is smaller for the analysis by region and is exactly 20%, yet the chi-square test suggests that that difference is significant (due to a larger sample size of 191). The Phi-value is approximately the same in the two analyses (.195 v. .209), as is the actual difference in percentages.

the purpose of comparing the answers by respondents from two different regions. The analysis confirmed these preliminary findings; while the majority of professional judges from the District Court of Zagreb, district state attorneys, and attorneys from the Zagreb Region classified the questions asked by lay judges as *not important* (54%; 71%; 58%, respectively), the majority of respondents from the Bjelovar Region had a more positive opinion about lay judges' questions: they most frequently said that these questions were *somewhat important* (48% of professional judges from district courts in the Bjelovar Region; 55% district state attorneys; 54% attorneys; χ^2=7.26, *d.f.*=1, *Phi*= -.195, *p* < .01).

7.7   Conclusion

This chapter examined the work of mixed tribunals during the trial stage of criminal procedure by focusing on three issues: participation in the group task, the importance of this participation, and opportunities to participate. Group participation of lay judges was measured by the perceived frequency of questions they asked during trial, whereas the importance of these questions was measured by the perceived importance of lay judges' explicit participation. Finally, opportunities for lay judges to participate in the tribunal were measured by the perceived frequency of instances in which the presiding professional judge invited lay judges to ask questions during trial.

Perceptions about the frequency with which professional judges asked questions during trial were not measured; the law normatively specifies that the examination by the presiding professional judge is the fundamental one, whereas the examination by lay judges or another professional judge is supplementary. Therefore, by the very nature of their role in the tribunal, presiding professional judges ask substantially more questions than other tribunal members do. The results reported in this chapter suggest that lay judges were not perceived as very active that in terms of perceptions about the frequency with which they asked questions during trial. Lay judges and other categories of respondents (professional judges, state attorneys, and attorneys) all agreed that lay judges asked questions very infrequently. These findings support theoretical developments discussed in Chapter 5 — tribunal member with low states on specific status characteristics (i.e., low status members) are not likely to be very active participants. An examination of several diffuse status characteristics revealed a clear pattern — broadly speaking, none of lay judges' demographic characteristics had a strong impact on the frequency with which they asked questions during trial.

As the theory predicted, the perceived importance of lay judges' participation, measured by perceptions about the importance of lay judges' questions asked during trial, was low — lay judges' questions were not perceived as particularly important by any of the categories of lawyers (professional judges, state attorneys, or attorneys), that is, persons with legal education and systematic training and experience in legal decision-making.[42]

The type of experience turned out to be important. Differences in opinion expressed by the respondents from district courts/offices and by the respondents from regional courts/offices suggested that seriousness of the cases and the experience of participation in large tribunals may have resulted in more positive opinions. Both professional judges and state attorneys from regional courts/offices evaluated lay judges' questions as more important than their counterparts from district courts/offices did.

Another issue examined in this chapter was that of lay judges' opportunities to participate. As discussed in Chapter 5, status characteristics theory predicts that lower status participants typically have fewer opportunities to participate (Balkwell, 1994). Moreover, above and beyond the issue of status in the tribunal, the *Criminal Procedure Law* (1993) provided presiding professional judges with more opportunities to participate by normatively specifying

---

[42]Lay judges were not asked about the importance of their own questions. The reasons are twofold: since lay judges generally asked questions infrequently, once they decided to ask a question, that question was probably very important to them; furthermore, it is unlikely that somebody would characterize their own statements as insignificant.

their examination as fundamental and lay judges' examination as supplementary.

The results suggested that professional judges from regional courts were perceived to have invited other members of the tribunal to ask questions more frequently than professional judges from district courts. Why? A possible explanation is that professional judges from regional courts, who presided over both small tribunals and large tribunals,[43] apply the same routine to both kinds of tribunals by inviting questions from other members of the tribunal. However, since large tribunals include another professional judge, it may be that professional judges in large tribunals primarily sought to present their colleagues, other professional judges (i.e., members with high status), with opportunities to ask questions. This may have created an atmosphere that seemed more conducive to asking questions even to lay judges. This perception was shared by lay judges from regional courts. However, these differences in opinion may also have been a result of the size of the decision-making group: presiding professional judges are less likely to ignore four additional members than to ignore only two. Finally, presiding professional judges at regional courts, that is, professional judges who presided over trials for more serious cases, may have wanted to incorporate heterogeneity into their courtrooms by providing for diverse perspectives.

In summary, the interaction of professional judges and lay judges during trial conforms with status characteristics theory; although mostly based on perceptions about lay judges' activity during trial, the picture about the opportunities lay judges were given to participate and their actual participation (painted by lay judges themselves, as well as by professional judges, state attorneys, and attorneys) is relatively uniform across the respondents from the same type of court/office. The description of lay judges' actual activity during trial (given by all four categories of respondents) is very similar across both types of courts: regardless of the frequency with which professional judges

---

[43] As mentioned earlier, the court registry from one of the regional courts suggests that the majority of trials by mixed tribunals are tried by large tribunals.

invited lay judges to ask questions, lay judges asked questions relatively infrequently. Moreover, and again consistent with status characteristics theory, lawyers (professional judges, state attorneys, and attorneys) generally regarded judges' comments as rather unimportant. It appears that, in expressing their opinion about the importance of lay judges' questions, lawyers generally did not take into consideration positive features of lay participation.

Chapter 8

Mixed Tribunals during Deliberation and Voting

The topic of this chapter is the interaction of professional judges and lay judges during deliberation and voting. Since deliberation is secret and only members of tribunals can be present, the questions concerning deliberation were asked only of the members of tribunals themselves.[1] The organization of this chapter follows the order of deliberation itself. The presiding professional judge usually summarizes the case at the beginning of deliberation; the tribunal then engages in the discussion of relevant issues; finally, the tribunal reaches a decision. Five crucial issues are examined: lay judges' competence to understand and evaluate evidence, lay judges' competence to understand legal issues, the frequency with which lay judges participate during deliberation, the importance of their participation, and the frequency with which lay judges disagreed with professional judges. At the conclusion of the chapter, key findings about deliberation and voting are placed into the theoretical framework from Chapter 5.

---

[1] State attorneys and attorneys were asked only for their general opinion about lay judges' ability to understand and evaluate evidence.

8.1 Legal Framework of Deliberation and Voting

Once the defendant(s), witnesses, and expert witnesses are examined and the examination of other evidence in the case is completed, the prosecutor, the victim, the defense attorneys and the defendant(s) give their closing statements (Article 339, *Criminal Procedure Law*, 1993). If upon hearing the closing statements the tribunal does not conclude that it is necessary to examine additional evidence, the presiding professional judge will declare that the trial has concluded and the tribunal will prepare for deliberation (Article 344, *Criminal Procedure Law*, 1993).

According to the *Criminal Procedure Law* (1993), the next part of the process consists of *deliberation and voting*. **Deliberation** is considered to be a discussion with the purpose of clarifying important issues in the case and reaching an agreement among the members of the tribunal with respect to the resolution of the case (Jemrić, 1987, p. 114). On the other hand, **voting** is considered to be the announcement of the verdict preferences by each tribunal member (Jemrić, 1987, p. 114). Decisions are made after oral discussion and voting (Article 116, *Criminal Procedure Law*, 1993). The vote of each member carries the same weight, regardless of whether the member is a lay judge or a professional judge. The presiding judge votes last (Article 116, *Criminal Procedure Law*, 1993).

A majority vote suffices for a valid decision (Article 116, *Criminal Procedure Law*, 1993). This rule provides an opportunity for lay judges, who outnumber the professional judge(s) in both small and large tribunals, to outvote the professional judge(s).

The presiding professional judge directs deliberation and voting and has the responsibility of ensuring that the tribunal discusses all the issues universally and thoroughly (Article 116, *Criminal Procedure Law*, 1993). The *Criminal Procedure Law* (1993) does not regulate the order in which the discussion during deliberation takes place.

8.2 Understanding and Evaluation of Evidence

The purpose of the criminal process is to determine the truth on the basis of the facts in the case. The application of the law on the basis of these facts then follows, as do the punishment of the guilty and the acquittal of the innocent. Members of mixed tribunals, lay judges and professional judges, need to decide factual issues and legal issues. The tribunal has the duty to determine truthfully and completely all the facts important for a lawful decision (Article 15, *Criminal Procedure Law*, 1993). According to the *Criminal Procedure Law* (1993, Article 347), the verdict can be based only on the evidence presented during the trial.

The tribunal can establish facts in two different ways: either through its own observation or through the evidence presented in the case (Bayer, 1989, p. 15). The broad definition of evidence, according to Bayer (1989, p. 19), includes testimony by the defendant(s), witnesses, and expert witnesses, as well as documents and technical recordings of the facts. In addition, evidence in a broader sense includes indirect evidence (*indicium*).

The use of evidence has been regulated either by common law or by statutory law throughout legal history. The tendency has been to eliminate arbitrariness and regulate the process of establishing facts by law. The legally regulated evaluation of evidence was dominant at the time when the inquisitorial procedure was blossoming in Europe (16th and 17th centuries). The statutes determined the number of pieces of evidence and the types of evidence required for a certain fact to be legally proven.

Starting from the second half of the 19th century, the European legal systems based on Roman law have used the principle of *free evaluation of evidence*.[2] This principle frees decision-makers from obligations imposed by any legal rules that might regulate the power of evidence for different types of evidence in advance. Exactly what evidence will be considered as important

---

[2]The Croatian *Criminal Procedure Law* (1993) states the principle of free evaluation of evidence in Article 16.

in order to accept a certain fact as proven depends on the decision-maker[3] and is not prescribed by the law.[4] Decision-makers are under no obligation to accept facts as proven because of the number of pieces of evidence or the mere existence of evidence, unless they have been *convinced* that these facts have been proven. This does not mean, however, that they are free to decide arbitrarily when to consider facts as proven; decision-makers need to follow the rules of logic and common sense.

The principle of free evaluation of evidence is present throughout the criminal process of Croatia, but it is emphasized especially strongly during trial and deliberation (Article 347, *Criminal Procedure Law*, 1993). Decision-makers have the responsibility to evaluate each piece of evidence separately and in comparison with other evidence in the case and, based on the results of these evaluations, to conclude whether a particular fact has been proven or not (Article 347, Item 2, *Criminal Procedure Law*, 1993). A decision by the Croatian

---

[3]Note that certain types of evidence are not allowed to be used in the courtrooms, for example, confessions obtained through torture, threats, or similar mechanisms (use of medical substances or medical procedures to elicit confessions; Article 218, Items 8 and 10, and Article 259, Item 3, *Criminal Procedure Law*, 1993), confessions obtained without the presence of a defense attorney when the defendant did not waive his/her right to have an attorney or when representation by a defense attorney is obligatory (Article 218, Items 9 and 10, *Criminal Procedure Law*, 1993).

[4]The *Criminal Procedure Law* (1993) lists exemptions from this rule in Article 404, Item 2, and Article 415. The final decision by the court can be changed if, among the other possibilities listed in Article 404 (*Criminal Procedure Law*, 1993), (1) the verdict was based on a false testimony by a witness, expert witness, or interpreter; (2) the verdict was a result of a crime committed by the professional judge, lay judge, or the person who conducted the investigation, or (3) the verdict that rejects the indictment was a consequence of the withdrawal of charges by the district attorney who abused his office. The acceptable proof in such cases is the final verdict that declares these persons to be guilty of crimes listed in Article 404, Item 2 (*Criminal Procedure Law*, 1993). If these persons died or the procedure may not be initiated because of the reasons that exclude the possibility of bringing criminal charges (e.g., statute of limitations), other evidence may be used to prove that they had committed the crime. Article 415 provides yet another example of the case in which the *Criminal Procedure Law* (1993) prescribed that the decision about a particular form of legal redress (extraordinary mitigation of punishment — "zahtjev za izvanredno ublažavanje kazne") may be changed if it can be proved (using the types of evidence listed in Article 404, Item 2) that the decision about the redress was based on a falsified document or false testimony of either witnesses or expert witnesses.

Supreme Court supported this viewpoint; in a case in which the defendant was declared guilty on the basis of indirect evidence, the appellate court stated that it was acceptable to base the guilty verdict on indirect evidence if there was a system, not a sum, of indirect evidence, and all the parts of the system were connected in a manner that excluded any possibility other than the one determined by the trial court (decision by the Supreme Court of Croatia, Kž. 1744/68–6, 01/29/1969, in Vasiljević and Grubač, 1987, p. 562).

Unlike the jury system, in which jurors are not required to explain the reasons for their decision, decision-makers in the system of mixed tribunals (lay judges and professional judges) have to explain the tribunal's decision in a (joint) written verdict. Therefore, decision-makers have the responsibility of explaining how they determined that the facts had or had not been proven and what the reasons that led them toward such a conclusion were (Article 357, *Criminal Procedure Law*, 1993). It is not satisfactory merely to state that some facts have been proven; decision-makers have to describe and explain the bases used to prove these facts and to list and analyze the evidence that convinced them that these facts were or were not proven (Jemrić, 1987, p. 396). There is a special obligation to explain the decision-makers' evaluation of contradictory evidence. This issue was regulated by Article 347 of the *Criminal Procedural Law* (1993).

If decision-makers do not furnish reasons in the verdict, give reasons that are contradictory or unclear, or allow contradictions between the reasons given in the verdict and the content of the documents or transcripts of the witness statements, an essential violation of the criminal procedure regulations will have been committed (Article 364, Item 1, Clause 11, *Criminal Procedure Law*, 1993). Consequences of such a violation are very serious; even if the defendant does not appeal this particular violation, the appellate court will examine whether any of the essential violations listed in Article 364 has been committed by the trial court *ex officio* in the case in which *any* of the two parties appealed regardless of the ground for appeal. If the appellate court determines that this violation occurred, it will vacate (i.e., reverse) the verdict and remand the case to the trial court (Article 385, *Criminal Procedure Law*, 1993). Therefore, correct understanding and evaluation of evidence is crucial for the quality and validity of decision-making.

As discussed in Chapter 1, critics of lay participation in the criminal justice system routinely argue that lay persons are not able to understand and evaluate evidence nor to apply legal norms. Although research studies suggest that, in general, jurors are competent fact-finders (Hans and Vidmar, 1986), some specific problems in evaluation of technical and expert evidence have been identified. The only existing study that examined this issue in the context of mixed tribunals (Casper and Zeisel, 1972) suggested that lay judges' ability to understand and evaluate evidence had some influence on the frequency of disagreement.[5]

8.2.1   Understanding of Evidence

Respondents were asked about judges' ability to understand evidence. However, due to the fact that the question concerns lay judges' competence, the wording of the question asked of lay judges was somewhat different from the wording intended for other categories of respondents.[6]

The respondents' answers were not uniform (Table 8.1); there were significant differences across various groups of respondents (χ^2=47.78, $d.f.$=8, Phi=.437, $p < .001$).[7] In general, respondents from regional courts/offices, both professional judges and state attorneys, had more positive opinion about lay judges' competence to understand evidence than respondents from district courts/offices or attorneys.[8] The pattern seems to be relatively clear;

---

[5]See Chapter 4 for more details on previous research studies on mixed tribunals.

[6]The question asked of *professional judges, state attorneys*, and *attorneys* was worded as follows: "Do you feel that lay judges are generally able to understand evidence?" The offered answers ranged from "always" to "never" on a five-point scale.

[7]The answers were recoded as follows: "always" through "frequently" into "often;" "sometimes" and "never" into "rarely."

[8]As discussed in Chapter 7, because of small sample sizes, the Marascuillo method (Glass and Hopkins, 1984, p. 391) identified as statistically significant only some of the differences I deem as substantively important. Specifically, I consider the opinion expressed by profes-

within a particular category of lawyers (professional judges, state attorneys), respondents from regional courts/offices were more likely to say that lay judges were frequently able to understand evidence than respondents from district courts/offices (χ^2=27.67, $d.f.$=1, Phi= -.432, $p < .001$). In other words, most respondents from higher hierarchical levels (80% of professional judges from the Supreme Court, 70% of professional judges from regional courts, and 71% of regional state attorneys) said that lay judges were able to understand evidence *frequently* or even *very frequently*, while most respondents from lower hierarchical levels (82% of professional judges from the District Court of Zagreb, 59% of professional judges from district courts in the Bjelovar Region, and 65% of district state attorneys) reported that lay judges were able to understand evidence only rarely. The opinion expressed by attorneys resembled the opinion expressed by professional judges and state attorneys from district courts/offices very closely — the majority of attorneys (78% of attorneys from Zagreb and 69% of attorneys from the Bjelovar Region) reported that lay judges were able to understand evidence only *rarely*.

In making assessments of lay judges' ability to understand evidence, professional judges could rely on the experience they acquired during actual deliberations (in which they had opportunities to discuss the evidence with lay judges and to get some feedback on lay judges' understanding and evaluation). State attorneys and attorneys, on the other hand, did not have such opportunities. They could only have had exposure to the (infrequent) questions lay judges

---

sional judges from the Supreme Court and from regional courts, as well as the opinion of regional state attorneys, to be substantively different from the opinion expressed by other groups of respondents. The opinion expressed by professional judges from the Supreme Court was significantly different from the opinion expressed by professional judges from the District Court of Zagreb (χ^2=18.27, $d.f.$=8, $p < .05$), attorneys from Zagreb (χ^2=19.06, $d.f.$=8, $p < .05$), and district state attorneys from Zagreb (χ^2=18.86, $d.f.$=8, $p < .05$). The opinion expressed by professional judges from regional courts was significantly different from the opinion expressed by professional judges from the District Court of Zagreb (χ^2=20.57, $d.f.$=8, $p < .05$) and from the opinion expressed by attorneys from Zagreb (χ^2=22.87, $d.f.$=8, $p < .05$). Finally, the opinion of regional state attorneys was *significantly* different from the opinion of district state attorneys from Zagreb (χ^2=18.70, $d.f.$=8, $p < .05$), from the opinion of attorneys from Zagreb (χ^2=22.87, $d.f.$=8, $p < .05$), and from the opinion of professional judges from the District Court of Zagreb (χ^2=18.25, $d.f.$=8, $p < .05$).

Table 8.1: Lay judges' ability to understand evidence as perceived by lawyers.[a]

	Prof. j. Dist. C. ZG	Prof. j. Dist. C. BJ	Prof. j. Reg. C.	Prof. J. Supr. C.	Dist. State a. ZG	Dist. State a. BJ	Reg. State a.	Att. ZG	Att. BJ
always	3.7%	0.0%	4.2%	0.0%	0.0%	0.0%	5.6%	2.6%	3.8%
very frequently	3.7%	13.8%	25.0%	10.0%	5.0%	10.0%	44.4%	5.3%	7.7%
frequently	11.1%	27.6%	41.7%	70.0%	10.0%	25.0%	22.2%	13.2%	15.4%
sometimes	81.5%	58.6%	29.2%	20.0%	70.0%	60.0%	27.8%	77.6%	69.2%
never	0.0%	0.0%	0.0%	0.0%	0.0%	0.0%	0.0%	0.0%	0.0%
N	27	29	24	10	20	20	18	76	26

[a]Question: "Generally speaking, do you feel that lay judges are able to understand evidence?"

Table 8.1: Continued.

	Prof j. All	State a. All R & D	Att. ZG & BJ
always	1.7%	1.7%	2.9 %
very frequently	13.5%	19.0%	5.9%
frequently	31.3%	19.0%	13.7%
sometimes	53.5%	53.4%	75.5%
never	0.0%	6.9%	2.0%
N	90	58	102

had asked during trial. Although it could be expected that such differences in actual experience might generate some differences between the evaluations furnished by professional judges and those furnished by state attorneys and attorneys, it turned out that the differences in the type of experience did not have significant influence. The pattern and direction of the opinion were very similar for all three categories of lawyers.

Respondents from regional courts/offices expressed a much more positive opinion about lay judges' ability to understand evidence than respondents from district courts. As discussed in Chapter 5, there are several plausible reasons that may explain these differences of opinion. In particular, cases tried at regional courts are more serious and tribunals are larger and of different composition — they feature an additional lay judge and another professional judge.

The analogous question asked of *lay judges* was worded as follows: "Do you feel that you have problems in understanding of evidence (statements given by defendants, witnesses, expert witnesses, material evidence)?" It is noteworthy that this question inquired about lay judges' *incompetence* to understand evidence, whereas the question asked of other groups of respondents asked about lay judges' *competence* to understand evidence.

Unlike lawyers, whose opinion differed by the type of court/office, the opinion of all four groups of lay judges (from the District Court of Zagreb, the District Court of Križevci, the Regional Court of Zagreb, and the Regional Court of Bjelovar) was quite similar ($\chi^2=1.15$, $d.f.=3$, $Phi=.072$, $p > .05$, n.s.).[9] The overwhelming majority of lay judges considered themselves competent to understand evidence (Table 8.2): between 80-90% of lay judges within each of the four groups said that they *did not have problems* at all or that they *sometimes* had problems in understanding of evidence. There were no differences with respect to the type of court ($\chi^2=1.05$, $d.f.=1$, $Phi=.069$, $p > .05$, n.s.), with respect to region ($\chi^2=0.01$, $d.f.=1$, $Phi=.001$, $p > .05$, n.s.), nor with

---

[9]For the purpose of these analyses, the answers "always" through "frequently" were merged into "often" and the answers "sometimes" and "never" were merged into "rarely."

Table 8.2: Lay judges' inability to understand evidence.[a]

	Lay j. Dist. C. ZG	Lay j. Dist. C. KŽ	Lay j. Reg. C. ZG	Lay j. Reg. C. BJ
never	12.9%	36.5%	23.8%	36.4%
sometimes	70.7%	51.9%	57.1%	51.5%
frequently	12.9%	5.8%	14.3%	9.1%
very frequently	2.6%	5.8%	4.8%	3.0%
always	0.9%	0.0%	0.0%	0.0%
N	122	53	21	33

[a]Question:"Do you feel that you have problems in understanding of evidence (statements given by defendants, witnesses, expert witnesses, material evidence)?"

respect to lay judges' educational level (χ^2=.131, $d.f.$=1, Phi=.024, $p > .05$, n.s.).

8.2.2   Evaluation of Evidence

Respondents were asked about judges' ability to evaluate evidence. The question asked of lawyers (i.e., professional judges, state attorneys, and attorneys) was somewhat different from the corresponding question asked of lay judges; while the former inquired about the ability of a group of respondents in general, the latter asked of each lay judge to assess his/her own ability.[10]

---

[10]The question asked of professional judges, state attorneys, and attorneys was worded as follows: "Generally speaking, lay judges evaluate evidence:" Possible answers ranged from "without any difficulty" to "not able to evaluate at all" on a five-point scale. The question asked of lay judges was worded as follows: "Generally speaking, you evaluate evidence:" Possible answers ranged from "without any difficulty" to "I am not able to evaluate evidence at all" on a five-point scale.

Table 8.3: Lay judges' evidence evaluation.[a]

	Prof. j. Dist. C. ZG	Prof. j. Dist. C. BJ	Prof. j. Reg. C.	Prof. J. Supr. C.	Dist. State a. ZG	Dist. State a. BJ	Reg. State a.	Att. ZG	Att. BJ
without any difficulty	0.0%	0.0%	0.0%	0.0%	0.0%	0.0%	0.0%	2.7%	0.0%
usually without any difficulty	7.4%	10.3%	33.3%	10.0%	5.0%	15.0%	29.4%	6.8%	7.7%
with some difficulty	51.9%	69.0%	58.3%	90.0%	35.0%	55.0%	58.8%	43.2%	34.6%
with serious difficulty	29.6%	13.8%	8.3%	0.0%	35.0%	20.0%	5.9%	35.1%	50.0%
not able to evaluate evidence at all	11.1%	6.9%	0.0%	0.0%	25.0%	10.0%	5.9%	12.2%	7.7%
N	27	29	24	10	20	20	18	76	26

[a]Question: "Generally speaking, lay judges/you evaluate evidence:"

Table 8.3: Continued.

	Lay j. Dist. C. ZG	Lay j. Dist. C. KŽ	Lay j. Reg. C. ZG	Lay j. Reg. C. BJ	Prof j. All	State a. All R & D	Att. ZG & BJ	Lay j. All R & D
without any difficulty	23.0%	22.6%	28.6%	30.3%	0.0%	0.0%	2.0%	24.5%
usually without any difficulty	36.9%	41.5%	42.9%	51.5%	15.5%	15.8%	7.0%	40.6%
with some difficulty	36.1%	22.6%	23.8%	18.2%	63.5%	49.1%	41.0%	29.3%
with serious difficulty	1.6%	1.9%	0.0%	0.0%	15.5%	21.1%	39.0%	1.3%
not able to evaluate evidence at all	2.5%	11.3%	4.8%	0.0%	5.5%	14.0%	11.0%	4.4%
N	122	53	21	33	90	58	102	229

While different wording could have caused some discrepancy, the results revealed remarkable differences (Table 8.3); about one-third or less within each group of professional judges, state attorneys, and attorneys reported that lay judges evaluated evidence "without any difficulty" or "usually without any difficulty" (10% of professional judges from district courts, 33% of professional judges from regional courts, 10% of professional judges from the Supreme Court, 10% of district state attorneys, 30% of regional state attorneys, 7% of attorneys), whereas more than 60% of lay judges in each group (61% of lay judges from district courts and 78% of lay judges from regional courts) selected these answers. Grouping the respondents by their role in the criminal justice system (professional judges, lay judges, state attorneys, and attorneys) revealed that the overwhelming majority of lawyers (84% of professional judges, 84% of state attorneys, and 91% of attorneys) reported that lay judges had problems in evaluation of evidence, while only one-third of lay judges reported the same ($\chi^2=138.04$, $d.f.=3$, $Phi=.539$, $p < .001$).

There was a similarity between the answers selected by lay judges and by other groups of respondents; respondents from regional courts/offices (professional judges, state attorneys, and lay judges) had a more positive opinion about lay judges' competence than respondents from district courts/offices (43% of respondents from district courts and 58% of respondents from regional courts reported that lay judges were able to evaluate evidence "without any difficulty" or "usually without any difficulty;" $\chi^2=6.43$, $d.f.=1$, $Phi= -.133$, $p < .05$). Regional differences were insignificant ($\chi^2=1.38$, $d.f.=1$, $Phi= -.057$, $p > .05$, n.s.).

Generally speaking, lay judges are expected not only to be able to understand evidence, but also to be able to evaluate it critically. The expectation was that the lay judges who said that they had no problems in understanding of evidence would be more likely to say that they had no problems in evaluating it either. When lay judges' responses to the question which inquired about their inability to *understand* evidence were compared to their responses to the question which inquired about their ability to *evaluate* evidence,[11] the chi-square test confirmed this expectation — the lay judges who said that they have not had *any* problems in understanding of evidence were significantly more likely to say that they had not had *any* problems in evaluation of evidence than the lay judges who said that they have had problems in understanding of evidence (43% *v.* 20%, respectively; χ^2=11.26, *d.f.*=1, *Phi*= -.225, $p < .001$).

Lawyers are generally assumed to be better evidence evaluators than lay persons — lawyers know how to "think like lawyers." One of the components of this ability to "think like lawyers," according to Mudd (1983), involves critical thinking common to all educated persons. Therefore, the expectation was (assuming that reporting would not be influenced by the respondents' educational level) that the more educated lay judges would report fewer problems in evaluation of evidence than their less educated counterparts. The results, however, indicated otherwise (χ^2=.053, *d.f.*=1, *Phi*= -.015, $p > .05$, n.s.).[12]

The discrepancy between the answers given by lawyers (professional judges, state attorneys, and attorneys) and the answers given by lay judges might be partially explained by the fact that lay judges may have tended to present their own abilities in a favorable light. The next question is what additional factors might explain this discrepancy. Moreover, are professional judges and lay judges using the same criteria when they evaluate evidence?

Respondents were asked to specify the factors which they viewed as the most important when they evaluated evidence. The question was worded as follows: "When you examine a statement given by a witness, the most important thing you take into consideration is: (a) how coherent the statement is, (b) how the whole statement is incorporated in the network of other evidence

---

[11]The answers to both questions were recoded in order to separate the responses which indicated that lay judges never had any problems in understanding or evaluation of evidence from the responses which indicated that lay judges sometimes or always had such problems.

[12]Lay judges' answers were grouped as follows: "without any difficulty" and "usually without any difficulty" *v.* "with some difficulty" through "I am not able to evaluate evidence at all."

in the case, (c) whether there exist some illogical points in the statement, (d) whether the witness is credible, and (e) whether you believe the statement given by the witness."[13]

The majority of both professional judges and lay judges (60% of professional judges and 53% of lay judges; $\chi^2=3.55$, $d.f.=4$, $Phi=.116$, $p > .05$, n.s.) selected the same answer — they said that the most important factor they were taking into consideration was "how the whole statement is incorporated in the network of other evidence in the case" (Table 8.4). This percentage varied from 52% for lay judges from the District Court of Zagreb to 67% for professional judges from regional courts. Furthermore, it seems that, while considering the remaining four answers, professional judges and lay judges from district courts were more likely to say that "credibility of the witness" itself was also an important factor they took into account when evaluating evidence, whereas professional judges and lay judges from regional courts afforded such a distinction to "illogical points in the statement."

Five professional judges offered some additional comments. Four professional judges, both from district and regional courts, said that they use all of these factors when they evaluate a particular piece of evidence, but the importance of each factor in a particular case depends on the case itself and on its circumstances. One of the lay judges from the District Court of Križevci had the same opinion, while another lay judge from the Regional Court of Zagreb emphasized the importance of intuition above all other factors. Two lay judges offered completely different approaches. One of them wrote that he chooses to believe one of the witnesses, meaning that all the witnesses who contradict the witness he believes are automatically discredited. The other lay judge wrote that he did not use these factors: there was no need for them, because professional judges volunteered their views of evidence evaluation (*sic!*).

---

[13]Respondents also had the option to write down additional comments. While answering this question, some respondents selected more than one answer. The results were not influenced by the exclusion of such multiple answers from the analysis. Therefore, only the results computed without multiple answers are presented.

Table 8.4: Factors in evidence evaluation.[a]

	Prof. j. Dist. C. ZG	Prof. j. Dist. C. BJ	Prof. j. Reg. C. ZG	Lay j. Dist. C. ZG	Lay j. Dist. C. KŽ	Lay j. Reg. C. ZG	Lay j. Reg. C. BJ	Prof. j. All	Lay j. All
coherency of statement	7.7%	3.6%	4.2%	6.2%	5.7%	0.0%	3.1%	5.0%	4.8%
fit into network of other evidence	38.5%	42.9%	50.0%	50.4%	49.1%	47.4%	53.1%	42.5%	48.0%
illogical points	7.7%	10.7%	12.5%	15.0%	5.7%	33.3%	21.9%	10.0%	14.8%
credibility	15.4%	17.9%	8.3%	21.2%	22.6%	9.5%	15.6%	13.8%	18.8%
believe the statement	0.0%	0.0%	0.0%	3.5%	7.5%	0.0%	6.3%	0.0%	4.4%
other	3.8%	10.7%	4.2%	0.0%	5.7%	0.0%	0.0%	6.3%	1.3%
2 or 3 answers	26.9%	14.3%	20.8%	3.5%	3.8%	9.5%	0.0%	20.0%	3.5%
N	27	29	24	122	53	21	33	80	229

[a]Question: "When you examine a statement given by a witness, the most important thing that you take into consideration is:"

8.2.3   Related Problems

What problems related to understanding and evaluation of evidence did the respondents single out? Professional judges, state attorneys, and attorneys were asked: "When lay judges experience problems in understanding and evaluation of evidence, they are related to:" The offered answers can be grouped around three issues: lay judges' incompetence to evaluate evidence ("inability of lay judges to evaluate evidence in general" and "inability of lay judges to evaluate certain types of evidence [statements by expert witnesses, for example]"), lay judges' lack of interest ("lay judges' lack of interest in the case" and "lay judges' lack of interest in participation in the criminal justice system in general"), and lay judges' lack of legal knowledge ("lay judges' lack of legal knowledge in general" and "lay judges' lack of procedural legal knowledge about evaluation of evidence").[14]

The answers provided by lawyers varied across groups (χ^2=24.69, $d.f.$=14, Phi=.336, $p < .05$). However, there seems to be a pattern (Table 8.5); the majority of professional judges and state attorneys from district courts/offices and the majority of attorneys (68% of professional judges from the District Court of Zagreb, 69% of professional judges from district courts in the Bjelovar Region, 51% of attorneys from Zagreb, 70% of attorneys from the Bjelovar Region, 83% of district state attorneys from Zagreb, and 55% of district state attorneys from the Bjelovar Region) attributed lay judges' problems in evaluation of evidence to "lay judges' lack of procedural knowledge about evaluation of evidence" or to " lay judges' lack of legal knowledge in general," while the majority of professional judges and state attorneys from regional courts/offices (52% of professional judges from regional courts and 56% of regional state at-

---

[14]The analogous question asked of lay judges was worded as follows: "If you feel that you (at least sometimes) have problems in understanding and evaluation of evidence, in your opinion, this is happening because: (a) evidence in general is difficult to evaluate, (b) certain types of evidence are very difficult to understand (statements by expert witnesses, for example), (c) the cases do not capture your interest, (d) there is lack of interest in participation in the criminal justice system in general, (e) there is a lack of procedural legal knowledge about evaluation of evidence, (f) there is lack of legal knowledge in general, and (g) I do not have any problems in understanding and evaluation of evidence."

torneys) pointed out "inability of lay judges to evaluate evidence in general" or "inability of lay judges to evaluate certain types of evidence." Moreover, it is noteworthy that approximately 40% of professional judges from regional courts and regional state attorneys also selected "lay judges' lack of legal knowledge in general." Not surprisingly, differences by the type of court/office were statistically significant (χ^2=15.14, $d.f.$=2, Phi=.345, $p < .01$), while differences by region were not (χ^2=1.14, $d.f.$=2, Phi=.080, $p > .05$, n.s.).

Lay judges from regional courts had a much better opinion about their ability to understand and evaluate evidence than their counterparts from district courts (χ^2=31.85, $d.f.$=3, Phi=.380, $p < .001$); while 65% of lay judges from regional courts said that they had no problems in understanding and evaluation of evidence, only 25% of lay judges from district courts said the same. This result was by no means surprising (Table 8.6). As reported in Chapter 7, lay judges from regional courts were more likely to say that they read the case file than lay judges from district courts; furthermore, both lay judges and professional judges from regional courts agreed that professional judges almost always provided a summary of the case (including the summation of the evidence) at the beginning of deliberation. In fact, when asked to specify the major purpose of this summation, the majority of respondents from regional courts replied that the purpose was to "present complex evidence in a way that is more *understandable* for lay judges."

Among the lay judges who reported having problems in understanding and evaluation of evidence (Table 8.6), the majority (69% of the lay judges from district courts who reported having problems in understanding and evaluation of evidence, which accounts for 52% of all lay judges from district courts; 84% of the lay judges from regional courts who reported having problems in understanding and evaluation of evidence, which accounts for 30% of all lay judges from regional courts) said that their problems existed either because "evidence in general is difficult to evaluate" or because "certain types of evidence are very difficult to understand," rather than because of "lack of legal knowledge in general" or "lack of interest in the case." Lay judges themselves,

Table 8.5: Lay judges' problems in understanding and evaluation of evidence as perceived by lawyers.[a]

	Prof. j. Dist. C. ZG	Prof. j. Dist. C. BJ	Prof. j. Reg. C.	Prof. J. Supr. C.	Dist. State a. ZG	Dist. State a. BJ	Reg. State a.	Att. ZG	Att. BJ
evidence in general	0.0%	0.0%	4.3%	0.0%	5.0%	5.0%	0.0%	9.3%	0.0%
certain types of evidence	11.1%	17.9%	47.8%	50.0%	5.0%	30.0%	55.6%	20.0%	19.2%
lack of procedural knowledge	7.4%	14.3%	4.3%	40.0%	35.0%	15.0%	27.8%	16.0%	7.7%
lack of legal knowledge	48.1%	50.0%	39.1%	0.0%	40.0%	40.0%	11.1%	30.8%	53.8%
no interest in the case	11.1%	3.6%	4.3%	10.0%	0.0%	10.0%	0.0%	9.3%	0.0%
no interest in participation	3.7%	7.1%	0.0%	0.0%	5.0%	0.0%	5.6%	6.7%	7.7%
2 or 3 answers	18.5%	7.1%	0.0%	0.0%	10.0%	0.0%	0.0%	7.9%	11.5%
N	27	29	24	10	20	20	18	76	26

[a]Question: "When lay judges experience problems in understanding and evaluation of evidence, the problems are related to:"

Table 8.5: Continued.

	Prof j. All	State a. All R & D	Att. ZG & BJ
evidence in general	1.2%	3.4%	6.9%
certain types of evidence	27.3%	29.3%	19.8%
lack of procedural knowledge	12.5%	25.9%	13.9%
lack of legal knowledge	40.9%	31.0%	36.6%
no interest in the case	6.8%	3.4%	6.9%
no interest in participation	3.4%	3.4%	6.9%
2 or 3 answers	7.9%	3.4%	8.9%
N	90	58	102

as well as other respondents, thought that " lack of interest in the case" and "lack of interest in participation in the criminal justice system" were not major problems. Thus, it is not the case that lay judges were not interested in participating; rather, the lay judges' answers suggested that their problems in understanding and evaluation of evidence should be attributed to both the complex task of understanding of evidence itself and the complexity of the evidence in the case.

Although the majority of lay judges from both regions reported having problems in understanding and evaluation of evidence,[15] lay judges from the Zagreb Region were less likely to report having no problems in understanding and evaluation of evidence than respondents from the Bjelovar Region (χ^2=10.76, $d.f.$=1, Phi=.225, $p < .01$). Again, this result should not be surprising because respondents from the Bjelovar Region reported that they were more likely to read the case file and that professional judges were more likely to provide a summation of the evidence at the beginning of deliberation (both of which may be significant factors for understanding and evaluation of evidence).

In summary, lay judges who reported having problems in understanding and evaluation of evidence and lawyers from higher levels of the hierarchy (regional courts/offices, the Supreme Court) most frequently said that lay judges' problems in understanding and evaluation of evidence were related to the complexity of the process of understanding of evidence itself, whereas lawyers from lower levels of the hierarchy (district courts/offices) and attorneys most frequently said that lay judges' problems in understanding and evaluation

---

[15]The majority of lay judges from regional courts reported having no problems in understanding and evaluation of evidence, while such was not the case for the majority of lay judges from district courts. Given that the number of surveyed lay judges from district courts far exceeds the number of surveyed lay judges from regional courts, when the answers by lay judges from regional and district courts from the same region were pooled for the purpose of the present analysis, lay judges from the two types of courts (district $v.$ regional) did not contribute with the same weight — the results were skewed toward the responses furnished by the respondents from district courts.

Table 8.6: Lay judges' problems in understanding and evaluation of evidence as perceived by lay judges.[a]

	Lay j. Dist. C. ZG	Lay j. Dist. C. KŽ	Lay j. Reg. C. ZG	Lay j. Reg. C. BJ	Lay j. All
evidence in general	15.7%	18.0%	14.3%	12.1%	15.4%
certain types of evidence	34.7%	34.0%	14.3%	18.2%	30.2%
lack of procedural knowledge	9.1%	6.0%	9.5%	0.0%	7.2%
lack of legal knowledge	13.2%	4.0%	0.0%	3.0%	8.5%
no interest in the case	4.1%	0.0%	0.0%	0.0%	2.3%
no interest in participation	2.5%	0.0%	0.0%	0.0%	1.4%
no problems	18.2%	36.0%	61.9%	66.7%	33.0%
2 or 3 answers	2.5%	2.0%	0.0%	0.0%	2.0%
N	122	53	21	33	229

[a]Question: "If you feel that you (at least sometimes) have problems in understanding and evaluation of evidence, in your opinion, this is happening because:"

of evidence were due to lay judges' lack of legal knowledge, both in general and about evaluation of evidence in particular. The respondents who emphasized problems in evaluation of evidence were more likely to pinpoint problems in evaluation of certain types of evidence than problems in evaluation of evidence in general.

Why did the lawyers' opinion about lay judges' competence to understand or evaluate evidence differ so considerably from the opinion expressed by lay judges? A related finding was that professional judges, state attorneys, and attorneys were more likely to say that lay judges had problems in understanding and evaluation of evidence than lay judges themselves. Furthermore, the most frequently selected reasons for lay judges' lack of competence differed across various group of respondents. Why did lay judges emphasize their problems in understanding of evidence itself over their lack of legal knowledge, while the majority of lawyers thought that lay judges' lack of legal knowledge, in particular the procedural rules concerning evaluation of evidence, was a very important, if not the most important reason? It may be that lay judges did not know the law and therefore could not have judged how important ignorance of the law was with respect to the process of understanding and evaluation of evidence. It is also quite possible that interpretations of what evidence evaluation meant were different; lay judges might have thought that they were competent to evaluate evidence as they understood that process, while professional judges might have considered lay judges incompetent to evaluate evidence within the framework of their rules, the rules of lawyers (that is, persons knowledgeable of legal rules).

8.3   Understanding of Legal Issues

As discussed in Chapter 1, critics of lay participation argue that lay participants are not able to understand and apply the law. The principal reasons that are regularly pointed out are that lay participants have neither legal education nor systematic training and experience in deciding legal cases. In the parlance of the theoretical developments from Chapter 5, lay judges possess low states of the two specific status characteristics that characterize the interaction in mixed tribunals.

The respondents in this study were asked to state their opinion about lay judges' competence to understand legal issues. The question asked of lawyers (professional judges, state attorneys, and attorneys) was worded differently from the question asked of lay judges; while the question asked of lawyers targeted their opinion about lay judges' ability in general, the question asked of lay judges focused on their own ability.[16]

The results indicated sharp differences; the majority of lawyers (83% of professional judges, 78% of state attorneys, and 89% of attorneys)[17] perceived lay judges as rarely able to understand legal issues in the case (Table 8.7), while the majority of lay judges (75%) thought that they understood legal issues often (χ^2=185.87, $d.f.$=12, Phi=.631, $p < .001$).[18] Regional differences were not important (χ^2=.225, $d.f.$=1, Phi= -.023, $p > .05$, n.s.), whereas differences in the type of court were: respondents from regional courts were more likely to say that lay judges understood legal issues than respondents from district courts (χ^2=6.92, $d.f.$=1, Phi= -.140, $p < .01$). Interestingly, while the differences with respect to the type of court persisted when separate analyses were performed for lay judges and state attorneys, such was not the case for the separate analysis performed for professional judges (χ^2=1.85, $d.f.$=1, Phi= -.143, $p > .05$, n.s.). On the other hand, lay judges from regional courts were more likely to report that they understood legal issues often than lay

---

[16]The question for professional judges, state attorneys, and attorneys was: "Do you feel that lay judges generally understand the legal issues involved in the case?" The question for lay judges was: "Do you feel that you understand the legal issues involved in the case?" The offered answers to both questions ranged from "always" to "never" on a five-point scale.

[17]The only exceptions were regional state attorneys, the majority of whom said that lay judges were frequently able to understand legal issues.

[18]The answers were recoded as follows: "always" through "frequently" as "often," and "sometimes" and "never" as "rarely."

judges from district courts (χ^2=5.46, $d.f.$=1, Phi= .159, $p < .05$). Similarly, regional state attorneys were more likely to report that lay judges understood legal issues often than district state attorneys (χ^2=16.49, $d.f.$=1, Phi= -.533, $p < .001$).

Such a discrepancy between the answers given by lawyers and lay judges can be at least partially explained by the fact that lay judges reported about their own behavior, while lawyers reported about the behavior of (a group of) others. Thus, although it may be that lay judges overestimated their own understanding of legal issues, and professional judges at the same time underestimated lay judges' ability, the fact that lay judges may have problems in understanding of legal issues nevertheless emerges. Moreover, due to the fact that lay judges do not know the law, their ability to evaluate whether they understood legal issues may have been weaker than that of professional judges.

In the arena of jury studies, the results of Doob's study (1979b) suggested that Canadian jurors overestimated their own ability to understand legal issues. Most of the jurors (96%) said that juries were generally able to understand legal instructions (Doob, 1979b, p. 62), but, when they were asked about a particular instruction given by the professional judge (standard limited use instructions regarding the defendant's criminal record), only one out of three jurors indicated that professional judges gave them this instruction.

The position of lay judges in mixed tribunals may be even weaker; they do not receive any legal instructions (like jurors do) nor do they receive a short seminar on legal issues (like magistrates do), yet they have to decide the legal issues jointly with a lawyer.

Table 8.7: Lay judges' understanding of legal issues.[a]

	Prof. j. Dist. C. ZG	Prof. j. Dist. C. BJ	Prof. j. Reg. C.	Prof. J. Supr. C.	Dist. State a. ZG	Dist. State a. BJ	Reg. State a.	Att. ZG	Att. BJ
always	0.0%	0.0%	0.0%	0.0%	0.0%	5.0%	0.0%	1.3%	0.0%
very frequently	0.0%	6.9%	8.3%	0.0%	5.0%	0.0%	5.6%	2.6%	3.8%
frequently	11.1%	6.9%	12.5%	30.0%	0.0%	5.0%	50.0%	9.2%	0.0%
sometimes	66.7%	86.2%	79.2%	60.0%	75.0%	85.0%	44.4%	77.6%	76.9%
never	22.2%	0.0%	0.0%	10.0%	20.0%	5.0%	0.0%	9.2%	19.2%
N	27	29	24	10	20	20	18	76	26

[a]Question: "Do you feel that lay judges/you generally understand the legal issues involved in the case?"

Table 8.7: Continued.

	Lay j. Dist. C. ZG	Lay j. Dist. C. KŽ	Lay j. Reg. C. ZG	Lay j. Reg. C. BJ	Prof j. All	State a. All R & D	Att. ZG & BJ	Lay j. All R & D
always	13.3%	19.6%	19.0%	31.3%	0.0%	1.7%	1.0%	18.0%
very frequently	13.3%	21.6%	28.6%	21.9%	4.4%	3.4%	2.9%	18.0%
frequently	44.2%	29.4%	33.3%	37.5%	12.2%	17.2%	6.9%	38.7%
sometimes	28.3%	25.5%	19.0%	9.4%	75.6%	69.0%	77.5%	24.0%
never	0.9%	3.9%	0.0%	0.0%	7.8%	8.6%	11.8%	1.4%
N	122	53	21	33	90	58	102	229

8.4 Deliberation

What happens between the summation at the beginning of deliberation (given by the presiding professional judge) and the moment the decision is reached by the tribunal? Reaching the verdict is a group task, and the expectation is that the tribunal will typically have spent some time discussing the important issues in the case before reaching the final decision.

This section examines the dominant subject of such discussions, as well as the frequency and importance of lay judges' contributions during discussions. Lay judges' participation is measured as the perceived frequency of lay judges' comments during discussions, while the importance of lay judges' contributions is measured as the perceived importance of lay judges' comments. In addition, the topics of lay judges' and professional judges' comments are compared, and possible problems with lay judges' comments are discussed.

The presiding professional judge leads deliberation and voting, and is responsible for a thorough and versatile discussion of all the relevant issues (Article 116, Item 2, *Criminal Procedure Law*, 1993). The law does not regulate the order in which discussion during deliberation is to proceed; rather, as a consequence of the principle of free evaluation of evidence, members of the tribunal decide that order. As the next section of this chapter shows, deliberation frequently starts with a summation given by the presiding professional judge.

Because the *Criminal Procedure Law* (1993) prescribed the order of issues the court has to decide/vote upon, presiding professional judges were likely to follow routinely these rules in determining the order of deliberation. Specifically, the order of issues that needed to be voted upon was determined by Article 117 (*Criminal Procedure Law*, 1993). The tribunal first needs to decide the preceding issues (*prethodna pitanja*), such as whether the court has jurisdiction over the legal case, and whether it is necessary to reopen the trial stage. Upon deciding the preceding issues, the tribunal will vote, if appropriate, on the principal issue. The tribunal will first decide whether the defendant committed the offense and whether he/she was criminally responsible. If the defendant has been found guilty and it thus becomes necessary to pass the sentence, the tribunal will determine the punishment and other criminal sanctions, expenses associated with the legal proceedings, and will decide all the remaining issues in the case.

These decisions are made by the majority vote (Article 116, Item 1, *Criminal Procedure Law*, 1993), which leaves the possibility for lay judges, who outnumber professional judges in both small tribunals and large tribunals, to outvote professional judges. Also, the presiding professional judge votes last. The law prescribes the way to obtain the majority vote (Article 116, Item 3, *Criminal Procedure Law*, 1993) if there is disagreement. Members of the tribunal are not allowed to refuse to vote on a particular issue when that issue is raised by the presiding professional judge, but the tribunal member who provides the minority vote for acquittal cannot be forced to vote on the punishment (Article 116, Item 4, *Criminal Procedure Law*, 1993). Interestingly, if there is disagreement about the sanction in such cases, the vote of the minority member who voted for acquittal and also refused to vote on the sanction would be counted toward the faction that voted for the option which is the most favorable for the defendant (Article 116, Item 4, *Criminal Procedure Law*, 1993).

The tribunal keeps a record of deliberation and voting. This record is kept in a separate envelope in the case file (Article 89, *Criminal Procedure Law*, 1993). If there is a separate minority opinion by one or more members of the tribunal, it is also recorded and kept in the same envelope. From my experience as a court apprentice (the presence of court apprentices during deliberations may be tolerated) and from the discussions I had with professional judges, I learned that these records do not contain the votes and opinions expressed during deliberation, and that they are simply official statements documenting that deliberation and voting have been carried out and what the final outcome(s) were (i.e., determination of guilt and, if appropriate, the decision regarding sanctions and other issues in the case). These records are not available to researchers;[19] in order to provide for a candid and unconstrained discussion, the records are kept secret. In fact, only higher courts may open this envelope when they decide appeals and other forms of legal redress, after which they must seal it again.

8.4.1 Summation at the Beginning of Deliberation

From experience as a court apprentice at the District Court of Zagreb and the Regional Court of Zagreb in the late 1980s, and from informal discussions with several professional judges in the course of carrying out this study, I learned that professional judges frequently started deliberation by summarizing the evidence, although they were not obligated to do so by the law. Similarly, Casper and Zeisel (1972, p. 152, Table 21) reported that three-quarters of the German mixed tribunals they studied began with such a summary: in the *Schöffengericht* (misdemeanors), summation was given in 68% of the cases, in the *Grosse Strafkammer* (felonies, less serious crimes, minor political offenses) in 100% of the cases, and in the *Schwurgericht* (serious felonies and serious political offenses) in 86% of the cases. Based on these experiences and prior research findings, the expectation was that the empirical findings of this study would confirm that professional judges typically started the deliberation process by providing a summary of the case.

Because state attorneys and attorneys may not be present in the courtroom during deliberation, questions about summation were asked only of the members of the tribunals — professional judges and lay judges. Professional judges and lay judges were asked about the frequency with which professional judges summarized the evidence at the beginning of deliberation.[20] As expected,

---

[19]See Chapter 6 for details.

[20]The wording of the question for professional judges was: "Do you usually summarize the evidence at the beginning of deliberation?" The offered answers were: "yes, always," "no, never," "sometimes, depends on the case," and "sometimes, depends on the lay judges." The question asked of lay judges, as well as the offered answers were analogous, with the obvious rewording. In addition, respondents were offered the opportunity to specify other reasons.

the overwhelming majority of professional judges (70% at district courts and 92% at regional courts) stated that they had always summarized the evidence at the beginning of deliberation (Table 8.8). In general, the majority of lay judges in three out of four groups of lay judges (53% of lay judges from the Regional Court of Zagreb, 62% of lay judges from the District Court of Križevci, and 88% of lay judges from the Regional Court of Bjelovar) agreed with professional judges and thereby confirmed that it was indeed unusual behavior when professional judges did not summarize evidence. The exception were lay judges from the District Court of Zagreb, only 21% of whom reported that professional judges always summarized the evidence, while the majority (79%) reported that this happened only occasionally. The chi-square test revealed that the answers were significantly different, which was especially the case when the answers provided by lay judges from the District Court of Zagreb were compared to the answers provided by any other group of respondents that was asked this same question (χ^2=89.14, $d.f.$=6, Phi=.540, $p < .001$). The answers by professional judges and lay judges differed significantly; professional judges were more likely to say that they always summarized the evidence than lay judges were (76% $v.$ 43%, respectively; χ^2=25.89, $d.f.$=1, Phi=.289, $p < .001$). It is noteworthy that only 1 lay judge out of 309 respondents (both professional judges and lay judges) said that professional judges *never* provided a summation of the evidence.

The estimates of the reported frequency of summation seemed to depend on the type of court: the percentage of professional judges who reported that they always summarized the evidence at the beginning of deliberation was higher for professional judges from regional courts (92%) than for professional judges from district courts (approximately 70%; χ^2=4.50, $d.f.$=1, Phi= $-.237$, $p < .05$). Similarly, lay judges from regional courts were more likely to say that professional judges summarized evidence on a regular basis than lay judges from district courts. In fact, while the majority of lay judges from district courts (66%) reported that summation of evidence was provided only occasionally, the majority of lay judges from regional courts (74%) reported

Table 8.8: Frequency of summation.[a]

	Prof. j. Dist. C. ZG	Prof. j. Dist. C. BJ	Prof. j. Reg. C.	Lay j. Dist. C. ZG	Lay j. Dist. C. KŽ	Lay j. Reg. C. ZG	Lay j. Reg. C. BJ	Prof. j. All	Lay j. All
yes, always	70.4%	69.0%	91.7%	21.3%	62.3%	52.4%	87.9%	76.3%	43.2%
no, never	0.0%	0.0%	0.0%	0.0%	1.9%	0.0%	0.0%	0.0%	0.4%
sometimes	29.6%	31.0%	8.3%	78.7%	35.8%	47.6%	12.1%	23.7%	56.4%
depends on case	25.9%	31.0%	8.3%	54.9%	24.5%	19.0%	12.1%	22.5%	38.5%
depends on LJs	3.7%	0.0%	0.0%	23.8%	7.5%	28.6%	0.0%	1.2%	17.0%
depends on other reasons	0.0%	0.0%	0.0%	0.0%	3.8%	0.0%	0.0%	0.0%	0.9%
N	27	29	24	122	53	21	33	80	229

[a]Question: "Do you/professional judges usually summarize evidence at the beginning of deliberation?"

that summation of evidence was *always* given (χ^2=26.41, *d.f.*=1, *Phi*= -.342, $p < .001$).

The influence of region was not important for professional judges, but it was important for lay judges. Virtually the same percentage of professional judges from district courts from the two regions reported that they always summarized the evidence (69% and 70%, χ^2=0.01, *d.f.*=1, *Phi*=.015, $p > .05$, n.s.). On the other hand, the majority of lay judges from the District Court of Križevci and lay judges from the Regional Court of Bjelovar were significantly more likely to report frequent summation of evidence by professional judges than lay judges from the other two courts, namely the District Court of Zagreb and the Regional Court of Zagreb (χ^2=50.86, *d.f.*=1, *Phi*= -.474, $p < .001$).

A glance at the lay judges' responses indicates that both the differences with respect to the type of court and regional differences in the lay judges' perceptions of frequency of summation were driven by lay judges from the District Court of Zagreb, only 21% of whom had reported that professional judges always summarized the evidence at the beginning of deliberation. While that percentage is considerably lower than that of any other group of lay judges, it is also true that there were many lay judges from the District Court of Zagreb (54.9%) who reported that professional judges summarized the evidence "sometimes, depending on the case." That percentage is considerably higher (by at least a 25% margin) than any corresponding percentage by another group of lay judges. Given that percentages of professional judges who reported that they always summarized the evidence at the beginning of deliberation did not vary as much, it seems that lay judges from the District Court of Zagreb may have interpreted more stringently what constitutes a (thorough) summary. Given the size of the court and the typical caseload, it would not have been unusual if summation were so speedy that many lay judges may not have appreciated it as such.

The respondents who stated that summation was not always given seemed to believe that whether it would be given depended more on the case itself than on the style of a particular professional judge or on other reasons.[21] The professional judges who said that they summarized the evidence occasionally mostly reported that their summation depended on the case (rather than on the lay judges sitting in the tribunal); ninety percent or more of the professional judges who emphasized that they did not provide summation in every case in each group said that whether they would provide the summation depended on the case. Lay judges from all four groups also said that summation most likely depended on the case; among the respondents who said that summation did not occur in every case, the majority in three groups[22] (70% of the lay judges from the District Court of Zagreb who reported that summation happened occasionally, 76% of the lay judges from the District Court of Križevci who reported that summation happened occasionally, and 100% of the lay judges from the Regional Court of Bjelovar who reported that summation happened occasionally) argued that this was a consequence of the case, rather than of the style of the presiding professional judge.

The next interesting question is why professional judges summarized the evidence at the beginning of deliberation; given that they do not have a legal obligation to do so, why did they do it so consistently? Respondents were asked why, according to their opinion, professional judges usually summarized the evidence at the beginning of deliberation.

The answers exhibited considerable variation (Table 8.9). It seems that there was a pattern which depended on the type of court. Professional judges and lay judges from district courts most frequently (49%) said that the purpose of summation was to "familiarize lay judges with the evidence in the case," while professional judges and lay judges from regional courts most frequently (43%) said that the purpose of summation was to "present complex evidence in a way that is more understandable for lay judges" (χ^2=9.57, *d.f.*=3, *Phi*=.181,

---

[21]The only exception were lay judges from the Regional Court of Zagreb.

[22]Lay judges from the Regional Court of Zagreb were the only group in which the majority of the respondents who said that summation did not occur in every case argued that whether summation occurred depended upon the professional judge, rather than on the actual case.

$p < .05$).[23] A similar comparison by region did not yield significant differences ($\chi^2 = 1.44$, $d.f. = 3$, $Phi = .073$, $p > .05$, n.s.), nor did the comparison of answers by the role in the criminal justice system (professional judges $v.$ lay judges; $\chi^2 = 2.27$, $d.f. = 3$, $Phi = .088$, $p > .05$, n.s.).

Cases tried at regional courts were more likely to include complex evidence and involve more serious offenses. However, importance may be attached not only to the complexity of the evidence and the seriousness of the case, but also to the lay judges' familiarity with the evidence in the case. Lay judges at both types of courts heard the evidence in each case; but, as the results presented in Chapter 7 show, they did not read the case file (and thus familiarize themselves with other evidence in the file) equally often — reading the case file was perceived to be more frequent at regional courts.[24] Therefore, it is not surprising that professional judges and lay judges from district courts, where the evidence in the case is less likely to be complex and lay judges are less likely to read the case file, reported familiarization of lay judges with the evidence in the case as the most frequent reason for summation. By the same token, it is not surprising that professional judges and lay judges from regional courts, where the evidence in the case is more likely to be complex, cases more serious, and lay judges are more likely to read the case file, reported most frequently that the purpose of summation was to "present complex evidence in a way that is more understandable for lay judges."

8.4.2 Dominant Subject of Deliberation

The tribunal is unlikely, on average, to spend much time discussing preceding issues. These are strictly legal issues and the professional judge will probably decide them and share his/her opinion with the tribunal. It is reasonable to

---

[23]Professional judges and lay judges were grouped into two groups: respondents from district courts and respondents from regional courts.

[24]Whereas 7.5% of lay judges from regional courts reported that they never read the case file, 28% of lay judges from district courts reported the same ($\chi^2 = 9.15$, $d.f. = 1$, $Phi = -.202$, $p < .01$); twenty-nine percent of professional judges from regional courts said that lay judges never read the case file, while as many as 48% of professional judges from district courts said the same.

Table 8.9: Reasons for summation.[a]

	Prof. j. Dist. C. ZG	Prof. j. Dist. C. BJ	Prof. j. Reg. C. ZG	Lay j. Dist. C. ZG	Lay j. Dist. C. KŽ	Lay j. Reg. C. ZG	Lay j. Reg. C. BJ	Prof. j. All	Lay j. All
familiarize lay judges with evidence	53.8%	51.7%	34.8%	47.9%	37.7%	30.0%	36.4%	46.3%	41.9%
present complex evidence	18.5%	10.3%	43.5%	22.3%	34.6%	38.1%	39.4%	22.5%	28.8%
repeat evidence content	26.9%	31.0%	17.4%	18.9%	21.2%	20.0%	12.1%	25.0%	18.3%
present own views	0.0%	6.9%	4.3%	4.1%	3.8%	5.0%	3.0%	3.8%	3.9%
N	27	29	24	122	53	21	33	80	229

[a]Question: "In your opinion, the purpose of summation is to:"

expect that most of the time spent on deliberation will be devoted to the major issues of the case — guilt and, if appropriate, punishment. Deciding guilt requires knowledge and understanding of the complex concept of criminal responsibility, while the determination of the sentence allows for more flexibility, the possibility of introduction of community values into the courtroom, and more negotiations among the members of the tribunal. In a study by Casper and Zeisel (1972), professional judges estimated the duration of typical deliberations by mixed tribunals in both cases with and without a full confession by the defendant. They concluded: "The deliberation time differs hardly at all, suggesting that the bulk of deliberation time is devoted to the sentencing issues" (Casper and Zeisel, 1972, p. 150).

In the present study, professional judges and lay judges were asked about the dominant topic of deliberation: "Considering deliberation as a whole, on what subject do your tribunals spend more time?" The offered answers were "guilt," "sentence," and "equally guilt and sentence."

The majority of lay judges within each group (63% of lay judges from the District Court of Zagreb, 65% of lay judges from the District Court of Križevci, 67% of lay judges from the Regional Court of Zagreb, and 55% of lay judges from the Regional Court of Bjelovar), which also translates into the majority of all lay judges (63%), said that tribunals spent approximately equal amounts of time on guilt and sentence (Table 8.10).

Professional judges most frequently (44%) selected the same answer as well. Their answers were significantly different from the answers provided by lay judges (χ^2=13.64, $d.f.$=2, Phi=.213, $p < .01$). Among the professional judges who reported that either subject drew more attention, the majority of professional judges from district courts[25] reported that tribunals spent more time on the subject of sentence, whereas the majority of professional judges

---

[25]Sixty percent of professional judges from the District Court of Zagreb reported that one subject was discussed at greater length, which constituted 33% of all professional judges from the District Court of Zagreb; 73% of professional judges from district courts in the Bjelovar Region reported that one subject was discussed at greater length, which constituted 35% of all professional judges from district courts in the Bjelovar Region.

Table 8.10: Dominant topic of deliberation.[a]

	Prof. j. Dist. C. ZG	Prof. j. Dist. C. BJ	Prof. j. Reg. C. ZG	Lay j. Dist. C. ZG	Lay j. Dist. C. KŽ	Lay j. Reg. C. ZG	Lay j. Reg. C. BJ	Prof. j. All	Lay j. All
guilt	22.2%	20.7%	33.3%	20.5%	25.5%	19.0%	35.5%	25.0%	23.6%
sentence	33.3%	34.5%	25.0%	16.2%	9.8%	14.3%	9.7%	31.3%	13.6%
equally	44.4%	44.8%	41.7%	63.2%	64.7%	66.7%	54.8%	43.8%	62.7%
N	27	29	24	122	53	21	33	80	229

[a]Question: "Considering deliberation as a whole, on what subject do your tribunals spend more time?"

from regional courts[26] reported that tribunals spent more time on the subject of guilt.

8.4.3   Lay Judges' Comments

Lay judges' comments are examined from several perspectives: their estimated frequency and possible influence of lay judges' demographic characteristics on the frequency of comments, topics of lay judges' comments, their perceived importance, and potential problems associated with them.

Frequency of Lay Judges' Comments

Professional judges were asked to determine the frequency of lay judges' questions and comments during deliberation in general, and in the last 10 deliberations in particular. The first question was worded as follows: "According to your experience, how frequently do lay judges ask questions and make comments, in addition to giving their vote, during deliberation?"[27]

Professional judges most frequently said that lay judges were not extremely active and that they only *sometimes* asked questions and made comments other than just stating their votes during deliberation (Table 8.11; 56% of professional judges from the District Court of Zagreb, 76% of professional judges from district courts in the Bjelovar Region, and 46% of professional judges from regional courts). There were some differences, however. In particular, professional judges from district courts in the Bjelovar Region were more likely to say that lay judges participated less actively than the other two groups of professional judges were (χ^2=5.27, $d.f.$=2, Phi=.257, $p > .05$, n.s.).[28]

---

[26]Fifty-seven percent of professional judges from regional courts who reported that one subject was discussed at greater length, which constituted 33% of all professional judges from regional courts.

[27]The offered answers ranged from "never" to "always" on a five-point scale.

[28]The answer "never" was omitted from the analysis because none of the professional judges had selected it. The answers "frequently" through "always" were merged and frequencies were compared to the frequencies of the answer "sometimes." Due to the fact that the group sizes were relatively small, the chi-square test was not sufficiently powerful to report statistical significance. However, the *Phi*-value suggested that there were important differences. Indeed, I consider the difference of 30% between the answers given by pro-

Table 8.11: Frequency of lay judges' questions and comments as perceived by professional judges.[a]

	Prof. j. Dist. C. ZG	Prof. j. Dist. C. BJ	Prof. j. Reg. C.
never	0.0%	0.0%	0.0%
sometimes	55.6%	75.9%	45.8%
frequently	33.3%	13.8%	37.5%
very frequently	7.4%	10.3%	12.5%
always	3.7%	0.0%	4.2%
N	27	29	24

[a]Question: "According to your experience, in addition to giving their vote, how frequently do lay judges ask questions and make comments during deliberation?"

A similar question, restricted to the experiences in the last 10 deliberations and focused on comments only, was asked of both professional judges and lay judges. The question asked of professional judges was worded as follows: "In how many of the last 10 deliberations in which you participated did lay judges make comments other than just stating their vote?" The corresponding question asked of lay judges was: "In how many of the last 10 deliberations in which you participated did you make comments other than just stating your vote?"[29]

The results show that lay judges reported making comments during deliberation significantly more frequently than professional judges gave them credit for (χ^2=5.27, $d.f.$=1, Phi= -.131, $p <$ .05);[30] while the majority of professional judges (63%) reported that lay judges made comments during deliberation infrequently, the majority of lay judges (52%) reported that they frequently made comments during deliberation (Table 8.12).

Interestingly, when the type of court was controlled for, the differences between professional judges and lay judges persisted only at district courts (professional judges from district courts were 25% more likely to say that lay judges made comments infrequently than lay judges from district court; χ^2=10.50, $d.f.$=1, Phi= -.214, $p <$ .01), while they disappeared at regional courts (the majority of professional judges and lay judges from regional courts were equally likely to say that lay judges made comments frequently; χ^2=0.22, $d.f.$=1, Phi= .053, $p >$ .05, n.s.).

Therefore, merging all professional judges into one group masked some important differences: the majority of professional judges from district courts (75%) said that lay judges made comments in less than one-half of the last 10 deliberations, while the majority of professional judges from regional courts

---

fessional judges from district courts in the Bjelovar Region and professional judges from regional courts to be substantively important.

[29]Six answers were offered to both questions, ranging on a six-point scale from "in all 10 deliberations" to "in none of the deliberations."

[30]The answers "in all 10 deliberations" through "in about one-half" were merged into "frequently," and the answers "in less than one-half" through "in none of the deliberations" were merged into "infrequently."

Table 8.12: Frequency of lay judges' comments in the last 10 deliberations.[a]

	Prof. j. Dist. C. ZG	Prof. j. Dist. C. BJ	Prof. j. Reg. C.	Lay j. Dist. C. ZG	Lay j. Dist. C. KŽ	Lay j. Reg. C. ZG	Lay j. Reg. C. BJ	Prof. j. All	Lay j. All
in all 10	3.7%	6.9%	37.5%	6.6%	13.5%	19.0%	24.2%	15.0%	11.9%
in more than one-half	11.1%	10.3%	20.8%	17.4%	19.2%	14.3%	37.3%	13.8%	18.9%
in about one-half	7.4%	10.3%	8.3%	23.1%	23.1%	19.0%	15.2%	8.8%	21.6%
in less than one-half	11.1%	10.3%	0.0%	9.1%	1.9%	19.0%	15.2%	7.5%	9.3%
in only a few	44.4%	55.2%	25.0%	38.0%	38.5%	23.8%	15.2%	42.5%	33.5%
in none	22.2%	6.9%	8.3%	5.8%	3.8%	4.8%	3.0%	12.5%	4.8%
N	27	29	24	122	53	21	33	80	229

[a]Question wording differed for professional judges and lay judges: **professional judges:** "In how many of the last 10 deliberations in which you participated did lay judges make comments, other than just stating their vote?"; **lay judges:** "In how many of the last 10 deliberations in which you participated did you make comments, other than just stating your vote?"

(67%) said that lay judges made comments much more frequently — in more than one-half of the last 10 deliberations (χ^2=12.44, $d.f.$=1, Phi= -.394, $p <$ .001). In fact, four out of ten professional judges from regional courts reported that lay judges made comments *"in all ten deliberations."* In other words, the type of court seemed to be important for professional judges, while such was not the case for lay judges (χ^2=2.14, $d.f.$=1, Phi= -.097, $p >$ .05, n.s.). These potential discrepancies will be discussed shortly.

Regional differences were important neither for lay judges nor for professional judges (χ^2=3.13, $d.f.$=1, Phi= -.117, $p >$ .05, n.s. for lay judges; χ^2=0.22, $d.f.$=1, Phi= -.062, $p >$ .05, n.s. for professional judges).

Demographic Characteristics and Frequency of Comments

Just as the preceding chapter discussed the impact of lay judges' demographic characteristics on the reported frequency of their participation (through the perceived frequency with which lay judges asked questions of defendant[s], witnesses, and expert witness), this chapter discusses the influence of lay judges' gender, age, education, occupational prestige, and mandate on the reported frequency of their participation during deliberation (through the perceived frequency with which lay judges made comments during deliberation). Chi-square tests were used to test for significant differences among demographic subgroups in the reported frequency with which lay judges made comments during deliberation.[31]

As mentioned earlier, previous studies on mixed tribunals did not systematically examine the effect of lay judges' demographic characteristics on the frequency of lay judges' participation. Studies on juries generally suggest that the variation in the frequency of group participation during deliberation is related to the characteristics of the individuals themselves: men, more edu-

---

[31] As before, the answers are grouped as follows: "in all 10 deliberations" through "in about one-half" as "frequently," and "in less than one-half" through "in none of the deliberations" as "infrequently." Due to small sample sizes, chi-square analyses will mostly be calculated for all lay judges; whenever feasible, however, separate analyses for lay judges from different courts will be conducted.

cated jurors, and those with higher-status occupations are more likely to speak (Hans and Vidmar, 1986, p. 108).

Predictions about the interaction during deliberation are made on the basis of theoretical developments from Chapter 5. Professional judges, tribunal members who have legal education and systematic training and experience in legal decision-making, will have a higher status in the tribunal than lay judges. Consequently, they will have more opportunities to participate and, once they participate, their contributions will be evaluated as more important. Lay judges, on the other hand, have neither legal education nor systematic training and experience in legal decision-making. The theory predicts that these specific status characteristics (i.e., legal education, systematic training and experience in legal decision-making) will be more important for the interaction among the tribunal members than diffuse characteristics will (e.g., age, gender). At the same time, not all diffuse status characteristics are expected to be equally important; appropriate hypotheses for each of the analyzed diffuse characteristics will be developed and tested. The logic behind each hypothesis stated here is similar to the logic behind the analogous hypothesis pertaining to trial (see Chapter 7 for details).

Studies on juries show that *gender* is an important factor; male jurors tend to speak more often during deliberation than female jurors do (Hans and Vidmar, 1986, p. 108). However, unlike the jury, in which there are typically no members who possess high states/levels of specific status characteristics and diffuse status characteristics thus become important, mixed tribunals are expected to give prominence to specific status characteristics. Gender is expected to induce minimal differences, if any, in the frequency with which lay judges participate during deliberation. Consistent with the analogous findings pertaining to trial, the results presented here indeed suggest that gender was *not* an important factor; differences in the self-reported frequency of comments by female and male lay judges were not statistically significant ($\chi^2 = .077$, $d.f. = 1$, $Phi = .018$, $p > .05$, n.s.); the majority of both female and male lay judges reported that they "frequently" made comments during deliberation. When the analysis was constrained to only lay judges from the District Court of Zagreb (where the percentage of female lay judges was much higher than in the other three courts — 49% $v.$ 9%-25%), the picture that emerged was quite the opposite: the differences were not only significant (χ^2=5.65, $d.f.$=1, Phi=.217, $p < .05$), but, contrary to the results of jury studies, female lay judges were more likely to say that they participated in deliberations actively than male lay judges. This is again consistent with the earlier finding related to trial — female lay judges from the District Court of Zagreb also reported being more active during trial than their male counterparts.

As for *age*, traditionally, lay participants were predominantly middle-aged or even older (Silberman, 1979, p. 368). This was also true for the majority of lay judges in this study: 57% were in the age group 51-65 years of age and an additional 22% were in the age group 36-50 years of age. As a result of socialization in different times, different degrees of self-esteem, and different senses of responsibility for participation in the legal decision-making process, it might be expected that the lay judges who were members of different generations would exhibit different frequencies of comments during deliberation. However, the results showed that, similar to the results for the reported frequency of asking questions during trial, none of the age groups of lay judges reported making comments during deliberation more frequently than any other age group (χ^2=4.68, $d.f.$=3, Phi=.145, $p > .05$, n.s.).[32] The chi-square test did not yield significant differences in the reported frequency of making comments during deliberation by various age groups of lay judges from the District Court of Zagreb either (χ^2=2.23, $d.f.$=3, Phi=.138, $p > .05$, n.s.).

According to jury studies, more educated jurors tend to speak more during deliberation (Hans and Vidmar, 1986, p. 108). In the context of mixed tribunals, *education* is an interesting characteristic; in the parlance of status characteristic theory, although it is not a specific status characteristic, it may be quite important for legal decision-making. Through their education, more

---

[32]Lay judges were grouped into four age groups: "35 and below," "36-50," "51-65," and "66 and above."

educated lay judges have grown accustomed to abstract ways of thinking and problem solving, they have met different people, and have become more sensitive to different ideas and viewpoints. In addition, because of their education, they were more likely to have obtained more prestigious jobs (occupational prestige is discussed in more detail shortly), and they may feel more comfortable talking to professional judges as their equals. In light of the theoretical developments from Chapter 5, the expectation was that, if there are differences at all, lay judges with higher educational levels will tend to participate more actively than lay judges who are less educated.

In contravention to these arguments, and in agreement with the findings from Chapter 7 on the effect of education on the reported frequency of participation during trial, the results show that less educated lay judges (high school diploma or below) reported participating in deliberation by making comments *more* often than more educated lay judges did[33] (χ^2=5.57, *d.f.*=1, *Phi*= -.157, $p < .05$); while the majority of less educated lay judges (58%) reported asking questions "frequently," the majority of more educated lay judges (59%) reported asking questions "infrequently." Very similar results were obtained for lay judges from the District Court of Zagreb — more educated lay judges reported lower frequency of comments (χ^2=4.54, *d.f.*=1, *Phi*=.195, $p < .05$).

People who have power and privilege are highly valued; therefore, *occupations* which are powerful and privileged are regarded highly (Treiman, 1977). As argued in Chapter 7, lay judges whose occupations are more prestigious are expected to be more accustomed to problem-solving group conversations in which their word is respected and valued. The expectation was, then, that lay judges whose occupations were more prestigious asked questions more frequently, because they felt that their questions and comments had been more appreciated and valued more highly by the professional judge, a person whose occupation is also on the higher level on the occupational prestige scale.

---

[33]Education was recoded as follows: "education below elementary school" through "high school diploma" as "less educated," and "some college" and "graduated from college" as "more educated."

The reported frequency of making comments during deliberation was not influenced by lay judges' occupational prestige (χ^2=1.21, $d.f.$=1, Phi=.079, $p > .05$, n.s. for all lay judges).[34] Lay judges from the District Court of Zagreb displayed substantively important differences (χ^2=3.57, $d.f.$=1, Phi=.186, $p > .05$, n.s.);[35] as was the case with the frequency of asking questions during trial, the above results suggested that the lay judges who had more prestigious occupations seemed to be somewhat more likely to say that they made comments during deliberation "infrequently" than the lay judges who had less prestigious occupations.

The *mandate* of lay judges was also examined as a factor that might have influenced the frequency of comments made by lay judges during deliberation. Although lay judges have not gone through systematic training in legal decision-making, they would have obtained experience in legal decision-making by participating in numerous trials and would thus have become more knowledgeable about the criminal process and their own role in the process.

The expectation was that the lay judges who were at the beginning of their mandate tended to make comments during deliberation less frequently than their more experienced colleagues. Novice lay judges (mandate below one year) did not know the rules and were still in the process of learning them. Experienced lay judges, that is, lay judges in the middle of their mandate (one to three years) would tend to ask questions most frequently, since they did know the rules and, at the same time, they did not succumb to the element of routine. Very experienced lay judges (mandate over three years) had considerable experience; they could have perceived that professional judges did not value their questions during trial and comments during deliberation highly and that

---

[34]Occupations were coded on the basis of Treiman's international occupational scale (Treiman, 1977) as those with lower prestige, which included occupations coded with numerical values from 10 to 45, and those with higher prestige, which included occupations coded with numerical values from 46 to 78. See Chapter 6 for a description of Treiman's occupational scale.

[35]Although the results of the chi-square test did not turn out to be significant, I regarded the difference of 19% to be substantively important. The *Phi*-value of .186 is consistent with that interpretation.

their input rarely made a difference. In addition, very experienced lay judges could have been influenced by an element of routine. All of these factors could easily have led toward a sharp decrease in the number of comments made by very experienced lay judges during deliberation.

The results revealed no significant impact of mandate on the reported frequencies of lay judges' comments during deliberation (χ^2=1.12, $d.f.$=2, Phi=.071, $p > .05$, n.s. for all lay judges; χ^2=1.34, $d.f.$=2, Phi=.109, $p > .05$, n.s. for lay judges from the District Court of Zagreb);[36] approximately one-half of lay judges from each group reported that they made comments during deliberation "frequently."

Another question about the influence of mandate on the frequency of lay judges' comments during deliberation was asked of both professional judges and lay judges. The question was worded as follows: "If you compare lay judges at the beginning of their mandate (first year) and lay judges in the latter part of their mandate with respect to their asking questions and making comments during deliberation, in your opinion, novice lay judges ask questions and make comments during deliberation:" The offered answers ranged from "much more frequently" to "much less frequently" on a five-point scale.

The opinions reported by professional judges and lay judges were similar;[37] the majority of respondents within most groups (64% for professional judges from district courts, 67% for professional judges from regional courts, 65% of lay judges from the District Court of Zagreb, and 56% of lay judges from regional courts) said that the frequency of lay judges' comments *did* change with their mandate;[38] the only exception were lay judges from the District Court of Križevci, the majority of whom said that the frequency of lay judges' comments was not related to their mandate (χ^2=8.33, $d.f.$=6, Phi=.169, $p >$

---

[36]Lay judges were grouped according to the length of mandate as follows: "novice" lay judges (up to one year), "experienced" lay judges (one to three years), and "very experienced" lay judges (over three years).

[37]The offered answers were recoded into three categories as follows: "much more likely" and "more likely" into "more likely," "equally likely" simply as "equally likely," and "less likely" and "much less likely" as "less likely."

[38]The answer "equally frequently" was compared to all the other answers.

.05, n.s.).[39] However, approximately equal percentages of respondents who said that there was a change in the frequency of comments during deliberation have reported that the frequency had increased/decreased. Thus, while a number of lay judges reported some change in the frequency of comments, there is little agreement on the direction of that change.

Finally, neither the type of court/office (district $v.$ regional) nor region (the Zagreb Region $v.$ the Bjelovar Region) had a significant impact on the reported frequency with which lay judges made comments during deliberation ($\chi^2=0.83$, $d.f.=2$, $Phi=.053$, $p > .05$, n.s. and $\chi^2=4.82$, $d.f.=2$, $Phi=.134$, $p > .05$, n.s., respectively).

Complexity of Evidence and Frequency of Comments

It is reasonable to expect that the frequency of lay judges' participation might vary with the complexity of evidence. Plausible arguments can be stated for both competing directions of the change. On the one hand, in the cases with complex evidence lay judges may be more active because there might be a larger number of unclear pieces of the evidence they would like to understand, clarify, and then discuss with other members of the tribunal. On the other hand, lay judges may try to avoid discussing issues they were not clear about in order to avoid embarrassment.

The question asked of professional judges was: "Lay judges are more likely to participate in the deliberation actively when the evidence is complex. Do you agree with this statement?" The corresponding question asked of lay judges was worded very similarly: "You are more likely to participate in the delib-eration actively when the evidence is complex (difficult to understand). Do you agree with this statement?"[40] The majority within virtually each group of

---

[39]The opinion of lay judges from the District Court of Križevci was substantially, but not statistically significantly, different from the opinions of several other groups — professional judges from the District Court of Zagreb (a difference of 24%), professional judges from district courts in the Bjelovar Region (a difference of 19%), professional judges from regional courts (a difference of 24%), and lay judges from the District Court of Zagreb (a difference of 21%).

[40]The offered answers were "strongly agree" through "strongly disagree" on a five-point

respondents — both professional judges (51% of all professional judges, 56% of professional judges from the District Court of Zagreb, and 52% of professional judges from district courts in the Bjelovar Region)[41] and lay judges (87% of all lay judges, 88% of lay judges from the District Court of Zagreb, 91% of lay judges from the District Court of Križevci, 86% of lay judges from the Regional Court of Zagreb, and 79% of lay judges from the Regional Court of Bjelovar) — thought that the complexity of evidence had influenced lay judges' activity during deliberation (Table 8.13; χ^2=85.53, $d.f.$=4, Phi=.535, $p < .001$).[42] Although the majority of professional judges from district courts and the majority of all lay judges said that the frequency of lay judges' comments and the complexity of evidence were related, professional judges seemed more likely to assert that there was no change in lay judges' behavior than lay judges were; specifically, 44% of professional judges and less than 11% of lay judges (9% of lay judges from district courts and 19% of lay judges from regional courts) said that there was no connection between lay judges' activity during deliberation and the complexity of evidence in the case.

In light of these preliminary results, it was by no means surprising that the differences in opinion by the type of court were significant for professional judges (χ^2=6.90, $d.f.$=2, Phi=.301, $p < .05$), but not for lay judges (χ^2=4.65, $d.f.$=2, Phi=.144, $p > .05$, n.s.). Furthermore, there were no significant regional differences when the answers by all lay judges and professional judges from district courts in the same region were merged (χ^2=0.10, $d.f.$=2, Phi=.019, $p > .05$, n.s.).

---

scale. In addition, respondents could also select "lay judges do not actively participate at all."

[41] The only exception were professional judges from regional courts, the majority of whom (54%) believed that the complexity of evidence did not have an impact on lay judges' activity during deliberation.

[42] The answers "strongly agree" and "agree" were merged, as were "strongly disagree" and "disagree," while the answer "lay judges do not actively participate at all" was omitted from further analysis. All professional judges were pooled, as were all lay judges from district courts and all lay judges from regional courts.

Table 8.13: Active participation in deliberation and complexity of evidence.[a]

	Prof. j. Dist. C. ZG	Prof. j. Dist. C. BJ	Prof. j. Reg. C.	Lay j. Dist. C. ZG	Lay j. Dist. C. KŽ	Lay j. Reg. C. ZG	Lay j. Reg. C. BJ	Prof. j. All	Lay j. All
strongly agree	3.7%	6.9%	12.5%	35.2%	37.7%	33.3%	27.3%	7.5%	34.5%
agree	11.1%	17.2%	25.0%	45.9%	47.2%	42.9%	45.5%	17.5%	45.9%
no difference	37.0%	41.4%	54.2%	11.5%	0.0%	14.3%	21.2%	43.8%	10.5%
disagree	40.7%	13.8%	8.3%	6.6%	5.7%	9.5%	6.1%	21.3%	6.6%
strongly disagree	0.0%	13.8%	0.0%	0.0%	0.0%	0.0%	0.0%	5.0%	0.0%
LJs do not participate actively at all	7.4%	6.9%	0.0%	0.8%	9.4%	0.0%	0.0%	5.0%	2.6%
N	27	29	24	122	53	21	33	80	229

[a]Question wording differed for professional judges and lay judges: **professional judges:** "Lay judges are more likely to participate in the deliberation actively when the evidence is complex. Do you agree with this statement?"; **lay judges:** "You are more likely to participate in the deliberation actively when the evidence in the case is complex (difficult to understand). Do you agree with this statement?"

Topics of Comments During Deliberation

As discussed earlier, critics of lay participation often argue that lay judges emphasize subjective elements (e.g., personality, appearance, credentials) when evaluating evidence and making decisions, while professional judges focus on objective elements (e.g., the content of the testimony and the relationship between the testimony and other evidence). Consistent with such arguments, observations of actual deliberations by mixed tribunals, conducted by law clerks in Poland, suggested that lay judges tended to consider the nature of the offense as less important than the personal circumstances of the defendant and the defendant's subjective fault (Pomorski, 1975, p. 206). The expectation was thus that the focus of lay judges' and professional judges' comments will be different: lay judges will tend to discuss subjective aspects more frequently than they discuss objective aspects, while the opposite will be true of professional judges.

To test this hypothesis, two questions were asked of professional judges and lay judges. The first question was worded as follows: "During deliberation, the majority of YOUR observations and comments are focused on the following issues:" The offered answers were "content of the evidence," "contradictions in and among the evidence," "credibility of the defendant, witnesses, and expert witnesses," and "personal characteristics of the defendant, witnesses, and expert witnesses."[43] The second question was worded very similarly. The crucial difference, however, was that the second question inquired about the behavior of members of the other group. That is, the wording of the question asked of professional judges contained "LAY JUDGES'" instead of "YOUR" and the wording of the question asked of lay judges contained "PROFESSIONAL JUDGES'" instead of "YOUR." The offered answers were the same as those offered for the first question.

The answers "content of the evidence" and "contradiction in and among the evidence," being more objective in nature, were recoded into "objective,"

---

[43]Respondents were also given an opportunity to add other issues they considered to be important. None of the respondents took advantage of the opportunity, however.

whereas the answers "credibility of the defendant, witnesses, and expert witnesses" and "personal characteristics of the defendant, witnesses, and expert witnesses" were recoded into "subjective."

The analysis turns to three related issues. First, how closely do professional judges' and lay judges' perceptions about the content of professional judges' comments match? Put differently, to what degree do professional judges and lay judges perceive the content of the comments by professional judges to be the same? Second, do the professional judges' and the lay judges' assessments of lay judges' comments differ? That is, to what degree do the professional judges' and lay judges' perceptions about the content of lay judges' comments coincide? Finally, does the perceived content of respondents' own comments match the perceived content of the comments by the other group of respondents? To address these questions, I performed three analyses: a comparison of the answers provided by lay judges and professional judges about the dominant topic of professional judges' comments, a comparison of the answers provided by lay judges and professional judges about the dominant topic of lay judges' comments, and a comparison of the answers provided by lay/professional judges about the dominant topic of their own comments and the dominant topic of the comments by their professional/lay counterparts in the tribunal.

All groups of respondents, except for lay judges from the Regional Court of Zagreb,[44] most frequently reported that *professional judges* focused on the "content of the evidence" (Table 8.14; 67% of professional judges from the District Court of Zagreb, 72% of professional judges from district courts in the Bjelovar Region, 61% of professional judges from regional courts, 57% of lay judges from the District Court of Zagreb, 44% of lay judges from the District Court of Križevci, 47% of lay judges from the Regional Court of Zagreb, and 69% of lay judges from the Regional Court of Bjelovar). The professional

---

[44]Lay judges from the Regional Court of Zagreb reported that professional judges focused on the "content of the evidence" as frequently as they reported that professional judges focused on the "credibility of the defendant, witnesses, and expert witnesses" (47% selected each answer).

judges' second most frequently selected topic of their own comments was another objective factor — "contradictions in and among the evidence." The lay judges' second choice of the topics of the comments most frequently mentioned by professional judges was "credibility of the defendant, witnesses, and expert witnesses."

In fact, a very high percentage of both professional judges and lay judges perceived that professional judges most frequently focused on the "objective" topics; eighty-six percent of professional judges and 68% of lay judges reported that professional judges focused on either "content of the evidence" or "contradictions in and among the evidence." Although it was clear that the majority of both professional judges and lay judges agreed on what topic professional judges discussed most frequently ("content of the evidence"), differences between the responses selected by professional judges and lay judges were still statistically significant (χ^2=10.55, $d.f.$=3, Phi=.189, $p < .05$).[45] Furthermore, respondents from district courts were as likely as respondents from regional courts (χ^2=1.09, $d.f.$=3, Phi=.061, $p > .05$, n.s.) and respondents from the Zagreb Region were as likely as respondents from the Bjelovar Region (χ^2=6.64, $d.f.$=3, Phi=.156, $p > .05$, n.s.) to say that the majority of professional judges' observations and comments during deliberation were focused on the content of the evidence.

When the same question about the topics of comments was asked about *lay judges'* comments, the results painted quite a different picture (Table 8.15). Professional judges and lay judges disagreed on what the most frequent subject of lay judges' comments was (χ^2=81.85, $d.f.$=3, Phi=.528, $p < .001$); while lay judges most frequently (51%) said that their own comments focused on the "content of the evidence," only 22% of professional judges said the same. On the other hand, 48% of professional judges and only 5% of lay judges said that lay judges' comments during deliberation focused on "personal characteristics of the defendant, witnesses, and expert witnesses." A more detailed

---

[45]For the purpose of this analysis, the four answers were considered separately. Respondents were grouped into two groups — professional judges and lay judges.

Table 8.14: Topics of professional judges' comments.[a]

	Prof. j. Dist. C. ZG	Prof. j. Dist. C. BJ	Prof. j. Reg. C. ZG	Lay j. Dist. C. ZG	Lay j. Dist. C. KŽ	Lay j. Reg. C. ZG	Lay j. Reg. C. BJ	Prof. j. All	Lay j. All
content	66.7%	72.4%	60.9%	56.9%	44.0%	47.4%	68.8%	67.1%	54.8%
contradictions	18.5%	17.2%	21.7%	10.3%	22.0%	0.0%	18.8%	19.0%	13.4%
credibility	14.8%	10.3%	17.4%	28.4%	28.0%	47.4%	12.5%	13.9%	27.6%
personal characteristics	0.0%	0.0%	0.0%	4.3%	6.0%	5.3%	0.0%	0.0%	4.2%
N	27	29	24	122	53	21	33	80	229

[a]Question wording differed for professional judges and lay judges: **professional judges:** "During deliberation, the majority of YOUR observations and comments are focused on the following issues:"; **lay judges:** "During deliberation, the majority of the comments made by PROFESSIONAL JUDGES are focused on the following issues:"

analysis wherein respondents were also divided by the type of court at which they served[46] yielded some additional insights (χ^2=94.15, $d.f.$=9, Phi=.566, $p < .001$); the majority of lay judges (51% of lay judges from both district courts and regional courts) reported that the majority of their own comments and observations during deliberation were focused on the "content of the evidence," while the majority of professional judges from district courts (55%) most frequently said that lay judges' comments were focused on "personal characteristics of the defendant, witnesses, and expert witnesses." The answers provided by professional judges from regional courts were equally divided among "content of the evidence," "credibility," and "personal characteristics;" they were also significantly different from the answers provided by professional judges from district courts (χ^2=10.84, $d.f.$=3, Phi=.370, $p < .05$). On the other hand, differences by the type of court were not significant for the lay judges' opinion (χ^2=1.18, $d.f.$=3, Phi=.074, $p > .05$, n.s.).

Interestingly, as was the case with the respondents' opinion about the most frequent comments made by professional judges, when professional judges and lay judges were pooled, neither the type of court (χ^2=1.16, d.f.=3, Phi=.074, $p > .05$, n.s.), nor region (χ^2=0.48, $d.f.$=3, Phi=.047, $p > .05$, n.s.) were related to the respondents' opinion about the most frequent comments made by lay judges.

The remaining piece of the puzzle is whether professional judges perceived that their most frequent observations and comments targeted the same kinds of issues as the comments made by lay judges did and, *vice versa*, whether lay judges perceived that their most frequent observations and comments targeted the same kinds of issues as the comments made by professional judges did. As it turned out, lay judges reported that their own comments did not differ significantly from those made by professional judges (χ^2=2.12, $d.f.$=1, Phi=.164, $p > .05$, n.s.) — both focused on "objective" issues. On the other hand, pro-

---

[46]That is, respondents were grouped into four groups: professional judges from district courts, professional judges from regional courts, lay judges from district courts, and lay judges from regional courts.

Table 8.15: Topics of lay judges' comments.[a]

	Prof. j. Dist. C. ZG	Prof. j. Dist. C. BJ	Prof. j. Reg. C. ZG	Lay j. Dist. C. ZG	Lay j. Dist. C. KŽ	Lay j. Reg. C. ZG	Lay j. Reg. C. BJ	Prof. j. All	Lay j. All
content	11.1%	24.1%	30.4%	52.2%	46.9%	35.0%	61.3%	21.5%	50.7%
contradictions	18.5%	20.7%	8.7%	19.1%	18.4%	20.0%	22.6%	16.5%	19.5%
credibility	7.4%	6.9%	30.4%	24.3%	26.5%	40.0%	16.1%	13.9%	25.1%
personal characteristics	63.0%	48.3%	30.4%	4.3%	8.2%	5.0%	0.0%	48.1%	4.6%
N	27	29	24	122	53	21	33	80	229

[a] Question wording differed for lay judges and professional judges: lay judges: "During deliberation, the majority of YOUR observations and comments are focused on the following issues:"; professional judges: "During deliberation, the majority of the comments made by LAY JUDGES are focused on the following issues:"

fessional judges reported that the two differed (χ^2=24.94, $d.f.$=1, Phi=.343, $p < .001$) — their own comments most frequently focused on "objective" issues while lay judges' comments most frequently focused on "subjective" issues.

Importance of Lay Judges' Comments

The frequency of lay judges' participation during deliberation and the most frequent topic of their comments may not tell the whole story. Another important aspect is the quality of lay judges' contribution, in particular the importance of their comments. There are only two groups of respondents who know what happens behind the closed doors during deliberation — professional judges and lay judges. Professional judges were asked to evaluate the importance of lay judges' comments, while lay judges were asked what opinion professional judges had about the importance of their comments.

The question asked of professional judges was: "Comments made by lay judges during deliberation are:" The corresponding question asked of lay judges was: "In your opinion, how do professional judges evaluate the comments you make during deliberation? They think your comments are:" The offered answers to both questions ranged from "very important" to "not important" on a four-point scale. Professional judges and lay judges furnished significantly different answers (Table 8.16; χ^2=42.24, $d.f.$=1, Phi= -.374, $p < .001$);[47] lay judges typically believed that professional judges would evaluate their comments more highly than professional judges actually did. While the majority of professional judges (88%) evaluated lay judges' comments as "somewhat important" or "not important," the majority of lay judges (55%) reported that professional judges would evaluate their comments as either "important" or "very important." The same discrepancy persisted when the type of court had been controlled for; the majority of professional judges from district courts (95%) evaluated lay judges' comments as "unimportant," while only approximately one-half of lay judges from district courts (52%) agreed with such an

---

[47]The answers "very important" and "important" were grouped together as "important;" "somewhat important" and "not important" were grouped together as "unimportant."

evaluation (χ^2=33.34, $d.f.$=1, Phi= -.385, $p < .001$). Similarly, the majority of professional judges from regional courts (71%) reported that the comments made by lay judges were "unimportant," while the majority of lay judges from regional courts (74%) said that professional judges evaluated their comments as "important" (χ^2=13.55, $d.f.$=1, Phi= -.420, $p < .001$).

Interestingly, statistically significant differences with respect to the type of court were also detected when the role in the criminal justice system had been controlled for. Specifically, professional judges from district courts were more likely to say that lay judges' comments were "unimportant" than professional judges from regional courts (95% $v.$ 71%, respectively; χ^2=8.71, $d.f.$=1, Phi= -.330, $p < .01$). Similarly, although the majority of lay judges shared the opinion about professional judges' estimates of the importance of their comments, lay judges from regional courts were less likely to say that professional judges evaluated their comments as "unimportant" than lay judges from district courts (26% $v.$ 52%; χ^2=10.22, $d.f.$=1, Phi= -.215, $p < .01$). It appears that these differences by the type of court were primarily due to lay judges from the Regional Court of Bjelovar, who believed more strongly than any of the three remaining groups of lay judges that professional judges would evaluate their comments as important (the corresponding percentages are 85% $v.$ 46%-55%).

Finally, region was not important for the answers by professional judges (the difference in percentages for the professional judges from the two regions was only 10% and was not statistically significant; χ^2=2.95, $d.f.$=1, Phi= -.230, $p > .05$, n.s.). On the other hand, lay judges from the Bjelovar Region were more likely to say that professional judges would evaluate their comments as "important" than their counterparts from the Zagreb Region (χ^2=8.06, $d.f.$=1, Phi= -.385, $p < .001$).[48]

In view of the apparent differences between what professional judges reported and what lay judges believed professional judges would report about

---

[48] Again, this result may have been primarily due to the responses given by lay judges from the Regional Court of Bjelovar.

Table 8.16: Professional judges' opinion on the importance of lay judges' comments.[a]

	Prof. j. Dist. C. ZG	Prof. j. Dist. C. BJ	Prof. j. Reg. C. ZG	Lay j. Dist. C. ZG	Lay j. Dist. C. KŽ	Lay j. Reg. C. ZG	Lay j. Reg. C. BJ	Prof. j. All	Lay j. All
very important	0.0%	0.0%	0.0%	15.3%	11.8%	5.0%	18.2%	0.0%	14.0%
important	0.0%	10.3%	29.2%	30.5%	43.1%	50.0%	66.7%	12.5%	40.5%
somewhat important	70.4%	65.5%	54.2%	49.2%	45.1%	35.0%	15.2%	63.7%	41.9%
not important	29.6%	24.1%	16.7%	5.1%	0.0%	10.0%	0.0%	23.8%	3.6%
N	27	29	24	122	53	21	33	80	229

[a]Question wording differed for professional judges and lay judges: **professional judges:** "Lay judges' comments made during deliberation are:", **lay judges:** "In your opinion, how do professional judges evaluate your comments made during deliberation? They think your comments are:"

the importance of lay judges' comments, it is interesting to explore whether there was a relationship between the lay judges' perceptions about the degree of courtesy with which professional judges behaved toward them and about the importance professional judges attached to lay judges' participation. Lay judges were asked to describe the behavior of professional judges toward them. The offered answers ranged on a five-point scale from "very courteous" to "very discourteous," with "indifferent" in the middle.[49] The results indicate that lay judges who perceived that they were treated with courtesy were more likely to report that professional judges would value their comments as "important" (χ^2=7.86, d.f.=1, Phi=.189, $p < .01$).

Is this conclusion true for both the lay judges who reported that they made comments "frequently" and the lay judges who reported that they made comments "infrequently?" For the lay judges who reported that they made comments "frequently," the percentages of lay judges who perceived that professional judges treated them with courtesy among the lay judges who believed that professional judges would evaluate their comments as important and among the lay judges who believed that professional judges would evaluate their comments as unimportant were similar (χ^2=1.96, d.f.=1, Phi=.129, $p > .05$, n.s.). On the other hand, those percentages differed significantly for the lay judges who reported making comments during deliberation "infrequently" (χ^2=4.31, d.f.=1, Phi=.205, $p < .05$); the lay judges who characterized the behavior of professional judges as "courteous" were at the same time more likely to report that professional judges would evaluate their comments as important than the lay judges who characterized the behavior of professional as "indifferent or discourteous."

The lay judges who perceived that professional judges would regard their comments as important were more likely to report that they made comments frequently than the lay judges who perceived that professional judges would re-

---

[49]For the purpose of statistical analysis, the answers "very courteous" and "courteous" were grouped into "courteous" and the remaining three answers were grouped into "indifferent or discourteous."

gard their comments as unimportant (χ^2=32.69, $d.f.$=1, Phi=.330, $p < .001$); while the majority of lay judges who perceived that their comments would be evaluated as important (60%) reported making comments frequently, the majority of lay judges who perceived that their comments would be evaluated as unimportant (73%) reported that they made comments infrequently. In addition, it is also important to consider the courtesy with which professional judges behaved toward lay judges. Specifically, the lay judges who said that the behavior of professional judges was courteous and that professional judges evaluated their comments as important were significantly more likely to say that they made comments frequently than the lay judges who evaluated professional judges' behavior as courteous and that professional judges evaluated their comments as unimportant (68% *v.* 38%, respectively; χ^2=17.70, $d.f.$=1, Phi=.301, $p < .001$). A similar analysis for the lay judges who evaluated the behavior of professional judges as "indifferent or discourteous" suggested that the lay judges who perceived that their comments were evaluated as important were more likely to say that they made comments frequently than the lay judges who perceived their comments as less important (71% *v.* 28%, respectively, χ^2=4.00, $d.f.$=1, Phi=.400, $p < .05$).

Why did professional judges attribute low importance to lay judges' comments? Put differently, what seemed to be the problem with lay judges' comments during deliberation? Professional judges were asked to select the problem they considered to be the most serious from the following list: "lay judges did not follow the trial carefully," "lay judges do not understand the evidence," "lay judges do not want to participate in deliberation," "lay judges do not know or understand the legal issues in the case," "other," and "there are no major problems."

Almost all professional judges (94%) reported the existence of at least some problems with lay judges' comments (Table 8.17). Professional judges typically did not blame lay judges for not following trials carefully, for their lack of interest to participate in deliberation, nor for their perceived (in)ability to understand evidence. Rather, the majority of professional judges (80% of professional judges from the District Court of Zagreb, 92% of professional judges from district courts in the Bjelovar Region, and 67% of professional judges from regional courts) attributed problems with lay judges' comments during deliberation primarily to their lack of legal knowledge ("lay judges do not know or understand the legal issues in the case"). Despite such convincing majorities, the type of court seemed to make a difference; professional judges from district courts favored "lay judges do not know or understand the legal issues in the case" more strongly than professional judges from regional courts did ($\chi^2=3.35$, $d.f.=1$, $Phi=-.220$, $p>.05$, n.s.).[50]

8.5   Voting

Deliberation ends with a verdict reached by the majority in the tribunal. In order to reach a verdict, members of the tribunal need to state their vote. In general terms, voting can be divided into voting on guilt and voting on sentence.[51]

Earlier studies on mixed tribunals (e.g., Casper and Zeisel, 1972) reported that initial disagreement on the sentencing issue was more frequent than initial disagreement on the issue of guilt. Furthermore, an analysis of disagreement in the *Grosse Strafkammer* cases, in which mixed tribunals were composed of nine members (three professional judges and six lay judges), revealed that lay judges disagreed on the issues of guilt and sentence more frequently in the cases in which professional judges disagreed among themselves (Casper and Zeisel, 1972, p. 153).

---

[50]For the purpose of this analysis, the answer "lay judges do not know or understand the legal issues in the case" was contrasted with all the other answers which indicated problems with lay judges' comments during deliberation. Although the chi-square statistic did not indicate statistical significance, I consider the difference of 20% to be substantively important. The *Phi*-value of -.220 is consistent with that interpretation.

[51]A more detailed description of these issues and the order in which the tribunal needs to decide them was provided earlier in this chapter.

Table 8.17: Problems with lay judges' comments as perceived by professional judges. [a]

	Prof. j. Dist. C. ZG	Prof. j. Dist. C. BJ	Prof. j. Reg. C.
did not follow the trial	3.7%	3.4%	4.2%
did not understand the evidence	14.8%	3.4%	16.7%
do not want to participate	0.0%	0.0%	4.2%
do not know or understand the legal issues	74.1%	82.8%	50.0%
no major problems	0.0%	3.4%	16.7%
2 answers	7.4%	3.4%	8.2%
other	0.0%	3.4%	0.0%
N	27	29	24

[a]Question: "The major problem, if any, with the comments made by lay judges during deliberation is:"

8.5.1   Disagreement

How frequently did disagreement occur and what issues did members of mixed tribunals disagree upon? This section examines the estimated frequency and perceived subject of disagreement between professional judges and lay judges during deliberation. The importance of summation given by the presiding professional judge at the beginning of deliberation is examined as a possible influence on the reported frequency of disagreement. Respondents from regional courts were also asked about the influence of disagreement among professional judges on lay judges' disagreement with professional judges, a situation that can arise only in large tribunals.

Frequency of Disagreement

Professional judges were asked about the frequency of disagreement in the following way: "According to your experience, how frequently do lay judges disagree with you during deliberation?" The companion question was asked of lay judges: "According to your experience, how frequently do you disagree with the professional judge during deliberation?" The offered answers ranged from "in almost all cases" to "never — we always agree" on a five-point scale.

Disagreements between lay judges and professional judges were not very frequent (Table 8.18); the majority of respondents, both professional judges and lay judges (96% of professional judges from district courts, 92% of professional judges from regional courts, 77% of lay judges from district courts, and 76% of lay judges from regional courts) said that lay judges disagreed with professional judges only infrequently.[52] Although the majority of respondents within each group reported that lay judges rarely disagreed with professional judges, there were differences among the opinions expressed by the four groups of respondents (χ^2=13.12, d.f.=3, Phi=.207, p < .01). Interestingly, professional judges from district courts were more likely to say that disagree-

---

[52]For the purpose of this analysis, the offered answers were grouped into "frequently" ("in almost all cases" through "in about one-half of the cases") and "infrequently" ("in less than one-half of the cases" through "never — we always agree").

ments occurred "infrequently" than lay judges from district courts (96% v. 77%; χ^2=10.45, $d.f.$=1, Phi= -.214, $p < .01$). Although the difference in the percentage of professional judges and lay judges from regional courts who reported that disagreements were "infrequent" (16%) was only slightly smaller than the corresponding difference detected at district courts (19%), the differences between the opinions expressed by professional judges and lay judges from regional courts did not reach the level of statistical significance (χ^2=2.65, $d.f.$=1, Phi= -.184, $p > .05$, n.s.).

Region did not seem to have an impact on the answers furnished by professional judges and lay judges. More than 90% of professional judges from district courts in both the Zagreb Region and the Bjelovar Region reported that disagreements occurred "infrequently" (χ^2=2.23, $d.f.$=1, Phi=.199, $p > .05$, n.s.). Similarly, lay judges from the Bjelovar Region were as likely to say that disagreements occurred infrequently as lay judges from the Zagreb Region (χ^2=5.74, $d.f.$=1, Phi=.159, $p > .05$, n.s.).

Three of the examined lay judges' demographic characteristics (gender, age, mandate) did not influence the reported frequency of disagreement (χ^2=0.23, $d.f.$=1, Phi=.032, $p > .05$, n.s. for gender; χ^2=1.37, $d.f.$=2, Phi=.078, $p > .05$, n.s. for age; χ^2=2.04, $d.f.$=2, Phi=.097, $p > .05$, n.s. for mandate). On the other hand, education and occupational prestige were significant for the reported frequency of disagreement. More educated lay judges were more likely to say that disagreement occurred infrequently than less educated lay judges (χ^2=5.57, $d.f.$=1, Phi=.158, $p < .05$). Similarly, lay judges who had more prestigious occupations were more likely to say that disagreement occurred infrequently than lay judges who had less prestigious occupations (χ^2=4.81, $d.f.$=1, Phi=.158, $p < .05$).

Casper and Zeisel (1972) reported that the frequency of disagreement among professional judges in nine-member tribunals was related to the frequency of disagreement between professional judges and lay judges, while such was not the case with smaller tribunals. In the present study, the influence of disagreement between professional judges was examined by focusing on large

Table 8.18: Frequency of disagreement.[a]

	Prof. j. Dist. C. ZG	Prof. j. Dist. C. BJ	Prof. j. Reg. C.	Lay j. Dist. C. ZG	Lay j. Dist. C. KŽ	Lay j. Reg. C. ZG	Lay j. Reg. C. BJ	Prof. j. All	Lay j. All
in all cases	3.7%	0.0%	4.2%	19.0%	9.8%	23.8%	12.1%	2.5%	16.4%
in more than one-half	3.7%	0.0%	4.2%	5.0%	2.0%	9.5%	0.0%	2.5%	4.0%
in one-half	0.0%	0.0%	0.0%	3.3%	0.0%	0.0%	6.1%	0.0%	2.7%
in less than one-half	0.0%	3.4%	8.3%	10.7%	3.9%	4.8%	0.0%	3.8%	7.1%
in a few cases	81.5%	72.4%	66.7%	33.9%	43.1%	47.6%	45.5%	73.8%	38.9%
never	11.1%	24.1%	16.7%	28.1%	41.2%	14.3%	36.4%	17.5%	31.0%
N	27	29	24	122	53	21	33	80	229

[a]Question wording differed for professional judges and lay judges: **professional judges:** "According to your experience, how frequently do lay judges disagree with you during deliberation?"; **lay judges:** "According to your experience, how frequently do you disagree with professional judges during deliberation?"

mixed tribunals. Professional judges and lay judges from regional courts were asked to compare the frequency of lay judges' disagreement in the cases in which the two professional judges agreed with the frequency of lay judges' disagreement that prevailed in the cases in which the two professional judges disagreed.[53]

Only 30% of professional judges and less than 10% of lay judges said that lay judges would be more likely to disagree when the two professional judges disagreed. Although most respondents in both groups (i.e., professional judges from regional courts and lay judges from regional courts) said that lay judges would not be more likely to disagree in such cases, it turned out that their answers were significantly different (χ^2=16.85, $d.f.$=2, Phi=.484, $p < .001$);[54] while the majority of lay judges (71%) said that they tended to disagree less frequently when there was disagreement between professional judges, approximately one-half of professional judges (50%) reported that the frequency of lay judges' disagreement with professional judges would not be affected by more frequent disagreement between the two professional judges.

It appears that lay judges found the atmosphere in which the two professional judges did not agree to be disturbing rather than stimulating: if two experts on law — persons with systematic training and ample practice in solving legal problems — understand a particular issue differently, then the problem must be very complicated, probably too complicated for lay persons to discuss. The usual *caveat* applies, however — this study examines perceptions; the results might be different if real disagreements were observed and compared. Overall, the effect of disagreement between professional judges was

---

[53]The question was worded as follows: "Compare the cases in which the two professional judges agree with the case in which the two professional judges disagree. According to your experience, in the cases in which the two professional judges disagree, lay judges will disagree, either among themselves, or with one or both professional judges:" The offered answers ranged on a five-point scale from "much more frequently" to "much less frequently."

[54]Lay judges from regional courts were merged into one group and their answers compared to the answers provided by professional judges from regional courts. The answers "much more frequently" and "more frequently" were merged, as were "less frequently" and "much less frequently," while the answer "equally frequently" remained as the third category in the analysis.

considerably weaker than the one reported by Casper and Zeisel (1972) for nine-member tribunals and was, at the same time, consistent with Casper and Zeisel's (1972) results for smaller tribunals (with fewer than nine members).

Subject of Disagreement

Determination of guilt requires knowledge and understanding of the complex concept of criminal responsibility, while determining the sentence allows more flexibility for the introduction of community values and for related negotiations among the members of the tribunal. The *Criminal Code* allowed for a more subjective input during the sentencing stage; following the principle of legality, the *Code* provided for each crime the minimum and the maximum sanction (or a range of sanctions), while the rules regulating the individualization of punishment (Article 41 of the *Criminal Code of the Socialist Federative Republic of Yugoslavia*, 1976) provided examples of factors to be considered in order to achieve the purpose of punishment. These factors included the degree of criminal culpability, motives, severity of the wrongdoing, circumstances surrounding the offense, prior life of the defendant (including prior criminal record), the defendant's personal circumstances, and the defendant's behavior upon committing the crime.[55] Some of these factors (e.g., motives, circumstances surrounding the offense, the defendant's personal circumstances) are more subjective in nature and are thus more likely to create a suitable outlet for discussions in which lay judges can take an active part.

Results of previous studies show that sentencing was the area where the tribunal spent more time (Casper and Zeisel, 1972) and where the influence of lay judges was stronger (Kubicki and Zawadzki, 1970). Kubicki and Zawadzki (1970) stated that the Polish study supported their hypothesis that sentencing was the area in which the influence of lay judges was more potent and the differences in opinion were most frequent. Borucka-Arctowa (1976, p. 291) pinpointed the elements lay judges bring into the deliberation room:

---

[55]Similar rules are provided in Article 37 of the *Basic Criminal Code of the Republic of Croatia* (1993) and Article 56 of the *Criminal Code* (1998).

They represent attitudes widespread among the public, stressing personal traits and circumstances of the offender, more than the professional judges, they tend to act on the basis of regard for special prevention of future misconduct of the offender, rather than with strict regard for general directives of current penal policy. Their attitudes may well contribute toward the individualization of punishment.

Professional judges and lay judges in this study were asked about the dominant topic of disagreement. The following question was asked of professional judges: "If and when disagreements occur, lay judges are more likely to disagree with you on the decisions concerning:" The corresponding question asked of lay judges was: "If and when disagreements occur, you are more likely to disagree with the professional judge on the decisions concerning:" The offered answers were: "guilt," "sentence," and "equally guilt and sentence." The results showed that professional judges and lay judges did not share the perceptions about the dominant topic of disagreement (Table 8.19; χ^2=21.44, $d.f.$=4, Phi=.270, $p < .01$);[56] professional judges most frequently (49%) said that disagreements about sentencing issues were the more likely ones, while lay judges most frequently reported that they were equally likely to disagree with professional judges on guilt and sentence (54% for three groups of lay judges and 50% for lay judges from regional courts in the Bjelovar Region).

Summation and Frequency of Disagreement

Lay judges are present during the entire trial and they listen to all the testimonies and examine all the evidence in the case. In fact, they may take an active role in this process. However, this is not the only source of information

---

[56]For the purpose of this analysis, the offered answers were not recoded, while the respondents were merged into larger groups: all professional judges from district courts and regional courts were merged into one group, as were most of the groups of lay judges. The exception were lay judges from regional courts in the Bjelovar Region, whose answers were quite different from the answers provided by the other three groups of lay judges; they were excluded from the group of all lay judges and were instead treated as a separate group of respondents.

Table 8.19: Topic of disagreement.[a]

	Prof. j. Dist. C. ZG	Prof. j. Dist. C. BJ	Prof. j. Reg. C. ZG	Lay j. Dist. C. ZG	Lay j. Dist. C. KŽ	Lay j. Reg. C. ZG	Lay j. Reg. C. BJ	Prof. j. All	Lay j. All
guilt	29.6%	6.9%	17.6%	26.1%	5.9%	9.5%	0.0%	17.7%	15.8%
sentence	48.1%	51.7%	47.8%	25.2%	25.5%	38.1%	50.0%	49.4%	39.2%
equally	22.2%	41.4%	34.8%	48.6%	68.6%	52.4%	50.0%	32.9%	54.0%
N	27	29	24	122	53	21	33	80	229

[a]Question: "If and when disagreements occur, lay judges/you are more likely to disagree with you/professional judges on the decisions concerning:"

for lay judges; they can also learn about the evidence in the case through the summation of the evidence (given by the presiding professional judge). The results showed that familiarizing lay judges with the evidence was regarded as the major purpose of summation by professional judges and lay judges from district courts, and was regarded to be among the most important purposes by respondents from regional courts. Professional judges did not necessarily just present the evidence; rather, they may have at the same time presented their views about the critical evaluation of that evidence, about the case, and about the defendant. That effort could have in turn resulted in fewer disagreements with lay judges. Therefore, the expectation was that there would be fewer disagreements in the cases in which summation was given than in the cases in which summation was not given.

The question asked of professional judges was: "In your opinion, are lay judges more likely to disagree with you during deliberation when summation is not given than when it is given?" The corresponding question asked of lay judges was: "In your opinion, are you more likely to disagree with professional judges during deliberation when summation is not given than when it is given?"[57] The majority of both professional judges and lay judges agreed that the perceived frequency of summation and the estimated frequency of lay judges' disagreement were related (53% of professional judges from district courts, 71% of professional judges from regional courts, 71% of lay judges from district courts, and 63% of lay judges from regional courts; $\chi^2=7.52$, $d.f.=6$, $Phi=.157$, $p > .05$, n.s.). Among the respondents who reported that summation and disagreement were related, the majority said that disagreement was more frequent when summation was not given than when it was given; more than 70% of the respondents within each of the four groups who reported that summation had an impact on the frequency of disagreement argued that the relationship was negative (80% of professional judges from district courts, 76% of professional judges from regional courts, 75% of lay judges from district courts, and 71% of lay judges from regional courts).

---

[57]The offered answers were "yes," "no," and "no difference."

Outvoting by Lay Judges

The purpose of deliberation is to provide for a discussion of important issues. Initial disagreements may or may not be resolved during that discussion. Members of mixed tribunals do not need to reach an agreement on all of the issues because the law provides that the decision is legally valid even if it is based on the majority vote. If disagreements are not resolved during the deliberation process, the majority verdict will be reached and those who disagree with it (and are thus outvoted) can enter their *votum separatum.*

Research studies show that the frequency with which lay judges outvote professional judges is low. Kubicki and Zawadzki (1970) reported that outvoting took place in only 6.3% of all the cases observed in the Polish study. Similarly, Casper and Zeisel (1972) reported that lay judges outvoted the professional judge in very few of the instances in which lay judges disagreed on the issue of guilt. The situation was somewhat different with sentencing issues; lay judges prevailed in 22.0% of the disagreements related to sentencing.

Professional judges in this study were asked to report the frequency with which they had been outvoted by lay judges. Analogously, lay judges were asked to report the frequency with which they outvoted professional judges.[58] Although it was possible for lay judges to outvote professional judges in both large and small tribunals (because they outnumber professional judges in both tribunals), the results showed that, as predicted, lay judges did not outvote professional judges very often (Table 8.20). In fact, less than 15% of professional judges and lay judges in each group reported that the frequency with which lay judges outvoted professional judges was higher than "in a few cases." In that sense, the opinion expressed by lay judges and professional judges was similar; the majority of respondents within each group (more than 85%) reported either that they had *never* been outvoted by lay judges/outvoted professional judges or that this occurred *in only a few cases.* However, some of

---

[58]The offered answers ranged from "very frequently" through "never" on a six-point scale.

the groups were more likely to say that lay judges *never* outvoted professional judges; (χ^2=12.25, $d.f.$=6, Phi=.200, $p > .05$, n.s.).[59]

Lay judges from regional courts perceived that they tended to outvote professional judges more frequently than lay judges from district courts (39.6% *v.* 56.4%, respectively; χ^2=4.57, $d.f.$=1, Phi= -.143, $p < .05$). Similarly, professional judges from regional courts perceived that lay judges tended to outvote them more frequently than professional judges from district courts did (41.7% *v.* 58.9%, respectively; χ^2=2.01, $d.f.$=1, Phi= -.159, $p > .05$, n.s.).[60]

8.5.2 Leniency

As discussed in Chapter 1, lay participants in mixed tribunals may perform a number of functions. For example, they may take part in individualizing the sanction by focusing on the defendant's personal factors. Indeed, the Polish study suggested that lay judges tended to consider official criminal policy or the nature of the offense as less important than the personal circumstances of the defendant and the defendant's subjective guilt (Pomorski, 1975, p. 206). Professional judges, on the other hand, are state officials and are oriented

---

[59]For the purpose of statistical analysis, the answer "never" was contrasted with "at least sometimes" (all other answers grouped together). Although the chi-square analysis did not yield statistically significant differences, some of the differences between the pairs were above 20% and I consider them to be substantively important. In particular, professional judges from the District Court of Zagreb were 22% more likely than professional judges from district courts in the Bjelovar Region, 28% more likely than professional judges from regional courts, 32% more likely than lay judges from the Regional Court of Zagreb, and 29% more likely than lay judges from the Regional Court of Bjelovar to report that lay judges had never outvoted them. Furthermore, professional judges from regional courts were 24% less likely to say that lay judges never outvoted professional judges than lay judges from the District Court of Križevci. Finally, lay judges from the District Court of Križevci were 28% less likely than lay judges from the Regional Court of Zagreb and 25% less likely than lay judges from the Regional Court of Bjelovar to say that they had outvoted professional judges.

[60]Although the difference between the answers provided by lay judges from the two types of courts was 16.8% and the difference between the answers provided by professional judges from the two types of courts was 17.2%, the former was statistically significant and the latter was not. Nevertheless, I regard both differences to be substantively important. This conclusion is supported by the respective *Phi*-values.

Table 8.20: Frequency of outvoting by lay judges.[a]

	Prof. j. Dist. C. ZG	Prof. j. Dist. C. BJ	Prof. j. Reg. C.	Lay j. Dist. C. ZG	Lay j. Dist. C. KŽ	Lay j. Reg. C. ZG	Lay j. Reg. C. BJ	Prof. j. All	Lay j. All
very frequently	0.0%	0.0%	0.0%	0.0%	1.9%	9.5%	0.0%	0.0%	1.3%
in more than one-half	0.0%	0.0%	0.0%	2.5%	0.0%	0.0%	3.1%	0.0%	1.8%
in one-half	0.0%	0.0%	0.0%	3.4%	1.9%	0.0%	0.0%	0.0%	2.2%
in less than one-half	0.0%	3.4%	0.0%	8.4%	0.0%	4.5%	0.0%	1.3%	5.0%
in a few cases	29.6%	48.3%	58.3%	33.6%	30.2%	47.6%	56.3%	45.0%	37.3%
never	70.4%	48.3%	41.7%	52.1%	66.0%	38.1%	40.6%	53.8%	52.4%
N	27	29	24	122	53	21	33	80	229

[a]Question wording differed for professional judges and lay judges: **professional judges:** "How frequently have you been outvoted by lay judges?"; **lay judges:** "In how many cases tried by mixed tribunals did you, lay judges, outvote the professional judge?"

toward following the official criminal policy; they need to strive toward consistency of punishment and to emphasize the principle of general prevention. Having both professional judges and lay judges in the same tribunal should serve as a correction that would both eliminate possible negative features of each decision-maker (routine justice by professional judges and biased justice by lay judges) and enhance positive features of joint decision-making.

Results of the Polish study (Kubicki and Zawadzki, 1970) and the German study (Casper and Zeisel, 1972) showed that, when lay judges disagreed with professional judges, lay judges were generally in favor of a more lenient sentence. However, as Borucka-Arctowa (1976, p. 290) pointed out, the degree of lay judges' leniency varies with the offense: there was a tendency by lay judges to reduce the punishment for petty economic offenses, while lay judges suggested harsher sentences for offenses against private property and offenses against socialized property of high value than professional judges did.

Professional judges and lay judges were asked a general question about harshness/leniency.[61] The opinion differed significantly across various groups of professional judges and lay judges (Tables 8.21 and 8.22; χ^2=36.01, $d.f.$=6, Phi=.352, $p < .001$);[62] while the majority of lay judges from both district courts and regional courts (70% and 63%, respectively) said that they were "equally likely" to vote for conviction as professional judges were, the majority of professional judges (61% of professional judges from district courts and 60% of professional judges from regional courts) picked answers other than "equally likely."

---

[61]The question asked of professional judges was worded as follows: "Generally speaking, do you think that you are more or less likely to vote for conviction than lay judges?" The corresponding question asked of lay judges was: "Generally speaking, do you think that you are more or less likely to vote for conviction than professional judges?" The offered answers ranged from "much more likely" to "much less likely" on a five-point scale.

[62]The offered answers were recoded into "more likely" ("much more likely" and "more likely"), "equally likely" (simply as "equally likely"), and "less likely" ("less likely" and "much less likely"). Respondents were grouped into professional judges from district courts, professional judges from regional courts, lay judges from district courts, and lay judges from regional courts.

Table 8.21: Lay judges' leniency.[a]

	Lay j. Dist. C. ZG	Lay j. Dist. C. KŽ	Lay j. Reg. C. ZG	Lay j. Reg. C. BJ	Lay j. All
much less likely	5.4%	7.7%	9.5%	3.0%	6.0%
less likely	17.8%	11.5%	23.8%	27.3%	18.4%
equally likely	67.0%	76.9%	57.1%	66.7%	68.1%
more likely	5.4%	0.0%	4.8%	3.0%	3.8%
much more likely	4.4%	3.8%	4.8%	0.0%	3.8%
N	122	53	21	33	229

[a]Question: "Generally speaking, do you think that you are more or less likely to vote for conviction than professional judges?"

There was a clear pattern among the respondents who selected answers other than "equally likely." The majority of professional judges who did not select "equally likely" said that they were more likely to vote for conviction than lay judges (Table 8.22; 52% of the professional judges from district courts who did not select "equally likely," which constituted 31% of all professional judges from district courts; 62% of the professional judges from regional courts who did not select "equally likely," which constituted 36% of all professional judges from regional courts). Consistent with this finding, the majority of lay judges from both district courts and regional courts who did not select "equally likely" said that they were less likely to vote for conviction than professional judges (Table 8.21; 74% of the lay judges from district courts who did not select "equally likely," which constituted 22% of all lay judges from district courts; 85% of the lay judges from regional courts who did not select "equally likely," which constituted 32% of all lay judges from regional courts).

Table 8.22: Professional judges' leniency.[a]

	Prof. j. Dist. C. ZG	Prof. j. Dist. C. BJ	Prof. j. Reg. C.	Prof. j. All
much more likely	0.0%	25.9%	9.1%	12.3%
more likely	12.5%	22.2%	27.3%	20.5%
equally likely	54.5%	25.9%	40.9%	39.7%
less likely	25.0%	11.1%	13.6%	16.4%
much less likely	8.3%	14.8%	9.1%	11.0%
N	27	29	24	80

[a]Question: "Generally speaking, do you think that you are more or less likely to vote for conviction than lay judges?"

Lay judges' leniency may have depended on their demographic characteristics. Previous research did not reach a consensus on the impact of *gender* on leniency. The Polish study reported that female lay judges (especially older ones) tended to be more lenient than male lay judges (Pomorski, 1975, p. 205), while the study by Casper and Zeisel (1972) indicated that female and male lay judges were equally likely to be more lenient/severe. The results of this study seem to side with those obtained by Casper and Zeisel (1972): neither female nor male lay judges reported being more lenient (χ^2=5.17, $d.f.$=2, Phi=.154, $p > .05$, n.s.).

Although both the study by Casper and Zeisel (1972) and the Polish study (Pomorski, 1975) suggested that leniency in sentencing increases with *age*, the results in this study uncovered no relationship between reported leniency and age of lay judges (χ^2=2.75, $d.f.$=4, Phi=.112, $p > .05$, n.s.). Furthermore, lay judges who were more *educated* in this study did not necessarily report being more lenient ($\chi^2=0.52$, *d.f.*=2, *Phi*=.049, $p > .05$, n.s.), as the Polish study might have suggested (Pomorski, 1975, p. 206). Similarly, neither *occupational prestige* nor the *mandate* of lay judges were important for the reported leniency of lay judges ($\chi^2=4.00$, d.f.=2, *Phi*=.135, $p > .05$, n.s. for occupation prestige; $\chi^2=8.02$, d.f.=4, *Phi*=.195, $p > .05$, n.s. for mandate).

Respondents were also asked a more specific question about lay judges' leniency in the instances in which there was disagreement.[63] The differences among the answers selected by professional judges and lay judges from different courts were statistically significant (Table 8.23; $\chi^2=40.6$, *d.f.*=12, *Phi*=.367, $p < .001$).[64] Professional judges were more homogeneous in their responses than lay judges; while each group of professional judges voiced a majority opinion (52% of professional judges from the District Court of Zagreb said that lay judges' opinion in the instances in which there was disagreement was "harsher" or "much harsher" than their own; 71% of professional judges from district courts in the Bjelovar Region and 68% of professional judges from regional courts said that lay judges' opinion in the instances in which there was disagreement was "more lenient" or "much more lenient" than their own), most categories of lay judges almost seemed to be equally likely to tell that their opinion in the instances in which there was disagreement was more lenient, harsher, or equally harsh as the opinion held by professional judges.[65]

Specifically, the breakdown of lay judges from the District Court of Zagreb was: 40% reported being "more lenient" or "much more lenient," 40% reported

---

[63]The question asked of professional judges was worded as follows: "When lay judges disagree with you, their opinion in general is:" The corresponding question asked of lay judges was: "When you disagree with the professional judge, your opinion in general is:" The offered answers ranged from "much more lenient" through "much harsher" on a five-point scale.

[64]The answers were recoded as follows: "much more lenient" and "more lenient" into "more lenient," "equally lenient" simply as "equally lenient," and "harsher" and "much harsher" into "harsher."

[65]The only exception were lay judges from the Regional Court of Bjelovar, the majority of whom (56%) reported that their opinion in the instances in which there was disagreement was "more lenient" or "much more lenient" than the opinion held by professional judges.

being "equally lenient," and 20% reported being "harsher" or "much harsher" than professional judges in the instances in which there was disagreement. The distribution was very similar for lay judges from the District Court of Križevci: 43% reported being "more lenient" or "much more lenient," 40% reported being "equally lenient," and 17% reported being "harsher" or "much harsher" than professional judges in the instances in which there was disagreement. Lay judges from the Regional Court of Zagreb featured the most uniform distribution among all four groups of lay judges (33% reported being "more lenient" or "much more lenient," 29% reported being "equally likely," and 38% reported being "harsher" or "much harsher" than professional judges in the instances in which there was disagreement), whereas lay judges from the Regional Court of Bjelovar seemed to voice a majority opinion in the direction of leniency (as many as 56% reported being "more lenient" or "much more lenient," 25% reported being "equally likely," and 19% reported being "harsher" or "much harsher" than professional judges in the instances in which there was disagreement).

When the answers by all lay judges were pooled, none of the examined demographic variables (gender, age, education, and occupational prestige), turned out to be significantly related to lay judges' leniency in the instances in which there was disagreement with professional judges ($\chi^2=0.25$, $d.f.=2$, $Phi=.033$, $p > .05$, n.s. for gender; $\chi^2=5.92$, $d.f.=6$, $Phi=.162$, $p > .05$, n.s. for age; $\chi^2=0.13$, $d.f.=2$, $Phi=.024$, $p > .05$, n.s. for education; $\chi^2=0.50$, $d.f.=2$, $Phi=.051$, $p > .05$, n.s. for occupation). The only variable that turned out to be important was mandate; although there were no important differences among novice (below one year), experienced (one to three years), and very experienced (above three years) lay judges in terms of the percentage of respondents who reported being harsher than professional judges (between 20% and 26%), there were important differences in the percentage of lay judges who reported that they were more lenient than or equally lenient as professional judges. Novice lay judges reported much more frequently (55%) that their severity was very similar to that of professional judges than either expe-

Table 8.23: Lay judges' leniency in disagreement.[a]

	Prof. j. Dist. C. ZG	Prof. j. Dist. C. BJ	Prof. j. Reg. C.	Lay j. Dist. C. ZG	Lay j. Dist. C. KŽ	Lay j. Reg. C. ZG	Lay j. Reg. C. BJ	Prof. j. All	Lay j. All
much more lenient	7.4%	25.0%	18.2%	7.4%	19.6%	0.0%	6.3%	16.9%	9.3%
more lenient	14.8%	46.4%	50.0%	33.1%	23.5%	33.3%	50.0%	36.4%	33.3%
equally lenient	25.9%	0.0%	18.2%	39.7%	39.2%	28.6%	25.0%	14.3%	36.4%
harsher	48.1%	28.6%	13.6%	19.8%	17.6%	38.1%	18.8%	31.2%	20.9%
much harsher	3.7%	0.0%	0.0%	0.0%	0.0%	0.0%	0.0%	1.3%	0.0%
N	27	29	24	122	53	21	33	80	229

[a]Question wording differed for professional judges and lay judges: **professional judges:** "When lay judges disagree with you, their opinion in general is:"; **lay judges:** "When you disagree with professional judges, your opinion in general is:"

rienced lay judges (34%) or very experienced lay judges (31%). On the other hand, more experienced lay judges (46% for experienced and 49% for very experienced lay judges) were more likely to say that their opinion in disagreement was more lenient than that of professional judges than novice lay judges were (19%; $\chi^2=9.44$, *d.f.*=4, *Phi*=.210, $p > .05$, n.s.).[66] The opinion held by more experienced lay judges (which was very similar for experienced lay judges and for very experienced lay judges) was based on a larger number of trials and deliberations than the opinion held by novice lay judges. These results would suggest that, as they become more experienced, lay judges become increasingly aware of professional judges' opinion and learn that it is very likely that professional judges' opinion about the severity of punishment differs from their own.

8.6 Conclusion

This chapter explored the interaction of professional judges and lay judges during the next stage of the criminal process — deliberation and voting. The topics of central interest were lay judges' competence to understand and evaluate evidence, lay judges' competence to understand legal issues, the frequency of lay judges' participation, and the importance of lay judges' participation.

As described in Chapter 1, lay participants have been criticized for not being competent to understand and evaluate evidence and for not being able to understand legal issues. Compared to professional judges, lay judges are disadvantaged both in the process of understanding of legal issues and in the process of understanding and evaluation of evidence because they do not know how to "think like lawyers" (Mudd, 1983). They have neither legal knowledge nor systematic training and experience in resolving legal issues, which are the two specific status categories important for the performance of the group task (legal decision-making). The implications of this disadvantaged position have

---

[66]Despite only marginal statistical significance ($p = .051$), I considered these differences, which amounted to at least 20%, to be substantively important. The *Phi*-value is consistent with this interpretation.

a direct impact, according to the theoretical developments in Chapter 5, on the frequency and importance of lay judges' contributions.

The theory predicts that professional judges would evaluate lay judges' *ability to understand evidence* as lower than their own. It seems that professional judges, as well as state attorneys and attorneys, indeed furnished such an evaluation. The differences in opinion between lawyers from the two types of courts/offices were substantial. The factors that likely contributed to these differences include the seriousness of the cases tried, the increased tribunal size (three *v.* five members), and a different composition of the tribunal (an additional professional judge in the tribunal). Not surprisingly, the lay judges' estimates of their own ability to understand evidence were higher than those provided by professional judges.

Interestingly, the important factor that both lay judges and professional judges most frequently focused on while evaluating evidence was how the whole statement was incorporated into the network of other evidence in the case. This result is by no means surprising; it is in accordance with the *story model* (Pennington and Hastie, 1993). Pennington and Hastie conducted a series of studies and concluded that jurors organized the evidence presented at the trial into a story that contained causal and intentional relations among various pieces of evidence (Pennington and Hastie, 1993). They also found that jurors who chose different verdicts had constructed different stories around the same pieces of evidence.[67]

Lay judges with higher educational levels (a characteristic that would in theory help lay judges achieve at least somewhat higher status) would likely have a greater general ability to solve problems, but would still lack legal knowledge and training and experience in legal decision-making. Therefore, the status of more educated lay judges would tend to be somewhat higher

---

[67]Pennington and Hastie (1993, p. 217) further wrote that, "the essence of this theory [the story model] is that the construction of a causal model of events, a story, is central in understanding the evidence and its implications. Other processes, such as understanding the judge's instructions and matching the story with a decision option are necessary to turn the juror's understanding of the evidence into a decision."

than that of less educated lay judges, but would still be lower than that of professional judges. The results show that education was not related to the lay judges' own perceptions of their ability to evaluate evidence.

The second issue concerns lay judges' *ability to understand legal issues*. While lay judges reported that they understood legal issues at least frequently, lawyers, consistent with the typical criticism of lay participation (lay judges are not able to understand the legal issues in the case), perceived that lay judges understood legal issues very rarely. Thus, it seems that lawyers attached considerable importance to the principal characteristics that differentiate between professional judges and lay judges — legal education and systematic training and experience in legal decision-making.

The third issue is the *frequency of* lay judges' *participation* during deliberation. Several aspects were looked into: perceptions of the frequency of lay judges' comments during deliberation, perceptions of the frequency of disagreement between lay judges and professional judges, and perceptions of the frequency with which lay judges outvoted professional judges.[68]

In terms of the frequency of lay judges' comments during deliberation, the results of this study suggest that professional judges did not perceive lay judges as very active during deliberation, while lay judges reported being much more active than professional judges gave them credit for. These differences were more pronounced at district courts (at which tribunals are smaller, of a different composition, and cases are less serious) than at regional courts. It may be that perceptions about the frequency of activity in larger tribunals (at regional courts), gathered through a larger number of participants voicing their opinion and a possibly intense participation by another professional judge,

---

[68]Perceptions about the frequency of professional judges' comments were not measured; since presiding professional judges are placed in the position of leadership by the law (they are assigned to coordinate the deliberation and are responsible for ensuring that all the relevant issues in the case be discussed thoroughly), and since they possess higher status in the tribunal, it is inevitable that they participated more frequently than other tribunal members.

contributed toward the overall perception that the activity in the tribunal in general and lay judges' contribution in particular are more intense.

Another measure of lay judges' contribution to deliberation was the frequency of disagreements between lay judges and professional judges. Professional judges and lay judges agreed that disagreements were not very frequent; they occurred in "a few cases" or "never." Lay judges who were more educated were more likely to say that they rarely disagreed with professional judges than lay judges who were less educated. In addition, lay judges who had more prestigious occupations were more likely to say that the frequency of disagreement with professional judges was low than lay judges who had less prestigious occupations.

The third aspect of the perceptions about lay judges' participation during deliberation is the perceived frequency with which lay judges outvoted professional judges. Because lay judges are perceived to have lower status in the tribunal, and because they tended to disagree with professional judges rarely, the expectation was that they would very rarely, if ever, have outvoted professional judges. The results strongly supported this hypothesis; lay judges were indeed perceived both by professional judges and by lay judges to influence the final decision by outvoting professional judges very rarely.

Finally, the fourth issue studied in this chapter was the *importance of* lay judges' *participation*. Both low- and high-status members were asked to evaluate how important professional judges perceived lay judges' comments to be. Lay judges thought that professional judges had a better opinion about their comments than professional judges reportedly did. It is quite possible that the lay judges' conclusion was based on verbal and nonverbal cues given by professional judges. Indeed, when lay judges perceived that professional judges had treated them with dignity and courtesy, they were more likely to feel that their comments were important. Furthermore, while professional judges claimed, in accordance with typical criticisms of lay participation, that lay judges focused primarily on subjective issues during deliberation (credibility and personal characteristics of defendant[s], witnesses, and expert witnesses in the case), lay judges argued that their own comments focused on more objective issues (content of the evidence and the relationship with other evidence in the case).

In summary, in accordance with theoretical developments outlined in Chapter 5, professional judges evaluated lay judges' comments as being neither very frequent nor important. Lay judges, whose frequency and importance of comments were inquired about, were likely to report that they participated more frequently and that their comments were perceived as more important than professional judges gave them credit for. Overall, although professional judges and lay judges disagreed about the frequency, importance, and content of lay judges' comments, they wholeheartedly agreed that disagreements between professional judges and lay judges were rare and that lay judges outvoted professional judges very rarely.

Chapter 9

General Opinions about Mixed Tribunals

The previous two chapters analyzed the perceptions of professional judges, lay judges, state attorneys, and attorneys about the work of mixed tribunals during trial and deliberation. This chapter is focused on a more global picture the respondents projected about mixed tribunals and the relationship between some of the specific issues related to the work of mixed tribunals and the respondents' overall opinion about mixed tribunals.

General opinions about mixed tribunals are probably not only a consequence of direct experience with mixed tribunals but also of what is learned through socialization into the legal culture. The expectation is, for example, that the respondents who were lawyers evaluated mixed tribunals on the basis of not only their personal experience but also on the basis of what they were taught in law school and what they have learned while being socialized into the legal profession (either as apprentices or in their current position).

The analysis starts with the determination of the respondents' general opinion about mixed tribunals. The possible influence of various factors (e.g., the respondents' role in the criminal justice system, the type of court, region, and the respondents' demographic characteristics) is discussed. Furthermore, it is hypothesized that general opinion is related to the respondents' opinions on other, more specific issues.

The reasons for the expressed opinion are discussed from the perspective of positive and negative features of trials by mixed tribunals. As a result of their general opinion, respondents suggested what the future of mixed tribunals should be and how mixed tribunals, if necessary, could be improved. Finally, mixed tribunals are compared with other forms of legal decision-making (a professional judge alone, professional tribunals, and the jury) is made.

9.1 General Opinion

According to Lapaine (1986), Croatian lawyers extended theoretical support to the system of mixed tribunals, but they were aware that the system had experienced many problems in practice. Kovačević (1973) emphasized that these problems reduced the quality of the system, so that the lay element in mixed tribunals had only a formal value, but not a substantial impact. However, while most authors who wrote about this topic (Bayer, 1955; Kovačević, 1973; Krapac, 1977; Bajić-Petrović, 1985a, 1985b; Lapaine, 1986a) discussed negative characteristics of trials by mixed tribunals, they all agreed that the political function of mixed tribunals *per se* was sufficiently important to justify the retention of the system of mixed tribunals.

This section starts with the examination of the respondents' general opinion and the way it was influenced by group factors and individual factors. Furthermore, the relationship between general opinion and the opinions about specific issues (raised earlier) is discussed.

Respondents were asked to provide their overall opinion about the system of mixed tribunals.[1] The results showed that the majority of respondents in all groups had a *favorable opinion* about mixed tribunals[2] (52% of professional judges from district courts in the Bjelovar Region, 65% of professional judges

---

[1] The question was worded as follows: "What is your view of the system of mixed tribunals in general?" The offered answers ranged from "very favorable" to "very unfavorable" on a six-point scale.

[2] The answers "very favorable" through "somewhat favorable" were merged into "favorable," while "somewhat unfavorable" through "very unfavorable" were merged into "unfavorable."

from regional courts, 70% of professional judges from the Supreme Court, 76% of lay judges from the District Court of Zagreb, 92% of lay judges from the District Court of Križevci, 100% of lay judges from regional courts, 62% of attorneys from the Bjelovar Region, 63% of district state attorneys from the Zagreb Region, 79% of district state attorneys from the Bjelovar Region, and 94% of regional state attorneys; Table 9.1); the exceptions were professional judges from the District Court of Zagreb and attorneys from the Zagreb Region, the majority of whom (63% and 53%, respectively) expressed an overall negative opinion about mixed tribunals (χ^2=83.85, $d.f.$=12, Phi = .424, $p < .001$).[3] The most frequent opinion about mixed tribunals among all groups of respondents was "somewhat favorable."

A few respondents added several sentences in the space provided for additional remarks and/or tried to explain their opinion. Two attorneys from Zagreb depicted their general opinions very vividly. One of them remarked:[4]

Mladen Kerstner, a Croatian author, wrote:

'Drašek: Tetec, what are lay judges?

Tetec: They are two heads of cabbage behind which
             is hidden the professional judge.'

The other attorney wrote that an ex-judge called lay judges "left and right pest," with which opinion he agreed. Comments provided by other respondents

---

[3]For the purpose of chi-square analysis, the answers "very favorable" through "somewhat favorable" were merged, as were "somewhat unfavorable" through "very unfavorable." When the analysis contrasting the opinion of those two groups with the opinions held by respondents from all the other groups was performed, differences were statistically significant; while 56% of the respondents from these two groups reported having a negative opinion about the system of mixed tribunals, 79% of the respondents from the other groups reported having a positive opinion about the system of mixed tribunals; χ^2=45.45, $d.f.$=1, $Phi = -.312, p < .001$.

[4]In Croatian:

Mladen Kerstner, hrvatski pisac, napisao je:
'Drašek: Tetec, kaj su to suci porotniki?
Tetec: To su dve glavice zelja iza kojih se skriva sodec!'

Table 9.1: General opinion about mixed tribunals.[a]

	Prof. j. Dist. C. ZG	Prof. j. Dist. C. BJ	Prof. j. Reg. C.	Prof. j. Supr. C.	Dist. State a. ZG	Dist. State a. BJ	Reg. State a.	Att. ZG	Att. BJ
very favorable	0.0%	3.4%	0.0%	0.0%	0.0%	5.3%	0.0%	2.7%	7.7%
favorable	3.7%	6.9%	8.3%	0.0%	15.8%	10.5%	0.0%	2.7%	3.8%
somewhat favorable	33.3%	41.4%	56.5%	70.0%	47.4%	63.2%	94.1%	41.1%	50.0%
somewhat unfavorable	29.6%	27.6%	30.4%	20.0%	10.5%	15.8%	5.9%	30.1%	15.4%
unfavorable	25.9%	17.2%	4.3%	10.0%	10.5%	0.0%	0.0%	11.0%	11.5%
very unfavorable	7.4%	3.4%	0.0%	0.0%	15.8%	5.3%	0.0%	12.3%	11.5%
N	27	29	24	10	20	20	18	76	26

[a]Question: "What is your view of the system of mixed tribunals in general?"

Table 9.1: Continued.

	Lay j. Dist. C. ZG	Lay j. Dist. C. KŽ	Lay j. Reg. C. ZG	Lay j. Reg. C. BJ	Prof j. All	State a. All R & D	Att. ZG & BJ	Lay j. All R & D
very favorable	15.3%	9.6%	19.0%	36.4%	1.2%	1.8%	4.0%	17.4%
favorable	16.1%	26.9%	19.0%	21.2%	5.5%	9.1%	3.0%	19.6%
somewhat favorable	44.9%	55.8%	61.9%	42.2%	46.2%	67.3%	43.4%	48.6%
somewhat unfavorable	18.6%	1.9%	0.0%	0.0%	28.1%	10.9%	26.3%	10.3%
unfavorable	4.2%	3.8%	0.0%	0.0%	15.6%	3.6%	11.1%	3.1%
very unfavorable	0.8%	1.9%	0.0%	0.0%	3.3%	7.3%	12.1%	0.9%
N	122	53	21	33	90	58	102	229

were less colorful, but more focused on the reasons underlying their responses. For example, a professional judge from the District Court of Zagreb wrote: "Mixed tribunals are necessary for the democratization of the society, but they are dangerous for the quality of the criminal justice system."

Respondents who discussed the reasons for their general opinion mostly focused on the issue of lay judges' competence to understand legal issues and to evaluate evidence. An attorney from the Bjelovar Region wrote:

> Everything boils down to 2 lay judges who do not possess legal knowledge at all and do not have the ability to evaluate evidence, but have the power to outvote the professional judge; therefore, they threaten both legitimacy and legal certainty, which, fortunately, does not happen too frequently.

One of the district state attorneys from Zagreb was more concerned about lay judges' competence in general. He wrote:

> The professional judge (educated, well paid, interested, ambitious, serious, conscientious, unburdened ...) is the only one competent to decide the future of a criminal case. In mixed tribunals, the professional judge *de facto* tries the cases, signs, and is responsible for the verdicts. Current lay judges either do not influence the decision at all or influence the decision insignificantly. There is no use keeping this current system.

One professional judge had an opportunity to work both in mixed tribunals (he decided more than 200 cases in mixed tribunals) and in professional tribunals, due to the fact that he had been working at the Military Court at the time this study was conducted:

> For the past year I have been working at the Military Court, where the tribunals are composed of professional judges. Comparing the work of these tribunals and mixed tribunals, I find it much easier to work in a tribunal composed of professional judges, because the possibility of mistakes is infinitely smaller, since the tribunal members participate actively both in fact-finding and in deciding legal issues.

In order to provide a more detailed analysis of general opinion about mixed tribunals, several factors are examined. These include, on the group level, the role in the criminal justice system (professional judges, lay judges, state attorneys, attorneys), the type of court/office (district, regional; not applicable to attorneys), and region (Zagreb, Bjelovar), and, on the individual level, age, gender, education (for lay judges), mandate (for lay judges), and occupation (for lay judges).

9.1.1 Group Factors

The **role in the criminal justice system** is an important factor affecting opinion about mixed tribunals (χ^2=59.54, $d.f.$=3, Phi = .357, $p < .001$); lay judges in this study tended to have a much more positive opinion about the system of mixed tribunals (86% of lay judges) than professional judges (53%) or attorneys (51%) did. Surprisingly, state attorneys (78%) had a much better opinion than either attorneys or professional judges.

The **type of court/office** was important too; respondents from regional courts/offices had a much better opinion about the system of mixed tribunals than respondents from district courts/offices did (72% of respondents from district courts/offices and 90% of respondents from regional courts/offices reported having a positive opinion about mixed tribunals; χ^2=13.26, $d.f.$=1, Phi = −.192, $p < .001$). While attorneys were omitted from the analysis because they represent clients at both regional courts and district courts, other respondents within the same role in the criminal justice system were grouped according to the type of court/office at which they served. The analysis suggested that lay judges from regional courts were more likely to have a positive opinion about mixed tribunals than lay judges from district courts (χ^2=11.86, $d.f.$=1, Phi = −.230, $p < .001$). Similarly, professional judges and state attorneys from regional courts/offices were more likely to have a positive opinion than their counterparts from district courts/offices (χ^2=2.76,

$d.f.=1$, $Phi = -.187$, $p > .05$, n.s. for professional judges; $\chi^2=3.66$, $d.f.=1$, $Phi = -.258$, $p > .05$, n.s. for state attorneys).[5]

Professional judges and state attorneys who served at district/regional courts/offices attended the same law schools and practiced at the same type of courts/offices. Thus, differences in their opinion about mixed tribunals were at best only partially a result of different ways of being socialized into the legal profession, but were probably due to the (very) different experiences they had had with trials by mixed tribunals. It seems that regional courts foster a more positive atmosphere for trials by mixed tribunals and are thus conducive to a more positive opinion about mixed tribunals in general. As discussed in earlier chapters, the reasons that might explain such differences include larger tribunal size itself, the presence of another professional judge (who is not the presiding professional judge), and the seriousness of cases tried at regional courts.

Region itself was a powerful factor. Respondents from the Bjelovar Region had a slightly more positive opinion about mixed tribunals than respondents from the Zagreb Region; sixty-five percent of respondents from the Zagreb Region and 80% of respondents from the Bjelovar Region had a positive opinion about mixed tribunals ($\chi^2=10.85$, $d.f.=1$, $Phi = -.161$, $p < .001$).[6]

9.1.2 Individual Factors

What are the influences of age (for all respondents), gender (for all respondents), education (for lay judges), mandate (for lay judges), and occupation (for lay judges) on the respondent's general opinion about mixed tribunals? For each of these variables, the data were first compared for all respondents,

---

[5] Although the results for professional judges and state attorneys turned out not to be statistically significant, this was primarily due to the fact that samples of professional judges and state attorneys were smaller than samples of lay judges. Differences for professional judges (20%) and state attorneys (23%) were larger than those for lay judges (19%). I consider these differences to be substantively important; *Phi*-values support this conclusion.

[6] As explained in Chapter 6, professional judges from regional courts and professional judges from the Supreme Court were omitted from this analysis, as were regional state attorneys, because their answers could not have been separated by region.

regardless of their role in the criminal justice system and/or their legal education. Next, respondents were divided into groups according to their role in the criminal justice system and/or their legal education.

Female and male respondents were equally likely to say that their opinion about mixed tribunals was positive (χ^2=1.05, $d.f.$=1, Phi = $-.048$, $p >$ .05, n.s.); **gender** was not an important factor in explaining differences of opinion, regardless of whether the respondents' opinion was analyzed together or separately for each role in the criminal justice system.[7]

Age showed an interesting property: when the answers by all respondents were pooled, there was a clear pattern indicating how age and opinion about mixed tribunals were related; when the answers within each group were compared, the pattern was different or it completely disappeared. The overall pattern seems to be that, as the respondents' age increased, the opinion about mixed tribunals became more positive (51% for the youngest group; 70% for the second youngest group; 78% for the second oldest group; 87% for the oldest group of respondents; χ^2=26.84, $d.f.$=3, Phi = .240, $p < .001$).[8] However, it is important to keep in mind that not all roles in the criminal justice system were equally represented in all age groups; two-thirds of the respondents in the oldest and the second oldest group were lay judges (66% and 68%, respectively), while the percentages were roughly reversed among younger respondents. The differences by age may have been detected simply because lay judges as a group had a more positive opinion about mixed tribunals than professional judges or state attorneys did. To shed further light on the matter, separate analyses were conducted for each of the four groups (lay judges, professional judges, state attorneys, and attorneys).

---

[7]The values of chi-square tests were as follows: for professional judges χ^2=1.00, $d.f.$=1, Phi = $-.106$, $p > .05$, n.s.; for lay judges χ^2=1.24, Phi = $-.075$, $p > .05$, n.s.; for state attorneys χ^2=.042, $d.f.$=1, Phi = .021, $p > .05$, n.s.; and for attorneys χ^2=.089, $d.f.$=1, Phi = $-.040$, $p > .05$, n.s.

[8]Respondents were grouped into four age groups: "35 and below," "36-50," "51-65," and "66 and above."

Lay judges' answers showed very little variation with age ($\chi^2=2.62$, $d.f.=3$, $Phi = .108$, $p > .05$, n.s.); the range of percentages of lay judges who had a positive opinion about mixed tribunals within each of the four age groups varied from 80% to 91%. Similarly, there were no significant differences among opinions of state attorneys of different ages ($\chi^2=1.56$, $d.f.=3$, $Phi = .126$, $p > .05$, n.s.),[9] nor were significant differences present for attorneys ($\chi^2=1.46$, $d.f.=1$, $Phi = .163$, $p > .05$, n.s.).[10]

Finally, older professional judges seemed to have a more positive opinion about mixed tribunals than younger professional judges; while the majority of older professional judges (72%) had an overall positive opinion about the system of mixed tribunals, only slightly below one-half (43%) of younger professional judges shared this positive opinion ($\chi^2=5.14$, $d.f.=1$, $Phi = .240$, $p < .05$).[11] The previous analysis suggests that the type of court/office (regional v. district) had an impact on the respondents' general opinion. Keeping in mind that professional judges at higher courts (regional courts, the Supreme Court) are older than professional judges at district courts (the promotion is made only after years of service at the district-court level), one may ask whether it is likely that the more positive opinion reported by older professional judges could have been reported primarily by professional judges from higher courts?

This was only partially the case; out of the 25 respondents who had a positive opinion about mixed tribunals, 15 (or 60%) were from regional courts or

---

[9]State attorneys were also grouped into only two age groups — "younger" and "older" — but the differences remained small; $\chi^2=0.32$, $d.f.=1$, $Phi = .057$, $p > .05$, n.s.

[10]Chi-square analysis could not have been performed on four age groups of attorneys because there were rather few respondents in some of the age groups, so respondents were grouped into only two groups — "younger" and "older."

[11]The analysis was also performed for the four age groups of professional judges, but due to a relatively large number of cells (4 × 2) and a sample of 90, the power of the test was limited and could not determine the 26.7% difference as statistically significant ($\chi^2=6.73$, $d.f.=3$, $Phi = .275$, $p > .05$, n.s.). Consequently, a large difference of 26.7%, which I consider to be substantively important, turned out not to be statistically significant. The *Phi*-value, which was even larger than the *Phi*-value computed during the analysis of two age groups, indicates that there is a relationship between the two examined variables.

the Supreme Court. Interestingly, when the type of court had been controlled for, differences by age appeared to be even stronger at the district-court level. Seventy percent of younger professional judges from district courts and only 39% of older professional judges from district courts had a positive opinion (χ^2=3.17, $d.f.$=1, Phi = .238, p > .05,, n.s.),[12] while they disappeared at the upper levels of the court hierarchy; the difference between older professional judges and younger professional judges from regional courts and the Supreme Court was only 12% (χ^2=0.55, $d.f.$=1, Phi = .129, p > .05, n.s.).

Also analyzed were education and occupational prestige. The analysis was conducted for lay judges only for a simple reason: all lawyers (professional judges, state attorneys, attorneys) are college graduates and have, consequently, the same educational level; furthermore, all lawyers belong to the same or very similar category on Treiman's scale of occupational prestige (Treiman, 1977). Neither lay judges' **education** nor their **occupational prestige** yielded significant differences in their general opinion about mixed tribunals (χ^2=.107, $d.f.$=1, Phi = −.022, p > .05, n.s., and χ^2=.222, $d.f.$=1, Phi = .034, p > .05, n.s., respectively);[13] regardless of their educational level or their occupational prestige, the great majority of lay judges (approximately 85%) reported that they had a positive opinion about mixed tribunals.

The influence of **the length of service** was measured by comparing the answers by groups of respondents with different lengths of service on the question about general opinion and by asking a separate question about the respondents' perceived influence of the length of service on their opinion. However, as a consequence of different types of experience (as discussed in Chapter 5), the analysis was performed separately for each of the roles in the criminal justice system (professional judges, lay judges, state attorneys, and attorneys).

---

[12]Since the sample size was only 56, the difference of 31%, which I consider to be substantively important, was not statistically important. In addition, I relied on the Phi-value of .238 to conclude that this difference was large.

[13]Respondents were grouped as those with "lower educational levels" (high school or below) and those with "higher educational levels" (above high school). Occupations were coded as "lower level" (10 through 45) and "higher level" (46 through 78) of occupational prestige according to Treiman's (1977) scale.

When the answers to the question about general opinion were compared based on the length of service, the conclusion was that the length of service was not an important factor for the opinion about mixed tribunals held by state attorneys (χ^2=.953, $d.f.$=1, Phi = .008, p > .05, n.s.), attorneys (χ^2=2.62, $d.f.$=1, Phi = −.163, p > .05, n.s.), and lay judges (χ^2=0.22, $d.f.$=1, Phi = .032, p > .05, n.s.).

The length of service was important only for professional judges; professional judges who had been professional judges five years or longer had a more positive opinion about mixed tribunals than professional judges who had been professional judges for less than five years. In fact, while the majority of professional judges who had been professional judges for more than five years had a *positive* opinion about mixed tribunals (54%), the majority of professional judges who had been professional judges for up to five years had a *negative* opinion about mixed tribunals (73%; χ^2=2.79, $d.f.$=1, Phi = −.188, p > .05, n.s.).[14] Although the majority of professional judges from both district courts and regional courts had been professional judges for at least five years (84% and 92%, respectively), the type of court may still be an intervening variable; less experienced professional judges were somewhat more likely to be serving at district courts, while more experienced professional were somewhat more likely to be serving at regional courts. Consequently, the observed differences between less experienced and more experienced professional judges may be due in part to the fact that professional judges from district courts, who had a more negative general opinion about mixed tribunals, were at the same time somewhat more likely to be less experienced. In order to explore the independent effect of the length of service, the same analysis was performed when the type of court had been controlled for. It turned out that, even when the type of court had been controlled for, the effect of the length of service persisted; less experienced professional judges from district courts were more likely to

---

[14]Despite the fact that the p-value did not show a statistically significant difference, I consider the difference of 27% to be substantively important. Furthermore, the Phi-value also implies that there is a relationship between the length of service and general opinion.

have a negative opinion about mixed tribunals than more experienced professional judges from district courts (89% *v.* 49%; χ^2=4.88, *d.f.*=1, *Phi* $= -.295$, $p < .05$).[15]

A separate question was asked about the opinion on the influence of the length of service on the lawyers' general opinion. Professional judges were asked: "What was your opinion about mixed tribunals at the beginning of your mandate as a judge in the criminal division?" Analogous questions, with obvious adjustments, were asked of state attorneys and attorneys.[16]

The expectation was that respondents would start at their positions as professional judges, state attorneys, and attorneys with a certain opinion about mixed tribunals. At that time they would have already been socialized into the legal culture (or a particular legal subculture) and, if their opinion about mixed tribunals had changed over time (since the time they had been appointed or started working in their current position), the change would have been a result of their experience with trials by mixed tribunals. Surprisingly, a very small percentage of respondents within each group (less than 10% within each group) thought that the experience in trials by mixed tribunals actually improved their opinion (Table 9.2). In fact, because so few respondents reported that the experience in trials by mixed tribunals improved their opinion, I excluded the two rarely chosen answers ("somewhat worse" and "much worse") from further analysis.[17] Interestingly, while approximately one-half or more than one-half of professional judges from regional courts and the Supreme Court (50%), state attorneys from regional offices (89%), and attorneys (58%) reported that their opinion remained the same, the majority of professional judges from

---

[15]The same analysis could not be performed for professional judges from regional courts and the Supreme Court for a very simple reason: not surprisingly, 92% of them reported being professional judges for more than five years.

[16]The offered answers ranged from "much better opinion" to "much worse opinion" on a five-point scale.

[17]When the answers "much better" and "better" were merged and the respondents who selected these answers were compared to the respondents who selected the answer "the same," the chi-square test showed significant differences (χ^2=18.52, *d.f.*=8, *Phi* $= .280$, $p < .05$).

district courts (65%) and state attorneys from district offices (51%) reported that their opinion about mixed tribunals became worse over time. As a group, professional judges were more likely to say that their opinion had become more negative than state attorneys and attorneys (χ^2=7.61, $d.f.$=1, Phi = .180, $p < .01$).

When the answers by all groups were pooled, the results suggested that the respondents who currently had an unfavorable opinion were more likely to say that their opinion had become more negative in comparison with their opinion at the beginning of their mandate than the respondents whose opinion was currently more favorable (χ^2=16.08, $d.f.$=1, Phi= -.264, $p < .001$).[18] In other words, the respondents whose current opinion about mixed tribunals was negative were more likely to say that their opinion had changed and had become more negative over time than the respondents whose current opinion about mixed tribunals was more positive. In fact, while the majority of respondents who had a current negative opinion (57%) said that their opinion had become negative over time, the majority of respondents who said that their current opinion was positive (69%) also reported that their opinion remained the same over time.

The expressed negative opinion about mixed tribunals might have been a result of the respondents' negative experiences with trials by mixed tribunals. Since the change of opinion, which was expressed by all the groups of respondents with different roles in the criminal justice system (professional judges, state attorneys, and attorneys), was not identical, it is important to discuss what type of experience helped change the already formed less negative opinion about mixed tribunals. For state attorneys and attorneys, there was

---

[18]The answers to the question about the general opinion on mixed tribunals were merged as follows: "very favorable" through "somewhat favorable" were merged into "favorable"; answers "somewhat unfavorable" through "very unfavorable" were merged into "unfavorable." Similarly, the answers to the question about the previously held opinion were recoded as follows: "much better opinion" and "better opinion" were merged into "better opinion," "the same opinion" was retained, while answers "worse opinion" and "much worse opinion" were omitted from the analysis because a very small percent of respondents had selected them.

Table 9.2: Opinion at the beginning of mandate.[a]

	Prof. j. Dist. C. ZG	Prof. j. Dist. C. BJ	Prof. j. Reg. C.	Prof. J. Supr. C.	Dist. State a. ZG	Dist. State a. BJ	Reg. State a.	Att. ZG	Att. BJ
much better	25.9%	34.5%	20.8%	0.0%	16.7%	26.3%	0.0%	13.3%	21.7%
somewhat better	37.0%	27.6%	25.0%	50.0%	27.8%	31.6%	11.1%	29.3%	13.0%
the same	33.3%	34.5%	45.8%	50.0%	55.6%	42.1%	88.9%	54.7%	60.9%
somewhat worse	0.0%	3.4%	8.3%	0.0%	0.0%	0.0%	0.0%	1.3%	4.3%
much worse	3.7%	0.0%	0.0%	0.0%	0.0%	0.0%	0.0%	1.3%	0.0%
N	27	29	24	10	20	20	18	76	26

[a]Question wording differed for professional judges, state attorneys, and attorneys: **professional judges:** "What was your opinion about mixed tribunals at the beginning of your career as a judge?"; **state attorneys:** "What was your opinion about mixed tribunals at the beginning of your career as a state attorney?"; **attorneys:** "What was your opinion about mixed tribunals at the beginning of your career as an attorney?"

Table 9.2: Continued.

	Prof j. All	State a. All R & D	Att. ZG & BJ
much better	24.4%	14.5%	15.3 %
somewhat better	32.2%	23.6%	25.5%
the same	38.8%	61.8%	56.1%
somewhat worse	3.4%	0.0%	2.0%
much worse	1.2%	0.0%	1.0%
N	90	58	102

no relationship between the opinion held currently (favorable, unfavorable) and a possible change in their opinion (better, the same; $\chi^2=1.81$, $d.f. = 1$, $Phi = -.140$, $p > .05$, n.s. for attorneys; $\chi^2=1.67$, $d.f. = 1$, $Phi = -.177$, $p > .05$, n.s. for state attorneys), while a relationship existed for professional judges: the professional judges who had a more negative opinion were more likely to say that their opinion had changed over time in the less favorable direction, while the professional judges who had a more positive opinion were more likely to say that their opinion remained the same over time (77% and 66%, respectively; $\chi^2=15.35$, $d.f. = 1$, $Phi = -.425$, $p < .001$). This result persisted when the type of court had been controlled for ($\chi^2=10.15$, $d.f. = 1$, $Phi = -.434$, $p < .01$ for district courts; $\chi^2=4.04$, $d.f. = 1$, $Phi = -.361$, $p < .05$ for regional courts). Since state attorneys and attorneys were present only during trials and their opinion was less likely to change and become more negative, it is likely that the experience of deliberations by mixed tribunals was the decisive factor that influenced the change in the professional judges' opinion by making it less positive over time.

9.1.3 Other Factors

In order to obtain a broader understanding of the changes in opinion, the analysis now turns to the examination of issues that influence general opinion and, at the same time, are influenced by general opinion. A number of these issues, including those pertaining to the estimates of lay judges' activity and those pertaining to the importance of lay judges' contributions, will be discussed in the order that closely mimics the chronological order of trial and deliberation.

General opinion about mixed tribunals and the perceived **frequency with which professional judges invited lay judges to ask questions** were related for state attorneys and attorneys, but not for professional judges and lay judges ($\chi^2=0.62$, $d.f.=1$, $Phi = .088$, $p > .05$, n.s. for professional judges; $\chi^2=0.11$, $d.f.=1$, $Phi = .022$, $p > .05$, n.s. for lay judges). The state attorneys and attorneys who had a more favorable opinion about mixed tribunals in general were more likely to say that professional judges invited lay judges to ask questions frequently (χ^2=4.49, $d.f.$=1, $Phi = .213$, $p < .05$ for attorneys; χ^2=5.77, $d.f.$=1, $Phi = .324$, $p < .05$ for state attorneys).[19] While the majority of the attorneys who had a negative general opinion (63%) reported that professional judges infrequently invited lay judges to ask questions, the majority of the attorneys who had a positive general opinion (58%) reported that professional judges frequently invited lay judges to ask questions. Similarly, the majority of the state attorneys who had a negative general opinion (83%) reported that professional judges infrequently invited lay judges to ask questions, while the majority of the state attorneys who had a positive general opinion (56%) reported that professional judges frequently invited lay judges to ask questions.

The reported **frequency of questions** asked by lay judges during trial was significantly related to general opinion held by professional judges and attorneys; the respondents who had an unfavorable opinion were more likely to say that lay judges never asked questions (χ^2=4.06, $d.f.$=1, $Phi = -.227$, $p < .05$ for professional judges; χ^2=3.84, $d.f.$=1, $Phi = -.198$, $p < .05$ for attorneys).[20] A similar analysis of lay judges' answers[21] and state attorneys' answers about the frequency of lay judges' questions showed no relationship (χ^2=.21, $d.f.$=1, $Phi = -.035$, $p > .05$, n.s. for lay judges; χ^2=0.48, $d.f.$=1, $Phi = -.093$, $p > .05$, n.s. for state attorneys).

General opinion was related not only to the reported frequency of lay judges' questions during trial, but also to the perceived **importance of lay**

---

[19]The answers to the question about the frequency with which professional judges invited lay judges to ask questions were recoded as "frequently" ("always" through "frequently") and "infrequently" ("sometimes" and "never").

[20]The answers to the question about the frequency of questions asked during trial were grouped as "never" *v.* all other answers. The answers to the question about general opinion about mixed tribunals were grouped as "favorable" ("very favorable" through "somewhat favorable") and "unfavorable" ("somewhat unfavorable" through "very unfavorable").

[21]The question about the perceived frequency of questions asked by lay judges was worded somewhat differently for lay judges; it inquired about the frequency with which they had asked questions in the last 10 trials. The answers were grouped as follows: "in all 10 trials" through "in about one-half of the trials" as "frequently," and "in less than one-half of the trials" through "in none of the trials" as "infrequently."

judges' questions (χ^2=25.55, $d.f.$=1, Phi = .337, p < .001);[22] the respondents who had a more favorable opinion about mixed tribunals in general were more likely to say that the questions asked by lay judges were more important than the respondents who had a more negative opinion about mixed tribunals in general. The relationship remained significant for each of the three groups of lawyers when their answers were examined separately (χ^2=12.05, $d.f.$=1, Phi = .393, p < .001 for professional judges; χ^2=13.74, $d.f.$=1, Phi = .519, p < .001 for state attorneys; χ^2=5.19, $d.f.$=1, Phi = .232, p < .001 for attorneys).

General opinion was significantly related to professional judges', state attorneys', and attorneys' judgments about **lay judges' understanding of evidence** (χ^2=29.72, $d.f.$=1, Phi = .350, p < .001); the respondents who had a more positive opinion about mixed tribunals in general were more likely to say that lay judges were generally able to understand evidence than the respondents who had a less positive opinion about mixed tribunals in general.[23] In fact, while the majority of respondents who had a positive general opinion about mixed tribunals (81%) reported that lay judges were able to understand evidence, the majority of respondents who had a negative general opinion about mixed tribunals (55%) reported that lay judges were able to understand evidence only occasionally. The pattern remained the same when their responses were analyzed separately, (χ^2=17.45, $d.f.$=1, Phi = .443, p < .001 for professional judges; χ^2=5.79, $d.f.$=1, Phi = .325, p < .05 for state attorneys; χ^2=8.11, $d.f.$=1, Phi = .286, p < .01 for attorneys).

Similarly, professional judges, state attorneys, and attorneys who had a more favorable opinion about the system of mixed tribunals in general were more likely to say that lay judges did not have problems or that they usually did

---

[22]The answers to the question about the importance of lay judges' questions were grouped as "important" ("very important" and "important") and "not important" ("somewhat important" and "not important").

[23]The answers to the question about understanding of evidence were grouped into "often" ("always" through "frequently") and "occasionally" ("sometimes" through "never").

not have **problems in evaluating evidence** (χ^2=33.84, $d.f.$=1, Phi = .270, p < .001).[24] The professional judges, state attorneys, and attorneys who said that lay judges could evaluate evidence without serious difficulty were more likely to have a positive opinion about mixed tribunals in general than their respective counterparts who said that lay judges had serious problems in evaluating evidence (χ^2=14.85, $d.f.$=1, Phi = .408, p < .001 for professional judges; χ^2=3.00, $d.f.$=1, Phi = .234, p > .05, n.s.[25] for state attorneys; χ^2=5.04, $d.f.$=1, Phi = .228, p < .05 for attorneys). A separate analysis for lay judges, in contrast with the analyses for the other three groups, showed that lay judges' general opinion about the system of mixed tribunals was not related to the reported frequency of problems in evaluating evidence (χ^2=0.65, $d.f.$=1, Phi = −.054, p > .05, n.s.).

The respondents who had a more favorable opinion about the system of mixed tribunals were more likely to say that lay judges **understood legal issues** than the respondents who a had less favorable opinion about the system (χ^2=37.62, $d.f.$=1, Phi = .288, p < .001).[26] Although this result persisted when separate analyses were carried out for all three groups of lawyers (professional judges, state attorneys, and attorneys), lay judges' general opinion about the system of mixed tribunals and the self-reported frequency with which they understood legal issues were not related (χ^2=5.35, $d.f.$=1, Phi = .245, p < .05 for professional judges; χ^2=4.75, $d.f.$=1, Phi = .294, p < .05 for

---

[24]The answers to the question about lay judges' ability to evaluate evidence were grouped as "no problems" ("without any difficulty" and "usually without any difficulty") and "problems" ("with some difficulty" through "they are not able to evaluate evidence at all"). Respondents were grouped by their role in the criminal justice system (i.e., professional judges, lay judges, state attorneys, and attorneys).

[25]As was the case on several occasions, I regard the difference of 26% to be substantively important although the chi-square analysis does not indicate statistical significance. The Phi-value confirms the existence of a relationship between the general opinion and the estimates of lay judges' ability to evaluate evidence.

[26]The answers to the question about the frequency with which lay judges understand legal issues were recoded as "frequently" ("always" through "frequently") and "infrequently" ("sometimes" to "never").

state attorneys; χ^2=2.95, $d.f.$=1, Phi = .173, $p > .05$, n.s.[27] for attorneys; χ^2=0.60, $d.f.$=1, Phi = $-.053$, $p > .05$, n.s. for lay judges).

The reported **frequency of lay judges' comments** during deliberation was also related to general opinion about mixed tribunals;[28] the respondents who had a more favorable general opinion about the system of mixed tribunals were more likely to say that lay judges made comments frequently than the respondents who had a less favorable opinion about the system. The same pattern persisted when the answers by lay judges and the answers by professional judges were analyzed separately (χ^2=3.76, $d.f.$=1, Phi = .218, $p > .05$, n.s.[29] for professional judges; χ^2=9.41, $d.f.$=1, Phi = .206, $p < .01$ for lay judges).

Not only did professional judges who had a more positive opinion about the system in general report that lay judges made comments more frequently, but they also attributed greater **importance to their comments** (χ^2=3.95, $d.f.$=1, Phi = .224, $p < .05$). On the other hand, lay judges' perceptions about the importance professional judges attached to their comments were not related to their general opinion about the system of mixed tribunals (χ^2=3.24, $d.f.$=1, Phi = .122, $p > .05$, n.s.)

The professional judges who perceived lay judges to be equally lenient or more lenient than the professional judges themselves were more likely to have a positive opinion about mixed tribunals than the professional judges who perceived lay judges to be harsher than the professional judges themselves (χ^2=4.13, $d.f.$=1, Phi = .233, $p < .05$). The analysis of lay judges' answers to

---

[27]Once again, although the difference of 30% was not statistically significant, I regard it to be substantively important.

[28]The answers about the frequency of lay judges' comments were merged as follows: "in all 10" through "in about one-half" as "frequently," and "in less than one-half" through "in none of 10" as "infrequently."

[29]In an already established pattern, while the difference of 22% for professional judges was not statistically significant, the difference of 14% for lay judges was (the sample of lay judges is three times larger than the sample of professional judges). In order to deal with these limitations of the chi-square test, the Phi-value is regarded as a benchmark. Based on the magnitude of the difference and the Phi value, I assert that the difference of 22% is substantively important.

the analogous question did not suggest such a relationship ($\chi^2=0.03$, $d.f.=1$, $Phi = .012$, $p > .05$, n.s.).

Voting was not related to the respondents' general opinion, neither to that of lay judges nor to that of professional judges ($\chi^2=0.02$, $d.f.=1$, $Phi = .008$, $p > .05$, n.s. for lay judges; $\chi^2=1.01$, $d.f.=1$, $Phi = .118$, $p > .05$, n.s. for professional judges).

The general conclusion is that professional judges, state attorneys, and attorneys exhibited stronger relationships between their general opinion about the system of mixed tribunals and other views of mixed tribunals than lay judges did. Having a more negative opinion about a specific issue, either the one dealing with the perceived frequency of lay judges' participation or the one dealing with the perceived lay judges' ability, seems to have been related to the overall negative opinion about the system of mixed tribunals. It may be the case that lawyers, more than lay judges, tended to evaluate lay judges' behavior in terms of the established opinion/stereotypes they held. However, there was probably an interaction between general opinion and views on a specific issue. How lawyers evaluated the importance of questions raised by lay judges seems to have been related to their general opinion about the system of mixed tribunals and lay judges; had their opinion been more positive, they would have been more likely to attribute greater importance to those questions and the perceptions of each separate issue would probably have influenced their general opinion.

As emphasized earlier, it does not seem that experience with mixed tribunals was the only factor important for the formation of general opinion. Another relevant factor may include the existing legal culture. The network of close friends and associates who are lawyers themselves may shape general opinion of professional judges, state attorneys, and attorneys. Therefore, it was expected that the lawyers whose close friends had a more negative opinion would also have been more likely to have a negative opinion than the lawyers whose friends expressed a less negative opinion. Three arguments come to mind: respondents tended to select friends whose opinion was similar to theirs; there was an interaction between the respondents' opinion and the opinion of their friends: their own opinion was shaped by their friends' opinion and, at the same time, their friends' opinion was shaped by theirs; and, finally, respondents perceived the opinion of their friends as more similar to their own than was objectively true.

The question that inquired about the perceived opinion of the respondents' friends on mixed tribunals was worded as follows: "What is the opinion about mixed tribunals most frequently expressed in the circle of lawyers you usually communicate with?"[30]

Two important conclusions surface from this analysis. First, the majority of professional judges, state attorneys, and attorneys (except for professional judges from the Supreme Court and regional state attorneys) had a network of friends whom they perceived to oppose the system of mixed tribunals (77% of professional judges from the District Court of Zagreb, 83% of professional judges from district courts in the Bjelovar Region, 73% of professional judges from regional courts, 65% of district state attorneys from the Zagreb Region, 56% of district state attorneys from the Bjelovar Region, 67% of attorneys from the Zagreb Region, and 61% of attorneys from the Bjelovar Region). The analysis of each response revealed a somewhat different picture. Most of the lawyers who had a very positive opinion about mixed tribunals ("somewhat favorable" or "very favorable") had friends whom they perceived to have a positive opinion about mixed tribunals. Similarly, the lawyers who had a negative opinion about mixed tribunals ("slightly unfavorable" to "very unfavorable") had friends whom they perceived to have a negative opinion about mixed tribunals. Interestingly, the lawyers who had an only somewhat positive opinion ("slightly favorable") had friends whom they perceived to have either a slightly favorable or a slightly unfavorable opinion.

Second, when the respondents' opinion was compared to the perceived opinion of their friends, the results suggested that the lawyers who perceived

---

[30]The offered answers ranged from "they strongly favor" to "they strongly oppose" mixed tribunals on a four-point scale.

that their friends opposed mixed tribunals were more likely to oppose mixed tribunals themselves (χ^2=8.76, $d.f.$=1, Phi=.317, $p < .01$ for professional judges; χ^2=24.51, $d.f.$=1, Phi=.522, $p < .001$ for attorneys; χ^2=10.63, $d.f.$=1, Phi=.466, $p < .001$ for state attorneys).[31] It is noteworthy that the lawyers who opposed mixed tribunals were more likely to have friends who also opposed mixed tribunals (that is, to perceive that their friends opposed mixed tribunals) than the lawyers who supported mixed tribunals. In other words, these results tell us that there was a relationship between the perceived opinion of one's friends and one's own opinion about mixed tribunals; but, it is very unlikely that only one impacts the other — it is more likely that "arrows go in both directions," resulting in constant reinforcement of these opinions.

9.2   Features of Trials by Mixed Tribunals

The results of the previous section showed that most of the groups of respondents expressed a generally positive opinion about mixed tribunals. What factors would they emphasize as positive or negative features of trials conducted by mixed tribunals in comparison with trials conducted by a professional judge alone? Respondents were asked about the features of trials by mixed tribunals they found to be the most positive and the most negative. These features, which were enumerated in the questionnaire, are based on the positive and negative features of trials by mixed tribunals discussed in Chapter 1.

9.2.1   Advantages

What are the advantages of trials by mixed tribunals? The discussion in Chapter 1 identified, among others, the tendency toward the independent and democratic legal process, the tendency to allow the citizens to exercise some

---

[31]The answers to the question about general opinion were grouped as "favorable" ("very favorable" through "somewhat favorable") and "unfavorable" ("somewhat unfavorable" through "very unfavorable"). The answers to the question about the friends' opinion were grouped as "favor" ("strongly favor" and "favor") and "oppose" ("oppose" and "strongly oppose").

control over decision-making in court cases, the tendency to involve citizens in the participation in government and state, and the tendency to educate the people about the operation of the criminal justice system. Introduction of lay participants can also be justified by emphasizing that lay participants focus on each particular case (they decide relatively few cases compared to professional judges) and bring community values into the case. In addition, greater legitimacy may be attributed to the legal decisions reached by lay persons, members of the community, than to those reached by professional judges. Lay judges are also perceived as mediators between the formalism of regular courts and the citizens.

Respondents were asked to select the positive features of mixed tribunals they considered to be the most important. The question was worded as follows: "Which of the following do you see as advantages of trials by mixed tribunals, as compared to trials by a professional judge alone? Put "1" next to the most positive feature, "2" next to the next most positive, etc., to the feature you see as the least positive." The answers were intended to capture the essence of the positive features typically used to advocate the use of lay persons in legal decision-making: "the public is involved in the work of the criminal justice system," "they educate the public about the criminal justice system," "they are a good way of introducing community values into the criminal justice system," "the decisions are more acceptable to the defendant and/or victim," "the decisions are more acceptable to the public," "the criminal process is democratic," "they protect the defendants against potential tyranny by government officials," "they provide closer attention to a particular defendant," and "other" (with the option of filling in other positive features).

Almost all respondents (87%) thought there were advantages of trials by mixed tribunals in comparison with trials by a professional judge alone (Table 9.3). Although the expectation was that the political function ("the criminal process is democratic") would be the most dominant, the results showed that the political function was only one among the three most frequently selected features. The other two were "the public is involved in the work of the criminal

Table 9.3: Positive features of trials by mixed tribunals.[a]

	Prof. j. Dist. C. ZG	Prof. j. Dist. C. BJ	Prof. j. Reg. C.	Prof. j. Supr. C.	Dist. State a. ZG	Dist. State a. BJ	Reg. State a.	Att. ZG	Att. BJ
public involved	48.0%	32.1%	33.3%	22.2%	71.4%	16.7%	13.3%	41.8%	22.7%
education	16.0%	17.9%	14.3%	0.0%	0.0%	5.6%	26.7%	7.3%	9.1%
community values	16.0%	7.1%	19.0%	66.7%	7.1%	44.4%	20.0%	21.8%	27.3%
acceptability for defendant and/or victim	4.0%	0.0%	4.8%	0.0%	0.0%	5.6%	6.7%	5.5%	0.0%
acceptability for public	0.0%	3.6%	4.8%	0.0%	7.1%	0.0%	0.0%	1.8%	4.5%
democratic	12.0%	28.6%	14.3%	0.0%	7.1%	16.7%	20.0%	9.1%	13.6%
safeguard	4.0%	10.7%	9.5%	11.1%	7.1%	5.6%	0.0%	12.7%	13.6%
focus on a particular defendant	0.0%	0.0%	0.0%	0.0%	0.0%	5.6%	13.3%	0.0%	9.1%
N	27	29	24	10	20	20	18	76	26

[a]Question: "Which of the following do you see as positive features of trials by mixed tribunals, as compared to trials by a professional judge alone?"

Table 9.3: Continued.

	Lay j. Dist. C. ZG	Lay j. Dist. C. KŽ	Lay j. Reg. C. ZG	Lay j. Reg. C. BJ	Prof j. All	State a. All R & D	Att. ZG & BJ	Lay j. All R & D
public involved	20.2%	22.0%	12.5%	13.8%	36.1%	34.5%	37.0%	19.0%
education	6.1%	4.0%	0.0%	3.4%	14.4%	10.2%	7.8%	4.7%
community values	27.2%	8.0%	12.5%	34.5%	19.6%	24.0%	23.2%	22.4%
acceptability for defendant and/or victim	1.8%	18.0%	0.0%	6.9%	2.5%	4.0%	4.1%	6.1%
acceptability for public	1.8%	2.0%	6.3%	0.0%	2.4%	2.4%	2.5%	2.0%
democratic	30.7%	28.0%	43.8%	37.9%	16.6%	14.4%	10.2%	32.3%
safeguard	7.9%	16.0%	25.0%	3.4%	8.4%	4.4%	12.9%	10.7%
focus on a particular defendant	4.4%	2.0%	0.0%	0.0%	0.0%	6.1%	2.3%	2.8%
N	122	53	21	33	90	58	102	229

justice system" and "lay participation is a good way of introducing community values into the criminal justice system." It seems that the respondents were not too concerned with either the acceptability of the decisions or the emphasis on a particular defendant. They also did not feel that protection against potential tyranny was an important role of mixed tribunals.

The primary choice of lay judges was the answer "the criminal process is democratic," that is, a political function. Lawyers (professional judges, state attorneys, and attorneys) tended to report more frequently "the public is involved in the work of the criminal justice system" and "lay participation is a good way of introducing community values into the criminal justice system" as their first choices than lay judges did (Table 9.3).

9.2.2 Disadvantages

Lay participants in criminal justice systems are usually attacked by the opponents of lay participation for numerous reasons. Negative features of lay participation were discussed at length in Chapter 1. In comparison with professional judges, lay judges are criticized for being less able to understand and evaluate evidence in general and certain types of evidence, such as expert testimony, in particular. Lay judges are further accused of being likely to base their decisions on personal characteristics of the defendants and other trial participants, as well as on other subjective issues. As a consequence of the fact that lay participants do not know the law, they have the tendency to focus on moral issues instead of legal issues and make decisions from the perspective of their values and personal opinion. Their decisions are less uniform because they are based on morality and tailored to suit a particular defendant. Lay participants also come under attack for being either harsher or more lenient than professional judges. In addition, one of the criticisms is that trials with lay participants are usually more expensive and, to a certain degree, slower than trials by a professional judge.

Respondents were asked to specify which of these problems they considered to be the most important. The question was worded as follows: "Which of the following do you see as serious problems with trials by mixed tribunals, as compared to trials by a professional judge alone? Put "1" next to the most serious problem, "2" next to the next most serious problem, etc., to the last item that you see as the least serious problem." The offered answers were "lay judges are less able to understand evidence and to weigh evidence properly than professional judges," "lay judges are unable to understand and apply the law properly," "the system of mixed tribunals is too costly," "lay judges are more likely to be influenced by personalities of various parties involved in the case than professional judges are," "lay judges are likely to base their decisions on prejudice or bias," "lay judges are unable to separate relevant and irrelevant issues in the case," "citizens are too often disillusioned or bored by their service as lay judges," "lay judges suggest very different decisions in similar cases, i.e., they are inconsistent," "the selection system for lay judges is very poorly organized and inefficient," "other" (with the option of filling in other negative features), and "there are no serious problems with trials by mixed tribunals."

The results suggest that the respondents did not think about mixed tribunals in "black and white" terms; a large percentage of respondents perceived trials with mixed tribunals as simultaneously having both positive and negative features. Just like a very small percentage of respondents reported that there were no positive features of trials by mixed tribunals, only a small percentage of respondents within each group thought that there were no problems with trials by mixed tribunals ("there are no serious problems with trials by mixed tribunals;" Table 9.4).[32]

It is quite remarkable that in the majority of these groups of respondents (10 out of 13 groups) respondents most frequently emphasized the same major problem — lay judges' inability to understand and evaluate evidence ("lay judges are less able to understand evidence and to weigh evidence properly

---

[32]The percentage is 6% or less for all groups of respondents, except for lay judges from the Regional Court of Zagreb, 15% of whom said that there were no problems with trials by mixed tribunals.

Table 9.4: Negative features of trials by mixed tribunals.[a]

	Prof. j. Dist. C. ZG	Prof. j. Dist. C. BJ	Prof. j. Reg. C.	Prof. j. Supr. C.	Dist. State a. ZG	Dist. State a. BJ	Reg. State a.	Att. ZG	Att. BJ
understanding of evidence	40.7%	48.3%	31.0%	33.0%	6.3%	42.1%	46.2%	32.8%	17.4%
understanding of the law	18.5%	20.7%	13.6%	0.0%	37.5%	21.1%	7.7%	18.8%	34.8%
too costly	3.7%	3.4%	4.5%	0.0%	0.0%	0.0%	0.0%	1.6%	8.7%
personality influence	14.8%	13.8%	22.7%	44.4%	6.3%	15.8%	23.1%	10.9%	13.0%
prejudice, bias	3.7%	0.0%	0.0%	0.0%	6.3%	5.3%	0.0%	3.1%	0.0%
irrelevant issues	7.4%	0.0%	13.6%	11.1%	6.3%	0.0%	15.4%	6.3%	4.3%
boredom	0.0%	3.4%	0.0%	0.0%	0.0%	5.3%	0.0%	7.8%	4.3%
inconsistency	0.0%	3.4%	0.0%	0.0%	0.0%	0.0%	0.0%	3.1%	0.0%
poor selection	7.4%	3.4%	13.6%	11.1%	31.3%	5.3%	7.7%	15.6%	13.0%
no problems	3.7%	3.4%	0.0%	0.0%	6.3%	5.3%	0.0%	0.0%	4.3%
N	27	29	24	10	20	20	18	76	26

[a]Question: "Which of the following do you see as serious problems with trials by mixed tribunals, as compared to trials by a professional judge alone?"

Table 9.4: Continued.

	Lay j. Dist. C. ZG	Lay j. Dist. C. KŽ	Lay j. Reg. C. ZG	Lay j. Reg. C. BJ	Prof j. All	State a. All R & D	Att. ZG & BJ	Lay j. All R & D
understanding of evidence	25.9%	40.8%	38.5%	48.0%	39.7%	31.2%	28.7%	33.2%
understanding of the law	17.9%	16.3%	15.4%	4.0%	15.8%	22.5%	23.0%	15.6%
too costly	12.5%	2.0%	0.0%	12.0%	3.4%	0.0%	3.5%	9.0%
personality influence	15.2%	18.4%	7.7%	28.0%	19.9%	14.7%	11.5%	17.1%
prejudice, bias	0.0%	2.0%	0.0%	0.0%	1.2%	4.0%	2.3%	0.5%
irrelevant issues	11.6%	6.1%	7.7%	4.0%	7.2%	6.9%	5.8%	9.0%
boredom	1.8%	0.0%	0.0%	0.0%	1.2%	1.8%	6.9%	1.0%
inconsistency	1.8%	6.1%	0.0%	0.0%	1.2%	0.0%	2.3%	2.5%
poor selection	11.6%	6.1%	15.4%	4.0%	8.2%	14.9%	14.9%	9.6%
no problems	1.8%	2.0%	15.4%	0.0%	2.2%	4.0%	1.1%	2.5%
N	122	53	21	33	90	58	102	229

than professional judges;" Table 9.4). Furthermore, among the three groups of respondents that selected another answer as their primary choice, this criticism of lay judges' lack of ability to understand and evaluate evidence was also a very frequent selection.

Interestingly, *all* groups of professional judges and lay judges, members of mixed tribunals, most frequently selected lay judges' inability to understand and evaluate evidence as their primary objection to the system of mixed tribunals. Members of the tribunals are at the same time the ones who were in the position that afforded them the most direct exposure to the problems experienced by lay judges, because they were the only ones who were present during deliberations, who observed how professional judges and lay judges related in the tribunal, and who had the best opportunity to learn about the level of lay judges' understanding of and ability to evaluate evidence. Such a close agreement between professional judges and lay judges strongly suggests that lay judges' ability to evaluate evidence was indeed among the most important problems, if not *the* most important problem of the system of mixed tribunals in Croatia.

Among frequently selected answers was the usual argument that lay persons are not able to understand and apply the law ("lay judges are unable to understand and apply the law properly;" Table 9.4).[33] It is interesting that lay judges themselves selected this answer rather frequently, although they generally perceived themselves as competent to understand and apply the law. On the other hand, it is not surprising that lawyers (professional judges, state attorneys, and attorneys) selected this answer frequently; however, most of them perceived lay judges as only sometimes able to understand the legal issues in the case.

Finally, the third frequently selected criticism of lay participation was that lay judges' decisions were based on bias and prejudice. Very few respondents emphasized this reason as important, although some respondents selected an answer that clearly represents its special case ("lay judges are more likely

---

[33]This issue was discussed in detail in Chapter 1 and in Chapter 8.

to be influenced by personalities of various parties involved in the case than professional judges are"; Table 9.4).

During informal discussions with professional judges at the District Court of Zagreb, I have learned that, in their opinion, one of the problems with trials by mixed tribunals was the poor selection process of lay judges. Research studies (Bajić-Petrović, 1985a, 1985b; Kamhi and Čalija, 1974) indeed suggested that some groups — particularly retired persons — were overrepresented in comparison with the general population and that they may not have been genuinely interested in participating. However, less than 15% of respondents within each group thought that the most important problem with the system of mixed tribunals was the fact that the "selection system for lay judges is very poorly organized and inefficient" (Table 9.4).[34]

Based on the literature (Kamhi and Čalija, 1974) and the objections that surfaced during informal discussions with professional judges from the District Court of Zagreb, two questions about the relationship between the selection process and the quality of trials by mixed tribunals were asked.

The first, more general question was asked about the quality of selection of lay judges and its influence on the quality of trials by mixed tribunals.[35] It was clear from the responses that very few respondents thought that the selection system enhanced the system of mixed tribunals; less than 10% of respondents in each group reported that the selection system had a positive impact on the quality of trials by mixed tribunals (the only exception were the Supreme Court Justices, 20% of whom said that the selection system made a positive impact). On the other hand, it is not clear whether the prevalent opinion was that the selection system in operation at the time had no impact or actually had a negative impact on the quality of trials by mixed tribunals. Attorneys

---

[34]The only group in which more than 15% of respondents (31%) thought that this was the most important negative feature of the system of mixed tribunals were (the rather inexperienced) district state attorneys from Zagreb (Table 9.4).

[35]The question was worded as follows: "The selection of lay judges as it is right now ..." The offered answers ranged from "significantly reduces the quality of trials by mixed tribunals" to "significantly enhances the quality of trials by mixed tribunals" on a five-point scale.

were the only group in which the majority (59% in the Zagreb Region and 52% in the Bjelovar Region) stated that the selection system had a negative impact on the quality of trials by mixed tribunals. While two out of three district state attorneys from the Zagreb Region reported the same, two out of three district state attorneys from the Bjelovar Region and regional state attorneys stated that the selection process had no impact on the quality of trials by mixed tribunals. Finally, the majority of professional judges from the District Court of Zagreb and from regional courts (59% and 58%, respectively) reported that the selection process and quality of trials by mixed tribunals were not related, while a slim majority of professional judges from district courts in the Bjelovar Region and from the Supreme Court said that the selection process had a negative impact on the quality of trials by mixed tribunals (52% and 50%, respectively).

The second, more specific question inquired about the influence of the number of retired persons in the tribunals on the quality of trials by mixed tribunals. The question was worded: "In your opinion, with a decrease of the number of retired persons participating as lay judges, that is, an increase of participation of other citizens, the quality of trials by mixed tribunals would:" The offered answers ranged from "significantly increase" to "significantly decrease" on a five-point scale.

While the majority of state attorneys (74%) and attorneys (74%) reported that a decrease in the number of lay judges who were retired would have had a positive impact on the quality of trials, professional judges were split. The majority of professional judges from the District Court of Zagreb and from regional courts (52% and 54%, respectively) said that the quality of trials and the number of retired lay judges were not related; the majority of professional judges from district courts in the Bjelovar Region and the Supreme Court (52% and 80%, respectively) reported that reducing the number of lay judges who are retired would improve the quality of trials by mixed tribunals.

However, it is important to keep in mind that, though noted as possible sources of some concern, overrepresentation of retired persons and the selection process in general were not perceived as very important in comparison with other negative features of trials by mixed tribunals.

9.3 Future of Mixed Tribunals

Despite theoretical support for the system of mixed tribunals, lawyers were generally aware that the system of mixed tribunals had been experiencing many problems in practice. As mentioned earlier, while most of the authors who wrote about mixed tribunals in Croatia (former Yugoslavia) discussed negative characteristics of trials by mixed tribunals (Bayer, 1955; Ljubanović, 1983, 1989; Kovačević, 1973; Kamhi and Čalija, 1974; Krapac, 1977; Bajić-Petrović 1985a, 1985b; Lapaine, 1986a), they all agreed that the political function of mixed tribunals by itself was so important as to merit retention of the system of mixed tribunals as a part of the criminal justice system. This did not mean, of course, that it was generally believed that the system could not have been improved. The need for modification was expressed, for example, by the majority of professional judges (70%) in Kamhi and Čalija's study (1974, p. 91) of mixed tribunals in Bosnia and Herzegovina.

Two questions inquired about the future of mixed tribunals. The first question asked respondents to state their opinion on whether mixed tribunals should be retained as a part of the criminal justice system or abolished completely. The second question inquired about the ways in which the respondents who wanted to retain the system mixed tribunals would want to improve it.

The question about the future of mixed tribunals was worded as follows: "What course of action about mixed tribunals would you like to see?"[36] The expectation was that lawyers would be more likely to suggest drastic changes than lay judges would. The reasons for this hypothesis were threefold: first,

---

[36]The offered answers ranged from "mixed tribunals should be abolished" to "mixed tribunals should remain unchanged." Respondents could also have responded that "mixed tribunals should be changed drastically" or "mixed tribunals should be improved only slightly," and could have specified their own suggestions about the ways in which mixed tribunals should be changed.

professional judges are more likely to perceive themselves as more competent to decide legal cases than lay judges are; second, the results of this study suggest that lay judges had a better opinion of mixed tribunals in general than professional judges did; and, third, lawyers may be more knowledgeable and feel more comfortable discussing legal changes than lay judges are.

Contrary to the opinion held by the majority of lawyers, who suggested that mixed tribunals should be changed drastically or abolished altogether (82% of professional judges from district courts, 70% of professional judges from the Supreme Court, 89% of district state attorneys, 75% of regional state attorneys, and 79% of attorneys),[37] the majority of lay judges (56% of lay judges from district courts and 67% of lay judges from the Regional Court of Zagreb)[38] suggested that the system of mixed tribunals should not be changed or should be changed only slightly (Table 9.5; $\chi^2=63.17$, $d.f.=12$, $Phi = .385$, $p < .001$).[39]

Not surprisingly, the results showed that the respondents who had a more favorable general opinion about the system of mixed tribunals were more likely to suggest that the system of mixed tribunals should remain the same or be changed only slightly ($\chi^2=48.74$, $d.f.=1$, $Phi = -.341$, $p < .001$).[40] In other words, while 50% of the respondents who had a positive opinion about mixed tribunals suggested that the existing system of mixed tribunals should not be

---

[37]The only exception were professional judges from regional courts, the majority of whom (60%) suggested either slight changes or no changes at all.

[38]The only exception were lay judges from the Regional Court of Bjelovar, the majority of whom (52%) suggested that mixed tribunals should be changed drastically or abolished altogether.

[39]The answers "mixed tribunals should remain unchanged" and "mixed tribunals should be changed only slightly" were merged, as were the answers "mixed tribunals should be abolished" and "mixed tribunals should be changed drastically."

[40]For the purpose of statistical analysis, the answers to the question about general opinion were grouped as "favorable" ("very favorable" to "somewhat favorable") and "unfavorable" ("somewhat unfavorable" to "very unfavorable"). The answers to the question about the changes of the system of mixed tribunals were grouped as follows: "abolished or changed drastically" ("mixed tribunals should be abolished" and "mixed tribunals should be changed drastically"), and "unchanged or changed slightly" ("mixed tribunals should be changed slightly" and "mixed tribunals should remain unchanged").

Table 9.5: Future of mixed tribunals.[a]

	Prof. j. Dist. C. ZG	Prof. j. Dist. C. BJ	Prof. j. Reg. C.	Prof. j. Supr. C.	Dist. State a. ZG	Dist. State a. BJ	Reg. State a.	Att. ZG	Att. BJ
abolished	56.0%	41.4%	30.0%	30.0%	31.3%	33.3%	0.0%	39.4%	38.1%
changed drastically	32.0%	34.5%	10.0%	40.0%	56.3%	55.6%	75.0%	42.3%	33.3%
changed slightly	0.0%	17.2%	50.0%	30.0%	12.5%	11.1%	18.8%	15.5%	0.0%
remain unchanged	12.0%	6.9%	10.0%	0.0%	0.0%	0.0%	6.3%	2.8%	28.6%
N	27	29	24	10	20	20	18	76	26

[a]Question: "What course of action about mixed tribunals would you like to see?"

Table 9.5: Continued.

	Lay j. Dist. C. ZG	Lay j. Dist. C. KŽ	Lay j. Reg. C. ZG	Lay j. Reg. C. BJ	Prof j. All	State a. All R & D	Att. ZG & BJ	Lay j. All R & D
abolished	20.0%	4.8%	0.0%	3.2%	41.5%	22.3%	39.1%	12.2%
changed drastically	26.4%	38.1%	33.3%	48.4%	27.8%	61.8%	40.0%	32.9%
changed slightly	10.0%	9.5%	0.0%	12.9%	22.2%	13.9%	11.5%	9.4%
remain unchanged	43.6%	47.6%	66.7%	35.5%	8.5%	2.0%	9.4%	45.5%
N	122	53	21	33	90	58	102	229

changed, only 11% of the respondents who had a negative opinion about the system reported the same. Interestingly, while the opinion about the changes was highly predictable for the respondents who had a negative opinion about the system of mixed tribunals in general (89% suggested drastic changes or abolition of the system), the answer was not as clear for the respondents who had a positive opinion about the system of mixed tribunals — approximately one-half of them voted for the abolition of the system or for drastic changes, while the other half preferred not to change it.

When their answers were analyzed separately, the same general conclusion regarding the relationship between the general opinion about the system of mixed tribunals and suggested changes to the system persisted for professional judges, lay judges, and attorneys, but not for state attorneys (χ^2=18.10, $d.f.$=1, Phi = $-.464$, $p < .001$ for professional judges; χ^2=4.42, $d.f.$=1, Phi = $-.150$, $p < .05$ for lay judges; χ^2=16.26, $d.f.$=1, Phi = $-.423$, $p < .001$ for attorneys; χ^2=.59, $d.f.$=1, Phi = $-.111$, $p > .05$, n.s. for state attorneys).

Lay judges were more likely to have a positive opinion about mixed tribunals in general, and were thus less likely to suggest drastic changes. In addition, although both professional and lay members of mixed tribunals most frequently selected the same major problem regarding trials by mixed tribunals ("lay judges' problems in understanding and evaluation of evidence"), lay judges perceived that they had fewer problems in understanding and evaluation of evidence than professional judges gave them credit for. It may be that lawyers thought that these problems were much more important for the high quality of trials by mixed tribunals than lay judges did, and, consequently, lawyers suggested more drastic changes than lay judges did.

The professional judges' suggestions about the future of mixed tribunals also depended on the type of court/office (χ^2=12.02, $d.f.$=1, Phi = .403, $p < .001$), while the same was true for neither lay judges nor state attorneys (χ^2=0.01 $d.f.$=1, Phi = .004, $p > .05$, n.s. for lay judges; χ^2=1.42, $d.f.$=1,

Phi = .168, p > .05, n.s. for state attorneys).[41] Differences between professional judges from the two types of courts were very clear; the majority of professional judges from district courts (82%) proposed drastic changes or the overall abolition of the system, while the majority of professional judges from regional courts (60%) proposed only minor changes or no changes at all. The fact that respondents from regional courts/offices required less drastic changes was consistent with their general opinion — respondents from regional courts/offices were more likely to have a favorable opinion than respondents from district courts/offices (Table 9.5).

A possible explanation for such differences is the experience respondents had. Since professional judges from both regional and district courts attended the same law schools and had been apprentices at the same courts, it seems likely that their different experiences with trials by mixed tribunals led them toward having a more/less favorable opinion and, as a consequence, toward requesting fewer/more changes to the existing system.

The selection process for lay judges at regional courts was identical to the selection process of lay judges at district courts; there were no special eligibility requirements that applied to the candidates for one type of court and, at the same time, did not apply to the candidates for the other. Therefore, the more favorable opinion expressed about the system of mixed tribunals at regional courts was likely due to the fact that the experiences with mixed tribunals at regional courts were different from the experiences with mixed tribunals at district courts. In other words, different experiences with trials by mixed tribunals at the two types of courts and the factors associated with the these differences (i.e., the size and composition of tribunals, seriousness of cases), as discussed earlier, may have had a significant impact on general opinion about mixed tribunals and, consequently, on the opinion about the future of mixed tribunals.

---

[41]The answers to this question were coded as "mixed tribunals should be abolished" and "mixed tribunals should be changed drastically" *v.* "mixed tribunals should be changed only slightly" and "mixed tribunal should remain unchanged." Respondents were grouped according to the type of court/office at which they served.

In answering the question about the future of mixed tribunals, respondents could add their own comments and specify how they would change mixed tribunals. Their comments focused on several topics: the selection process, seminars for lay judges, "blue-ribbon" lay judges, more thorough explanations by professional judges, and limitations of the jurisdiction of mixed tribunals.

Lawyers frequently emphasized that they would like to work with lay judges who are professionals in certain fields and whose specialized knowledge would help the tribunal resolve the case. One of the professional judges from district courts in the Bjelovar Region suggested detailed changes in this direction:

> Mixed tribunals are a positive feature of our legal system, but it is necessary to elect lay judges more selectively and to dispatch them to tribunals depending on their education and occupation. For example,
>
> - Violent offenses — an average person from the community
> - White-collar offenses — persons who were employed in the same occupation
> - Traffic offenses — persons who are drivers
> - Juvenile delinquency — persons whose occupations are related to children

Comments about the selection process can be grouped as those dealing with the selection process itself and those dealing with the underrepresentation/overrepresentation of a certain demographic group of lay judges. When respondents discussed the selection process itself, they frequently mentioned that this process should be organized in a manner that would eliminate the possibility of selecting lay judges who are not genuinely interested in participating in the criminal justice system and are thus very likely not contribute to the trial actively. Selection of younger and more educated lay judges were among the most frequently mentioned changes the respondents would like to see implemented.

One of the attorneys from Zagreb explained why he believed it was important to increase the educational level of lay judges. His explanation echoed some of the arguments employed in analyzing the theoretical underpinnings of interaction in mixed tribunals (Chapter 5).

> Lay judges most frequently do not have the most elementary level of knowledge to decide a particular case, be it legal knowledge or education in general ... Furthermore, I think that they are not even familiar with their rights and duties, and they cannot stand up to the professional judge. I see them as absolutely unimportant for the course of the trial and the decision.

Respondents targeted not only the low education of lay judges but also their lack of legal knowledge. Not surprisingly, lawyers were more explicit in advocating this point. One of the attorneys from Zagreb stated:

> Mixed tribunals do not fulfill their function primarily because lay judges do not have adequate general education and knowledge of criminal law. Understanding of criminal law requires a high level of general education, and its application in a particular case requires familiarity with legal terminology and their meaning, and a developed legal logic.

Some respondents wanted not only to see an increase in the educational level of lay judges in general but to introduce short seminars about the law (criminal law and criminal procedure law) as well. Finally, a small number of respondents (mostly lay judges from the District Court of Zagreb) said that they would like to receive more thorough explanations by professional judges about both factual and legal issues in the case. Lawyers also suggested that the jurisdiction of mixed tribunals should be restricted permanently to offenses with imprisonment over five years, as had been set temporarily by the 1991 *Presidential Decree* (1991b).[42]

These suggestions are very revealing, especially in light of the next question: "What would you suggest as the most important improvement to the system of mixed tribunals?" Respondents were asked to select from a list of

---

[42]This *Decree* was still in effect at the time when the data were collected — in June 1993 — but was subsequently abolished in 1996.

offered answers; they were also given the option of writing down additional improvements.

The results suggested that there was an agreement among professional judges and lay judges that "short seminars about criminal law and procedure" would have provided the most important improvement to the system of mixed tribunals. All four groups of lay judges selected this answer most frequently (Table 9.6), as did two out of three groups of professional judges who conducted trials with mixed tribunals (the third group of professional judges, those from the District Court of Zagreb, selected the same answer as their second most frequent choice).

That the lay judges' most frequent choice turned out to be short seminars about criminal law and procedure was surprising, since most lay judges reported that they frequently understood the legal issues involved in the case (with which opinion professional judges disagreed). It may be that lay judges would rather rely more heavily on their own knowledge of the law than constantly listen to and accept the professional judges' interpretation of the law. Specifically, it may be that lay judges wanted to be more thoroughly familiar with the legal issues in the case, so they could feel better equipped to understand the issues involved in the case, to follow the professional judges' comments, and to make legal decisions.

It is not reasonable to assume that a short seminar would enable lay judges to acquire legal knowledge comparable to that possessed by professional judges; professional judges would continue to be responsible for almost all procedural issues. However, they would benefit by spending less time introducing the basics of legal concepts to lay judges and having more time to discuss facts and more advanced legal issues. This suggestion is akin to the changes introduced for lay magistrates in the United Kingdom; they are now required to take an introductory seminar about the law and their rights and duties.

The lay judges' second most frequently selected improvement was "more thorough explanations given by the professional judge about the evidence in the case." Since the most frequently selected negative characteristic (selected

Table 9.6: Improvements to the system of mixed tribunals.[a]

	Prof. j. Dist. C. ZG	Prof. j. Dist. C. BJ	Prof. j. Reg. C.	Prof. j. Supr. C.	Dist. State a. ZG	Dist. State a. BJ	Reg. State a.	Att. ZG	Att. BJ
short seminar about law	22.2%	50.0%	43.5%	20.0%	14.3%	26.3%	25.0%	27.7%	30.4%
explanations by prof. judge	18.5%	3.6%	4.3%	50.0%	28.6%	15.8%	25.0%	23.1%	17.4%
taking notes	0.0%	0.0%	0.0%	0.0%	0.0%	0.0%	6.3%	0.0%	0.0%
selection	11.1%	10.7%	8.7%	0.0%	7.1%	10.5%	0.0%	10.8%	8.7%
"blue-ribbon"	48.1%	28.6%	26.1%	30.0%	42.9%	36.8%	37.5%	33.8%	30.4%
seminar about rights & duties	0.0%	7.1%	17.4%	0.0%	7.1%	10.5%	6.3%	4.6%	13.0%
N	27	29	24	10	20	20	18	76	26

[a]Question: "What would you suggest as the most important improvement to the system of mixed tribunals?"

Table 9.6: Continued.

	Lay j. Dist. C. ZG	Lay j. Dist. C. KŽ	Lay j. Reg. C. ZG	Lay j. Reg. C. BJ	Prof j. All	State a. All R & D	Att. ZG & BJ	Lay j. All R & D
short seminar about law	57.7%	46.0%	37.5%	50.0%	36.6%	22.4%	28.4%	52.2%
explanations by prof. judge	17.1%	32.0%	31.3%	13.3%	13.4%	22.5%	21.6%	21.2%
taking notes	3.6%	6.0%	6.3%	6.7%	0.0%	2.1%	0.0%	4.8%
selection	2.7%	2.0%	6.3%	20.0%	9.1%	6.1%	10.2%	5.3%
"blue-ribbon"	1.8%	2.0%	0.0%	3.3%	33.9%	38.7%	32.9%	1.9%
seminar about rights & duties	17.1%	12.0%	18.8%	6.7%	7.0%	8.2%	6.9%	14.6%
N	122	53	21	33	90	58	102	229

by both professional judges and lay judges) was that lay judges had problems in understanding and evaluation of evidence, respondents probably felt that more thorough explanations by professional judges would be beneficial for lay judges.

Another answer that lawyers tended to select most frequently was not nearly as popular with lay judges ("selection of lay judges who are professionals in certain fields [economists for fraud cases, for example]"). Why would respondents want to introduce "specialist" lay judges? The immediate answer is that lay judges who are specialists in certain areas would help professional judges by clarifying issues in areas which are not the professional judges' specialty. "Specialist" lay judges would thus complement the professional judge in the process of legal decision-making, but, this would come at a cost: their contribution would be different from that of "regular" lay judges. While "regular" lay judges are primarily intended to bring community values into the courtroom and to fulfill other functions discussed in Chapter 1, "specialist" lay judges would bring their specialized knowledge. Their role is shaped as consultants or experts in their area of experience. It is quite possible that such tribunals would depart from the idea of mixed tribunals and would *de facto* become professional tribunals.

Most respondents did not believe that giving lay judges the option to take notes would be a significant improvement. Also, obtaining a more representative sample of the general population in the pool of lay judges was not a particularly popular choice. In other words, respondents were not as concerned about the selection process (which takes place before lay judges arrive to the courtroom) as they were concerned about potential problems during trials themselves (e.g., problems in understanding and evaluation of evidence, understanding of legal issues). Finally, only lay judges thought that seminars about their rights and duties as lay judges would improve the system of mixed tribunals. The percentage of lay judges who selected this answer as the most important one varied from 7% for lay judges from the Regional Court of Bjelovar to 17% for lay judges from the District Court of Zagreb.

9.4 Mixed Tribunals and Other Decision-Makers

Despite numerous suggestions about the improvements to the system of mixed tribunals, the majority of respondents expressed a positive opinion about mixed tribunals. Generally, lawyers suggested changes to the system of mixed tribunals, while lay judges advocated no change. Would some respondents go as far as suggesting the replacement of mixed tribunals with some other types of decision-makers? To address this issue, respondents were asked in a series of questions to state their preference between mixed tribunals and a professional judge alone, professional tribunals, and the jury, respectively.

Respondents were first asked whom they favored as the decision-maker in the criminal process — mixed tribunals or a professional judge alone?[43] The expectation was that lawyers would prefer trials by a professional judge alone over trials by mixed tribunals (since they would probably reason that professional judges are better fact-finders and are better equipped to apply the law), while lay judges would prefer trials by mixed tribunals (which would offer them a chance to retain social control over the work of professional judges).

As expected, the majority of lawyers (with the exception of regional state attorneys, one-half of whom favored mixed tribunals) and, unexpectedly, the majority of lay judges from district courts, favored trials by a professional judge alone over trials by mixed tribunals (85% of professional judges from district courts, 83% of professional judges from regional courts, 70% of professional judges from the Supreme Court, 54% of lay judges from district courts, 68% of district state attorneys, and 62% of attorneys), while the majority of lay judges from regional courts (68%) and regional state attorneys (50%) favored trials by mixed tribunals (Table 9.7). A very small percentage of respondents (less than 15% in each group) favored mixed tribunals and professional judges equally.

---

[43]The offered answers ranged from "strongly favor mixed tribunals" to "strongly favor a professional judge alone" on a five-point scale.

Table 9.7: Mixed tribunals [MT] v. a professional judge alone [PJ].[a]

	Prof. j. Dist. C. ZG	Prof. j. Dist. C. BJ	Prof. j. Reg. C.	Prof. j. Supr. C.	Dist. State a. ZG	Dist. State a. BJ	Reg. State a.	Att. ZG	Att. BJ
strongly favor MT	3.7%	3.4%	4.2%	0.0%	0.0%	5.3%	11.1%	5.3%	3.8%
slightly favor MT	3.7%	13.8%	8.3%	30.0%	31.6%	10.5%	38.9%	26.7%	15.4%
no preference	3.7%	0.0%	4.2%	0.0%	5.3%	10.5%	11.1%	6.7%	15.4%
slightly favor PJ	33.3%	44.8%	54.2%	50.0%	26.3%	57.9%	22.2%	34.7%	42.3%
strongly favor PJ	51.9%	37.9%	29.2%	20.0%	36.8%	15.8%	16.7%	26.7%	23.1%
N	27	29	24	10	20	20	18	76	26

[a]Question: "Whom do you favor as a decision-maker in the criminal process?"

Table 9.7: Continued.

	Lay j. Dist. C. ZG	Lay j. Dist. C. KŽ	Lay j. Reg. C. ZG	Lay j. Reg. C. BJ	Prof j. All	State a. All R & D	Att. ZG & BJ	Lay j. All R & D
strongly favor MT	15.7%	11.5%	28.6%	36.4%	3.4%	5.4%	5.0%	18.9%
slightly favor MT	18.2%	26.9%	38.1%	33.3%	11.2%	26.8%	23.8%	24.2%
no preference	13.2%	3.8%	9.5%	9.1%	2.2%	8.9%	8.9%	10.1%
slightly favor PJ	31.4%	53.8%	19.0%	18.2%	44.5%	35.7%	36.6%	33.5%
strongly favor PJ	21.5%	3.8%	4.8%	3.0%	37.8%	23.2%	25.7%	13.2%
N	122	53	21	33	90	58	102	229

The expectation for the respondents who preferred trials by a professional judge alone is that they would be more likely to vote for the abolition of mixed tribunals. When asked specifically about the future of mixed tribunals, most lawyers actually suggested either abolition or drastic changes in the system of mixed tribunals, while lay judges advocated the opposite: slight changes or no changes at all. Although lay judges from district courts favored trials by professional judges over trials by mixed tribunals, they, surprisingly, did not ask for abolition or drastic changes in the then current system of mixed tribunals.

Respondents from regional courts/offices were more likely to favor mixed tribunals than respondents from district courts/offices were (χ^2=15.98, $d.f.$=2, $Phi = .210, p < .001$).[44] Such was the case for lay judges (χ^2=19.69, $d.f.$=2, $Phi = .294, p < .001$) and state attorneys(χ^2=4.40, $d.f.$=2, $Phi = -.280$, $p < .05$), while there were no significant differences by the type of court for professional judges (χ^2=0.06, $d.f.$=2, $Phi = -.027, p > .05$, n.s.). Regional differences were not important (χ^2=0.36, $d.f.$=2, $Phi = -.081, p > .05$, n.s. for professional judges; χ^2=0.55, $d.f.$=2, $Phi = -.049, p > .05$, n.s. for lay judges; χ^2=0.49, $d.f.$=2, $Phi = .113, p > .05$, n.s. for state attorneys; χ^2=0.14, $d.f.$=2, $Phi = .037, p > .05$, n.s. for attorneys).

Following the same logic, the expectation was that lawyers would prefer professional tribunals and lay judges would prefer mixed tribunals. The corresponding question was worded as follows: "How would you evaluate mixed tribunals in comparison with tribunals composed only of professional judges, that is, professional tribunals?"[45]

As expected, all groups of lawyers (except regional state attorneys) favored professional tribunals (85% of professional judges, 72% of attorneys, and 84%

---

[44]The answers were grouped as "favor mixed tribunals" ("strongly favor mixed tribunals" and "favor mixed tribunals"), "no preference" (simply as "no preference"), and "favor a professional judge alone" ("favor professional judge" and "strongly favor a professional judge alone").

[45]The offered answers ranged from "strongly favor mixed tribunals" to "strongly favor professional tribunals" on a five-point scale.

district state attorneys), while lay judges had a different opinion[46] (Table 9.8) — they favored mixed tribunals (53% of lay judges from district courts and 85% of lay judges from regional courts). The percentages of lawyers who favored professional tribunals ranged from 67% for professional judges from the Supreme Court to 90% for professional judges from district courts in the Bjelovar Region and district state attorneys from the Bjelovar Region. Lay judges from regional courts (who at the same time had a more positive opinion about mixed tribunals) tended to favor mixed tribunals more than lay judges from district courts did (who had a less positive opinion about mixed tribunals).

The type of court/office was important; lay judges and state attorneys from district courts/offices were more likely to say that they favored professional tribunals than their counterparts from regional courts/offices (χ^2=5.34, $d.f.$=1, $Phi = -.154$, $p < .05$ for lay judges; χ^2=11.87, $d.f.$=1, $Phi = -.460$, $p < .001$ for state attorneys).[47] There were no significant differences for professional judges; nine out of ten professional judges from both district and regional courts replied that they preferred professional tribunals (χ^2=0.00, $d.f.$=1, $Phi = .000$, $p > .05$, n.s.)

It also turned out that lawyers from the Zagreb Region and the Bjelovar Region were equally likely to "favor professional tribunals" (χ^2=0.26, $d.f.$=1, $Phi = .068$, $p > .05$, n.s. for professional judges; χ^2=0.79, $d.f.$=1, $Phi = .144$, $p > .05$, n.s. for state attorneys; χ^2=0.12, $d.f.$=1, $Phi = -.011$, $p > .05$, n.s. for attorneys).[48] Region turned out to be important only for lay judges; although both groups preferred mixed tribunals over professional tribunals, lay

---

[46]When the opinions by professional judges, state attorneys, attorneys, and lay judges were compared, the differences were statistically significant (χ^2=197.55, $d.f.$=6, $Phi = .649$, $p < .001$).

[47]Since very few lawyers reported that they did not favor professional tribunals, the answers that favored mixed tribunals and neutral answers were merged.

[48]The offered answers were grouped as "favor mixed tribunals" ("strongly favor mixed tribunals" and "favor mixed tribunals"), "no preference" (simply as "no preference"), and "favor professional tribunals" ("favor professional tribunals" and "strongly favor professional tribunals").

Table 9.8: Mixed tribunals [MT] v. professional tribunals [PT].[a]

	Prof. j. Dist. C. ZG	Prof. j. Dist. C. BJ	Prof. j. Reg. C.	Prof. j. Supr. C.	Dist. State a. ZG	Dist. State a. BJ	Reg. State a.	Att. ZG	Att. BJ
strongly favor MT	0.0%	3.4%	0.0%	0.0%	0.0%	5.3%	22.2%	6.7%	0.0%
slightly favor MT	14.8%	6.9%	4.2%	33.3%	15.8%	5.3%	27.8%	17.3%	25.0%
no preference	0.0%	0.0%	8.3%	0.0%	5.3%	0.0%	11.1%	4.0%	4.2%
slightly favor PT	22.2%	41.4%	50.0%	22.2%	47.4%	57.9%	27.8%	46.7%	37.5%
strongly favor PT	63.0%	48.3%	37.5%	44.4%	31.6%	31.6%	11.1%	25.3%	33.3%
N	27	29	24	10	20	20	18	76	26

[a]Question: "How would you evaluate mixed tribunals in comparison with tribunals composed only of professional judges, that is, professional tribunals?"

Table 9.8: Continued.

	Lay j. Dist. C. ZG	Lay j. Dist. C. KŽ	Lay j. Reg. C. ZG	Lay j. Reg. C. BJ	Prof j. All	State a. All R & D	Att. ZG & BJ	Lay j. All R & D
strongly favor MT	22.9%	13.2%	28.6%	30.3%	1.2%	8.9%	5.1%	22.2%
slightly favor MT	33.9%	32.1%	52.4%	57.6%	11.5%	16.1%	19.2%	38.7%
no preference	35.6%	20.8%	9.5%	12.1%	2.2%	5.4%	4.0%	26.2%
slightly favor PT	6.8%	24.5%	9.5%	0.0%	35.8%	44.6%	44.4%	10.2%
strongly favor PT	0.8%	9.4%	0.0%	0.0%	49.3%	25.0%	27.3%	2.7%
N	122	53	21	33	90	58	102	229

judges from the Zagreb Region were more likely to say that they favor mixed tribunals than lay judges from the Bjelovar Region (92% v. 79%, respectively; $\chi^2 = 8.02$, d.f.=1, Phi = .189, p < .01).

Finally, respondents were asked to compare mixed tribunals to the jury: "How would you evaluate mixed tribunals in comparison with the jury (where 6 to 12 lay persons decide the case without the presence of a professional judge)?"[49] It is noteworthy that, although Croatians have had extensive exposure to many TV- and film-courtroom dramas in which the jury had a prominent role, their knowledge about the actual work of the courtroom workgroup (especially the jurors) in common-law systems is rather limited.

The expectation was that lay judges and lawyers would both prefer trials by mixed tribunals, albeit for different reasons. Lay judges, being familiar with the system of mixed tribunals and its problems, nevertheless held a positive general opinion about it. Furthermore, three out of four groups of lay judges did not ask for substantive changes in the existing system of mixed tribunals. Therefore, it was assumed that lay judges would tend to prefer the system of mixed tribunals, a system that is familiar to them and about which they have a positive opinion, over a system unfamiliar to them — the jury system. On the other hand, although professional judges (and other groups of lawyers) tended to have a less positive opinion about mixed tribunals than lay judges did, they would still prefer mixed tribunals over the jury because the former system (unlike the latter) presents professional judges with an opportunity to exert direct influence over lay judges' opinion during deliberation.

The results support the hypothesis: the most frequently selected answer by all groups of respondents — professional judges, lay judges, state attorneys, and attorneys — was that they favored mixed tribunals over the jury (71% of professional judges, 50% of lay judges, 60% of attorneys, and 80% of state attorneys; Table 9.9).[50]

---

[49]The offered answers ranged from "strongly favor mixed tribunals" to "strongly favor the jury" on a five-point scale.

[50]The offered answers were grouped as follows: "favor mixed tribunals" ("strongly favor mixed tribunals" and "favor mixed tribunals"), "no preference" (simply as "no preference"),

Table 9.9: Mixed tribunals [MT] v. the jury [J].[a]

	Prof. j. Dist. C. ZG	Prof. j. Dist. C. BJ	Prof. j. Reg. C.	Prof. j. Supr. C.	Dist. State a. ZG	Dist. State a. BJ	Reg. State a.	Att. ZG	Att. BJ
strongly favor MT	33.3%	13.8%	16.7%	30.0%	50.0%	31.6%	55.6%	24.7%	26.1%
slightly favor MT	44.4%	48.3%	54.2%	50.0%	27.8%	52.6%	22.2%	32.9%	43.5%
no preference	3.7%	0.0%	8.3%	0.0%	16.7%	5.3%	11.1%	4.1%	13.0%
slightly favor J	14.8%	17.2%	12.5%	10.0%	0.0%	5.3%	11.1%	31.5%	17.4%
strongly favor J	3.7%	20.7%	8.3%	10.0%	5.6%	5.3%	0.0%	6.8%	0.0%
N	27	29	24	10	20	20	18	76	26

[a]Question: "How would you evaluate mixed tribunals in comparison with the jury (where 6 to 12 lay persons decide the case without the presence of a professional judge)?"

Table 9.9: Continued.

	Lay j. Dist. C. ZG	Lay j. Dist. C. KŽ	Lay j. Reg. C. ZG	Lay j. Reg. C. BJ	Prof j. All	State a. All R & D	Att. ZG & BJ	Lay j. All R & D
strongly favor MT	14.3%	11.3%	19.0%	27.3%	43.8%	45.5%	35.0%	15.9%
slightly favor MT	24.4%	37.7%	57.1%	51.5%	36.2%	34.5%	35.4%	34.5%
no preference	29.4%	22.6%	14.3%	18.2%	9.7%	10.9%	6.3%	24.8%
slightly favor J	21.8%	24.5%	9.5%	0.0%	6.0%	5.5%	28.1%	18.1%
strongly favor J	10.1%	3.8%	0.0%	3.0%	4.3%	3.6%	5.2%	6.6%
N	122	53	21	33	90	58	102	229

The opinions of professional judges and state attorneys from district and regional courts/offices were very similar (χ^2=0.01, $d.f.$=1, $Phi = -.012$, $p > .05$, n.s. for professional judges; χ^2=0.08, $d.f.$=1, $Phi = .039$, $p > .05$, n.s. for state attorneys). On the other hand, the majority of lay judges from regional courts favored mixed tribunals, while the majority of lay judges from district courts favored the jury (78% v. 58%; χ^2=21.21, $d.f.$=1, $Phi = -.306$, $p < .001$).

Finally, regional differences were not important for state attorneys and attorneys (χ^2=0.24, $d.f.$=1, $Phi = -.082$, $p > .05$, n.s. for state attorneys; χ^2=1.06, $d.f.$=1, $Phi = -.105$, $p > .05$, n.s. for attorneys). Interestingly, while professional judges from district courts were 16% more likely to vote for mixed tribunals than professional judges from regional courts (χ^2=1.63, $d.f.$=1, $Phi = .171$, $p > .05$, n.s.), lay judges from district courts were 17% *less* likely to vote for mixed tribunals than lay judges from regional courts (χ^2=5.58, $d.f.$=1, $Phi = -.157$, $p < .05$).[51]

9.5 Conclusion

The previous two chapters examined perceptions about the behavior of lay judges and professional judges during trial and deliberation. This chapter is focused on the more general opinions the respondents expressed about mixed tribunals, positive and negative features of trials by mixed tribunals, future of mixed tribunals, and possible improvements to the then existing system of mixed tribunals.

In general, lay judges had a more positive opinion about mixed tribunals than lawyers did (professional judges, state attorneys, and attorneys). Con-

---

and "favor the jury" ("favor the jury" and "strongly favor the jury"). Respondents were grouped as professional judges, lay judges, state attorneys, and attorneys (χ^2=22.40, $d.f.$=3, $Phi = .219$, $p < .001$).

[51] The 16% difference for professional judges was not statistically significant, while the 17% difference for lay judges was. As usual, this was probably due to the fact that the sample of lay judges is larger; at the same time, the Phi-value was larger for professional judges than for lay judges.

sistent with that finding, lay judges suggested either no changes or only minor changes to the system of mixed tribunals, while lawyers suggested drastic changes or abolition of the system of mixed tribunals altogether. Lawyers evaluated the contribution made by lay judges, members of the tribunal with lower status (based on low states of specific status characteristics), in a less favorable light and, therefore, had a less positive opinion about mixed tribunals. Lay judges, on the other hand, attributed greater importance to their own participation; as a result, they were more satisfied with the system of mixed tribunals.

It is quite possible that stereotypes about lay participation and its benefits and drawbacks may have influenced general opinion about mixed tribunals. In addition, it may be the case that lawyers, at least to some degree, accepted and advocated the view that they are the only ones who can make high-quality legal decisions regarding the facts and the law. In fact, the majority of the lawyers who participated in this study preferred trials by professional tribunals over trials by mixed tribunals and trials by a professional judge alone over trials by mixed tribunals — the surveyed lawyers sent a clear message about their views on who legal decision-makers should be.

This study shows that the type of experience lawyers had determined whether or not their opinion will change as they gain more experience. For professional judges, their experience with mixed tribunals further reinforced their negative opinion or changed their positive opinion toward a less positive one. State attorneys and attorneys reported that they had not changed their opinion over the years.

It was expected that all young lawyers, future professional judges, state attorneys, and attorneys initially held a similar general opinion about mixed tribunals (since they attended the same law schools). The type of experience they obtained during their service, however, was different: professional judges were present during both trials and deliberations, while state attorneys and attorneys were present only during trials. Therefore, the reported changes in the opinion since the beginning of lawyers' careers (the opinion of professional judges became more negative, while the opinion of state attorneys and attorneys reportedly remained the same) can be attributed to the different types of experience respondents had been exposed to. The results show that experience with mixed tribunals was an important factor that influenced the general opinion held by professional judges, but not the general opinion held by state attorneys and attorneys.

Opinion about mixed tribunals differed by the type of court/office. It seems that the experience with trials at regional courts — through the experience of trials in mostly larger tribunals, the presence of another professional judge, and the seriousness of the cases tried — facilitated a more positive opinion on mixed tribunals. Respondents from regional courts/offices, in comparison with respondents from district courts/offices within the same group of respondents (professional judges, state attorneys, and lay judges), reported a more positive account of the following issues: a higher frequency of lay judges' participation, a greater importance of lay judges' participation, and a greater degree of lay judges' competence to understand and evaluate evidence and legal issues. Since respondents from regional courts perceived all of these issues more positively, it is logical that they also voiced a more positive general opinion about mixed tribunals than their counterparts from district courts.

Almost all respondents considered some of the functions of lay participation as advantages of trials by mixed tribunals. Among the more popular themes were the democratization of the criminal process, participation in government, and introduction of community values into the criminal justice system. When asked about negative features of trials by mixed tribunals, lay judges and lawyers both focused on the issue of lay judges' competence as decision-makers and emphasized lay judges' problems in understanding and evaluation of evidence and understanding of legal issues. Lawyers perceived that the competence of lay judges (lower status members) depended precisely on the specific status characteristics identified in Chapter 5 — lay judges' lack of legal knowledge and systematic training and experience in resolving legal issues. Lay judges perceived that their greatest problem was understanding and evaluation of evidence; their lack of legal knowledge was not singled out as frequently.

Professional judges and lay judges agreed that the most beneficial improvement to the then existing system of mixed tribunals would have been the introduction of seminars about criminal law and criminal procedure. In other words, both professional judges and lay judges agreed that the most troublesome issue related to lay participation is lay participants' lack of legal knowledge or familiarity with the law — the *lay* element that lay judges are bringing to the process of legal decision-making.

It is also quite interesting that the second most frequently selected improvement lay judges asked for (which was, at the same time, not nearly as popular with professional judges) was more thorough explanations by professional judges. Lay judges probably felt that more thorough and detailed explanations would help them understand and evaluate evidence, and would also reduce the problem of dealing with unfamiliar legal concepts and issues.

The final topic of this chapter was an overview of the respondents' opinion about the comparison of mixed tribunals to other forms of legal decision-making. Lawyers, who generally perceived that professionals are more competent decision-makers than lay judges are, preferred both trials by a professional judge alone and trials by professional tribunals over trials by mixed tribunals. Lay judges from regional courts, who were valued more highly than their counterparts from district courts (both in terms of their level of activity and assessed importance of contribution), formed a more positive opinion about mixed tribunals and tended to prefer mixed tribunals over a professional judge alone more frequently than lay judges from district courts did.

When the respondents were asked to compare mixed tribunals to professional tribunals, most lawyers selected professional tribunals, while most lay judges selected mixed tribunals. Again, lawyers perceived that professionals are more competent decision-makers than lay judges are. Lay judges, on the other hand, preferred mixed tribunals; although they were aware that there were occasional problems with their own competence, they probably viewed trials by professional tribunals as a potentially serious threat to the independent and democratic criminal trial.

Professional lawyers and lay judges both considered mixed tribunals as a more acceptable form of lay participation in legal decision-making than the jury, although the reasons for such a choice may have been different. Lay judges were aware that they did not know the law; they did know, on the other hand, that their legal decisions, unlike those reached by the jury, needed to follow the letter of the law. Therefore, lay judges may have felt that they needed the help of lawyers to resolve legal issues. While such help was readily available in mixed tribunals, this would not be the case with the jury. Furthermore, lay judges may also have wanted to retain the system of mixed tribunals because it was familiar to them. Despite their generally negative opinion about mixed tribunals, professional judges probably preferred the system of mixed tribunals because it allowed them at the very least to interact actively with lay participants and to influence their opinion; such an interaction would not be possible in the context of jury trials and professional judges may have felt reluctant to relinquish direct control over the decision-making process.

Chapter 10

Conclusion

Before the existence of the state and its apparatus, the disputes and wrongs among people were resolved by the decisions reached by members of the community. Since those ancient times lay participation in decision-making has been present in different forms and has enjoyed varying levels of success and acceptance. The sense of community participation and the desire to achieve democracy contribute toward the (re)establishment of lay participation. Being judged by one's peers, having a safeguard against an overzealous prosecutor or a biased judge, and providing citizens with the opportunity to become actively involved in and learn about legal decision-making are among the most prominent reasons used to motivate the introduction of lay participation in the criminal justice system. Furthermore, research studies show that the involvement of lay participants increases levels of satisfaction with and perceptions of fairness of the overall criminal justice system and the government.

Despite the fact that lay participants are frequently criticized for being biased, prejudiced, and unable to critically evaluate evidence and understand the law, positive features of lay participation prompted a large number of countries around the world to utilize lay participation in their contemporary criminal justice system. With the increased openness and orientation toward the building of democratic societies, lay participation has the potential of expanding even further, as was recently the case in Russia and Spain.

European countries whose legal systems are based on Roman law often utilize mixed tribunals as the predominant form of lay participation. Mixed tribunals have existed for many centuries and are currently widespread in countries of both Western and Eastern Europe, as well as in other parts of the world.

The theoretical foundation used in this book to explain the interaction in mixed tribunals is based on **status characteristics theory**. Mixed tribunals are formal, heterogeneous groups whose members differ in terms of their status in the group and develop expectations about the contribution of the group members. Professional judges, educated in law and systematically trained and experienced in legal decision-making, are expected to have a higher status in the tribunal than lay judges, members who have neither legal education nor systematic training and experience in legal decision-making. As a consequence of their pre-specified role in the legal proceedings and attributed higher status, professional judges are expected to be more active and more persuasive in the discussions among tribunal members. All characteristics of an individual, both those related to the task directly (specific status characteristics) and those related to the task only indirectly (diffuse status characteristics), are expected to have an impact on the formation of expectations about the status of and the contributions by the group members, although the weight attached to specific status characteristics is expected to greatly exceed the weight attached to diffuse status characteristics.

Results of this study suggest that professional judges did not perceive lay judges as very active during trials and deliberations. Lay judges themselves reported that they asked questions during trials only infrequently. However, lay judges argued that they were substantially more active during deliberation than professional judges gave them credit for. As for the importance of lay judges' questions during trial and comments during deliberation, professional judges did not perceive it to be high.

In accordance with stereotypes about *lay* persons' ability to understand the law, lawyers (professional judges, state attorneys, and attorneys) were not impressed with **lay judges' ability to understand the law**. Rather, they perceived that lay judges rarely understood the legal issues in the case. On the other hand, lay judges themselves reported that they were frequently able to understand legal issues.

Consistent with typical criticisms of lay participation, lawyers did not think highly of **lay judges' ability to evaluate evidence**: they perceived that lay judges had problems in evaluating evidence. Again, lay judges themselves reported that they were generally able to evaluate evidence. Furthermore, professional judges reported that in the process of evidence evaluation lay judges typically focused on subjective issues, such as the personality of the defendant, and were thus more likely to entertain frequent visits by Mr. Prejudice and Mrs. Sympathy than to focus on objective issues. In an already familiar pattern, lay judges themselves reported that they focused on objective issues. At the same time, professional judges seemed well above reproach — both lay judges and professional judges reported that professional judges focused on objective issues in the process of evidence evaluation.

These discrepancies may be partially driven by the so-called *self-serving bias*. For example, studies clearly show that respondents describe themselves to be above the group average when surveyed about their driving skills (Svenson, 1981), ethical issues (Baumhart, 1968), managerial prowess (Larwood and Whittaker, 1977), productivity (Cross, 1977), and health (Weinstein, 1980). In this sense, a lay judge may tend to estimate his/her own ability to participate or the frequency and importance of his/her own participation as higher than he/she would evaluate the ability of other lay judges to participate or the frequency and importance of their participation. Furthermore, Doob (1979b, p. 62) suggested that lay participants have the tendency to overestimate their own general ability to understand the legal issues in the case; while the majority of jurors in Doob's study (1979b) reported being generally able to understand legal instructions, they had problems remembering that professional judges gave them a particular legal instruction. Similarly, the effect of self-serving bias was observed in jury studies; while more than 80% of jurors reported that they understood most of the instructions, 45% of them said that their *fellow jurors* did not (Tsongas *et al.*, 1986, p. 9). The dilemma that remains is whether lay judges are able to describe accurately the degree to which they understood the legal issues in the case if they do not know the law. Results of Ellsworth's study (1989) make this issue particularly troublesome: jurors in that study were not able to recognize the correct answer in regard to the legal issues when they heard it — during deliberation, they were as likely to substitute the correct answer with an erroneous one as they were to substitute an erroneous answer with the correct one.

Lawyers, on the other hand, may lean in the opposite direction — they may actually underestimate the **frequency and importance of lay judges' participation,** as well as lay judges' ability to understand the law and evaluate evidence. As members of mixed tribunals who enjoy higher status, professional judges will have the tendency to evaluate lay judges' contribution and ability as lower than their own. This can be coupled with the notion that the professional judges' general opinion on mixed tribunals (which was either mildly positive or negative) reinforces their perceptions about lay judges' contribution and its importance and, in turn, is reinforced by these perceptions. At the same time, consistent with the phenomenon of self-serving bias, professional judges will tend to overestimate their own ability compared to the ability and contribution by an average professional judge.

Possible overestimates by lay judges and underestimates by professional judges still leave portions of these discrepancies unexplained. The opinions held by professional judges and lay judges were in agreement about the frequency with which lay judges asked questions during trials, while they differed about the frequency with which lay judges made comments during deliberation. That difference, however, was only present for a subset of professional judges and lay judges — those from district courts. Professional judges from district courts (unlike professional judges from regional courts) had a negative opinion about the system of mixed tribunals in general and it is quite possible that they evaluated the actual behavior of lay judges through the lenses of that opinion and, at the same time, that the actual behavior of lay judges (which in reality may include less frequent participation in deliberations at district courts than at regional courts) reinforced their general negative opinion.

The discrepancies in the estimates of the importance of lay judges' participation, the content of their comments, and their ability to evaluate evidence may reflect differing perspectives on what the key issues in the case are and how to evaluate them. Professional judges, being skilled professionals, may have believed that all tribunal members should follow the legalistic approach. Lay judges, on the other hand, may have perceived that their role is more social in nature and more open toward the humanitarian, emotional aspects of the case than toward the strict enforcement of the law. Indeed, the majority of lay judges in the Polish study thought that lay judges served a function in counteracting the tendency of statutory law to ignore the realities of life (Borucka-Arctowa, 1976).

Furthermore, each member's choice to focus on and discuss a particular piece of evidence is heavily influenced by the member's level of knowledge about that piece of evidence and other evidence in the case. Professional judges, as results of this and other studies (Kulcsár, 1972; Borucka-Arctowa, 1976) suggested, have a distinct advantage over lay judges; while professional judges have not only an opportunity but also an obligation to read the case file in order to prepare for the trial (e.g., to determine the order of evidence presentation; to prepare questions for the defendant[s], witnesses, and expert witnesses), lay judges typically do not have such an opportunity either because of technical barriers (e.g., they do not know in advance in which case they will participate on the day they come to court) or because of the informal tendency to withhold the case file from the lay judges. Hale (1973, p. 99) described such an advantage of professional judges over the jury:

> Any system will work well or ill according to the quality of the persons administering it, but it is suggested that in a case of any complexity a judge is likely to be a more reliable finder of fact than a jury. This is not because a judge is necessarily more

intelligent than a juror or combination of jurors: nor does it rest on the judge's greater familiarity with the work because facility of decision is not synonymous with correctness of decision. The great advantage possessed by a judge sitting alone is that he is able to go back and back to the documents and the transcript, and to take as long as he needs to reach his conclusions: he has the better means of being right.

Finally, there is a realistic possibility that lay judges indeed overestimated their ability to understand legal issues and that the "true" evaluation of the ability of lay judges to understand legal issues is closer to the estimates furnished by professional judges. Results of research studies on jurors' understanding of legal instructions in their usual form suggest that there may be some merit to this viewpoint (Charrow and Charrow, 1979; Elwork *et al.*, 1977; Elwork *et al.*, 1982; Hastie *et al.*, 1983; Severance and Loftus, 1982). However, it is important to keep in mind that there are several crucial differences between jurors and lay judges in mixed tribunals: upon receiving oral and/or written legal instructions from the professional judge jurors are sent to deliberate by themselves, while lay judges do not receive *any* legal instructions before the deliberation with the professional judge begins. Therefore, whether the lay judges will understand the legal issues in the case depends to a great degree on the professional judge(s) in the tribunal, that is, on the availability of time and willingness to explain the law to the lay judges.

Professional judges and lay judges shared the opinion that lay judges rarely **disagreed** with professional judges. This finding is consistent with status characteristics theory: since professional judges enjoy a higher status in the tribunal than lay judges do, professional judges' opinion is evaluated as more important (and thus followed more frequently) than that furnished by lay judges.

Because the professional judges' formal position is determined by the law and because of the tendency of humans to attribute the leadership position to those who participate in discussions more frequently (Regula and Julian, 1973), professional judges will be perceived not only as members of higher status, but also as leaders in the group. Quantity and quality of verbal contributions affect the opinion the group members develop about the speaker's competence, influence, and leadership ability (Sorrentino and Boutillier, 1975; Carli, 1991). Research studies showed that members of higher status in the group are more likely to interrupt and are more successful in interrupting when they interact with lower status members than when they interact with higher status members (Rogers and Jones, 1975; O'Barr, 1982; Roger and Nesshoever, 1987). Lay judges, being the members of lower status, will not feel comfortable contradicting professional judges (whom they perceive as experts on the subject matter of the group task), which in itself creates a propensity toward low rates of disagreement.

That both professional judges and lay judges reported relatively low frequencies of disagreement is not surprising because the great majority of respondents stated that professional judges usually started the deliberation with summation of the evidence (which is not required by law). To a significant degree, summation of the evidence prevents disagreements which might result from the fact that professional judges and lay judges are afforded different levels of availability of information about the case. It also provides an opportunity for professional judges to present their views on the evidence in the case by either explicitly commenting on a particular piece of evidence or by deciding to discuss or omit certain pieces of evidence during summation. It is quite possible that the professional judge's view on a particular piece of evidence will become clear during summation even if is not explicitly stated. Kennedy (in Cheang, 1973, p. 125-126) described how the presiding professional judge in the case of Dr. Stephen Ward carried out summation to the jury:

> It was not that the judge had omitted what was favourable to Ward — the record belied that. It was simply a question of emphasis. When the judge was pointing out to the jury those things in favour of Ward, he often did so in a flat, matter-of-fact voice. He appeared so uninterested in what he was saying that one could not be interested oneself: the mind automatically shut off from him. Yet when it came to matters which told against Ward,

> his tone changed: his voice and bearing became brighter, livelier,
> he held the attention where elsewhere he had lost it.

Indeed, respondents in this study, including both professional judges and lay judges, clearly agreed that disagreements were less frequent when summation of evidence was performed than when it was not. In other words, as the professional judges in Klausa's study (1972) argued, there are methods of persuading lay judges (and summation may be one of them).

On the other hand, infrequent disagreements may be surprising from a different perspective. If the roles played by lay judges and by professional judges are not identical (the former being primarily "social" and the latter being primarily "professional"), occasional disagreements of opinion are bound to happen. Willingness to express one's opinion is typically related to the perceptions about the likely reaction by other group members. The results of earlier studies (Casper and Zeisel, 1972; Frassine *et al.*, 1979; Ljubanović, 1983) suggested that the overwhelming majority of disagreements between professional judges and lay judges were resolved in a specific way: the disagreeing lay judge changed his/her opinion. Not surprisingly, group interaction was important for the lay judges' willingness to express their disagreement; lay judges who perceived that their opinion was more likely to be accepted by the professional judge were more likely to say that they expressed their disagreement (Kulcsár, 1982, p. 97).

An interesting question is whether this difference of opinion would become a verbalized disagreement; there still may be plenty of room left for lay judges to try to persuade professional judges indirectly, that is, without explicitly stating their differing opinion. Indeed, the results of Kulcsár's study (1982) suggested that the majority of lay judges who said that they disagreed with the professional judge did not *express* their disagreement explicitly. It is, therefore, quite plausible that lay judges have an opinion that differs from the professional judges' opinion substantially more frequently than lay judges actually choose to reveal. Such a decision may be motivated by their experience: they may have formed an impression that professional judges would not accept their opinion. Consequently, they may decide either to "go with the flow" or to try to persuade other members of the tribunal without voicing an explicit disagreement.

Demographic characteristics of the lay judges who participated in this study were often not significant predictors of the way they perceived their work in the tribunal. A notable exception was the importance of education and occupational prestige of lay judges for the reported frequency of disagreement. Lay judges who were more educated and/or who held more prestigious occupations had a status that was somewhat higher than that of lay judges who were less educated and/or held less prestigious occupations. While such a status differential suggests that the former group of lay judges would feel less inhibited to express their disagreement with professional judges, the results of this study suggest that more educated lay judges and lay judges holding more prestigious occupations were actually *less* likely to say that they disagreed with professional judges. There are at least two factors that contribute to such a finding. First, assuming that political orientation has been controlled for, it is quite possible that more educated lay judges and lay judges holding more prestigious occupations have indeed *disagreed* with professional judges *less frequently* because they were more likely to belong to the same social class as professional judges do and thus to share the same system of values, which in turn may have led to more similar opinion in general, especially on sentencing issues. Second, more educated lay judges and lay judges who hold more prestigious occupations are likely to be more persuasive and more convincing in *implicitly* getting their point across and thus avoiding explicit disagreement.

A variable that frequently plays an important role in the analysis of the respondents' opinion is the **type of court/office** at which the respondents serve or perform their role. In the instances in which the type of court/office was important, the respondents from regional courts/offices evaluated lay participation more positively (regardless of whether these were the estimates of lay judges' activity, importance of that activity, or general ability) than the respondents from district courts/offices. Since there is no reason to believe that there were differences in the ability and skill of lay judges who served at the two types of courts, explanations for this discrepancy are likely to lie elsewhere. To begin with, because the cases tried at regional courts are more serious, it is possible that lay judges may be more interested in the case and more active because the stakes are higher and professional judges may be more willing to discuss the case with other tribunal members. Second, the size and the composition of tribunals are not identical for the cases tried at district courts and regional courts. It appears that the vast majority of trials by mixed tribunals at regional courts are tried by large tribunals (see Chapter 4), which may provide an atmosphere that is more conducive toward real group discussion of the case than that which prevails in small tribunals. To adopt Ellsworth's terminology (1989), not only may five heads be better than three, but the presence of two professional judges in large mixed tribunals may also stimulate a more lively exchange of opinion among professional judges, which in turn has the potential to induce increased levels of participation by lay judges. Similarly, Casper and Zeisel (1972, p. 152) pointed out that the size and the composition of mixed tribunals had influenced the frequency of disagreement; the frequency of disagreement among the tribunal members was higher in tribunals composed of nine members than in the tribunals composed of three or five members. Furthermore, the rate of lay judges' disagreement was higher when professional judges disagreed among themselves (Casper and Zeisel, 1972, p. 153).

General opinion about lay participation is an interesting subject for study in itself. Research studies found that professional judges in common-law countries voiced strong support for the jury system. For example, the results of Doob's study (1979c) found that most of the surveyed Canadian professional judges had a very favorable opinion about the jury system. Similarly, Harris *al.* (1987, p. 79-80) reported that three-quarters of the surveyed federal and state professional judges in the United States agreed that, "for routine civil cases, the right to trial by jury is an essential safeguard which much be retained."

However, when researchers made further inquiries, they found the level of enthusiasm was not as high as the above results would seem to suggest. For example, when professional judges in Doob's study (1979c) were asked to compare jury verdicts and verdicts by professional judges, their enthusiasm for the jury system turned out to be less overwhelming: professional judges perceived themselves as more likely to come up with just and fair verdicts than juries were. Similarly, two-thirds of professional judges in the study by Harris *et al.* (1987, p. 79-80) agreed that, "a serious study should be made of alternatives to trial by jury for certain types of cases."

Previous research studies on mixed tribunals indicated that professional judges in civil-law countries reported an entire range of opinion. Professional judges expressed an overall positive opinion about mixed tribunals (Kubicki and Zawadzki, 1970; Klausa, 1972), voiced an overall positive opinion and offered sharp criticisms on specific issues (Görlitz, 1970; Kulcsár, 1972, 1982; Ljubanović, 1983, 1989), or had a negative overall opinion (Kamhi and Čalija, 1974; Klami and Hämäläinen, 1992). For example, although six out of ten professional judges in the study by Görlitz (1970) said that their overall opinion was positive, almost one-half of the professional judges said that lay judges contributed *nothing* or almost nothing to the verdict. Similarly, despite the fact that professional judges in Kulcsár's study (1972, 1982) and Ljubanović's study (1983, 1989) expressed a positive opinion about lay participation, they said that they would have reached a wrong verdict rarely, if ever, without the presence of lay participants.

Although this study generally found that lay judges held a much more positive opinion about mixed tribunals than lawyers did, professional judges, state attorneys, and attorneys expressed a *positive* opinion about mixed tribunals and reported that trials by mixed tribunals had positive features. However, the majority of these lawyers at the same time reported that the system of mixed tribunals should be abolished or changed drastically and that they preferred professional judges alone or professional tribunals (but not the jury) over mixed tribunals. In other words, the stereotypes which maintain that only skilled professionals are able to make legal decisions came to surface once again.

Perceptions about the frequency and importance of lay judges' activity, as well as perceptions about lay judges' ability to evaluate evidence and understand legal issues, were evaluated through the prism of the evaluators' general opinion about lay judges; their general opinion was reinforced by the observed frequency and importance of lay judges' activity and their observed ability to evaluate evidence and understand legal issues. Indeed, the respondents who perceived the questions and comments raised by lay judges to be less frequent and less important, as well as those who perceived lay judges to be less able to evaluate evidence and understand legal issues, were at the same time more likely to say that their opinion about mixed tribunals was negative.

Respondents evaluated Croatian mixed tribunals positively because of the political function they perform, the opportunity for citizen participation, and the potential for the introduction of community values into the criminal justice system. The most frequent criticism of mixed tribunals, voiced by both professional judges and lay judges, was lay judges' (in)ability to understand and evaluate evidence. Not surprisingly, respondents believed that the most important improvements to the system of mixed tribunals included items related to lay judges' ability to understand evidence. Lay judges asked for more detailed explanations by professional judges, while professional judges, state attorneys, and attorneys asked for lay judges who are experts in certain fields ("blue-ribbon" lay judges). Finally, professional judges and lay judges agreed that one of the most important improvements would be the introduction of short seminars about criminal law and procedure.

Lay judges do not receive systematic information about their rights and duties or about criminal trials. Typical novice lay judges are probably not very familiar with the flow of a typical trial and their roles in it. It appears, then, that a readable, introductory booklet that would aim to prepare lay judges for their duty by presenting them with relevant information would be more than welcome.

Interestingly, while no such attempt was undertaken in recent times, five decades ago, that is, a few years after the end of World War II, the Yugoslav Ministry of Justice published a booklet titled *The Role of Lay Judges in Our Administration of Justice* (1948). The purpose of the booklet was to familiarize lay judges with their role and their rights and duties. It was written at a level accessible to literate lay audiences. Upon stating the purpose of the booklet, the authors discussed the roles of people's courts and put positive features of lay participation in the context of the Yugoslav system. The booklet next featured a description of criminal and civil trials, which was followed by a discussion of the organization of justice administration and the courtroom workgroup. Particular emphasis was put on lay judges' rights and duties and positive functions they could achieve (*The Role of Lay Judges in Our Administration of Justice*, 1948, p. 30-31):

> In the course of the trial itself, lay judges have the duty to monitor the proceedings carefully, to familiarize themselves with the case completely, and to later participate in decision-making actively. Lay judges are not summoned to the court merely to observe and listen to what others do and say and ultimately merely to confirm what the presiding professional judge proposes. They are equal tribunal members and decisions reached by the tribunal are their deeds as well. They should thus participate in decision-making actively and with interest.

Finally, the appendix to this small booklet includes a shortened version of the then applicable statute that regulated the organization of the system of justice administration in general and lay judges' rights and duties in particular. While little is known about how successful the application of the booklet in practice really was, the booklet by all means had the potential to be a very useful tool. Interestingly, no such booklet has been available to lay judges in recent times.

Unlike juries, which typically do not have to apply the law and even have the right to bend the law, lay judges in mixed tribunals have the responsibility to apply the law. In order to be able to perform this task, they first have to be familiar with the relevant legal rules and to understand them. Short courses or informative booklets (not unlike the one designed by the Yugoslav Ministry of Justice in 1948) about their rights and duties and about the basic elements of trial would inform lay judges *before* the actual trial and would thus prepare them for it. Having a basic level of familiarity with one's rights and duties, that is, knowing "the rules of the game" before the game starts, eliminates a large part of the guessing from the lay judges' effort and allows lay judges to spend more energy on substantive issues. Being provided with relevant legal statutes (describing both the lay judges' role and the most important aspects of trial) before the trial would undoubtedly be very useful for lay judges both during the trial itself and, especially, during deliberation, just like it was useful for the jurors in Diamond's study (Diamond, 1993, p. 296).

Lay judges typically do not receive relevant legal information before the trial. Kubicki and Zawadzki (1970, p. 104) reported that lay judges received information about the legal issues in the case from the professional judge *before* the trial started in only 20% of the cases; this study and other studies suggested that lay judges rarely read the case file (Kubicki and Zawadzki, 1970; Klausa, 1972; Kulcsár, 1982). However, any consideration of the introduction of obligatory pre-trial legal information should be carried out with due caution.

First, short seminars about criminal law and criminal procedure for lay judges would not transform lay judges into lawyers, neither should such a transformation be the purpose of these seminars; professional judges would still be the experts on the subject of law. However, discrepancies between the states/levels of specific status characteristics would be lessened, since lay judges would be perceived as more competent by professional judges and would feel more competent (and more confident!) to detect important issues in the case and to apply the rules of evidence evaluation. Furthermore, lay judges would be familiar with the flow of the criminal process; they would also know that they are supposed to participate in the process actively. Professional judges, on the other hand, might be more satisfied with the lay judges' contribution, since they would need to invest less time introducing basic legal concepts to lay judges and would instead be able to spend more time discussing other issues in the case.

Second, the timing of these seminars or of the distribution of booklets may be important. Jury studies suggest that jurors who received preinstruction both before the evidence was presented and afterwards appeared to like being given the preinstruction (Heuer and Penrod, 1989, p. 426). However, the danger associated with such a practice is that jurors might form their opinion before the last piece of evidence is presented and try to evaluate each piece of evidence in accordance with their opinion ("hypothesis-confirming search"). The same problem might surface with lay judges, who may become overly confident in their legal skills and, based on the simplified version of criminal procedure they have been exposed to, may "lock in" their vote/opinion without considering the possibility that additional legal details (of which they are presently unaware of) might change the whole outcome. Furthermore, lay judges might develop the tendency to rely more heavily on the law and on their knowledge of the criminal justice system (i.e., to perform the professional function) and to thereby neglect their social function.

Another suggestion by professional judges was to introduce "specialist" lay judges. Currently, the Croatian legal system recognizes certain criminal cases in which only "specialists" can sit as lay judges — the criminal cases that concern juveniles. The basic idea behind this rule is to attain the highest possible quality of legal decisions by utilizing decision-makers who are trained in child and adolescent psychology and pedagogy. The introduction of lay judges who possess specialized professional knowledge may also increase the status lay judges have in the tribunal and affect directly the frequency and importance of their participation — specialist lay judges would take more floor time and their comments would be evaluated as more important than the comments made by "regular" lay judges. For example, the results reported by Krystufek (1976) suggested that if lay judges possessed specialized non-legal technical knowledge about the issues in the case, they usually expressed their opinion and tribunals tended to rely on their expertise.

There are at least two problems associated with this idea. First, the line between the role of a fact-finder and an expert witness would be blurred. While the professional judge (who is a lay person in that particular field of expertise) would have an easier time while making a decision (as would the whole tribunal), the question that remains is whether other evidence and other issues in the case would be perceived by the "expert" lay judge through the lens of this particular piece of evidence or issue.

Second, some of the basic principles that govern the introduction of lay participation (e.g., providing *all* citizens with the opportunity to participate in the government, ensuring that community voices and values be heard) would be violated. Peers would no longer participate in legal decision-making and cases would instead be decided by a professional tribunal composed of experts in law (professional judges) and experts in other fields (economists, engineers, physicians). Although the level of understanding of expert evidence by such professional tribunals would without any doubt be higher than the level attainable by "ordinary" mixed tribunals and "blue-ribbon" lay judges would have a higher status in the tribunal than "average" lay judges, other values (some of which may be of crucial importance for the defendants) would inevitably be sacrificed.

Furthermore, the results of this study and other studies (Kubicki and Zawadzki, 1970; Kulcsár, 1982) suggest that lay judges rarely read the case file, either because they were not given sufficient time and adequate opportunity (e.g., the case file is locked in the professional judge's file cabinet), or because they were not interested in reading it. Furthermore, Kulcsár (1982) reported that the frequency of asking questions of merit and reading the case file were positively related; lay judges who read the case file were more likely to ask questions and make comments of merit than lay judges who did not read the case file. Just like professional judges always read the case file in advance, reading the case file would provide an opportunity for lay judges to familiarize themselves with the case before the trial starts. Reading the case file would probably increase the frequency of lay judges' participation; however, it may also have an undesirable effect of creating the potential for lay judges to reach a decision before the trial is over.

Many of the problems encountered in the work of mixed tribunals have been experienced by **other heterogeneous decision-making bodies** — mixed groups composed of members who differ with respect to specific status characteristics. It follows, then, that the study of mixed tribunals has broader implications.

Mixed tribunals are somewhat similar to *occupational licensing boards*, a heterogeneous small task-oriented group utilized in the United States. Similarities lie in the fact that both groups contain professional members and lay members and are charged with making their decisions jointly. While lay judges are typically in the majority in mixed tribunals, lay members in occupational licensing boards may be either in the majority or in the minority. The introduction of lay participants in occupational licensing boards fulfills a function which also motivates the introduction of lay participation in legal decision-making — the political function. In the context of occupational licensing boards, this political function is often formulated as the tendency to provide the consumers with an additional layer of protection from incompetent service providers by increasing lay participation on the board. Interestingly, one of the arguments for keeping lay members on boards echoes the latent function of lay judges in mixed tribunals: "If nothing else, it may be that the presence of public members in increased numbers on occupational regulatory boards has prevented the erosion of the consumer point of view that might have occurred without their presence" (Schutz, 1983, p. 515).

Mixed tribunals and occupational licensing boards also share certain negative features. It seems that any attempt to introduce a form of lay participation in the groups in which professionals make decisions unleashes comments about lay participants' lack of technical expertise and, as a consequence, their incompetence to make decisions. Critics of lay participation in occupational licensing boards argue that, "it is risky to concentrate responsibilities requiring technical expertise among fewer licensee members, and that licensees may re-sent being governed by individuals with limited technical knowledge" (Schutz, 1983, p. 505).

Finally, the direct impact of lay members in mixed tribunals and occupational licensing boards is similar: studies on occupational licensing boards (Schutz, 1983; Schneider, 1987; Graddy and Nichol, 1989) also suggest that the direct impact of lay members on the work of occupational licensing boards is not significant. One of the studies (Schutz, 1983) reported that the increase in lay participation made little difference with respect to the tasks occupational licensing boards perform.

Social security appeal tribunals in the United Kingdom are another example of a heterogeneous group in which group members differ with respect to the levels of specific status characteristics they possess. A series of research results known as "The Bell Report" (Bell *et al.*, 1974; Bell *et al.*, 1975; Bell, 1982) led to the introduction of a law that required all chairmen of social security appeal tribunals to be legally qualified. Gradual transition took place over a five-year period (1984-1989), during which these tribunals were presided over either by legally qualified chairmen or by lay chairmen. This provided a unique opportunity for social scientists to study and compare the underlying dynamics of the two varieties of social security appeal tribunals.

Results of research studies (Jackson *et al.*, 1987; Wikeley and Young, 1992) suggested that professionalization, judicialization, as well as greater reliance on rules and regulations, resulted in the marginalization of lay members in the tribunals presided by legally qualified chairmen. It was clear that lay chairmen were more likely to invite contributions from other members than legal chairmen were (85% *v.* 67%, respectively; Jackson *et al.*, 1987, p. 249-250); lay members in the tribunals presided over by lay chairmen were more likely to ask questions of appellants and representatives than lay members in the tribunals presided over by legal chairmen (Jackson *et al.*, 1987, p. 250). Wikeley and Young (1992, p. 138) further reported that lay members were not very active in the work of tribunals; they "often fail to participate actively in the deliberations," the majority of deliberations took five minutes or less, and the decision was unanimous in 98% of the cases.

Wikeley and Young (1992) found additional evidence of marginalization of lay members by comparing the results of their study (conducted after the period of transition was over) to the results of the study by Jackson *et al.* (1987). While Wikeley and Young (1992) found that approximately one-half of all lay members were entirely silent throughout the appeal hearings conducted by professionalized tribunals, Jackson *et al.* (1987) reported that lay members made no contribution in approximately one-fifth of the hearings. Wikeley and Young (1992, p. 139) explained the lay members' marginalization by appealing to the advantages legal chairmen have over lay members. These advantages were analogous to the specific status characteristics possessed by professional judges (and lacked by lay judges) in mixed tribunals: "a legal background, superior training and an expertise built up through their more frequent attendance at hearings" (Wikeley and Young, 1992, p. 139).

A similar conclusion may be drawn when mixed tribunals are compared to the *grand jury* in the United States. Although the grand jury is composed only of jurors and professional judges do not take part in their decisions, there is another lawyer who, although not officially a member of the group, has a significant impact on the group's decision — grand jury proceedings are *ex parte* procedures headed by the prosecutor.

Results of research studies on the grand jury (Carp, 1975; Rowland, 1979) showed that the prosecutor, a professional lawyer, exerts a high degree of influence on the decisions reached by the grand jury; in nearly one-half of the cases, the grand jury took on cases solely on the basis of what the district attorney claimed the defendant's file contained, without actually examining the file itself. Furthermore, the grand jury refused to follow the district attorney's recommendations in only 6% of the cases, and in 80% of the cases it voted with no discussion whatsoever. In other words, in reaching their decisions about indictments, jurors tend to rely heavily on the skill and integrity of the district attorney (Carp, 1975, p. 868):

Perceived as an expert, as a professional, the district attorney is constantly looked to for guidance and information as to the proper disposition of cases and as to the legitimate functions of the grand jury. The prosecutor is fully aware of the grand jury's reliance on him in this regard and his subsequent behavior fully verifies the maxim that knowledge is power.

Carp (1975) listed several reasons for such seemingly surprising results. First, the composition of the grand jury was highly non-representative, which, according to Carp (1975), resulted in a low level of internal conflict among the grand jurors. Second, grand jurors do not learn about their duties, functions, and prerogatives from an independent source; the prosecutor has the primary role in their training and indoctrination. Third, the enormous size of the caseload creates pressure on grand jurors to decide cases quickly. The last but not the least important issue discussed by Carp (1975) deals with the factors that establish the prosecutor's dominant position. As novices, grand jurors learn from the prosecutor about their rights and duties; since they do not have a full understanding of these issues until the third session, as Carp reported (1975, p. 867), "there exists the strong potential that they will become 'rubber stamps' of the district attorney's staff." The question then remains to what degree do grand juries actually perform their role — that of protecting criminal defendants from overzealous prosecutors (Carp, 1975; Rowland, 1979).

While the analogy with mixed tribunals is admittedly not perfect — the prosecutor is not a member of the decision-making body and, furthermore, has been the one who trained the jurors — it is nevertheless very strong. Similar to mixed tribunals, the grand jury features a dominant entity (the prosecutor) who overshadows the jury members with the level of legal knowledge and experience.

In a broad context, every heterogeneous decision-making body composed of professional and lay members, be it the mixed tribunal, licensing board, social security appeal tribunal, or student disciplinary board, will experience similar kinds of problems. If lay members are to be members of such decision-making bodies because of all the positive functions these bodies may achieve, then they need to be provided with an atmosphere conducive to their participation and with an adequate opportunity to participate. Lay judges who are familiar with their rights and duties in the proceedings, who face well-intentioned and respectful professional judges, who are well-informed about the circumstances of the case, and who have the time and the opportunity to read the case file, will likely participate more actively and, as a result, contribute toward emphasizing the positive functions of lay participation. Failure to provide such a conducive environment not only creates a fertile soil for sharp criticism, but also undermines the very intent and purpose of lay participation.

Bibliography

Abel, R. L. (1985). Comparative sociology of legal professions: An explanatory essay. *American Bar Foundation Research Journal*, 8, 5-79.

Abramson, J. (1994). *We, the Jury*. New York: Basic Books.

Allen, J. L. (1977). Attitude change following jury duty. *Justice System Journal*, 2, 246-257.

Allison, J. (1990). In search of revolutionary justice in South Africa. *International Journal of the Sociology of Law*, 18, 409-428.

Allot, A. N. (1957). The judicial ascertainment of customary law in British Africa. *The Modern Law Review*, 20, 244-263.

Anderson, S. (1990). Lay judges and jurors in Denmark. *The American Journal of Comparative Law*, 38, 839-864.

Aries, E. (1976). Male-female interpersonal styles in all male, all female, and mixed groups. In A. G. Sargent (Ed.), *Beyond Sex Roles*. St. Paul, MN: West Publishing Co.

Arzt, G. (1982). Review of Der Laienrichter im Strafprozess. Vier empirische Studien zur Rechtsvergleichung, by Casper G. & Zeisel H. *The American Journal of Comparative Law*, 30, 154-155.

Bajić–Petrović, L. (1985a). Odlike i osobenosti sudija porotnika u sudskoj praksi. *Pravo*, 2, 48-56.

Bajić–Petrović, L. (1985b). Učešće gradjana u ostvarivanju sudske funkcije u opštinskim i višim sudovima SAP Vojvodine. *Komuna*, 27, 43-47.

Baldwin, J. (1974). Magistrates and their training. *Justice of the Peace*, 138, 715-717.

Baldwin, J. (1975). The compulsory training of the magistracy. *Criminal Law Review*, 22, 634-643.

Baldwin, J. & McConville, M. (1979a). Trial by jury: Some empirical evidence on contested criminal cases in England. *Law and Society Review*, 13, 861-890.

Baldwin, J. & McConville, M. (1979b). *Jury Trials.* London: Oxford University Press.

Balkwell, J. W. (1994). Status. In M. Foschi & E. J. Lawler (Eds.), *Group Processes: Sociological Analyses.* Chicago: Nelson-Hall Publishers.

Balkwell, J. W. & Berger, J. (1996). Gender, status, and behavior in task situations. *Social Psychology Quarterly*, 59, 273-283.

Barada, M. (1952). *Hrvatski vlasteoski feudalizam po Vinodolskom zakonu.* Zagreb, Croatia: Jugoslavenska akademija znanosti i umjetnosti.

Baumhart, R. (1968). *An Honest Profit.* New York: Prentice-Hall.

Bayer, V. (1940). *Problem sudjelovanja nepravnika u savremenom kaznenom sudovanju.* Zagreb, Croatia.

Bayer, V. (1955). Suci porotnici. *Zbornik Pravnog fakulteta u Zagrebu*, 5, 142-156.

Bayer, V. (1988). *Jugoslavensko krivično procesno pravo.* Knjiga prva. Uvod u teoriju krivičnog procesnog prava. 8th ed. Zagreb, Croatia: Narodne novine.

Bayer, V. (1989). *Jugoslavensko krivično procesno pravo.* Knjiga druga. Pravo o činjenicama i njihovom utvrdjivanju u krivičnom postupku. 5th ed. Zagreb, Croatia: Narodne novine.

Bayer, V. (1995). *Kazneno procesno pravo - odabrana poglavlja.* Prepared by D. Krapac. Zagreb, Croatia: Ministry of the Interior.

Bell, K. (1982). Social security tribunals: A general perspective. *Northern Ireland Legal Quarterly*, 33, 132-47.

Bell, K., Collinson, P., Turner, S., & Webber, S. (1974). National insurance local tribunals: A research study - Part I. *Journal of Social Policy*, 3, 289-315.

Bell, K., Collinson, P., Turner, S., & Webber, S. (1975). National insurance locall tribunals: A research study - Part II. *Journal of Social Policy*, 4, 1-24.

Benz, U. (1982). *Zur Rolle der Laienrichter im Strafprozess*. Lübeck, Germany: Schmidt Römhild.

Berger, J., Fişek, M. H., Norman, R. Z., & Zelditch, M., Jr. (1977). *Status Characteristics and Social Interaction: An Expectation–States Approach*. New York: Elsevier.

Berger, J., Rosenholtz, S. J., & Zelditch, M., Jr. (1980). Status organizing process. In A. Inkeles, N. J. Smelser, & R. H. Turner (Eds.), *Annual Review of Sociology*, 6. Palo Alto, CA: Annual Reviews.

Berger, J., Webster, M., Jr., Ridgeway, C., & S. J., Rosenholtz, S. J. (1986). Status cues, expectations, and behavior. In E. J. Lawler (Ed.), *Advances in Group Processes*, Volume 3. Greenwich, CT: Jai Press, Inc.

Berman, J. (1969). The Cuban popular tribunals. *Columbia Law Review*, 69, 1317-1354.

Beuc, I. (1989). *Povijest država i prava na području SFRJ*. Zagreb, Croatia: Narodne novine.

Block, B. P. (1996). Justice and justices. *Justice of the Peace & Local Government Law*, 160, 887.

Bond, R. A. & Lemon, N. F. (1981). Training, experience, and magistrates' sentencing philosophies. *Law and Human Behavior*, 5, 123-139.

Borucka-Arctowa, M. (1976). Citizen participation in the administration of justice: Research and policy in Poland. In L. Friedman & M. Rehbinder (Eds.), *Zur Soziologie des Gerichtsverfahrens. Jahrbuch für Rechtssoziologie und Rechtstheorie*, 4, 286-299. Opladen: Westdeutscher Verlag.

Buchholz, I. (1986). The role of the lay assessors in the German Democratic Republic (GDR). *International Journal of Comparative and Applied Criminal Justice*, 10, 215-222.

Bundesministerium der Justiz. (1997). Geschlechts- und Berufsstruktur der Schöffen im Bundesgebiet im Vergleich mit der Bevölkerungsstruktur. Bonn: *Bundesministerium der Justiz.* Unpublished report.

Burman, S. (1989). The role of street committees: Continuing South Africa's practice of alternative justice. In H. Corder (Ed.), *Democracy and the Judiciary.* Mowbray, Capetown: Institute for a Democratic Alternative for South Africa.

Burns, P. T. (1973). A profile of the jury system in New Zealand. *Western Australian Law Review*, 11, 105-110.

Butler, W. E. (1972). Comradely justice in Eastern Europe. *Current Legal Problems*, 25, 200-218.

Carli, L. L. (1991). Gender, status, and influence. In E. J. Lawler, B. Markovsky, C. Ridgeway, & H. A. Walker (Eds.), *Advances in Group Processes*, Volume 8. Greenwich, CT: Jai Press, Inc.

Carp, R. A. (1975). The behavior of grand juries: Acquiescence or justice? *Social Science Quarterly*, 55, 853-870.

Casper, G. & Zeisel, H. (1972). Lay Judges in the German Criminal Courts. *The Journal of Legal Studies*, 1, 135-191.

Cecil, J. S., Lind, E. A., & Bermant, G. (1987). *Jury Service in Lengthy Civil Trials.* Washington, DC: Federal Judicial Center.

1981 Census of Population, Households, and Residences; Active Population and Employed Workers. Popis stanovništva, domaćinstava i stanova 1981; aktivno stanovništvo i zaposleni radnici (1986). Zagreb, Croatia: Republički zavod za statistiku Republike Hrvatske.

Chang, D. H. & Janeksela, G. M. (1996). An analysis of the Korean criminal justice system. In C. B. Fields & R. H. Moore, Jr. (Eds.), *Comparative Criminal Justice.* Prospect Heights, IL: Waveland Press.

Charrow, R. & Charrow, V. (1979). Making legal language understandable: A psycholinguistic study of jury instructions. *Columbia Law Review*, 79, 1306-1374.

Cheang, M. (1973). Jury trial: The Singapore experience. *Western Australian Law Review*, 11, 120-132.

Clark, J. P. (1989). Conflict management outside the courtrooms in China. In R. J. Troyer, J. P. Clark, & D. G. Rojek (Eds.), *Social Control in the People's Republic of China*. New York: Praeger.

Collins, B. E. & Guetzkow, H. (1964). *A Social Psychology of Group Processes for Decision Making*. New York: Wiley.

Consolini, P. M. (1992). *Learning by Doing Justice: Jury Service and Personal Attitudes*. Unpublished Ph.D. dissertation. University of California, Berkeley.

Croatia: Facts and Figures. (1997). Available at http://web.lexis-nexis.com.

1997 Croatian Almanac. (1998). Available at http://www.hina.hr/almanah97.

Cross, K. P. (1977). Not can, but will college teaching be improved? *New Directions for Higher Education*, 17, 1-15.

Costantini, E. & King, J. (1980/1981). The partial juror: Correlates and causes of prejudgment. *Law & Society Review*, 15, 9-39.

Čulinović, F. (1946). *Pravosudje u Jugoslaviji*. Zagreb, Croatia: Nakladni zavod Hrvatske.

Čulinović, F. (1954). Porota u Jugoslaviji. *Zbornik Pravnog fakulteta u Zagrebu*, 4, 40-58.

Dabinović, A. (1940). *Hrvatska državna i pravna povijest*. Zagreb, Croatia: Matica Hrvatska.

David, R. & Brierley, J. E. C. (1968). *Major Legal Systems in the World Today*. London: The Free Press.

Davis, J. A. & Smith, T. W. (1990). *General Social Surveys, 1972-1990: Cumulative Codebook*. Chicago, IL: National Opinion Research Center.

Dawson, J. P. (1960). *A History of Lay Judges.* Cambridge, MA: Harvard University Press.

Dawson, J. P. (1968). *The Oracles of the Law.* Ann Arbor, MI: The University of Michigan Law School.

Dean, M. (1995). Trial by jury: A force for change in Japan. *International and Comparative Law Quarterly,* 44, 379-404.

Diamond, S. S. (1990). Revising images of public punitiveness: Sentencing by lay and professional English magistrates. *Law and Social Inquiry,* 15, 191-221.

Diamond, S. S. (1993). What jurors think: Expectations and reactions of citizens who serve as jurors. In R. E. Litan (Ed.), *Verdict: Assessing the Civil Jury System.* Washington, DC: The Brookings Institution.

Diamond, S. S. & Stalans, L. J. (1989). The myth of judicial leniency in Sentencing. *Behavioral Sciences and the Law,* 7, 73-89.

Doob, A. N. (1979a). Public's view of the criminal jury trial: A report to the Law Reform Commission of Canada. In *Studies on the Jury.* Ottawa: Law Reform Commission of Canada.

Doob, A. N. (1979b). Canadian juror's view of the criminal jury trial: A report to the Law Reform Commission of Canada. In *Studies on the Jury.* Ottawa: Law Reform Commission of Canada.

Doob, A. N. (1979c). Canadian trial judges' view of the criminal jury trial: A report to the Law Reform Commission of Canada. In *Studies on the Jury.* Ottawa: Law Reform Commission of Canada.

Dow, P. E. (1981). *Discretionary Justice: A Critical Inquiry.* Cambridge, MA: Ballinger.

Dressel, P. L. & Mayhew, L. B. (1954). *General Education: Explorations in Evaluation.* Westport, CT: Greenwood Press.

Duff, P. (1990). The role of the jury in Hong Kong. *Hong Kong Law Journal,* 20, 367-380.

Duff, P., Findlay, M., & Howarth, C.(1990). The Hong Kong jury: A microcosm of society? *International and Comparative Law Quarterly*, 39, 881-891.

Duff, P., Findlay, M., Howarth, C., & Tsang-fai, C.(1992). *Juries: A Hong Kong perspective.* Hong Kong: Hong Kong University Press.

Eighty-Fifth Parliament Session (1874). Notes from the Parliament session held on October 13, 1874. Croatian Parliament.

Ellsworth, P. C. (1989). Are twelve heads better than one? *Law and Contemporary Problems*, 52, 205-223.

Elwork, A., Sales, B. D., & Alfini, J. (1977). Juridic decisions: In ignorance of the law or in light of it? *Law and Human Behavior*, 1, 163-180.

Elwork, A., Sales, B. D., & Alfini, J. (1982). *Making jury instructions understandable.* Indianapolis: Michie/Bobbs-Merrill.

Elwork, A. & Sales, B. D. (1985). Jury instructions. In S. Kassin & L. Wrightsman (Eds.), *The Psychology of Evidence and Trial Procedure.* Beverly Hills, CA: Sage.

Estey, F. N. (1951). The *scabini* and the local courts. *Speculum*, 26, 119-129.

Exline, R. V. & Ziller, R. C. (1959). Status congruency and interpersonal conflict in decision making groups. *Human Relations*, 12, 147-162.

Exner, F. (1933). Development of the administration of criminal justice in Germany. *Journal of the American Institute of Criminal Law and Criminology*, 24, 248-259.

Felkenes, G. T. (1989). Courts, sentencing, and the death penalty in the PRC. In R. J. Troyer, J. P. Clark, & D. G. Rojek (Eds.), *Social Control in the People's Republic of China.* New York: Praeger.

Felstiner, W. L. F. & Drew, A. B. (1978). *European Alternatives to Criminal Trials and Their Applicability in the United States.* Washington, D.C.: National Institute of Law Enforcement and Criminal Justice.

Field, H. (1979). Rape trials and jurors' decisions: A psychological analysis of the effects of victim, defendant, and case characteristics. *Law and Human Behavior*, 3, 261-284.

Fisher, B. A. (1974). *Small Group Decision Making: Communication and the Group Process.* New York: McGraw-Hill Book Company.

Fisher, E. A. (1975). Community courts: An alternative to conventional criminal adjudication. *The American University Law Review*, 24, 1253-1291.

Forsyth, W. (1875). *History of Trial by Jury.* New York: James Cockcroft & Co.

Frank, J. (1963). *Courts on Trial.* New York: Atheneum.

Frassine, I., Piska, K., & Zeisel, K. (1979). Kapitel: Österreich. In G. Casper & H. Zeisel (Eds.), *Der Laienrichter im Strafprozess.* Heidelberg, Germany: C. F. Müller Juristischer Verlag.

Friedgut, T. H. (1979). *Political Participation in the USSR.* Princeton: Princeton University Press.

Galanter, M. (1993). The regulatory function of the civil jury. In R. E. Litan (Ed.), *Verdict: Assessing the Civil Jury System.* Washington, DC: Brookings Institution.

Gergen, K. (1974). *Social Psychology: Explorations in Understanding.* New York: Random House.

Gerken, J. (1988). Bürger als Richter. Über Jugendschöffen und den Erziehungsanspruch des Jugendstrafrechts. In J. Gerken & K. F. Schumann (Eds.), *Ein trojanisches Pferd im Rechtsstaat.* Pfaffenweiler, Germany: Centaurus-Verlagsgessellschaft.

Germany: Facts and Figures. (1997). Available at http://web.lexis-nexis.com.

Gillespie, D. F. & Mileti, D. S. (1981). Heterogeneous samples in organizational research. *Sociological Methods & Research*, 9, 375-388.

Glass, G. V. & Hopkins, K. D. (1984). *Statistical Methods in Education and Psychology.* Boston: Allyn and Bacon.

Gneist, R. (1967). *Die Bildung der Geschworengerichte in Deutschland.* Reprint. Aalen, Germany: Scienta-Verlag.

Goldberg, R. (1968). Are women prejudiced against women? *Transaction,* 5, 28-30.

Goodman, J., Greene, E., & Loftus, E. F. (1985). What confuses jurors in complex cases. *Trial,* November, 65-74.

Gomard, B. (1976). *Studier i den Danske Straffeproces.* Copenhagen: Juristforbundet.

Görlitz, A. (1970). *Verwaltungsgerichtsbarkeit in Deutschland.* Neuwied am Rhein, Germany: Luchterhand.

Gottschall, J. (1983). Carter's judicial appointments: The influence of affirmative action and merit selection on voting on the U.S. courts of appeals. *Judicature,* 67, 165-173.

Graddy, E. & Nichol, M. B. (1989). Public members on occupational licensing boards: Effects on legislative regulatory reforms. *Southern Economic Journal,* 55, 610-625.

Grant, B. & Schwikkard, P.(1991). People's courts? *South African Journal on Human Rights,* 7, 304-316.

Gray, J. (1958). Opinions of assessors in criminal trials in East Africa as to native custom. *Journal of African Law,* 2, 5-18.

Green, T. A. (1985). *Verdict According to Conscience: Perspectives on the English Criminal Trial Jury 1200-1800.* Chicago, IL: University of Chicago Press.

Griffiths, J. (1997). Dutch political culture reflected in the mirror of the jury. *Maastrichts Journal of European and Comparative Law,* 4, 153-160.

Gross, S. R. (1991). Expert evidence. *Wisconsin Law Review,* 1991, 1112-1233.

Gruhl, J., Spohn, C., & Welch, S. (1981). Women as policymakers: The case of trial judges. *American Journal of Political Science,* 25, 308-322.

Gryski, G. S., Main, E. C., & Dixon, W. J. (1986). Models of state high court decision making in sex discrimination cases. *Journal of Politics, 48,* 143-155.

Hale, J. (1973). Juries: The West Australian experience. *Western Australian Law Review,* 11, 99-104.

Hammel, E. A. (1970). *The Ethnographer's Dilemma: Occupational Prestige in Belgrade.* Unpublished paper. University of California, Berkeley, Department of Anthropology.

Hans, V. P. & Doob, A. N. (1976). Section 12 of the Canada Evidence Act and the deliberations of simulated juries. *Criminal Law Quarterly,* 18, 235-253.

Hans, V. P. & Vidmar, N. (1986). *Judging the Jury.* New York: Plenum Press.

Harding, S. (1986). *The Science Question in Feminism.* Ithaca: Cornell University Press.

Harris, L. (1987). *Judges' Opinions on Procedural Issues: A Survey of State and Federal Judges Who Spend at Least Half Their Time on General Civil Cases.* New York: Aetna Life & Casualty.

Hastie, R., Penrod, S. D., & Pennington, N. (1983). *Inside the Jury.* Cambridge, MA: Harvard University Press.

Heath, T. J. (1993). God, man and the stipendiary. *Justice of the Peace,* 157, 137-138.

Heinz, J. P. & Laumann, E. O. (1982). *Chicago Lawyers: The Social Structure of the Bar.* New York: Russell Sage Foundation.

Henley, N. (1977). *Body Politics: Power, Sex, and Nonverbal Communication.* Englewood Cliffs, NJ: Prentice-Hall.

Herrmann, R. (1957). *Die Schöffen in den Strafgerichten des kapitalistischen Deutschland.* Berlin: Veb Deutscher Zentralverlag.

Heuer, L. & Penrod, S. D. (1989). Instructing jurors: A field experiment with written and preliminary instructions. *Law and Human Behavior,* 13, 409-430.

Hoffman, L. & Maier, N. (1961). Quality and acceptance of problem solutions by members of homogeneous and heterogeneous groups. *Journal of Abnormal and Social Psychology*, 62, 401-407.

Howard, B. E. (1904). Trial by jury in Germany. *Political Science Quarterly*, 19, 650-672.

Humphrey, R. (1985). How work roles influence perception: Structural-cognitive processes and organizational behavior. *American Sociological Review*, 50, 242-252.

Izraeli, D. (1985). The attitudinal effects of gender mix in union committees. *Industrial and Labor Relations Review*, 37, 212-221.

Jackson, M., Stewart, H., & Bland, R. (1987). Tribunals hearing supplementary benefit appeals: The members' role. *Policy and Politics*, 15, 245-251.

Jearey, J. H. (1960). Trial by jury and trial with the aid of assessors in the superior courts of British African Territories: I. *Journal of African Law*, 4, 133-146.

Jearey, J. H. (1961a). Trial by jury and trial with the aid of assessors in the superior courts of British African Territories: II. *Journal of African Law*, 5, 36-47.

Jearey, J. H. (1961b). Trial by jury and trial with the aid of assessors in the superior courts of British African Territories: III. *Journal of African Law*, 5, 82-98.

Jemrić, M. (1987). *Zakon o krivičnom postupku.* 5th ed. Zagreb, Croatia: Narodne novine.

Jolliffe, J. E. A. (1961). *The Constitutional History of Medieval England: From the English Settlement to 1485.* London: Adam and Charles Black.

Jovanović, M. (1958). *Porota u pravosudju Jugoslavije.* Beograd, Yugoslavia: Priručna biblioteka za pravna i društvena pitanja.

Kalven, H., Jr. & Zeisel, H. (1966). *The American Jury.* Chicago, IL: The University of Chicago Press.

Kamhi, S. & Čalija, B. (1974). *Sistem porote u našoj zemlji i problemi vezani za učešće gradjana u vršenju pravosudja*. Sarajevo, Bosnia and Herzegovina: Svjetlost.

Kapardis, A. & Farrington, D. P. (1981). An experimental study of sentencing by magistrates. *Law and Human Behavior*, 5, 107-121.

Kawaley, I. (1989). The fair cross-section principle: Trial by special jury and the right to criminal jury trial under the Bermuda Constitution. *International and Comparative Law Quarterly*, 38, 523-546.

Kaznin, (1963). A court of comrades (Sud Tovarishchei), *Pravda*, Nov. 13, 1963, p. 4.

Kerr, N. L., Harmon, D. L., & Graves, J. K. (1982). Independence of multiple verdicts by jurors and juries. *Journal of Applied Social Psychology*, 12, 12-29.

Klami, H. T. & Hämäläinen, M. (1992). *Lawyers and Laymen on the Bench*. Helsinki: Suomalainen Tiedeakatemia.

Klami, H. T. & Hämäläinen, M. (1993). Judges and lay judges in Sweden and Finland. In A. Aarnio, S. L. Paulson, O. Weinberger, G. H. von Wright, & D. Wyduckel (Eds.), *Rechtsnorm und Rechtswirklichkeit*. Berlin: Duncker & Humblot.

Klami, H. T., Hämäläinen, M., Hatakka, M., & Sorvettula, J. (1990). Nonprofessional judicial reasoning. *Rivista Internazionale di Filosofia del Diritto*, 67, 93-114.

Klausa, E. (1972). *Ehrenamtliche Richter*. Frankfurt: Athenäum Verlag.

Kovačević, M. (1973). Porota u našem sistemu sudovanja. *Pravna misao*, 4, 3-6.

Krapac, D. (1977). Neki osnovni problemi u vezi sa sudjelovanjem gradjananepravnika u vršenju sudske funkcije prema odredbama novog krivičnog zakonodavstva SFRJ. *Naša zakonitost*, 31, 13-27.

Krapac, D. (1987). Lecture notes on Criminal Procedure. Unpublished.

Kregar, J., Smerdel, B., & Šimonović, I. (1991). Novi Ustav Hrvatske: Nastanak, osnovne ideje i institucije. *Zbornik Pravnog fakulteta u Zagrebu*, 45, 130-150.

Krüger, F. K. (1914). The judicial system of the German Empire with reference to ordinary jurisdiction. *California Law Review*, 2, 124-136.

Krystufek, Z. (1976). The function of the lay judge in Czechoslovakia. In L. Friedman & M. Rehbinder (Eds.), *Zur Soziologie des Gerichtsverfahrens. Jahrbuch für Rechtssoziologie und Rechtstheorie*, 4, 301-306. Opladen: Westdeutscher Verlag.

Kubicki, L. & Zawadzki, S. (1970). Lay assessor judges in penal proceedings in the light of empirical research. In S. Zawadzki & L. Kubicki (Eds.), *Udział Lawników W Postępowaniu Karnym*. Warszawa: Wydawnictwo Prawnicze.

Kühne, H. H. (1985). Laienrichter in Strafprozess? *Zeitschrift für Rechtspolitik*, 18, 237-239.

Kulcsár, K. (1972). Lay participation in organizational decision making. In P. Halmos (Ed.), *Hungarian Sociological Studies. The Sociological Review, Monograph 17*. Keele, United Kingdom: University of Keele.

Kulcsár, K. (1982). *People's Assessors in the Courts*. Budapest: Akadémiai Kiadó.

Lamb, T. A. (1981). Nonverbal and paraverbal control in dyads and triads: Sex or power differences. *Social Psychology Quarterly*, 44, 49-53.

Lampe, J. R. (1996). *Yugoslavia as History: Twice There was a Country*. Cambridge, United Kingdom: Cambridge University Press.

Langbein, J. H. (1974). *Prosecuting Crime in the Renaissance*. Cambridge, MA: Harvard University Press.

Langbein, J. H. (1977). *Comparative Criminal Procedure: Germany*. St. Paul, MN: West Publishing.

Langbein, J. H. (1981). Mixed court and jury court: Could the continental alternative fill the American need? *American Bar Foundation Research Journal*, 4, 195-219.

Lapaine, M. (1986). Neka razmišljanja o sudjelovanju sudaca porotnika u našem krivičnom postupku. *Naša zakonitost*, 40, 605-612.

Larwood, L. & Whittaker, W. (1977). Managerial myopia: Self-serving bias in organizational planning. *Journal of Applied Psychology*, 62, 194-198.

Lempert, R. (1992). A Jury for Japan? *The American Journal of Comparative Law*, 40, 37-71.

Leng, S. C. and Chiu, H. (1985). *Criminal Justice in Post-Mao China*. Albany: State University of New York Press.

Litan, R. E. (1993). Introduction. In R. E. Litan (Ed.), *Verdict: Assessing the Civil Jury System*. Washington, DC: Brookings Institution.

Ljubanović, V. (1983). *Sudjelovanje gradjana u suvremenom jugoslavenskom krivičnom sudjenju*. Unpublished doctoral dissertation. Zagreb, Croatia: University of Zagreb, Croatia.

Ljubanović, V. (1984). Osnovna obilježja ostvarivanja i mogući pravci daljeg razvoja sudjelovanja gradjana u krivičnom sudjenju. *Naša zakonitost*, 38, 1315-1326.

Ljubanović, V. (1989). *Demokratizacija krivičnog pravosudja*. Osijek, Croatia: Pravni fakultet Sveučilišta u Osijeku.

Lloyd-Bostock, S. M. (1989). *Law in Practice*. Chicago, IL: Lyceum Books.

Lockheed, M. E. & Hall, K. P. (1976). Conceptualizing sex as a status characteristic: Application of leadership training strategies. *Journal of Social Issues*, 14, 77-88.

Loftus, E. L. (1974). The incredible eyewitness. *Psychology Today*, 8, 116-119.

Loftus, E. L. (1996). *Eyewitness Testimony*. Cambridge, MA: Harvard University Press.

Luginbuhl, J. (1992). Comprehension of judges' instructions in the penalty phase of a capital trial. *Law and Human Behavior*, 16, 203-218.

Macan, T. (1992). *Povijest hrvatskog naroda*. Zagreb, Croatia: Nakladni zavod Matice Hrvatske.

MacCoun, R. J. & Tyler, T. R. (1988). The basis of citizens' perceptions of the criminal jury. *Law and Human Behavior*, 12, 333-352.

Makamure, K. (1985). A comparative study of comrades' courts under socialist legal systems and Zimbabwe's village courts. *Zimbabwe Law Review*, 3, 34-61.

Marder, N. S. (1987). Gender dynamics and jury deliberation. *The Yale Law Journal*, 96, 593-612.

Martin, P. Y. (1985). Group sex composition in work organizations: A structural-normative model. *Research in the Sociology of Organizations*, 4, 311-349.

McCabe, E. J. (1989). Structural elements of contemporary criminal justice in the People's Republic of China. In R. J. Troyer, J. P. Clark, & D. G. Rojek (Eds.), *Social Control in the People's Republic of China*. New York: Praeger.

McCloskey, H. & Brill, A. (1983). *Dimensions of Tolerance: What Americans Believe about Civil Liberties*. New York: Russell Sage Foundation.

McCormick, P. & Job, T. (1993). Do women judges make a difference? An analysis by appeal court data. *Canadian Journal of Law and Society*, 8, 135-148.

Meeker, B. F. & Weitzel-O'Neill. (1977). Sex roles and interpersonal behavior in task-oriented groups. *American Sociological Review*, 42, 91-105.

Menkel-Meadow, C. (1989). Exploring a research agenda of the feminization of the legal profession: Theories of gender and social change. *Law and Social Inquiry*, 14, 289-319.

Merry, S. E. (1993). Sorting out popular justice. In S. E. Merry & N. Milner (Eds.), *The Possibility of Popular Justice: A Case Study of Community Mediation in the United States*. Ann Arbor, MI: The University of Michigan Press.

Merry, S. E. & Milner, N. (1993). *The Possibility of Popular Justice: A Case Study of Community Mediation in the United States*. Ann Arbor, MI: The University of Michigan Press.

Mischel, H. N. (1974). Sex bias in the evaluation of professional achievements. *Journal of Educational Psychology*, 66, 157-166.

Mjesečnik Pravničkog društva u Zagrebu. (1884). 12, 696-699.

Mnookin, R. & L. Kornhauser (1979). Bargaining in the shadow of the law: The case of divorce. *Yale Law Journal*, 88, 950-997.

Moore, L. E. (1973). *The Jury: Tool of Kinds, Palladium of Liberty.* Cincinnati, OH: Anderson Publishing Co.

Moore, R. H., Jr. (1996). Islamic legal systems: Traditional (Saudi Arabia), contemporary (Bahrain), and evolving (Pakistan). In C. B. Fields & R. H. Moore, Jr. (Eds.), *Comparative Criminal Justice.* Prospect Heights, IL: Waveland Press.

Moore, R. H., Jr. (1987). Courts, law, justice, and criminal trials in Saudi Arabia. *International Journal of Comparative and Applied Criminal Justice*, 11, 61-67.

Mudd, J. O. (1983). Thinking critically about "Thinking like a lawyer." *Journal of Legal Education*, 33, 704-711.

Murray, P. L. (1998). A comparative law experiment. *Indiana International and Comparative Law Review*, 8, 231-259.

Nelson, A. (1987). Sweden. In G. F. Cole, S. J. Frankowski, & M. G. Gertz (Eds.), *Major Criminal Justice Systems: A Comparative Systems.* 2nd ed. Newbury Park, CA: Sage.

van Niekerk, B. (1972). The police in the apartheid society. In P. Randell (Ed.), *Law, Justice, and Society.* Johannesburg: Study Project on Christianity in Apartheid Society, SPRO-CAS Publication.

O'Barr, W. (1982). *Linguistic Evidence: Language, Power, and Strategy in the Courtroom.* New York: Academic Press.

O'Connor, M. (1993). Lay justices or stipendiaries? *Justice of the Peace*, 157, 453-454.

Ogorelica, N. (1899). *Kazneno procesualno pravo.* Zagreb, Croatia: Naklada Kraljevske hrvatsko-slavonsko-dalmatinske Zemaljske vlade.

Pabst, W. R., Munsterman, G. T., &. Mount, C. H. (1976). The myth of the unwilling juror. *Judicature*, 60, 164-171.

Packwood, W. T. (1974). Loudness as a variable in persuasion. *Journal of Counseling Psychology*, 21, 1-2.

Paicheler, G. (1979). Polarization of attitudes in homogeneous and heterogeneous groups. *European Journal of Social Psychology*, 9, 85-96.

Parker, H., Sumner, M., & Jarvis, G. (1989). *Unmasking the Magistrates.* Milton Keynes, Great Britain: Open University Press.

Pennington, N. & Hastie, R. (1993). The story model for juror decision making. In R. Hastie (Ed.), *Inside the Juror.* Cambridge: Cambridge University Press.

Penrod, S. D. & Cutler, B. L. (1989). Eyewitness expert testimony and jury decisionmaking. *Law and Contemporary Problems*, 52, 43-83.

Perić, I. (1995). *Godine koje će se pamtiti.* Zagreb, Croatia: Školska knjiga.

Piliavin, J. A. & Martin, R. R. (1978). The effects of the sex composition of groups on style of social interaction. *Sex Roles*, 4, 281-296.

Plato (1970). *The Laws.* Transl. with an Introduction by Saunders, T. J. Harmondsworth: Penguin Books.

Pomorski, S. (1975). Lay judges in the Polish criminal courts: A legal and empirical description. *Case Western Reserve Journal of International Law*, 7, 198-209.

Provine, D. M. (1981). Persistent anomaly: The lay judges in the American legal system. *Justice System Journal*, 6, 28-43.

Provine, D. M. (1986). *Judging Credentials.* Chicago, IL: University of Chicago Press.

Rácz, A. (1972). People's assessors in European socialist countries. *Acta Juridica Academiae Scientiarum Hungaricae*, 14, 395-415.

Ramundo, B. A. (1965). The comrades' court: Molder and keeper of socialist morality. *The George Washington Law Review*, 33, 693-727.

Rashotte, L. S. & Smith-Lovin, L.(1997). Who benefits from being bold: The interactive effects of task cues and status characteristics on influence in mock jury groups. *Advances in Group Processes*, 14, 235-255.

Regula, C. R. & Julian, J. W. (1973). The impact of quality and frequency of task contributions on perceived ability. *Journal of Social Psychology*, 89, 115-122.

Reichel, P. L. (1994). *Comparative Criminal Justice Systems: A Topical Approach*. Englewood Cliffs, NJ: Prentice Hall.

Reichert, I. F. (1973). The magistrates' courts: Lay cornerstone of English justice. *Judicature*, 57, 138-143.

Reichert, J. (1979). Lay judges and assessors: A comparative perspective. In L. Silberman (Ed.), *Non-Attorney Justice in the U. S: An Empirical Study*, New York: Institute of Judicial Administration.

Richert, J. P. (1977). A new verdict on juror willingness. *Judicature*, 60, 497-501.

Richert, J. P. (1983). *West German Lay Judges: Recruitment and Representativeness*. Gainesville, FL: University Presses of Florida.

Richings, F. G. (1976). Assessors in South African criminal trials. *Criminal Law Review*, 23, 107-116.

Ridgeway, C. L. (1981). Nonconformity, competence, and influence in groups: A test of two theories. *American Sociological Review*, 46, 333-347.

Ridgeway, C. L. (1982). Status in groups: The importance of motivation. *American Sociological Review*, 47, 76-88.

Ridgeway, C. L., Berger, J., & Smith, L. (1985). Nonverbal cues and status: An expectation states approach. *American Journal of Sociology*, 90, 955-978.

Roger, D. & Nesshoever, W. (1987). Individual differences in dyadic conversational strategies: A further study. *British Journal of Social Psychology*, 26, 247-255.

Rogers, W. T. & Jones, S. F. (1975). Effects of dominance tendencies on floor holding and interruption behavior in dyadic interaction. *Communication Research*, 1, 113-122.

The Role of Lay Judges in Our Administration of Justice. Uloga sudaca porotnika u našem pravosudju (1948). Beograd, Yugoslavia: Službeni list FNRJ.

Ross, S. D. (1973). A comparative study of the legal profession in East Africa. *Journal of African Law*, 17, 279-299.

Rowland, C. K. (1979). The relationship between grand jury composition and performance. *Social Science Quarterly*, 60, 323-327.

Rueschemeyer, D. (1987). Comparing legal professions cross-nationally: From a professions-centered to a state-centered approach. *American Bar Foundation Research Journal*, 10, 415-446.

Sachs, A. (1984). Changing the terms of the debate: A visit to a popular tribunal in Mozambique. *Journal of African Law*, 28, 99-106.

Salman, S. M. A. (1983). Lay tribunals in the Sudan: An historical and socio-legal analysis. *Journal of Legal Pluralism*, 21, 61-128.

Sarat, A. (1977). Studying American legal culture: An assessment of survey evidence. *Law and Society Review*, 11, 427-488.

Sawer, G. (1965). *Law in Society*. Oxford: The Clarendon Press.

Schlesinger, R. B., Baade, H. W., Damaška, M. R., & Herzog, P. E. (1988). *Comparative Law*. 5th ed. Mineola, NY: The Foundation Press.

Schneider, S. K. (1987). Influences on state professional licensure policy. *Public Administration Review*, 47, 479-484.

Schorn, H. (1959). *Der Richter im Dritten Reich*. Frankfurt: Vittorio Klostermann.

Schreiber, H. L. (1974). Akteneinsicht für Laienrichter. In G. Stratenwerth (Ed.), *Festschrift für Hans Welzel zum 70. Geburtstag am 25. März 1974*. Berlin: Walter de Gruyter.

Schutz, H. G. (1983). Effects of increased citizen membership on occupational licensing boards in California. *Policy Studies Journal*, 11, 504-516.

Severance, L. & Loftus, E. F. (1982). Improving the ability of jurors to comprehend and apply criminal jury instructions. *Law and Social Review*, 17, 153-198.

Silberman, L. (1979). *Non-Attorney Justice in the U. S.: An Empirical Study*, New York: Institute of Judicial Administration.

Sirotković, H. & Margetić, L. (1990). *Povijest država i prava naroda SFR Jugoslavije*. Zagreb, Croatia: Školska knjiga.

Skvoretz, J. (1981). Extending expectation status theory: Comparative status models of participation in N person groups. *Social Forces*, 59, 752-770.

Smaus, G. (1985). *Das Strafrecht und die Kriminalität in der Alltagssprache der deutschen Belölkerung*. Opladen: Westdeutscher Verlag.

Smend, R. (1911). *Das Reichskammergericht*. Weimar: Hermann Böhlaus Nachfolger.

Smith, D. N. (1968). Native courts of Northern Nigeria: Techniques for institutional development. *Boston University Law Review*, 48, 49-82.

Smith, G. (1974). Popular participation in the administration of justice in the Soviet Union: Comrades' courts and the Brezhnev regime. *Indiana Law Journal*, 49, 238-252.

Smith, A. W. (1981). Racial tolerance as a function of group position. *American Sociological Review*, 46, 558-573.

Smith, L. & Malandro, L. (1985). *Courtroom Communication Strategies*, New York: Kluwer Law Book Publishers.

Solaim, S. A. (1971). Saudi Arabia's Judicial System. *The Middle East Journal*, 25, 403-407.

Sorrentino, R. M. & Boutillier, R. G. (1975). The effect of quantity and quality of verbal interaction on ratings of leadership ability. *Journal of Experimental Social Psychology*, 11, 403-411.

Sourcebook of Criminal Justice Statistics 1997 (1998). Washington, DC: U.S. Department of Justice, Bureau of Justice Statistics.

Spohn, C. (1995). Decision making in sexual assault cases: Do black and female judges make a difference? In B. Raffel Price & N. J. Sokoloff (Eds.), *The Criminal Justice System and Women.* New York: McGraw-Hill.

State Court Organization 1993 (1995). Washington, DC: U.S. Department of Justice, Bureau of Justice Statistics.

Statistical Calendar of Yugoslavia. Statistički kalendar Jugoslavije, 1989. (1989). Beograd, Yugoslavia: Savezni zavod za statistiku.

Statistical Abstract of the United States. (1993). Washington, DC: U.S. Department of Commerce, Bureau of the Census.

1979/80 Statistical Yearbook (1981). New York: United Nations, Department of International Economic and Social Affairs, Statistical Office.

Statistical Yearbook of the Republic of Croatia. Statistički godišnjak Republike Hrvatske, 1991. (1991). Zagreb, Croatia: Republički zavod za statistiku Republike Hrvatske.

Statistical Yearbook of the Republic of Croatia. Statistički ljetopis Republike Hrvatske, 1992. (1993). Zagreb, Croatia: Republički zavod za statistiku Republike Hrvatske.

Statistical Yearbook of the Republic of Croatia. Statistički ljetopis Republike Hrvatske, 1993. (1993). Zagreb, Croatia: Republički zavod za statistiku Republike Hrvatske.

Statistical Yearbook of the Republic of Croatia. Statistički ljetopis Republike Hrvatske, 1997. (1997). Zagreb, Croatia: Republički zavod za statistiku Republike Hrvatske.

Strauss, G. (1986). *Law, Resistance, and the State: The Opposition to Roman Law in Reformation Germany.* Princeton, NJ: Princeton University Press.

Strauss, S. A. (1973). The jury in South Africa. *Western Australian Law Review,* 11, 133-139.

Strodtbeck, F. L. & Hook, L. H. (1961). The social dimensions of a twelve-man jury table. *Sociometry*, 24, 397-400.

Strodtbeck, F. L., James, R. M., & Hawkins C. (1957). Social status in jury deliberations. *American Sociological Review*, 22, 713-719.

Svenson, O. (1981). Are we all less risky and more skillful than our fellow drivers? *Acta Psychologica*, 94, 143-148.

Šulek, B. (1952). *Izabrani članci*. R. Maixner & I. Esih (Eds.), Zagreb, Croatia: Jugoslavenska akademija znanosti i umjetnosti.

Taps, J. & Martin, P. Y. (1990). Gender composition, attributional accounts, and women's influence and likability in task groups. *Small Group Research*, 21, 471-491.

Terrell, F., Terrell, S. L., & Golin, S. (1977). Language productivity of black and white children in black versus white situations. *Language and Speech*, 20, 377-383.

Thaman, S. C. (1995). The resurrection of trial by jury in Russia. *Stanford Journal of International Law*, 31, 61-274.

Thaman, S. C. (1998). Spain returns to trial by jury. *Hastings International and Comparative Law Review*, 21, 241-537.

Thibaut, J. & Walker, L. (1975). *Procedural Justice: A Psychological Analysis*. Hillsdale, NJ: Erlbaum.

Thompson, W. C. (1989). Are juries competent to evaluate statistical evidence? *Law and Contemporary Problems*, 52, 9-41.

de Tocqueville, A. (1966). *Democracy in America*. Lawrence, G. (Transl.), New York: Harper & Row.

Trajković, J. (1984). *The Judicial System of Yugoslavia*. Beograd, Yugoslavia: Jugoslavenski pregled.

Treiman, D. J. (1977). *Occupational Prestige in Comparative Perspective*. New York: Academic Press.

Troyer, R. J. (1989). Chinese social organization. In R. J. Troyer, J. P. Clark, & D. G. Rojek (Eds.), *Social Control in the People's Republic of China.* New York: Praeger.

Tsongas, J. E., Anderson, B. F., & Monson, A. D. (1986). *The Ninth Circuit Courts: A View from Jury Box.* Unpublished manuscript.

Tuzlak, A. & Moore, J. C., Jr. (1984). Status, demeanor and influence: An empirical reassessment. *Social Psychology Quarterly,* 47, 178-183.

Tyler, T. R. (1990). *Why People Obey the Law.* New Haven, CT: Yale University Press.

Ugwuegbu, D. (1979). Racial and evidential factors in juror attributions of legal responsibility. *Journal of Experimental Social Psychology,* 15, 133-146.

Urabe, M. (1976). A study on trial by jury in Japan. In H. Tanaka & M. D. H. Smith (Eds.), *The Japanese Legal System.* Tokyo: University of Tokyo Press.

Vasiljević, T. & Grubač, M. (1987). *Komentar Zakona o krivičnom postupku.* 3rd ed. Beograd, Yugoslavia: Savremena administracija.

Vasiljević, T., Lazarević, Lj., Grubač, M., & Kuhajda, V. (1975). *Učešće gradjana u sudjenju na teritoriji SAP Vojvodine.* Novi Sad, Yugoslavia: Zavod za naučno-istraživački rad Pravnog fakulteta u Novom Sadu.

Vidmar, N. J. & Schuller, R. A. (1989). Juries and expert evidence: Social framework testimony. *Law and Contemporary Problems,* 52, 133-176.

Wagner, W. (1974). *Der Volksgerichthof im Nationalsozialistischen Staat.* Stuttgart: Deutscher Verlags-Anstalt.

Walker, T. G. & Barrow, D. J. (1985). The diversification of the federal bench: Policy and process ramifications. *Journal of Politics,* 47, 596-617.

Wassermann, R. (1982). Der Bürger als Richter: ehrenamtliche Richter in der Justiz. *Recht und Politik,* 17, 117-125.

Weinstein, N. D. (1980). Unrealistic optimism about future life events. *Journal of Personality and Social Psychology,* 39, 806-820.

Wigmore, J. H. (1936). *A Panorama of the World's Legal Systems*. Washington, DC: Washington Law Book Company.

Wikeley, N. & Young, R.(1992). The administration of benefits in Britain: Adjudication officers and the influence of social security appeal tribunals. *Public Law*, 1992, 238-262.

Wolf, M. (1987). *Gerichtsverfassungsrecht Aller Verfahrenszweige*. München: C. H. Beck'sche Verlagsbuchhandlung.

Wolfe, N. T. (1996). An alternative form of lay participation in criminal adjudication: Lay judge courts in the Federal Republic of Germany. In C. B. Fields & R. H. Moore, Jr. (Eds.), *Comparative Criminal Justice*. Prospect Heights, IL: Waveland Press.

The World Factbook (1995). Available at http://web.lexis-nexis.com

Yakolev, A. (1988). A truly independent court. *Moscow News*, 43.

van Zyl Smit, D. & Isakow, N.(1985). Assessors and criminal justice. *South African Journal on Human Rights*, 1, 218-235.

COURT CASES:

Apodaca v. Oregon (1972). 406 U.S. 404, 92 S.Ct. 1628, 32 L.Ed.2d 184.

Ballew v. Georgia (1978). 435 U.S. 223, 98 S.Ct. 1029, 55 L.Ed.2d 234.

Burch v. Louisiana (1979). 441 U.S. 130, 99 S.Ct. 1623, 60 L.Ed.2d 96.

Cargill v. State (1986). 255 Ga. 616, 340 S.E.2nd 891.

Duncan v. Louisiana (1968). 391 U.S. 145, 88 S.Ct. 1444, 20 L.Ed.2d 491.

Powers v. Ohio (1991). 499 U.S. 400, 111 S.Ct. 1364, 113 L.Ed.2d 411.

Singer v. US (1965). 380 U.S. 24, 85 S.Ct. 783, 13 L.Ed.2d 630.

Strauder v. West Virginia (1879). 100 U.S. 303, 25 L.Ed. 664, 10 Otto 303.

Taylor v. Louisiana (1975). 419 U.S. 522, 95 S.Ct. 692, 42 L.Ed.2d 690.

Williams v. Florida (1970). 399 U.S. 78, 90 S.Ct. 1893, 26 L.Ed.2d 446.

Witherspoon v. Illinois (1968). 391 U.S. 510, 88 S.Ct. 1770, 20 L.Ed.2d 776.

R. v. Mwita (1948). 15 E.A.C.A. 128.

King Emperor v. Tirumal Reddi (1901). 24 Madras 523.

LEGAL SOURCES:

Argentina:

Code of Criminal Procedure Law of the Province of Cordoba (1992). Law No. 8123 of the Providence of Cordoba, *Official Bulletin*, January 16, 1992.

Constitution of the Republic of Argentina. La Constitución de la Nación Argentina y los Derechos Humanos; Un Análisis a la Luz de la Reforma de 1994. (1995). F. Salvioli (Comp.).

Criminal Judiciary Act (1991). Law No. 24050. *Official Bulletin*, December 30, 1991.

Criminal Procedure Code (1991). Law No. 23984. *Official Bulletin*, September 9, 1991.

Project Concerning the Organization of Criminal Justice and the Office of the Attorney General (1988). *Doctrina Penal Law Review*, 1988, 340-383.

Croatia:

Attorneys Law. Zakon o odvjetništvu (1972). Narodne novine, 53/72, 8/90, 31/90.

Attorneys Law. Zakon o odvjetništvu (1994). Narodne novine, 9/94.

Austro-Hungarian Compromise of 1867. Hrvatsko-ugarska nagodba iz 1876.

Basic Law on the Courts of General Jurisdicton. Osnovni zakon o sudovima opće nadležnosti (1965). Službeni list, 7/65.

Basic Criminal Code of the Republic of Croatia. Osnovni krivični zakon Republike Hrvatske (1993). Narodne novine, 31/93, 39/93, 108/95, 16/96, 28/96.

Civil Procedure Law. Zakon o izmjenama i dopunama Zakona o parničnom postupku (1965). Službeni list, 12/65.

Code Concerning the Compilation of Lists of Jurors. Zakon o sastavljanju porotničkih listinah (1875). Sbornik zakonah i naredabah.

Code Concerning the Use of Press. Zakon o porabi tiska (1875). Sbornik zakonah i naredabah.

Code of Criminal Procedure for Offenses by the Press. Kazneni postupak u poslovima tiskovnih za kraljevine Hrvatsku i Slavoniju (1875). Sbornik zakonah i naredabah.

Commentary Concerning the Criminal Procedure Law. Objašnjenja Zakonika o krivičnom postupku (1953). Beograd, Yugoslavia: Arhiva za pravne i društvene nauke.

Commerce Courts Law. Zakon o privrednim sudovima (1954). Službeni list, 31/54.

Commerce Courts Law. Zakon o privrednim sudovima (1965). Službeni list, 7/65.

Constitutional Law. Ustavni zakon (1953). Službeni list, 3/54, 4/54.

Constitutional Law. Ustavni zakon (1990). Narodne novine, 2/90.

Constitution. Ustav (1946). Službeni list, 10/46.

Constitution. Ustav (1963). Službeni list, 14/63.

Constitution. Ustav (1974). Službeni list, 9/74.

Constitution of the Republic of Croatia. Ustav Republike Hrvatske (1990). Narodne novine, 56/90.

Courts Law. Zakon o sudovima (1954). Službeni list, 30/54.

Courts Law. Zakon o sudovima (1967). Narodne novine, 21/67.

Courts Law. Zakon o sudovima (1994). Narodne novine, 3/94.

Criminal Code of the Socialist Federative Republic of Yugoslavia. Krivični zakon SFRJ (1976). Službeni list, 44/76, 36/77, 56/77, 34/84, 74/87.

Criminal Code. Kazneni zakon (1998). Narodne novine, 110/97.

Criminal Procedure Law. Zakon o kaznenom postupku (1875). Sbornik zakonah i naredabah.

Criminal Procedure Law. Zakon o sudskom krivčnom postupku (1929). Službene novine, 47/29.

Criminal Procedure Law. Zakon o krivičnom postupku (1948). Službeni list, 97/48.

Criminal Procedure Law. Zakonik o krivičnom postupku (1953). Službeni list, 40/53.

Criminal Procedure Law. Zakon o izmjenama i dopunama Zakonika o krivičnom postupku (1967). Službeni list, 15/67.

Criminal Procedure Law. Zakon o krivičnom postupku (1977). Narodne novine, 36/77, 60/77, 14/85, 26/86, 74/87, 57/89, 3/90, 52/91, 34/93, 38/93, and 28/96. Restated in 1993.

Criminal Procedure Law. Zakon o kaznenom postupku (1998). Narodne novine, 110/97.

Criminal Procedure Law for Offenses by the Press. Zakon o kaznenom postupku u poslovih tiskovnih za kraljevine Hrvatsku i Slavoniju (1875). Sbornik zakonah i naredabah.

Decree Concerning Honorable Judges. Uredba o počasnim sudijama (1933). Službene novine, 174/33.

Dubrovnik Statute. Dubrovački statut (1332).

Fundamental Law Concerning Management of State Companies by the Workers' Council. Osnovni zakon o upravljanju radnih kolektiva državnim privredinim poduzećima (1950). Službeni list, 43/50.

Judicial Criminal Procedure Law. Zakon o sudskom krivičnom postupku (1954). Službeni list, 30/54.

Judicial Proceedings Act. Sudski poslovnik — Pravilnik o unutrašnjem poslovanju redovnih sudova (1988). Narodne novine, 45/88.

Juvenile Courts Law. Zakon o sudovima za mladež (1998). Narodne novine, 111/97.

Law Concerning Judicial Authority. Zakon o vlasti sudačkoj (1874). Sbornik zakonah i naredabah.

Law Concerning the Organization and Jurisdiction of Military Courts in the Yugoslav Army. Zakon o organizaciji i nadležnosti vojnih sudova u Jugoslavenskoj armiji (1945). Službeni list, 65/45.

Law Concerning the Organization of the People's Courts. Zakon o uredjenju narodnih sudova (1945). Službeni list, 67/45.

Law Concerning the Organization of the People's Courts. Zakon o uredjenju narodnih sudova (1946). Službeni list, 51/46.

Law Concerning Amendments and Supplements to the Criminal Procedure Law. Zakon o izmjenama i dopunama Zakonika o krivičnom postupku (1965). Službeni list, 12/65.

Military Courts Law. Zakon o vojnim sudovima (1954). Službeni list, 52/54.

Military Courts Law. Zakon o vojnim sudovima (1965). Službeni list, 7/65.

Poljice Statute. Poljički statut (1440).

Presidential Decree. Uredba o organizaciji, radu i djelokrugu sudbene vlasti u slučaju ratnog stanja ili neposredne ugroženosti neovisnosti i jedinstvenosti Republike Hrvatske (1991a). Narodne novine, 67/91.

Presidential Decree. Uredba o primjeni Zakona o krivičnom postupku u slučaju ratnog stanja ili neposredne ugroženosti neovisnosti i jedinstvenosti Republike Hrvatske (1991b). Narodne novine, 73/91.

Presidential Decree. Uredba o stavljanju izvan snage uredbi iz oblasti pravosudja (1996). Narodne novine, 103/96.

Public Prosecutor Law. Zakon o državnom odvjetništvu (1977). Narodne novine, 17/77, 17/86, 27/89, 16/90, 41/90, 14/91, 66/91, 22/92, 39/92, 58/93.

Regular Courts Law. Zakon o uredjenju redovnih sudova za Kraljevinu Srba, Hrvata i Slovenaca (1929). Službene novine, 20/29.

Regular Courts Law. Zakon o redovnim sudovima (1977). Narodne novine 5/77, 17/87, 27/88, 32/88, 16/90, 41/90, 14/91, 66/91. Restated in 1988.

Regulations Concerning Compensation and Awards of Lay Judges. Pravilnik o naknadama i nagradama sudaca porotnika (1996).

Regulations Concerning Court Organization. Uputstva o postupku pred narodnim sudovima (1943). 1/44.

Regulations Concerning Court Organization. Uputstva o preuredjenju sudova (1944). 1602/44.

State Attorneys Law. Zakon o državnom odvjetništvu (1977). Narodne novine, 75/95.

State Judicial Council. Zakon o državnom sudbenom vijeću (1993). Narodne novine, 58/93.

Vidovdan Constitution — The Constitution of the Kingdom of Serbs, Croats, and Slovenians. Vidovdanski Ustav — Ustav Kraljevine Srba, Hrvata i Slovenaca (1921). Službene novine, 28. Jun 1921.

Vinodol Statute. Vinodolski statut (1288).

France:

Criminal Procedure Code. Code d'instruction criminelle (1808).

Germany:

Constitutio Criminalis Carolina (1532).

Constitution. Grundgesetz (1949). BGBI S. 1; BGBI I S. 3146, BGBI III 100.1.

Court Organization Act. (1877).

Court Organization Act. Gerichtsverfassungsgesetz (1975). BGBI. I S. 1077.

Criminal Procedure Law. Strafprozessordnung (1987). BGBI. I S. 1074.

German Judicial Code. Deutsches Richtergesetz (1972). BGBI. I S. 713.

Juvenile Court Code. Jugendgerichtsgesetz (1974). BGBI. I S. 3427.

Hong Kong:

Basic Law of the Hong Kong Special Administrative Region of the People's Republic of China (1990).

Ordinance for the Regulation of Jurors and Juries (1843).

Israel:

Courts Law (1984). Consolidated Version. 38 L.S.I. 271.

Japan:

Jury Law (1923). Law No. 50 of 1923.

Russia and the former USSR:

Constitution of the Soviet Union (1936).

Decree on Courts (1918). 7. March 1918.

A New Stage in the Activity of the Comrades' Courts. Novyi Etap v Deiatel'nosti Tovarishcheskikh Sudov (1964). Sovetskaia Iustitsiia, 23.

Statute on Comrades' Courts (1961). Transl. *XIII Current Digest of the Soviet Press.*

Spain:

Law on Trial by Jury. Lay Del Jurado (1995). In M. Catena (Ed.), *Ley Del Jurado.* Victor ed., 2nd ed.

The United States:

Amendment VI of the U.S. Constitution (1791).

Index

TEXAS A&M UNIVERSITY - TEXARKANA